A NEW CRIT
OF THEORETICAL

A NEW CRITIQUE OF THEORETICAL THOUGHT

BY

HERMAN DOOYEWEERD Dr jur.
Professor of Philosophy of Law, Free University of Amsterdam
Fellow of the Royal Dutch Academy of Sciences

TRANSLATED BY

DAVID H. FREEMAN
Assistant Professor of Philosophy, Wilson College

AND

H. DE JONGSTE
English Master in the Ist Christian Secondary School of Rotterdam

VOLUME III

THE STRUCTURES OF INDIVIDUALITY OF TEMPORAL REALITY

PAIDEIA PRESS LTD.
1984

PAIDEIA
PRESS

This book was originally published in four volumes.

First published by The Presbyterian and Reformed Publishing Company in 1969. This edition published in 1983 by special arrangement.

Paideia Press Ltd., P.O. Box 1000, Jordan Station, Ontario, Canada LOR ISO.

ISBN 978-0-88815-297-8
Fourth printing, 2021

Printed in the United States of America.

CONTENTS

Page

Page

Page

PART II (CONTINUATION) - THE STRUCTURES OF THE DIFFERENTIATED INSTITUTIONAL COMMUNITIES WITH A TYPICAL HISTORICAL FOUNDATION

Page

PART II (*CONCLUSION*) - THE STRUCTURES OF VOLUNTARY ASSOCIATIONS AND THE INTER-INDIVIDUAL AND INTER-COMMUNAL RELATIONSHIPS IN A DIFFERENTIATED SOCIETY

PART III - INTRODUCTION TO THE THEORY OF THE ENKAPTIC INTER-STRUCTURAL INTERLACEMENTS

PART I

THE STRUCTURES OF INDIVIDUALITY OF TEMPORAL THINGS

Chapter I

THE MISINTERPRETATION OF NAÏVE EXPERIENCE BY IMMANENCE-PHILOSOPHY

§ 1 - THE METAPHYSICAL CONCEPT OF SUBSTANCE AS A SPECULATIVE EXAGGERATION OF A DATUM OF NAÏVE EXPERIENCE.

It is undoubtedly true that in the pre-theoretical attitude we continue to experience the identity of a thing, while observing it to be susceptible to change. The tree in front of my house may change and vary in its visible form in the process of growing and with the various seasons; nevertheless, we are sure that it persists in being the same tree. The book in my hand is no longer new. Its cover is loose and its margins are filled with notes, yet in my experience, it is the same book I originally purchased.

Chemistry and biology give us theoretical understanding of the continual changes occurring in the molecular combinations of matter and in the cells and tissues of a living organism, but our knowledge of the things mentioned above is supplied by our naïve experience, before we acquire theoretical insight into physico-chemical or bio-chemical changes. Naïve experience may be deepened through this natural scientific knowledge, but cannot be *destroyed* by it.

There is, however, a limit to the amount of change that is compatible with our experience of the identity of a thing. When I throw a book into a fire and it is consumed, the *thing itself* is consumed. Chemistry cannot teach anything concerning the annihilation of this thing, as such. For, as a special science, it must eliminate the things of naïve experience from its theoretical field of vision, at least insofar as they are not qualified by a physical-chemical structure. Otherwise, it could not give theoretical insight into the functional coherence of events, presenting themselves in the modal aspect of reality which it examines.

The naïve perceiver, bound to what we have previously called the plastic horizon of experience, cannot account for the latter.

His pre-theoretical *concept* of a thing is bound to sensory perception. He experiences things without being able to gain a theoretical insight into their typical structures of individuality.

When asked why the tree planted in his garden a few years ago is still the same tree, a man capable only of naïve experience will soon appeal to sense perception, if he is at all willing to consider such a difficult question. And so he will necessarily get muddled in a problem which cannot be solved by the test of the senses.

When forced to explain what he experiences, the naïve perceiver thus seemingly corroborates the philosophical theory which interprets the essential data of naïve experience as mere sense phenomena.

Since philosophy was convinced that nothing permanent may be found in „sense phenomena", it began to pose the problem of identity and change on a metaphysical basis. Because the things of naïve experience are *transient*, and every process of change must nevertheless be related to an identical subject, metaphysics began to seek a supra-temporal *substance*, possessing a permanence unaffected by the process of becoming and decay.

Without first obtaining a correct insight into what is actually given in naïve experience, as the identical whole in the changing things, metaphysical immanence-philosophy thus began to search for the *οὐσία*, the imperishable substance which alone can truly be called "being."

This metaphysical problem of the *οὐσία* originated in a speculative exaggeration of a datum of naïve experience. What is strictly given in our experience of the identity of temporal things, does not provide a sufficient reason to seek supra-temporal *substances* behind the latter. Our experience of the identity of a thing is always *temporal*.

A speculative exaggeration and misconception of this datum was already implied in the metaphysical type of cosmonomic Idea lying at the foundation of this philosophical search for the true being.

In the final hypostasis of its deification, philosophical thought itself appears to be the *ἀρχή* of the idea of supra-temporal substance.

Metaphysical thought theoretically separated the structure of reality into the real metaphysical *noumenon* and the deceptive *phenomenon*. Thus, it turned away from what is strictly given in naïve experience.

By seeking true reality in eternal, unchangeable, unmoved being, PARMENIDES, the Eleatic, declared all becoming and change to be a sensory phenomenon, which does not correspond to true Being. But the real origin of this Being is theoretical thought which identifies itself with its product: *Τὸ γὰρ αὐτὸ νοεῖν ἐστίν τε καὶ εἶναι·* (For thinking and being is one and the same).

Substance as the personal point of reference of temporal being in AUGUST BRUNNER.

Since the idea of a metaphysical substance in the sense explained above has, as such, nothing to do with the things of naïve experience, it might have another origin. The question may be raised as to whether metaphysics, in seeking the supra-temporal point of reference of all changeable things, is perhaps primarily concerned with the transcendental basic problem of the radical identity of the I-ness, as the concentration-point of human existence and human experience. The neo-scholastic philosopher, AUGUST BRUNNER [1], who is strongly under the influence of existentialism and modern phenomenology, has to some degree interpreted the idea of substance in this sense. According to him this idea should in the first place be related to the personal centre of experience, since only the human person as subject corresponds in an adequate sense to the definition of substance as "*ens in sē stans*". The concrete unity of the selfhood is always the same notwithstanding the change of its ontical relations. The accentuation of the selfhood is thus supposed to be responsible for the philosophy of substance in Greek and medieval thought. From this central viewpoint BRUNNER also tries to explain the concept of substance in its reference to the "lower levels of being". Availing himself of HEIDEGGER's existentialistic conception of "concern" *(Sorge)*, he supposes that in the material levels of being the selfhood, in its concerned struggle for possession, seeks permanent things on which it can rely: 'So the concept of substance reveals its true meaning: a fixed thing with a certain permanency'. This permanency is of primordial importance in cultural objects, since the latter are only serviceable in a steady and durable state. From the cultural objects the property of permanency and unchangeableness was transferred to the

---

[1] A. BRUNNER S.J. *Der Stufenbau der Welt.* Ontologische Untersuchungen über Person, Leben, Stoff. (München-Kempten, 1950).

"forms". So the *οὐσία* is a permanent kernel, which is the essence of cultural things and BRUNNER thinks that this is the origin of the conception of unchangeable essence, in respect to which changes are only accidental. Accidental in this sense are also the relations which, in their typical realization on infra-personal levels, are opposed to the selfhood. One should, however, avoid any absolutization of the "essence" and take the latter, with the accidental relations, as a structural whole, especially in the case of the selfhood.

BRUNNER's view is doubtless interesting, but it cannot be accepted as a serious interpretation of the metaphysical concept of substance in its classical and medieval sense, nor in that of modern Humanistic metaphysics. BOETHIUS [1] has indeed defined personality with the aid of the classical concept of substance as "*naturae rationalis individua substantia*", and this definition has had a great influence in scholastic theology [2]. But the origin of this metaphysical concept has nothing to do with the modern personalistic view of being, and *a fortiori* it cannot be related to the Christian view of the I-ness as the individual religious centre of human existence and experience. The idea of an "*ens in sē stans*" is, on the contrary, entirely incompatible with the Christian conception of the human selfhood as a spiritual centre, which is nothing in itself, but whose nature is a "*stare extra sē*", a self-surrender to its true or its fancied Origin.

As long as the human person in its central kernel is conceived as a "substance", it is impossible to understand the profound Biblical meaning of the creation of man after the image of God. BRUNNER himself contradicts the conception of the selfhood as a "substance" when he remarks: 'It is the mode of being of the selfhood to transcend itself and in this very transcending to be a self and with itself".[3] His distortion of the real metaphysical concept of *οὐσία* clearly appears from his view that in the material sphere the cultural object is the original proto-type of a "substance". For cultural objects have never been conceived as real "substances" in a metaphysical sense. This very fact proves

---

[1] *De duabus naturis et una persona Christi* c. 3.

[2] THOMAS AQUINAS accepted it in his *Summa Theol.* I qu. XXIX, cap. 3.

[3] *Op. cit.* p. 184: "Es ist die Seinsweise des Selbst, über sich hinaus zu sein und gerade darin selbst und bei sich zu sein". Cf. MICHAEL FR. J. MARLET S.J.: *Grundlinien der Kalvinistischen Philosophie der Gesetzesidee als Christlicher Transzendentalphilosophie* (Karl Zink Verlag, München, 1954) p. 115.

that the identification of this metaphysical concept with the naïve notion of a "thing" must rest on a fundamental misunderstanding of the latter.

The concept of substance in Greek metaphysics.

Metaphysical immanence-philosophy has turned away from the transcendent religious horizon of human experience. Its concept of substance is rooted in an absolutization of the theoretical antithesis implied in the theoretical attitude of thought. It rests upon the antithesis between a noumenal being, as a true reality *in itself*, and a merely phenomenal world. Metaphysical substance is conceived of as a "thing in itself" and this "noumenal thing" is opposed to "sensible things". Under the influence of PARMENIDES' idea of the true "being", enclosed in a spherical form, pre-Aristotelian metaphysics conceived of substance [1] as a supra-temporal and unchangeable entity. As long as this view was maintained a confusion with the things of naïve experience was impossible. Substance was conceived exclusively as a supra-sensible "form" of being in its opposition to "matter" as the principle of becoming and decay.

As far as we are informed by authentic fragments, we may establish that the Ionian philosophy of nature, which before ANAXAGORAS held to the religious primacy of the matter-motive, never called the eternally flowing Stream of life the true *οὐσία*. ANAXIMANDER opposed the *ἄπειρον*, as the divine origin, to *τὰ ὄντα* (the existing things). Although this form-less origin was conceived as the ever-lasting principle of all perishable things, it lacked the very character of a "substance". For, as remarked above, in pre-Aristotelian metaphysics the idea of *οὐσία* was exclusively oriented to the supra-sensible *form* of being [2].

---

[1] The term "substance", as shown by PRANTL *(Gesch. der Logik* I, p. 514), first appeared in QUINTILIANUS *Instit. orat.* 3, 6.

[2] In the first Book (ch. 3) of his *Metaphysics* ARISTOTLE ascribes to the Ionian philosophers of nature the opinion that the origin of existing things is their *οὐσία* (substance). This is doubtless incorrect. But this manner of interpretation of the Ionian thinkers can be explained from ARISTOTLE's method of debating, which starts from his own conception concerning the relation of form and matter in natural substance. According to him "matter" can only become *actual* by assuming a form in an individual substance. To demonstrate the untenableness of the opinion that the matter-principle as such is the actual origin of existing things, he interprets this opinion in the sense of his concept of *οὐσία*. But the philosophical concept of permanent being does not appear in Greek thought

This was even the case in pre-Socratic atomism, which was certainly no materialism in the pre-Socratic Greek sense [1], nor in the modern sense of the word. The "atoms" are nothing but minimal geometric forms of "elements". DEMOCRITUS called them ἰδέαι. They are not sensible but intelligible. In PLATO's *Timaeus* they belong to the intelligible world of the οὐσίαι and are opposed to the chaotic material of the χωρά, in which the "elements" still lack these limiting forms of being and consequently may not be properly called fire, air, water, and earth. The Platonic *eidè* are also οὐσίαι in the sense of imperishable ideal forms of being which, however, belong to a different area of the *noumena*.

It was in fact ARISTOTLE who in his concept of natural substance made the first attempt to synthesize the principles of form and matter to an ultimate substantial unity. But at the same time he paved the way for a fundamental confusion of the concept of substance and that of the thing of naïve experience, by conceiving the former in two different senses.

After his abandonment of the Platonic χωρισμός (separation) between the noumenal world of the οὐσίαι and the sensible world of becoming and decay, ARISTOTLE's primary concern was to conceive of substance as the immanent point of reference in the process of change itself. Only individual things are liable

---

before PARMENIDES: and then it is immediately opposed to the principle of matter. Therefore the interpretation of ANAXIMANDER's ἀρχὴ τῶν ὄντων (origin of the being things) as the οὐσία (substance) of the things is scientifically impossible. It is remarkable that in this context of his argument ARISTOTLE does not mention ANAXIMANDER. The reason is perhaps that ARISTOTLE saw that ANAXIMANDER's clear distinction between the ἄπειρον (the formless Origin) and τὰ ὄντα (the things which have *being*) was not serviceable to his interpretation of the Ionian thinkers.

[1] ARISTOTLE (*Met.* I, 4, 985 b) says that LEUCIPPUS and DEMOCRITUS conceived the πλέον (the full) and the κένον (the void) as principles of being in the mode of matter. As I have explained in more detail in the first volume of my *Reformatie en Scholastiek in de Wijsbegeerte* this is a misinterpretation of the view of the atomists. The "atoms" are called "full" (of being) in contrast with the flowing air which, as the principle of matter, is conceived as void of being (τὸ κένον is called the μὴ ὄν, *i.e.*, the non-being). The conception of the flowing air as the void was taken over from the older Pythagoreanism. ARISTOTLE interprets both the atomistic πλέον and the κένον as "material principles of being". This misinterpretation is due to the fact that in ARISTOTLE's metaphysics the geometrical forms are conceived of as "intelligible matter". Cf. *Met.* VII, 1036a 12 sqq.: 'Matter, however, is partly sensible, partly intelligible; ...intelligible is the matter which is present in the sensible without being sensible: of this nature is the mathematical'.

to becoming and decay. So the individual natural entity (τόδε τι) as the individual unity of matter and essential form, is conceived as πρώτη οὐσία (primary substance). But, in addition, the term οὐσία (substance) is applied to the intelligible specific εἶδος of a natural thing which comprehends its "essence" (τὸ τί ἦν εἶναι). This general essence of the existing individual thing is called οὐσία δεύτερα (substance in a secondary sense). It is also called ἡ κατὰ τὸν λόγον (or κατὰ τὸ εἶδος) οὐσία (noumenal substance) in contradistinction to the οὐσία αἰσθητή or the individual sensible thing as an actual concrete substance. The latter is liable to "substantial change", as such it is capable of generation and destruction. But the general εἶδος as the pure intelligible "essence" of a thing, in its specific characteristics, is not capable of temporal change, since it has only an abstract mode of being in the intellect [1]. In the individual substance the essential form is always materialized and individualized. The specific essence of a natural substance doubtless comprehends the components of matter and form, but only in a generic and specific sense, not in their actual individuality [2].

It cannot be denied that ARISTOTLE's conception of primary substance has a deceitful resemblance to the naïve conception of things with their relative permanency in their accidental changes. It is, therefore, necessary to subject this idea of primary substance to a closer analysis.

A more detailed critical analysis of ARISTOTLE's concept of primary substance.

Substance (οὐσία) in Aristotelian metaphysics always means the primary category of being, which lies at the foundation of

---

[1] Compare the statement in *Met.* Z 15, 1039 b where the 15th chapter is introduced as follows: 'The οὐσία as concretum, however, is distinguished from the *eidos* (I mean that the *eidos* is at one time taken with the individual matter, at an other time the *eidos* is taken in its generality). *Ousia* in the former sense is capable of destruction (for it is capable also of generation), but there is no destruction of the *eidos* in its generality, neither is it generated; the being of a house is not generated, but only the being of this house; but *eidè* are without generation and destruction... for it has been shown that no one begets... nor makes them'. The essential form of the sensible things is, as such, no more liable to generation and destruction (Cf. *Met.* Z, 8, 1033 b 5 sqq). Sometimes this form is also called εἶδος.

[2] Cf. *Met.* Z. 1035 b: 'So matter is a part of the εἶδος, as well as of the (individual) composite of form and matter; εἶδος, however, means the essence' (the species, not the form only).

all accidental categories (such as quantity, quality, place, relation, *etc.*). As such, this primary metaphysical category has always an exclusively intelligible character. The distinction between sensible and noumenal *οὐσίαι* can, therefore, never mean that the former *as substances* are perceptible by the senses.

Primary substance (*τόδε τι*) is conceived of as a "thing in itself", which as such is not related to the sensory and intellectual functions of human experience. The sensibility of this thing has only an epistemological meaning. It exclusively means a relation of human sensory perception to the "things in themselves", not an intrinsic relation of the latter to the former. Even the qualities of the things to which the subjective sensory perception is related (such as light or heavy, red or blue, cold or warm) are conceived as "accidents" of the substance which are independent of possible perception.

It is clear that such "*qualitates occultae*" are meaningless not only from the viewpoint of modern natural science, but also from that of naïve experience. This is a strong indication that the Aristotelian idea of primary substance cannot be identical with that of a pre-theoretically conceived thing. For the latter is always bound to the subject-object relation, which has no room for a metaphysical "thing in itself".

What can then be the real meaning of the Aristotelian primary substance? As observed, ARISTOTLE never abandoned the Greek conception of *οὐσία* as a *noumenon*. This implies that "primary substance" is nothing but the supposed first temporal "*Gegenstand*" of the theoretical-logical function of thought. Metaphysics is of the opinion that the antithetical "*Gegenstand-relation*" corresponds to true reality. Thus the "true being" of a natural thing, as the supposed "*Gegenstand*" of theoretical thought, is hypostatized to a "substance", as the independent bearer of the changeable and accidental properties of this thing. As long as this primary *οὐσία* is not affected by change, a natural thing remains the same notwithstanding all accidental alterations.

But how can the primary substance guarantee this identity of a changeable thing? The former is thought of as a whole (*σύνολον*) combining the form and matter of a thing into an ultimate unity. As such it is called an *οὐσία σύνθετος* (a composite substance) [1]. But this very idea of a substantial unity of form and matter implies the crucial dialectical basic problem of

---

[1] *Met.* VIII 3, 1043 a 30.

Greek metaphysics. We have explained in the Prolegomena of the first Volume that the form-matter motive is the real religious starting-point of Greek thought and that as such it contains an insoluble religious antithesis. PLATO introduced the dialectical Idea of being which would synthesize the antagonistic principles of form and matter by means of a dialectical logic. ARISTOTLE has taken over this dialectical Idea of being by conceiving matter in its general sense as a pure potentiality of being which can acquire actuality only by assuming a form. But this dialectical synthesis between form and matter lacked a real starting-point in which the two antithetical principles of being could find concentric unity. In PLATO the dialectical synthesis remains restricted to the ideal sphere of the transcendent *eidè*. Even the genus (generic *eidos*) of the *genesis eis ousian* (the becoming a being), which is introduced in the dialogue *Philebus*, belongs to this sphere. Only by means of the mathematical principle of a numerical series (the *peras*) is it related to the material world of becoming. But the *οὐσία* as such is never identified with a perishable thing. ARISTOTLE does so in his conception of primary substance. This conception is nothing but the consequence of his abandonment of the Platonic *χωρισμός* between the intelligible world of the *eidè* and the ideal *mathematical forms*, on the one hand, and the phenomenal world of becoming and decay, on the other. The dialectical *eidos* of the composite substance is now conceived of as a secondary *οὐσία*; it is nothing but an ideal abstraction from the primary substance and this latter belongs to the world of becoming and decay. Nevertheless this changeable and material substance continues to be conceived as a *noumenon*, a purely intelligible "thing in itself". But how can a pure *noumenon* be an individual perishable entity?

Here the intrinsical antinomy of this substance-concept is clearly shown. The primary *οὐσία* is charged with a task which could not be fulfilled by the dialectical idea of being in its general metaphysical sense. It is supposed to realize the pseudo-synthesis between the antithetical principles of form and matter in an individual perishable unity. This unity is thought of as an absolute being. It cannot be a mere relation between form and matter since in Aristotelian metaphysics and logic the category of substance functions as the independent point of reference of all ontical relations. The category of relation is an accidental one which pre-supposes substance. It is true that ARISTOTLE has conceived this category in a particular restricted sense. But it is undeniable that his whole conception of the πρώτη οὐσία would become meaningless if it did not imply more than a dialectical relation between form and matter [1].

The idea of a composite substance contains a *contradictio in terminis* if this relation is conceived as the ultimate unity of the primary οὐσία itself. For though the synthesis as such is nothing but a relation, the substance in itself must be a unity independent of all relations. THOMAS AQUINAS was fully aware of this supposed absolute character of the οὐσία when he acknowledged that substance in itself is unknowable since all human knowledge is restricted to relations. So he rightly concluded that it is only knowable from its accidental properties in which it *reveals* itself [2].

But what may be this absolute X which guarantees the ultimate unity of an individual natural composite? In the 17th chapter of Book VII of his *Metaphysics* ARISTOTLE tries to answer this question. Here he starts from the thesis that the οὐσία is a principle and a cause. His argument proceeds as follows: That which is a composite in such a way that the whole is a unity, not as a disorderly heap but as a syllable, has, as such, an independent being. For a syllable is not the same as its elements, the letters. If the whole were itself an element or a composite of elements, its definition would be involved in a *regressus in infinitum*. That which makes a natural thing an individual whole distinct from its components, is the first cause of its being. And this is the substance. Many things lack the character of substance. But everything that exists as a substance

---

[1] This is also established by THOMAS AQUINAS: *De ente et essentia* cap. 2: 'Non etiam potest dici quod essentia significet relationem quae est inter materiam et formam vel aliquid superadditum illis, quia hoc de necessitate esset extraneum a rē, nec per eam rēs cognosceretur'.

[2] Cf. *De ente et essentia* cap. II: 'Sed quia ens absolute et primo dicitur de substantiis, et posterius secundum quid de accidentibus, inde est quod essentia proprie et vere est in substantiis, sed in accidentibus est quodammodo et secundum quid'. *Summa c. gent.* IV, 14: 'in rebus creatis comparatur relatio ad absolutum sicut accidens ad subjectum'. Compare with these two quotations. *Summa Theol.* I qu. XXIX art. 1 ad 3um: 'quia substantiales differentiae non sunt nobis notae, vel etiam nominatae non sunt, oportet interdum uti differentiis accidentalibus loco substantialum'. Cf. also in V *Met.* 9. A. D. SERTILLANGES O.P. *S. Thomas d'Aquin* (Paris 1910) (translated by R. Grosche *Der hl. Thomas von Aquin* (1928) p. 111 remarks: 'With Thomas, too, the substance in itself is doubtless unknowable since every knowledge is based on relations and it cannot reveal the absolute but by means of the relative which manifests it'.

according to and through nature, is a natural whole which is different from its elements and is the principle of being of this thing.'

This argument is a typical example of a metaphysical conclusion drawn from logical reasoning. But the latter, as such, can never lead to a metaphysical *absolutum.*

That in a logical sense the whole is different from its elements, and that every attempt to reduce the former to elements implies a *regressus in infinitum,* can never lead to the conclusion that there must exist a substance as an absolute point of reference of all of its ontical relations. Logic alone cannot furnish a principle of unity which transcends the dialectical form-matter motive of Greek thought. And ARISTOTLE has not really done so. Apparently the question concerning the primary substance, as a really *metaphysical* and not merely physical-sensible *"Gegenstand"* [1], has troubled him and he was not able to find a univocal solution. The argument summarized above is the continuation of a previous reasoning which led to the conclusion that the question concerning the principle of being of a thing refers to the cause of its matter. And ARISTOTLE says that this cause is the form and that this form is substance. This solution contradicts the immediately following argument that the cause of individual being must be the whole of the composite and that this whole is substance. For it cannot be doubted that the form of a natural composite cannot be the whole of the latter. In addition it cannot be a substance in the metaphysical sense because the form of a composite needs matter for its realization.

Since JAEGER's genetic analysis of the *Metaphysics* it is not difficult to explain this contradiction. In the *Urmetaphysik* the *οὐσία* as a *Gegenstand* of metaphysical research was still conceived in a transcendent sense. This original conception is most clearly revealed in Book *K* (1—8), which therefore was erroneously considéred by NATORP as non-authentic. This was also

---

[1] In his splendid analysis of the *Metaphysics,* WERNER JAEGER (*Aristoteles* p. 171 ff) has convincingly demonstrated that in the original project (the '*Urmetaphysik*'), to which belong the Books *A—E,* 2 before their later revision, the problem concerning the sensible substance could not yet appear, since here the *οὐσία* is still conceived in the Platonic transcendent sense. The Books *Z, H* and *Θ* (V, VI en VII) in which ARISTOTLE explains his conception of primary substance, belong to the later period characterized by the definitive break with the Platonic separation between the sensible world and the intelligible world of the *οὐσίαι.* We shall return to this point in the text.

the conception lying at the foundation of the first five Books, before their partial revision by which they were adapted to the new view developed in the later inserted Books *Z*, *H*. and *Θ*, concerning the primary substance [1]. The transcendent unchangeable *οὐσία* was conceived as the Unmoved Mover, not in the sense of the Platonic *eidè*, and so the original metaphysics was nothing but a philosophical theology. This appears from Book *A* which in this respect completely reproduces the view of the earlier writing *Περὶ Φιλοσοφίας*. But the Platonic *χωρισμός* between the intelligible *οὐσίαι* and the sensible and changeable things was still sharply maintained. This implied that the theoretical research of the latter was viewed as the task of physics alone.

But since the introduction of the metaphysical concept of primary (sensible) substance it was necessary to delimit the metaphysical view of the changeable things from the physical field of inquiry. This is done by stating that the task of physics as to the sensible substances is restricted to the investigation of their matter, whereas the consideration of the forms and the actual being is reserved to metaphysics [2]. Therefore it was necessary to introduce also the forms of the natural composites as *οὐσίαι* (substances) in addition to the actual whole and the *eidos*. This was done in Book *E*, 8. Here ARISTOTLE explains the different meanings of *οὐσία*: '*Οὐσίαι* are called the elementary bodies as earth, fire, water and the like, as well as bodies in general and the living beings consisting of them and the demons inclusive of their parts. All this, however, is called substance, because it is not predicated of a subject but conversely it is the subject of which something is predicated.

'In a different sense one calls substance that which is inherent in a thing that is not predicated of a subject, and is the cause of its being, such as the soul in an animal.

'Furthermore one calls substance the parts of substances which limit the latter and indicate a "this" whose elimination results in the elimination of the whole, such as the planes of a body, as some people say, and the planes with the line. And in general some thinkers suppose the numbers are substances in this sense,

---

[1] As a connective link is to be considered the later inserted second chapter of book *E*, in which the different meanings of being are explained.

[2] *Met.* VII, 11, 1037 a 20 sqq.: *εἴρηται ... ἐν μὲν τῇ μεθόδῳ τῇ τῶν φυσικῶν περὶ τῆς ὕλης, ὕστερον δε περὶ τῆς κατ' ἐνέργειαν·* Cf. JAEGER *op. cit.* p. 214.

because after their elimination nothing continues to exist and they limit everything.

'In addition the essence, whose concept is a definition, is also called the substance of the thing concerned.

'So it appears that the term substance is used in two ways: first it is understood as the ultimate subject that is not predicated of an other subject, secondly it is understood as that which is a "this" and separate; such, however, is the shape and form of a thing'.

Thus the qualification of the forms of natural composites, as substances in the sense of the (formal) causes of their being, was introduced in close connection with the new concept of primary substance. But the elevation of these forms to the rank of *οὐσίαι* contradicted the Aristotelian view that these forms cannot have an independent being. Only the deity and the pure spirits are conceived of as actual forms without any matter. Therefore they satisfy the metaphysical conception of substance.

The introduction of the forms of natural composites as *οὐσίαι* has caused a general confusion in ARISTOTLE's arguments, especially in the 7th Book of the *Metaphysics*. In the 11th chapter of this book the soul is even called *πρώτη οὐσία* (primary substance). Here (1037 a 8 sqq) we read: 'One sees, however, also that the soul is a primary substance, the body matter, whereas man is the composite of soul and body, viewed as the general characteristics of its essence'.

From all this it will appear that the definition of a primary substance, as the actual whole of a natural composite different from its matter and form, implied an impasse.

This actual whole is supposed to unite the antagonistic principles of matter and form into a radical and absolute unity. But such a unity was excluded by the very basic motive of Greek thought. Even the general metaphysical basic concept of being was affected by the intrinsic dualism of this religious motive. The new concept of primary substance as an actual whole of form and matter could not appeal to a higher principle transcending the dialectical basic antithesis.

Is the primary substance to be interpreted as a structure of being? The view of MICHAEL MARLET.

In his important book *Grundlinien der Kalvinistischen Philosophie des Gesetzidee* [1] MICHAEL MARLET has suggested that the

[1] *Op. cit.* p. 112 ff.

Aristotelian-Thomistic substance-concept may be interpreted in the sense of a structure of being. He acknowledges that in Aristotelian metaphysics this concept has been over-estimated and has played the rôle of an absolute centre of individual reality *(Wirklichkeitszentrum)*.[1] This was due to the fact that the Greek philosopher lacked the Christian idea of creation. And so the conception of substance as a structure of individuality, as it is understood in the philosophy of the cosmonomic Idea, was almost completely lacking in the original Aristotelian view. In the Thomistic version, however, the idea of primary substance should be understood exactly in this structural sense.

Starting from AUGUST BRUNNER's interpretation, mentioned above, MARLET thinks that the only concern of THOMAS is to explain that an individual thing presupposes a structure which embraces both substance and accidents as structural principles. In virtue of its substantial principle the individual thing must have a being in itself *(esse in se, subsistere)*. And this principle has also the rôle of substance, in the sense of *substratum* in virtue of which the individual being is in the condition of potentiality with respect to further accidental determinations.

Granted that this interpretation of the Thomistic conception is correct, I cannot see that it contains a real solution of the crucial problem implied in the metaphysical concept of primary substance. This problem is not the relation between the latter and its accidental properties but rather that concerning the deeper unity of the irreducible ontical principles of form and matter.

As to the essence of primary substance THOMAS clearly explains that it is nothing but a composite of matter and form and that only the latter is the cause of its being, whereas the specific matter of the composite (*materia signata*) is the principle of its individuality[2]. This view does not add any essential moment to

---

[1] *Ibid.* p. 112. As to this view of the Aristotelian concept ot primary substance, which agrees with my interpretation, MARLET refers also to S. MANSION: *La première doctrine de la substance* (Rev. néoscolastique 44 (1946) p. 363.

[2] *De ente et essentia* cap. 2: 'Relinquitur ergo quod nomen *Essentiae*, in substantiis compositis, significat illud quod est ex materia et forma compositum... Unde oportet ut essentia, qua res denominatur ens, non tantum sit forma nec tantum materia, sed utrumque, quamvis huiusmodi esse sive essentiae sola forma suo modo sit causa... Sed, quia individuationis principium est materia, ex hoc forte videtur sequi quod essentia, quae complectitur in se simul materiam et formam, sit tantum particularis et

the Aristotelian conception of *primary* substance as an individual whole. And it is not able to explain what this ultimate unity of form and matter may be.

That it cannot be a real *structure* of individuality appears from the fact that the *principium individuationis* is sought in "matter" alone; in the Thomistic version — according to the most plausible interpretation of THOMAS' view — matter is here taken in the sense of '*materia quantitate signata*'. This accentuates the dialectical tension between form and matter in the concept of primary substance to a still higher degree, since the substantial form, as such, lacks any individuality and can receive from matter only a *quantitative* individualization. We have shown in an earlier context [1] that this means a fundamental depreciation of individuality, since in the Aristotelian view matter is the principle of imperfection.

THOMAS accepted the Aristotelian view of the *principium individuationis*. At the same time he accepted the Augustinian conception that in the Divine Logos there are creative Ideas of individual beings as St. Peter, St. John, *etc*. But this Augustinian view contradicted the Aristotelian conception of individuality and could not be accommodated to the latter. This caused insoluble antinomies in the Thomistic explanation of the individual immortality of the human soul, which I have demonstrated in detail in my treatise on the *Idea of the Structure of Individuality and the Thomistic Substance-concept* in the Review, *Philosophia Reformata* [2].

In the Aristotelian-Thomistic doctrine of being the dialectical dualism between the principles of form and matter even penetrates the metaphysical explanation of the categories. The categories of quantity are ascribed exclusively to matter. So the conception of *materia quantitate signata* as the origin of individuality must result in precluding any real structural and integral view of the temporal individual things. If *matter* is the *principium individuationis*, the metaphysical-logical idea of the whole cannot be a real idea of the structure of individuality. And so we can only conclude that the Aristotelian concept of primary substance has nothing to do with the naïve conception of indivi-

---

non universalis. Et ideo sciendum est quod materia non quomodolibet accepta est principium individuationis, sed solum materia signata'.

[1] Vol. II pp. 417 ff.

[2] Phil. Ref. 8 (1943) p. 65—99; 9 (1944) p. 1—41; 10 (1945) p. 25—48 en 11 (1946) p. 22—52.

dual things notwithstanding its deceitful resemblance to the latter.

From the very beginning of Greek speculative thinking, there existed a fatal tendency to confuse the metaphysical concept of substance with the concept of a thing (*Ding-Begriff*). But in ARISTOTLE this confusion received its explicit formulation and it has persisted to the present day. The modern conflict between the concept of function and the concept of substance has thus become a meaningless alternative between a theoretical concept of function and the concept of a thing. And this struggle is carried on as if the concept of substance explained the essence of our naïve experience of things!

BERTRAND RUSSELL's identification of substance and the thing of naïve experience.

This fundamental confusion may be illustrated by BERTRAND RUSSELL's explanation of the concept of substance in his book *The Analysis of Matter*[1].

According to RUSSELL substance is a category which is natural to common sense, although without the attribute of indestructibility added by the metaphysicians. Substance, whether indestructible or not, is of great importance in primitive thought, and dominates syntax, through which it has dominated philosophy down to our own day. At a primitive stage there is no distinction between "substance" and "thing"; both express, first in language and then in thought, the emotion of recognition. To an infant, recognition is a very strong emotion, particularly when connected with something agreeable or disagreeable. When the infant begins to use words, it applies the same word to percepts on two occasions, if the second rouses the emotion of recognition associated with the memory of the first, or perhaps merely with the word which was learnt in the presence of the first. Using a given word as a response to stimuli of a certain kind, is a motor habit, like reaching for the bottle. Two percepts to which the same word applies are thought to be identical, unless both can be present at once: this characteristic distinguishes general names from proper names. The basis of this whole process is the emotion of recognition. When the process, as a learning of motor habits, is complete, and reflection upon it begins, identity of name is taken to indicate identity of substance — in one sense in the case of proper names, in another sense in the case of

[1] *The Analysis of Matter* (London, New York, 1927) pp. 151 ff.

names applicable to two or more simultaneous percepts — *i.e.* general names (Platonic ideas, universals). A substance or thing is supposed to be identical at different times, although its properties may change. The conception of substantial identity is embedded in language, in common sense, and in metaphysics.

According to RUSSELL this is useful in practice but harmful in theory. It is harmful if taken as metaphysically ultimate: what appears as one substance with changing states should be conceived as a series of physical occurrences linked together in some important way. This conception is based on the general theory of relativity. This means that in RUSSELL's philosophical view of the world the whole problem concerning the structure of individuality of things and events, as they are experienced in the pre-theoretical attitude of human mind, has been eliminated. The structure of empirical reality is considered from the functional viewpoint of modern physics alone.

But how is it possible that RUSSELL thinks the naïve conception of things has been conquered by the evolution of modern physics? The reason is that to him these things are identical with the metaphysical view of destructible substances as found in ARISTOTLE's conception of the primary *οὐσία*. Apparently RUSSELL sees no fundamental difference between this conception of substance and that of the persistent material units of classical mechanistic physics founded by GALLILEO and NEWTON.

We shall show presently that there is an essential difference between these two conceptions and that both are fundamentally opposed to the naïve experience of things. But it is doubtless true that the classical mechanistic view considered the supposed persistent material units as substances filling up the absolute three-dimensional space and that these substances were conceived of as the points of reference for all natural events happening in time.

From the above we can understand why in his criticism of this classical-physical view of substance RUSSELL thinks he hits both the metaphysical substance-concept and the naïve concept of a thing. Both may have seemed to be plausible at an earlier stage of physics, when time and space were considered separately. But since the introduction of time as the fourth dimension of world-space they have lost any verifiable meaning: 'The conception of one unit of matter — say one electron — as a

---

[1] *Op. cit.* p. 248.

"substance", *i.e.* a single simple entity persisting through time, is not one which we are justified in adopting, since we have no evidence whatever as to whether it is true or false. We define a single material unit as a "causal line", *i.e.* as a series of events connected with each other by an intrinsic differential causal law which determines first-order changes, leaving second-order changes to be determined by extrinsic causal laws. (In this we are for the moment ignoring quantum phenomena). If there are light-quanta, these will more or less fulfil this definition of matter, and we shall have returned to a corpuscular theory of light; but this is at present an open question. *The whole conception of matter is less fundamental to physics than it used to be, since energy has more and more taken its place.*' (Italics are mine.)

In order to link also the curious facts of interval and quantum into this functionalistic total view of empirical reality RUSSELL suggests that the world consists of steady events, accompanied by rhythms, like a long note on the violin while arpeggios are played on the piano, or of rhythms alone. Steady events are of various sorts, and many sorts have their appropriate rhythmic accompaniments. Quantum changes are supposed to consist of "transitions", *i.e.* of the substitution, suddenly, of one rhythm for another. When two events have a time-like interval, if space-time is discrete, this interval is the greatest number of transitions on any causal route leading from the one event to the other. The definition of space-like intervals is derived from that of time-like intervals. The whole process of nature may, so far as present evidence goes, be conceived as discontinuous; even the periodic rhythms may consist of a finite number of events per period. The periodic rhythms are required in order to give an account of the quantum principle. A percept, at any rate when it is visual, will be a steady event, or system of steady events, following upon a transition.

'Percepts are the only part of the physical world that we know otherwise than abstractly. As regards the world in general, both physical and mental, everything that we know of its intrinsic character is derived from the mental side, and almost everything that we know of its causal laws is derived from the physical side. *But from the standpoint of philosophy the distinction between physical and mental is superficial and unreal*' [1].

---

[1] *Op. cit.* p. 402.

RUSSELL's concept of an event. RUSSELL's debate with WHITEHEAD.

The final statement of this quotation, which I have italicized, is only understandable from RUSSELL's concept of events which is supposed to be "metaphysically neutral", *i.e.* neutral with reference to the distinction between material and mental occurrences. Both, "matter" and "mind" are conceived of as logical structures of relations between events. RUSSELL's concept of logical structure will be considered presently. Provisionally we shall exclusively pay attention to his view of events.

Whereas WHITEHEAD, his collaborator in the *Principia Mathematica,* distinguishes between events, as the dynamical elements of the universe, and the permanent "objects" which, in contradistinction to the former, return in the perceptions as identical with themselves [1], RUSSELL ignores this distinction. With him the relatively permanent and identical element in the objects of perception is represented by what he calls "steady events". As events in a primary sense are regarded the percepts whose objective contents are completely abstracted from the subject-object relation, and in a secondary sense also what may be logically derived from the latter, *viz.* the physical, not directly perceptible events.

The physical object to be inferred from perception is a group of events, rather than a single "thing". Percepts are always events, and common sense is rash when it refers them to "things" with changing states. RUSSELL thinks the connection between physics and perception can throw a surprising light on the *notion of substance. According to him, there is, therefore,* every reason, from the standpoint of perception, to desire an interpretation of physics which dispenses with permanent substance [2].

WHITEHEAD is of the opinion that the different events which constitute a group — whether those which make up a physical object at one time or those which make up the "history" of a physical object — are not *logically* self-subsistent, but are mere "aspects", implying other "aspects" in some sense which is not merely causal or inductively derived from observed correlations. RUSSELL thinks this view is perhaps nearer to common sense than his own conception. But he considers it impossible on purely logical grounds, and empirically useless. As to the latter

---

[1] Cf. for instance his book *Process and Reality* (1929).

[1] *Op. cit.* p. 247.

point his argument is as follows: Given a group of events, the evidence that they are "aspects" of one "thing" must be inductive evidence derived from perception, and must be exactly the same as the evidence upon which we have relied in collecting them into causal groups. The supposed logical implications, if they exist, cannot be discovered by logic, but only by observation; no one, by mere reasoning, could avoid being deceived by the three-card trick. Moreover, in calling two events "aspects" of one "thing", we imply that their likeness is more important than their difference; but for science both are facts, and of exactly the same importance. One may say that the theory of relativity has grown up by paying attention to small differences between "aspects". So RUSSELL concludes that the "thing" with "aspects" 'is as useless as permanent substance, and represents an inference which is as unwarrantable as it is unnecessary'.

RUSSELL's identification of naïve experience with the ontological theory of naïve realism.

We must notice that this Russellean view of substance and thing is dependent on the fundamental misconception already encountered in the first explanation of our transcendental critique of theoretical thought and to be considered in more detail presently. We mean the identification of naïve experience with the ontological theory of naïve realism and the lack of insight into the essential difference between the antithetical "*Gegenstand-relation*" of theoretical thought and the subject-object relation of the pre-theoretical conception of reality. The real datum of naïve experience is reduced to the theoretical abstraction of objective sense-impressions. So RUSSELL does not observe the pitfall hidden in the supposed epistemological and natural scientific "refutation" of naïve experience. He thinks that for common sense (identified with naïve experience) the *percepts* are identical when two people see the sun, whereas for the causal theory of perception they are only similar and related by a common causal origin. Starting from this sensualistic theoretical misunderstanding of the pre-theoretical experience of reality he continues: 'It would be a waste of time to recapitulate the arguments against the common-sense view. They are numerous and obvious, and generally admitted. The laws of perspective may serve as an illustration: where one man sees a circle, another sees an ellipse, and so on. These differences are not due to anything "mental", since they appear equally in photographs from different points of view. Common sense thus becomes involved in contradictions. These do not exist for solipsism, but that is a desperate remedy. The alternative is the causal theory of perception'[1].

The causal theory of perception seems thus to be clearly opposed to the common-sense view, and the "naïve realism" of the latter should be replaced by the former: 'it appears that the world of each person is partly private and partly common. In the part which is common, there is found to be not identity, but only a greater or less degree of similarity, between the percepts of different people. It is the absence of identity which makes us reject the naïve realism of common sense; it is the similarity which makes us accept the theory of a common origin for similar simultaneous perceptions'[2]. But if naïve experience is to be interpreted as a naïve realistic theory, its opposition to a causal theory of perception cannot be fundamental. So we are not surprised by the fact that immediately after the last quoted statement RUSSELL remarks that the inference made in the causal theory from what is experienced to what can never be experienced is made plausible by the strength of "the common-sense arguments for an external cause of perception"!'

As to RUSSELL's criticism of the substance-concept of classical mechanistic physics I can completely agree with his argument that this concept has become useless since the older mechanistic conception of matter appeared to be untenable[3]. The constants of modern physics have indeed nothing to do with the rigid "material units" which in NEWTON's system were assumed as the ultimate substantial points of reference for all natural events. We may establish that this conception of substance lay at the foundation of the whole mechanistic view of reality, construed according to the classical Humanistic science-ideal. The main point, however, is that, just as the Aristotelian idea of primary *οὐσία*, it was fundamentally different from the naïve concept of a thing. The same thing may be said with respect to the substance-concept in modern biological theory which has only caused a fundamental confusion in the scientific manner of posing prob-

---

[1] *Op. cit.* p. 198.
[2] *Op. cit.* p. 207.
[3] This is also the opinion of BERNARD BAVINK *Ergebnisse und Probleme der Naturwissenschaften* (9th ed. 1948), pp. 210 ff.

lems. In the third part of this volume [1] I shall show this in detail with regard to DRIESCH's concepts of entelechy and "psychoid", and WOLTERECK's hypothesis of a substantial "matrix" of "living matter".

Therefore we may conclude that RUSSELL's confusion between the pre-scientific thing-concept and the essentially metaphysical concept of substance testifies to a fundamental misinterpretation of naïve experience.

RUSSELL's logical mathematical concept of structure.

The idea of a logical structure of relations between events by which RUSSELL wants to replace both the concept of a thing and that of substance is an extremely functionalistic construction. For this idea of structure is no other than that which was laid at the foundation of a general kind of arithmetic in RUSSELL's and WHITEHEAD's *Principia Mathematica* (Vol. II, part IV). It was identified with the notion "relation-number" and defined as "the class of all relations similar to the given relation". When two relations have the same structure (or relation-number), thus RUSSELL argues, all their logical properties are identical. Logical properties include all those which can be expressed in mathematical terms.

The inferences from perception to physics, made in the causal theory, depend mainly upon the assumption of a certain similarity of structure between cause and effect where both are complex. Moreover, they are concerned mainly, if not exclusively, with logical properties. From this point of view RUSSELL thinks psychological time of perception may be identified with physical time. For neither is a datum, but each is derived from data by inferences which allow us to know only the logical or mathematical properties of what we infer. The conclusion is that, wherever we infer from perceptions, it is only structure that we can validly infer; and structure is what can be expressed by mathematical logic, which includes mathematics [2]. The only restrictions RUSSELL makes with respect to the similarity of structure between percepts and the groups of events constituting physical "objects" is that the relations which are nearer an "object" to those which are further from it are many-one, not one-one.

---

[1] Cf. also my treatise *Het Substantiebegrip in de Moderne Natuurphilosophie en de Theorie van het Enkaptisch Structuurgeheel* (Phil. Ref. 15th Year, p. 66—139).

[2] *Op. cit.* p. 254.

If we are observing a man half a mile away, his appearance is not changed if he frowns, whereas it is changed for a man observing him from a distance of three feet. It is obvious as a matter of logic that, if our correlating relation S is many-one, not one-one, logical inference in the sense in which S goes is just as feasible as before, but logical inference in the opposite sense is more difficult. That is why we assume that differing percepts need not have exactly similar stimuli. If we have xSx^1 and ySy^1, where S is many-one, and if y and y^1 differ, we can infer that x and x^1 differ; but if y and y^1 do not differ, we cannot infer that x and x^1 do not differ. We find often that indistinguishable percepts are followed by different effects — *e.g.*, one glass of water causes typhoid and another does not. In such cases we assume imperceptible differences — which the microscope may render perceptible. But where there is no discoverable difference in the effects, we can still not be sure there is not a difference in the stimuli which may become relevant at some later stage.

When the relation S is many-one, RUSSELL calls the two systems which it correlates "semi-similar". This consideration makes all physical inference more or less precarious. We can construct theories which fit the known facts, but we can never be sure that other theories would not fit them equally well.

All this may suffice to give a clear idea of RUSSELL's functionalistic view of empirical reality; it has no room for the things of naïve experience because the typical and integral structures of individuality lying at the foundation of this experience have been replaced by mathematical-logical relation-numbers. WHITEHEAD's idea of a thing with different aspects is rejected from the functionalistic viewpoint saying that it lacks the foundation of an inductive evidence derived from perception and which is exactly the same as the evidence upon which we have relied in collecting the given "events" into causal groups.

When, however, the act of perception, as a real event, has itself different modal aspects, this whole argument appears to rest upon a *petitio principii*. We should not be led astray by the apparent modesty which masks this prejudice. RUSSELL says that there is no theoretical reason why a light-wave should not consist of groups of occurrences, each containing a member more or less analogous to a minute part of a visual percept. 'We cannot perceive a light-wave, since the interposition of an eye and brain stops it. We know, therefore, only its abstract mathematical properties. To assert that the material *must* be very different from percepts is to assume that we know a great deal more than we do in fact know of the intrinsic character of physical events... The gulf between percepts and physics is not a gulf as regards intrinsic quality, for we know nothing of the intrinsic quality of the physical world, and therefore do not know whether it is, or is not, very different from that of percepts'.

Real scientific modesty, however, should begin with a clear distinction between theoretical abstractions and the integral structures of human experience. The attempt to reduce the latter to the former is no real scientific modesty. On the contrary, it testifies to a hidden *hybris,* which replaces the real data by abstract "elements" of a so-called physico-psychical world which may be controlled by mathematical and natural-scientific thought, and identifies this theoretical construction with the whole of empirical reality.

The fundamental difference between the Aristotelian-scholastic and the modern Humanistic concept of substance.

The mathematical-logical concept of function is made serviceable to a methodical obliteration of the modal and the plastic horizon of human experience. We have granted that the modern development of natural science must lead to an abandonment of the substance-concept as it was conceived in classical physics. But this was only possible because this latter notion — in sharp contrast with the things of naïve experience — was itself of a theoretical origin. And we should not forget that since the rise of the classical Humanistic science-ideal the concept of substance had assumed a meaning fundamentally different from that ascribed to it in Aristotelian-scholastic metaphysics.

Whereas the Aristotelian idea of primary *οὐσία* was at least intended to account for the structures of individuality as they are realized in the concrete things of human experience, the modern concept of substance was meant to eliminate them. The Humanistic science-ideal in its classical deterministic sense was inspired by the secularized creation-motive, which was incompatible with the form-matter-motive in its original Greek and scholastic sense. It had the clear intention to destroy the world of naïve experience in order to reconstrue reality after the pattern projected by creative mathematical-mechanical thought.

Since DESCARTES the metaphysical concept of material substance is nothing but the hypostatization of the general functional coherence between physical phenomena which can be conceived in mathematical equations giving expression to causal laws. The answer to the question whether in addition to a material substance a mental substance should be accepted was in the last instance dependent on the influence of the practical freedom-motive in pre-Kantian Humanistic metaphysics. In the second part of the first volume we have shown that the development of the Humanistic concept of substance gives an exact expression to the development of the dialectical tensions between the motives of personal freedom and domination of nature.

It was this concept of substance which HUME criticized from a sensationalistic psychological viewpoint. This critique, which to a high degree has influenced RUSSELL, tried to explain this concept as a false hypostatization of functional relations of resemblance and contiguity between successive impressions. These natural associations were supposed to explain also the naïve belief in relatively constant things, a belief which lacks this false theoretical hypostatization and thus, according to HUME, is quite legitimate.

Although HUME acknowledged that naïve experience cannot be a theory of reality, he reduced in this way the integral structures of individuality realized in the things of naïve experience, to a functional coherence between abstracted elements of sensory perceptions. This testified to a psychologistic turn in the Humanistic science-ideal.

The critical concept of substance as a synthetical *a priori* concept of function and the misconception of the naïve experience of a thing as experience of a *"Gegenstand"*.

In order to save the belief in ethical freedom of the human personality KANT's *Critique of Pure Reason* reduced "natural substance" to a transcendental category of experience, limited to sensory phenomena. The practical Idea of substance, on the contrary, became the main-stay of the Humanist *ideal of personality:* the idea of the *autonomous homo noumenon.*

Substance, as a category of relation (*substantia et accidens*), is assumed to be closely connected with both of the other two categories of this class (*causality and interaction*), and as such, to be the universally valid transcendental prerequisite for the experience of natural things. But, in this category of substance, KANT functionalistically misinterpreted our naïve experience of a thing's identity. In a temporal scheme, KANT theorized this experience of identity to the functional substance-concept of classical mathematical physics: the concept of the quantitatively constant matter! In this way the "things" of naïve experience were simply identified with the "*Gegenstände*" of natural scientific thought.

This procedure immediately resulted in the elimination of the datum of naïve experience. In KANT's footsteps the whole critical epistemology considered the transcendental-logical category of substance as the origin of the experience of things.

A quotation from P. H. RITTER's *Schets eener critische Geschiedenis van het Substantiebegrip in de nieuwere Wijsbegeerte* will suffice to characterize this so called critical view: 'sensorial impressions are received by us, but a thing is made by us. We experience the qualities of a thing, but the thing itself is not given in experience; it is put there by us. A thing is a hypothesis; through it we try to supplement what is given and make it intelligible [1]. This hypothetical thing is what is called substance' [2].

§ 2 - THE NAÏVE ATTITUDE TO REALITY AND ITS MISCONCEPTION AS AN "ABBILD-THEORIE" (COPY-THEORY). THE UNTENABILITY OF FUNCTIONALISTIC INTERPRETATIONS.

So it appears that various philosophical speculations attempt to explain away identical thing-hood as it is experienced in the naïve attitude. One theory interprets it in terms of a transcendental formation of sensory material by means of the concept of substance, as a category of relation; another, relates it to a metaphysical concept of substance; a third, considers identical thing-hood as a product of fantasy, a fictitious union of merely associated sensory impressions; a fourth, views it as a constant system of functional relations. To all of these speculative misunderstandings naïve experience implicity takes exception by persisting in its pre-theoretical conception of things, events and social relationships in their integral structures of individuality. It stands to reason that this protest is not theoretically founded. Naïve experience cannot account for it in a philosophical way. But it intuitively rejects every theoretical interpretation that mis-

[1] The writer here follows LAND's *Inleiding tot de Wijsbegeerte*, 123.
[2] *Schets*, p. 9.

understands its data and tries to deprive it of the integral structures of its plastic horizon.

Because it experiences reality in the indivisible meaning-coherence of its modal aspects, common sense intuitively repudiates any attempt to divide its experiential world into theoretically abstracted independent spheres. It takes exception to any idealistic volatilization of essential structural traits of concrete temporal reality, and does not allow the world of things to be reduced to pure sensory phenomena.

In an unsophisticated non-theoretical attitude we experience reality in an indivisible *coherence of cosmic time.* The functionalistic view offered by scientific thought does not satisfy this integral experience any more than the metaphysical concept of substance of speculative philosophy. Both are equally foreign to the naïve view.

Naïve experience is not neutral with respect to the religious position of the I-ness.

Our present comments are valid for all naïve experience. Nevertheless there is a fundamental difference between the Biblical-Christian attitude and the apostate attitude of this experience. This is due to the religious basic motives which are operative in the centre of human existence and which in the temporal horizon determine the direction of the function of faith.

It may be that naïve experience is not liable to an absolutization of theoretical abstractions; but this does not protect it from mythological aberrations when the transcendent religious dimension of the experiential horizon is shut to the light of Divine Word-revelation. This is the case when the religious attitude of the experiencing I-ness is ruled by an apostate basic motive.

In the Biblical attitude of naïve experience the transcendent, religious dimension of its horizon is opened. The light of eternity radiates perspectively through all the temporal dimensions of this horizon and even illuminates seemingly trivial things and events in our sinful world.

In this attitude the experiencing I-ness is necessarily in the I-we relation of the Christian community and in the we-Thou-relation with God, Who has revealed Himself in Christ Jesus. This is why this naïve experiential attitude cannot be uninterested and impersonal.

This should not be misunderstood. It would be an illusion to suppose that a true Christian always displays this Biblical attitude in his pre-theoretical experience. Far from it. Because he is not exempt from the solidarity of the fall into sin, every Christian knows the emptiness of an experience of the temporal world which seems to be shut up in itself. He knows the impersonal attitude of a "Man"[1] in the routine of common life and the dread of nothingness, the meaningless, if the tries to find himself again in a so-called existential isolation. He is acquainted with all this from personal experience, though he does not understand the philosophical analysis of this state of spiritual uprooting in Humanistic existentialism.

But the Christian whose heart is opened to the Divine Word-revelation knows that in this apostate experiential attitude he does not experience temporal things and events as they really are, *i.e.* as meaning pointing beyond and above itself to the true religious centre of meaning and to the true Origin.

And now I must emphatically protest against any attempt to interpret the basic Biblical attitude of experience in the sense of some theological *theory*, which, as such, is irrelevant to naïve experience. In so doing one would only replace an indisputable datum of Christian naïve experience by a theoretical reflection of the Christian which, as such, may be ignored in a purely "objective" description of what is really experienced in the pre-theoretical attitude. Apart from our selfhood naïve experience is no more possible than theoretical thought. Both proceed from the heart, the religious root of our temporal existence. A purely "objective" experience is a contradictio in terminis. And so we may not eliminate a fundamental difference resulting from the central sphere of human consciousness, if we want to do justice to the real data in discussion here.

Does a person of modern culture still have a really naïve experience?

There is, however, a primordial question which we have to consider in order to cut off a misconception with regard to the true meaning of the naïve atitude.

Can we still legitimately speak of naïve experience in modern culture? Has not education deprived us of a truly naïve attitude? Are we not accustomed to certain scientific concepts? Have we not all of us acquired a more or less theoretical disposition in

---

[1] *i.e.* one like many; cf. *Existence and Being* by Martin Heidegger (Vision Press Ltd; London, 1949), p. 45.

our thinking? Is not the naïve attitude of experience a "lost paradise" still inhabited perhaps by children and primitive people, but irrevocably abandoned by civilized adult humanity?

However understandable such questions may be, they betray a lack of insight into the true structural meaning of naïve experience.

It is true that by modern education common thought more or less has been penetrated by concepts which originate from modern science and have found expression in common speech. We have been accustomed to the practical use of elementary arithmetic and geometry, to the use of an abstract chronology; our naïve experience of the starry sky has undergone the historical influence of modern astronomy; we have some idea of natural laws, *etc.*

In general theoretical education varying from elementary instruction to methodical scientific tuition has influenced our mode of thinking and widened our experiential horizon. Nevertheless naïve experience, as such, does not assume the typical theoretical attitude with its abstract *Gegenstand-relation*. Even its concepts which originate from modern science have changed their meaning and assumed a concrete and practical sense. The naïve attitude cannot be destroyed by scientific thought. Its plastic horizon can only be opened and enlarged by the practical results of scientific research. It does not cease to be naïve because it undergoes certain historical formation due to the practical influence of science on social life.

One should not forget that such an influence is not possible unless the results of theoretical research are made accessible to naïve experience. This is to say, they must be integrated into the full plastic horizon of the latter.

To mention only some examples: telegraph, telephone, trains, aviation, the technical application of gas, electricity, and, since the last world-war, also the practical application of atomic energy, belong to the *opened* temporal reality of modern human experience and are not theoretical abstractions. They are now a part of our world's concrete coherence, because they have been *realized* in integral structures of individuality. As long as we conceive them in these concrete structures without theoretical reflection on this integral experience, our attitude toward such things is naïve. It becomes theoretical only when we seek to give it a theoretical explanation. To become familiar with reality opened by modern culture, our experience must undergo a certain forming, but this forming does not affect the naïve attitude, as such.

On seeing an airplane for the first time, a savage does not grasp the concrete reality of this object of culture. The plastic horizon of his experience has not yet been sufficiently disclosed and enlarged. Lacking the necessary formation, he fails to understand it and is unable to experience an airplane as we do. To him it will have a magical character.

The savage's experience would be the same as our own if the really mythological conception were right that our experiential horizon is limited to what is perceptible by the senses. The truth is that both the plastic and the theoretical horizon have their historical aspect. The only difference is that the former is integral and presents reality in typical total-structures of individuality, whereas the latter is bound to the theoretical ἐποχή of cosmic time and to the theoretical *Gegenstand-relation.*

Naïve experience and social praxis. The so-called primitive attitude and the complicated problem of animism.

Naïve experience is doubtless first formed by social praxis. It is, therefore, a fundamental error to seek the pure pattern of this experience in infants who have not yet learned the practical function of things and events in social life. Experience in its proper sense presupposes a sufficient development of the typical act-structure of human existence and a practical acquaintance with the things of common life which is not acquired by animal instinct.

Essential to the pre-theoretical mode of experiencing is the subject-object relation conceived in the integral structures of individuality apart from any theoretical abstraction. This point was already stressed in our first confrontation of the theoretical attitude with the naïve mode of experience.

But is the latter compatible with animistic and magical representations, which are not only met with in primitive cultural areas, but repeatedly reappear in certain popular conceptions among highly cultivated nations? This question is very complicated and cannot be answered so simply as BERTRAND RUSSELL does.

According to him, common sense does not initially distinguish as sharply as civilized nations do between persons, animals, and things. Primitive religion affords abundant evidence of this. A thing, like an animal, has a sort of power residing within it: it may fall on our head, roll over in the wind, and so on. It is only gradually that inanimate objects become sharply separated from people, through the observation that their actions have no purpose. But animals are not separable from people on this ground, and are in fact thought by savages to be much more intelligent than they are [1].

If RUSSELL's opinion were right, it would be incomprehensible that animistic conceptions can reappear in highly civilized people and even in prominent systems of metaphysics. The supposition that in primitive experience the animistic view of things is due to a defective observation of their behaviour does not agree with the fact that primitive men are in general excellent observers in a practical sense.

To avoid a fundamental confusion it will be necessary to distinguish different forms of animism.

Animistic representations may belong to an infantile and consequently pre-experiential phase of human development. Such representations are due to a provisional inability to conceive subject-object relations.

This infantile animism should not be confounded with an animistic mythology ruled by the basic motive of a primitive religion of life, nor with an animistic metaphysics oriented to the transcendental problems of the theoretical *Gegenstand-relation*. The latter has nothing to do with the naïve attitude of experience. The former is indeed related to the aspect of belief in the pre-theoretical attitude. It does not affect the naïve experience in its plastic subject-object relations. It does not prevent a sharp practical distinction between things, plants, animals, and people in the common familiar sphere of social life. In general it does not even imply the ascription of mental and vital qualities to inanimate things [2]. And where this is done, it is restricted to particular things. If this is due to the influence of mana-belief, it is not certain that the mysterious power ascribed to some things is viewed as *vital* power. It might be a residue of pre-animistic belief.

The opinion of LEVY-BRUHL concerning the primitive mind according to which it has nothing in common with ours, except

---

[1] *Op. cit.* p. 151.

[2] Cf. P. S. G. MOELIA: *Het primitieve denken in de moderne wetenschap* 1933) pp. 111 ff.

the sensible impressions of the outer-world, has appeared to be untenable [1].

The truth is that primitive animism, just as the mana-belief, belongs to a mysterious social sphere of experience with which the primitive adolescent is not made acquainted before his initiation as a member of the tribe [2]. It refers only to the mysterious causes of events which especially influence primitive life and whose supposed deeper sense transcends the common sphere of experience. This confirms our statement that the sacral sphere concerns only the *aspect of belief* of the experiential world and does not affect the typical structure of the naïve attitude. So it becomes understandable that primitive animistic and magical conceptions may reappear in the naïve experience of modern Western people as a specific form of superstition.

The reason is that in the naïve attitude even of modern people, the functionalistic natural-scientific concept of causality does not play an intrinsic rôle. The causal question implies rather the problem concerning the final meaning of a concrete event that strikes us in an emotional manner, and that we cannot believe to be a mere accident. Whereas the Christian belief relies on Divine Providence, pagan superstition seeks for super-natural causes in the temporal horizon of experience. It is only due to the fact that such superstition has lost the guiding rôle in modern culture that it no longer prevents the opening of our experiential horizon. For the latter has undergone a cultural formation which far exceeds that of primitive people.

Once again the misinterpretation of naïve experience as a copy theory (*Abbildtheorie*).

If we bear in mind the theoretical interpretations which immanence-philosophy has given to our naïve experience of the identity of a thing, we will not be surprised that from this point of view the typical attitude and structure of this experience have been exposed to the most singular misconceptions. These misconceptions culminate in the opinion that naïve experience is to be considered as a specific theory concerning the relation of our consciousness to reality. This supposed theory is called the "*Abbild*"- or "copy"-theorie of "naïve realism". Accor-

---

1 Cf. Vol. II, pp. 329 ff.

2 Cf. Marg. Mead: *An Investigation of the Thought of Primitive Children, with Special Reference to Animism.* Journ. Royal Anthr. Inst. Vol. LXII (1932), pp. 173 ff.

ding to it our perception furnishes us with an exact image of reality; perceiving is like taking a photo. We have met with this interpretation already in our *Prolegomena.* It reappeared in RUSSELL's explanation of the relation between the concept of a thing and that of substance.

A quotation from WINDELBAND may serve to typify this theorization of naïve experience: 'This most current meaning of truth (*i.e.* as a correspondence between a representation and reality) has no doubt been derived from naïve empirical thought, in which it is related to the representations of things and their activities. This concept of truth pre-supposes a relation to exist between human representations and reality similar to that between a thing and its copy. The representation is related to reality as its *Gegenstand*. Here we have perhaps the most complete expression of the naïve picture of the world, which assumes that the representing mind is placed in a surrounding world, which must in some way repeat itself in this mind' [1].

Widely propagated by the *critical* school, this view makes naïve experience something amazingly contradictory. It is called naïve, which should mean non-theoretical, yet it is alleged to be rooted in an epistemological theory, to be refuted by the "*critical*" analysis of knowledge.

This entire theorization of naïve experience can only result in

---

[1] *Einleitung in die Philosophie* (2e Aufl. 1920) p. 197/8: 'In der Tat ist jene geläufigste Bedeutung der Wahrheit' (namely that truth consists of a correspondence between a representation and reality) 'wohl zuerst aus dem naiven empirischen Denken entnommen und darin auf die Vorstellung von den Dingen und ihren Tätigkeiten bezogen worden. Dieser Wahrheitsbegriff setzt ein Verhältnis der Abbildlichkeit zwischen der menschlichen Vorstellung und der Wirklichkeit voraus, auf die sie sich als auf ihren Gegenstand beziehen soll: wir haben darin vielleicht den vollständigsten Ausdruck der naïven Weltansicht, welche den vorstellenden Geist in einer Umwelt befindlich annimt, die sich in ihm irgendwie wiederholen soll'.

See also *Gesch. der neueren Phil.* (4e Aufl.) 11: 'Der naïve Realismus der gemeinen Denkens... meint, die Dinge spazierten so in den erkennenden Geist hinein, druckten sich in ihm ab, spiegelten sich in ihm...' (The naïve realism of common thought supposes that things, as they really are, enter into the knowing mind, impress themselves in it, are reflected in it...).

Compare also NATORP: *Die logischen Grundlagen der exacten Wissensch.* (2e Aufl. 1921). p. 8, who views the basic error of naïve realism in the assumption 'dasz die Dinge auf dem Wege der Wahrnehmung, als einer Art Abspiegelung der Gegenstände in unserer Vorstellung gegeben sind'. [that things are given in our representation, through observation, as a kind of reflection of the objects...].

a meaningless struggle against something incapable of being combated theoretically.

For the very essence of the naïve attitude appeared to be that in it thinking lacks the theoretical *Gegenstand-relation*. Consciousness is here directed toward full reality; it is systatic [1], and grasps reality as reality offers itself, *i.e.* in a plastic structure.

No matter how constructed, any establishment of a dualism between our functions of consciousness and reality, has nothing to do with naïve experience, but is rather a specific theory.

The conception that the psychical and logical functions of consciousness are opposed, as a kind of sensitive plate, to a closed and self-contained natural reality is foreign to the data of naïve experience.

§ 3 - THE SUPPOSED REFUTATION OF NAIVE EXPERIENCE BY THE RESULTS OF SPECIAL SCIENCES. THE THEORY OF THE SPECIFIC ENERGIES OF SENSE ORGANS.

The opinion that naïve experience, as a primitive form of naïve realism, has been definitively refuted by science, is especially based upon the unreliability of the sensory aspect of perception as to the "objective" states of affairs in reality. "Objective" is meant here in the sense of corresponding to the experimental results of natural science. What appears to lack objectivity in this sense is supposed to be merely subjective sensory appearance.

In earlier epistemological arguments against the "naïve realistic" view an appeal was made especially to the famous distinction between the so-called primary and secondary qualities of things. But even in recent works this appeal can be found. The German philosopher of nature, BERNARD BAVINK, for instance, observed in the 5th ed. of his work *Ergebnisse und Probleme der Naturwissenschaften*: 'The doctrine of the subjectivity of the so-called secondary qualities (sensory qualities such as colours, tones, temperatures, pressure, *etc.*) is pretty well the only thesis about which all philosophers are agreed. The refutations of naïve realism are too obvious not to convince every one who has given them a moment's thought' [2].

How have these convincing refutations of naïve realism been

[1] The reader will remember that this obsolete word is meant to indicate the factual immediacy of our integral experience of reality.

[2] *Ergebnisse und Probleme der Naturwissenschaften* (5e Aufl. 1933) p. 73: 'Die Lehre von der Subjektivität der sog. sekundären Qualitäten

accomplished? Has modern physics delivered the fatal blow, as BAVINK apparently wishes to suggest?[1] Such a suggestion is in itself naïve; physics exists as a result of a process of elimination. To be a special science, it must eliminate from its field of research all non-logical modalities of experience except the mathematical-physical aspects. Objective sense-phenomena are here only important as analogical perceptible objectivations of original physical states of affairs. In this sense they are no more to theoretical physics than symbols referring to the pre-sensory aspect of energy. Sensory colours, for instance, refer to electro-magnetic waves, lying at their foundation. It is not the sensory modality, as such, which concerns physics; but it makes no sense to suppose that electro-magnetic waves of a certain wave-length are sensorily perceptible, if they lack an objective sensory aspect. How then can physics refute naïve experience?

THEODOR HEARING[2] correctly points out that modern physics not only eliminates the secondary qualities of matter, but the so-called primary qualities, as well. And BAVINK himself has stressed the undeniable fact that modern physics has in principle abandoned any visible model of its formulae. Physics was obliged to do so since the physical phenomena appeared not to correspond to the classical mechanistic view. It must restrict itself to a mathematical formulation of the physical functions as such, which lack any sensory character.

The opinion, however, that these abstract mathematical-physical formulae, at least in principle, would exhaust the objective contents of human experience, is no better than a pseudo-scientific mythology.

(Empfindungsqualitäten, wie Farben, Töne, Temperaturen, Drucke usw.) ist seit LOCKE so ziemlich der einzige Satz, über den sich alle Philosophen einig sind, denn die Widerlegungen des naiven Realismus sind zu schlagend, als dass sie nicht einen jeden überzeugen muszten, der einmal darüber nachdenkt'.

In the posthumous 9th ed. (1948) this passage has been left out.

[1] *Op. cit.* 'Es ist gerade der eigentlichste Zweck der Physik, dasz wir uns in ihr von den Beschränktheiten und Irrtümer der direkten Sinneserfahrung losmachen...'. And later on: 'An die Stelle der Töne und der Farben treten Schwingungszahlen, an die Stelle der unmittelbaren Wärmeempfindung tritt die Molekularbewegung usw.' [The most essential purpose of physics is to get rid of the limitations and errors of our direct sense-experiences... The numbers of vibrations replace musical tones and colours, the movements of molecules replace the direct impressions of heat, *etc.*].

[2] *Philosophie der Naturwissenschaft* (1923) pp. 328 ff.

It is simply unscientific to combat the existence of objective sensory qualities in their original modal sense with natural-scientific arguments. This whole criticism of naïve experience lacks a true insight into the modal diversity of subject-object relations. And it misinterprets this experience fundamentally by ignoring the plastic horizon of the structures of individuality. It is doubtless true that in the naïve attitude we accept objective sensory qualities. But we experience them in the concrete context of our plastic horizon. We do not identify them with our subjective sensory impressions; we are always willing to complete or to correct a superficial perception by a more exact observation of the objective sensible image of a thing or an event, if it draws our special attention and if we are not in an emotional condition impeding a quiet verification of our subjective sensations. *But the sensory aspect of perceiving does not at all play that preponderant rôle in naïve experience which the current epistemological opinion ascribes to it.*

In general naïve human perception shows a strongly anticipating character. Especially the symbolical anticipations are important through which the sensory impressions evoke a name designating a thing or event in its typical structure of individual totality.

It is this structure, expressing itself in the sensory image without being itself of a sensory character, which determines the things and events experienced in the naïve attitude. This structure embraces the whole modal horizon of this experience as an implicit component of the plastic horizon. Within the latter there is a great variety in the degrees of clarity in the individual awareness of the experiential world. The relatively small sphere of full clarity is surrounded by a much larger sphere which forms the background of our experience and whose vagueness increases with its distance from the circle of our special attenttion. In the naïve attitude the latter is in principle determined by practical interests. In this whole plastic horizon the sensory subject-object relation has its proper restricted function.

The denial of the objective sensory functions of empirical reality is tantamount to the denial of empirical reality itself.

As to physics, this would mean the destruction of the basis of its experiments. It is true that the objective sensory phenomena can have no other importance for physics than that they present an *analogical* sensory objectivation of original physical states of affairs, which, as such, lack a sensory character. But without their unbreakable coherence with these sensorily perceptible phenomena the energy-functions could not be experienced. It is meaning-less to say that the latter cannot be experienced because we do not know *what* they are. As *modal* functions they do not correspond to a *what*, but to a *how*, a *modus quo*. And this *modal* sense belongs to the horizon of our experience.

The *what* is always determined by structures of individuality which exceed the boundaries of a single aspect.

The theory of the specific energies of the sense-organs.

The arguments against the existence of objective sensory qualities have acquired a seemingly more solid basis in the physiology of the sense-organs. By his doctrine of the specific sense-energies JOHANNES MÜLLER transformed LOCKE'S doctrine of the subjectivity of the so-called secondary qualities into a physiological theory. And, not long ago, as ALOIS RIEHL observes [1], this theory was fervently believed in physiology.

MÜLLER assumes that the nerves of our sense organs are endowed with innate, inherent energies. The optic nerve, for instance, has within itself the energies of light, darkness, and colour. It does not enable us to see because the retina comes into contact with something physically called "light". Light is not the first and chief impulse that gives birth to sense impressions of light and colour. 'If set vibrating by sonic waves the retina would only give an impression of light, and the auditory nerve would only produce sound, if it were accessible to physical light' [2].

The sensations received from the "things of the external world" do not present the properties of the things themselves. What they show rather are the real qualities of our senses: 'It is quite immaterial what kind of stimuli affect the sense-organs, their operation is always in conformity with the particular energies of the senses: the nerve-core gives itself light here, causes itself to sound there, here it feels itself, there it smells itself and tastes itself' [3].

In short, the "law of the specific energies of the sense organs"

---

1 *Der Philosophische Kritizismus* II (2e Aufl. 1925) p. 66. I borrow the following summary of this theory from RIEHL.

2 'Schwingend vielmehr wurde die Netzhaut nur leuchten, der Hörnerv, wenn er dem physikalischen Lichte zugänglich wäre, nur tönen'.

3 'Es ist ganz gleichgültig von welcher Art die Reize auf den Sinn sind, ihre Wirkung erfolgt immer in den Energien der Sinne. Das Nerven-mark leuchtet hier sich selbst, dort tönt es sich selbst, hier fühlt es sich selbst, dort riecht und schmeckt es sich'.

affirms that external stimuli do not influence the nature of our sensory impressions. To substantiate this contention MÜLLER appeals to the well-known fact that sensory impressions may originate without an adequate or specific stimulus. And, therefore, he concludes that they do not need an adequate external cause, but can be obtained by having a sensation of the conditions of the nerves of our sense-organs without any external cause.

Here we are first confronted with the question what is meant by "external causes". If the latter are taken in a physical sense, I can agree with the thesis that such causes can never have sensory effects. It makes no sense to assume that the impression of sensory colours is caused by light-waves *in their abstract physical aspect*. If light-waves are taken as real events in an empirical sense, they must have an objective sensory modality, and then cause and effect are to be conceived in the *sensory* subject-object relation.

MÜLLER, however, means the term "external causes" in the sense of biotical stimuli originating from light-waves, sonical waves *etc., i.e.* as biotical causes which themselves are caused by external events, physically called electro-magnetic waves. Indeed, biotical stimuli excercised on the nerves of the sense-organs can no more be caused by the external events concerned, if the latter lack an objective biotical aspect. And biotical stimuli, as such, cannot cause sensory psychical impressions, if the term "biotical" is taken in a non-psychical sense. This is to say, it is necessary from a scientific point of view to distinguish the different modal aspects of the causal problem if we want to escape a pseudo-scientific mystification.

We do not explain anything when we assume a causal relation between events *which are viewed under different modal aspects.*

This holds good also with respect to MÜLLER's own theory which considers the specific energy of our sense-organs as the first and chief cause of our sensory impressions. In what sense is the term "energy" meant here? If the latter were to be understood in a functional physical sense, the whole theory would be a mystification.

But in general physiologists are not very exact in their terminology. They speak the language of materialism and often their manner of posing problems betrays indeed a materialistic view of empirical reality. MÜLLER, for instance, says that the optic nerve "sees".

For the present I will not dwell further on this singular terminology. Let us assume that the sense-organs are viewed in their typical structure of an individual whole, in which the different modal functions within the general cadre of their own law-spheres are kept in mutual correspondence by the typical structural principle of totality. Let us leave alone for a moment the fact that these organs can exercise their specific sensory-psychical functions only within the context of the typical structural whole of the body; and also that the latter, if it is human, is extremely complicated and also embraces a typical act-structure referring to a central I-ness.

We may then interpret MÜLLER's theory in this sense that, owing to their typical total structure, the sense-organs answer a biotical stimulus with the production of a typical sensory impression, which is independent of the specific nature of the stimulus and determined by the specific nature of the sense-organ alone. We have to investigate if this view has a sufficient ground in the facts alleged.

The problem of the so-called inadequate stimulus.

LOTZE and E. H. WEBER have already ascertained that there is no conclusive proof supporting MÜLLER's theory. They have sought an objective explanation of the inadequate stimulus, and, in most instances, they have succeeded in showing that the latter is only seemingly inadequate (*e.g.*, the stimulation of the taste nerves by galvanic stream causes, by an electrolitic process, a simultaneous stimulus which furnishes a stimulus adequate to produce the experienced sensation of taste).

The rareness of the occurrence of really inadequate stimuli in comparison with the normal cases has been pointed out by WEINMANN. Unless produced artificially, inadequate stimuli appear to be the result of a chance event, a violent encroachment (*e.g.*, a blow on the eye), disease or disorder and change in the bodily organs, such as a feeling of cold accompanying fever and high skin temperature.

It is an established methodological principle that one should not abandon an established law because of an apparent exception. The presence of an extraordinary and abnormal case is explainable in terms of unusual conditions.

The main point, however, is that the distinction between adequate and inadequate stimuli pre-supposes the existence of objective sensory qualities, whose perception corresponds to adequate specific stimuli: If MÜLLER*'s theory were right we would never be able to establish inadequate stimuli. And so his view is refuted by the very empirical facts which are supposed to confirm it.*

The occurrence of a really inadequate stimulus proves thus the very contrary of MÜLLER's conclusion that the specific nature of the stimuli is indifferent for the type of sensation experienced. What follows is rather that a specific sensory activity is so strongly and indissolubly accommodated to its homogeneous stimulus that even abnormal interference cannot change the senses' normal pattern of functioning.

A person who is born blind does not experience a phosphene, and someone who becomes blind at an early age does not have visual phantasies in his dreams. This indicates that an adequate stimulus is necessary and indispensable for the normal activity or our sense organs.

Naïve consciousness views the impressions experienced without adequate stimulation as unnatural; and when in possession of healthy sense organs, it does not allow such impressions to lead to false judgments. RIEHL correctly points out that if MÜLLER's theory were true, the bond would be broken between the "objective" and the "subjective world" [1].

The conclusion would be inescapable that objective sensory perception is impossible. One should also consider the untenable consequences of this theory with respect to animal life. Smell and taste play an important rôle in an animal's struggle for survival, but if it be true that all sense organs react in their specific way to each arbitrary stimulus, animals would be unable to survive.

Our experiments with inadequate stimuli are to a high degree limited in their scope. Optic sensations, for instance, can be evoked through mechanical and electrical stimuli from the periphery only; but it has not been proven that light sensations can be produced from the root of the optic nerve. These sensations therefore do not arise independently of the locality of action of the stimuli, as was supposed by MÜLLER.

What remains of MÜLLER's evidence?

According to the physiologist NAGEL, the experiments to which

---

[1] We would rather speak of the internal modal bond between subjective and objective psychical functions and the interfunctional bond between the psychical function and the pre-psychical functions.

MÜLLER can rightly appeal are restricted to those made on the "*chorda tympani*" in the opened tympanic cavity. And RIEHL correctly observes in this connection: 'It is impossible to base a law on one single, unexplained exception... The view held by HELMHOLTZ that physiological experiences have established MÜLLER's law, as far as experiments were possible, cannot be maintained in the face of recent findings in physiology' [1].

The theory of HELMHOLTZ

HELMHOLTZ intended to present a more detailed physiological foundation of MÜLLER's theory, but instead furnished proof that physiology, as such, is not competent to establish the exclusive subjectivity of our sensory impressions of the outer-world. In his famous and much disputed theory of optic and tone sensations, HELMHOLTZ, following TOURTUAL, made a sharp distinction between two kinds of differences between sensory impressions. The first embraces those originating from the specific nature of our sense-organs (*e.g.*, the specific difference between a sensation of sound and a sensation of colour). They are called *differences of modality*. The second kind embraces the differences between sensations of the same sense-organ and are called *qualitative*. There is, *e.g.*, a *qualitative* difference between the sensations red and blue, high tone and low tone. Modality, or modal difference in sensation is exclusively dependent upon the specific energy of the sense organ in question, while its particular quality is also determined by the kind of stimulus received. Thus each physically simple tone of a certain pitch and frequency of vibration causes a simultaneous vibration in only one section of the ground-membrane, composed of a system of cords. The simultaneous vibration arises only in that part of the ground-membrane which is tuned to receive the tone in question, and the nerves related to the part set in vibration receive this vibration as a stimulus. In the same way the pitch of a tone depends upon the nature of physical sound waves; the quality of a sensation of colour depends upon the nature of the light which stimulates the retina.

It is not necessary to follow HELMHOLTZ's theory in further

---

[1] RIEHL, *op. cit.* p. 71: 'Auf eine einzige, noch unerklärte Ausnahme laszt sich kein Gesetz gründen... Die Behauptung von HELMHOLTZ, die physiologische Erfahrung habe, soweit Prüfung möglich war, das Müllersche Gesetz bestätigt, läszt sich den Ergebnissen der neueren Sinnesphysiologie gegenüber nicht aufrechterhalten'.

detail. The summary given above is sufficient to show that it fundamentally limits the validity of MÜLLER's so-called law of the specific energy of sense-organs. According to HELMHOLTZ, the "quality" of sensations is not affected by MÜLLER's law. But the kernel of MÜLLER's theory lies in its very affirmation that stimuli do not in any way influence the generation of sensations. RIEHL correctly goes a step further: if the particular qualities of sensations are co-determined by the nature of the stimulus (as HELMHOLTZ's investigations have demonstrated), then their modality can no more be independent of the latter. We can make a distinction in our thinking between a sensation's modality and its quality, but in reality the modality and quality of a sensation cannot be separated.

Finally, MÜLLER's theory clashes with modern biological conceptions, according to which the sense-organs only gradually become differentiated and adapted to the different stimuli. Especially the anatomical and physiological connections between optic, auditory and tactile organs have been emphasized. Sensations of heat and touch, *e.g.*, are not clearly distinguishable when our perceptive organs are affected by minimal stimuli. In the light of all these modern investigations RIEHL concludes: 'There is a necessary relation between stimulus and sensation. The qualities of sensations are the more fully developed properties of things in the outer world. Consequently common sense is insofar right to follow the compulsory force of the sense-impressions and to have no doubt about their objectivity. Only in this respect is common sense in error that it assumes the exclusive objectivity of sensation. This is inadmissable, because in every product of interaction the nature of the operator as well as that of the reactor makes itself felt'[1].

The misunderstanding in RIEHL's interpretation of naïve experience.

We disagree with RIEHL only on one point. RIEHL's "critical realism" prejudices his judgment and causes him to assert that *common sense or naïve consciousness* sets forth such a "theory" concerning the exclusive objectivity of sensory impressions.

Starting from the metaphysical antithesis between the "world in itself" and the "world as it appears to us", he neglects the pre-theoretical subject-object relation which is essential to naïve

---

[1] *Op. cit.* p. 79.

experience. The latter does not confound the subjective sensory impressions with the objective sensory qualities of the things perceived.

It is aware of the possibility of subjective illusions and subjective inexactness in its perceptions. And it does not ascribe its sensations to "things in themselves". This is exactly what RIEHL imputes to the naïve attitude. This is to say that the latter is again interpreted in terms of an "*Abbild-theorie*", though this misinterpretation does not appear at first sight. RIEHL has not actually penetrated to the objective sensory functions of things [1]. This is why in the last instance he gives a nominalistic interpretation of the relation of our sensory percepts to the things perceived. This may appear from the following quotation: 'Sensations are, of course, signs, if one wants to call them so, and not copies. They are even signs by means of which we express our own bodily nature rather than that of the rest of the physical world, although the latter does not essentially differ from the former. These signs develop with the increasing activity of our senses, and although from the start determined by the viewpoint of our apprehension, they are not arbitrary, but natural signs' [2].

We are here confronted with a distinction, already made by OCCAM, between natural and arbitrary signs. This supposed difference falsifies both the meaning of language and a thing's objective-psychical aspect [3]. Rooted in a conception which opposes reality and consciousness, this form of nominalism shatters the temporal coherence of reality, thereby involving itself in an irreconcilable conflict with the data of naïve experience.

This conflict does not arise because naïve experience holds to a dogmatic "*Abbild-theorie*", requiring the correction of critical realism. It arises, rather, because the simple data of selfcon-

---

[1] He considers the qualities of things to be only physiological reactions.

[2] *Op. cit.* p. 79: 'Die Empfindungen sind also allerdings wenn man sie so nennen will, "Zeichen", nicht Abbilder, sie sind sogar Zeichen, durch die mit der zunehmenden Entwicklung der Empfindungstätigkeit und schon zufolge des Standpunktes unserer Auffassung mehr die Natur unserer eigenen Körperlichkeit, die freilich von der übrigen körperlichen Natur nicht wesentlich verschieden sein kann, zum Ausdruck gelangt, als die Natur der äusseren Dinge selbst. Aber sie sind keine willkürlichen Zeichen, sondern natürliche'.

[3] In the nominalistic theory of OCCAM the objective-logical aspect of a thing is also misinterpreted.

sciousness are no longer intelligible to the hypostatizing attitude of critical realism.

It may be that from a natural-scientific view-point objective sensory phenomena are only "symbols" referring to imperceptible physical relations. But this does not entitle us to deny the real events an objective sensory aspect and to reduce the sensory subject-object relation to a symbolic reference of sensory impressions to a metaphysical "world in itself".

The interpretation of our naïve experiences of a thing by RIEHL, RICKERT and NATORP.

RIEHL *seeks to qualify the 'realism of common sense' in this* way that it takes the representations of outward things for these things themselves, so that it does not distinguish observation from the object of observation [1]. RIEHL's misinterpretation of the meaning of naïve experience is understandable, if we consider that he unquestioningly accepted the "*Satz des Bewusztseins*" or "*Satz der Phänomenalität*", in terms of which he arbitrarily interpreted the attitude of "common sense".

It is, however, this very thesis with its critical realistic counterpart, the assumption of a formally knowable "world in itself", which is irreconcilable with the naïve experiential attitude. This should call a halt to such an epistemology. Naïve experience cannot be rightly understood from the view-point of a representational phenomenalism. Critical realism fails to recognize that synthetical thought pre-supposes *enstatic-systatic* [2] thought, with which it should never come into conflict.

Our naïve experience does not teach us to believe in metaphysical "*Dinge an sich*" [3], existing independently of the functions of our consciousness, so that the latter is onesidedly dependent upon them. The basic tenet of RIEHL's critical realism is that the transcendental synthetic categories of human understanding (taken in the Kantian sense) are accommodated to the forms of a reality in itself, which is opposed to our consciousness. On such a basis, only an abstract formal knowledge of things can be acquired [4]. Because of the very nature of naïve

---

[1] Op. cit. II p. 3: 'die Vorstellungen äuszerer Dinge für die äuszere Dinge selbst nimmt und also Wahrnehmung und Wahrnehmungsgegenstand nicht unterscheidet!

[2] Cf. our explanation Vol. II pp. 468 ff.

[3] RIEHL *op. cit., ib.*

[4] *Op. cit.* p. 26.

experience, it can never be reconciled with this epistemological view of reality.

The pre-theoretical attitude is incompatible both with critical realism and critical idealism, because both fundamentally curtail the integral structure of reality. On the basis of a critical epistemology, rooted in immanence philosophy, RIEHL seeks to arrive at a synthetical construction of the horizon of empirical reality. With him theoretical philosophy [1], therefore, exhausts itself in "science and in a critique of knowledge" [2]. In accordance with KANT, he seeks the unity of self-consciousness in a transcendental logical unity of the cogito, which, as the necessary pre-requisite for all synthesis, determines all experience. Thus, RIEHL involves himself in the same antinomy with respect to the problem of synthesis as did KANT. He also posits the Kantian thesis: 'In the narrow sense of the word there are only laws of nature for the understanding that conceives of nature. It is only the understanding that assumes the permanency and uniformity of the phenomena as a universal premise, and consequently as a law of nature. Talking of the laws of nature outside of the understanding means a lapse into logical anthropomorphism, which is as little founded as teleological anthropomorphism' [3].

It is apparent that from this epistemological viewpoint naïve experience must be misunderstood.

An important moment in RIEHL's conception of the reality of a thing (*Ding-wirklichkeit*).

Although we must fundamentally reject this critical realism, RIEHL is to be credited with a rehabilitation of the sensory aspect of human experience which had been depreciated by KANT. He tries to bridge over the rigid gulf which in the Kantian epistemology separated the world of the "things in themselves" and the world as it appears to us.

According to him, the "things in themselves" undergo an en-

---

[1] RIEHL accepts KANT's distinction between theoretical and practical philosophy.

[2] *Der Phil. Kritizimus* III (2e Aufl. 1926) pp. 15 ff.

[3] *Op. cit.* III p. 43/44: 'Gesetze der Natur in der genaueren Bedeutung des Wortes gibt es sogar nur für den Verstand, der die Natur denkt. Erst der Verstand macht Beständigkeit und Gleichförmigkeit der Erscheinungen zur allgemeinen Prämisse und damit zum Gesetze der Natur und auszer dem Verstande von Gesetzen der Natur reden heiszt in einen logischen Anthropomorphismus verfallen, der nicht weniger grundlos ist als der teleologische.'

richment by the qualities assumed in their sensory appearance. To quote his own words: 'The immediate objects of perception are occasionally called by KANT mere phenomena, depreciated as mere appearances, as if things as such must necessarily mean more than their operations on our senses. If in theoretical philosophy evaluating judgements were to the point, the relation between the value of phenomena and things in themselves would have to be reversed. The phenomenal world, pre-supposing conciousness, is not inferior to things as such; it is rather an enriched kind of reality. The world of things and our consciousness to which they appear, form one totality of reality, which is only supplemented and completed by our "consciousness"'[1].

Important is also RIEHL's view that the attributes of things in the "outer" world and the qualities in our sensations are mutually related as potential to actual reality. Consequently the world of the senses may be said 'to exist only as a process of becoming'[2]. *It is true that* by viewing the sensory qualities of things as nothing but physiological reactions[3] and considering only our subjective sensory consciousness of them as psychical, RIEHL fails to do justice to the essence of their psychical object-function. Nevertheless, he clearly asserts: 'Things and consciousness, to which they appear, form one totality of reality, which is not completed and perfected but by consciousness'[4].

We may object that even this view is not sufficient to conceive the integral horizon of empirical reality. It maintains the metaphysical opposition between a "world in itself" and a "world of phenomena". It assumes that the first is only knowable in terms of mathematical-physical formulae. And the completion and per-

---

[1] *Op. cit.* II p. 18/19: 'Die unmittelbaren Objekte der Wahrnehmung werden von KANT gelegentlich nur Erscheinungen genannt, zu bloszen Erscheinungen "herabgewürdigt", als müszte das Ansich der Dinge notwendig mehr bedeuten als ihre Wirkungen auf unsere Sinne. Eher liesze sich das Wertverhältnis zwischen den Erscheinungen der Dinge und diesen selbst umkehren, wenn in der theoretischen Philosophie Werturteile überhaupt am Platze waren: die Erscheinungswirklichkeit könne, eben weil sei Bewusztsein voraussetzt, nicht als herabgeminderte, sie müsse vielmehr als gesteigerte Wirklichkeit betrachtet werden. Die Dinge und das Bewusztsein, dem sie erscheinen, bilden eine Gesamtheit des Wirklichen, das erst durch das Bewusztsein ergänzt und vollendet wird'.

[2] *Op. cit.* II p. 87: 'dasz sie nur dadurch ist, dasz sie wird'.

[3] *Op. cit.* II p. 80.

[4] 'Die Dinge und das erscheinen, bilden eine Gesamtheit des Wirklichen, das erst durch das Bewusztsein ergänzt und vollendet wird'.

fection of this metaphysical world of "things in themselves" is supposed to be performed by the sensory function of human consciousness alone. The normative aspects of empirical reality are eliminated in accordance with the Kantian dualism between "nature" and "freedom", or theoretical and practical reason.

Nevertheless, notwithstanding all these serious objections, it should be granted that RIEHL has taken a step in the right direction; his view of the relation between the psychical and the prepsychical functions is doubtless better than that of KANT [1].

RICKERT's criticism of "critical realism".

RICKERT is of the opinion that RIEHL's critical realism simply formulates the *problem* of a transcendent being of the objective thing-world. And he objects to this "realism" that it is not warranted to include a problem in the presuppositions of epistemology [2]. Insofar as RIEHL shares RICKERT's epistemological prejudice, this criticism is justified, but when the dogmatism of this prejudice is seen, it loses all of its force. Epistemology is founded in a transcendental Idea of the horizon of human experience and empirical reality. Starting from a functionalistic *"Satz des Bewusztseins"* (RICKERT speaks of a *Satz der Immanenz*) epistemology cannot comprehend its own basic problem of the inter-modal synthesis of meaning. RICKERT's thesis that a *problem* may never be included in the pre-suppositions of epistemology, is equally applicable to his own transcendental-idealistic epistemology, based on the problematic assumption of a transcendental-logical subject of knowledge. This *presupposition* conceals the basic problem of theoretical synthesis, insoluble on the immanence standpoint.

RICKERT's attitude toward naïve experience.

RICKERT's evaluation of naïve experience strengthens our impression that this so-called critical idealism approaches the pre-theoretical attitude with a prejudice which precludes a true understanding. It is true, RICKERT agrees with the view that naïve realism is not an "*Abbildtheorie*" that can be scientifically combated. But the real attitude of "critical Idealism" toward pre-theoretical experience appears from the qualification of the latter as 'a complex of rash and vague opinions, sufficient

[1] Cf. *Op. cit.* II, p. 45.

[2] RICKERT *Der Gegenstand der Erkenntnis (3rd ed. 1915)* p. 28.

in daily life, and which should be left alone in people who only want to live'[1].

This haughty treatment of naïve experience as a "*quantité négligeable*" for epistemology rests on a basic misinterpretation of its meaning. RICKERT thought he did naïve experience justice in his interpretation that 'the component parts of the spatial-temporal world of the senses, so familiar to us all, form the only reality'[2]. The epistemology of transcendental idealism is supposed to disagree with "naïve realism" only by adding the thesis: 'The being of every reality must be viewed as an immanent being, as a being in consciousness, or as an object to which a conscious subject necessarily belongs'[3].

But the truth is that RICKERT approaches naïve experience with a pre-conceived functionalistic schema of empirical reality. Instead of examining the pre-theoretical horizon of experience as it is given, he attempts to construe it according to his own schema.

He does therefore not notice that, in spite of his acknowledgement that naïve experience is no "copy-theory", he does convert it into a theory which identifies the abstract sensory aspect with the integral whole of empirical reality.

I do not forget that in his *System der Philosophie* RICKERT speaks of a pre-theoretical "*Erleben*" of the unity of "value" and "reality", which he wishes to approach theoretically in a subjective-idealistic *Sinn-Begriff*[4] (as a synthesis of "value" and "reality"). But this does not bring him any closer to a correct interpretation of the actual data of naïve experience. What RICKERT calls "naïve realism" is exclusively a *view of empirical reality*. And this "reality" is understood here as the phenomenal world of nature in the Kantian sense. What RICKERT calls "*Erleben*" is not the same as his Kantian conception of experience. But even if we leave this difference alone for a moment and consider the question as to whether his view of "*Erleben*" is acceptable as an adequate interpretation of the

---

[1] 'ein Komplex von undurchdachten und unbestimmten Meinungen, die zum Leben ausreichen, und die man denen, die nur leben wollen, ruhig lassen kann'.

[2] 'dasz die Bestandteile der uns allen vertrauten räumlich-zeitlichen Sinnenwelt die einzige Wirklichkeit bilden'.

[3] *Op. cit.* p. 119: 'Das Sein jeder Wirklichkeit musz als ein immanentes Sein, als ein Sein im Bewusztsein oder als ein Objekt angesehen werden, zu dem notwendig ein bewusztes Subjekt gehört'.

[4] Concept of 'meaning'.

pre-theoretical attitude, the answer must be in the negative. The schema, "value" and "reality", rests (as we have seen in Vol. I pp. 127 ff) upon the metaphysical division of the temporal horizon into a *"noumenon"* and a *"phenomenon"*, thereby theoretically destroying its structural meaning. Naïve experience cannot be approached as a *"begriffloses, irrationelles, und namenloses Erleben"* [1] of a unity between two theoretically construed worlds, corresponding to the dialectical basic-motive of nature and freedom. It lacks neither a logical, nor a linguistic aspect. And it is fundamentally foreign both to RICKERT's idea of reality and to his world of unreal values.

NATORP's view of the naïve experience of a thing as a logical synthesis lacking *"Reinheit"* (purity).

The Marburg school among the neo-Kantians has completely caricatured naïve experience, as a quotation from NATORP will illustrate: 'We hold the conviction so aptly expressed by KANT: Where the understanding has not united anything beforehand, it cannot analyse anything. Consequently, he concludes that in our knowledge synthesis is the first requirement for logical comprehension, and analysis is only significant as its pure reverse. The things given beforehand, insofar as it is in any way meaningful to speak of them, are rather syntheses of a primitive understanding, accomplished beforehand, but far from always in a pure and therefore correct manner' [2].

PLATO said that philosophy begins with wondering. I would like to add that in taking cognizance of NATORP's view of the pre-theoretical conception of things, wondering changes into understanding when the cosmonomic Idea of his philosophical system is discovered. For, one unacquainted with the logicistic cosmonomic Idea of the Marburg school will indeed be amazed at its distorting interpretation of naïve experience. That in this

---

[1] *System der Philosophie* p. 258: 'a conceptless, irrational and nameless experience'.

[2] *Die logischen Grundlagen des exakten Wissenschaften* (2th ed. 1921) p. 9: "wir halten an der Überzeugung fest, der KANT den fast sinnfälligen Ausdruck gegeben hat: 'Wo der *Verstand* zuvor nichts verbunden hat, da kann er auch nichts auflösen'. Also folgert er, sei vielmehr Synthesis für das logische Verständnis des Erkennens notwendig das Erste, die Analysis von Bedeutung nur als deren reine Umkehrung. Die vorausgegebenen Dinge, soweit von solcher zu reden überhaupt Sinn hat, sind vielmehr voraus vollzogene, aber entfernt nicht immer rein und daher nicht immer richtig vollzogene Synthesen eines primitiven Verstandes".

respect NATORP's interpretation even exceeds KANT's is obvious when we remember that for the Marburg school, the "laws of synthesis", at the foundation of analysis, have really only a transcendental-logical meaning.

The naïve experience of a thing is thus lodged in the vestibule of mathematical logicism, and is supposed to be only a "logical synthesis" of a primitive understanding, whose constructions are "far from always pure and consequently not always exact".

This brings to an end our discussion of erroneous views of naïve experience. We must now direct our full attention to the "plastic horizon" in which the latter grasps the extremely interlaced structures of things and their relations. Those of social communities and inter-individual social relations will be treated later on.

CHAPTER II

THE STRUCTURE OF A THING

§ 1 - INTRODUCTION.

Our first problem is: how can we gain theoretical access to the structures in which things present themselves to our naïve experience? We have shown that each theorization of the latter results in a misunderstanding. The very intention to give a satisfactory theoretical account of the naïve experiential attitude, must consequently keep us from theorizing it.

As far as I know, immanence philosophy, including phenomenology, has never analysed the structure of a thing *as given in naïve experience.*

We do not forget that SCHELER in his posthumous treatise *Lehre von den drie Tatsachen* has undertaken an important attempt to explain the different character of natural, specific scientific, and phenomenological experience [1]. As an opponent of KANT's transcendental synthetical *a-priorism,* he agrees with us in his protest against any view that considers natural things in our naïve experience as the products of a theoretical synthesis. Just as we have done, he warns against every imputation of theories to the naïve attitude.

But he fails to offer any positive insight into the plastic horizon of naïve experience. SCHELER only presents a somewhat impressionistic image of the latter, whose difference from the theoretical attitude is indicated in a negative rather than in a positive manner. In any case, he does not explain what a thing of naïve experience actually is.

On the basis of my previous critical sketch of phenomenology [2], I feel justified in saying that SCHELER was unable to penetrate to the actual structure of a thing of our naïve experience. To represent the latter correctly, he would have been obliged to

---

[1] Included in Vol. I of *Schriften aus dem Nachlasz* (1933) p. 329 ff.

[2] Cf. Vol. II pp. 485 ff. and pp. 584 ff.

abandon his immanence point of view and his Idea of cosmic reality, which furnish him an *a-priori* starting-point.

We have already seen how HUSSERL misinterpreted the thing-structure of reality, as one of the "regions of the "material" sphere, *next to* the sphere of functional-sensory *qualities, spatial figures etc.* [1].

We must therefore resume the discussion of the problem: what procedure must be followed to gain the desired theoretical access to the structure of things in naïve experience? Since this access cannot be acquired without theoretical analysis, we must obviously seek a point of contact in the theory of the modal spheres.

We must first see how far we can use the modally defined concept of function, and at what critical point it is insufficient in our present enquiry.

Let us begin with a functional analysis of a natural thing. Take as an example: this budding linden before my window. It is of great methodological importance to point out that by limiting my theoretical attention to this concrete natural thing, I am actually engaged in a theoretical abstraction. In veritable naïve experience, things are not experienced as completely separate entities. This point is ignored or rather denied by SCHELER [2]. It must be emphasized, however, if we are to understand the plastic horizon of reality, and if we are to avoid a naturalistic and atomistic interpretation of the latter. Nevertheless, I will provisionally begin with the abstraction in question. Theoretical analysis ought to proceed from the simple to the complex. It will become apparent in the sequel that the "simple" only occurs in the full complexity of a universal interlacement of structures.

In addition, we should be aware of the fact that what appears to naïve experience as a simple structural whole will appear not

---

[1] Cf. Vol. II pp. 17 ff.

[2] Cf. SCHELER: *Die drei Tatsachen* p. 361: 'Nichts ist gewisser, als dasz natürliche Wahrnemung alle Gegenstände die Sie uns gibt, als einzelne und individuelle Gegenstände gibt'. [There is nothing more certain than the fact that all the objects given in natural observation, are given as singular and individual objects].

But with regard to the direction of our perceptual attention, this statement certainly ascribes to naïve experience a theoretical abstraction which is contradictory to its essence. While intending to give the quintessence of non-theoretical observation, SCHELER has already theorized it.

to be simple at all from a theoretical point of view. Really simple structures are not to be found in the macro-world of human experience. Even in its inner structure of individuality everything in this world shows a more or less complicated interlacement of typical structures. But this is a subject of later examination. For the present we must leave it alone.

The tree before my window undoubtedly has subject-functions in the modal spheres of number, space, motion and energy. In its numerical aspect, it is subject to arithmetical laws; as a spatial figure, it is subject to original spatial laws; as a moving figure and as a mass of energy it is subject to kinematical laws and those of energy, in the original modal sense intended by phoronomy [1] and physics.

But as long as the tree is viewed only in these abstract aspects, it is theoretically meaningless to speak of a linden. Neither does it make sense in this case to appeal to the individualization of the modal functions concerned (explained in Part I ch. VII of the second Volume), in order to discover in them the expression of a typical structure of individuality corresponding to a linden. If within their field of research physics and chemistry meet with typical structures of individuality, such structures will certainly not be those of living things, so long as the biotical aspect of experience is eliminated. Rather they will be typical structures of atoms, molecules, crystals, *etc.* And the modal individuality the latter show within the mathematical and physical aspects, as such, displays nothing that can evoke the idea of a linden.

A fortiori a merely functional viewpoint discloses nothing within the mathematical and physical aspects by which a tree delineates itself as an individual thing, in the general functional coherence within the modal law-spheres concerned. Instead, this functional coherence, guaranteed by the modal meaning-structure of a law sphere, seems completely to absorb the individual functions of the tree as a thing.

A purely mathematical-physical analysis of the latter must necessarily eliminate its typical structure as an individual whole and replace it by a system of interactions between energy-functions. And in this functional system there is no room for a distinction between internal and external processes of energy-

[1] Phoronomy is the purely geometrical theory of motion, also called "kinematics".

exchange with reference to a tree. The ultimate points of reference of the physical system are atoms, electrons, protons, neutrons, deuterons, photons, *etc.*, and electro-magnetic fields and fields of gravitation, which are no "things" in the sense of naïve experience. Chemistry, too, has nothing to do with the structure of the tree as such, as long as it restricts itself to the viewpoint of inorganic and organic chemistry and eliminates the biotical anticipatory sphere of the physical-chemical aspect.

But, when we observe the organic vital aspect of our linden, the situation changes. It is evident that this tree has a central function in the biotical sphere which, no matter whether or not it will appear to have an original or nuclear type of individuality [1], is in any case characteristic of the structure of the individual whole. It is a subject-function which is the ultimate functional point of reference for the internal structural coherence of the tree in the typical groupage of its different modal aspect-functions.

The qualifying function in the structure of a linden.

Because it occupies a central position in its structure, this biotical subject-function may be called the *qualifying* function of the tree. *In no other modal aspect can* we find a modal function capable of qualifying a linden as a structural whole. And, it is also important to notice that this qualifying biotical function is the last subject-function of the tree's temporal structure.

Does this mean that the temporal reality of our linden is completed in the biotical modality? If such were the case we would indeed be confronted with an individual *"Ding an sich"* in its metaphysical sense, or to be more exact, the tree would not at all exist "for us". A thing existing in a pre-psychical modal isolation would be excluded from the inter-modal temporal coherence of meaning, necessary for human experience.

The impossibility of terminating the reality of an individual thing in a specific modality. The typically qualified object-functions.

The *thingness* of a linden does not allow itself to be fundamentally enclosed in any single modal aspect within the temporal order. In the psychical modality, a tree functions as a typically

[1] The expression "original or nuclear type of individuality" is used in the same sense as in the general theory of the modal spheres. Cf. Vol. II, part 1, chapt. VII, § 3, pp. 423 ff.

qualified[1] individual sensorily perceptible image. It has, in other words, a typically qualified modal object-function in this modal aspect. In the logical modality, a tree functions as the qualified individual object of a possible concept, and as such it contains the objective logical characteristics of the thing; in the historical aspect it functions as a qualified individual object of possible culture; in the linguistic modality as an individual object of symbolical signification; in the social[2] modality, it has a potential individual social object-function (consider trees in parks, along streets, *etc.*); in the economic sphere, it has the function of a qualified object of economic valuation; in the aesthetic sphere it is a qualified individual aesthetic object (object of aesthetic appreciation); in the juridical aspect it functions as a qualified individual legal object (*rēs*), even if as yet it were a *rēs nullius;* in the ethical modality it functions as a qualified individual object of our love or hate; and finally in the sphere of faith, a tree functions as an object of our belief (*e.g.*, we believe it has been created by God, or is merely a product of nature, or — in the case of an animistic belief — it is inhabited by a demon or a good spirit).

A tree does not have a subject-function in any post-biotical modal law-sphere. In such spheres it has only object-functions, whose structural character is typically related to its qualifying biotic subject-function. We have repeatedly observed that in the naïve attitude the various modal aspects of an individual thing are experienced only implicitly, without our articulately being conscious of them, and without our executing a theoretical analysis of its modal functions, as accomplished above. Nevertheless the elimination of any one of the modal functions of the linden here before my window results in an abstraction foreign to our naïve experience, and which our cosmic self-consciousness refuses to identify with this concrete tree. The elimination of the logical object-function of the linden, for example, would make it impossible for us to have any experience of it as an individual thing. The latter would then also be deprived of all the object-functions it possesses in the subsequent modalities. It could not be named or play an objective rôle in human cul-

[1] "Qualified", namely by the qualifying function, in the entire structure of this natural thing.

[2] The term "social" is meant here in the modal sense of the aspect of intercourse.

ture, in human intercourse, economy, aesthetic enjoyment, juridical life, *etc.*

Seemingly this would result in a falling back into an animal manner of awareness of things belonging to an animal's bio-milieu; and this mode of awareness cannot be called *experience* since it lacks any relation to a selfhood. But, in fact, the result would be quite different, because the attempt to eliminate the logical object-function of a thing in our experiential world can be made in theoretical thought alone, and cannot affect our actual experience. We are only confronted with the theoretical result of a theoretical abstraction.

Our theoretical experiment must lead to the elimination of a thing's entire structure. If I theoretically eliminate the logical object-function of a tree, the tree itself is necessarily lost to my theoretical glance. An appeal to the subjective synthetical function of the Kantian categories will not be of any avail. The most that they could do would be to clarify the functional view of reality, employed in classical physics, but we have already seen that they cannot even do that. And in any case, they have no bearing on our naïve experience of things in their typical structures of individuality.

But did we already grasp the typical thing-structure of our linden in our theoretical view? No, we did not yet arrive at a theoretical idea of an individual whole. Our previous analysis has been restricted to the functional domain of the theory of modalities; but the latter, by its doctrine of modal structure, modal subject-object relation, functional opening-process [1], and individualization of modal meaning, could furnish the necessary point of contact, needed to find a theoretical access to a thing's structure of individual totality.

The typical structure of the internal opening-process and its coherence with the functional structure of the modal aspects.

The key to our problem is supplied by the tree's *qualifying function.* We have established that the latter is its last subject-function, and the ultimate functional point of reference for the entire internal structural coherence of the individual whole in the typical groupage of its aspects. This description is, however, not exhaustive; the qualifying function is also the tree's *charac-*

---

[1] Also termed: unfolding process, and process of disclosure.

teristic leading or guiding function. It plays the central rôle in the tree's internal unfolding process. The latter reveals an *internal* totality-structure and is, therefore, essentially different from the merely functional unfolding-process treated in the first part of Volume II.

Under the guidance of the qualifying organic vital function the anticipatory spheres in the tree's earlier modal functions are opened and directed *in a typical manner.* This is to say that this unfolding-process is no longer understandable from the general modal structure of the pre-biotical functions. The fact that the latter have biotical anticipations in a general modal sense is not sufficient to explain why the opening-process in the pre-biotical aspects of the linden exhibits a *typical biotic qualification* which is characteristic of this tree, as such. This state of affairs appears to depend upon the structure of individuality of this tree *as a whole,* in which the biotical function, in a special type of individualization, has the central rôle of a *qualifying* function. This is not understandable from the general temporal order of the aspects, which finds expression in their general modal structure. This general temporal order is maintained in every structure of individuality. But the latter belongs to a different dimension of our experiential horizon, which is not reducible to that of the modal spheres, though it pre-supposes the general order of modalities. Through the typical structure of our linden, as an individual living whole, the earlier functions acquire an *internal* inter-modal structural coherence, which is distinct from the *external* functional coherence of the *different types of individuality* within the modal aspects.

In the theory of the modal spheres we concentrated solely on the *functional* structure of the opening-process and learned nothing of the typical *internal structure* of the latter as found in the things of naïve experience. But we can now see the close relationship between these structures. The internal structure of a thing pre-supposes a functional structure of its modal aspects and an inter-functional coherence of the latter.

I do not mean to say that naïve experience is based upon a theory of modal spheres. I have continually warned against such a misunderstanding. The functional structure of reality is not based upon theoretical thought, the latter is rather based upon the functional modal structure of reality, of which there is an implicit, although inarticulate awareness in our naïve experience.

Within the typical total structure of our linden, the internal unfolding-process is executed so completely that the tree, as an individual thing (marked by its qualifying function), exhibits an *integral* internal unity [1]. This is the reason why this typical structure can express itself in all of its modal aspects, even in its post-biotical object-functions. All of them are related to an individual whole whose typical internal structure lies at the foundation of the typical internal coherence of its modal functions. It is this typical totality-structure which also determines the central rôle of the biotical function in this temporal coherence of internal functions.

The qualifying function indicates the intrinsic destination of a thing in the temporal world-order.

The qualifying function indicates the intrinsic destination of a thing in the temporal world-order, which should not be confounded with an external teleology, nor with a metaphysical entelechy of a "natural substance". An external teleology cannot explain the veritable internal structure of a thing. The qualifying function of our linden, indicating its intrinsic destination, is an essential factor of the internal structure of this tree. External teleological relations, on the contrary, can only concern its reference to other beings. To the question: 'What end or purpose can our linden serve?' the answer may be, *e.g.*: 'We can enjoy its shade, and birds can build nests in it'.

Such *ends* lie outside of the internal structure of the actual thing. It is true that they play an essential part in our naïve experience, because the latter does not separate a thing from its context with other beings. But in the structural subject-object relations of naïve experience the object-functions of our linden are bound to the internal structure of individuality of the latter. This is why in the naïve attitude we do not confound the inner nature of the tree with the needs of other beings which it may satisfy. Its inner destination as a linden is implicitly distinguished from its external teleological relations.

Apparently this intuitive distinction can be satisfactorily accounted for by the metaphysical concept of entelechy introduced by ARISTOTLE. The entelechy of a living being is conceived of as the *inner telos* (end) of its internal material process of

---

[1] We shall see that this internal unity cannot be guaranteed by the leading biotical function.

becoming, and, as such, it is clearly distinguished from any external teleological relation. But our critical analysis of the Aristotelian concept of substance[1] has shown that this apparent accordance with naïve experience cannot detract from the fundamental difference between the naïve conception of a thing and a natural *οὐσία*. It is the very structure of individuality which appeared to be imcompatible with the latter. And, since our view of the qualifying function of the linden, as that typical internal function which indicates the intrinsic destination of the whole, is unbreakably bound to this structure, it cannot be conceived in terms of an Aristotelian entelechy.

§ 2 - THE UNITY OF THE THING-STRUCTURE AND THE MODAL SPHERE-SOVEREIGNTY.

The modal sphere-sovereignty of the different aspects of a thing is not affected by the internal structural principle of the individual whole.

We have now to consider the question if the internal unity of a thing guaranteed by its structure of individuality is indeed compatible with the general theory of the modal spheres. In the previous section we have stressed the inner connection between the modal structures of the different functions of a linden and the typical internal structure of the individual whole. Nevertheless, at first sight this connection implies a difficulty, still accentuated by the fact that every attempt at a theoretical analysis of a whole seems to destroy it.

This difficulty concerns the modal sphere-sovereignty of the aspects, which cannot be affected even by the internal opening-process of the pre-biotical functions of our linden under the guidance of its qualifying function.

Metabolic processes, for instance, occurring within the internal structure of a living organism, have doubtless a physical-chemical aspect. As such, they are processes of exchange of energy subjected to physical-chemical laws. Nevertheless, metabolism in its typical inner structure is bound to the individual whole of a living organism. Its energy-aspect is opened under the typical guidance of the qualifying function of this organism and thus it shows a typical biotic qualification.

Does this mean that in the internal structure of the living organism the modal boundaries between the energy-aspect and the

---

[1] Cf. pp. 9 ff. of this Volume.

biotical aspect are levelled out? The general theory of the modal law-spheres decidedly denies such a supposition. It maintains the modal sphere-sovereignty and consequently rejects every idea of a *causal* relation between the aspects concerned. There is not a hidden "entelechy" or "vital force" which can explain the metabolic processes in their physical-chemical aspect. Nor can the biotical aspect be reduced to the energy-aspect. The biotic anticipations of the energy-functions, disclosed in the internal opening-process of the living organism, retain their physical-chemical character. The assumption of a causal encroachment of vital energy upon the physical-chemical aspect of metabolism would only result in a pseudo-explanation. The different modal aspects of a real causal process ought to be accurately distinguished.

But this very view-point of the general theory of the modal spheres seems to contradict the idea of an individual whole introduced by the theory of the structures of individuality. And this is why the South-African philosopher H. G. STOKER was of the opinion that we need a concept of substance, since the theory of the modal law-spheres does not explain the absolute internal unity of a thing, as guaranteed in God's creative plan. It is therefore necessary to consider the relation between the modalities and the structures of individuality in greater detail. It will be shown that the contradiction alleged exists only in appearance.

As to STOKER's objection it should be primarily observed that from the very beginning we have acknowledged the insufficiency of the theory of the modal spheres to account for the internal structural unity of a thing. We have, however, proceeded from this theory to that of the typical structures of individuality. It is true that for the sake of a theoretical analysis of these plastic structures we were obliged to make use of our previous analysis of the functional structures of the modalities. But we have stressed the fact that the structures of individuality belong to another dimension of our experiential horizon. It was therefore to be expected by anticipation that we should arrive at the critical point where the theory of the modal aspects cannot help us any further.

Nevertheless, we must maintain the thesis developed in the second Volume that there exists an unbreakable coherence between the functional structures of the modal aspects and the internal structures of individuality by virtue of which the things of naïve experience present themselves as individual wholes.

Even in the internal structure of a thing the modal sphere-sovereignty of its different functions is not abolished. *The reason is that this modal irreducibility appeared to be founded in the same temporal order which is also the basis of the plastic horizon of human experience.* But a thing is more than the sum of its individualized modal functions. It shows the typical structure of an individual whole, in which the continuous unbroken coherence of its structural functions is guaranteed by cosmic time. The appearance of an inner contradiction between modal sphere-sovereignty and the internal unity of a thing is only due to the *Gegenstand-relation.* It is due to the theoretical ἐποχή of this cosmic temporal continuity, which is necessary to grasp the inner structure of a thing with its typical groupage of modal functions in our analysing theoretical view.

The inter-modal character of the unity of a thing and the internal individual thing-causality.

The individual unity in the diversity of modal functions is essential to the thing's internal structure, but this unity cannot be of a modal character. We have established that within its modal boundaries the qualifying biotic function cannot exercise any causal influence upon the physical-chemical functions of the living organism. But the real causal processes occurring in the internal structure of this organism proceed after the pattern of an individual whole, which lies at the foundation of all its modal functions and expresses itself in each of them in a specific-modality. The different modalities of the internal causal relations are never *real, as such.* They are nothing but modal aspects of a real whole which has a continuous duration in cosmic time. Every modal function of this individual whole must have a bottom layer in the continuous inter-modal coherence of cosmic time in which any temporal reality is embedded [1].

The internal thing-causality is neither to be explained in terms of a theory of parallelism, nor in terms of a theory of interaction between the modal functions.

It should be clear that this conception of internal thing-causality is neither to be explained in terms of a theory of parallelism, nor in terms of a theory of interaction between the modal functions.

---

[1] Cf. Vol. II pp. 473 ff.

Both of these theories are of a metaphysical origin. This is already evident from the fact that they have been devised to solve the metaphysical problem concerning the relation between "soul" and "material body", conceived of as different substances. And this pseudo-problem was born from the very lack of insight into the continuity of cosmic time and from an absolutization of the theoretical *Gegenstand-relation*. It is unmasked as a pseudo-problem as soon as we have seen that metaphysical substances in this sense do not exist and that every real causal process occurs in the continuity of cosmic time.

A closer examination of STOKER's argument.

STOKER has pointed out that time cannot operate causally, as such. If, consequently, a thing is only the sum of its functions plus time, then, as yet, no real explanation of the *individual internal unfolding-process* has been given. And, if the question is so put, STOKER's remarks are doubtless correct, although STOKER rejects our Idea of cosmic time.

Time, abstracted from empirical reality, cannot work causally. But it is fundamentally incorrect to suppose that a thing is nothing more than the sum of its functions plus time. Time is not an external something that joins itself to the various functions. But, as previously established in the general theory of the modal spheres, the various functions are *intrinsically temporal in* character. Even in the modal structures of meaning, cosmic time is always present in anticipating and retrocipating functions. The temporal horizon lurks behind and in the modal horizon of reality.

Temporal reality does not end in the modal functions; it is not shut off in the modal horizon of the law-spheres. Rather, it has — if I may use this image — its inter-modal prolongation in the continuity of the cosmic coherence.

The continuity of cosmic time is not empty. *Reality* is present in the continuous intermodal temporal coherence.

My answer to STOKER's argument may therefore be summarized as follows: the continuity of cosmic time is inter-modal, but not empty. Time, in its continuity, may not be cut off from reality, as a floating abstraction, and then joined to reality by means of a plus sign. Reality, in its typical thing-structure, is present in time's continuous coherence.

In fact, reality has its inter-modal bottom-layer in the continuity of cosmic time.

And it is only in this cosmic temporal bottom-layer of every thing-structure that the individual whole of a thing is realized. Its individual identity receives its determination from its internal structural principle. It is this *identity* that is intuitively experienced in naïve experience.

This identity is consequently *more* than functional. And this "more" does not mean an empty temporal coherence (as STOKER has apparently interpreted my viewpoint), but it lies, within time, in the reality of the thing itself, as an individual and integral whole. The philosophy of the cosmonomic Idea does not first break up a thing's unity into modal law-spheres, and then, in *retrospect,* seek *unity* in a thing. *The transcendental Idea of the individual whole precedes the theoretical analysis of its modal functions. It is its pre-supposition, its cosmological a-priori.*

The identity of a thing, rooted in the continuity of cosmic time, is, however, not the metaphysical identity of a *substance,* as the absolute point of reference of its different "accidental properties". Nor can it be the radical identity of the different modal functions of the thing concerned. The modal aspects of reality find their deeper identity in the central religious sphere alone. But temporal things are perishable, they do not have a supra-temporal selfhood; their thing-identity is only that of a temporal individual whole, *i.e. of a relative unity in a multiplicity of functions.*

Why the temporal identity of a thing cannot itself become a '*Gegenstand*' of theoretical analysis.

It is impossible to make the structural continuity of a thing, which guarantees its relative identity, into a *Gegenstand* of theoretical analysis. Any attempt to do so results in intrinsic antinomies. By means of theoretical analysis we can only establish that the temporal duration of our linden, as an identical whole, is bound to the maintenance of its realized internal structure, qualified by its typical leading biotic function. But in this way we do not penetrate to the inter-modal continuity of the individual whole.

We are no more able to isolate the cosmic temporal bottom-layer of a thing-structure, than we can theoretically isolate our intuitive faculty. All theoretical isolation pre-supposes the inter-modal continuity of cosmic time.

This was why I wrote in an earlier work that the way in which the internal unfolding-process in a tree, in its inter-modal structure of individuality, is possible, is an unsolvable problem, both for philosophy and the special sciences [1].

Theoretical thought here reaches its limits and thereby reveals that it is not self-sufficient. To grasp a thing's temporal unity within the functional diversity of our cosmos, it must appeal to the naïve experience of time. Theoretical thought can only approach it by means of a transcendental Idea, a limiting concept. By so doing it explicitly accounts for this unity as a transcendental pre-supposition of the philosophical analysis of a thing's structure. The philosophy of the cosmonomic Idea thus gives a theoretical explanation of naïve experience but does not replace it.

Is this a deficiency of this philosophy? Must our view be augmented here by an Idea of creation which, apart from the modal horizon of our experience, conceives of the unity of a thing in a new concept of substance? Is STOKER right in thinking that from the very need of such a concept it clearly appears that created reality does not exist in the mode of meaning, but only *possesses* meaning?

Let me begin with repeating that our Christian cosmonomic Idea contains the Idea of creation and is completely permeated with it. But, I deny that it is possible for theoretical thought to eliminate the modal dimension of our experiential horizon, without entangling itself in meaningless and antinomical absolutizations. I deny that the unity of a thing, as presented in naïve experience, can be *theoretically comprehended,* if we merely view it in another "conic section" of the cosmos [2], *viz.* that of substances.

Even though STOKER has not yet developed his viewpoint in greater detail, I foresee that his effort will lead to an illegitimate extension of the task of philosophical thought.

STOKER speaks of a substantial causality in the internal structure of things. I speak of *individual thing-causality* in the sense that there exists a typical structural coherence between directing and directed functions in the continuous real bottom-layer of a thing as an individual whole. We both are seeking to account

---

[1] *De Crisis in de Humanistische Staatsleer* (1931), p. 109.

[2] Cf. STOKER: *Die Wijsbegeerte van die Skeppingsidee* (1933, p. 44). I have borrowed STOKER's term "conic section" *(kegelsnede)* from this writing.

for a state of affairs which within the thing's internal structure exceeds the boundaries of the modal spheres. It is not my intention to quibble with STOKER over the *word* "substance". I must assume on the ground of his writings and on personal correspondence that he does not intend to defend a *metaphysical* concept of *οὐσία*. Nevertheless, I do not yet see what new philosophical perspectives are opened by attempting to grasp inter-modal continuity in a supposedly non-metaphysical concept of substance. Even the temporal *identity* of a thing cannot be experienced apart from the diversity of its modal functions; it is a *relative* identity, pointing beyond and above itself to the inter-modal meaning-coherence of time and the radical unity of meaning in the central religious sphere of our experiential horizon. STOKER apparently distinguishes the thing's "substantial" unity from meaning. Sometimes he calls this substantial unity: "force", "dynamic reality", "will" or "love" [1]. In my opinion this use of analogical terms without any modal qualification of their meaning is only confusing.

It betrays, at least in a terminological respect, the influence of an irrationalistic metaphysics; and I suppose it shows an after-effect of Schelerian ideas in STOKER's thought, an after-effect incompatible with his present rejection of a *metaphysical* concept of substance. If this supposition is right, it explains also STOKER's maintenance of the neo-scholastic conception that the "substance" of created things is to be conceived as a *being* which cannot be identified with *meaning*. In this case we are once again confronted with the analogical idea of being, which pretends to embrace both God and His creatures, though in a different sense. Then we must again seek for an independent point of reference for meaning in a created "substance". Then it also becomes understandable why STOKER cannot agree with our rejection of any dichotomy of human existence within the temporal horizon. For he holds to the scholastic conception of a material substance and a soul-substance, which is not intrinsically compatible with the central religious meaning of the "heart" as the single and integral concentration-point of human existence.

---

[1] These terms are to be found in *Die Wijsbegeerte van die Skeppingsidee* p. 25.

A closer analysis of STOKER's substance-concept as he has provisionally explained it.

In the face of all these implications of STOKER's substance-concept I fear that he has not succeeded in conceiving it in a non-metaphysical sense. Indeed, what could it add to our conception of the thing-structure, explained above, if it really lacked any metaphysical implication? STOKER ascribes to substance a *dynamical* being. We have constantly emphasized the dynamical character of all created reality in its dependent existence as *meaning*. STOKER is not satisfied with this. He seeks for a hidden energy, will or love in the substantial core of all created things lying *behind* meaning; consequently lying also behind the essential meaning-*coherence* which determines the existence of all things within the temporal and religious horizon of human experience. I cannot see how this attempt may escape from landing in genuine metaphysics, which tries to transcend the horizon of meaning by absolutizing analogies presenting themselves within this horizon. Energy (force), will and love cannot be one and the same within the temporal horizon of meaning. Every analogy is bound to an original meaning-kernel which determines its specific sense. But, when we take the terms concerned in an undefined analogical sense, we can operate with them in a speculative way. Then we may assume that the substantial being of our linden is force, will or love, and so on, and nobody is able to deny it on experiential grounds, because one does not know in what sense these terms are meant. In poetry the aesthetical imagination may seek expression in pregnant metaphors which have no other rôle than evoking a visionary picture of nature. But in philosophy we are not concerned with the visionary world of the poet. Here we are obliged to explain the meaning of our words in their theoretical use, and this meaning is bound to the theoretical dimension of our temporal horizon, although this theoretical dimension points beyond and above itself to the pre-theoretical and supra-theoretical dimensions.

Within the integral meaning-coherence of cosmic time, energy and love are original meaning-kernels of two different modal aspects, *viz.* the physical and the moral modality. The analogies of these meaning-kernels, implied in other modalities, have a different sense determined by the modal nuclei of their own spheres. This state of affairs is not affected by the structures of individuality. The radical unity of all the different modalities in which they coalesce, is not to be found in a supposed ontical sphere of substances which, as such, is sought *beyond* and *behind* the horizon of meaning. On the contrary, it is the concentration-point of meaning in the *imago Dei,* which is nothing in itself, but rather the reflection of the Divine Being in the central human sphere of creaturely meaning. And since the fall of mankind this *imago Dei* is only revealed in its true sense in Jesus Christ.

As to "will,' as the supposed substantial kernel of "created being" we must remark that it is a specific direction of human "acts", which have different modal aspects and may assume different structures of individuality. In any case it is impossible to ascribe volitional acts to inorganic things, to plants or animals, because they lack a self-hood.

We must thus conclude that a substance-concept which seeks the substantial kernel of all created beings in force or energy, will or love, can only result in a general confusion with respect to the specific nature of created things.

STOKER, who wants to base philosophy on the Idea of creation, should guard against this confusion, since the Idea concerned implies that everything has been created after its proper nature. The cause of this lack of clear distinction is to be sought in the very attempt to find a substantial kernel of created things beyond the horizon of meaning. Such an attempt is indeed *meaning-less,* because this horizon delimits the very nature and mode of existence of everything created. Beyond this horizon there exists nothing except the Divine Being which is the Origin of all meaning.

This is the reason why philosophical thought which tries to discover a substantial being of created things as the independent *bearer* of meaning, must always land in meaningless absolutizations of theoretical abstractions. And since these abstractions are taken from the very meaning-coherence of our temporal horizon of experience, this attempt dissolves itself in intrinsic antinomies. But the absolutization, as such, which is inherent in this attempt, is incompatible with the Biblical conception of creation and reveals the influence of un-Biblical dialectical basic motives.

A return to neo-Scholasticism?

STOKER denies the metaphysical character of his concept of substance. And, indeed, as far as I can see, he has not borrowed this concept from Greek or medieval scholastic metaphysics. But I have already observed that his terminology clearly betrays the influence of modern irrationalist trends of thought and I supposed this might be due to an after-effect of Schelerian ideas.

In SCHELER, as well as in French spiritualistic neo-Scholasticism, we can observe a strong influence of some ideas, borrowed from LEIBNITZ' monadology, but transformed in an irrationalist-dynamical sense.

With STOKER this influence may be noticed especially in his conception of the substantial kernel of things as "force". We have remarked that within the theoretical horizon the concept of "force" immediately requires a delimitation of its modal meaning. Naïve experience is also aware of "force". But it is entirely foreign to the idea that it would be the hidden "essence" of all things; it experiences energy in its original modal sense only implicitly; "force", however, is experienced explicitly as a particularly strong manifestation of energy (in its coherence with sensory feeling) in concrete natural events, or in a human or animal body.

In the non-theoretical experiential attitude, no one seeks the "essence" of a picture, a table, a statue, a plant, or hill in "force", but one experiences the force of a storm, the force of muscles, the force of a water-fall, of a moving body, *etc.* And this naïve experience of force always occurs in an unbreakable meaning-coherence with other "qualities" of things and events. Only in the aspect of faith can the naïve experience of force be related to a revelation of God's Being. But when this is done without conceiving force in the integral meaning-coherence of the temporal order, one lands in a primitive mythology.

In his conception of monads as "metaphysical concentration-points of force" LEIBNITZ hypostatized the theoretical concept of force as it was introduced in NEWTON's physics. Trying to penetrate to the hidden "substantial kernel" of created reality, lying at the foundation of the merely phenomenal world, he elevated an undefined physical concept (which had only sense in the whole meaning-context of NEWTON's system) to the rank of a metaphysical attribute of monadic being. Here, too, the result was only mythological. In our critical analysis of this metaphysics in the second part of Volume I we have shown that the dynamical conception of the monads (implied in the metaphysical concept of force) was inspired by the autarchy-motive of the Humanistic ideal of personality.

As to the voluntaristic turn of this Leibnitzian conception in STOKER's concept of substance, we must remark that it is also found in French neo-scholastic spiritualism. Whereas in LEIBNITZ "force" was supposed to be the hidden autarchical stimulus of the representations within the monads, spiritualist neo-scholasticism conceived it as a *volitional* energy, the impulse of "action".

And STOKER's identification of this "volitional force" with "love" may be influenced by the modern irrationalistic reáction against the scientialist view of the world. The "controlling attitude" of natural science, which furnishes only external and formal mathematical knowledge of the universe, is opposed to the "loving attitude", which penetrates to the internal essence of things which is love and a longing for completion (cf. also GRÜNBAUM's book *Herrschen und Lieben*).

All this may evoke a feeling of aesthetical pleasure, but it can hardly be maintained that it is inspired by the Biblical motive of creation, nor that it could aid in deepening our philosophical insight into the inner nature and structure of temporal things. I agree that in its central religious sense love is the fulfilment and radical unity of all temporal meaning in the Divine plan of creation. But a Christian philosopher should remember that this radical love can only be found in the *imago Dei*, which has been radically obscured by the fall of mankind and is only revealed to us in Jesus Christ as the Redeemer.

It is meaningless to seek this love in an independent substantial *being* of the things of our naïve temporal experience and to identify it with a metaphysical "volitional force". This is nothing but a vain speculation originating from a neo-romantic turn in the Humanist freedom-motive. A Christian neo-scholasticism may try to accommodate this mystical metaphysics to the Idea of creation, but this is not the way in which we can arrive at a real reformation of the philosophical attitude of thought through the Biblical basic motive.

In this context it strikes me that STOKER thinks his conception of substance gives a better expression to "the autonomous being and value of the cosmos with respect to God" [1]. For it is this very autonomous being and value of the created world in itself which must be denied from the radical Biblical viewpoint of

---

[1] The South-African text of this quotation reads: 'die eien zijn en die eienwaarde van die kosmos teenover God'.

creation. Here we are confronted with the core of the question if we can ascribe to created things a mode of existence which is *being* in the traditional metaphysical sense of the word.

It deserves special attention that in their discussion with the philosophy of the cosmonomic Idea, Roman Catholic philosophers avail themselves of the same argument which STOKER alleges in favour of the maintenance of the concept of substance and the metaphysical idea of being. But they also acknowledge that here an ultimate difference is at issue between Roman Catholicism and the Reformation, especially the Calvinist Reformation [1].

In my opinion, the maintenance of the traditional metaphysical idea of being and of the substance-concept implied in it, is only understandable from the dialectical scholastic basic-motive of nature and grace (super-nature). I agree that recent Roman Catholic neo-scholasticism which as much as possible seeks to interpret this theme from an Augustinian point of view, has seriously tried to purify it from its dualistic character.

Especially MARLET's interpretation deserves particular attention. Nevertheless even he, who has shown such a great sympathy with the philosophy of the cosmonomic Idea, is of the opinion that in the last analysis this philosophy, because of its rejection of the substance-concept, fails to do sufficient justice to the autonomous being of the creature in its relation to God.

He, too, ascribes this to the theological influence of CALVIN. In his struggle against SERVET's pantheistic interpretation of God's immanence in the created world, this Reformer is supposed to have emphasized the transcendence of the Divine essence with regard to the creature to such a degree that he denied to the latter the principle of existence which metaphysically is called *being*. On the other hand, he accentuated the immanence of God's activity in the world so strongly that the activity of the creature no longer could be viewed as a consequence of its

---

[1] In the recent thesis of O. J. L. ALBERS O.E.S.A. *Het Natuurrecht volgens de Wijsbegeerte der Wetsidee* (1955, drukkerij Gebr. Janssen), defended at the University of Utrecht, this difference is laid at the foundation of a comparative study of the Philosophy of the Cosmonomic Idea and Thomistic metaphysics. It is striking to observe that this Roman Catholic author raises the same objection against my conception of the religious concentration of the meaning of our temporal world in the *imago Dei* in man, as can be found in STOKER. This criticism, however, is lacking in Roman Catholic authors who display an accentuated Augustinian inspiration.

proper being. In the philosophy of the cosmonomic Idea this has led to a theoretical absolutization of the "religious moment" in the relation between God and creature, with the neglect of the ontical relation implied in the analogy of being. And here, so MARLET concludes, is to be sought the fundamental difference between the transcendental Idea of analogical being and the three-fold cosmonomic Idea of Calvinistic philosophy, notwithstanding every deeper unity of Christian inspiration [1].

I cannot agree with this reduction of the difference to a theological problem. Therefore we had better leave this question alone as to whether MARLET has done justice to CALVIN's theological view of the relation between God and creature [2]. The only point at issue here is the religious basic motive of the scholastic metaphysical theory of analogical being and the concept of substance implied in it. And it cannot be denied that it is the motive of nature and grace that we have found to be of a dualistic origin.

It is impossible to reverse this relation, as the Dutch neo-Thomistic philosopher ROBBERS has done in his discussion with the philosophy of the cosmonomic Idea [3]; one cannot maintain the thesis that the Idea of analogical being is the real basic motive of neo-scholastic thought, while the motive of nature and grace is only secondary and dependent on the former. Our transcendental critique has shown that the dialectical Idea of *analogia entis* originated from Greek philosophy and was ruled here by the dialectical religious basic motive of form and matter. It could not be accommodated to the ecclesiastical doctrine of creation except by the scholastic basic motive of nature and grace. One should not obscure this essential point by transforming the religious basic motive into a metaphysical or theological Idea. The latter is dependent on the former. It is not metaphysics or theology which rules the religious basic motive

---

[1] *Grundlinien der Kalvinistischen Philosophie der Gesetzesidee als Christlicher Transzendentalphilosophie* (München, 1954) p. 133/4. MARLET appeals here to J. L. WITTE S.J. *Het Probleem Individu-Gemeenschap in Calvijn's Geloofsnorm* (1949) Vol. I p. 136.

Cf. also Dr P. SCHOONENBERG S.J. *Een Gesprek met de Wijsbegeerte der Wetsidee,* in the philosophical chronical of the review '*Streven*' (Year VIII Vol. 1 nr 2, 1954).

[2] Cf. Prof. G. BERKOUWER, *Identiteit of Conflict?* (Phil. Ref. 21 Year 1956, pp. 1—44).

[3] *De Wijsbegeerte der Wetsidee in Gesprek met het Thomisme,* Studia Catholica 24 (1949) pp. 161—171.

of philosophical thought. The latter is its supra-theoretical starting-point, its central spiritual impulse.

By denying created things a metaphysical substantial being we have not detracted anything from their proper reality and activity, which is fundamentally distinct from the Divine Being of the Creator. We have only stressed that this reality is of the character of meaning, which cannot be independent and self-contained. The real value of every creature is implied in its meaning-character, not in a supposed "being in itself". The very intention of metaphysics to find a substantial kernel of created things outside of the horizon of meaning leads to "nothingness", to meaningless absolutization. Neo-scholasticism, no matter whether it is found in Protestant or in Roman Catholic thought, may assimilate important parts of the philosophy of the cosmonomic Idea. Nevertheless, its ultimate spiritual impulse is not that of this philosophy. The scholastic basic motive of nature and grace, however much accommodated to the radical Biblical starting-point, is incompatible with the radical antithetical attitude with respect to the un-Biblical basic-motives of philosophical thought. It is obliged to seek a compromise with them. Therefore, it is always inclined to assimilate Greek or Humanist motives by accommodating them to Christian belief. This is the final difference between Reformation and Scholasticism in philosophy.

A summary of my provisional objections against STOKER's substance-concept.

I can now summarize my provisional attitude toward STOKER's introduction of a supposedly non-metaphysical concept of substance as a supplement to the theory of the modal law-spheres.

1. After conducting a modal examination of reality, based on the theory of the modal spheres, STOKER wishes to take a closer view of the things of naïve experience. With this desire I am in full agreement; however, I believe this examination is the very task of the theory of the structures of individuality, which cannot be replaced by a theory of substances in the line of STOKER's provisional hints.

2. I object to any view which does not conceive of meaning as the exclusive mode of existence of all of the things created, unless this difference should turn out to be merely a question of terminology. But apparently this is not the case since STOKER's view appears to result in a fundamental criticism of the whole

content of my cosmonomic Idea, especially of the Idea of a religious concentration point of our temporal world. STOKER rejects the central position of mankind in our "earthly cosmos" and wants to view everything "in its immediate relation to God" without the intermediary of Jesus Christ. This is why he raises a serious objection against the entire "Christocentric" direction of the philosophy of the cosmonomic Idea. And this is indeed a serious point of difference.

3. I consider it incorrect and intrinsically contradictory to maintain that there are two entirely different ways to contemplate reality, corresponding to different "conic sections of the cosmos", and *excluding any mutual connection.* If the theory of the modal spheres and the theory of the structures of individuality are not arbitrary constructions but are grounded in the cosmic order, they cannot exist without an intrinsic coherence or connection. Anyone who accepts the theory of the law-spheres, as STOKER does, cannot eliminate the modal viewpoint in his theoretical examination of the structures of things, even though the theory of the law-spheres is admittedly inadequate to explain naïve experience without the supplement of a theory of the typical structures of individuality. It is true that STOKER does not intend to deny an inner connection between the modalities and his idea of substance. But he believes his concept of substance enables him to grasp an absolute ontical unity of a thing which lies byond the horizon of meaning, and is really *being,* independent of its modal functions, whereas the latter are dependent on substance. And I deny that he is able to do so.

4. I do not simply object to the term "substance", but to the danger that — contrary to STOKER's own wishes — such a concept will make it easy for speculative motives to gain an entrance into re-formed philosophy.

The temporal non-modal unity and identity of things cannot be grasped in a theoretical concept. This *unity* and *identity* has its foundation in cosmic time, which alone makes all experience and theoretical thought possible.

5. STOKER has shown with great acuteness that if a thing is only a complex of its functions plus cosmic time, then no explanation can be given of the opening-process within its total structure. I am very grateful to STOKER for this criticism. It has caused me to clarify a point, presumably not sufficiently developed in my earlier writings. This misunderstanding arises from thinking that the continuity of cosmic time, which cannot

be grasped in a theoretical concept, is not filled with reality. The consequence would be that reality is resolved in its modal functions within the law-spheres. I hope my closer explanation has cleared away such a fundamental misinterpretation.

Finally I want to stress that my critical remarks concerning the implications of STOKER's substance-concept do not detract in any way from my appreciation of his important attempt to enlarge the prospects of our reformed philosophy. My only intention is to warn against the danger of assimilating this philosophy to a neo-scholastic trend of thought which holds to the traditional metaphysical Idea of being with all of its religious and philosophical implications. And these implications are the more critical if STOKER means to emancipate his transcendental basic Idea of creation from its Biblical coherence with the motive of fall into sin and redemption by Jesus Christ in the communion of the Holy Spirit. For by so doing his "philosophy of the Idea of Creation" would land in a "theistic thought" which is even decidedly rejected by those prominent Roman Catholic trends of neo-scholasticism which move in the Augustinian line of a *philosophia Christiana.*

§ 3 - THE INNER ARTICULATION OF STRUCTURAL TYPES. RADICAL TYPES, GENO-TYPES AND VARIABILITY TYPES.

The structural principle of a linden, in whose analysis we were engaged, appeared to exceed the boundaries of the modal spheres. In the modal dimension of our experiential horizon we could establish the typical biotical qualification of the tree's structure of individuality. But this structure itself appeared to embrace all of the modal aspects in subject-object relations characteristic of naïve experience. It individualizes the modal functions and groups them together in a typical way within the cadre of an individual whole. The idea of the internal structural unity of this real whole, guaranteed by the inter-modal continuous coherence of its functions in cosmic time, *precedes* every analysis of the modal diversity of these functions. This is the fundamentally new viewpoint that the theory of the structures of individuality has opened.

In which dimension of the horizon of human experience does this internal unity have its foundation? Here we have the first question pertaining to the theory of the structures of individuality.

In our treatment of epistemology we discovered three transcendental dimensions in the experiential horizon arranged in perpective levels.

The temporal horizon appeared to be the foundation of the modal horizon. And both appeared to form the perspective in which arises the horizon of the structures of individuality. If the internal unity of a thing is grounded in this last dimension, it follows that it can only be a *temporal unity in the modal diversity of the functions.* As long as we keep this fundamental point in mind we will not fall back into the speculative metaphysical concept of substance. Nor can we be entrapped by a modern vitalistic "holism" [1] which seeks to grasp the individual whole of a living organism by reducing its physico-chemical aspect to a modality of its central bio-psychical sphere [2].

In the plastic horizon of cosmic time, a thing's modal functions are neither joined together into a metaphysical "substance", nor into a functional identity of modal functions. But they only come together in the continuous *operational coherence* of a *structural unity of irreducible modal functions,* a coherence which as such is necessarily *inter-modal and temporal in character.*

This structural unity possesses a law- and a subject-side. We propose to show in greater detail that the modal functions of a thing can only become its internal structural functions insofar as they are the expression of its structural unity as an individual whole.

The cosmic temporal order of the modal aspects could only be theoretically approached by an analysis of their modal structures, in which this order finds expression. Similarly we can obtain a theoretical insight into the typical total structures of individuality only by analyzing their internal structural functions in the different modal aspects, as they are typically grouped within an individual whole.

It is in vain to seek for another theoretical access to these structures, because theoretical thought is bound to the *Gegenstand-relation.*

---

[1] 'Holism' (derived from the Greek word "*holon*", *i.e.* a whole, a totality) signifies: view of totality.

[2] The biotical and the psychical aspects are not distinguished here as irreducible modal spheres.

The structures of individuality as typical structures of temporal duration.

The cosmic temporal order expresses itself, according to its functional structure, in the modalities of meaning, and according to its structures of individuality, in the internal typical groupage of the modal aspects within structural totalities.

In the Prolegomena we have said that all the basic structures of temporal reality are grounded in the order of cosmic time. We assumed that all of them are specific structures of time and as such are necessarily related to the factual duration of transitory things, events, processes, acts, social relationships, and so on [1].

This might seem to be a bold thesis so long as it could not yet be tested in its confrontation with the real states of affairs.

Meanwhile the general theory of the modal spheres has shown the rightness of this hypothesis with respect to the modal structures, at least insofar as it appeared possible to show a temporal succession in their realization in genetic processes. In addition the analysis of the opening-process of the modal spheres appeared to confirm our hypothesis.

But in the nature of the case this evidence remained bound within certain limits. In the first place we should remember that the modal aspects are only realized in structures of individuality, which in principle function in all the modal spheres of our temporal horizon. This is to say that when we establish that organic life could only develop after the realization of an inorganic world adapted to its needs, we can only mean that this inorganic world (our earth as a part of the solar system), in its typical structure of individuality, is *typically qualified* by a physico-chemical energy-constellation. Nevertheless, this earth had already *potential* object-functions in the biotical and the later aspects. These potential functions were only opened and actualized after the appearance of living organisms, plants, animals and man.

Similarly, when we establish that in the genetic process of human life the development of feeling precedes that of the logical function, and the development of the latter that of the cultural function of controlling formation, which in its turn precedes that of the lingual function *etc.*, we can only mean a process of actualization of potentialities already present in the structural principle of human bodily existence. In the

[1] Vol. I, p. 29.

temporal order of the modal aspects there cannot be a *real* succession. We could only show that this order has a temporal character because it is necessarily related to a genetic process of realization which reveals successive phases of actualization of the different modal aspects in accordance with this order. But these successive phases of realization are bound to structures of individuality which exceed the boundaries of the modal aspects. As such, these typical total structures have no real duration, since they belong to the law-side of cosmic time. But the individual things, processes, *etc.* in which they are realized, do have it.

This is to say that the temporal character of the order of the aspects expressed in their modal structures can only be proved indirectly in their theoretical abstraction.

Secondly, it follows from this indirect character of the evidence that it cannot be applied to the three mathematical aspects of our temporal horizon of experience. For it will appear that there are not to be found any structures of individuality whose typical qualifying function is of a numerical, spatial or kinematic modality. We could only show that the factual temporal duration of individual things and events has mathematical aspects and that in these aspects the factual duration of realized numerical, spatial and kinematic relations follows the modal temporal order of their law-spheres concerned. From the analysis of their modal structures we could then conclude *per analogiam* that these aspects are arranged in the general cosmic order of time.

On the other hand the thesis that the structures of individuality are really typical structures of cosmic time, may be proved in a direct way. This is very important, because in this way, too, it convincingly appears that they have nothing to do with metaphysical "substances". *In general we can establish that the factual temporal duration of a thing as an individual and identical whole is dependent on the preservation of its structure of individuality.*

The duration of a book or a picture is typically different from that of our linden, or from that of a radio-active element or a machine, *etc.* This will become clear in the course of our further investigations, when we have analysed their typical structures of individuality in greater detail. We may, therefore, conclude that these structures are really typical structures of temporal duration.

The inner articulation of structural types.

The internal structural principle determines the subjective or objective individuality of the whole. It belongs to the law-side of cosmic time; it is a *typical law of individuality,* which rules the structural coherence of the different functions within the individual totality. As such it is an inter-modal *law,* a typical *unity of order in the modal diversity of its aspects,* just as the individual whole, as its factual subjective or subjective-objective correlate, is an *individual factual unity* in the modal diversity of its functions. Every structural type exhibits an inner articulation of typicalness, descending from an ultimate irreducible general type to an ultimate species which embraces no further specific types. But we cannot theoretically approach this inner articulation of the structures of individuality in the current way, which is only a method of logical classification. For this method ignores the very problem in which we are concerned here, *viz.* the typical groupage of irreducible aspects within a structural unity of order.

In general its view-point is determined by a specific scientific field of research. In addition there appears to exist a great divergency and confusion with respect to the foundation of a classificatory system in the different branches of science which have need of a typology.

The concept of species in modern biology.

A striking example of this divergency and confusion is to be found in modern biological systematism. Since the rise of genetics and phylogeny the concept of species has lost that unity of meaning which it possessed in the Linnaean system. Diagnostic, genetics and phylogeny avail themselves of different criteria, which are not to be combined. This confusion expresses itself even in terminology. Diagnostic speaks of *taxon* in the sense of a collection of isoreagent individuals; phylogeny defines a species as a *phylon* in the sense of a phyletic series; genetics calls a species an *isogenon* or isogenetic unity and defines this concept as a collection of individuals having the same genotypical composition. In addition genetics has developed another concept of species, *viz.* that of the "*reine Linie*" (JOHANSSEN), which it defines as the collection of all individuals descending from one or two isogenetic-homozygotic parents, no matter whether they have become also homozygotic or heterozygotic [1].

[1] Cf. AD. MEIJER, *Logik der Morphology* (1926) and J. LEVER and H.

A great many modern biologists are of the opinion that the higher generic classifications of plants and animals lack a natural basis and are only artificial categories, products of a generalizing logical abstraction. Consistent evolutionistic students of phylogeny consider also the concept of species as a conventional construction of the human mind. The influence of philosophical and religious pre-suppositions is manifest in these views.

The difference between a classificatory and a typological method in modern psychology and psychiatry.

In modern psychology and psychiatry there is an increasing insight into the fundamental insufficiency of a rigid classificatory method. The reason is that the traditional class-concept implies a sharp distinction between the groups encompassed by the different classes, whereas any attempt at a psychological typology of human personalities is confronted with the impossibility to establish rigid limits between the types. The characteristic properties of the latter appear to be manifold and gradual; there exist "flowing transitions" from one type to another, mixed types, intermediary forms which contradict the class-concept. The famous psychologist W. STERN has therefore established that a psychological type is sharply to be distinguished from a class: 'The limits between a type and its neighbour-types are always flowing; ...Transitional forms necessarily belong to the structure of the type-division' [1].

This may have a close connection with the essentially unfixed character of the temporal act-structure of human nature, which will ask our attention presently.

But the chief point is that the different attempts at a psychological typology show a similar divergency with respect to their foundation as appeared to exist in the biological classifications.

DOOYEWEERD, *Rondom het Biologisch Soortbegrip II* (Phil. Ref. 14th Year 1949, p. 33 ff).

[1] W. STERN, *Die differentielle Psychologie in ihren methodischen Grundlagen* (Barth, Leipzig, 3rd ed. 1921) pp. 173 ff.

Compare also CARL G. HEMPEL and P. OPPENHEIM, *Der Typusbegriff im Lichte der neuen Logik* (Leiden, 1936), who have made an interesting attempt at a logistical foundation of the type-concept as an *"Ordnungsbegriff"*, in contrast to the class-concept. This formal-logical treatise, however, is not serviceable in our theory of the structures of individuality.

Cf. also A. SEIFFERT, *Die kategoriale Stellung des Typus* (1953).

The so-called ideal-typical method in modern sociology and the typological concepts of dogmatic jurisprudence.

In the so-called cultural sciences we meet with a typological method which clearly betrays its origin from a historicist view of temporal reality. We mean the ideal-typical method introduced in sociology by the German scholar MAX WEBER. Historism denies in principle that the different types of modern social relationships such as marriage, family, State, Church, trade, or those of a primitive society, are founded in constant structural principles which determine their inner nature. From the absolutized historical viewpoint it can discover nothing but individual transitory cultural phenomena involved in a continuous change and development. In this line of thought WEBER conceived the typological concepts of sociology as relatively arbitrary constructions of the human mind, in which certain empirical historical traits of the different social relationships are intentionally exaggerated to gain an "ideal type". For the historian such ideal types are only auxiliary concepts, which can help him to understand the subjective social meaning of human actions and to give a causal explanation of their probable issue.

In dogmatic jurisprudence and the general theory of law the generic and specific type-concepts are preponderantly viewed as means of legal technique. In the footsteps of RUDOLPH v. JHERING it is denied that they have any foundation in the order of reality and they are considered to be only serviceable to an economic-logical classification of the legal material.

Similar to modern sociology, legal theory lacks any foundation in a theory of the social structures of individuality. The result is that it also lacks any deeper theoretical insight into the inner nature of the different types of legal spheres, whose internal character is determined by the structural principles of the social spheres in which they function. Dogmatic jurisprudence shows a traditional tendency to absolutize the typical legal spheres of the State (private civil law and public law). It is only due to this state of affairs that, generally speaking, the current unscientific concept of sovereignty could maintain itself in the dogmatical theory of the sources of law.

Sociology of law, on the other hand, has often the tendency to ignore the inner nature of the legal spheres of the State and to absolutize economically qualified law originating from the social spheres of industry and trade.

*

This is sufficient to explain why the current methods of forming generic and specific type-concepts cannot be serviceable in our theory of the structures of individuality. Leaving alone their specific scientific orientation, we must conclude that they lack a sufficient foundation in the structural temporal order of created reality.

For an analysis of the inner articulation of the structural types of individual totalities we need in the first place a criterion to establish the ultimate irreducible *genera,* which form the foundation of their further structural articulation. This criterion ought to be founded in the plastic dimension of the temporal order. It is only to be discovered in the typical structural groupage of the modal aspects within the structural whole.

Radical types and the kingdoms of individual things, events, or relationships circumscribed by them.

The first and most fundamental difference between the structural types is determined by the modality of their typical leading function, which gives the structural whole its typical qualification and internal destination.

This criterion delimits the ultimate *genera* of the structures of individuality, which, as such, are not enclosed in higher generic types. Because of their elementary and fundamental character they circumscribe invariable structural orbits of individuality whose further typical articulation is dependent on them.

We shall designate these elementary *genera* by the term *radical types,* and the structural orbits of things or other individual totalities encompassed by them, we shall call *kingdoms.*

In the macro-world of naïve experience our plastic horizon shows three radical types of a pre-logical qualification. They delimit three kingdoms, *viz.* 1) that of inorganic kinds of matter, things and events, all of which have a typical qualification in the energy-aspect; 2) that of plants and their bio-milieu, which kingdom has a typical biotic qualification; 3) that of animals, inclusive of their typical symbiotic relationships, their form-products and animal milieu, a kingdom which is typically qualified in the psychical aspect.

Naïve experience is generally not confronted with the difficulty due to so-called border-cases, where the biologist may be in doubt whether the entity in question belongs to the inorganic kingdom or to the vegetable or animal kingdom. Most of these border-cases present themselves in the micro-world, which is not directly accessible to pre-theoretical experience. For the present they may be left alone, because they do not affect the existence of the three kingdoms concerned[1]. The latter are

---

[1] I do not overlook the problem concerning the nature of the various kinds of virus, particularly the specific virus which causes the mosaic disease in tobacco-plants. The American scholars STANLEY and WIJCKOFF discovered that this virus is an albuminous matter of an extremely high molecular weight and fit to be crystallized. Thus it seems that a non-living "substance" possesses the capability of assimilation, which up till now was considered to be an exclusive property of a living organism. A virus-molecule of this specific type is apparently able to multiply by transforming the specific kinds of matter present in the tobacco leaves.

B. BAVINK *(Ergebnisse und Probleme der Naturwissensch.* 9th ed. 1948, p. 360) is of the opinion that we are here confronted with a discovery of an extremely important significance for our entire view of the relation between inorganic and living "substances". I do not believe so, though I do not deny in any respect the high scientific importance of STANLEY's and WIJCKOFF's discovery. The chief point is that the virus concerned has appeared to be a non-living "substance", which is only able to multiply in a "parasitical" connection with the living tobacco-plant. This is to say that the boundaries between the radical types are not levelled out by the assimilatory phenomena concerned. The question as to whether the assimilation itself is to be considered as an internal process of the living organism, in which the virus has only a catalytic rôle, or as a physico-chemically qualified process, is of a secondary concern. BAVINK's opinion that STANLEY's and WIJCKOFF's discovery has already proved that the latter solution is right, is certainly premature. It is hardly acceptable that the multiplication of the virus-molecule would occur apart from the internal reaction of the living organism, since mosaic disease can only develop in the living plant. In addition, BAVINK overlooks the problem how albuminous molecules of so highly complicated a structure can originate apart from a living organism. To solve this difficulty some biologists have supposed that a virus is perhaps a micro-organism which has degenerated to a parasite and has retained nothing of all its particular vital capacities but that of assimilation. (Cf. the inaugural address of H. J. STAUDINGER, Freiburg 1946).

In any case BAVINK's premature conclusion is doubtless connected with his so-called emergent evolutionism. According to this theory, life emerges from inorganic matter when the latter attains to an extreme complexity of physico-chemical constellation. In the same way mind is supposed to be a new product of evolution emerging from non-mental life when the latter has risen to an extreme complexity of organisation (Cf. C. LLOYD MORGAN, *Emergent Evolution*).

We have argued in Vol. II (pp. 107 ff.) that life in its original sense is not a "substance", but an irreducible modality of our experiential horizon, which cannot be defined by secondary phenomenal criteria. The philosophical theory of emergent evolution does not explain anything when it assumes that life is an emergent evolutional result of dead matter.

generally accepted also in biological diagnostic, which has established specific criteria for the distinction of plants and animals; these criteria are also applicable to the micro-world of protozoa and protophyta. As such, they cannot be of a radical typical character because they concern only sensorily perceptible characteristics, referring to physico-chemical properties (*e.g.*, the presence of chlorophyll and a cellulose-membrane in vegetable cells). But though these criteria are not valid without exception, they are related to the foundational radical types of our plastic experiental horizon.

It should not be objected that there is a pan-psychistic view in the philosophy of nature which ascribes to plants and even to inorganic matter some kind of feeling-life. This is a metaphysical assumption which cannot be verified by experiential data and lacks any foundation in the plastic horizon of our temporal world. It cannot be seriously doubted that in the macro-world of naïve experience there is a radical difference between animal behaviour and merely vegetative reactions upon physiological stimuli, and that this difference is due to the typical leading psychical function of the animal structure. Animal psychology has shown this even with *protozoa,* such as *infusoria,* notwithstanding their lack of a differentiated central nervous system[1]. Naturally the psychological experiments concerned cannot prove anything if it is *a-priori* denied that the objective sensory aspect of animal behaviour gives verifiable expression to subjective animal feeling functions. But such a prejudice is tantamount to denying the possibility of animal psychology. A materialistic behaviourism cannot account for the facts as they are critically established. Its "objectivism" is meaningless and contradictory since it ignores the truth that every objective phenomenon is bound to the subject-object relation, and outside of this relation dissolves itself into nothingness.

Animal psychology and behaviourism.

Animal psychology should doubtless guard against an anthropomorphic interpretation of animal behaviour. But we have explained in the second Volume that the feeling-aspect is a general modality of our experiential horizon, which may not be

---

[1] Cf. the very critical analysis of the psychological experiments concerned with J. A. Bierens de Haan, *Die tierischen Instinkte und ihr Umbau durch Erfahrung* (Leiden, publ. E. J. Brill, 1940) pp. 274 ff., esp. pp. 278—281.

identified with any typical structure that expresses itself in it. It embraces both animal and human emotional sensations and we are able to distinguish them after their typical structures of individuality. No single structural type can transcend our experiential horizon because all structures of individuality belong to its plastic dimension. Behaviourism ignores this horizon. Therefore it has a false and meaningless view of human experience.

Animal behaviour cannot be experienced as such outside of the radical type which delimits the animal kingdom from that of plants and that of the inorganic world. This is to say that this behaviour has a psychical qualification, which cannot be neglected without eliminating its typical animal nature. Indeed, the specific scientific criteria which the biologist handles to distinguish animals and plants, presuppose the radical types which alone can make this distinction meaningful. For, why should biology seek for material criteria if the difference between the animal and the vegetable kingdom were not presupposed in the plastic structures of our experiential horizon?

Differences in the physico-chemical properties of the cell-bodies could, as such, never evoke the idea of these kingdoms. It is only because of the border-cases, where at first sight the individuals do not betray their radical type, that the biologist seeks for secondary empirical criteria of a natural scientific character. But these criteria themselves show their true meaning only in the context of the radical types to which they refer. The usual lack of a cellulose-membrane in the animal cells may hang together with the psycho-motor structure of the animal body, in contradistinction to the vegetative structure of that of plants. For this psycho-motor structure requires a complete plasticity of the cells. Even the lowest kind of *protozoa, viz.* the amoeba shows this trait, though it should be granted that this criterion cannot be applied without exception.

As a rule (though not without exception) plants are enabled by means of their chlorophyll and sunlight to produce the most complicated combinations of their bodily matter from very simple kinds of matter in the inorganic world, whereas animals have to take organic matter from their food to assimilate it. This fact betrays an inner coherence with the temporal order of their types. The animal kingdom could not develop before the inorganic world and the vegetable kingdom had begun their temporal evolution. The vegetable kingdom had even to produce the typical physical-chemical constellation of the atmosphere necessary for the development of animal life, by delivering a sufficient quantity of free oxygen. In the modal horizon this genetic succession of the kingdoms appeared to correspond to the temporal order of the aspects, in which the energy-aspect precedes the biotical, and the latter modality precedes the psychical.

The denominator of comparison of the radical types.

Since the radical types are the ultimate *genera* in the inner articulation of the structures of individuality, it makes no sense to seek for a higher "logical" genus of "living beings", which is supposed to embrace plants, animals, and man [1]. Nor is it meaningful to construe a higher genus of "sensory beings", as ARISTOTLE does in his *Metaphysics.*

Such a method of forming generic concepts betrays a fundamental lack of insight into the structures of individuality, as they are grounded in the plastic order of cosmic time. We are here confronted with the same state of affairs as has already been discussed in the general theory of the modal spheres, *viz.* that every distinction of the different fundamental structures of our temporal horizon of experience presupposes a basic denominator of comparison [2]. We cannot theoretically distinguish the different modal aspects without such a basic denominator. Similarly we cannot distinguish the different structures of individuality if we have not an *a-priori* Idea of their common basis of comparison. Every absolutization of the theoretical *Gegenstand-relation* implies the necessity to seek this basis in theoretical thought itself. By so doing the irreducible character of the radical types cannot be acknowledged and a pseudo-logical genus-concept must replace the cosmic temporal order, which indeed is the only legitimate basic denominator of these radical types.

Why there does not exist a human radical type.

Mankind is not enclosed in a temporal kingdom of individual beings. I have explained in another work [3] that the human body, as the individual whole of a man's temporal existence, shows a very complicated interlacement of different typical structures

---

[1] Naturally this objection does not pertain to the use of a collective *name*, but to the method of *theoretic concept-formation.*

[2] Compare Vol. I p. 47 and Vol. II pp. 18 ff.

[3] *Reformatie en Scholastiek* Vol. III (not yet published).

which are combined in a form-totality, qualified by the so-called act-structure. This act-structure is successively founded in an animal, a vegetative and a material structure. It gives the human body its proper human character. But this act-structure, though it functions in all of the modal aspects, lacks, as such, a typical qualifying function within a temporal sphere. It is the immediate temporal expression of the human I-ness, which transcends the cosmic temporal order. The reason is that human existence is not restricted to the temporal world, and does not find its ultimate internal destination in the latter. Every radical type, qualified by a typical leading function, implies an inner restriction and limitation of the internal temporal destination of the individual beings enclosed in it. But man is created after the image of God, as the lord of the "earthly" temporal world. Therefore his body lacks any trait of specialization which would bind it to a specific milieu. The erect gait, the spiritual expression of the human face, the human hand formed to labour after a free project, testify to the fact that the human body is the free plastic instrument of the I-ness, as the spiritual centre of human existence.

The act-structure of this body is neither qualified by a logical, nor by an ethical function. It is not even qualified in the faith-aspect. If it were, human act-life would be either enclosed in a typical theoretic radical type, or in a typical ethically or pisteutically qualied[1] structural frame. But the truth is that human acts, with their threefold intentional direction *(viz.* the knowing, the volitional and the imaginative directions), may assume the most different structures of individuality. The act of praying is typically qualified as an act of faith. The act of scientific or philosophical reflection is typically qualified by the theoretical-logical function of thought, the act of aesthetical imagination is typically qualified in the aesthetical aspect of experience, *etc.* But the act-structure of the human body lacks, as such, any typical qualification. It is this very structure which makes the human body the field of free expression for the human spirit, *i.e.* for the religious centre of human existence.

This is why the traditional scholastic qualification of man as a rational-ethical being is unacceptable, as is the metaphysical dichotomistic view of body and soul, in which it is rooted. The

---

[1] In this context "pisteutic" (from Gr. πιστευτικός) means *qualified by faith.*

unqualified act-structure of the human body is quite different from the traditional conception of a "rational soul", in the sense of an immortal spiritual substance which is the metaphysical "form" of the "material body". Nor is the human body to be conceived as a "material substance" distinct from the soul, or, in the genuine Aristotelian sense, as the "matter" of the "soul", which has only actuality through the soul as its "form". The human body is man himself in the structural whole of his temporal appearance. And the human soul, in its pregnant religious sense, is man himself in the radical unity of his spiritual existence, which transcends all temporal structures.

No better than the traditional-scholastic conception of man as a rational-ethical being is the modern historicistic view that man is qualified by his cultural activity. Although it is undeniable that the latter has a human character and cannot be ascribed to animals, the cultural function can no more qualify man than the logical or the ethical modalities of his temporal existence. As explained in Volume II, it is only due to the absolutization of the historical aspect that the modal character of the cultural function has been overlooked.

If man lacks a specific temporal destination, it follows that the typical differences of race, nation, *etc.*, and those of temperament and character-disposition can never result in a division of mankind similar to the division found in the vegetable and animal kingdoms. The exaggeration of racial differences is only due to racial ideologies which lack a scientific foundation and are anti-Christian and inhuman in their political application.

But the further explanation of this subject belongs to philosophical anthropology, which we have reserved for a separate work. In the present context our only concern was to show that mankind is not enclosed in a radical type of the plastic temporal order. Man belongs neither to the animal kingdom, nor to a specific human kingdom of "rational-ethical" or "cultural beings".

Radical types of a secondary order which are typically related to human social life.

We shall see, however, that in the plastic dimension of the temporal order there are to be found radical types of a secondary order which are essentially related to the societal life of man, and in this sense have a typical human character. Their very plurality shows that they cannot give a radical typical determination of man himself. The secondary structural types, on the contrary, which we shall meet with in the animal kingdom, are implied in the radical type of the latter. This state of affairs already found expression in our circumscription of this radical type.

The leading function and the foundational function of a structural whole.

The radical type appeared to be the elementary and most fundamental structural principle for the typical groupage of the different modal functions within an individual whole which lacks a supra-modal centre. It determines the modality of the leading or guiding function, which qualifies every individual totality belonging to the same kingdom. But it does not inform us of the further inner articulation of a structure of individuality.

How can we theoretically approach this articulation in the descending series of divergent structural types with their complicated bifurcations according to the principles of similarity and diversity? This is a problem which since PLATO's dialogues *Sophistes* and *Politicos* has repeatedly been discussed in philosophy, without having found an ontologically well founded solution.

The general theory of the modal spheres has laid bare an inter-modal structural coherence between types of individuality which present themselves in different law-spheres [1]. It appeared that this structural coherence reveals a surprising analogy of the architectonic construction of a modal structure. There are modal types of an original or nuclear character, there are others which appear to be typically founded in nuclear types of a preceding modality, and still others which refer forward to original types of a later arranged modality. This state of affairs is very important for our further analysis of the inner articulation of the structures of individuality. It is well founded in the plastic dimension of the temporal order. And thus we are not in danger of falling back into arbitrary methods of logical classification, when here we seek a methodical point of connection for our following investigations.

The radical types remain our starting-point. But now we proceed from the modal determination of the leading function of an individual whole to the types of individuality which this function assumes in the inner articulation of a structural principle. If these modal types lack an original character, we have

[1] Cf. Vol. II, pp. 414—425.

to seek the modal aspect of the structural whole in which the latter displays its nuclear type of individuality. If this aspect precedes that of the leading or guiding function, it appears that the structural whole is characterized by two functions, *viz.* its leading function and a foundational function which has the nuclear type of individuality.

The anticipatory structure of the foundational function does not affect its nuclear type of individuality.

But here we are confronted with a difficulty which at first sight assumes the semblance of an antinomy. In the structural whole the foundational function cannot be in a closed condition. In its own modality it must express the structural unity of the whole in its qualification by the leading function.

This implies that the foundational function can only be conceived in an anticipatory coherence with the leading function; and this state of affairs must also reveal itself in its type of individuality. Does this not result in a cancellation of the distinction between anticipatory and nuclear types within the modal spheres?

When we consider this difficulty we should remember that we have met with a similar *aporia* in the analysis of the opening-process of the normative anticipatory spheres of the modal aspects. It has appeared that this opening-process is founded in the historical sphere, but in the last analysis is guided by the modal function of faith. In this context we have observed that the question in which modal sphere the process of disclosure takes its start, is only to be answered by distinguishing the two correlative directions of the cosmic order of time. In the foundational direction the historical sphere appeared to be the starting-point, in the anticipatory direction it could only be the modal sphere of faith. The circumstance that in the last analysis the opening of the historical or cultural aspect is itself guided by faith does not detract from the foundational rôle of the former in the process of disclosure.

In an analogous way we must solve the difficulty regarding the relation between the foundational and the leading function in the structures of individuality. The fact that the former can only be conceived in an anticipatory coherence with the latter does not affect the nuclear character of the type of individuality of the foundational function. In the retrocipatory direction of cosmic time this type shows no specific foundation in another type of a preceding modality. The leading function, on the contrary, does show such a retrocipatory typicalness. In other words, the original or nuclear type of the foundational function reveals itself only in the retrocipatory direction of time. In the anticipatory direction it does not appeal to another original type of a later arranged modality. It is consequently not the nuclear type itself which anticipates the leading function, it is rather the foundational function to which it belongs, that does so. The latter shows an anticipatory coherence with a leading function of a non-original type. This anticipatory structure of the foundational function, however, cannot give its type of individuality an anticipatory character.

The appearance of two characteristic structural functions in the further inner articulation of a structure of individuality turned out to be bound to the condition that the guiding function lacks an original type. It may be asked whether there are also structural totalities whose qualifying function shows an anticipatory type of individuality. This question is not to be answered in an *a-priori* way. I can only say that so far as my inquiry has extended I have not met with them.

Geno-, or primary types and variability types.

If the foundational function exhibits a morphological type of a specific modality, this may be an indication that we are confronted with a structural whole in which different structures are interlaced and combined into a typically qualified form-totality. The presence of such a foundational function may also indicate interlacements of different structures which lack such a combination into a morphological whole.

Both possible states of affairs will demand our attention in the course of our further investigations.

In the present introductory phase of our inquiry the interlacement, as such, gives us a criterion for a general division of the structural types presenting themselves within the same radical type. This division is founded in the plastic dimension of the temporal order, because the structures of individuality are interlaced in the cosmic coherence of time and cannot realize themselves in their theoretical abstraction. This is a state of affairs similar to that which we have observed in the modal structures. In the modal horizon the inner structural coherence of a modality is to be distinguished from the inter-modal coherence between the different aspects. Similarly, in the plastic horizon the inner coherence of the structural functions within a typical structural whole is to be distinguished from the inter-structural coherence due to its interlacement with other types of individual totalities.

But here the analogy ends. For, whereas the inter-modal coherence of the aspects finds expression exactly in their internal modal structures, a similar state of affairs in the plastic horizon is precluded by the very nature of the structures of individuality. Here the interlacements between structures of a different type only find expression within the latter in special types of individuality which are clearly distinct from those belonging to the irreducible inner structure of the whole.

Insofar as structural particularities in the descending inner articulation of a radical type are to be ascribed to the *internal structure* or inner nature of the individual whole, we shall style them *geno-* or *primary* types. Insofar as these structural particularities are dependent on morphological interlacements of an individual whole with individual totalities of a different radical- or geno-type, we shall speak of *variability-* or *pheno-types.*

The latter pre-suppose the geno-types and are consequently not to be viewed as a complex of external traits impressed upon an individual whole by another totality, *independent of the inner nature of the former.* This would be a mechanical view which does not fit to the structures of individuality. We can only say that the variability-types give expression to a variety of types of interlacement which, as such, cannot determine the inner nature of the totalities interlaced.

It may be that specific types of interlacement with other individual totalities are injurious to the natural unfolding of an individual whole. But it is indubitable that, generally speaking, interlacements are a necessary requirement for the realization of the inner nature of a thing. In other words, it is the geno-typical nature of an individual whole itself which is the ultimate standard of the distinction between natural and unnatural interlacements, consequently also of the distinction between natural and unnatural variability-types.

Within the vegetable and animal kingdoms we are, in addition, confronted with the enigmatical state of affairs that there are inter-structural interlacements which are natural to one of the interlaced individuals, and unnatural with respect to the internal structure of the other. A striking example of this state of affairs is to be found in the parasitical forms of symbiosis.

The internal differentiation of geno-types.

Geno-types may exhibit an immense internal differentiation of structural, mutually cohering larger and narrower *sub-types*, which retain their internal geno-typical character and are not reducible to variability-types.

Within a geno- or primary type the descending inner articulation will end in ultimate sub-types which show no evidence of further internal differentiation.

Within the radical type animal, for example, many geno-types can be distinguished: mammal, bird, fish, coelenterat, mollusc, insect, and so on. And within the geno-type insect, systematical zoology further distinguishes coleopteron, neuropteron, dipteron and others. The dipteron-type is again differentiated into culicide, tabanide, chironomide, *etc.* while the culicide-type permits a further distinction into the culex and the anopheles-type. The latter is composed of a great number of types, one of which is the maculipennis. This maculipennis, in turn, includes the messeae type, the typicus type and the labrianchiae type, the latter of which appears to contain the atroparvus and the elutus-type. Here we have arrived at final sub-types, which themselves again admit of numerous pheno-typical mutable variations, dependent upon the environment in which the animals live.

It is not the task of the theory of the structures of individuality to develop a typological system of this differentiation on its own account. It has only to lay bare the foundation of such a system in the plastic dimension of the temporal order and to analyze the problem of the structural whole in the diversity of its modal aspects. Special sciences are in a constant danger of surrendering to an evolutionistic or historicistic view which results in an elimination of the structures of individuality. Therefore it is necessary to emphasize that every genetic viewpoint pre-supposes these structures. The latter cannot be subject to genesis and evolution, it is only their *realization* in changeable individuals which permits a genetic investigation according to specific scientific viewpoints. Ideovariations (mutations) which occur within the vegetable or animal kingdoms cannot give rise to new *structural principles,* but only to *individuals* which exhibit a specific geno-type not yet realized before.

Every attempt at a causal genetic explanation of the geno-types and the radical-types themselves is meaningless. Every *phylon* which phylogeny seeks to establish, pre-supposes the radical types and their inner articulation in different geno-types whose successive realizations in individuals it arranges in a phyletic series. These realizations are dependent on specific conditions, but these conditions can never be constitutive of the structural principles whose realization was subject to the process of genesis. The great process of cosmic-temporal becoming presupposes the Divine creation of all things after their proper inner nature. And it is the temporal world-order which in its plastic dimension determines the inner nature of all individual totalities which are subject to genesis and decay in time.

The philosophical implications of evolutionism.

A consistent evolutionism must begin with a theoretical destruction of the modal structures before it can proceed to a theoretical destruction of the structures of individuality. It cannot accept irreducible modal aspects of the genetic process, because this would contradict the very pre-suppositions of evolutionism. The older Darwinistic theory was obliged to construe the process of genesis after the pattern of the classical Humanist science-ideal.

The continuous coherence of the modal structures and the structures of individuality in cosmic time, as well as their successive genetic realization in conformity to their temporal order, was replaced by the construction of a gap-less continuous mechanistic system of phylogenetic series; no single structure was supposed to be irreducible and the modal boundaries between the physico-chemical, the biotic, the physical and the post-physical aspects were completely levelled out.

The modern conception of emergent evolutionism rejects the mechanistic materialism of DARWIN and HAECKEL. But it has not abandoned the basic tenet of the latter, *viz.* that the biotic, psychical and so-called "mental" modalities of temporal reality have originated from physico-chemical constellations in a process of continuous evolution. Nevertheless it tries to maintain the proper nature of the "higher levels" of reality resulting from this process. This implies antinomies which we shall examine in the last chapter of this volume.

Evolutionism is not a specific scientific theory; it is a philosophical view. The discoveries of palaeontology which furnish the chief direct test of this view, refer to a genesis and evolution within the cadre of irreducible basic structures of individuality. They do not show that evolutionistic image of the development of the vegetable and animal kingdoms and of mankind which nowadays is to be found, *e.g.*, in the works of J. HUXLEY and SIMPSON. Even the facts established by embryology, to which HAECKEL appealed as the convincing proof of his famous "biogenetic basic law", have nothing to do with the philosophical basic tenet of evolutionism. The same remark must be made with respect to the results of the so-called "blood-reaction", which are interpreted as indirect proofs of the theory of descent. In the explanation of our anthropology we shall return to these questions and treat them in greater detail. In the present context we had only to lay bare the philosophical implications of the evolutionistic view of the genetic process.

The distinction between radical types, geno- or primary types and variability types is not limited to the kingdoms of natural things.

The division between geno- and pheno- or variability types calls to mind the distinction, current in the biological doctrine of heredity, between geno- and phenotypical factors [1], respectively traced back to intrinsic genetic predispositions and environmental influences.

Nevertheless, our division is not oriented to a specific scientific viewpoint. It pertains to the structures of individuality, as such, which should be presupposed in every specific scientific typology and cannot be replaced by the latter. This must be evident from the fact that the very problem in which a philosophical analysis of these structures is concerned, *viz.* the typical unity or order in the diversity of modal aspects of an individual whole, exceeds every specific scientific viewpoint.

But it might be that a cautious philosophical analysis of this fundamental problem can lay the foundation for a scientific revision of the classificatory concepts of systematic biology in a really structural-typological sense.

The distinction between radical types, primary types and variability types in the sense explained above, was applied to biology by Dr J. H. DIEMER [2], whose promising life ended in a German concentration camp. In an important thesis and different later writings he tried to demonstrate that the acceptance of this structural principle of individuality, in its correlation with the modal principle of function, can furnish a satisfactory solution to the controversial biological problem of structure. According to him, the traditional concept of species has lost its scientific value, since it has appeared that it is impossible to define it by means of sharp and generally serviceable criteria.

---

[1] In biology the word "*genotype*" has two meanings: 1. the fundamental constitution of an organism in terms of its hereditary factors; 2. a group of organisms each having the same combinations of hereditary characteristics. A *phenotype* is one that is distinguished by visible characteristics rather than by hereditary or genetic traits; the word also denotes all the individuals belonging to such a type.

[2] *Over Biotypen van Anopheles Maculipennis* (thesis, Leiden, 1935); *Het Soortbegrip en de Idee van het Structuurtype in de Biologie* (Phil. Ref. 1st Year, 1936 pp. 30 ff); *De Totaliteits-idee in de Biologie en de Psychologie* (Phil. Ref. 4th Year 1939); *De nieuwe holistische Biologie* (1936).

The relation of structural type and subjective (or objective) individuality of a thing.

We have observed that a *type*, as a *structure* of individuality, has the character of a law. Within the ultimate sub-types of geno-types, no further internal differentiation is evident, but these types, too, can never pass over into the a-typical subjective (or objective) individuality of the whole determined by them.

In our naïve experience the identity of the whole is retained throughout all transformation within its so-called "accidental" properties. If this identity were to be viewed as that of the *internal structural principle* only (*i.e.* of the geno-type in its inner articulation and in its enclosure by the foundational universal radical-type), then the datum in naïve experience would not yet be accounted for in a sufficient way.

This datum is not only the constant identity of an individualized geno-type, but very definitely of this individual whole which exhibits it in the context of its variability-types.

Our contention is that the identity in question must possess its law- and subject-sides in a mutual, unbreakable correlation; in other words, it must be both a-typically individual, and determined in conformity with its internal structural principle.

Let us again return to the first example of our analysis: the structure of a linden tree. In its radical type, its biotical function is its directing, leading, or qualifying function.

The ultimate sub-type of its geno-type is the boundary of the internal differentiation of its structural principle. And, since our tree will appear to be a typically qualified form-totality, in which different structures are interlaced, we may expect that its total structure has a typical foundational function. In addition, as an object of human culture, it shows a variability-type in its interlacement with my garden. It has become a garden-tree whose appearance typically differs from that of an un-cultivated individual of the same geno-type.

But this typological approach of our linden remains focused on the law-side of its individuality. As soon as we direct our attention to its individual subject-side, we must establish that also its subjective identity cannot be guaranteed by any of its modal functions, not even by its radical function in its ultimate a-typical individuality.

No cell remains the same in a living organism. But neither the inner changes in the individual biotical aspect of these micro-structures, nor the constant changing of the cells taken as a whole, can violate the individual identity of a tree. This clearly testifies to the fact that the latter is not based upon the modal horizon of our experience but upon the structurally determined individual whole. The only material point is that the qualifying function (in that individual manner, proper to this linden in my garden) continues to lead and direct its earlier functions, especially the physico-morphological pattern of the whole, as the foundational function; and that the inner operational coherence of this thing continues to reveal itself as an individual totality, in which every changed part continues to play its proper rôle.

And this individual totality, in its determination within the plastic horizon, furnishes the foundation of the internal structural functions of the three, and not *vice versa!* It is inter-modal in principle and expresses itself in each of its internal modal functions. This implies that a structural-theoretical examination of the latter presupposes the foundational transcendental Idea of the individual totality.

Theoretical thought does not dominate the plastic horizon; the reverse is true; the latter is the foundation of a correct Idea of totality. Only by bearing this in mind can the truth about the inner structure of things be discovered.

§ 4 - STRUCTURES OF INDIVIDUALITY HIDDEN TO NAÏVE EXPERIENCE AND DISCLOSED THROUGH THEORETICAL INVESTIGATION.

Our first introduction to the analysis of structures of individuality has chosen as an example a living natural thing, accessible to our naïve experience, without further qualification.

The sensory aspect of a tree presents itself in an objective macroscopic perceptional image in which its numerical, spatial, kinematic, physico-chemical and biotic functions (with their macro-processes) are objectified in relation to our subjective-sensory perceptive function.

A scientific structural investigation, however, that is not one-sidedly restricted to a theoretical concept of function, can disclose structures of individuality in the micro-world, which have not been objectified in the macroscopic perceptional world of naïve experience.

Why can we not find any original types of individuality in the mathematical modalities?

In this context we have to explain more precisely why original types of individuality are not present in the numerical, spatial and kinematic spheres. The reason is that in these three mathematical aspects no single qualifying or foundational function is to be found characteristic of the structure of an individual real whole. No single real thing or event is typically qualified or founded in an original mathematical aspect.

The energy-aspect appears to be the first modality in which the radical function of a kingdom of individual totalities presents itself.

Modern physics and chemistry have been confronted with the inner structure of atoms and molecules (as typical combinations of atoms) not in an *a-priori* manner, but after long inductive investigation. The positivist view that atoms are nothing but economical scientific fictions, since they are not perceptible to the eye of sense, has proved to be untenable. The reality of atoms and molecules has been definitely established from their perceptible operations. What is real cannot be resolved into bare modal functions, even though physics and chemistry focus their attention exclusively upon the physical and mathematical aspects of these micro-structures.

Radio-active investigations, for instance, succeeded in making the operations of individual atoms directly perceivable. It is now possible to view their activity objectively by means of the senses. Photography enables us to follow the path taken by an *individual particle in the encompassing gas-filled space*. The number of individual electrically charged atoms, thrown off by a radium quantum in a specific time, can be counted. This demonstrates that the theoretical investigations of physics have reached a real individuality-structure of the micro-world, which cannot be enclosed in the physical law-sphere, even though its qualifying function belongs to the latter. Physics teaches that the visibility of a body is dependent upon its relationship to light waves that touch it (whose wave length lies between 760 to 380 milimicron — a milimicron equals 0,000001 mM). We know, however, that the objective sensory aspect of reality is itself not physical in character.

Physics alone, from its modal physical point of view, cannot teach us what atoms really are, what they are as real micro-totalities.

A purely physical "*Ding an sich*", still referred to in philosophic discussion, is an intrinsically contradictory metaphysical construction. Modern wave-mechanics may resolve the old rigid material corpuscles into so-called "*Wellenpakete*" (packets of waves), but the most this concept can do is making the physical aspect of atoms accessible to us.

Classical mechanics conceived of matter as rigid, not capable of being added to or decreased. KANT viewed it as the space-filling substance in all physical changes. This conception of matter has been definitively discarded by modern physics as useless; the latter no longer recognizes an actual concept of substance [1]; but to infer from this that the transcendental Idea of an individual whole is hereby affected, is to confuse reality with its physical aspect [2].

Neither the reality of macro-things nor that of atoms can be exhausted in one or more law-spheres. The temporal unity of an individual whole (no matter whether it is to be conceived as a thing or as an event), in the diversity of its modal functions, is not modal in character, and can, therefore, not be grasped in any physical concept of function.

In the radio-active phenomena, physics encounters the physically qualified internal structural principle of radio-active elements, displaying a purely internal disintegration process, which cannot even be influenced by external, purely functional factors.

The internal structure of so-called chemical elements.

And does not each chemical "element" display an internal structure of individuality, differing fundamentally from a functionalistic concept of substance?

The presumably final or elementary "building blocks of matter", namely, electrons and protons (as well as the newly discovered neutrons, positive electrons, deuterons, mesons) viewed physically, exhibit in their free state the general energy function of mass and charge.

---

[1] Constant typical operational quanta are not "substantial".

[2] B. BAVINK, too, appears to fall into this error in his cited work p. 209. He stretches the physical concept of function too far in his thesis: 'Die Welt besteht aus lauter einzelnen Wirkungsquanten *h*, die in... einer vierdimensionalen "Ordnung" (x, y, z, t) verteilt sind'. [The world consists of merely single quantums of energy *h*, divided into... a four dimensional order (x, y, z, t)].

In the relationship of an internal atomic structure, however, they have a typical spatial order (according to the new wave mechanics, quantified wave paths around a centre) and possess typical chemical-physical totality-properties, related to a specific number and to a typical order of electronic paths. The atom, as *an individual totality, is not* to be deduced from the bare modal functional properties of its more elementary elements. It possesses a veritable structure of individuality in the radical type of the kingdom of physically qualified totalities.

A more complicated structure is to be found in molecules and crystals. But, just as in the case of a macro-whole like our linden-tree, a closer analysis of these structural complications must be put off till we have arrived at a special investigation of the enkaptic interlacements of different structural types, and especially of the figure of the enkaptic structural whole. The reader has not yet been prepared for a closer consideration of these complications in the present, merely introductory phase of our enquiry.

Observation: Modern physics now realizes that it cannot teach us *what* fills its modal functional schema x, y, z, (*ci*)t. It can only teach us *how* it is filled in the modal sense of the energy-aspect, though this "how" implies the typical quantum-structure of energy-operation. Even though physics itself was obliged to renounce the concept of substance, metaphysics is again ready to reconstruct it as a speculative basis for the physical concept of function. The neo-Thomistic philosophy of nature clings to the ether as a necessary substantial bearer of energy-operations, though since EINSTEIN's theory of relativity this ether can no longer play its classical rôle as an absolute system of reference. But even outside of the neo-Thomistic trend of thought we can notice a remarkable revival of the substance-concept in philosophically interested scientists. I need only indicate EDDINGTON's hypothesis that there is a world-substance unknown to physics, which can fill the formal schema x, y, z, t. It is supposed to be psychical in its nature. "Matter" is then considered to be only a formal modus, in which this world-soul appears to one of its parts, namely, to a conscious human spirit or to an animal. This is a complete restoration of metaphysical psycho-monism as it was earlier defended by HEYMANS in the Netherlands.

"Materialism", which could always place itself as an antipode against this spiritualism, is supposed to be refuted by the recent evolution of physics. And the hypothesis in question is assumed to be corroborated by the fact that the physical world-formula is purely mathematical in character, and mathematical forms are of an "undoubtedly spiritual" character. As if PLANCK's "*Wirkunsquantum*" *h* had a modal mathematical meaning! Naturally with respect to such an idealistic metaphysics, physics had best maintain a wise silence. But physics, when it is confronted with phenomena which do not allow themselves to be purely functionally explained, may not ignore the structures of individuality which express themselves in the latter. As these structures appear to be structures of cosmic time, they have nothing to do with the rigid concept of substance, as an absolute point of reference for its accidental relations.

The internal structure of a living cell.

Biology has discovered the cell as the last independent viable unity of a living mass, without being able on its own account to solve the philosophical problem of its structure of individuality. And in this case, too, it is true that — even though the qualifying function of this thing-structure, at least in plant cells, is of a biotical modality — the thing-structure itself is not resolved in this function. The reality of the cell is beyond doubt, though it is not directly accessible to naïve experience.

The individual organic vital function of a cell, in the internal thing-structure, directs the numerical, spatial, kinematic and physical-chemical functions. And the thing-structure expresses itself objectively in the theoretically opened sensory image of perception, in its objective logical function, and so on. But here, too, we are confronted with structural complications which can only be treated in a later phase of our inquiry. Therefore we cannot yet subject the internal structure of the cell to a closer analysis, but must restrict ourselves to some general remarks.

Electrons, protons, *etc.*, may freely move outside of the atomic structures; similarly the biotical function, as such, also reveals itself outside of the typical cell-structure. Modern histology has made evident that at least more developed bodies, in particular those of animals and men, contain many living, non-cellular combinations. But, apart from their relation to living cells, the so-called exoplasmic constituents of the organism, do not appear any more viable than the so-called endoplasmic particles within a cell deprived of its nucleus [1].

Both structural totalities remain hidden to naïve experience; only theoretical investigation unfolds them to us [2]. In both cases

---

[1] Cf. Dr R. WOLTERECK, *Grundzüge einer allgemeinen Biologie* (1932) pp. 313 ff.

[2] It stands to reason that natural science also reveals to us macro-thing-structures which, because of their gigantic distances from our earth and spatial circumference, are just as much hidden to naïve experience. Naïve experience is bound to the natural field of perception though we have seen that it is by no means restricted to the sensory aspect of its experiential world.

we are struck by the indissoluble coherence between the internal thing-structure and the external functional relations, and by the enormous intricacy due to the fact that the simple structures function in evermore complicated totalities.

Both states of affairs will be in the centre of our later investigations concerning the study of mutually interconnected structures. Before conducting such an investigation it is necessary for us to institute a schematic investigation with respect to other radical and geno-types of individuality.

Unless we have gained such a schematic synopsis, we cannot acquire an insight into the nature of the intertwinements of the different thing-structures.

CHAPTER III

THE SUBJECT-OBJECT RELATION IN THE THING-STRUCTURE OF REALITY

§ 1 - THE INNER STRUCTURAL CHARACTER OF THE SUBJECT-OBJECT RELATION IN A THING.

Up until now we have examined only the structures of things which, with respect to their radical type, are qualified by an internal subject-function in the physical and biotic modality respectively [1].

The temporal reality of things determined by these structures is not completed in the modality in which they have their leading or qualifying function.

A brief modal analysis of the thing-structure of a tree (a macro-thing), discloses that in all later modal aspects it possesses possible object-functions. The latter are as yet unopened in full temporal reality. For their disclosure they depend on corresponding subject-functions, which are not found in the tree itself.

Again we are confronted here with he subject-object relation within the temporal horizon of reality. Previously, in our theory of the modal spheres, we were able to examine only the abstract modal significance of this relation. But now, in our theory of the structures of individuality, it takes on a new aspect, determined by the *plastic horizon* of human experience, within which we must re-examine the subject-object relation.

The structure of a thing expresses itself in each of its modal aspects of meaning.

In this investigation, too, our leading viewpoint is that the structure of a thing expresses itself in each of its modal aspects.

The modal subject-functions of our linden-tree are not objectified without plastic structure in the tree's objective-sensory

[1] We have already noted that the animal kingdom has a psychical qualification in its radical type.

perceptional image. Rather, it is the biotically qualified natural thing which, according to the full plasticity of its internal structure and variability-type, expresses itself within the psychical object-side of reality in the sensorily perceptible image familiar to us [1].

The internal structure of our tree in its variable realization expresses itself also in all the later modalities in which it functions as this individual living natural thing.

Only after we have gained a theoretical insight into this continuous expression of a thing's internal structure and variability-type in all its modal aspects, can justice be done to our naïve experience.

The actual subject-functions of our linden are objectified in its object-functions in such a way that the latter betray the structural architecture of the whole, in the typical groupage of its aspects. In its sensorily perceptional image, for example, the qualifying function, as such, delineates itself in an objective modal analogy, which hereby acquires a dominant position in the total image. In naïve experience this immediately distinguishes the objective sensory image of a living tree from that of a dead thing though doubt may arise with respect to trees affected by disease. And similarly the objective sensory total image of an animal, generally speaking, expresses the leading psychical function of the latter. If we do not consider theoretical borderline cases, we are almost directly conscious whether or not a sensorily perceived image belongs to an inorganic or an organic living thing, to an animal or a plant.

In such instances the internal structural functions of a thing display an extremely complicated character. If the thing-structure actually expresses itself in every one of these functions, then in the first place its leading function must be the expression of the structural totality.

The internal structural-character of the qualifying function.

If we return to the micro-structure of the atom, we may thus establish that the leading function of the latter will display an internal structural individuality in the physical modality.

Qualified by the nuclear moment of the modal structure of

---

[1] Earlier empiricistic psychology erroneously resolved this sensory total image into functionally distinct impressions only subjectively associated by our function of perception.

energy, the modal analogies of number, space and motion individualize themselves within an internal typical structure in the leading function of the micro-whole we call an "atom". In this internal structure they are determined by the nuclear moment individualized in the leading function.

The entire complex system of modal foundations [1], examined in the theory of modal spheres, reappears in a new complication in the modal aspects of a structural whole. And what applies to the theoretically disclosed micro-totalities is valid *a fortiori* for the macro-things of naïve experience, whose individuality-structure is much more directly accessible to us. It is profitable to penetrate this extremely intricate state of affairs, so that we are fully aware of the distortion of naïve experience by a functionalistic conception which bypasses the problem of a thing-structure, and by abstract simplification theoretically demolishes what is given in the pre-theoretical experiential attitude.

The structural principles are not dependent on the genesis of individuals in which they are realized.

We have seen that the structural principles, which appeal to the continuity of the cosmic temporal order, are, as such, in no way dependent upon the genesis of individuals in which they are realized. As we saw in Volume II, they rather belong to the plastic dimension of the temporal world-order.

It is of course impossible to determine in a subjective *a priori* manner what actual individual things exist in our cosmos. But the typical structural principles of things are not subjective, but are of a structural *a priori* determining character [2]. This does not mean that our *theoretical knowledge* of these structural laws of individuality is *a priori*. Their *a priori* character only refers to the *ontical temporal order*. This is to say that they are the structural frame in which alone the process of genesis and decay of individual beings is possible.

Objective thing-structures qualified by a psychical structural function.

It is indeed the various types of *structural principles of indi-*

---

[1] The Dutch text has the term "*funderingen*", which means that the retrocipatory analogies in a modal structure in the last instance are founded in the original modal nuclei to which they refer.

[2] Cf. Vol. II p. 478 for the distinction between structural and subjective *a priori*.

vidual totalities that are here being subjected to a theoretical analysis.

Our present interest is with the subject-object relation in connection with a thing-structure. Our investigation will be concerned, in the first place, with the question whether or not there are structures of individuality in which a thing is not qualified by a leading subject-function, but rather by an individual object-function.

Provisionally limiting our investigation to natural things, and temporarily leaving alone the more complex normatively qualified products of human formation, we can in fact establish the existence of natural things, qualified by a structural object-function.

All things of nature, formed or produced by animal activity, are to be considered as objective natural things. The macro-world of naïve experience, as well as the micro-world show a very varied wealth of such animal products: ant hills, bird nests, honey-combs, spiders' webs, beaver dams, shells of molluscs, silicious forms produced by *protozoa,* and the numberless other amazing formations produced by animal instinct.

With respect to their internal structure, these things undoubtedly have individual subject-functions in the mathematical and physical aspects, but their qualifying function is not in these spheres. The subjective vital instinct of animals has formed them into objects of animal life, qualified by a typical animal-psychical object-function, which has the leading rôle in the structure of this thing. The actualization of this object-function is dependent on animal subjectivity.

This state of affairs clearly shows the secondary character of these form-products, which lack an independent radical-type and can only exist and be experienced in their subject-object relation to the animals which have produced them.

Nowhere else is the intrinsic untenability of the distinction between meaning and reality so conclusively in evidence as in things whose structure is objectively qualified.

Anyone who theoretically restricts the reality of these animal products to the pre-biotic modalities, is left with a theoretical abstraction in which the actual natural thing does not structurally express itself. The mistake, inherent in the distinction between created reality and meaning, is nowhere more apparent than in things whose qualifying function is only given in a subject-object relation.

For it is really impossible to ascribe their typical nature to an independent "substance". Their very nature is meaning, realized in a structural subject-object relation. A bird's nest is not a "thing in itself", which *has* a specific meaning in the bird's life. It has *as such* no existence apart from this meaning.

Anyone who theoretically eliminates the latter does not retain the objective reality of a bird's nest, but an aggregate of materials of different structure, which lacks the very nature of this animal form-product as an individual whole. Such things are united with the animal creatures which formed them in an individual bio-psychical relationship. Even when detached from the latter they remain qualified as objective animal formations.

To account for many remarkable phenomena in this domain, science, in the narrow sense, must have an insight into this state of affairs.

The protoplasm of rhizopodes, for example, produces firm formations which consist of minerals (in particular silicic acids, as in the case of radiolaria and the diatoms, and calciumcarbonate, as in the case of foraminiferes and calc-algae). The siliceous lattices, -tubes and -radii, or the calc-shells, -lattices and -spiculae formed in this way, display different shapes and patterns from type to type, which are unrelated to the physico-chemically qualified crystalline forms of silicic acid and calcium carbonate.

WOLTERECK observes that if the $Si\ O_2$-formations of radiolaria were composed of $Si\ O_2$-crystals, these animal products could be conceived of as aggregate forms, whose law-conformity would be based on the crystallization laws of silicic acid. Actually the plasm of these protozoa produces thousands of specific siliceous forms which all deviate from the formational laws of the mineral silicic acid anhydrite [1].

Typical mathematical structural functions of these formations are here revealed, which have an unbreakable coherence with the physico-chemical, the biotic, and (with the radiolaria) the psychical functions of the *protophyta* and *protozoa* concerned. Their total-structure appears to be of a typical biotical and

---

[1] WOLTERECK, *op. cit.*, pp. 118 and 119.

psychical qualification respectively, which reveals itself in a typical subject-object relation.

And the reality of these natural things cannot even be restricted to the pre-logical aspects. In connection with subjective human existence, these natural things have closed structural object-functions in all the normative modalities. These object-functions can be disclosed and actualized by subjective human activity.

Reality as a continuous process of realization.

For the reality of a thing is indeed dynamic; it is a continuous realization in the transcendental temporal direction.

The inner restlessness of meaning, as the mode of being of created reality, reveals itself in the whole temporal world. To seek a fixed point in the latter is to seek it in a "*fata morgana*", a mirage, a supposed thing-reality, lacking meaning as the mode of being which ever points beyond and above itself. There is indeed nothing in temporal reality in which our heart can rest, because this reality does not rest in itself.

§ 2 - THE OBJECTIVE THING-STRUCTURE OF A SCULPTURE.

Our provisional analysis of the typical structures of objective natural things made us aware of manifold interweavings between things. Consider for instance the heterogeneous constituents of a bird's nest, joined by a typical form-totality resulting from animal shaping. These materials have their own internal structure, which may be very complicated and which differ radically from that of a bird's nest. Beaver dams, ant hills, and honeycombs are themselves the objective products of co-operation carried on in a subjective animal societal relationship. The latter has itself been organized by a group instinct into a real unity amidst the diversity of individual animals.

In our subsequent treatment of *enkapsis* we shall examine, in a more inclusive and basic manner, these structural interlacements. They become increasingly complex if we focus our attention upon the normatively qualified thing-structures, instead of upon those belonging to the three natural radical types.

For the present we are considering the subject-object relation in the thing-structures of reality and our immediate concern is with *things qualified by a normative object-function.* Enkaptic structures will be dealt with, therefore, only insofar as it is necessary to do so in the context of this enquiry.

As a first example of a normatively qualified objective thing we shall examine a work of fine art of the primary-type sculpture[1]: Hermes with the boy Dionysus, the master-piece of the Greek sculptor PRAXITELES.

Do all works of fine art actually have an objective thing-structure? If they do not, can we still speak of "works of art" as a secondary radical-type?

It would be incorrect to assume that all works of fine art display the structure of objective things. This will be obvious if we compare plastic types (*i.e.* painting, sculpture, wood carvings, *etc.*) with music, poetry and drama.

Works of art belonging to the last category lack the constant actual existence proper to things in the narrower sense. They can only be constantly objectified in the structure of scores, books, *etc.* And we shall show later on that such things as scores and books, are, as such, symbolically qualified. They can only *signify* the aesthetic structure of a work of art in an *objective* way and cannot *actualize* it.

This is why artistic works of these types are always in need of a subjective actualization lacking the objective constancy essential to works of plastic art. Because of this state of affairs they give rise to a separate kind of art, *viz.* that of *performance,* in which aesthetic objectification and actualization, though bound to the spirit and style of the work, remain in direct contact with *the re-creating individual conception of the performing artist.* The latter's conception, as such, cannot actualize itself in a constant form, though modern technical skill has succeeded in reproducing musical sound-waves by means of a phonograph.

In the third section of the preceding chapter we have introduced the term "secondary radical types" to denote the ultimate *genera* of the different human societal relationships. The secondary character of these radical types appeared from the fact that they are of a human character and therefore pre-suppose human nature, without being able to define the latter. The objectified products of the human "mind" are in addition of a secondary typical character, since they can only exist in a structural subject-object relation.

---

[1] *Translator's note:* "Primary types" are geno-types. Pheno-types are "variability-types".

A radical type, as such, cannot imply an answer to the question whether or not the individual totalities belonging to its "kingdom" are to be viewed as "things" in a narrower sense [1].

Therefore, there cannot be raised any justified objection against the assumption that all works of fine art (inclusive of such which can only be constantly objectified in a symbolically qualified structure) show the same radical type.

And this assumption, quite familiar to naïve experience, is well founded from an ontological viewpoint.

A work of art *qua talis* is not a mere general logical concept resulting from an arbitrary abstraction. It is a radical type of a strictly *a priori* character. It is firmly rooted in the plastic horizon of our experience and the plastic dimension of the cosmic-temporal order. As such it embraces constant geno-types and variability-types.

Analysis of the internal typical structure of PRAXITELES' Hermes with the boy Dionysus.

We shall now examine the structure of individuality of PRAXITELES' sculptural master-piece: Hermes with the boy Dionysus. If our first concern is with an analysis of the modal functions of its internal thing-structure, it might, at first glance, seem that the whole inter-modal foundational relationship, previously examined in the theory of modal spheres, breaks down at a critical point.

Unquestionably the last modal subject-function of this marble statue is found in the physico-chemical aspect. Equally certain is the fact that with respect to its radical type it is qualified by an objective-aesthetic function. And unless endowed with an internal structure of individuality, anticipating the aesthetic object-function, the physico-chemical subject-function could not be the expression of the internal structure of the objective work of art, as a thing.

The first difficulty, however, arises when we try to re-discover the temporal order of the modal aspects, explained in the second Volume, within the internal structure of the statue. At first sight the latter seems to lack an actual function in the biotic modality.

---

[1] A thing in its proper sense implies a relatively constant realization of its individuality-structure. A poem, a musical composition or a drama are imaginative totalities of an aesthetic qualification which can be reproduced only in a coherent series of mental acts and acts of performance, with the aid of their symbolical objectification in books and scores.

This would contradict the theory of the modal law-spheres, according to which the aesthetic object-function is founded in all its substratum functions, inclusive of the biotic aspect. If the structure of Hermes lacks a biotic function, the entire foundational relationship becomes highly problematical.

That all post-physical structural functions of the statue must possess an *objective* character and stand in an unbreakable *coherence* with the corresponding subject-functions of human temporal experience is clearly evident.

Beginning with the psychical modality it is no trouble to analyse these objective structural functions in the work of art. It is just the biotical modality that seems to be a stumbling block.

The artist was obliged to work with an inorganic material and as a consequence the statue seems to lack a biotic object-function. For in the context of the work of art there can in the nature of the case be no question of marble as a "means of life", which objective biotic function we really may ascribe to water and other in-organic matter. So we seem to be confronted by a thing-structure lacking an essential modal aspect of reality, if the theory of law-spheres be true.

Is this really the case? Generally speaking we can say that the sculpture must have a biotic object-function because without the latter it could not be sensorily perceptible. We refer to our earlier statement that biotic stimuli excercised on the nerves of the sense-organs cannot be caused by external things and events, if the latter would lack an objective biotic aspect[1]. But in the present context we are not satisfied with this general statement since we are engaged in the analysis of a particular structure of individuality.

We wish to gain an insight into the typical structure of PRAXITELES' Hermes even in its objective biotic function, whose presence in a general sense may be granted. In the work of art under consideration the living body of the god and that of the boy Dionysus are objectively represented in a sensorily perceptible image. This is doubtless a structural particularity which is not proper to all sculptures. We might just as readily have chosen as an example an abstract sculptural work, exclusively dominated by the harmony of lines, the proportional configuration of planes, *etc.*

---

[1] Cf. p. 40 of this Vol.

The complicated representational relation in the objective-sensory aspect of sculpture.

Nevertheless, let us pause a moment to consider the abovementioned particularity of PRAXITELES' sculpture in more detail. For in its objective sensory aspect it contains the interesting "*Abbild-relation*", whose modal structure we have analysed in Volume II [1]. Yet it might be that from this structural particularity we get a deeper insight into the inner coherence between the modal aspects of the sculpture's total structure.

Let us suppose that the artist had used a living model. The objective sensorily perceptional image of the marble statue is certainly not a simple copy of that of the living pattern. Although possessing an individual aesthetic aspect, the human body is not *qualified* aesthetically; properly speaking, it is not a work of art; it has not the typical inner destination of the latter. The artist, in his subjective aesthetic conception, rather visualized his Hermes as a product of his aesthetic fantasy in the body of his living model. He was concerned essentially with the individual, aesthetically qualified total structure of his conception, to which he must give expression also in the visual sensory form of the sculpture.

In this respect the critical idealism of RICKERT loses sight of the actual situation. It restricts the empirical reality of a work of art to a matter of sensory impressions in time and space formed by the understanding into the synthesis of a thing, which our aesthetical judgment only relates in a subjective individualizing manner to an "aesthetic value". But the qualifying individuality of the Hermes in its full empirical reality is really aesthetic in nature. If the realization of PRAXITELES' aesthetic conception as such were not of an incomparable artistic individuality, the individuality of this work of art would be ascribable to a "sensory material" only. For an abstract ideal world of values, as such, lacks any individuality.

Our contention, on the contrary, is that the proper sensory "*Urbild*" reproduced in PRAXITELES' Hermes, is *not the sensory form of the living model*. In the individual "*Abbild-relation*" the sensory image of the marble statue is much rather directly related to the ideal harmonious sensory shape evoked in the productive fantasy of the artist by the contemplation of his living model.

---

[1] Vol. II, pp. 375 ff.

Lacking an *original* sensory objectivity[1], the sensory form of the marble Hermes has thus the objectivity of an aesthetically qualified structural "*Abbild*". To understand the structural subject-object relation implied in PRAXITELES' master-piece, an insight into this state of affairs is of the utmost importance. The relation in question is in principle different from a merely *natural "Abbild-relation"* (such as is implied in the inverted image of a thing on the retina of the eye).

The structural-sensory object-aspect of a natural thing (in its individual beauty) is not necessarily related to the individual productive fantasy of the perceiving subject. And it does not have an inner aesthetically qualified structure, but expresses the structure of a *natural thing.*

This is why the "natural" beauty of such a thing is also not especially related to the productive fantasy of the artist. Rather it pertains to the subjective aesthetic experiential function of everybody who is receptive to beauty. We can only say that this objective beauty, which is present in the thing in a latent objective function, is made manifest, *i.e.* disclosed, in the actual subject-object relation to the receptive aesthetical appreciation of the observer. But there is no question here of the realization of an aesthetic conception in an artistic thing-structure.

In PRAXITELES' Hermes, in contrast, we are really confronted with such a structure. With respect to its sensory form, this thing is actually an image or copy of the visionary sensory shape, originally born in the productive fantasy of the artist.

Productive and reproductive fantasy respectively in the creation and appreciation of a work of art.

To comprehend the objective reality of this work of art, the observer must contemplate it as the structural objective realization of the subjective aesthetic conception of the artist. By deepening and enriching his natural aesthetic vision, he must actually acquire a reproductive aesthetic fantasy. When this is lacking, he can view the objective aesthetic structure of a work of art only as a more or less close resemblance of the beautiful "living model" and in consequence judge it solely in terms of its similarity to natural beauty. The objective reality of the *work of art* entirely escapes him, since he does not experience its individual structural *meaning.*

---

[1] Vol. II, pp. 374 ff.

To say that such an observer does experience the actual thing, *viz.* as an individual natural entity, while losing sight only of the aesthetic "idea" realized in it, is inaccurate. The thing presented here *is the work of art.* A natural thing is not given at all in this structure. PRAXITELES' Hermes does not have any real existence apart from its incomparable aesthetically qualified structure. By viewing the real work of art as a copy of a beautiful natural object, the observer lacks a real experience of this sculpture.

The merely intentional character of the object of fantasy.

In this context we have still to consider a question concerning the objectification of an aesthetic conception.

We noticed, in our analysis of the modal subject-object relation, that a transcendental modal subject-function cannot objectify itself within its own modality [1]. If this be true, how can the subjective aesthetic conception be aesthetically objectified in a work of art? To answer this question the productive aesthetic fantasy must be studied more closely.

In Volume II (p. 425/6) we have explained that the latter is typically founded in the sensory function of imagination, which in a restrictive sense is also to be observed in animal psychical life, at least in that of the higher organized animals.

Sensory imagination really exhibits a productive objectifying function.

And a peculiar subject-object relation is disclosed in the visual fantasm. Our theory of the modal spheres did not yet permit us to investigate this subject-object relation in more detail. The latter is only intelligible in connection with the intentional structure of a fancied thing or event.

The sensory fantasm is not really related to the pre-psychical subject- or subject-object functions of an actually existing thing or actually occurring event; it is rather the objective sensory aspect of the product of our imagination. In the aesthetically qualified conception of PRAXITELES this productive imagination has *projected* the sensory image of his Hermes as a merely *intentional* visionary object.

In our productive fantasy we are thus indeed confronted with an *intentional* object, in the sense explained in the modal analy-

[1] Cf. Vol. II, part I, p. 370.

sis of the subject-object relation in context with the scholastic logical conception of the *objectum intentionale*[1]. In itself this object does not have any relation (except an intentional one) to the concrete object-side of temporal reality, presented in the structure of a thing.

This intentional object is nevertheless bound to the modal and the plastic dimensions of the temporal horizon of experience and of reality. And just because it is bound to the transcendental horizon of experience, the fancied objective structure of a thing is a *potential* structure capable of being represented in a real thing. *And it is essential to the reality of the latter that it be a representation of the fancied thing-structure.*

Viewed modally, it is therefore incorrect to speak of an aesthetic objectification of the aesthetic subject-function of the artist.

The aesthetic object-function of the work of art is only the aesthetic representation, in the objectively-aesthetically qualified structure of a real thing, of a merely intentional aesthetic object of the fantasy of the artist. Nevertheless, this intentional object can only function in an intentional subject-object relation of aesthetic modality. And so its aesthetical objectification in the sculpture is an implicit objectification of this intentional relation. It is not, however, an objectification of the aesthetic subject-function *as such, i.e.* apart from a particular intentional relation to the Hermes, as an object of PRAXITELES' aesthetic fantasy[2]. And this was meant by the term "transcendental modal subject function".

*

With our present background, let us examine more closely the coherence of structural functions inherent in PRAXITELES' work of art. First, observe that the vital function of Hermes and the boy Dionysus was objectively *intended* in the artistic conception

---

[1] Cf. Vol. II, part I, pp. 387 ff.

[2] It is absolutely necessary to make our analysis as careful as possible here, although the modal distinctions made are extremely hard to follow. The modal import of the concepts is sharply defined, but they are unintelligible unless an insight is gained into the theoretical states of affairs under investigation. *The difficulty connected with a clear analysis of the modal aspects of a structure of individuality originates from the fact that every aspect is an expression of the structural whole.* Thus it must seem that the aspects pass into each other, if we lose sight of their different modality.

of these figures. In the aesthetically qualified structure of his artistic conception, the artist indeed had a productive vision of two living deified human bodies. The organic vital function of Hermes and the boy Dionysus was thus undoubtedly implicitly intended in his productive fantasy. This aesthetic *intention* is realized in the objective structure of the statue, as a thing.

The marble Hermes does not *live subjectively,* as does a living model. But, in its aesthetic structure, the intentional vital function has been objectively represented or depicted. *And this objective representation belongs to the reality of the marble Hermes with the boy Dionysus. The artist must have viewed the anatomic structure of the living bodies, but in its individual disclosure and deepening by the productive aesthetic fantasy.*

This is undoubtedly a peculiarity of PRAXITELES' Hermes which other works of art need not have. It is of essential importance, however, for an understanding of the internal structure of this particular work of art.

The typical foundational function of a sculptural work of art and the problem of its modal determination.

According to the structural principle of PRAXITELES' Hermes, the *leading* appears to belong to a typical aesthetic object-function of an internal structural character; namely, *to the harmonious objectification of an intentional (imagined) aesthetically qualified, Hermes- and Dionysus-figure.* And, the aesthetic expression of the vital function of the sculptured bodies appears to be *essential* in the typical leading structural function.

Of course the artist could also have given a sculptural expression to an aesthetic vision of two dead bodies. But then the character of the work of art would have been entirely different. The essential character of the intended vital function is directly evident if you consider the wonderful technique PRAXITELES employed to acquire such a life-like effect in marble. Consider the inimitable position of the head of Hermes; the dreaming-pensive expression of the face; the tender warm tone of de body achieved by rubbing the surface with wax; the application of a refined technique of painting to the hair and eyes; and the gracious position of the left arm, bearing the boy Dionysus, while the right arm[1] playfully shows a bunch of grapes to the child.

---

[1] The damaged statue present in the Louvre at Paris shows only a fragment of this arm.

A closer examination immediately reveals that *a structurally unbreakable relationship with a typical foundational or substratum-function* is expressed in the leading structural function of Hermes. The type of individuality of the leading aesthetic function is not *original,* but has its final typical foundation in an *earlier* modal type, in a manner generally explained in Volume II, Chap. VI, § 3 (pp. 423 ff.).

This peculiar feature of a structural principle was already encountered in our earlier investigation of structures of individuality in natural things. We were, however, obliged to defer a closer analysis of this state of affairs because it appeared to cohere with an intricate complication in the structure of a natural whole displaying the character of a so-called enkaptic form-totality.

But in the present context we must proceed to a first reconnoitering of such internal structural interlacements insofar as they are revealed in PRAXITELES' sculptural work of art. For we cannot penetrate any further into the structure of individuality of this masterpiece apart from a provisional investigation of these interlacements. In addition we need such a provisional enquiry for the structural analysis of all the other products of human formation. But the necessity of this enquiry in the present context cannot appear before we have discovered the orginal or nuclear modal type of individuality in which the typicalness of the leading aesthetic object-function of PRAXITELES' Hermes is founded. For, since the latter does not show this nuclear type, the internal geno-type of this work of art must have a typical foundational function and consequently be characterized by two typical structural functions.

But, in which modal law-sphere is this foundational function enclosed? What modality of meaning does it have? This problem is extremely difficult and of great importance for our subsequent investigations.

If our thinking were conditioned by the Aristotelian form-matter schema, our inclination would be to seek the typical foundational function of the work of art in the marble material. It is, however, certain that this material itself possesses a *natural* structure of individuality and is therefore not to be comprehended in a merely modal-functional manner.

Why the typical foundational function of the work of art cannot be found in the natural leading function of the marble.

The internal structure of individuality of the unfinished marble is undoubtedly qualified by its typical physico-chemical structural function (as the "leading" function). The type of individuality revealed in the qualifying energy-aspect of its structure can only be brought to light by a physico-chemical analysis. As we shall see presently, this analysis shows that, as to its chemical structure, marble is nothing but a variability type of an original geno-type of inorganic matter.

Is the typical foundational function of PRAXITELES' Hermes to be found in this leading function of the natural marble?

A seemingly strong case can be made against an affirmative answer to the above question. In the treatment of the problem of modal individuality, in our general theory of law-spheres, we discovered that the subjective aesthetic conception, with its merely intentional objectivity, is typically founded in the sensory function of fantasy. Doesn't this imply that the objective fully-realized work of art must find its typical objective foundation in the same modality; namely, the modality of feeling? In other words, is it not the sensory objectified fantasy-form which is to be viewed as the typical substratum function of Hermes, rather than its pre-sensory, physico-chemical structural function?

But we should not overlook an essential fact, *viz.* that the objective sensory fantasy-form of the Hermes is not a merely intentional one, in the same sense as that of the subjective artistic conception. This fantasy-form has been depicted and realized in the marble material. Therefore we may ask: does not this fantasy-form refer to the original meaning-individuality of the physico-chemical function of the marble?

It is impossible, however, for the internal leading function of the natural product, as such, to be the typical original substratum function of the marble Hermes. The raw marble, as a natural product, does not yet have within itself anything that can serve as the typical original foundation of the individuality of this work of art.

As an object of human moulding, the marble is fully a *δυνάμει ὄν*, *i.e.* a material that can assume every possible cultural form, and can just as well be made into a thing entirely lacking the inner structure of a work of fine art.

The physico-chemical aspect of the marble Hermes cannot contain the leading structural function of a natural thing, but only an internal structural function of this specific sculptural work of art. But, as such, it can no more be considered as the *typical foundational function* of the latter, because, even in its internal physico-chemical function *within* the work of art, the marble continues to be a bare *material* for the aesthetic expression.

The sensory structural function of PRAXITELES' Hermes does not have an original individuality.

The marble statue, as such, is the objective plastic *representation* of an aesthetically qualified intentional fantasy-object, which itself appeared to be typically founded in a sensory fantasm. Since the physico-chemical function of the marble-material appears to be eliminated as a possible typical foundational function of the Hermes, it may seem once again that this rôle is only to be ascribed to the objective sensory image of this sculptural work. On closer observation, however, it is evident that such a solution does not touch the real state of affairs.

For on the one hand, the objectivity of this sensory image is not *original* but representational; and on the other the artist's plastic activity is an *original free formation*, as such pointing beyond the sensory aspect.

To be an adequate typical foundation of the aesthetic typicalness of the marble statue, the sensory image should have to be *given* in nature, and it has been conclusively demonstrated that it is not.

The sensory figure of the Hermes is not a *natural* form of marble, but is only the sensory expression of an aesthetically qualified controlling formation of the material after the artist's own free project. It is, in other words, not *original* in its own typical individuality, but anticipatory.

The typical historical foundational function of a sculpture in connection with the stylistic element. Style as a differentiating factor in its geno-type.

Our conclusion is that the real typical foundational function of PRAXITELES' work of art is found solely in the historical law-sphere, modally qualified by free formative control [1].

---

[1] Cf. Vol. II, Part I, pp. 192 ff.

The nuclear type of individuality of the statue is thus to be ascribed to its objective historical structural function, and not to its physico-chemical or objective sensory functions: the objective-technical depictive form given to the marble material by the hand of the artist, is in truth the typical modal substratum of the statue's aesthetic individuality.

This conclusion may appear strange at first, but it undeniably explains states of affairs essential to this plastic work of art.

If we consider the inner articulation of the geno-type: plastic work of art, we first meet with the pictorial, the mimic and the sculptural types[1]. The latter embraces the narrower type of sculptured figures of deities and, as a sculptural type, it shows the variability-type of marble-sculpture which we shall examine presently.

The type "sculptured figures of deities" doubtless finds its modal nuclear type of individuality in the cultural or historical aspect.

The entire further differentiation of the narrower geno-type "sculptured figures of deities" is dependent upon a style-moment; and from our general theory of modalities we know that a style-moment is a typical historical analogy (already endowed with a type of individuality) in the aesthetic modality.

This moment, too, typically points back from the aesthetic modality to the historical. A style-moment is essential only to the aesthetic typicalness of *art* and is naturally absent in the beauty of *nature*.

It must be acknowledged, moreover, that also in naïve experience the technical form appears as the typical bearer of the entire aesthetic structure of the free work of art[2], even though this foundational function is here theoretically unanalysed.

Technical form and the leading aesthetic expression of the artist's conception are the two aspects characterizing our experience of every sculptural work of art. Their inner structural unity is a requirement of every good and mature sculpture.

---

[1] Cf. p. 123, note of this vol.

[2] A work of fine art is free, when it is not enclosed in an *enkaptic* structural whole which lacks an aesthetic qualification. We shall subsequently elaborate this point.

The secondary radical-type of a work of art reconsidered. Why all secondary radical types of man-made complete things imply two radical functions.

Is it only the *geno*-type "sculptural art-work" that has a typical historical foundation, or does the *radical type* of the entire "kingdom of works of art" imply such a typical cultural basis?

If we take the term radical-type in its orginal sense defined previously, this question must cause some surprise. For a radical-type in this original sense was conceived as the ultimate genus of a structure of individuality, in which the qualifying function of the whole is only determined in its general modal meaning. The typical foundational function did not make its entrance into our investigation before we had considered the gradual types of individuality which the leading or qualifying function assumes in the inner *differentation* and *articulation* of a radical type.

In the present context, however, we are not concerned with *original* radical-types, but with such of a secondary character as pertain to human societal life. And here we are confronted with the particular state of affairs that the different objective products of human formation as well as the typical spheres of a differentiated human society exhibit a radical difference of qualifying functions, which precludes the possibility to ascribe them to the same radical type. At the same time it appears impossible to conceive the different "kingdoms" of these secondary human structures without taking account of their typical modal foundational functions. Every attempt in this direction would land us in an arbitrary method of classification, lacking any foundation in the plastic dimension of the temporal order. This will clearly appear from our further investigations. We are, therefore, obliged to acknowledge kinds of secondary radical types implying two radical functions, which, as such, are as yet only determined as to their general modal meaning.

After this explanation of the modified sense in which the term radical type is used with respect to works of art and other products of human formation, we may return to the question raised above.

The answer must be that indeed all works of fine art exhibit the same secondary radical type with a typical aesthetic qualification and a typical historical foundation. With respect to their internal structure of individuality, musical and literary works are no more based on an original-typical physical or sensory natural substratum than the different types of plastic art appeared to be. Musical compositions are typically founded in a free controlled rhythmic formation of musical sounds, as a cultural tonal substratum of the leading aesthetic conception of the composer. And literary works of art show a typical foundation in a cultural formation of lingual means of expression, which is modally different from the formative moment inherent in the aspect of symbolic signification as such. The cultural formation intended belongs to the technique of literary art.

The interwovenness of a natural and an aesthetically qualified structure in a sculptural work of art, as an enkaptic binding of the former.

We must now consider a further point of essential importance to plastic art, because a work of art, included in this geno-type[1], actually displays an objective thing-structure.

In our analysis of the internal modal functions of the Hermes of PRAXITELES, we concluded that the natural structure of individuality of the marble cannot play a *constitutive* rôle in this artistic work. Nevertheless, the question arises how the structure of the latter is related to the internal structure of the natural material.

Naturally it cannot be denied that the material, however much moulded by the artist, continues to be marble, and that the actual qualifying function of the latter is still physico-chemical in nature.

Is it not necessary, therefore, to distinguish two structures closely interwoven in the statue itself, *viz.* that of the natural product, marble, and that of the marble work of art, Hermes? And could not we say that the natural product marble functions separately as an individual whole so as to form the typical substratum of the statue as a sculpture?

If the preceding questions are to be answered in the affirmative, our analysis of the two radical-functions of the internal structure of individuality of Hermes is still correct. However, we must supplement this analysis by an investigation of the

---

[1] Primarily differentiated according to the ancient classification into architectonic, sculptural, and pictorial art. We have replaced the architectural type by that of the mimic art (of dancing, *etc.*), because architecture, as such, does not belong to the radical type: work of fine art. The reason is that a work of architecture, however beautiful it may be, is, as such, not aesthetically qualified. This will appear from our later investigations.

close relation sustained by this latter structure with another structure, presenting itself as its foundation.

This new problem, now requiring our full attention, was not solved in our earlier structural analysis.

We are unaware of any objection that could vitiate our argument that the qualifying physico-chemical function of the natural product marble is unable to ground the type of individuality of the statue, revealed in the internal leading structural function of the latter. Nor can our analysis of the objective cultural form, as the typical foundational function of the aesthetic individuality of Hermes, be effectively argued against.

Nevertheless, this does not refute the thesis that the objective marble-form necessarily pre-supposes the natural structure of individuality of the marble, as a natural product, and that for the reality of the statue a close connection is essential between the natural material and the work of art.

Homogeneous aggregate and a non-homogeneous individual whole.

What is the nature of this relationship? According to its natural structure of individuality marble is a granular crystalline aggregate of calc-spar crystals; and its objective sensory feature, colour, *etc.*, depend upon the particular kind of material. The work of art itself, however, is not an aggregate, but an unbreakable *non-homogeneous whole.* Its parts are not indiscriminate pieces of marble but the members of the moulded marble bodies. They are determined by the inner structural law of the sculpture and can only function in the individual totality of the latter.

The natural aggregate condition of the marble is under certain geological conditions (*e.g.*, a volcanic soil and contact metamorphosis) determined by the crystallization laws of calcium carbonate ($CaCo_3$). Because of the dependence of its formation upon such external geological conditions, marble is to be viewed as a variability type of calcium carbonate. The aggregate is a homogeneous whole, in which atoms are arranged in specific directions to form a stable lattice-work, held together in a balanced state of firm material by very strong electro-magnetic forces.

In the structure of the work of art, in contrast, the marble does not function as a homogeneous aggregate, but in an aesthetically qualified cultural form, whose parts are not homogeneous, but each of which has its own plastic function in the total composition. To the artist the marble is important solely as a medium of expression.

The natural physical-chemical processes in the marble do not play the leading rôle in the structure of the work of art, but only in the natural product. Nevertheless, by the artist's technical procedure they may be directed in an anticipatory way to the expression of his aesthetic conception.

In other words, we encounter here a typical example of an *enkaptic* interlacement in which a natural structure of individuality is bound by the structure of a work of art [1].

In such an enkaptic union there ought not to be any dualism observable between the natural and the aesthetically qualified structures. In its enkaptic functions, the natural material ought not to appear as a resistance to aesthetic representation; instead it should be completely opened to the expression of the artist's conception. Consequently, the natural physico-chemical and the objective sensory functions of the statue, directed toward the leading aesthetic structural function of the work of art, ought to be opened, thereby enriching their own structural functional meaning. To the degree that the marble strikes us as a resistive natural material, not completely controlled by the artistic technique, the work of art is a failure, or at least lacking in perfection. The internal structural unity, *intended* in the aesthetic conception, is then not fully realized objectively in the marble statue. An obtrusive dualism exists between the enkaptically bound natural structure of individuality of the marble and the objective expression of the aesthetic project.

The internal unity of the art-work is also disturbed by a dualism between the typical foundational and the leading function.

Neither should a dualism exist between the typical foundational and the typical leading function of a sculpture. The technical formative function ought not to obtrude at the expense

---

[1] Part III of this volume is devoted to a detailed investigation of such enkaptic interlacements. Provisionally, I can only circumscribe the meaning of the term "*enkapsis*" as follows: *enkapsis* takes place, when one structure of individuality restrictively *binds* a second structure of a different radical- or geno-type, without destroying the peculiar character of the latter.

of the leading aesthetic structural function, instead of becoming the full *expression* of the latter.

The musical counterpart of such a dualism is found in a musical performance when the technique of the performer obtrudes at the expense of the *musical expression*, or when the tonal waves (which bear the musical structure) obtrude at the expense of the unity of musical harmony.

The natural structure of individuality of the marble material is not abolished but its meaning is enriched and opened in its enkaptic function within the inner structure of the work of art.

Thus it appeared that the natural structure of individuality of the marble functions in the objective thing-structure of the sculptural art work as an enkaptically bound structure only. And this enkaptic relation is subject to the normative law requiring that in the inner structure of the work of art the marble can only function as a material for the expression of the artistic conception.

This does not imply that the natural structure of the material is eliminated or abolished. The artist cannot transform marble into flesh and blood. His plastic aesthetic activity remains bound to the natural structure of his material.

The task of the artist is to open or disclose the natural structure of his material through the aesthetic structure of the work of art, so that the natural structure itself (although only in its enkaptic functions) becomes a complete expression of this aesthetic structure.

The enkaptic intertwinement of these two structures of individuality can no more be explained by the metaphysical Aristotelian form-matter schema than the inner structure of the art-work itself can. In fact ARISTOTLE did not recognize a substantial form proper to a work of art. The reason is that he did not consider a work of art, as such, to be an individual substance[1]. From this metaphysical viewpoint ARISTOTLE is obliged

---

[1] An opposite contention is still defended by those who hold that ARISTOTLE mistook the art forms for substantial forms. This view is refuted by the entire 2nd Chapter of the 8th Book of the *Metaphysics*. In Z 2, 1943a, ARISTOTLE explicitly states that art products, as such, even in their union with matter, are not substances, but only *analogies* of substances:

'Now none of these things mentioned (*viz.* art-products such as a

to view PRAXITELES' sculpture only as an *accidental* form of the "natural substance" marble. By so doing the internal structure of the work of art and the enkaptic function of the marble-material in the latter cannot be accounted for. In addition, the conception that a "natural substance" may become "matter" with respect to an "accidental form" implies an intrinsical antinomy. For the marble is supposed to retain its proper "substantial form" and the latter cannot become "matter" of a merely accidental form. Substance is the absolute point of reference for all its accidental properties. How then can marble become "matter" with respect to the art-form?

Naturally, I am not opposed to the *terms* "form" and "matter", but only to their dualistic metaphysical connotation. The metaphysical concepts of form and matter do not fit to the structures of individuality and their enkaptic interlacements.

As such the moulded marble is a variability- or phenotype of the sculptural art-work.

The reader can now understand why we previously characterized marble-plastic as a variability-type of the geno-type "sculptural art work" [1].

The structure of individuality of the marble, as such, is that of a natural product, and *qua talis* never enclosed in the structural principle of the sculptured art work, nor in the internal differentiation of this geno-type.

But the variability-type always points to an enkaptic interwovenness of structural principles.

---

honey-drink, a book, a cupboard, a threshold, a house, *etc.*) is substance, even when coupled with matter, yet it is what is analogous to substance in each case'. (I have made use of W. D. Ross's translation here. D.H.F.).

With respect to PRAXITELES' Hermes, ARISTOTLE's conception implies that the marble statue is a substance only insofar as it is a piece of marble, but not insofar as it is an aesthetically formed figure. The essence of the material is not changed by its being formed into a figure.

This agrees with the interpretation of ALEXANDER OF APHRODISIAS in his commentary on the *Metaphysics*.

Our conception is in no way vitiated by the fact that in Book VII, the contrast between matter and form is illustrated by pointing to the relation between the ore and the form of a statue. This illustration does not concern substantial forms. This does not detract from our view, explained in an earlier context, that in ARISTOTLE's religious basic motive the cultural form-motive of the Olympian religion has acquired the primacy.

[1] Cf. § 3, where we provisionally applied the distinction between radical-, geno- and variability-types to work of art.

And the enkaptic relation, analysed in the sculptural art-work, has the peculiarity that an irreversable foundational relationship exists between the natural and the aesthetically qualified thing-structures. The marble can function separately from its enkaptic interlacement with the sculptural work of art, Hermes of PRAXITELES, but the reverse is impossible. This is why the structural principle of the marble statue is founded in that of the marble as a natural product.

In our general analysis of *enkaptic intertwinements* we shall notice a great many of such irreversible foundational relationships between structures of individuality belonging to the most different kingdoms.

§ 3 - RADICAL TYPES OF OTHER NORMATIVELY QUALIFIED OBJECTIVE THING-STRUCTURES.

We will now examine normatively qualified object-structures — entirely different in character from those inherent in works of fine art —, in which we shall discover new structural peculiarities. In this context we shall analyze the structure of some ordinary everyday utensils, such as chairs, tables, *etc.*

This may seem to be a trivial subject. Does it really imply philosophical problems? It may be granted that the analysis of a work of art is a subject worthy of philosophic discussion. But must a serious philosophy concern itself with the endless multiplicity of structures inherent in the most ordinary things of everyday life? Is it not sufficient to qualify this entire category of objects simply as "cultural things", in which man has formed a natural material in relation to specific values of life? Is it, in other words, necessary for philosophy to lose itself into a detailed examination of the typical structures of such things as these?

We can reply that our philosophy cannot neglect the things of naïve experience, as its attitude toward the latter is quite different from that of modern immanence philosophy. Any resemblance of triviality is the result of the attitude of apostate human self-consciousness casting its shadow over the richness of God's creation and levelling out its structural particularities in the monotonous uniformity of general schemes. Naïve experience, when viewed in the light of Divine Revelation, becomes rich in meaning. It becomes a caricature when the things of daily life are no longer experienced in the perspective of meaning, pointing to its Divine Creator.

In PLATO's dialogue *Parmenides,* the aged founder of the Eleatic School warns the young SOCRATES that he should not disdain relating the seemingly most trivial things, as *e.g.*, hairs and mud, to ideal forms *(eidè)*.

Modern philosophy will, generally speaking, leave a closer examination of "hairs and mud" to natural science, and that of chairs, tables, lamps and other utensils to technology. Philosophical problems, however, will not be discovered in such things because modern thought has lost the interest in structures of individuality presenting themselves in pre-theoretic experience. The latter, as such, is viewed as a triviality.

It is this very attitude with respect to naïve experience which our philosophy rejects in principle.

The radical type of everyday utensils and the enkaptic interwovenness of their structure of individuality with the natural structure of the materials.

What thing-structure does a table or chair display? Such utensils are also formed out of specific materials in accordance with a free human project. Both organic and inorganic matter may furnish the raw material. And again we can ascertain that the natural structure of the material is enkaptically bound to the internal structure of the utensil. The latter is irreversably based on the natural structure.

In modern life, materials are technically formed into semi-manufactured products, before they are again formed into utensils.

The primary natural structure of wood used in the construction of furniture is found in the trunk of a living tree. This structure is, as we have seen, typically qualified by a biotic subject-function. The tree, as an individual thing, must be destroyed in order to make planks out of its trunk.

Certain agglomerations of cells (*viz.* the parenchymal wood-cells) may continue to live for a certain time, but they are separated from the individual total unity of the tree. Thus, when it is no longer bound in this non-homogeneous whole but detached from it, the *wood tissue* is in an entirely different condition. Of course, as a type of wood, it still displays a *secondary-natural structure* of individuality, but it no longer discloses its *original natural structure.* This does not detract from the fact that it continues to reveal a typical relation to its natural origin. The tree produces its wood-cells out of cambium, and the wood remains qualified as the organic product of the tree, even after it has been separated from the total structure of the living tree and after its cells have died.

It is not easy to establish what in this condition is its qualifying or leading function. At first sight we might be inclined to consider the latter as a biotic object-function since the wood is a product of the tree. Are not also the shells of molluscs typically qualified by an object-function in the modal aspect in which the leading function of the animals concerned is found?

But, on second thought, this conclusion *per analogiam* appears to be unsound. The typical biotic and the psychical subject-object relations which are bound to specific structures of individuality pre-suppose that the object-functions concerned are either actual or at least potential, so that they may be actualized by a biotic or psychical subject-function to which they are typically related in a qualifying manner.

With respect to wood originating from a destroyed tree this is not the case. It cannot function in a biotic subject-object relation able to *qualify* its structure of individuality.

The dead wood is nothing but a physico-chemically qualified kind of matter, which is no longer enkaptically bound in a living organism. Left to itself it would be subject to a physico-chemical process of dissolution. What then is its qualifying function so long as it retains its typical structure as wood, produced by a typical kind of tree? One should not think that this is an artificial question resulting from our concern to bind the empirical phenomena to a pre-conceived system of modalities. The different modal spheres are not *construed* by us. They are *given* in the temporal horizon of empirical reality and do not permit themselves to be levelled out by a supposedly simplifying reduction of reality to a so-called physico-psychical scheme. The plastic dimension of the temporal horizon is bound to the modal dimension; and a theoretical destruction of the latter results in a destruction of the structures of individuality.

Therefore we must insist on a satisfying answer to the question raised. If we must conclude that wood, in its condition as dead matter, is necessarily of a physico-chemically qualified structure, the difficulty remains how to account for its relation to the tree from which it originates.

This difficulty can only be solved when we consider that the matter of the wood, which as such is qualified by a typical physical combination of atoms, has assumed a variability-type by its enkaptic interlacement with the living organism of this particular kind of tree. This variability-type reveals itself so long as the wood in its separate condition exists. Wood of oak is clearly distinct from wood of the beech and from any other kind of this matter. And it is in its variability-type that the wood maintains its relation to the tree from which it originates.

The material forms of the organs, which betray the original enkaptic function of the wood-matter in the living organism, have lost their typical meaning. Although still retaining water, after their separation from the total structure of the tree, the woody fibres and woody ducts can no longer fulfil their proper function of conducting water to the top. Similarly, the still living parenchymal wood cells remain storage centres of reserve materials, but this function is no longer the original structural function in the total structure of the living tree.

The structural type of the so-called semi-manufactured products.

These reserve materials, which have become useless and harmful to the material, must now be eliminated from the wood by a technical refining process. After being sawed into planks and treated against decay, the wood becomes a technical product. As such it has its objective foundational function in the historical modality; but it is only a *semi-formed* technical product, in which the secondary natural structure of the wood is enkaptically bound.

The relation between the structure of individuality of the wood and that of the planks is an irreversable *foundational relation.*

A characteristic of the structural type of these so-called semi-products is that they do not possess an internal typical leading function.

The structural leading function of the enkaptically bound natural structure of the material cannot be considered that of the semi-product. The most that can be based upon enkaptic structural interwovenness are the variability-types.

It is much rather characteristic of the structure of technical materials that their *potential historical-technical destination* can only acquire a more precise specification (but no longer an internal one) in relation to the types of utensils or other kinds of man-made products in whose structure they are to function enkaptically.

As appeared from our analysis of the structural interlacement between the marble material and the sculptured art-work, the material, considered in itself, is completely *δυνάμει ὄν*. Its natural leading function can never be the typical foundational function in the structure of a work of art.

The structural type of a technical semi-product is thus by nature semi-defined. This is why I no longer speak of a radical type of these materials, as was done in the first (Dutch) edition of this work. For a radical-type, even a secondary one, requires an internal leading function, which is lacking in the material as a semi-product.

Having investigated the typical incomplete structure of the material as a "semi-product", we must observe that he foundational function of this structure is *not* that of things formed out of such material. The technical form of a plank or a slab of marble does not possess any other nuclear type of individuality than that of a semi-manufactured material. It is only the technical form which the material assumes in the structures of the end-products that can found the individuality-type of the leading structural functions of the latter. But this technical form does not belong to the internal structure of the material, neither to that of the technical semi-product nor to that of the secondary natural product. It belongs to the internal structure of the work of art or the utensil, or any other end-product of human formation. The material is only bound by this technical form in the manner of an enkaptic interlacement with the art-work, the utensil, *etc.*

A thing formed out of semi-manufactured materials is thus founded on at least two structures of individuality, enkaptically bound in its own structure. A parallel state of affairs is not found in things directly formed out of raw material; in such things only the raw material is enkaptically bound.

Analysis of the internal structural functions of a chair in relation to the modal foundational system of law-spheres.

Having completed our analysis of the structural type of raw and of semi-manufactured material, we can return to our original problem: What is the thing-structure of a table or chair?

It must be clear that this structure pre-supposes that of the materials, without being identical with the latter.

The material employed must of course be suitable for the objective destination of these utensils. Nevertheless, the natural structures of individuality of the various materials and those of the semi-products made out of them can be very different. Wood, metal, leather, wool, *etc.*, can be utilized in the same chair, and thus function in the same enkaptic interlacement.

This state of affairs re-emphasizes the fact that the inner structures of the materials remain clearly distinct from the internal structure of the chair as an individual whole.

A chair has internal structural functions in all the modal law-spheres. However, the functions preceding the typical foundational function in the cosmic temporal order do not have an *original type of individuality,* but only an *anticipating* one. We shall show this by a methodical analysis of these different modal functions.

The typical numerical and spatial relations in the structure of a chair are necessary conditions for its typical technical form. But the mathematical figures of the seat, back, arms, and legs of a chair are typically determined by the internal structural principle of such furniture, in which the cultural function of technical formation has again the foundational rôle.

It stands to reason that these spatial figures, modally based on numerical relations, are not given in the materials, neither in their structure as semi-products, nor in that of the natural product. Rather they are freely projected in the internal conception of their designer, and are realized in the actual thing by a free formative activity.

In the project, the structural functions in question (*i.e.* the numerical and spatial) are intentionally directed to the typical leading function of the chair. In the realization of this project they must open their anticipatory possibilities and give expression to the entire structure of the object.

The other structural functions of the chair, preceding the objective historical function in the inter-modal order, are also essential to the individual reality of the chair's totality.

The internal physico-chemical function of this thing is its last subject-function. Its later functions are not *subjective* but *objective* in nature [1].

[1] *Translator's note.* The terms "*subjective*" and "*objective*" are used in the sense previously defined in Vol. II, Part I, Ch. V. Cf. pp. 366 ff. D.H.F.

The physico-chemical structure of the individual whole is not that of the separate materials, though the latter have an enkaptic function in the thing's energy-aspect. Bound by the cultural form of the individual totality, the materials in their enkaptic physico-chemical function are no longer *qualified* by the internal energy-function of their natural structure. They are freely arranged after the project of a typically qualified whole, whose internal structure is also expressed in its energy-aspect.

This internal structural energy-aspect of the chair is opened in its anticipatory possibilities and directed to the leading function of this thing. Its typical weight and bearing power are brought into accordance with its typical objective destination by rational consideration and calculation. This may suffice to understand that its typical physico-chemical constellation is not that of a natural thing, though it continues to be subject to the general laws of the energy-aspect. Human technical activity has realized those typical structural anticipatory potentialities in physical-chemical constellations which cannot be actualized in a natural way without human leading.

A chair should be accommodated to the sitting posture of the human body to give it rest and support. Periodic rest is a biotic need in human life and thus it is evident that the chair must have a biotic object-function related to the subjective biotic function of man. But it stands to reason that this biotic object-function cannot be of the typical restrictive character found in the vegetable and animal kingdoms.

It has a strongly anticipatory structure and cannot be experienced apart from the typical total structure of the chair expressing itself in this modal function. A chair satisfies a biotic-*cultural* [1] need of man, a need which in addition is *qualified* by a post-historical function, whose modality we shall examine presently. This typical qualification is objectified in the leading function of the chair's total structure.

The same state of affairs presents itself in the sensory image of this thing. Referring to our explanation of the analogous state of affairs in the sensory image of PRAXITELES' Hermes, we may establish that the objective sensory function of the chair is not given in nature. It anticipates the two typical radical functions of this piece of furniture and can only be experienced as the

---

[1] This means a cultural anticipation in the modal structure of the biotic aspect.

sensory objectification of the intentional subject-object relation present in the free project of the designer. The sensory structural image of the chair is related to the sensory human feeling of rest and support. And these subject-object relations also exhibit a typical anticipatory character.

The objective logical modality of the chair's typical structure is related to the subjective logical idea of the latter in human thought as a result of an implicit (pre-theoretical) or explicit (theoretical) analysis. As an inherent aspect of this thing it gives expression to the logical coherence of the structural plan of the whole by which the latter is clearly distinct from any natural product. The structural type of individuality revealed in this logical object-function is no more originally logical than that of the preceding functions is original in their pre-logical modalities. It exhibits an anticipatory character since it appeals to the post-logical radical functions of the chair's structure.

The typical foundational function of utensils and the problem of the individual identity of a thing.

We shall now try to make it still clearer that the typical foundational function of this type of utensils can only be found in their cultural (historical) aspect. The implicit concept that we have of a chair in our naïve experience does not adequately explain its inner structure of individuality. It clings to sensorily perceptible characteristics, though the latter are implicitly conceived in an anticipatory sense. The current explanation of the lingual meaning of the word chair as denoting a seat which may have different forms, does in principle not exceed this implicit naïve concept. It cannot satisfactorily account for the internal structure of individuality revealed by this thing.

Numerous other things, which no one would call a chair, are made to sit on, *e.g.*, a saddle, a piano stool, a cushion, a bench, *etc.*

However much attention be focused on the sensory form, this cannot serve as a foundational function in the structure of the chair. The type of individuality revealed in the sensory image appeared to lack an original character in this aspect of the thing in question. Rather it immediately suggests a cultural human formation (of a material) by which an intentional sensory image is objectively represented in the sensory figure of an actual thing.

Naïve experience is involved in the difficulties indicated in the first chapter of this Volume, when asked to explain what part of the sensory form of a chair can change without destroying its individual identity. Such a problem cannot be coped with by the employment of a subjective, sensorily limited, general concept of a chair. Neither is this question answered by pointing to sensory form as a whole. This simply raises a new problem, because this entirety or whole appeals to the *internal structural totality* of the thing concerned. And this structural whole only finds *expression* in its sensory image, without being identical with it.

Is the identity of a chair, for example, destroyed by the recovering of its seat and back with tissue of the same or somewhat different pattern or by the replacement of a broken leg? Of course not. Nevertheless, several such partial modifications can give it a completely "new face". So it appears that the individual identity of the parts cannot be essential to that of the whole.

But suppose that the wooden or wicker seat of an ordinary kitchen chair is replaced by a well springed bottom covered with expensive upholstery; this certainly would affect its individual unity. And certainly the typical "style" of a parlour chair cannot be altered without affecting its individual identity. These facts will appear to be relevant for tracing the inner structural principles of these things.

The presence of a seat is of course essential to the primary type chair. But even this characteristic is not related to the sensory form only. A dog choosing a beautiful easy chair as a resting-place, certainly perceives a sensory form associated with the satisfaction of his sensory desire for rest. But a dog does not really perceive the sensory form of a "chair". His power of perception is limited to the sensory psychical function. An animal cannot relate the *perceived form* to its total *underlying structure*. To the dog the only essential point is that the sensory figure of the seat affords satisfaction to his sensory desire for rest.

With man it is quite different. Even without engaging in a theoretical analysis, he is able to experience such things as tables and chairs, as individual totalities, in accordance with their typical structural meaning.

The only condition is the historical opening of his experiential horizon by a proper cultural education.

A primitive man does not need tables and chairs to meet his natural or social requirements. When he is tired, the ground or a tree trunk provide an adequate resting place. The introduction of furniture and the cultivation of its habitual societal use are dependent on a historical disclosure of human society.

We cannot doubt, therefore, that these utensils have a typical historical foundation, also when considered from the standpoint of human subjectivity (*i.e.* in the structural subject-object relation in which they are necessarily included).

As to their foundational function such things as chairs and tables are rightly called "cultural objects" belonging to a higher level of civilization. But what modality is to be ascribed to the typical leading function of their structure of individuality?

This question cannot be escaped by the traditional reference to specific human aims to which these things are serviceable. Such teleological characterizations may suffice in practical life, but they do not satisfy the requirements of a due theoretical analysis of the structures of individuality. This already appeared from the current teleological definition of a chair as a cultural object made to sit on.

Though it is undeniable that the presence of a seat is essential to this piece of furniture, this characteristic appeared to be insufficient to distinguish a chair from other things made to sit on.

The typical qualifying function in the radical type of utensils.

How then shall we discover the qualifying function of such things with respect to their radical type? First, we must observe that the geno- or primary types, tables and chairs, although susceptible to further structural determination, are already differentiated, since they belong to the more inclusive geno-type furniture.

The relation between the concept table or chair to the concept furniture is not that of the *logical particular* to the *logical universal* without any reference to the structural order of temporal reality. Much rather a fixed structural articulation of the type of individuality is here given, which is well founded in this order.

With respect to their *inner structure,* the utensils in question are furniture with an individualized leading function.

The typical objective destination of furniture is inseparably interwoven with the entire arrangement of a human dwelling. The further differentiation of the structural type, table or chair, depends upon whether they are to furnish a living-room, kitchen, garden, library, restaurant, office, *etc.*

This differentiation does not pertain to merely *external* structural peculiarities of furniture or to merely subjective purposes in human consciousness. A parlour chair is objectively different from a kitchen- or garden chair. The various intentional structures of the objects, according to which they are fashioned, have been objectively *realized* in the material.

The individual identity of a kitchen chair is destroyed when the latter is re-upholstered and embellished in a manner that makes it out of place for kitchen service.

With respect to its radical type, the individualized leading function of such furnishings is enclosed in the modality of social intercourse. Within the structural subject-object relation [1] it is subject to the norms of sociability, class or rank obligations, style, and so on.

In a work of fine art there should not be any dualism between its technical form and its leading structural function. This principle also applies to furniture. A good piece of furniture ought to be of a reliable build. Whether factory or hand made, its technical construction should be adequate and its material durable. Quite similar to this requirement is the demand made of the artist that he show ability in the technical side of his craft. However, in works of art as well as in furniture, the leading structural function is not found in technical form.

The relation between free and applied or bound art [2].

A comparison between the internal structure of a piece of furniture and that of a work of fine art gives rise to a difficult problem, a problem which has played an important part in modern aesthetics. The same difficulty is encountered in our theory of the relation between the radical type "work of fine art" and the radical types of all other objective thing-structures in which an aesthetic structure plays a special rôle.

Historically viewed, the plastic arts grew out of hand work, or to state it more accurately — so as to avoid the misunderstanding caused by any evolutionism eliminating the structural principles —, hand work served as an historical occasion for the rise of independent plastic art.

---

[1] All things qualified by a normative object-function are necessarily included in this relation.

[2] Cf. also SUSANNE K. LANGER, *Feeling and Form*, Scribner's, New York 1953, pp. 303 ff.

Applied art should, however, be sharply distinguished from free art. The former has recently succeeded in reconquering an increasing domain of architecture which in the process of mass fabrication had been left to bad taste and the pursuit of gain.

The architecture of buildings constructed for a practical purpose can never be "pure fine art". The wellknown views of the famous Dutch architect BERLAGE on the task of the artist in this field — apart from their special elaboration — are classic rather than modern.

Although the terms leave much to be desired, what do we mean by "pure" art in contrast to "applied" art?

The word "*Reinheit*"[1], in its general philosophical usage, has become suspect for us. It has often been employed to express the tendency of immanence philosophy to absolutize a specific modal aspect of experience. Both the modal functions of meaning and the structures of individuality were theoretically eliminated from the cosmic coherence of the temporal order and rendered independent, assumed to exist "*an sich*", which deprived them of their very *meaning*!

Christian aesthetics cannot recognize any "pure art" in this sense. The slogan of last century '*l'art pour l'art*' (art for art's sake) [2] is simply the expression of a deification, because it absolutizes the aesthetic modality. Our objection to this slogan, however, does not concern its intention to defend the right of free artistic expression against those who intend to make art always serve a specific utilitarian or moral purpose. Our opposition is only directed to the absolutization of the aesthetic modality by restricting a work of art to its leading structural function and ignoring its post-aesthetic aspects. We shall therefore define the term "pure art" in such a way that any misunderstanding as to the meaning of the adjective is precluded.

By "pure art", in contrast to "bound" and "applied" art, we will understand such artistic works whose inner structural principle has really an *aesthetic qualification* and has been detached from any enkaptic inclusion by the structural principle of things not aesthetically qualified, whereas, conversely, the *internal* structural principle of a work of pure art binds things of an other qualification. This view of "pure art" enables us to comprehend

---

[1] *i.e.* purity.

[2] In the so-called "movement of the eighteen eighties" in Dutch belles lettres.

a state of affairs not fully intelligible to modern trends of aesthetics whose vision of the structure of temporal experience is enmeshed in the immanence-standpoint.

When commissioned to design a bank building or city hall, an architect should first realize that the structural principle of his architectonic work does not have an aesthetic qualification. The aesthetic structural function of such a building must remain bound to the structure of the latter according to its own typical leading and foundational functions. This is to say that the aesthetic function should itself give an adequate expression to the structural principle of the building which, as such, is not a work of fine art.

This does not mean that in the design and construction of the building, aesthetic requirements must be minimized. It does imply, however, that the artist is not engaged in the production of a free aesthetically qualified object. The aesthetic aspect of his conception is here subordinate to the proper structural principle of the building.

The beauty of a natural thing, that of a free work of art, and that of a building or a piece of furniture lacking as such an aesthetic qualification, is quite different in each instance.

It should now be clear that "pure art" in principle pre-supposes a differentiated civilization. Generally speaking, the aesthetic aspect of all human products in undifferentiated cultural life remains entirely bound to the structure of things not qualified aesthetically; but this need not in any way detract from the possibility that such products show real beauty.

The structural function of furniture styles and the pompous character of the style Louis XIV.

The above explanation has in principle clarified the relation between the structural principle of furniture and that of a work of fine art. It has appeared that the aesthetic function can never have the leading and qualifying rôle in the structure of furniture.

The artistic beauty of such things and of other useful objects is properly *bound* beauty. It ought itself to be the expression of the internal structural principle of the thing in question. Of course a work of fine art can function in an enkaptic condition within the structure of a piece of furniture.

The latter, for example, may possess independently constructed carvings, which, when separated from it, must be considered as free works of art. But, in its enkaptic condition, such carving has a structural function within a whole that is not aesthetically qualified, and it ought not to obtrude at the expense of the proper character of the latter.

This also brings to light the nature of furniture-style. Furniture-style is a typical aesthetic structural function of a bound character. It can never be a leading or foundational function, but ought to express within itself the inner structural principle of furniture, in the typical context of a collectivity to which it belongs.

Style inseparably binds an individual piece of furniture to the entire interior for which it is intended, as long as it serves its proper function. And as a subjective-objective structural function, style is subject in a normative sense to a structural principle.

Consider the massive and imposing arm-chairs in the style Louis XIV, as designed by A. LEPAUTRE! They form a structural whole, with the heavy tables decorated in overwhelming detail with festoons and carvings and their consoles, garnished with rare marble and other materials; a whole, with the many-branched crystal crowns, and monumental mirrors, designed for the repeated reflection of the rich decoration; with the ebony secretaires, inlaid with rich mosaics, garnished with arabesques in engraved copper; with the ceilings and wainscots, whose frames were decorated with white and gold ornaments exhibiting shell-motifs and rosettes, and with the rich tapestries, whose soft tints had to temper the extreme brilliance of the furnishings!

In this entire style is expressed the splendour and pride of the social milieu of Louis XIV, based on a culture marked by unrestricted lust for power.

This is not a mere subjective view of objects, in themselves existing only as natural things. Rather it is a typical social function of intercourse that is objectively expressed in this furniture and in the whole interior to which it belongs. And it is exactly this social function which qualifies the entire structure of the interior of this style and completely determines the character of the arrangement as it really *is*; furniture in the style Louis XIV does not exist apart from this function.

From this it clearly appears that things belonging to such a typical, socially [1] qualified collective are themselves qualified

---

[1] The term "social" is used in this context in the modal sense of the aspect of human intercourse.

by a leading object-function of social modality. They necessarily function in structural subject-object relations which make them subject to norms.

The style Louis XIV cannot be uncritically accepted as being its own self-sufficient norm (a typically irrationalistic view).

Our admiration of the art in evidence in the furnishings, gardens and buildings in the style Louis XIV, is accompanied by the critical reserve that the pride and apostate tendencies of the court of the "*roi soleil*" gave rise to unbalance and disharmony. The inner unity and proper character of things were often sacrificed to the desire for monumentality and ostentation.

The colonnade of the Louvre, and various church buildings, such as LEMERCIER's chapel at the Sorbonne, illustrate what we mean. CLAUDE PERRAULT, the artist responsible for the colonnade of the Louvre, seems to have intentionally disregarded the bound character of building-style. For the sake of monumentality, he sacrificed the inner unity of the architecture and disregarded the fact that his task was not to create an entirely new building. As a result the Louvre shows a dualism between the architectural work of PIERRE LESCOT and that of PERRAULT.

In the chapelle de la Sorbonne, the heavy set monumental dome seems to press down the entire external architecture of the church.

The furniture style Louis XIV betrays the inner tendency to erase the structural difference between furniture and architecture. Following EMILE BAYARD[1], we can call it a *façade style*.

The disharmony in the opening process, discussed in Vol. II in connection with the functional modal structure of reality, is here very clearly seen in connection with the individuality-structure of things.

This style cannot be comprehended in terms of abstract aesthetic standards, but only in relation to the entire historical context of the cultural sphere in which it is formed. Historicism irratonalistically misinterprets this connection between style and history; it ignores the entire plastic horizon of empirical reality and its non-arbitrary structural principles. In contrast, our contention is that these plastic structural principles are the necessary pre-requisites of all objective products of human formation executed in a specific style.

---

[1] EMILE BAYARD *L'art de reconnaître les styles* (Paris) p. 232.

A reconsideration of the difference between the objective leading structural function of things and the merely subjective purposes to which they can be made serviceable. A new problem.

One peculiarity of the narrower geno-type furniture examined by us is that these useful objects[1] belong to a structural collective relationship which ought to express itself objectively in their own thing-structure.

Once again we wish to establish that the objectively realized leading function of these everyday utensils is not to be confused with the subjective ends for which they can be used. The merely subjective teleological concepts, generally employed to distinguish cultural objects theoretically, is inadequate here.

There is nothing to prevent my using a parlour chair as a kitchen chair, a table as a seat, or a tea-cup as a wine-glass. However, no matter what abnormal subjective end I may use an object for, I am always conscious that, according to its entire inner structure, it is not objectively destined for such arbitrary aims. Normal subjective use is inseparably bound to the objective qualifying function of the object itself. And this function is not eliminated by a haphazard usage deviating from the norms of intercourse.

This raises a new problem. It is undeniable that in the course of time the objective social destination of various utensils seems to change. An antique shawl, for example, can now be used as a wall decoration. How can we account for this? This problem brings us to the consideration of a new theme, requiring separate attention.

§ 4 - ACTUALIZATION AND INACTUALIZATION[2] OF THE OBJECTIVE QUALIFYING FUNCTION OF OBJECTS TYPICALLY FOUNDED IN THE HISTORICAL ASPECT.

Let us notice first of all that, functioning in their typical structural subject-object relation, the things of this radical type can be so narrowly bound to a certain office, social status, family or

[1] This group type belongs to the radical type: the kingdom of historically founded and objectively and socially qualified utensils. This kingdom includes innumerable primary types and sub-types.

[2] *Translator's note.* "Inactualization" means the condition in which something is rendered no longer actual, no longer in operation or in effect. D.H.F.

person, that apart from such they cannot be used in accordance with their individual qualifying function.

This structural peculiarity is thus due to the subject-object relation without which these things cannot function according to their objective destination. It may be that for every subject able to experience their structure, these things are the same, but they are not, therefore, *useable* for each of these subjects (consider for example, a throne, a chair of honour, a smoking jacket, an admiral's uniform, a family portrait, a wedding ring, and so on).

It is in some instances possible for the subjective individualization of the destination of a thing to be objectively expressed in its symbolic aspect in a manner that is only external to its inner structure, *e.g.*, by the carving of initials or a family-blazon. In such cases this objective symbolical indication of the thing's individual destination can generally be removed, so that such objects are no longer bound to a special office, family, or person.

Such is not the case, however, in the various specific types of things that we discussed first, because in these instances, the individualization of the social destination is objectively expressed in a thing's entire inner structure.

The radical type of things qualified by an object-function in the faith aspect.

An identical observation can be made with respect to other radical types of useful objects, whose foundational function is historical, but whose objective qualification is not enclosed in the social modality (*i.e.* the aspect of intercourse).

The entire structure of an altar, a chapel, a temple, a crucifix or rosary, betrays their objective destination for worship. The majority of such things are connected with the sacred character of the subjective community to which they belong, which is obviously qualified by the function of faith.

Such unbreakable coherence between a specific subjective "societal group" and things qualified by an object-function were already encountered in the animal kingdom. But how much more complicated and richer are they revealed in human society!

When such things as these are no longer used according to their objective destination, and placed in a museum, for example, they more or less continue to express their original societal destination, in accordance with their objective structure of individuality. Their objective reality, however, cannot really be experienced unless one is sympathetically aware of the typical group-structure to which they belong, including their qualifying subject-object relation [1].

Otherwise, even though we know their names, they continue to be as strange to us as an airplane, or a telephone would be to an uncivilized primitive, or a performance of BEETHOVEN'S Heroica to a man unreceptive to music.

The routine view of modern daily life may not be confused with actual naïve experience. A restatement of the relation between intuitive and symbolic knowledge according to modern phenomenology.

It must be recognized, however, that in the routine of modern daily life, we are usually satisfied if we can name a thing that is strange to our normal experience. The most that we ordinarily demand is that we can form a notion of its immediate utility. Modern phenomenology undoubtedly has this in mind in its desire for more than an impersonal merely symbolical knowledge of things. Hence, its insistence on an intuitive "*Wesensschau*", designed to eliminate entirely the symbolical aspect of experience, in order to penetrate to a full view of its essence. In Vol. II, we have shown why this view is not acceptable.

The symbolical aspect of meaning cannot be detached from the individual reality of a thing. Its elimination results in a theoretical abstraction, in which a theoretical "*Gegenstand*" replaces a thing's full reality.

Nevertheless, it is true that in the routine of daily life, the knowledge of a thing's name and its utility does not penetrate to its empirical reality. We simply cannot speak of naïve experience here, but only of an abstract technical mode of inculcation. Unfortunately, the enormous extensiveness of modern society often leads to an inevitable loss in the intensity of "naïve experience".

Fortunately, however, this routine does not affect our experience of things essentially familiar to us. As we demonstrated earlier, a person of modern culture does still have naïve experience.

---

[1] This point is important for the ethnological ascertainment of the objective destination of primitive utensils, in whose technical form the qualifying function is not always clearly expressed. Cf. F. GRAEBNER *Methode der Ethnologie* (Heidelberg 1911) pp. 56 ff.

The inactualization of the objective leading function of useful objects.

The above observations imply, first of all, that in the subject-object relation to which the radical types of the things in question are necessarily bound, a sharp distinction must be made between the *objective empirical reality* of things and the *subjective actualization of their objective qualifying function.*

It may be that the actualization in question has become impossible in any way because historical development has given a new cultural form to human society. The unbreakable coherence between the typical leading function and the typical foundational function of these things is here disclosed in an extremely pregnant manner.

Whether or not historically founded useful objects of earlier times can still be used nowadays in accordance with their original objective destination, primarily depends upon the question whether they still fit to the present historical milieu. As to some kinds of things which are typically qualified by a subject-object relation in the aspect of social intercourse, the powerful influence of fashion can bring about that really antiquated objects, especially antique furniture, are even preferred in certain social circles to modern products. It may be that this preference is also caused by the solidness and beautiful forms of the objects concerned. But as a matter of fact it may be established that imitation antique furniture is readily accepted when one has no money to pay for the original.

In any case, antique furniture, glasses, *etc.*, can still be used according to their original objective destination, though nowadays they are perhaps not always practical. And their seemingly fitting to the present cultural milieu is to be ascribed to the influence of fashion already mentioned.

As to things which do not satisfy this condition, the possessor will try to give them another actual destination. Old shawls, which as articles of dress have got out of fashion, may be used as wall-decoration. Old armours and weapons may be preserved or collected for their decorative value or historical interest.

The splendid patrician houses of the 17th century's merchant families along the wonderful canals of Amsterdam are for a great deal transformed into offices.

Medieval castles have lost any capability to be used according to their original objective destination. Insofar as they have not retained the function of dwelling-houses, they are only preserved as cultural curiosities of particular historical interest. For the same reason a great many preserved things belonging to earlier times, have found a place in museums.

The adage, *Tempora mutantur et nos in illis* may rightly be extended to include these socially qualified products of human formation because of their typical historical foundation. At the end of the preceding section we provisionally described this state of affairs as a *change* or *shift* in the *objective destination.*

What do we really understand by this shift? Does it imply a real change in the structure of a thing? No, in empirical reality the objective structure of a thing is constant so long as the latter exists. The clothing of knights, nowadays on view in museums, is still the same dress previously worn as attire distinctive of a privileged social class. But, if I may use the expression, because of modern cultural development, the objective qualifying function of such costumes has been *in-actualized*; it is no longer in operation. In the medieval feudal society knighthood had an actual military function. Since the end of the Middle Ages it lost any military significance but it retained its position as a rank endowed with political power. The French revolution destroyed this position and thereby knighthood disappeared as a particular privileged social rank. The present generation can still experience knightly attire as objective socially qualified things of a by-gone historical period. Their objective qualifying function is the objectification, in the real clothing material, of an intentional conception of the designer of these costumes. This state of affairs remains unchanged by the transitions of cultural development. But the socially qualified objective destination of knightly costumes can no longer be actualized by the present generation, because the feudal class-system has disappeared.

The qualifying subject-object relation implied in radical types of the thing-structures here discussed, thus displays a special peculiarity.

The three figures in the subject-object relation of these thing-structures: the intentional representational relation, the unfolding relation, and the actualization relation.

The "shift in the objective destination" of historically founded utensils is really only a shift in a specific aspect of the subject-object relation in which these things stand. To be specific, it is only a change in the actualization relation between their objective qualifying function and human usage.

We must, therefore, sharply distinguish the following modes in the subject-object relation of these things.

1. The *objectification,* in the structure of a real object, of the intentional object, as the latter is conceived in the *design* of a thing *(intentional representational relation).*
2. The subjective *unfolding* or *opening* in human experience of the closed objective thing-structure (*unfolding* or *opening relation*).
3. The actualization of the objective thing-structure by human activity, which uses the thing according to its objective and opened qualifying function (*actualization relation*).

If our analysis is correct, a "shift in the objective destinatiou" does not affect a thing's original structure; it leaves intact both the intentional representational relation and the unfolding relation; it is exclusively concerned with the actualization relation. A thing's objective destination is inactualized, *i.e.* its original destination can no longer be practically realized. However, its qualifying function can still be understood in our experience.

The actualization relation shifts from a thing's qualifying function to its historical or aesthetic object-function. Knightly attire, for example, can still only be actualized in an historical pageant, a historical spectacle, or a play, whereas it otherwise belongs in a museum as a cultural curiosity.

This shift in the actualization relation between a thing's subjective use and its objective qualifying function is, moreover, in no way dependent upon the subjective whims of human intention. It provides no basis for a subjective teleological view of the reality of these things.

An old shawl is properly used for decorative purposes if, and only if, it possesses an objective attractive harmony expressing its beauty as an antique piece of dress.

Old knightly garb is a museum piece only because an historical feature of a certain cultural period is objectively expressed in its typical foundational function. It is a cultural curiosity because the freely designed form of the clothing and the accompanying weapons objectively reflect the powerful socially qualified position of knighthood in former times.

The shift in the actualization relation, in other words, continues to be connected with the internal structure of real things and does not merely depend upon the subjective human arbitrariness of changing purposes.

§ 5 - THE RELATION BETWEEN THE INTERNAL STRUCTURAL PRINCIPLE AND THE MODAL FOUNDATIONAL SYSTEM IN THE SUBJECT-OBJECT RELATION OF SYMBOLICALLY QUALIFIED THINGS. THE BIOTIC STRUCTURAL FUNCTION IN THE UNFOLDING- AND ACTUALIZATION RELATIONS.

Having gained an insight into various radical types of the structural principles of normatively qualified objective things, we can now engage in a more detailed examination of the way in which the temporal order of the modal aspects is maintained in the subject-object relation, to which these things are bound.

From the outset it had to be made clear that this general order of modalities cannot be dependent upon a thing's internal structural principle, but that the latter must express itself in the former.

Our problem is simply to gain a clear insight into this state of affairs with respect to things whose structural principles do not immediately disclose their connection with the modal dimension of our experiential horizon.

In our analysis of the structural functions of the plastic work of art, Hermes of PRAXITELES, we, at first, had difficulty in locating its biotic structural function. And this difficulty seemed to return with regard to all the other things formed out of inorganic material.

Though a closer analysis of some structural principles of such things has shown the indubitable presence of a biotic object-function, yet it might seem that this presence is only due to certain structural peculiarities of the types of things explicitely examined. We shall, therefore, now pay attention to a secondary radical type of historically founded objects which at first sight does not betray any connection with the biotic aspect of experience.

We wish to demonstrate that a biotic structural function is as such necessarily included in the subject-object relation of these things, both with respect to the unfolding-relation, whereby they are related to human experience, and with respect to the actualization relation, whereby they are related to subjective human usage.

From the analysis of this type of objects it will become completely clear that the biotic object-function concerned is necessarily inherent in all products of human formation, irrespective of their structural peculiarities.

The biotic structural function of things in the unfolding relation of their objective empirical reality.

We have already observed that objects produced by man must necessarily function in the biotic subject-object relation, because they are sensorily perceptible. A house, a candelabrum, or a chair must function objectively in our biotic space, if their objective sensory image is to be disclosed to our subjective perception. The reason is that our sense perception pre-supposes the biotic stimulation of our visual nerves and, in the biotic subject-object relation, nothing can affect these organs which does not itself function subjectively or objectively in the biotic modality.

All things, however, function in the biotic modality *in their own typical structure*. It is only in this structure that things are related to human experience.

Thus, it is first the previously analysed *unfolding relation* in objective empirical things that pre-supposes their having a function in the biotic subject-object relation.

Upon a little reflection it is also clear that without an objective-biotic structural aspect, things qualified by a normative object-function could not be actualized in this qualifying function according to their objective inner destination. All these things belong to the objective *human environment,* which in comparison to the milieu of plants and animals, is incomparably richer. By actualizing their objective destination, man enlarges his environment and frees it from its static dependence on the physico-chemical functions given in *nature.* And thereby he places his natural vital requirements under the direction of a *free formative control.*

In their inner structure, things objectively symbolically qualified and historically founded, lack the previously analysed representational relation to an intentional object that itself is not symbolically qualified.

To illustrate this state of affairs just described we have chosen a primary group belonging to a radical type, as yet unanalysed. Our example is a book intended solely for reading.

Such a book belongs to the kingdom of historically founded and symbolically qualified things (letters, scores, signs, banners, flags, monuments, and so on, also belong to this kingdom).

In contrast to those previously analysed, thing-structures of this radical type do not depict an intentional object not symbolically qualified. At the utmost depictions of an non-symbolically qualified intentional object are *enkaptically* contained in their own structure (cf. the illustrations in the text of a book, the depiction of a historical figure or event in a monument).

The objective material letters are realized in a symbolically qualified structural relation on the pages and cover of a book. In this coherence the intentional conception of the author is only *signified* in an objective thing structure; it is not really *depicted* or *represented.*

Of course the connection with the thoughts signified, or the musical or literary conception respectively, of the author is essential in the objective symbolical qualification of the book. The entire internal differentiation of the primary type of the latter is always bound to the nature of the ideas and conceptions signified, thus determining whether or not a book is of a scientific, literary, musical or some other type. This intentional relation, however, is not objectified in the formerly analysed *depicting or representational relation;* instead, it remains *symbolical* in character. It is given only in the inseparable coherence between the objective sign, the subjective signification and the signified idea or conception, which intentionally points to a specific state of affairs.

From our earlier investigations we may conclude that the typical foundational function of the book is neither to be found in the leading function of the natural structure of the raw materials, nor in the cultural foundational function of the semi-manufactured technical materials out of which it is formed.

These materials belong only to the variability types of a book. A great diversity of materials, *e.g.*, paper, silk, leather, may be used in its construction, and can enkaptically function in its proper structure.

The internal structure of individuality of a book, however, cannot possess any other foundational function than the cultural *book-form* constructed according to an intentional technical design. And this *book-form* includes the size and binding of its pages as well as the symbols printed, drawn or (type)written on them [1].

---

[1] ARISTOTLE has tried to explain the structure of a book with the aid of his form-matter schema. Though he agrees that this scheme in its proper sense is only applicable to natural substances, he thinks it can analogically be applied to cultural products. But he views the form of a book — which according to the form-matter scheme determines its essence

It is only by taking into account the full structural coherence of this foundational function with the symbolical qualifying or leading function that the structural principle of such a book can be theoretically approached.

Objectifying realization of the intentional project, unfolding of the leading object-function to human experience, and actualization of the book's objective destination can be clearly distinguished in the subject-object relation in which this thing functions.

As soon as the author's ideas or his artistic conception are symbolized in the objective letters (or notes) of a book, the symbolical objectifying realization is complete — and, as observed, this occurs without an essential depiction of the intentional subject-object relation inherent in the conception of the author. This objectifying realization can occur through the agency of persons to whom the meaning of the letter- or note-combinations is entirely inaccessible or closed. Of course the author is the sole agent of this realization in his hand-written manuscript.

The objective linguistic function, in a still latent condition inherent in the thing-structure of the book, is opened by every reader (in his subjective, historically founded linguistic function) who understands the meaning of the objective letter- (or note-) combinations.

It is not necessary that he himself uses the book. It may be read to him so that he has only to listen.

The actualization of the book, according to its objective symbolical destination, is possible only if we pick it up, turn its pages, and so on. In other words, both its opening to human experience and its actualization demands that we use our body in its organic vital function.

But then it follows that a book must have an objective structural aspect in the biotic modality. This structural aspect cannot be theoretically eliminated without at the same time losing sight of the book as a thing. Modally viewed, the sensory objectivity of a book, its sensorily perceptible image, is necessarily grounded in its biotic objectivity, through which it is objectively *at hand* for our use and able to stimulate our sense-organs by the material signs which fill its pages.

— exclusively in the glued material sheets. This is to say that its leading structural function, namely the symbolic, is completely overlooked (Cf. *Met.* H, 2, 1042 b). From this it appears again that this form-matter scheme is unserviceable to explain the structures of individuality.

In this modal function of the book, however, the entire objective thing-structure of the latter is expressed. It is not an abstract biotic function, but much rather this concrete thing which by the material symbols contained in its pages exercises a physiological influence upon our sense-organs.

The same statement applies to the entire inter-modal coherence of meaning to which the plastic structure of the book is bound.

It must be evident that especially the objectively-symbolically qualified things tremendously enrich and enlarge man's individual life.

By means of books our horizon is broadened and enriched; lifted out of our actual natural environment, we are brought into intentional contact with imaginary or real human life of the past or the present. These things furnish us with an intensive intentional contact with the immense societal experience of mankind, signified in their symbolically qualified structure. By means of books our subjective individual experience is permeated with a perspective of the richness of human society in the past and the present.

PART II

STRUCTURES OF INDIVIDUALITY OF TEMPORAL HUMAN SOCIETY

CHAPTER I

THE BASIC PROBLEM IN THE STRUCTURAL PRINCIPLES OF TEMPORAL HUMAN SOCIETY

§ 1 - INTRODUCTION. THE STRUCTURAL PRINCIPLES OF HUMAN SOCIETY AS THE TRANSCENDENTAL CONDITIONS OF OUR EXPERIENCE OF VARIABLE FACTUAL SOCIETAL RELATIONSHIPS. THE BASIC PROBLEM OF SOCIOLOGY AS A TOTALITY-SCIENCE.

Our investigation of the structures of individuality is now to be focused upon the structural principles of the various typical relationships in human society. We may establish that this part of our inquiry is to be viewed as foundational for any special science which examines these societal relationships under a specific theoretically abstracted modal viewpoint. In the first place, however, it is foundational for empirical sociology, which lays claim to the scientific investigation of societal relationships *as such*, either in the totality of their appearance, or in the sense of a supposed specific sociological viewpoint which is to be distinguished from the psychological, historical, economical, juridical and other specific scientific points of view.

This cannot become clear so long as our theoretical experience of these relationships is not made into a critical problem. Under the influence of the Humanistic science-ideal both in its natural scientific and its historicist conceptions. Modern sociology of the last century has supposed it could, as a theoretical science, establish and examine human societal relationships as pure facts, apart from any normative view starting from the order of divine creation. Insofar as positive societal norms were taken into consideration, they were usually viewed as subjective axiological psychical or mental reflections of "objective" factual relations in human society, as such capable of "causal explanation". And insofar as at present a "normative sociology" is acknowledged, it is emphasized that it can only set forth the ideal socio-cultural world as it *ought to be*, whereas theoretical sociology studies the societal universe as it *is* [1].

It stands to reason that this familiar separation between social facts and "ideal" social norms leaves no room for structural principles of human society lying at the foundation of the factual societal relationships. Since these structural principles can only be of a normative qualification and, as such, are not subject to historical change, they are in principle eliminated from theoretical sociology. Any idea that they determine the very nature of the different communal and inter-communal or inter-individual relationships is foreign to this current view.

The historicist conception of "socio-cultural phenomena" does not permit the acceptance of societal structures of individuality which, as such, are not subject to historical development, since they are exactly the transcendental conditions for every possible experience of factual societal relationships. As a result, the whole question concerning the inner nature of the different types of societal "groups" and inter-communal or inter-individual relationships is eliminated.

The pseudo-natural scientific concept of structure in modern sociology.

Instead, sociologists operate with "ideal types" in the sense of subjective generalizing constructions, as explained in an earlier context of our inquiry. And insofar as theoretical sociology speaks of structures of society, this term is not meant in our transcendental sense, but much rather in the pseudo-generic sense of "constellation" or "composition" of different "elements".

Such conception of structure betrays its origin from natural scientific thought, even with those sociologists who emphasize the methodological difference between natural sciences and cultural sciences. It precludes the insight into the basic problem of sociology, which lays claim to a theoretic total view of human society, in contradistinction to all special socio-cultural sciences. For in what sense is this total view to be understood? It cannot be a simple addition of the viewpoints from which human society is examined. Theoretical sociology has often referred to biology, as an example of a theoretic science giving a real synthesis of all specific natural scientific viewpoints. Sociology should do the

---

[1] F. OPPENHEIMER, *System der Soziologie* I, I, p. 69. Normative sociology is called here *"social philosophy"*.

same with respect to all specific socio-cultural sciences [1]. But this argument fails if it is viewed as a real solution of the basic problem of sociology as a total science of society.

As a specific science, biology cannot solve the basic problem of the structural unity of a living organism in the modal diversity of its different aspects. It cannot, as such, explain the inner structural relation between the vital aspect and the mathematical and physico-chemical aspects of the living whole. This is a genuine philosophical problem, whose solution is dependent upon the cosmonomic basic Idea lying at the foundation of every theoretical total view of temporal reality, though it is to be tested by its confrontation with experiential states of affairs. Neither can the basic problem of theoretical sociology be solved by referring to a presumed causal interaction between the different modal aspects of human society. We have seen in an earlier context that the structural relation between the different aspects of an individual whole cannot be viewed as a mutual causal encroachment of one modal function upon the modal spheres of the others. Any assumption of the contrary necessarily lands us in a kind of mythology. If a structural causality is meant within and between individual societal totalities, it should be observed that such an integral causality pre-supposes the total view of theoretic sociology, which appeared to be exactly the basic problem of the latter. In any case one should be aware that such an integral structural causality exceeds the boundaries of theoretical thought. It can only be handled as a transcendental Idea, not as a specific scientific concept. It can never yield a scientific explanation of a structural whole.

Thus it is nothing but a scientific mystification when it is assumed that the structural unity of a society as a whole, and of every specific "group", is the result of a causal interaction between its "components". Even when these "components" are taken in a "socio-cultural" sense, as is done by the famous social scientist Sorokin, and are conceived as a structural constellation of interacting subjects (persons), meanings-values-norms, and social "vehicles" or "conductors", the assumption of a causal interaction can never explain the structural unity of the individual totality. In fact it can be established that Sorokin handles the notion of socio-cultural causality in different specific scientific meanings (psychological, historical and even mechanical

---

[1] Cf. for example, Fr. Oppenheimer, *op. cit.*, I, 1, pp. 132 ff.

concepts of causality are used promiscuously!). He does not know the transcendental Idea of a structural causality, according to which the real internal causal processes within an individual societal whole of typical structure occur in conformity to the typical groupage of its different aspects, without any encroachment upon the modal sphere-sovereignity. And this is the more deplorable because Sorokin, in contradistinction to most positivistic social scientists, is fully aware of the indispensible rôle of norms and values in human society, and his sociological system is admirable in many respects.

Sorokin's over-estimation of the rôle of legal norms in all organized groups.

The fundamental lack of a philosophic foundation of his sociology in a theory of the structures of individuality, in the sense explained in this Volume, is clearly seen in his over-estimation of the rôle of legal norms in *all "organized groups", irrespective* of their inner nature. According to him the central trait of an organized interaction (group, institution, or social system) is the presence in it of law-norms 'as the conduct-regulating and behavior-controlling aspect of the component of meaning-values' [1]. It may be granted that every organized community has its own legal norms, which regulate the conduct of its members and organs *in the juridical aspect.* But it is a quite different thing to say that these legal norms are the central characteristic of all of the organized "groups". It will appear from the examination of different structural types of organized communities that it is only a particular secondary radical type, in whose inner structure the juridical aspect plays indeed the central and leading rôle. It is not possible to ascribe the same qualifying trait to organized communities of a radically different type without levelling out in principle their typical inner nature. A similar lack of structural analysis is revealed in Sorokin's other typological classifications of "socio-cultural interactions" and in his more detailed analysis of the different societal "groups". This must be established even with respect to a sociological system which shows a clear awareness of the constitutive rôle of norms in the societal relationships. Thus this statement will be all the more applicable to systems which try to reduce the social norms to natural laws.

---

[1] *Society, Culture and Personality* (New York and London, 1947) p. 70.

This fundamental lack of insight into the real societal structures of individuality coheres with a factual elimination of the modal structures of the different aspects of human society. This is the very reason why the typical sociological problem of totality could not be viewed in its proper sense. This problem primarily includes that of the philosophical basic denominator under which the different modal aspects of human experience are to be grasped in the theoretic view of totality. This is clearly shown by the fact that all the -isms in the philosophical view of empirical reality which our transcendental critique has laid bare as a consequence of the immanence-standpoint, reappear in the different sociological systems.

In his system of general sociology SOROKIN tries to explain these -isms from the many-sided character of the "socio-cultural universe": 'Since the universe itself is many-sided', so he remarks, 'there must logically be several standpoints, each of which specializes in the study of one of the main aspects. Such a specialization is found, as a matter of fact, in any basic science, from physics and chemistry to biology'. According to him, the net result of such divergence is a more adequate and many-sided knowledge of man's socio-cultural world. And he thinks this must be emphasized in order to avoid the frequent mistake of interpreting this diversity as a sign of the immaturity of sociology [1]. Exaggerations of a specific viewpoint in the mechanistic or biologistic schools are to be corrected by the criticism of other sociologists.

But this very minimizing of the divergence between the different sociological schools betrays a fundamental lack of insight into the real character of the totality problem in sociology. If the appearance of the different -isms were to be nothing but a specialization in the study of one of the main aspects of human society, their divergence could be reduced to that of the specific viewpoints of the different special sciences concerned with the study of societal relationships. But the various sociological -isms are exactly characterized by the *absolutization* of a specific modal aspect *in order to grasp human society in the theoretical view of totality*. Such absolutizations cannot be corrected by other absolutizations. The very problem is how a general sociology may avoid them; this is to say, from what standpoint a sociological view of the totality of the different modal aspects is possible.

[1] *Op. cit.* p. 24.

SOROKIN's solution of the totality-problem in general sociology.

SOROKIN himself tries to solve this problem from the philosophical standpoint of H. RICKERT. He is of the opinion that sociology is a cultural science which, in contradistinction to the natural sciences, has to deal with the "super-organic" or "mental" vital phenomena to be found only in man and the man-made world. The socio-cultural universe is constituted by meaning, values and norms, which are superimposed upon the biotic properties of man and which, though different from the two other "components" of this universe (*viz.* the human subjects of social interaction and the material vehicles of this interaction), none the less also give the latter their socio-cultural sense.

As a generalizing cultural science, sociology is distinct from the individualizing science of history. By its view of totality it differs from the other generalizing social sciences, as economics, politics, and the science of religion, each of which deal only with a specific compartment of the socio-cultural universe.

In our analysis of the modal structure of the historical aspect in Vol. II we have already subjected this neo-Kantian view of culture and human society to a detailed critique. We have seen that it is destructive to the insight into the different modal aspects of human society. In fact we may establish that, in his confrontation of sociology with the other "socio-cultural sciences", SOROKIN nowhere pays attention to these modal aspects, but only to concrete societal phenomena. He observes that 'economics studies only business organizations as a variety of society; political science analyzes the state as a specific kind of society; the science of religion investigates the church as a special form of society. General sociology, on the other hand, is concerned with society as a genus(!), with the properties and relationships that are found in any society, be it a business firm, a church, a state, a club, the family, or anything else'.

It must be clear that by thus posing the problem of the total view of sociology, its very kernel is lost to sight. This problem is just as well present in a scientific analysis of a particular societal whole, as a business organization, a State, a family, a Church, *etc.*, as it is in a theoretical research of the interrelations between "all the main varieties of society with one another". A scientific research of a business organization as an individual totality is sociological in its nature, as well as that of a State, a family, a club or a Church. Special social sciences such as economics, jurisprudence, philology, ethics, theology and so on, can never grasp the total structures of these societal figures on their own hand, since their scientific viewpoint is determined by a specific modal aspect of our social experience.

On the other hand, sociology is confronted with the problem of a theoretical total view of human society when it studies the various interrelations between the particular types of societal relationships. Can we speak of human society in the sense of an individual whole encompassing all the particular societal types as it parts? This problem shows a close relation to that regarding the theoretic total view of the modal meaning-aspects of our social experience and is, just like the latter, of a transcendental character. It is really the same problem which in the one case refers to the modal structures, in the other case to the typical structures of individuality. Thus it must be clear that it cannot be solved by sociology on its own account, but only by the transcendental critique of theoretical thought in its application to the theoretical total view of the structural types of societal relationships.

The uncritical character of sociological universalism.

From the outset this transcendental basic problem has been overlooked by sociology. SAINT-SIMON and AUGUSTE COMTE introduced a universalistic view of human society and they supposed they could do so, without any metaphysical or religious prejudice, from a genuine positivistic standpoint. Society was proclaimed to be an "organic whole" encompassing all particular societal relationships as its parts. This universalistic view was taken over from the irrationalistic freedom-Idealism with its historical mode of thought, but combined with the rationalistic and naturalistic science-ideal of the Enlightenment, which contradicted it in principle. Thus the individualistic natural law view of human society was criticized and rejected seemingly only for its lack of insight into the societal facts and laws. But is it really a fact that human society in its temporal horizon shows the character of an individual whole encompassing all the specific societal relationships as its parts? This question is not to be answered by referring to the universal coherence of all societal relationships within a "cultural community". The latter restriction implies a new problem, namely whether in our disintegrated and secularized modern Western culture there can be any question of a genuine cultural community as was found in medieval Christian society. COMTE realized this problem and was of the opinion that his positivistic philosophy was destined to solve it, because the positivistic ideas were able to reintegrate Western culture by assuring it a mental solidarity. But in his time this was not a fact, but a belief.

Apart from this question it should be considered that a cultural community (taken not in its abstract modal sense, but as a real social whole), can at best be a whole of a particular radical type which shows a historical qualification. As such, it cannot assume the universalistic rôle of an all-embracing societal community. That this truth was overlooked is only to be explained from the historicistic idea of culture, which appeared to lack any tenable definition of its meaning. As to the universal coherence of the different societal relationships I must observe that this interrelation implies the very problem of the theoretical total view of human society. The universal interlacements of all *temporal societal* relationships cannot detract from the irreducibility of their different radical and geno-types. It is not to be understood how in a highly differentiated modern society there could exist any temporal societal whole able to encompass all of these radically different types as its parts. It will appear that even in a primitive undifferentiated society this cannot be the case.

GURVITCH's universalist construction of all-inclusive societies.

Since such *all-inclusive societal* wholes are not *given in the* temporal horizon of human experience, universalistic sociologists are obliged to *construe* them. GEORGES GURVITCH has introduced the distinction between functional or particular, and super-functional or all-inclusive groups, and proclaimed that the latter are historically realized in all-inclusive societies. As all-inclusive groups are regarded the nation, the "international society", and "humanity"(?), and in "backward societies" the tribe, the city(?) and the empire. These super-functional groups are distinguished from the "all-inclusive societies" in the sense that the latter represent "total social phenomena", while the former are only groups of super-functional character. There is no other explanation given of all-inclusive societies than that their types are more concrete than the nation, the international society and humanity, which can be treated more *in abstracto* as general types, just as the groups which are parts of them.[1] It is already completely obscure what is meant by all-inclusive or super-functional groups in a differentiated society. What, for instance, have we to understand by "the international society" as a collective unit of all-inclusive character, what by humanity? And is a nation really an all-inclusive social whole? Can it for instance include the Roman Catholic Church, or even a kinship whose members have a different nationality, or a State with different national groups, or industrial world-concerns as the Royal Dutch Shell Corporation and the Philips companies? And wherever has "humanity", as a super-functional "group", been integrated into an all-inclusive temporal society? The latter is, according to GURVITCH, the historical integration of all particular groups which are its constitutive "elements" and receive from it "its historical characteristics". 'Groups of the same kind integrated, for example, in archaic, capitalist, fascist or other societies, vary not only as functions of the instable equilibria, constituted by the forms of sociality immanent in them, but also as functions of definite historic epochs of cultural spheres (Oriental, Occidental, *etc.*), to which belong the inclusive social types'.[2]

Thus it appears that an all-inclusive society is to be understood as a cultural community of a definite historical epoch, which is supposed to integrate all particular groups that are its "elements". But as soon as we try to realize this historical conception by means of the given examples, it turns out to be completely confused. A fascist or a capitalist "society" is hardly to be conceived as a cultural unity encompassing all types of societal relationships. Fascism is a totalitarian political ideology, which is quite different from societal reality. It could only be realized in the structure of a State which, according to GURVITCH himself, is only a functional or particular group. As an *ideological community* it was restricted to the circle of its adherents, which by no means can be identified with a totality of societal relationships as meant by sociological universalism. The concept "capitalist society", on the other hand, is oriented to the absolutization of the economic-technical viewpoint in the Marxian system of sociology. It may be granted that a capitalist mode of industrial production, in its realization, exercizes a powerful in-

---

[1] *Sociology of Law* (Londen, 1947) p. 184.

[2] *Op. cit.* p. 183.

fluence upon social life in its non-industrial structures insofar as the latter have enkaptic functions in industrial relationships. But this does not mean that "capitalism" is to be conceived as the qualifying characteristic of an *all-inclusive society* which integrates all kinds of particular societal relationships into an individual whole. The latter assumption is nothing but a historicist and universalist construction which lacks any foundation in our experiential horizon.

OPPENHEIMER's universalist construction of human society.

We will consider another universalist construction of human society, that of the German sociologist FRANZ OPPENHEIMER. We have already mentioned his attempt to explain the possibility of general sociology, as a non-philosophical empirical total science of human societal life, by reference to biology. All special natural sciences could be integrated into biology 'because they all, without exception, in the last analysis are related to the *same object (Gegenstand): viz.* to the process of life in general. This enormous immortal *individuum, life,* extending itself in space and time, is their "*Gegenstand*"'.

In the same way sociology has to become the total science of the "social process". According to OPPENHEIMER, the latter is the activity of "human masses" (*Betätigung menschlicher Massen*). Human mass is the substance of this process and its activity is the expression of its moving force [1]. A human mass, however, is not to be viewed as a mass of individuals. There exists, strictly speaking, only one single individuum in an absolute sense, *viz.* "Life" in its one-ness, disclosing itself in the innumerable forms of plants, animals, and men. From this single and all-inclusive "Life" originate the species as rather separate unities. And a society, as a human mass, is nothing but a species, living socially, *i.e.* united by psychical interactions. It is therefore a "piece of life", which lives in a better and higher sense than an individual man. For, the latter is subject to death, while species and human society are "immortal", enjoy "eternal life", because in the change of generations they renew themselves continually.

Thus the universalist construction of human society is founded upon the metaphysical substance-concept. "Life" is elevated to a metaphysical entity, an immortal "individuum", and "human

[1] *System der Soziologie* (Jena, 1922) Vol. I, 2 p. 443.

society" is considered a secondary immortal substance, originating from the primary substance, just as the vegetable and animal species!

We may observe once again that the metaphysical substance-concept precludes any insight into the modal dimension of our experiential horizon. After having been hypostatized to an immortal substantial individuum, the biotic modality is deified to the absolute origin of plants, animals, mankind and human society in its all-inclusive sense. Thus OPPENHEIMER is not aware of the analogical character of the life-concept in its application to human society. Through the elimination of the modal aspects he arrived at the untenable thesis that in the last instance physics, chemistry and biology have the same "*Gegenstand*", *viz.* the "immortal individuum", *life*. Thereby he overlooked the fact that the living organism of a cell has a structure of individuality, whose different aspects are irreducible in their modal meaning, so that the physico-chemical aspect is never to be subsumed under the biotical modality. Similarly he does not consider that if human society is to be an individual temporal whole, it must have a structure of individuality in which the different modal aspects are united in a typical groupage. As a result, the transcendental problem concerning the possibility of a theoretical total view of human society is eliminated by a dogmatic metaphysical vitalism, and the universalist construction of human society ends in pure mythology!

The three forms of universalism.

A consistent sociological universalism cannot be satisfied by the conception of a particular human society as an all-inclusive whole, embracing all types of societal relationships as its parts. It must necessarily proceed to the assumption of an all-inclusive temporal community of *mankind*. This was already the opinion of COMTE.

It may be that this sociological universalism is founded in an ontological universalism which considers all that exists within the temporal horizon as a part of the "universe", whereas the latter is conceived as an individual whole endowed with actual, or at least potential being.

It may also be that sociological universalism is accompanied by an axiological universalism, which ascribes a higher value to the assumed whole of temporal human society than to the individual man.

But it is not necessary that these three forms of universalism present themselves in mutual combination. PLATO, for instance, was a consistent universalist in an ontological sense. But in his view of human society he only appeared to be an inconsistent universalist, since he considered the Greek *polis* as the all-inclusive whole of social relationships.

And in his dialogue *Phaedo* he clearly rejected the axiological universalistic view of this polis by arguing, in a mythical depiction of the life after death, that the philosopher has a higher value than the good citizen. Therefore it is necessary to insist on a sharp distinction between these three forms of universalism.

As to the universalistic view of mankind as the all-inclusive temporal whole of human society, we must establish that this view is incompatible with the plastic dimension of the temporal world-order. We cannot accept it without abandoning in principle the irreducible structures of individuality of societal life and the modal structures of its different aspects, pre-supposed in them. This view lacks any foundation in our experiential horizon and is nothing but an *a priori* philosophical construction.

Christian thought has often fallen prey to this sociological universalism by considering it as a consequence of the Biblical vision that mankind has originated "from one blood". From the latter is was concluded that mankind is a great family community bound by the ties of universal kinship and including in principle all kinds of societal relationships. This is a serious error to which we shall recur in a later context.

The three transcendental problems of a theoretical total view of human society.

For the present we must restrict ourselves to an elucidation of the transcendental problems involved in a theoretical total view of human society. We may formulate them as follows:

1. Where is the basic denominator to be found needed for a comparison of the different types of societal relationships, set apart and opposed to one another in the antithetic *Gegenstand-relation* of theoretical thought?
2. How is their mutual relation and coherence to be viewed?
3. Where do they find their radical unity and totality of meaning, or in other words, from which starting-point can we grasp them in the theoretical view of totality?

Our general transcendental critique of theoretical thought has brought to light that the philosophical immanence-standpoint can only result in absolutizations of specific modal aspects of human experience. Similarly we may establish that on this standpoint every total view of human society is bound to absolutizations both of specific modal aspects and of specific types of individual totality. This will appear from our following structural analysis.

From the Christian transcendence-standpoint the radical unity and meaning-totality of all temporal societal structures of individuality is only to be found in the central religious community of mankind in its creation, fall and redemption by Jesus Christ. This starting-point excludes in principle every universalist sociological view, which seeks the unity and all-embracing totality of all types of societal relationships in a temporal community of mankind. Neither a nation, nor the Church in the sense of a temporal institution, nor the State, nor an international union of whatever typical character, can be the all-inclusive totality of human social life, because mankind in its spiritual root transcends the temporal order with its diversity of social structures.

This was the firm starting-point from which Christianity by the spiritual power of its divine Master broke through the pagan totalitarian view of the Roman empire, and cleared the way for a veritable and salutary revolution of the social world-view. The radical meaning of this Christian revolution would be frustrated by identifying it with the Stoic idea of mankind as a temporal community of all-inclusive character. It is true that the natural law doctrine of HUGO GROTIUS used this Stoic idea as a foundation for international law and that this idea broke through the classical Greek absolutization of the *polis*. But it could never become the starting-point for a social world-view which hits any absolutization of temporal societal life at its *roots*. It could not clear the way for a theoretical examination of the basic structures of individuality determining the inner nature of the different types of societal relationships.

It is only from the Biblical Christian transcendence-standpoint that the three transcendental basic problems formulated above can be solved in a way which precludes absolutizations. The basic denominator for a theoretical comparison of the different structural types of human society can here only be the temporal world-order rooted in the divine order of creation. The mutual relation between the social structures of individuality is only to be viewed as that of an inner sovereignty of each structure within its own orbit, balanced by its coherence with the other structures in cosmic time; the latter guarantees enkaptic external functions of any particular social relationship in all the others, insofar as their different structural principles are realized.

And this theoretical total view is only possible from the starting-point that the different societal structures of individuality find their radical unity and meaning-totality beyond cosmic time in the central religious community of mankind.

It is indeed our transcendental basic Idea in its application to the theoretical total-view of the societal structures of individuality which gives this solution to the three transcendental problems formulated above.

The principle of structural sovereignty of every type of societal relationship within its own inner orbit, and the undifferentiated societies.

But when we try to apply this Idea to the factual societal relationships realized in the different phases of the evolution of human social life, there seems to arise a serious difficulty.

At first sight it might appear that this Idea presupposes a differentiated condition of human society which, as explained in Vol. II, is dependent upon the opening-process of its historical or cultural aspect. How then can we apply it to primitive or undifferentiated societies? Does not it appear from this difficulty that our whole view concerning the validity of constant structural principles for the factual societal relationships is at best of an ideal-normative character, and should be eliminated from any explanation of society as it factually *is*?

I think this conclusion would be quite premature. When we establish that a matrimonial community, a State, a Church, *etc.* have a constant inner nature, determined by their internal structural principles, we do not mean that *all* of these societal structures of individuality have been realized in every phase of development of mankind. We only mean that the *inner nature* of these types of societal relationships cannot be dependent on variable historical conditions of human society. This is to say, as soon as they are realized in a factual human society, they appear to be bound to their structural principles without which we could not have any social experience of them. We shall see presently that this does not detract anything from the great variability of the social forms in which they are realized.

As to undifferentiated societies, this implies that their types of societal relationship also have structural principles, determining their inner nature, and differing fundamentally from those of differentiated types.

This view is doubtless ruled by the Biblical Idea of divine creation of all things after their proper nature. But it is again and again confirmed by the social facts themselves.

The inner nature of a matrimonial bond urges itself upon man because it is not his own creation. Doubtless the factual matrimonial relationship between a man and a wife may be bad enough. Man and wife may break the marriage bond. But it is impossible to make such a factual behaviour into a social norm, because it contradicts the very nature of a matrimonial relation and the latter is a fundamental institution of every human society. The bolshevist authorities were obliged to capitulate to the "logic of the social facts" when they saw that the communist doctrine of marriage as a free companionship, dissoluble at any moment by the will of each of the parties, in its practice led to a fundamental desintegration of the Russian society.

In the same way the inner nature of a State, of a university, of a Church, of an industrial enterprise, or, in an undifferentiated society, of a sib, a tribe, or a guild, cannot be identified with the variable and changing factual relationships in which their internal structural types are realized. The latter urge themselves upon man and cannot be transformed by him. This is why the real structural principles of human society can never be replaced by constructed "ideal types", in the sense of MAX WEBER.

The only reserve to be made with respect to the application of our transcendental Idea of social totality to undifferentiated societies, is that the societal basic principle of the sovereignty of each structural type within its own inner orbit cannot be applied to the mutual relation of undifferentiated types which appear to have *the same inner nature.* But this does not detract from the universal validity of this principle as such, which only refers to the relation of structural types of a different *radical or geno-type.*

§ 2 - THE SOCIETAL FORMS AND THEIR RELATION TO THE STRUCTURAL PRINCIPLES OF THE DIFFERENT TYPES OF SOCIETAL RELATIONSHIPS.

The totality-character of the societal forms is disregarded by the so-called formal sociology.

All typical structures of individuality of human societal relationships are of a normative qualification. This is what distinguishes them in principle from animal types of symbiosis. This also implies that they require a human shaping on a cultural basis and can only be realized in particular societal forms which differ with the various cultural areas and the level of historical development of the latter. These societal forms are the social products of the process of human shaping and exhibit the same typical totality-character as the typical structural principles to which they give a positive form. This is to say that in principle they function in all the modal aspects of our social experience and are not exhausted in their historical or cultural modality, though they are always typically founded in the latter.

This is why any attempt at a delimitation of the sociological field of research from that of the specific social sciences by restricting the former to the forms of human societal life, was doomed to fail. We have explained this in detail in our analysis of the modal structure of the historical aspect in the second Volume. In addition it appeared that in the so-called formal sociological school of SIMMEL, V. WIESE and other sociologists, the concept "social form" was conceived in the pseudo-natural scientific sense of a more or less constant "element" of every complicated societal relationship whatever. The latter was supposed to be composed of such "elements" in more or less intricate combinations. But even these "*elementary*" societal forms, if they are to be really understood in a societal sense, turn out to exhibit a typical totality character involving the transcendental problems explained in the preceding section. This is why they cannot be examined in an abstract general way, but only within the typical structures of individuality and their mutual interrelations. Apart from the latter, they are nothing but pseudo-generic concepts which, combined with their erroneous interpretation as "social elements", necessarily lead sociology astray.

The difference between the transcendental structural principles of human society and the subjective socio-political principles (maxims).

The typical structural principles to which the social forms give a positive shape should be sharply distinguished from the subjective socio-political pinciples. The latter are results of human reflection on the fundamentals of human society and the maxims of their concrete formation in accordance with a particular cultur-historical situation. In this sense one speaks of liberal, socialistic, fascistic, communistic, Roman Catholic, Calvinistic, *etc.* principles for societal life. These subjective social principles are always to be tested to the normative structural principles founded in the temporal divine world-order, which determine the inner nature of the different societal relationships and the mutual relations between the latter.

It is undeniable that the process of formation of human society is influenced to a high degree by the subjective social principles which have acquired a socio-cultural control over the majority of the members of a cultural community. But it would be incorrect to overestimate their rôle. Subjective social principles may contradict the essential structural principles of human society founded in the divine world-order. The latter is the *order of reality,* which can never be set aside without destructive consequences for human societal life. *This is also the reason why veritable positive structural norms are constitutive for the factual societal relationships. They are not merely "ideal" standards for valuating the latter, but really give a positive form to their inner nature.* It is true that this formation can occur in a better or worse way in proportion to its being guided by better or worse subjective social principles. But apart from the typical structural principles which determine the inner nature of the different societal relationships, there can be no question of real positive societal norms.

The societal forms and the factual societal relationships. The temporal duration of both.

The societal forms are therefore nothing but the forms which the typical structural principles assume in the process of their positivization. As such they are not identical with the individual factual societal relationships, since they belong to the law-side of human societal life. But they are the necessary link between the structural principles and the factual transitory societal relationships subject to them. As products of human formation, and in contradistinction to the structural principles, they themselves have a certain temporal duration, which is distinct from that of the factual relationships presenting themselves within their positive social frame.

Though they have a typical historical foundation and, as such, are variable in time, they must have a relative constancy because otherwise they would not be able to maintain a positive order in the configuration of the factual societal relationships.

The societal forms do not only positivize the inner radical- and geno-types of the latter. *They are also the real nodal points of the complicated interlacements between the positivized structural types.* For we have seen that no single structure of individuality can be realized in isolation and that everywhere the intertwinements between the different structural types, already guaranteed on the law-side by the cosmic order of time, are *realized* within typical forms.

Constitutive or genetic, and existential social forms.

Social forms are to be distinguished in proportion to their having a genetic or an existential character.

Genetic forms are such which constitute a social relationship; existential forms determine the pheno-typical traits of a constituted social relationship during its existence. Both give rise to different variability-types of the structural types, which receive from them their positive figures. A family, for instance, is genetically interlaced with the matrimonial community of the parents. This conjugal community is interlaced with the State by its modern genetic social form of the civil nuptial performance and the marriage-contract and (in preponderantly Roman Catholic countries) with the Church by the genetic social form of the ecclesiastical performance and nuptial benediction[1]. In this sense we speak of a civil or an ecclesiastic marriage. In an undifferentiated society, marriage often has a close interlacement with the sib-structure by its constitutive genetic form of a contract of sale.

Through their modern existential social forms both the matrimonial and the family communities exhibit a great number of variability-types, which determine the pheno-typical traits of matrimonial and family life. An industrial labourer-family shows a different pheno-type from that of a farmer-family in

[1] In England the Anglican Church, as the Established Church, has also the competence to perform or "celebrate" a marriage.

which a certain patriarchic trait is conserved, as a consequence of the close intertwinement of family-life with the farm-business. Both differ considerably from a pastoral family, *etc.* An industrial or agrarian business in its turn is interwoven with the life of the city or the village, with the State and the Church, with international life, *etc.*, both in its genetic and its existential forms.

So it must be evident how much the social scientist will be at fault in this intricate system of enkaptic interlacements, if he considers only the variable forms of societal relationships, without paying attention to the constant transcendental structural types realized in them. And it is no wonder that a positivistic sociology is not able to detect any constant difference in nature between the various structural types of societal relationships. As the social forms, both in their constitutive and existential functions, vary with the historical development and bring the different societal structures into interlacement, it is impossible from them alone to gain any insight into the inner structural differences between the various types.

If, for example, we consider the former Dutch East- and West-Indian companies, we observe that in the social form of trade-companies, constituted with the consent of the States General, they exercized a genuine State-authority in the settled areas and possessed a fleet and an army.

When we consider the medieval existential form of the Church, we must conclude that the latter was so much interwoven with the secular government and with the administration of secular justice that at first sight it showed all the traits of a State.

Add to this the modern variability-types of State, Church, industrial business, school, university, *etc.*, originating from the typical genetic and existential forms in which they are realized. All this may suffice to establish that it is impossible to detect firm boundaries between the different types of societal relationships if we do not penetrate behind the social forms to the internal structural principles positivized by them.

So it is quite understandable that in his work *De la Division du Travail* DURKHEIM, led astray by the evolution of the social forms, concluded that the modern State is involved in a process of inner transformation from a primitive "segmentary" to a differentiated "organic" type. This was supposed to occur by replacing the antiquated uniform territorial divisions through a functional system of divisions according to the different branches of socio-economic service, organized in autonomous syndicates.

This is also the reason why MAX WEBER restricted his "ideal type" of the State to the modern State forms, because, from his historicist point of view, he did not see the possibility of construing an "ideal type", embracing also the antique and medieval forms of "political life". Historicism does not raise the primordial question whether the medieval feudal system could indeed realize the State-idea, if, in other words, the *feudal regna* may be considered as "real States". Historicism lacks any transcendental criterion of the body politic and must consequently also speak of the old Germanic, Greek and Roman "gentilitial States", because the ancient sibs and *gentes* doubtless exercised political functions.

If we consider a beautiful embroidery from behind, we do not discover any pattern in the confused criss-cross of the interlacements. Similarly we cannot discover the structural patterns of the different types of societal relationships if we pay attention only to the genetic and existential forms in which they are interlaced with one another.

§ 3 - SOME PRELIMINARY TRANSCENDENTAL DISTINCTIONS.

As our examination is primarily concerned with the *structural principles* of the various types of subjective societal relationships, the current general concept of "social groups" and their general classifications are not available to us. The reason is that this current concept, and the various current criteria of a general classification of "groups" lack any transcendental foundation in the plastic dimension of the temporal order. They are, therefore, arbitrary from the transcendental viewpoint and preclude a real insight into the social structures of individuality [1].

This is why we must try and find some other preliminary distinctions of a general character which will enable us to gain a systematic survey of the various structural types of societal relationships. It would certainly be premature to suppose that they are exhaustive. But, to my mind there should be no doubt that they are serviceable for a provisional division of the main types. Their transcendental relation to the societal structures of individuality will be explained in a later context.

[1] If the term group is to have any scientifically delineated sense, it should only be applied to the positivized societal relationships on the basis of a transcendental distinction of the latter according to their internal structural types.

Communal relationships and inter-individual or inter-communal relationships. Their correlativity.

In the first place we have to pay attention to the structural distinction between communal and inter-individual or inter-communal relationships, inherent in every temporal human society as such, as its transcendental condition. In the first (Dutch) edition of this work this distinction was denoted by the Dutch terms "*gemeenschaps*"- and "*maatschapsverhoudingen*", corresponding to the German terms "*Gemeinschaft*" and "*Gesellschaft*", though the current meaning of these German words is quite different from that intended in my own distinction.

It is impossible to render the Dutch terms adequately by the English words "*community*" and "*society*", because especially the latter has quite different meanings from that of the Dutch word "*maatschapsverhouding*". Although the English term "community" is no more an exact equivalent of the Dutch word "*gemeenschap*" in the sense intended by me [1], I have retained it for lack of a better suitable word. But it is all the more necessary to define the meaning which I shall ascribe to it.

By "community" I understand any more or less durable societal relationship which has the character of a whole joining its members into a social unity, irrespective of the degree of intensity of the communal bond.

By inter-individual or inter-communal relationships I mean such in which individual persons or communities function in coordination without being united into a solidary whole. Such relationships may show the character of mutual neutrality, of approachment, free cooperation or antagonism, competition or contest.

It is doubtless possible that within communal relationships, too, such traits may reveal themselves in the factual attitude of the members with regard to one another. But the intrinsic difference is that, as long as the communal bond exists, these traits occur between members of the same whole, so that the

[1] Most Anglo-Saxon social scientists use the term community especially in the sense of a "territorial group". Cf. for example H. P. FAIRCHILD, *Dictionary of Sociology* (1944), p. 52; R. M. MAC IVER, *Community* (1917), p. 22; REUTER and HART, *Introduction to Sociology* (1933), p. 129; A. MCCLUNG LEE, *New Outline of the Principles of Sociology* (1946), p. 248, all quoted bij J. P. KRUYT, *Gemeenschap als Sociologisch Begrip*, p. 6 (Mededelingen der Kon. Ned. Akademie v. Wetensch., Nieuwe Reeks, Dl. 18 no. 3, 1955).

factual behaviour of the latter continues to be subject to the positivized structural principle of the community, and continues to be experienced as such. If within a marriage bond, husband and wife factually behave as if they were only in a neutral or antagonistic inter-personal relationship of a particular type, this has a quite different societal significance from that of the behaviour of a man and woman who are really so related to one another. This is why any idea according to which all typical societal relationships are supposed to be composed of the same elementary social relations or forms of interactions, though in different combinations, is destructive to the insight into the real structures of individuality within a human society.

Our general systematic distinctions are by no means to be interpreted in this sense.

In addition it should be observed that there exists a strict correlation between communal and inter-communal or inter-personal relationships. This is to say that in the temporal order every communal relation has a counterpart in inter-communal or inter-personal relationships, and conversely. The same individual persons who in one respect are members of the same community may in another respect be in an inter-personal or inter-communal relation to one another.

In considering the factual societal behaviour of people it should not be overlooked that it occurs within the cadre of an intricate net-work of typical structures of correlated communal and inter-communal or inter-personal relationships. By eliminating the structural principles of the latter, positivistic and historicist sociology must necessarily arrive at an erroneous view of the societal facts. This has given rise to superficial and untenable generalizations, especially in the dynamic theory of society.

We refer, for instance, to SUMNER MAINE's theory, according to which the developmental line of societal life is to be described as an evolution from *status* to *contract*; or to DURKHEIM's above mentioned view of the fundamental transformation of society; or to TÖNNIES' theory concerning the evolution of human society from *"Gemeinschaft"* to *"Gesellschaft"*, to which we shall return presently.

Organized and un-organized communities ("*Verbände*" and natural communities).

If a community is typically founded in a historical power-formation which is organized, we speak of an *organized com-*

munity. The German sociological term denoting such communities, is "*Verband*".

The organization provides a community that lacks a natural foundation with a more or less continuous existence, whereby it becomes independent of the duration of life of its individual members. Unorganized communities, on the other hand, have a *typical biotic foundation*. They are *natural communities*; and since they lack a typical historical foundation they are to be found at all times, though they may show very different social forms, and in a primitive society may be intersected by artificial systems of kinship. Natural communities in this sense are marriage, cognate family (in the narrow sense of the bond between a set of parents and their children) and the cognate family bond in its broader sense, which, as we shall see in our analysis of its typical individuality-structure, has natural boundaries with respect to its extent (the degrees of natural kinship belonging to it).

It may be that neighbourhood also gives rise to a natural community, especially in the case of colonists. But one should guard against confounding such a natural community with an undifferentiated organized vicinage, which is doomed to disappear in the process of societal differentiation and which has a quite different structural type, *viz.* that of a guild or an artificial brotherhood.

The concept "natural community" requires a sharp delimitation if it is t obe scientifically applicable. It loses any distinct meaning if it is oriented to the Aristotelian conception of the "social nature" of man. In this case even the State is called a "natural community" because man is conceived of as a *ζῷον πολίτικον*, which can realize his substantial human form only through the cultural education of the *polis*.

For the same reason I shrink from calling a friendship a natural community, because the term friendship (with its confusing difference of degrees) lacks a univocal sense. If friendship is typically founded in a feeling of sympathy, we must remark that feeling, insofar as it is not of a biotically founded instinctive character, can be hardly viewed as a typical firm basis of a *natural* community. And a typical biotical foundation of friendship is certainly lacking [1]. Similarly the term "natural

[1] Cf. DIETRICH BONHOEFFER's poem *Der Freund* (Widerstand und Ergebung, Briefe und Aufzeichnungen aus der Haft, München, 1952, p. 269):

Nicht aus dem schweren Boden
wo Blut und Geschlecht und Schwur

community" loses any definite sense if it is applied to the social relation between all of the individual undertakings belonging to the same branch of industry or agriculture in order to construe a "natural foundation" for a public legal organization of such a branch.

We have observed that communities which are typically founded in a historical power-formation with a durable organization, by means of the latter have a continuous existence independent of the lease of life of their members. A natural community, such as a cognate family and a kinship bond in its broader natural sense, may have a restricted continuous existence, but this continuity lacks the supra-individual character of an organized community. It is only an *organization* which can make a community independent of the lease of life of all its individual members. This is not so in the case of the natural family as a bond between parents and children. By the death of the parents this bond is irrevocably broken leaving only the bond of kinship, which equally lacks the supra-individual character of an organized community.

Durable organization necessarily implies the *societal relation of authority and subordination* in its different modal aspects. This relation is also found in the matrimonial community and the family in its narrowest sense. But here it lacks, as such, the typical historical foundation of a power-organization. Once again

---

mächtig und heilig sind,
wo die Erde selbst
gegen Wahnsinn und Frevel
die geweihten heilgen uralten Ordnungen
hütet und schützt und rächt, —
nicht aus dem schweren Boden der Erde,
sondern aus freiem Gefallen
und freiem Verlangen des Geistes,
der nicht des Eides und des Gesetzes bedarf,
wird der Freund dem Freunde geschenkt.
[A friend is a gift to a friend
not from the heavy soil where blood and
race and oaths are mighty and holy,
where the earth itself watches over the sacred
hallowed and ancient ordinances
and defends and avenges them,
not from the heavy soil of the earth,
but from free choice and the free desire
of the heart, which are not in need of
an oath or a law.]

we must reject the conception of this authoritative relation as an "element" of all "compound" societal relationships. The truth is that it is only found in organized communities in the sense defined above, and in addition in some natural communities (not for example in the natural kinship community in its broader sense, nor in a natural community founded in neighbourhood). Moreover the relation of authority and subordination is only to be understood from the structural types of the different communities in which it is inherent. The natural authority of the husband or the parents, for example, is radically different from that of a magistrate in a State, or from that of a manager of a factory. One cannot level out these differences in nature without losing sight of the most fundamental states of affairs in human society.

In the inter-individual and inter-communal relationships any relation of authority and subordination is lacking. This does certainly not mean that here the individuals and communities are coördinate to one another in a position of social equality. The natural law ideas of freedom and equality have an abstract juridical meaning and could only be realized in the civil law aspect of the inter-individual and inter-communal relationships. In any other respect these relationships show a great inequality in the position of the parties, caused by age, sex, class or rank, disposition, trade or profession, fortune, political or industrial power, *etc.*

All these differences in social position lack a real integration within the inter-individual and inter-communal relationships. As to the former, they are to a more or less considerable degree also due to the difference in function or position which the individual persons hold within organized communities. This is to be explained from the unbreakable correlation between communal and inter-individual relationships and the enkaptic functions of the former within the latter. It is, for example, undeniable that a prime Minister, a cardinal or the chief manager of an industrial world-concern occupy a much stronger position in the inter-individual relationships than a mine-labourer or a simple bank-employee. But, whereas in a community all individual differences in position are in the last instance integrated into the unity of a societal whole, the inter-individual and inter-communal relationships present the picture of a non-integrated inequality and diversity in social position between the different parties.

This is the reason why no single inter-personal or inter-communal relationship can occur without finding its counterpart in a communal bond. A human society cannot exist as an unintegrated diversity alone. The unbreakable correlation between unity and diversity is founded in the temporal world-order itself.

But this transcendental correlation, which is a condition of any possible human society, should not be confounded with the relation of a societal whole and its parts, as is done by a consistent sociological universalism. A community in the sense defined above is indeed an individual whole, which embraces its parts and integrates any social diversity occurring within its internal structure into a higher communal relationship. But if an inter-communal or inter-individual relationship is conceived of as a part of an all-embracing societal whole, this is tantamount to its theoretical transformation into a communal relation. This is to say that its inner nature is eliminated and its enkaptic interlacement with communal relationships is misunderstood.

Sociological individualism as an absolutization of the inter-individual relationships.

While sociological universalism is to be understood as an over-estimation of the communal relationships, the absolutization of the inter-individual relationships is characteristic of the individualist view of human society. The latter will always seek to construe society from its supposed "elements", *i.e.* from elementary interrelations between human individuals. From this standpoint the reality of communities (especially of organized communities) as societal unities is generally denied. The latter are only considered as fictitious unities resulting from a subjective synthesis of manifold inter-individual relations in human consciousness.

This sociological individualism may be founded in an ontological and axiological individualism. But this is no more necessary than the combination of a sociological universalism with an ontological and axiological universalism. A genuine ontological individualism is, for example, found in LEIBNITZ' metaphysical monadology, which was doubtless combined with an axiological individualism rooted in the individualist conception of the Humanistic ideal of human personality. But it may occur that such a monadic ontological individualism is accompanied by a universalist view of temporal human society.

HOBBES was doubtless a sociological individualist. Nevertheless he ascribed axiological primacy to the State as a fictitious super-person construed by a compact between the individuals.

One should especially guard against an all too frequently occurring identification of the contrast between sociological individualism and sociological universalism with that between nominalism and realism in the famous contest concerning the reality of "*universalia*". Though it is true that sociological individualism is usually accompanied by a moderate or extreme nominalism, the latter may also occur with sociological universalism. In itself the contest between nominalism and realism is not concerned with the question whether human society is to be viewed as a whole with parts or as a constellation of interrelations between individuals.

If the correlativity between communal and inter-individual or inter-communal relationships is indeed a transcendental condition of every human society, it follows that both sociological individualism and universalism must result in an elimination of the societal structures of individuality.

As to individualism we must observe that it can never arrive at the transcendental Idea of a genuine communal whole lying at the foundation of its structural parts. As soon as it is attempted to construe a community from elementary relations between individuals, the whole dissolves itself into a plurality of elements and its structural principle is lost to sight.

According to its structural principle community in its different types doubtless belongs to the law-side of human society. It is not a natural fact but a normative task, which can be realized in a better or worse way. For this reason it is quite understandable that in our time the adherents of a consistent a-normative conception of empirical sociology in the sense of MAX WEBER show a tendency towards the complete elimination of the idea of community from their field of research [1]. It is true that these sociologists especially mean the idea of community as it was understood by FERDINAND TÖNNIES, whose conception we shall criticize presently. But their arguments for the rejection of the idea mentioned clearly show that they implicitly reject the conception of community in our sense.

It should, however, be borne in mind that the elimination of

---

[1] Cf. KRUYT in his above mentioned treatise published in the *Mededelingen* der Kon. Ned. Akademie van Wetenschappen.

the normative idea of community implies that of the inter-communal and inter-individual relationships insofar as the latter can no more be conceived in their proper societal sense apart from their normative structural principles. This is due to the very correlativity of these two foundational kinds of relationships. Apart from its structural principle no single societal relationship can be theoretically established and examined in its factual realization without denaturing its societal meaning.

TÖNNIES' conception of *"Gemeinschaft"* and *"Gesellschaft"*.

As our fundamental distinction between communal and interpersonal or inter-communal relationships differs in principle from TÖNNIES' antithetic conception of *"Gemeinschaft"* and *"Gesellschaft"*, it is necessary to consider the latter more in detail. For it is TÖNNIES' connotation of these German terms which has been epochal in continental European sociology since the appearance of his book in which he first introduced his conception [1]. TÖNNIES employs the terms *"Gemeinschaft"* and *"Gesellschaft"* respectively [2]) to bring out a contrast between an essential "social organism", on the one hand, in which the individual is *"naturwüchsig"* (*i.e.* arising spontaneously, as in an organic process) ingrown, and the mechanical aggregate of transitory social ties and relations, on the other, which must be viewed as the artificial products of human arbitrariness.

The members of a true *"Gemeinschaft"* are essentially and intrinsically united, and remain so in spite of external separation. The members of a *"Gesellschaft"*, in contrast, are intrinsically separated, and this in spite of all artificial bonds.

To characterize the opposition between *"Gemeinschaft"* and *"Gesellschaft"* TÖNNIES coined the pregnant terms *"Wesenswille"* and *"Kürwille"*.

---

[1] *Gemeinschaft und Gesellschaft* (1st ed. 1881; this book has already appeared in a 6th and 7th ed., Verlag Karl Curtius, Berlin). In his work *Soziologie als Wirklichkeitswissenschaft* the German social scientist HANS FREIJER observed that the influence of TÖNNIES' fundamental distinction has been so universal that it operates almost in an anonymous and underground way. Cf. also TÖNNIES' *Einführung in die Soziologie* (Stuttgart 1931), p. 14.

[2] *Gemeinschaft* is something like *community*; *Gesellschaft* resembles *"association"*, but there is no exact rendering of these terms possible. Cf. SOROKIN, *Society, Culture and Personality*, pp. 116—117 (Harper Bros., New York, 1947).

The "*Wesenswille*" is the natural unity of volition in all the members of a "*Gemeinschaft*". Building on natural instincts it is formed in an inner community of feelings, love and hatred, likes and dislikes, ideas and beliefs. The "*Kürwille*" or "arbitrary volition", in contrast, is a merely external agreement made in order to reach a specific external goal. In it the mutual profit *(do ut des)* is paramount and an inner unity of will is lacking [1].

True "*Gemeinschaften*" are found in marriage and the family (in the narrower sense of the bond between a couple of parents and their children), in domestic relationship and mark-community, in sibs and villages, in ancient and medieval cities, with their guilds and religious community, and in the medieval Church. They always precede the individualistic "*Gesellschaft*" and are either authoritarian or associatory in character or show a combination of both types. "*Gesellschaft*" is a modern rationalistic factor in human society, excercising a destructive influence upon the foundations of culture. It marks the decline of civilization and is antagonistic to all real "*Gemeinschaft*". There are two main periods of cultural development: a period of "*Gemeinschaft*" is followed by a period of individualistic "*Gesellschaft*". The former is characterized by concord, customs, and religion. The latter is characterized by convention, politics and public opinion, as expressed in typical forms of "*Gesellschaft*": in a large modern city, with its trade and industry; in national life, with its calculating politics; and in cosmopolitan life, consciously proclaimed in concepts by rationalistic science, adopted by literature and the press, and passing in this way into public opinion.

In the modern rationalized Western society there are only residues of true "*Gemeinschaft*" in family-life, in the State, in the Church, in the trade-unions, *etc.* Nevertheless the period of "*Gemeinschaft*" is over. We are now in the period of "*Gesellschaft*" with its prospect of the dissolution and decline of human culture. Thus it appears that with Tönnies the contrast between "*Gemeinschaft*" and "*Gesellschaft*" assumes the character of a central theme in the philosophy of history, a theme which dominates his whole view of cultural development.

It is evident that this view implies an axiological standard incompatible with the Idea of historical development explained in

---

[1] Cf. F. Tönnies *Fundamental Concepts of Sociology*, Engl. translation by C. Loomis, New York 1940, p. 17.

our analysis of the opening-process of the historical law-sphere.

The glorification of the undifferentiated medieval corporations and the depreciation of the process of differentiation and integration inherent in the disclosure of human culture show a strong influence of Romantic philosophy. And the pessimistic view of the period of "*Gesellschaft*" is doubtless inspired by the Marxian conception of the dialectical development of the capitalist society. The idea according to which true "*Gemeinschaft*" grows as a natural "organism" is taken from SCHELLING and the Historical School. It is a strongly deceptive trait in this view that really natural communities, such as marriage and the cognate family, are bracketed with undifferentiated organized communities as the sibs, the guilds, the medieval cities, the medieval vicinages, *etc.* For it is evident that the latter cannot maintain themselves in the historical process of differentiation and integration of human society; whereas really *natural* communities may disclose their inner nature all the more purely when they are freed from the artificial intersections caused by the primitive sibs and patriarchal domestic communities. Of course this does not detract from the fact that in the modern highly differentiated, but at the same time strongly secularized Western society the natural communities are threatened by other serious dangers. Insofar TÖNNIES' view indeed contains an important moment of truth that we shall be better able to examine at the close of our examination of the structural principles of the different societal relationships. But this cannot make his conception of "*Gemeinschaft*" and "*Gesellschaft*" acceptable as such. This conception is destructive to the insight into the transcendental correlativity between communal and inter-individual or inter-communal relationships. By reducing all organized communities which do not correspond to his romantic idea of "*Gemeinschaft*" to mere contractual relations, TÖNNIES in principle eliminates any examination of their inner nature and structural principles.

The transcendental significance of the general distinction between differentiated and un-differentiated societal relationships for the historical examination of human society.

We have to add some further general systematic distinctions to those introduced and explained above. They will also appear to be indispensable if we wish to do justice to the element of truth in TÖNNIES' conception.

In the first place the difference between *differentiated* and *undifferentiated* societal relationships appears to be foundational for every examination of the historical development of human society (usually styled: "social dynamics", in contradistinction to "social statics").

That this distinction is really of transcendental significance has been shown in detail in the analysis of the opening-process of the modal structure of history in the second Volume. Though the distinction as such is generally accepted in sociology, there is a great divergence in its interpretation, elaboration and historical-philosophical appreciation. In this respect the view of TÖNNIES, for example, is diametrically opposed to that of SPENCER or DURKHEIM. The main defect of the current views is their pseudo-biological or -mechanistic foundation. Nowhere is the distinction oriented to the societal structures of individuality founded in the plastic dimension of the temporal world-order.

Institutional communities and voluntary associations.

Secondly we have to introduce the systematic distinction between *institutional* and *non-institutional communities.* As the terms "institute" or "institution" lack a univocal meaning in sociology (especially since DURKHEIM's extremely broad interpretation of the words), it is again necessary to give a sharp, definition of the sense in which I shall use them.

By "institutional communities" I understand both natural and organized communities (in the sense defined above) which by their inner nature are destined to encompass their members to an intensive degree, continuously or at least for a considerable part of their life, and such in a way independent of their will. According to the Christian view their differentiated basic types are founded in a special divine institution.

The natural familistic community (both in its broader and in its narrower sense) is one into which man is *born.* The same holds good with respect to the State; although one can get citizenship also in other ways, no citizen is able to change his nationality at will. The institutional community of the Church receives the children of Christian parents as its members by baptism and as such they continue to belong to this community through a bond independent of their will, until they reach their years of discretion. This institutional trait is lacking in the sects which reject infant-baptism and are sometimes even without any institutional organization.

Similarly the institutional conjugal community embraces husband and wife by a bond independent of their will. According to its inner structural principle it is a bond which is destined to unite them for life. When there are particular circumstances which make it necessary to dissolve it, it is the institutional character of the conjugal community which requires supra-individual rules for divorce. In any case the inner nature of this institution is independent of the subjective conceptions of the matrimonial bond, which in course of time may strongly vary. A scientific examination of the development of such conceptions and their influence upon the formation of the positive norms regulating this institution presupposes the supra-arbitrary structural principle of the latter. By eliminating this principle scientific research lacks any point of reference which alone makes it possible to relate the different conceptions to the same institution [1]. The institutional character of the conjugal bond precludes any possibility of transforming the latter into a voluntary association.

In a secondary sense the institutional character must also be ascribed to the undifferentiated organized communities, which also embrace their members by a bond independent of their will. The reason is, as we shall explain in a later context, that in their undifferentiated societal form, in which different structural principles are interlaced, an institutional structural principle always has the leading rôle, either that of kinship or that of a political community.

As observed, the term "institution" is usually taken in a much broader sense, especially by French sociologists.

EMILE DURKHEIM viewed the "institutions" as the specific field of research of sociology [2]. He identifies them with the whole of the "social facts", conceived as facts which, independent of the consciousness of the individuals, originate from a "collective consciousness" *(conscience collective)*, and as such impose themselves upon the individuals. He distinguishes the corporative institutions *(insti-*

---

[1] It is in vain to seek for some common characteristics in the different subjective conceptions which science might combine to a so-called "empirical" concept of the marriage bond. The so-called "common traits" are, as such, quite arbitrary and can never determine the inner nature of the institution.

[2] *Les Règles de la Méthode Sociologique* (9th ed. 1938, Préface p. XXIII): 'La sociologie peut être définie: la science des institutions, de leur génèse et de leur fonctionnement'. [Sociology may be defined as the science of institutions, of their origin and functioning].

tutions corps) from the durable collective manners of behaviour *(institutions choses)*, such as law, morals, language, occupational customs, *etc.*, and the collective modes of existence (such as styles of building, traffic, *etc.*). The all-inclusive "*institution-corps*" is society as a whole, endowed with a collective consciousness.

The famous Roman Catholic social scientist and jurist MAURICE HAURIOU, founder of the so-called institutional school of law, followed DURKHEIM in this broad conception of the term institution.

He, too, calls all organized and un-organized communities "*institutions-corps*", in contradistinction to the "*institutions-choses*". But he rejects DURKHEIM's conception of the collective consciousness, which this sociologist employs to account for the independent existence of the institutions with respect to the individuals.

HAURIOU tries to base this supra-individual rôle of the social institutions on metaphysical *Ideas*, conceived in a neo-Platonic sense. With him these Ideas play more or less the rôle of the structural principles of societal relationships in our sense, though HAURIOU has not at all analyzed the social structures of individuality. To account for their influence in the positive formation of the corporative societal relationships HAURIOU takes refuge to ALFRED FOUILLÉE's conception of "*idées-forces*" (operative ideas in a psychological sense) [1]. The metaphysical Ideas of corporative relationships are historically realized by means of operative ideas *(idées d'oeuvre)* which exercize a psychological influence upon an élite of "entrepreneurs", thereby stirring them to concentrate their energy for the purpose of realizing them. The metaphysical Ideas concerned are themselves called "institutions" or "institutional Ideas". By means of the operative ideas they are "embodied" or "incorporated" in the factual institutions of human society as soon as their influence has expanded from the élite to the whole of individuals to be embraced by the corporation.

Naturally I shall not deny that sociologists are entitled to employ the terms "institution" and "institutional" in a more extensive sense than I do, provided that they define what they understand by the words. But this terminology actually gives rise to serious objections if it leads to a levelling out of the fundamental structural difference which we express by the distinction between *institutional* and *non-institutional* or voluntary communities.

Among the differentiated organized communities only the State and the Church have an institutional character in the sense defined above. All the others display the nature of voluntary associations, though we shall see that some of them may be realized in forms impeding the full disclosure of this voluntary character. They originate from the free differentiated interpersonal and inter-communal relationships, though with respect

---

[1] FOUILLÉE, too, rejects the conception of a collective consciousness of human society, distinct from the consciousness of the individuals.

to their inner structure they are not reducible to the latter. They are, consequently, based on the principle of *freedom to join and leave.* A compulsory membership, whereby they become compulsory organizations can never be derived from their inner nature. It may be the consequence of a specific kind of enkaptic interlacement with the State, exceeding their internal structural sphere, whereby they assume a public law function and are endowed with a public authority delegated by the State. It stands to reason that this can only occur with associations of a very important societal character, such as, for example trade-unions, which can be used in a so-called functional decentralization of the public administration.

As long as this is only a question of an *enkaptic binding* in the structure of the State, the compulsory character will not extend beyond the public law sphere, whereas the joining and leaving of the members of the association as such remains free. The compulsion then only has an indirect character and means that in the event of his not joining, a man lacks any influence upon public legal regulations or decisions affecting his interests, and will perhaps also be deprived of other advantages. Should, however, the compulsion to join assume a direct character and the organization as such consequently be transformed into a compulsory association, it would at the same moment lose its original inner nature and become a part of the State. Its qualifying or leading function is then modified in principle; it has assumed a radically different structure. And we have seen that the structural principles of societal relationships are not *created* by man but are founded in the divine order of creation.

Associatory and authoritarian forms of association. Indirectly compulsory organizations.

The non-institutional organizations which in modern differentiated society show an immense diversity in nature and formation, have either an *associatory*[1] *("genossenschaftliche")* or an *authoritarian ("herrschaftliche")* form of government.

In the first case the highest authority is vested in all the members together. In the second case authority does not derive from the latter but is imposed upon them. Consider, for example, the

[1] I intentionally avoid the adjective "democratic" since this term pertains to the governmental form of the State only, and its extension to radically different organized communities implies the danger of levelling out the structural principles of the societal relationships.

relation between employer, manager and labourers in a modern factory. As an organized community with its essential structural subject-object relation to the buildings and machines, a factory is not to be viewed as an organization with an associatory form of government. This might only be justified in the exceptional case that the labourers themselves have founded the factory and instituted the authoritative organs. But, as a rule, the organization intended shows an authoritarian form.

In addition it must be observed that the formal freedom of the labourers to join and to leave such an industrial organization is often frustrated by the situation of the "labour-market", by their factual economic position and one-sided skill and training. This is why the authoritarian economically qualified labour organization in the modern Western forms of industrial life can hardly be considered as completely voluntary associations. They rather show some resemblance to institutional communities. Nevertheless it would lead to a fundamental confusion if we should bracket them with the latter. For it is not the *structural principle* of an economically qualified authoritarian labour organization which as such precludes a complete realization of the freedom to join and to leave. Much rather it is the *positive social form* in which it is realized on the historical basis of the modern capitalistic forms of production, which has given rise to a factual societal situation hardly to be justified. Here we are confronted with another form of indirect compulsion, a form not originating from the enkaptic interlacement of the organization with the State. When we call them *indirectly compulsory organizations* one should remember that this term cannot have a transcendental sense as is the case with our former systematic distinctions, since its meaning does not pertain to the structural principles of human society.

The State is the only differentiated community to which belongs a compulsory organization in its proper sense *in accordance with its inner nature.* This will become clear from our analysis of its structural principle.

Associatory and authoritarian forms of voluntary and indirectly compulsory organizations may be enkaptically interwoven with one another in the genetic form of a free association. This will be the case when the established "purpose" of the latter embraces the foundation of an organized labour-community, an instructional community, *etc.* We shall examine such interweavings in a later context.

§ 4 - THE NAÏVE EXPERIENCE OF THE CONTINUOUS UNITY AND IDENTITY OF SUPRA-INDIVIDUAL (ORGANIZED) COMMUNITIES AND OF NATURAL COMMUNITIES EXCEEDING THE TWO-ONENESS RELATION. THE FUNDAMENTAL DIFFERENCE BETWEEN THE STRUCTURE OF A MULTIPLE HUMAN COMMUNITY AND THAT OF A THING.

It is undeniable that in naïve experience we conceive of organized (supra-individual) communities as being continuous and identical unities, which persist as such in spite of the change in their members.

The same holds good with respect to unorganized or natural communities exceeding the two-oneness relationship. But in this case with the restriction that the continuity of the whole is not experienced as a supra-individual bond, but as being bound to the life of particular members. It is certain that in naïve experience such a continuous whole presents itself only in the *full inter-modal coherence* of temporal reality, in which a rôle is also played by the actual subject-object relations between the community and the complexes of things objectively destined for its use.

A parochial or other local church-relationship, for example, is never experienced naïvely apart from its buildings, the relationship of a family in its narrowest sense is usually connected with its dwelling (cf. the Dutch term "*huisgezin*" [1] and the English term household), and an industry with its factory buildings.

In naïve experience, however, we are fully conscious of the variable nature of these subject-object relations, which are obvious *actualization relations* in the formerly defined sense [2]. A change of buildings, for example, which objectively correspond to the destination of a multiple community, no more affects our naïve experience of the identity of the latter than the complete or respectively partial change of its members does. And if a typical subject-object relation (actualization-relation) is lacking temporarily or permanently, we still retain a notion of *subjective* relationship, as a continuous unity amidst the change in members. It must be admitted that the pre-theoretical attitude meets with some difficulty when there is no point of contact to be found in the objective reality of things. But this does not detract from the fact that the naïve experience of a multiple communal relationship is falsified in principle if it is inter-

[1] "*Huisgezin*" means a family sharing the same home.
[2] Cf. pp. 147 ff. of this Volume.

preted exclusively in terms of sense perception, as if it could consider only an objective sensorily perceived image (*e.g.*, of people in a building) as a unity.

It is also erroneous to believe that only theoretical thought is able to comprehend a multiple community as a continuous whole and that naïve experience is only aware of *individuals*. Nothing is closer to naïve experience than the reality of the unifying communal bond, at least within institutional communities; and nothing is more foreign to it than the resolving of such relationships into *individuals*.

The fundamental error involved in the interpretation of the naïve experience of a communal whole in terms of a sociological individualism.

It is impossible to interpret the naïve experience of a multiple communal whole in terms of sociological individualism without transforming this pre-theoretical experience into a theory. And we have shown in detail in the first part of this Volume that this is tantamount to a fundamental misunderstanding of its inner nature.

Of course naïve experience is no more able to explain the continuous internal unity of a societal whole than it is able to explain that of natural things, works of art or other normatively qualified objective things.

GIERKE points out, for example, that the medieval Germanic pre-theoretical conception of organized communities identified them with the totality of their united members [1]. This identification was made even though medieval juridical sources clearly show a thorough awareness that the identical unity of a mark-community, for example, is not affected if the number of its inhabitants is reduced to 2 or 3.

Among primitive tribes the individual man is never considered apart from the communal whole to which he belongs. Very often

[1] A parallel of this naïve conception of totality is furnished by the pre-theoretical view of the totality of a man's inheritance as including all separate objects belonging to it. Thus GAIUS states in his *Institutiones* II, 54: "Olim rerum hereditariarium possessione velut ipsae hereditates usucapi credebantur, scilicet anno; lex enim XII tabularum soli quidem res biennio usucapi jussit, ceteras vero anno, ergo hereditas in ceteris rebus videbatur esse, quia soli non est, quia neque corporalis est, et quamvis postea creditum sit ipsas hereditates usucapi non posse...".

the sib or clan is the real unity taken into account within the tribal community. This is to say that here the inter-personal relationships are completely embedded in communal and inter-communal relationships, and are determined by the latter. The individual man *as such, i.e.* viewed apart from his particular sib and tribe, is here only known in the sense of the *outcast,* the *outlaw.* And where sibs are lacking, the natural families are the primordial social unities and never the individuals.

In the pre-theoretical attitude the members of a community are always viewed as embraced by the unifying bond of a whole. The latter is simply experienced without reflection, but always distinguished from the inter-individual or inter-communal relationships which are their correlates. It is meaningless to suppose that this experience is the result of a subjective synthesis of a given manifold of social interactions between individuals. *A fortiori* it makes no sense to assume that the communal whole as it presents itself to the naïve experiential attitude may be reduced to an "economical" fiction of human thought. As the naïve experience of the social whole of a community precedes any reflection or theoretical analysis, it is an irreducible *datum.*

And it is this very datum which is unexplainable from the standpoint of a sociological individualism.

Why sociological universalism cannot account for the data of naïve experience.

This does not mean that sociological universalism would be in a better position to account for this datum of the pre-theoretical experience of communal relationships. For although this universalism departs from the idea of the societal whole and its inner articulation in individual parts, it eliminates in principle the experiential datum of the unbreakable correlativity between communal and inter-communal or inter-personal relationships. This very correlativity is essential in the naïve experience of both of the latter, irrespective of the differentiated or undifferentiated condition of human society.

When, living in a modern Western society, we retire into the intimate sphere of our family, our experience of the close community with our wife and children is co-determined by the contrasting experience of the inter-individual intercourse with persons not belonging to this intimate circle. Conversely, our experience of isolation in a foreign city or in a circle with which we are not acquainted is co-determined by the lack of those typical communal relationships experienced in our own city or in a familiar circle.

Similarly in an undifferentiated primitive society the experience of societal relationships is completely determined by the correlativity of "blood-friendship" and tribal community on the one hand, and the relationships with persons of another sib or family, or with an inimical tribe on the other.

Any idea that this contrast between communal bonds and inter-individual or inter-communal relations is to be bridged by a universalist scheme of the whole and its parts, is foreign to naïve experience.

But this does not at all mean that this contrast lacks a deeper solution. It is the Biblical Christian starting-point alone which offers this solution by relating all temporal societal relationships in a concentric sense to the radical spiritual solidarity of mankind in creation, fall into sin, and redemption by Jesus Christ in the religious communion of the Holy Spirit. We have already observed that it is this very starting-point which precludes any absolutization either of the communal or of the inter-communal and inter-individual relationships, as they present themselves within the temporal order.

When we examine the latter kind of relationships more in detail it will appear that in the light of the central commandment of love, their typical structures of individuality lose any appearance of antagonism to the radical communal unity of the human race.

The dangerous implications of any sociological universalism.

The seemingly more Christian character of sociological universalism in its consistent sense, in comparison with sociological individualism, is only due to the fact that the former seeks an ultimate community in which all temporal divergences in the societal relationships are integrated, and in which the unity of mankind finds expression.

This seems to be a sublime ethical view especially captivating in a time which strives after an international integration of the world. It is readily forgotten that temporal communities are as much affected by sin as non-communal relationships and that in general more extensive communities show a lower level of morality than those of a more intensive character.

The chief point, however, is that the universalistic view is a false ideology because of its absolutization of the temporal communal relationships and its replacing the radical unity of mankind by a theoretically devised temporal one. Therefore it is in fact much more dangerous than the individualist view, since it is in principle a totalitarian ideology which implies a constant threat to human personality. It may be that in a universalist sociological system these implications seem to be completely avoided by very beautiful explanations of the "organic" character of the societal whole and its inner articulation in autonomous individual parts and members. Universalism will always stress that true freedom and self-disclosure of human personality is only guaranteed by its "organic" conception, in contradistinction to the "mechanical" individualist view, in which the individual lacks true individuality.

But one should not be led astray by these biological analogies, notwithstanding any assurance on the part of the universalists that they are to be understood in a cultural scientific or *„geisteswissenschaftliche"* sense.

The truth is that the human I-ness transcends every temporal societal relationship and that it is therefore impossible to conceive of the human person in its totality as an "organic" member of a temporal societal whole.

In other words, *the biological analogy fails at the critical point of the transcendental Idea of totality.* Human society is neither to be viewed as an "organism" nor as a "mechanism". Both views affect the very *human* character of the societal relationships.

One should not object that the Christian view is at least universalistic with respect to the *religious* conception of the solidarity of mankind. This conception has nothing to do with sociological universalism in its proper sense. This appears convincingly from the fact that the membership of the "*corpus Christi*" is completely independent of all temporal communal relationships, so that the latter are never to be viewed as "organic parts" of this transcendent spiritual communal whole. This confirms our earlier statement that this religious conception is indeed incompatible with any form of sociological universalism.

The structural character of an organized communal whole. Its difference from a thing-structure.

The above considerations give rise to the question: what is the proper structural character of a multiple communal whole and particularly of an organized community?

For it cannot be denied that at first sight an organized societal whole seems to show a surprising resemblance to the internal whole of a thing-structure, whose various types have been examined in the first part of this volume. Similar to the latter, an organized communal whole possesses a real continuous identity in spite of a complete change in its parts. It functions, just like the typical totality-structure of a thing, as a real unity in all of its modal aspects. And, in the same way as a plant or an animal, it has its own internal sphere of life.

This resemblance to a thing-structure is completely lacking in an inter-communal or inter-individual relationship; and to a much lower degree it is found in a natural multiple community, such as a family.

So it is no wonder that especially in the biologist trends of sociology the substance-concept was employed to explain the character of an organized communal whole as a living „super-organism". In KJELLEN's famous book *Der Staat als Lebensform*, for example, this substantialist view is applied to the State in an extremely consistent way. And since we have shown in the first part of this volume that the concept of substance is usually identified with that of a thing, this view led to a fundamental confusion between the societal structure of an organized community and the thing-structure. We shall return to this confusion in a later context.

In earlier publications preceding the first (Dutch) edition of this work I myself applied the term "thing-structure" to organized communities precisely to emphasize the fundamental difference of my conception from any functionalist, substantialist, or dialectical structural view of such societal wholes. But this terminology was to a high degree inadequate and confusing; and therefore I abandoned it in all my later publications. I shall briefly account for this terminological change.

Although we have shown in detail that a thing-structure as it is experienced in the pre-theoretical attitude has nothing to do with a metaphysical substance-concept, the term "thing", at least in its philosophical use, has an intrinsically restricted meaning. It is applicable only to a structural whole of a relatively permanent character which lacks subject-functions in the logical and post-logical aspects and therefore can be only an "object" in the typical human societal relationships.

One might even prefer a more restrictive conception of the term, according to which it pertains only to "dead objects", *i.e.*

to structural wholes lacking a subject-function in the biotic aspect, irrespective of their typical qualification. But, in my opinion, no serious objection can be raised against a definition of the term which includes plants and animals.

An organized human community, on the other hand, has a radically different type of existence from that of a "thing". This radical difference is not to be found in its lack of a "material body" or in its supposed restriction to the "mental" sphere. The human body is no more to be viewed as a "thing" than a human community is, because it is qualified by the general act-structure in the sense briefly explained in an earlier context [1]. And the temporal communal human relationships are not restricted to the so-called "mental" aspects but function in the pre-logical modalities as well. This will be shown in detail in the sequel of our examinations.

The only radical difference between a human community and a "thing" is to be found in the fact that the former has subject-functions in all the modal aspects of human experience and human social existence. This implies that a communal whole can never be a societal object. It can only be realized in a more or less durable social coherence of typical human acts and typical modes of human behaviour which are determined and unified by the inner structure of individuality proper to this community. This realization is doubtless bound to objective social "vehicles" or "conductors" in the sense meant by SOROKIN, and especially to the structural lingual subject-object relation. But such is not only a condition of the realization of a community but of all human societal relationships.

§ 5 - THE PROBLEM CONCERNING THE UNITY AND IDENTITY OF AN ORGANIZED COMMUNITY IN GREEK AND MEDIEVAL REALISTIC METAPHYSICS.

In the preceding section we have established the data of naïve experience, with regard to the conception of a community as an identical whole and its correlativity with the inter-communal and inter-individual relationships. We shall now engage in a more detailed inquiry into the development of the philosophical conceptions of the unity of organized communities.

---

[1] Cf. this Volume pp. 87 ff. Naturally a human body is not to be identified with a corpse.

The influence of the form-matter motive upon the Greek conception of the *polis*. PROTAGORAS' depreciation of the gentilitial organization.

In Greek philosophy the view of human society was in the last instance ruled by the form-matter motive. After the rise of a real State-institution which destroyed the political power of the undifferentiated gentilitial and tribal organizations, the Greek *πόλις* or city-state was generally considered as the all-inclusive whole of Greek society. This was due to the fact that this *polis* had become the centre of the cultural religion of the Olympian Gods and the centre of Greek culture. By the formative power of the city-state the Greek citizen was supposed to be elevated in principle above the uncivilized barbarian.

It was doubtless PROTAGORAS, the founder of the sophistic trend of thought, who gave this common view its first philosophical expression.

By depreciating nature as the unfolding of an orderless vital process in the sense of the Greek matter-motive, he at the same time depreciated the ancient gentilitial and tribal organizations. As the centres of the older natural religions, the latter had preceded the State-formation. PROTAGORAS viewed them as unstable social products of nature lacking law and morality. According to him legal and ethical norms can only originate from the *nomos* (legislation) of the *polis*, not from *nature*.

It should also be observed that PROTAGORAS, insofar as we can reconstrue his views, rejected an individualistic conception of the *polis*. He conceived of the latter as a real communal whole whose laws, viewed as the expression of the *general opinion* of the democratic community, impose themselves upon the citizens irrespective of their *individual* opinion.

It is only with the later sophists that a radical individualist conception of the *polis* is found. And this radical individualism as it is represented by POLOS, THRASYMACHOS and KALLIKLES, had its background in a shift of the primacy from the *nomos* to *nature*. But the latter is conceived in PROTAGORAS' sense of an orderless vital process in which the stronger individuals have a natural right to oppress the weaker. It is the Greek matter-motive unchecked by the form-motive which dominates this radical individualism.

The dialectical tension of the form-matter motive in PLATO's universalist conception of the ideal State.

In order to secure the *polis* and its laws against this ethical nihilism PLATO and ARISTOTLE combated the sophistic opposition between *nature* and *nomos.* They sought to found the political order of the city-state in a metaphysical way. Both of them held to the (inconsistent) universalist view of the *polis* as the all-inclusive whole of Greek society. They understood that it is impossible to conceive of the State in its factual existence without a normative principle which determines its essential nature. They were, in other words, completely aware of the impossibility of a purely positivistic concept of human societal relationships. And both of them held to the dialectical basic-motive of Greek thought in their conception of the relation between the factual development of the *polis* and the normative principle of its nature. They viewed the deformation of factual political life as a necessary consequence of the *Anangkè* (fate) of the matter-principle, whose power is opposed to that of the formative divine Reason. Both of them were especially concerned with the problem of the identical unity of the societal whole in the diversity of its parts, without finding a satisfactory solution.

In his construction of the ideal State in his dialogue *Politeia* PLATO sought this unity in a harmonious hierarchical order of the three ranks of Greek society. This order should be in an analogous conformity to his construction of the harmonious order of the three parts of the human soul, and in accordance with his conception of the idea of justice in its concentric relation to the central Idea of the Good.

But, as I have shown in detail in the first volume of my *Reformatie en Scholastiek in de Wijsbegeerte,* his trichotomistic construction of the human soul was itself penetrated by the dialectical dualism of the form-matter motive. It could not actually account for the idea of a whole.

Similarly there remains an unsolved tension, in his idealist conception of the *polis,* between the idea of the political whole, as a public order on the one hand, and the private relationships in the conjugal and family-communities and the private agricultural and commercial business, on the other.

In fact the problem of the societal whole was insoluble in the universalist conception of the Greek *polis* because of the radical difference in nature between the State and the non-political communities and inter-individual relationships.

Nevertheless ARISTOTLE seemingly succeeded in a consistent universalist construction. But this could only occur at the cost of a complete levelling out of the structures of individuality of human society.

The metaphysical foundation of the universalistic view of the *polis* in ARISTOTLE.

ARISTOTLE viewed human society, from its smallest unity, the "household", to the city-state (πόλις), as founded metaphysically in the substantial form of human nature. The complete unfolding of this essential form is the natural end of man's existence. But as the individual man is not able to realize this essential end in isolation, the disposition to communal life is implied in his rational nature. This innate social impulse (ὁρμή) is realized in a hierarchy of lower and higher levels of communal life, in which every lower community strives for its perfection in a higher association. The ultimate perfection of communal life is found in the *polis*, which is therefore the perfect human society and embraces all the other communities as well as the individual men, as its *parts* determined by the *whole*.

This implies that, according to the teleological order of human nature, the State is prior to the household and the village (as an association of households) and also prior to the individual man. This does not detract from its being posterior to the lower communities in terms of time.

According to its essential aim, as it is founded in the substantial form of human nature, the State ought to provide its citizens with all things belonging to a good (*i.e.* a perfect) human life (τὸ εὖ ζῆν).

Every community is established for some good end, since men always act to obtain a good. The State, however, though being a species of the general concept "community" (κοινωνία), and as such, logically distinct from other species of this genus, is in the natural ethical order the highest, embracing all the others. The reason is that it aims at the highest human good, *i.e.* the perfection of man's rational-ethical nature.

The household as an economic community and its three forms of authority.

Viewed according to its development in time, the State originates from the household (*οἰκία*), but this is only possible because in this lowest community the germ of State-formation is already implied. As the form-principle takes priority over the matter-principle and consequently in the teleological order the perfect community is prior to the imperfect, the nature of the household can only be conceived in a part-whole relation to the *polis*.

This is an inevitable consequence of the universalist view of human society. But at the same time it is a consequence which in principle precludes any insight into the radical difference in nature between a natural and an organized institutional community. The State is conceived of as the perfect *natural* association of villages, which themselves are nothing but associations of households.

One should keep in mind that ARISTOTLE does not consider the conjugal bond and the natural family in its narrowest sense as different (though closely genetically interwoven) communities. His philosophic explanation of the nature of the State takes its starting-point in the *οἰκία*, *i.e.* the Greek domestic community forming an individual household. The relationship of husband and wife and that of parents and children are only viewed as parts of the domestic community, whose primordial relationship is that of master and slave.

This is due to the fact that the household is in the first place considered as an economical unity concerned with providing man with the basic material means of well-being; and secondly as a community serviceable to the propagation of the "human species". The science of domestic management is economics (*oiko-nomia, i.e.* the laws of the household). According to ARISTOTLE, politics shows an analogy to "economics". It is true that he warns against losing sight of the specific difference between the State and the household. But in his universalist view of the *polis* this difference cannot be of a radical character. It is in the first place a difference in scale and secondly a difference in governmental form. As to the latter the household is a monarchy (although including aristocratic and despotic relations, as we shall see), ruled by one head, whereas the Greek *polis* has a number of rulers.

But this is nothing but a question of extent and number. The only qualitative difference to be found in ARISTOTLE's political theory is taken from his metaphysical view of the teleological natural order. The State is the perfect community directed to the good life[1] and should be "autarchical"[2], *i.e.* self-sufficient, whereas the lower communities are by nature non-autarchical since they require their perfection by the State.

According to the teleological natural order, the essential nature of a community is determined by the natural purpose to which it is directed. The household as the most primitive and lowest community is the natural association for supplying the lower daily needs and sexual propagation. Several households sooner or later unite in order to supply more than this. The village, however, is itself only adequate to supply the minimal material needs of this enlarged community. Therefore the State arises from a union of villages to provide men with a good or perfect cultural and ethical life. Its citizens are the heads of the particular households.

The universalist view of the conjugal and family-bond.

By viewing the household as the germ of the State, ARISTOTLE emphasizes its inherent relation between the natural ruler and the natural subject, which he supposes to be first of all the relationship of master and slave. In comparison to this relation that of husband and wife and that of parents and children are not equally specific. In order that the race may exist at all there must be a union of male and female, which are driven by instinct to mate and produce posterity. Such mating and propagation, however, is not peculiar to men and does not differentiate them from the animals.

It is true that ARISTOTLE recognizes that the human conjugal bond is also a moral relation, at least among free persons, where it involves friendship and mutual service. But he does not consider the irreducible typicalness of this relation, neither does he pay attention to the irreducible character of the natural moral affection between parents and their children. It is the universalist view which leads him to the conclusion that these moral relations require their expansion and perfection in the community of the State. They are not ends in themselves but only means to the formation of good citizens.

---

[1] Cf. *Pol.* I, 1280b: *κοινωνία τοῦ εὖ ζῆν.*

[2] That this autarchy is meant as a normative requisite appears from the fact that ARISTOTLE recognizes the possibility that a state lacks this property. In *Pol.* VI, 1291a, for example, he remarks that a polis which has too small a number of subjects is not autarchical.

To him friendship is a general condition of every communal life. It can, therefore, attain to perfection in the State alone [1].

For the same reason ARISTOTLE stresses the relation between authority and obedience, even in the conjugal and kinship bonds, in terms of political forms of government. So he speaks of the aristocratic character of the husband's authority over his wife and the monarchical character of the paternal authority over the children, whereas the authority of the master over his slave is of a despotic nature. Consequently the chief characteristic of the household is found in its being an organization that keeps persons of incomplete capacity or development in proper order. Its unity is guaranteed by the general relation of ruler and ruled, to which we shall return presently. Its head directs the activities for the getting and spending of wealth. He is the economist and has to concern himself not only with production but with the use of what is produced, with a wise administration of his property. Property is necessary both to existence and to citizenship. But as it is only a means to the end of a good life, it appears once again that the household, as an essential economic unity, requires its completion and perfection by the State.

This may suffice to show the destructive consequences of ARISTOTLE's universalist construction for the insight into the structures of individuality of human society. The truly natural communities of marriage and family are conceived of as dependent parts of an economically qualified organized whole, which in its turn is considered as a constituent part of the State. I do not overlook that his view of the conjugal bond has its background in the common Greek conception of a married wife as a children-bearer and domestic drudge, and, viewed from this background, is even to be called progressive in an ethical respect. But this cannot detract from its fundamental failure with regard to the inner nature of this natural community.

Is there a connection between ARISTOTLE's universalist view of the *polis* and the undifferentiated structure of the earlier Greek society?

In a later context we shall examine the question in how far the Aristotelian view of human society is influenced by the un-

---

[1] Cf. *Pol.* III, 1280b: *διὸ κηδεῖαι τ' ἐγένοντο κατὰ τὰς πόλεις καὶ φρατρίαι καὶ θυσίαι καὶ διαγωγαὶ τοῦ συζῆν· τὸ δὲ τοιοῦτον φιλίας ἔργον· ἡ γὰρ τοῦ συζῆν προαίρεσις φιλία. Τέλος μὲν οὖν πολέως τὸ εὖ ζῆν, ταῦτα δὲ τοῦ τέλους χάριν. Πόλις δὲ ἡ γενῶν καὶ κωμῶν κοινωνία ζωῆς τελείας καὶ αὐτάρκους.* Cf. also *Eth. Nicom.* VIII c. 9 and 11.

differentiated condition of the former gentilitial and tribal organization and of the ancient agrarian domestic community. This influence might explain why his universalist construction of the *polis* does not show the dialectical tensions of PLATO's *Politeia,* which doubtless takes into account the radical difference between the State as a public institution and all private communities. It might explain why ARISTOTLE, in contradistinction to PLATO, views the undifferentiated agrarian domestic community as the primary foundation of the *polis* and exclusively considers the heads of the households as citizens endowed with political competence. It might finally explain why the Aristotelian view of human society, with its "organic" construction of the *polis* from lower communities, so admirably suited the scholastic conception of the undifferentiated medieval society; and why even contemporary scholastic theories of the State which consider the medieval society as the admired model of their organic anti-absolutistic view of the State-institution, appeal to ARISTOTLE.

It is readily forgotten that ARISTOTLE's universalist view of the *polis,* however "organically" it was construed, was no less absolutistic than PLATO's. The conception of the household as a part of the political community, for example, led him to the consequence that the *polis* should regulate human procreation. PLATO was of the same opinion.

The corporative occupational classes in ARISTOTLE's ideal State.

It is true that ARISTOTLE treated only the households and the villages as *essential* parts of the organism of the State. He considered voluntary associations only as contingent organizations with special ends. Nevertheless, in his ideal State he proposed an *absolutistic division of its citizens into compulsory corporative occupational classes and after the Spartan pattern would have the government regulate common meals in which all citizens* should be obliged to participate [1].

Just like PLATO, ARISTOTLE is of the opinion that a well ordered State should be based upon a division of labour among the different occupational classes. But, whereas PLATO in his project

[1] See GIERKE, *Deutsches Genossenschaftsrecht* I, p. 30. Also cf. K. HILDENBRAND, *Geschichte und System der Rechts- und Staatsphil.* Bnd. 1, p. 335 and A. MENZEL, *Griechische Staatssoziologie* Z.F. öff. R. Bnd. XVI, 1936, p. 23.

of the ideal State denies to the governors any private household and property, ARISTOTLE, on the contrary, makes the latter an essential condition of the governmental functions.

According to him, the rulers need an independent private economical position which allows them leisure to devote themselves to political affairs. As a consequence, ARISTOTLE considers it as a corruption of the governmental system if the supreme authority is in the hands of a majority of poor citizens, since the latter are inclined to seek their own profit and to oppress the other classes. We shall see that this viewpoint led him to the introduction of non-political criteria for the distinction of intrinsically political forms of government. From his universalist standpoint PLATO also did so. But in ARISTOTLE this confusion was co-determined by his view of the "household" as the primordial part of the State.

The conception of the organized societal whole as a real unity whose identity is guaranteed by its constitution *(taxis)*. The State as a unity of political order *(unitas ordinis)*.

If the *polis* is to be viewed as the whole of all societal relationships, what then guarantees its inner unity and identity?

It stands to reason that realistic Greek metaphysics, in its universalist view of human society, held to the *reality* of the all-embracing whole of the *polis*. But this reality is to be understood as the reality of its normative *eidos* or essence, in ARISTOTLE founded in an objective teleological world-order. Although, as explained earlier, sociological universalism as such is not to be identified with a realistic view of the *eidè*, the latter doubtless rules the Platonic and Aristotelian conception of the reality of a social whole.

This clearly appears when we compare the Platonic and Aristotelian conceptions with the modern so-called transpersonalist universalistic view of an organized community.

PLATO and ARISTOTLE certainly did not conceive of the inner unity of the *polis* as a "collective person", nor were they familiar with a juridical concept of an organ. GIERKE, KARL HILDENBRAND [1], REHM and others have demonstrated this convincingly. The

[1] K. HILDENBRAND, *Geschichte und System der Rechts- und Staatsphil.* Bnd. I (1860), p. 23 ff. The place in PLATO's *Crito* cited by MENZEL (*Beiträge zur Gesch. der Staatsl.* 1929, p. 164) does not speak of the State as a person, but rather identifies State and laws.

speculative-universalistic construction of an organized community as an *"Überperson"* or *"Gesammtperson"*, which we shall discuss later on, does not originate in Greek realistic metaphysics; it is a modern irrationalistic product of Romanticism, with its dialectical view of the relation between the individual and the community. It presupposes the universalist turn in the conception of the Humanistic personality-ideal, explained in the second part of the first Volume.

In our *Prolegomena* we learned that irrationalism rests upon an absolutizing of the individual subject-side of temporal reality at the cost of the general law-side. Such a view cannot be joined with the depreciation of individuality inherent both in Platonic and Aristotelian metaphysics. An organized community is in realistic metaphysics a composite structural order, metaphysically grounded in an objective *Idea* or *eidos*.

In PLATO's dialogue *Politeia* the State is conceived of as a real *mesokosmos* connecting the *mikrokosmos* of the individual man with the *makrokosmos*, the universe. As observed above, the inner unity of the ideal State is guaranteed by the harmonious hierarchical order of the three ranks of Greek society: the wise rulers, the military rank, and the rank which has to provide society with the necessary material means. This order is conceived of as an order of justice according to which every rank fulfils its proper task, without interfering with that of the others, in order to guarantee an harmonious cooperation in the interest of the whole. In the dialogue, *The Laws*, PLATO intends to project a scheme of government which is realizable in the necessarily imperfect condition of real men and as much as possible approaches the ideal outlined formerly. Here the unity of the whole is sought in a well balanced constitution combining the monarchical and the democratic principles of government under the supreme rule of the law. By such a constitution conflicts between the different social groups may be eliminated and thereby the stability of the whole ensured. In other words, PLATO considers the unity of the *polis* only under the viewpoint of the relatively best system of government. He does not consider it in the light of the inner typical structure of the State as such. His only concern is to answer the question by what kind of political governmental form the unity of human society, as a supposed all-inclusive whole, may be ensured.

The Aristotelian solution of the problem and its influence upon the Stoic construction.

In the last instance this is also ARISTOTLE's concern. But he tries at the same time to give a general solution to the problem concerning the unity and identity of the State, irrespective of the question by what kind of governmental form this unity may be best realized.

This solution is no more than in PLATO oriented to the inner typical nature of the State as such. Rather it is applicable to any species of the genus "organized community". According to ARISTOTLE it is the generic relation of ruler and subject that joins a plurality to the unity of a community. From his explanation of this relation it clearly appears that he does not even restrict it to human society. Much rather he conceives it as a general metaphysical relation which is also applicable to composite substances, such as plants, animals and individual men, whose material bodies are ruled by a soul as substantial form[1]. We shall see presently that this conception was taken over in the Stoic construction of the organized communities. It has doubtless a point of contact in PLATO's construction of the unity of the three ranks of his ideal State, in correspondence with the relation of ruling and being ruled in the three parts of the rational soul.

In an organized community the ordering of the relation between the ruling part and the subjects is called *taxis* *(τάξις)*. ARISTOTLE understands this term in the sense of a law *(nomos)* [2] concerning the distribution of political authority and benefits. It is this *taxis* which, according to him, guarantees the identity of the State, although the individuals who are its citizens may change.

When this *taxis* or constitution, undergoes a fundamental change, because the control in the State shifts to another social group, the identity of the community is lost and another State arises [3].

---

[1] Cf. *Pol.* I, 1254a 28: *ὅσα γὰρ ἐκ πλειόνων συνέστηκε καὶ γίνεται ἕν τι κοινόν, εἴτε ἐκ συνεχῶν εἴτε ἐκ διῃρημένων, ἓν ἅπασιν ἐμφαίνεται τὸ ἄρχον καὶ τὸ ἀρχόμενον;*
Pol. I, 1254a 24: *καὶ εἴδη πολλὰ καὶ ἀρχόντων καὶ ἀρχομένων ἐστίν.*

[2] *Pol.* III, 1257a 18: *ἡ γὰρ τάξις νόμος.*

[3] *Pol.* III, 1276b 2: *εἴπερ γάρ ἐστι κοινωνία τις ἡ πόλις, ἔστι δὲ κοινωνία πολιτῶν πολιτείας, γινομένης ἑτέρας τῷ εἴδει καὶ διαφερούσης τῆς πολιτείας ἀναγκαῖον εἶναι δόξειεν ἂν καὶ τὴν πόλιν εἶναι μὴ τὴν αὐτήν.*

In this sense the τάξις is the εἶδος of a *polis*, its *essential form*, though the State is not a natural substance.

ARISTOTLE is obviously not thinking in terms of a *functional juridical point of view*. His concern is rather with a structural change in what modern political theory calls: "*Verfassung im materiellen Sinn*"[1] (SCHMITT, SMEND, HELLER and others), the *politeia*, as ARISTOTLE calls it.

This *taxis*, or constitution, however, is itself conceived in a universalist sense. Properly speaking, it is not meant as the inner political order of the *State*, but much rather as that of society in its totality, whose identical unity the *taxis* is supposed to ensure. The distribution of political power is only a means to the realization of the end of the perfect society, *viz.* the good or perfect life of its members. As this ultimate end embraces human life in its *totality*, there is not any inner material restriction of the competence of the *polis* as the supreme legislator. Such a restriction can only be established by the inner structural principle of the State-institution, which determines the inner nature of the latter. But the universalist view of the *polis* is to be maintained only by eliminating this structure of individuality.

It is true that ARISTOTLE, just like PLATO in his dialogue on the *Nomoi*, emphasizes that the aiming at perfect virtue requires the rule of law or of principle, which is reason. But, since this law is not conceived of in the inner limitation of the typical structural principle of the State, it cannot guarantee any restriction of the typical sphere of competence of the latter. Instead, ARISTOTLE as well as PLATO, only pay attention to the ideal postulate that the distribution of political competence among the citizens should occur in conformity to the principle of a just division of labour, according to the different abilities of the individuals. It should occur in such a way that persons of equal virtue have equal competences, and those who are unequal, unequal competences. Thus is justice secured. No actual State entirely conforms to this principle. Nevertheless its *taxis* may more or less approach to the rule of reason. So the governmental forms can be classified into two groups. Those which aim at the good of the community as a whole are relatively acceptable, whereas those which aim at the good of the rulers alone are corrupted.

[1] "Material constitution", opposed to "formal juridical constitution".

The influence of the universalist view upon ARISTOTLE's theory of the governmental forms of the State.

Generally in accordance with PLATO, ARISTOTLE assumes three forms of relatively good government, each of which has its corresponding perversions. They are monarchy, aristocracy and timocracy (in which latter those who have adequate property qualification equally share in political power). Their perversions are tyranny, oligarchy or plutocracy, and democracy, respectively.

We shall not engage here in a detailed enquiry into this theory of governmental forms. Instead, we will in the present context only point to the fact that the universalist conception of the *taxis* or constitution results in the introduction of unpolitical criteria of the governmental forms of the State.

This is the reason why neither PLATO nor ARISTOTLE were able to do justice to the democratic form. ARISTOTLE based his distinction between oligarchy and democracy upon the criterion of nobility and wealth, on the one hand, and freedom and poverty, on the other. He assumes that a democracy which attributes equal political power to all free citizens, irrespective of their abilities and economic measure of possession, must necessarily result in a rule of the poor, who misuse their authority for their own profit. So he overlooks the fact that a democratic form of government is not intrinsically connected with the socio-economic distinction between the haves and the have nots. Nor does democracy, as such, imply that all citizens have an equal share in the government of the State, irrespective of their abilities. It is in itself an intrinsically *political* form of government, which, like any other, is liable to deformation, but cannot be justly characterized by its corruption. A temporary connection between democracy and a political rule of the proletariat is a phenomenon which can only be explained from an enkaptic interwovenness between the structure of the State and that of the non-political, economically qualified relationships. But this interlacement can never determine the inner political nature of democracy, nor does it necessarily imply a misuse of political power. During the Persian wars the Athenian democracy gave a splendid example of patriotism and public spirit. In the days of ARISTOTLE it was doubtless in a condition of decline.

But ARISTOTLE's universalist view of the Greek *polis* did not permit him to distinguish the inner political organization of power and its enkaptic interlacement with non-political relationships. This is why he rejects the political criterion according to which in a democracy, in contrast to a monarchy, aristocracy, and oligarchy, the influence of the people is guaranteed by the principle of majority. In his opinion the latter is only a usually occurring consequence of the rule of the poor, and not the primary criterion of the democratic form of government. When the rich rule on the ground of their socio-economical position, oligarchy is the necessary result, and when the poor, as such, have the political power, democracy follows [1]. Because, generally speaking, a small minority is rich and the majority poor, democracy is generally the rule of the majority, and oligarchy that of the minority. In other words, even the rule of a rich majority would remain oligarchic and that of a poor minority democratic. Here the confusion of political and non-political criteria is clearly evident [2].

Was ARISTOTLE aware of the fundamental difference and correlativity of communal and inter-individual relationships? His distinction between commutative and distributive justice.

We have seen that the concept of *taxis,* by which ARISTOTLE sought to account for the inner unity and identity of an organized community, has the character of a general metaphysical idea. Its application appeared not to be restricted to the human societal relationships. Much rather it was also intended to explain the unity of a composite substance which has the nature of a community of non-substantial (and consequently not separately existing) components (*κοινωνία ἐκ συνεχῶν*). It should be observed that in the discussion of the substance-concept in ARISTOTLE's *Metaphysics* the concept of *taxis* does not occur in this terminology. Nevertheless, in its material meaning it does occur when ARISTOTLE points to the relation of soul and material body in his argument that the substantial unity of the whole is guaranteed by its "essential form", which rules its "matter".

---

[1] Cf. *Pol.* III, 1279b 11, and in particular 1280a, 1: *ἀναγκαῖον μὲν ὅπου ἂν ἄρχωσι διὰ πλοῦτον ἄν τ' ἐλάττους ἄν τε πλείους, εἶναι ταύτην ὀλιγαρχίαν, ὅπου δ' οἱ ἄποροι, δημοκρατίαν.*

[2] This very kernel of ARISTOTLE's view of democracy is apparently overlooked by REHM, *Geschichte der Staatsrechtswissenschaft* (Handbuch des öffentlichen Rechts, Einleitungsband, 1e Abt.), pp. 96 ff., where he opposes ARISTOTLE's supposed purely political conception of the criterion of democracy to that of constitutional law.

This is to say that the concept of *taxis,* in its application to an organized community, was nothing but the metaphysical idea of the essential form in an analogous application. In consequence, the inner difference between a human societal community and a natural substance is only sought in the former's composition of substantial unities. In fact an organized community is considered as an analogy of a natural substance and in this way the insight into the real nature of a human community was precluded.

Nevertheless the question arises whether Aristotle has not shown a real insight into the fundamental difference between communal and inter-individual relationships. In the first (Dutch) edition of this work I thought so on the ground of the sharp distinction made by him between two forms of justice, *viz.* commutative and distributive justice. Aristotle, I argued, sharply distinguishes between the justice to be exercised in the internal relationships between subjects and rulers, and that which has to find expression in the inter-individual relationships between coordinate persons in contracts and private wrongs. The former he called δίκαιον διανεμήτικον or *justitia distributiva,* and the latter he styled δίκαιον διορθώτικον or *justitia commutativa.*

Is this really so? Let me begin with recognizing that the individualist trend in the Humanist doctrine of natural law has indeed never acknowledged that distributive justice has a juridical sense. Hugo Grotius already remarked that it pertains to the distribution of benefits, which are not the object of a really juridical obligation. Therefore, he was of the opinion that this form of justice does not belong to the strict legal sphere, but rather to morality. And the four main principles in which he summarizes natural law in its strictly juridical sense [1], are indeed only legal principles pertaining to inter-individual relationships. *A fortiori* the juridical sense of distributive justice is denied by Hobbes. And, generally speaking, we may establish that in modern philosophy of law all the trends that have lost the insight into the fundamental difference between communal law and inter-individual private law, have no room for Aristotle's distinction between commutative and distributive justice.

Nevertheless, it may be seriously doubted that Aristotle him-

---

[1] In the Prolegomena of his work *De Jure Belli ac Pacis.*

self had a real insight into the fundamental difference and correlativity between communal and inter-individual relationships. If so, this would have meant an abandonment in principle of his universalist view of human society. And this cannot be supposed.

Let us, therefore, consider his conception more in detail. It takes its start from ARISTOTLE's general concept of justice in its application to societal life.

In general, justice requires the application of the principle of equality (*τὸ ἴσον*) in giving each his due. But *justitia distributiva* demands that in the distribution of honours and benefits we take into account the inequality of personal properties and conditions. It requires the employment of a geometrical proportion determining the relation of value between unequal terms. *Justitia commutativa,* on the other hand, guards that in exchange transactions (*ἐν τοῖς συναλλάγμασι*) the objective value of the exchanged commodities is equal, which equality only consists in an arithmetical proportion. The same holds good with respect to the retribution of a wrong, in which case the exchange of value and counter-value is of a compulsory character.

In fact it does not appear that this distinction between commutative and distributive justice was inspired by a clear insight into the difference between communal and inter-personal relationships. It is true that the former kind of justice, in addition to the retribution of wrong, especially pertains to voluntary transactions of exchange. But in the Aristotelian view, these transactions, however inter-individual in character, are in principle a component of the all-embracing communal life in the *polis.*

The whole Aristotelian conception of commutative justice has its background in his aversion to commercial trade and interest. In his opinion the latter threaten the virtue of the community, because they are to be viewed as unnatural methods of enrichment and are not primarily directed to mutual and equal service, which is a communal duty. Interest *(tokos)* cannot rightly arise from money, because the latter, being inanimate, is not able to beget *(tokouein).* And commercial trade which has its aim in profit making is unworthy of a citizen since it stimulates the striving for wealth as an end in itself, whereas wealth can only be a means to the fulfilment of the task of the good citizen. Viewed in this light, the Aristotelian distinction between commutative and distributive justice can indeed have nothing to do with the fundamental difference between communal and inter-individual relationships.

Naturally the terms may be retained to signify the different standards of justice which should be employed with respect to private relationships in the sphere of civil law and to public law relations of a communal character. But in this case the terms assume a quite different meaning from that intended by ARISTOTLE. The Aristotelian conception of commutative justice, implying a fundamental condemnation of commercial trade and interest, is by no means serviceable in a modern society. It presupposes the Aristotelian ideal of an autarchical all-inclusive *polis,* based on the economy of undifferentiated agrarian households.

*

In the High Middle-Ages the Aristotelian theory of the organized communities was accommodated to the Christian conception of the human race, reborn in Christ, and profoundly described by the apostle PAUL as the "body of Christ", with its Head and individual members. This synthesis was performed by THOMAS AQUINAS within the cadre of the scholastical basic motive of nature and supra-natural grace. Such a procedure must result in a partial subversion of the Christian view by Greek immanence-philosophy. But the scholastic synthesis was prepared by an infiltration of Greek societal conceptions in the patristic time. To gain a sharp insight into this methodical deformation of the religious starting-point of the Christian view of human society, we shall once again confront the latter with the Greek metaphysical conception of a perfect community.

The radical opposition between the Christian view of the body of Christ and the Greek view of the perfect community.

We have seen that the Christian religion struck a decisive blow at the very foundation of the entire ancient view of human society.

Behind all the temporal societal relationships it revealed the religious root of the human race. It disclosed the transcendent religious bond of unity of the latter in the creation, the fall into sin, and the redemption by Jesus Christ, the Head of the reborn human race, who in the mystery of the incarnation is truly God and truly man.

This was not a metaphysical theory of a temporal human community, but was the death blow to the Aristotelian view of a perfect community. The latter implied a transformation of the divine world-order into a metaphysical order of reason and, in its theory of the substantial form of human nature, it arrested the transcendental societal Idea of mankind in the Idea of a rational and moral perfection, attainable in the State alone.

The Christian view did not place a new community (the Church in its transcendent religious sense) on a parallel with, or if need be, above all temporal relationships, as a merely higher level in the development to human perfection. Nor did it project a cosmopolitical temporal community of mankind beyond all boundaries of families, races and States, in the Stoic fashion.

Instead, it laid bare the religious meaning-totality of all social relationships, each of which ought to express this meaning-totality according to its own inner structure. Without this insight into the radical spiritual foundation of human societal life, the differentiation of structural principles of temporal society cannot be understood in its true meaning.

The critical point in any Christian view of this temporal society is the question what position is to be ascribed to the Church, as an organized institution. It is beyond doubt that the latter, in its inner nature, is not to be viewed apart from the *corpus Christi* in its transcendent religious sense as the radical communion of reborn mankind in Jesus Christ.

Nevertheless, it may neither be identified with the religious fulness of the body of Christ, nor with the temporal expression of the latter in those societal relationships which as such have a radically different type from that of the organized Church-institution. We shall return to this question when we engage in a detailed analysis of the structural principle of this institutional community. In the present context we have only to point to the serious danger of a totalitarian view of the Church-institution after the pattern of the Greek universalist conception of the *polis*. The former would then be conceived as the "perfect" society of the whole of Christian life, just as the State, according to the Greek conception, was viewed as the perfect society of natural rational and ethical life.

This danger was all the more serious because, with respect to pagan society, the Church-institution was indeed an entirely new figure. This society could not but view this Christian institution as the centre of a new Christian empire, which was a threat to that of the Roman emperor. Jesus' solemn declaration that His Kingdom is not of this world could not be comprehended since this Kingdom appeared to have a mighty influence upon the view of secular authority.

In contrast to the absolutistic idea of the Roman empire, the proclamation that God must be obeyed rather than man was indeed a radical innovation. For the first time, fundamental limitations were imposed upon the competence of the State-authority, limitations both with respect to the new Church-institution and to the natural family-life of the Christians, who laid claim to the freedom of a Christian education of their children; limitations above all with respect to the spiritual centre of personal human life, which was conceived of as being independent of any temporal societal condition of the individual person.

It is undeniable that this Christian standpoint, rooted in the confession of God's sovereignty as Creator, the apostasy of the "natural man", and Christ's kingdom in the hearts of the members of a new mankind, implied a radical revolution in the entire view of temporal human society. If from the very beginning this religious starting-point in its pure and original sense had also ruled the theoretical Christian view of the societal relationships, there might have been no question of a partial falling back into the universalist conceptions of Greek immanence-philosophy.

Even in its partial compromise with the latter, Christian thought brought a real gain to the philosophy of human society by contributing new and undestructible ideas.

It broke in principle the shackles of the immanence standpoint by its insight into the impossibility of restricting the social bond of mankind to the temporal horizon of earthly life, and by viewing the latter in the central light of the "*corpus Christi*". No one can deny the enormous influence of the Christian idea of office, in its contradistinction to the ancient conception of authority; the significance of the delimitation of the competences of the Church and the State, already sharply enunciated in the theory of GELASIUS; the significance of the religious elevation of manual labour, the value of the application of AUGUSTINE's antithesis between the *civitas Dei* and *civitas terrena*, and so on.

Why this religious basic Idea could not be successfully worked out in a radical Christian theory of social relationships during the Middle-Ages. The universalist view of the holy Roman empire.

And yet, with TROELTSCH, we must frankly admit that the Christian theory of society, as it developed in the High Middle Ages, in a more or less closed form, must not be viewed as more Christian than it really was.

Various factors prevented the basic Christian Idea of the kingdom of Christ from being developed purely.

The Church fathers had already synthesized Christian thought with the Stoic-Aristotelian view of man as a rational social animal, with Stoic ethics and natural law doctrine.

The historical development of the temporal Church during the Middle Ages led to its elevation to a top position of power. Transformed into a hierarchical sacramental institution of grace, it arrogated to itself absolute authority over the souls of its members, and gradually identified itself with the "invisible Church" in its central religious sense as the "body of Christ".

Add to this the undifferentiated condition of the medieval secular society after the dissolution of the Carolingian empire, already discussed in the second volume. In this historical condition the Church institution was indeed the only integrating factor of Western culture. The feudal system caused a close interlacement of spiritual and secular authority. In the period of the so-called ecclesiastically unified culture, this whole complex of historical causes resulted in a factual supremacy of the hierarchical ecclesiastic authority over the entire political and social life.

At this time a view of society developed which ascribed a really universalistic position to the temporal institutional Church (wrongly identified with the Church as a religious-transcendent "organism"). This universalist view of the ecclesiastic institution pertained to the spiritual side of social life. But it was combined with a universalist conception of the secular social relationships. This view was to a high degree influenced by the idea of the holy Roman empire introduced in the Carolingian period. This empire was supposed to embrace Christianity as a whole, both in its spiritual and secular social relationships. In consequence it must have a spiritual and a secular head and the only question was to which of them was to be ascribed the supremacy, to the pope or to the emperor? The debate about this problem was not concerned with the relation between the Church and the State as two separate institutions. The universalist view of the holy Roman empire did not allow such a distinction, apart from the fact that after the decline of the Carolingian empire a real State-institution no longer existed. It was rather the conception of the *Corpus Christianum* transformed in a temporal sense which ruled the discussion. The famous theory concerning the two swords is a clear evidence of this state of affairs.

In this respect Thomistic philosophy posed a new problem by combining the universalist view of the ecclesiastical institution with the Aristotelian conception of the State as the whole of natural society. This problem presupposed the new scholastical basic motive of nature and grace.

THOMAS AQUINAS' synthesis of the Christian idea of the *corpus Christi* with ARISTOTLE's metaphysical theory of society.

The theory of the organic character of human society and of the development of the social and political disposition in man was already familiar to patristic thought. But here it was conceived in a predominantly Stoic-Christian manner. In THOMAS AQUINAS it acquires its foundation in the Aristotelian conception of the "substantial form" of human nature.

On the basis of the Aristotelian metaphysico-teleological idea of development, the household was proclaimed to be the germ of the State. The medieval guilds, corporatively closed occupational groups, were theoretically conceived as organic components of the city State. The State (both the city State and the holy Roman empire) was again viewed as a perfect, autarchical community *(societas perfecta)*.

Of course, in THOMAS AQUINAS the State is only *societas perfecta* in the natural sphere. In all matters relating to salvation it is subordinate to the sacramental institute of grace; but even this relation between State and Church is formally conceived of according to the metaphysical rational order of matter and form.

Both the institutional Church and man's function of faith are hypostatized in the "sphere of grace".

Within the "sphere of nature" the rational and moral nature of man is hypostatized, and in the essential form of man, as its implication, the State, conceived of as an organic "*unitas ordinis*" [1],

---

[1] Man is also conceived of as a "*unitas ordinis*". P. E. KURZ, in his *Individuum and Gemeinschaft beim Hl. Thomas Aquinas* (1932) is of the

of which all other forms of society are merely dissimilar components.

THOMAS accepts the entire Aristotelian view concerning the *taxis*, as the principle of unity of organized communities. In consequence he also considers the controlling part as the lawful factor which holds the various components of the corporative organism in a continuous coherence and unity, leading them to the immanent goal of the bond, the communal good [1].

Unhesitatingly THOMAS subordinates all non-political natural relationships to the State, which, as the perfect natural community, is higher than all others known and produced by reason [2]. The State includes them as its organic — although heterogeneous — constituents.

In the Church fathers the view was still prevalent that the State is based upon the power of the sword, instituted by God because of sin to restrain the wickedness of man. THOMAS gave this view a strongly Aristotelian turn.

In ARISTOTLE the State was necessarily based upon the rational and moral essential form of man, because he conceived of the volitional activity of the soul as exclusively belonging to its affective and desiring activity, which in itself is not inclined to follow the leading of reason in choosing the mean (μεσότης) between two extremes. By means of its laws the State must help to accustom the individual to virtue [3]. This conception was adopted by THOMAS in his commentary on ARISTOTLE's *Politica* and it does not appear that he abandoned it in his later works [4].

Within the cadre of this teleological and metaphysical view of human society, THOMAS was no more in a position than was ARISTOTLE to investigate the internal structural principles, which,

---

opinion that this concept does not have an ontological significance. Cf., however, A. MENZEL, *Griechische Staatssoziologie* (Z.f. öff. R. XVI, 1936) pp. 7 ff, and our explanation of the Aristotelian concept of *taxis*, pp. 206 ff. of this Volume.

[1] *De regimine principum* I, cap. 1. In complete accordance with ARISTOTLE, the social concept of unity of order is conceived here in analogy to the *unitas ordinis* to be found in the human body, the universe and the individual, in which latter the soul rules over the body and in the soul the rational part rules over the affective and desiring impulses.

[2] The Commentary on ARISTOTLE's *Politica* (Parmenser ed., Bnd. 21), p. 266.

[3] *Eth. Nicom* X, cap. 10, pp. 1180a 29 ff.

[4] *Comm. Arist. Pol.*, pp. 367, 370, 371, 400, 424.

grounded in the divine world-order, prescribe its own internal typical law to each societal relationship.

The Thomistic theory of organized communities has no room for sphere-sovereignty, but only for the autonomy of the lower communities. The difference between these two principles.

This realistic metaphysical theory does not have any room for the principle of the internal sphere-sovereignty of each typical structural relationship of human society after its own inner nature. It can at the utmost allow for the autonomy of non-political relationships within the State and for the autonomy of the State with respect to the Church.

In accordance with ARISTOTLE, the goal of the State is sought in the universal good of perfection. And we have already established that in the universalist view of "natural society" this idea does not possess any inner structural limitation. Placed in the cadre of THOMAS' scholastical motive of nature and grace, it includes the supplying of citizens with all temporal goods, which as necessary or desirable commodities form a natural basis for the striving after the eternal good of salvation. The only formal limitation of the task of the State lies in the reserve that it only has to supply what its citizens cannot acquire individually or in the lower associations.

But just as the State is the perfect society in the natural sphere, the Church-institution is the *societas perfecta* in the supra-natural sphere of grace. And, in accordance with THOMAS' conception of the relation between nature and grace, the State is subordinate to the Church, which alone can elevate natural life to the supra-natural level of perfection. So the universalist view of human society, already expressed in the pre-Thomistic idea of the holy Roman empire, acquires its typical elaboration within the new scholastical basic motive of nature and supra-nature.

The supremacy which in this Thomistic view is ascribed to the Church-institution implies that to the State is in principle denied any competence of interfering with ecclesiastical affairs. But in addition, the final judgment concerning the question which affairs pertain to the natural and which to the supra-natural sphere, can only belong to the Church. Since in the Thomistic view the autonomy of natural reason is only of a relative character and human nature is in need of its supra-natural perfection, it is the supra-natural ecclesiastical institution which alone can establish the Christian principles of government. And, as the infallible interpreter of natural ethical law, this Church alone is in a position to pass judgment concerning the limits of competence of the State [1].

This is how THOMAS seeks to evade the absolutistic consequences of the Aristotelian conception of the *polis*. And it is indeed undeniable that by its transplantation in THOMAS' scholastical cadre of thought with its basic motive of nature and grace, the Greek absolutization of the State is broken through.

THOMAS recognized unassailable subjective natural rights of the individual man apart from the State. To the Aristotelian thesis that the individual and the lower natural communities are parts of the *polis*, he adds the reserve: "insofar as they belong to the same order as the latter". Positive law, which, according to THOMAS, can only be formed by a perfect society, is, in his opinion, bound to natural law and cannot be valid if it is in contrast with the latter.

But, in the natural sphere, the individuals and the lower communities are not in a position to establish such a violation of natural law by the legislator. If the State is of the opinion that its laws are in conformity to natural law, the citizen has to give precedence to the judgment of the political authority. It is only the Church to which belongs the final judgment if the citizens of the State pretend that their natural rights are violated.

Moreover, the above mentioned reserve added to the Aristotelian conception of the individuals and the lower communities as parts of the State, has only significance with respect to the "supra-natural order". It does not mean that THOMAS assumes an internal *natural* sphere of the lower communities which is exempt from the legal authority of the State. The latter view would have in principle contradicted his universalist conception of human society.

Taking into account the privileges and customary freedom of the medieval corporations, THOMAS could accept their autonomy. But autonomy is not identical with internal sphere-sovereignty of the different types of societal relationships. The fundamental difference between the two is that autonomy only occurs in the relation of a whole and its parts, whereas sphere-sovereignty pertains to the relation between social structures of a different

---

[1] *De reg. princ.* I, 14 ff. Cf. also *Summa contra Gentiles* 3, 17, 19.

radical or geno-type, which in principle lacks the character of a part-whole relation. Sphere-sovereignty is only determined and limited by the inner nature of the social relationship itself and is thereby grounded in the divine world-order. The limits of autonomy belonging to the parts of the State, on the contrary, cannot be grounded in the inner nature of these parts. The reason is that this nature is dependent on that of the whole itself. We shall recur to this point in detail.

§ 6 - THE PROBLEM CONCERNING THE IDENTICAL UNITY OF ORGANIZED COMMUNITIES IN THE OLDER INDIVIDUALISTIC AND UNIVERSALISTIC NOMINALIST THEORIES [1].

In opposition to metaphysical realism, nominalism, at least in its rationalistic-individualist trend of sociological thought, must deny the metaphysical foundation of social relationships.

---

[1] In his *Gesellschaftslehre* (3e ed. 1930, p. 98) OTHMAR SPANN considers it illegitimate to oppose individualism and universalism, except in a metaphorical sense, as nominalism and realism: "Denn nicht um die ontologische und logische Frage des Allgemeinbegriffes (der Idee) handelt es sich hier, sondern um eine Zergliederung gesellschaftlicher Erfahrungstatsachen". [For this contrast is not concerned with the ontic or logic problem of the universal idea, but with the analysis of social matters of experience.]

This observation is incorrect in two respects, although we ourselves have established in an earlier context that the sociological contrast between individualism and realism is quite different from that between nominalism and realism.

In the first place we shall subsequently show that in its view of human society not all nominalism is individualistic. In the course of its development nominalism has brought forth numerous trends which often formed polar contrasts. Modern irrationalistic nominalism, for example, has developed its own method for the so-called *Geisteswissenschaften* and is predominantly universalistic in a sociological sense. And in the view of human society held by the nominalistic Stoa, we shall also discover a universalistic undercurrent.

In the second place SPANN overlooks the fact that every theory concerning the structure of human society is based upon a specific conception of the basic structure of reality. What he calls the ontological question really lies at the foundation of every analysis of empirical societal facts. Human society belongs to reality.

It is correct to speak of nominalistic and realistic theories of society, but it is illegitimate to identify the former with individualism. The realistic metaphysical theories analysed above appeared in fact to imply a universalist view of society.

The older individualistic nominalism, in PLATO's dialogue *Politeia* represented by GLAUCON, only conceived of the individual sensory thing as really existing. It could only stigmatize the realistic conception of an organized community as mystical metaphysics. The individual was conceived here as an *in-dividuum,* as a being, enclosed within itself and preceding every societal relationship. The State could then only be considered an aggregate of individuals, not an "organic whole" whose unity is guaranteed by a metaphysically founded order of ruling and obeying.

Insofar as individualistic nominalism did not simply repudiate social life, as did the radical Sophists and the Cynics, it had to seek a construction to justify any bond between the individual and the requirements of communal life. Especially the compulsory authority of the State was in need of such a construction.

The rationalistic-nominalistic concept of function in the theory of organized communities, in opposition to the Aristotelian metaphysical realistic concept of substance.

The Aristotelian theory, based on a teleological and metaphysical order of reason *(lex naturalis),* viewed authority as a necessary pre-requisite of every community and grounded it in the essential nature of man as a "social animal". Communal life, as such, is implied (metaphysically) in this essential human nature. According to the teleological world-order, everything is justified that is necessary for the existence of a community; to this end authority is of primary importance, since without it no "unity of order" is possible.

In this way the authoritative structure of organized communities also received its metaphysical foundation in the substantial form of human nature.

This metaphysical concept of substance cannot be employed as an ontological foundation in a nominalistic theory of society. The latter is *ex origine* functionalistic; it seeks to comprehend an organized community in a theoretical concept of function.

The Aristotelian concept of substance tried to explain the *structure of an individual whole,* although it did so in an inadequate manner. The nominalistic concept of function, as demonstrated in volume I, part II, is not in any way concerned with such structures of individual totality; it is exclusively oriented toward abstract modal aspects of reality, not comprehended in their cosmic coherence.

Functionalism must thus construe human society in terms of a specific modal viewpoint, for example, as a functional psychical interaction between individuals, or in terms of a legal contract (the so-called social compact).

The Aristototelian theory of the social impulse in the essence of human nature could be readily transformed into a theory of a non-metaphysical naturalistic or functionalistic-idealistic stamp. In this denatured form it could be made the starting-point of a nominalistic construction of organized communities.

This was already done in the Stoic theory of the *appetitus socialis,* which was founded in a universalistic ontology. So did also the Averroistic nominalism of the late Middle Ages, as found for example in JOHN of Jandun and MARSILIUS of Padua, who grounded the authority of the State, together with the entire legislation, in the general will of united individuals.

The universalist theory of societal relationships of the Roman Stoa and their functionalist and nominalist conception of the unity of the *corpora ex distantibus.*

The Stoics denaturalized the Aristotelian *εἴδη* to the naturalist and nominalist *λόγοι σπερματικοί* [1]. The Aristotelian transcendent divine *Nous,* the unmoved mover of the cosmos, was replaced by the immanent world-logos. The materially conceived cosmic *πνεῦμα* (pneuma) of the world-logos permeates matter and binds the cosmos into a unity; it is at the same time the basic principle of the *forming and moving ποιοῦν, i.e.* the causal activity of the world-logos. And through the *ποιότητες*, or special qualities, the latter forms the "matter" (the *ὑποκείμενον,* as the basic principle of the *πασχεῖν* , *i.e.* the passive undergoing), which itself lacks qualitative properties, into individual things.

In his theory of entelechies ARISTOTLE conceived of the cosmos as a hierarchical structure of materially realized forms, which through the teleological and metaphysical order reveal a striving *(ὄρεξις)* toward the highest form of perfection. The Stoics transformed this metaphysical *ὄρεξις* into a naturalistic *σύνδεσμος* (material coherence) [2].

---

[1] *Logoi spermatikoi, i.e.* material germinal forms originating from the divine world-logos.

[2] Cf. J. SAUTER, *Die philosophischen Grandlagen des Naturrechts* (Wien 1932) p. 47: "Die Welt ist ja hier kein compositum substantiale, sondern

The levels of cosmic being are now reduced to mere evolutionary modalities of the world-logos, of the cosmic *πνεῦμα*, which with a peculiar tension (*τόνος*) permeates matter internally and limits it externally into individual things. This *πνεῦμα* expresses itself in inorganic nature as *ἕξις* (cohesive power), in the vegetable world as *φύσις* (growth) and in the animal and human sphere as *ψυχή* (soul), which in man includes the *λόγος* (reason).[1]

The human *λόγος* is, however, no longer the metaphysical essential form of man; it is only the product of a progressive development, which is gradually concentrated (*συναθροίζεται*) out of perceptions and representations [2].

All the emphasis is laid on the individuality of all that exists. The Stoics gave expression to the notion of the absolute diversity of all things. In modern times this was formulated by LEIBNITZ as the *principium identitatis indiscernibilium* and was incorporated into his monadology.

The interesting nominalistic theory of organized communities, developed on this philosophical basis by the middle and late Roman Stoa [3], acquired considerable influence among Roman jurists.

This theory joins with the well-known division of things into three classes, *viz.* *σώματα ἡνωμένα* *(corpora unita, continua)*, *σώματα σύνημμενα* *(corpora coniuncta, composita)*, and *σώματα ἐκ διεστώτων* *(corpora ex distantibus)*.

This division is nothing but a naturalistic transformation of the one made by ARISTOTLE in his general doctrine of *taxis*, as the unifying bond of every community [4].

The first class contains the things whose unity is constituted by a simple revelation of the world-soul or deity *(spiritus unus)* respectively in the *ἕξις*, or the *φύσις*, or the *ψυχή*, or the *logos*, of things determined by sensory qualities (*ποιότητες*), *i.e.* inorganic things, plants, animals and men.

The second class, that of the *corpora coniuncta* or *composita* includes all inorganic things, composed of various *corpora unita*,

---

eine Substanzeinheit, bestehend aus "causa et materia"". [The world here is not a *compositum substantiale*, but a substantial unity consisting of *causa et materia*.]

[1] Cf. JOH. VON ARNIM, *Stoicorum veterum fragmenta* II, nr 458.

[2] *Ibidem*.

[3] Since it does not affect the topic under discussion I will not go into the important differences between the middle and older Stoa.

[4] Cf. the preceding section pp. 208 ff.

and whose unity lies in the ψυχὴ τοῦ τεχνίτου, *i.e.* the conception of their creator (*e.g.*, buildings, wagons, ships, and so on).

The συνήμμενον, viewed from a physical standpoint, ("physical" in the organological-stoical sense, not in the sense of mathematical physics!), does not display an inner fusion of parts (κρᾶσις δι' ὅλων), as in the case of the ἡνωμένον. Its parts are coordinate to each other (παράθεσις), and without the concept of its creator it cannot exist as a unity [1]. Consequently the unity of the *corpora coniuncta* lies in the concept that the craftsman had of it and which he incorporated into his work.

The ψυχή assigns in the concept the proper place to each part. A component of the συνήμμενον is that which functions in the way in which the craftsman had conceived of it.

The class of the *corpora ex distantibus,* the *universitates rerum aut personarum,* includes all things which, without mutual sensory points of contact, naturally exist as *corpora singula et finita,* and yet can be called by a single name *(uni nomini subjecta)* [2].

This class includes the communal relationships of human society, as well as objective *collections* made up of things or animals, *e.g.* a flock of sheep (as a commercial object), a library, *etc.*

The single name that can be used to characterize such relationships is then the formal expression of the τόνος (tenor) which binds the individual members into a unity.

The identity of an organized community is conceived of by the Stoics in a predominantly functional-juridical sense.

Although, with respect to organized communities, the late Roman Stoics speak of an internal social instinct in this τόνος, it is evident that they lay the emphasis on the functional-juridical bond, externally holding the individuals together [3].

---

[1] For the linguistic significance of the term συνήμμενον cf. BREHIER, *Theorie des incorporels dans l'ancien Stoicisme* (Paris, 1928).

[2] Cf. for example, POMPONIUS 1. 30 D. 41, 3. For a complete survey of the source material of the *Corpus Juris Civilis* see GÖPPERT, *Über einheitliche, zusammengesetzte und Gesammtsachen nach römischem Recht,* 1871.

[3] P. SOKOLOWSKI in his *Sachbegriff und Körper in der klassischen Jurisprudenz und der modernen Gesetzgebung* (1902), p. 48 ff, rightly opposes the view of GIERKE *(Genossenschaftsrecht* III, 1881, p. 32/3) and GÖPPERT, that the *corpora ex distantibus* are limited to human communities and animal herds, only developed and held together by the psychical social impulse.

Thus in his *Epist.* 102 (bib. XVII, 2) SENECA writes: "*Quaedam (corpora) ex distantibus, quorum adhuc membra separata sunt, tanquam exercitus, populus, senatus, illi enim, per quos ista corpora efficiuntur, jure aut officio cohaerent, natura diducti et singuli sunt.*"

Undoubtedly the reference is here to the legal order which as an external bond brings unity to the individuals.

In a similar sense CICERO (*republica* 1, 39) writes: "*res publica res populi, populus autem non omnis hominum coetus... sed coetus multitudinis juris consensu et utilitatis communione consociatus*" [1]. And further: "*Lex civilis societatis vinculum, jus autem legis aequale; quid enim est civitas nisi juris societas?*" (*Ibid.* 49).

Why the Stoic conception of the social nature of man cannot explain the inner unity and authoritative structure of organized communities. How it differs from the realistic-metaphysical theory.

The theory of the social *τόνος*, working internally in all individuals, doubtless introduced a universalistic motive in the Stoical theory of society. Although it was thus oriented to the idea of the whole and its parts, it could not explain the inner typical unity and authoritative structure of the organized communities.

On the one hand, this theory of the inner *tonos* originated in a pantheistic universalism which, in keeping with a naturalistic monism, permits the *essences* of all individual things to fuse together [2].

---

[1] This definition is formally the same in THOMAS AQUINAS, but its material sense is different. Cf. also HEINRICH WIEGAND, *Die Staatslehre des Thomas von Aquin* (Rechtsidee und Staatsgedanke 1930), p. 213.

[2] According to the Stoics, the individuality and the particular properties of things are not determined by the *inner tonos,* but rather by the *external tonos.* Cf. NEMESIUS, *De natura hom.* c. 2, p. 29: *εἰ δὲ λέγοιεν, καθάπερ οἱ Στωϊκοί, τονικὴν τινα εἶναι κίνησιν περὶ τὰ σώματα, εἰς τὸ ἔσω ἅμα καὶ εἰς τὸ ἔξω κινουμένην, καὶ τὴν μὲν εἰς τὸ ἔξω μεγεθῶν καὶ ποιοτήτων ἀποτελεστικὴν εἶναι, τὴν δὲ εἰς τὸ ἔσω ἑνώσεως καὶ οὐσίας.* The inner *tonos* consequently only determines the being and the inner union of things, not their individuality and particular qualities (*ποιότητες*).

In sharp opposition to realistic metaphysics, with its plurality of substantial forms, the Stoics, in their naturalistic monism, taught the *substantial unity of all things* in accordance with their foundational view of being.

In a similar sense SIMPLICIUS wrote in his *In Categorias Arist.* 68 E:

The consequence is that, when applied to human society, this view cannot recognize in the *natural order* of the world any structural boundaries between the different types of communities which delimit their inner specific nature. Rather it reveals an evident cosmopolitan tendency [1].

And, on the other hand, the autarchical sage, the ideal man of Stoic ethics, does not require any *external* means for his happiness. His subjective ethical inclination to live in accordance with the *lex naturalis* is supposed to make him completely independent of positive human social relationships. This ethical ideal worked together with the afore-mentioned cosmopolitan tendency. It deprived the State, as well as the other particular societal relationships, of the position they held in ARISTOTLE. It was in particular diametrically opposed to the Platonic ideal State, with its three classes and its absolute orientation of individual ethos to State ethos.

According to DIOGENES LAERTIUS and PLUTARCHUS, ZENO, CLEANTHES and CHRYSIPPUS devoted considerable attention to the State and generally valued the beneficial operation of positive law in the laws of the body politic [2]. In spite of this, however, they relegated all specific social relationships, including the State, to a lower position. The autarchical sage did not need the State for his perfection. In fact he was permitted to break the positive laws of the body politic, if he was able to justify his action on the ground of the eternal natural law.

Stoic philosophy never abandoned its cosmopolitan idea of a kingdom including both gods and men; an idea which recognized no boundaries between the various relationships of society. In keeping with the Stoical monistic-pantheistic world picture,

---

οἱ δὲ Στωϊκοὶ δύναμιν, ἢ μᾶλλον κίνησιν τὴν μανωτικὴν καὶ πυκνωτικὴν τίθενται, τὴν μὲν ἐπὶ τὰ ἔσω, τὴν δὲ ἐπὶ τὰ ἔξω· καὶ τὴν μὲν ἐπὶ τοῦ εἶναι, τὴν δὲ τοῦ ποιὸν εἶναι νομίζουσι αἰτίαν.

This firmly establishes the fact that in Stoicism the *appetitus socialis*, as the inner working *tonos* in the individuals, can never be the foundation of social relationships *in their particular inner structure*. The Stoics can only seek the construction of the latter *in terms of an external functional point of view.*

[1] The remark of TROELTSCH in his *Die Soziallehren der Christlichen Kirchen und Gruppen* (1919) p. 68: "Der radikale Individualismus und Universalismus ist an sich gliederungslos", is of importance here, although TROELTSCH wrongly relates it to the Christian idea of human community.

[2] DIOGENES LAERT, VII 433, PLUTARCHUS, *de Stoic. rep.* 2.

only this universalist idea could serve as the ideal of society.

According to PLUTARCHUS, the main idea in ZENO's *Politeia* (written under Cynic influence) is that, without any distinction between particular States, nations and laws, humanity is to form a united society and world-kingdom, enabling men to live together under the common law as a grazing herd [1]. In this kingdom of sages there will not be any marriage, family, temple and judicature.

The imperial idea, as first realized in the Macedonian kingdom, and later in the Roman empire, can only find favour with the Stoics insofar as it broke through the limits of the closed city State. In this form, too, the idea of the State was placed on a lower level than the idea of a kingdom, including gods and men, without any political organization. When the Roman Stoics spoke about the inner social instinct of living beings, out of which the various social groups arise, they thereby viewed veritable organized communities, such as *gentes* and States, in the same way as the coordinate inter-individual societal relations [2].

The Stoics were unaware of the peculiar *inner structure* of organized communities as *corpora*, with a typical continuous unity amidst change in membership [3]. When the Roman Stoics wished to develop a theory of organized communities, they obviously had to seek the proper ground of the latter's specific unity in the *external tonos* of the functional legal order, which they undoubtedly viewed as being grounded in the *lex naturalis.*

The Stoic doctrine concerning the *appetitus socialis* appeared to be unable to account for the structural unity of a *specific* social whole. Especially the compulsory authority of the State lacked any foundation in this doctrine, since the Stoical theory of natural law taught the original freedom and equality of all men in the "golden age of innocence", which was considered as the natural condition of mankind [4].

---

[1] PLUTARCHUS, *Alex. M. fort.* I, 6.

[2] Cf. ANTONINUS in his *Inner Dialogues (ad se ipsum)* 9, 9.

[3] Cf. SOKOLOWSKI, *Op. cit.* E 512, Anm. 128, who in my opinion lays too much emphasis upon the inner *tonos* as the foundation of communal organizations.

[4] As is generally known, the old legend of the "*aureum saeculum*" was developed in detail in PLATO. SENECA developed the idea of an uncorrupted natural state, which he says he had taken from POSIDONIUS in his

It is true that the natural state of innocence, without property and inequality, was not the final goal for the Stoics. It is certain, however, that with them the State, founded on the power of the sword, is not based upon nature but upon convention.

That the Stoics thought the State existed for the purpose of bridling human dissoluteness, caused their political theory to be favoured by the Church-fathers.

We have seen that the case was entirely different in the metaphysical teleology of the Aristotelian theory of the State. In it the relation of authority and subordination was implied in the social nature of man, grounded in his substantial essential form. And PLATO, too, considered this relation to be founded in the metaphysical order. PLATO's and ARISTOTLE's entire philosophy of the State and of law was based upon the principle of inequality of individual men.

Slavery was, therefore, justified in principle and the distinction between the ruling and the ruled classes was considered to be essential also to the ideal State.

The structure of authority was not in any way conceived of in a functional juridical way. As explained in the previous section, both PLATO and ARISTOTLE viewed the relation of authority and subordination as a general characteristic of every composite organism[1]. ARISTOTLE introduced the distinction between *τὸ ἄρχον* and *τὸ ἀρχόμενον* for all organisms *ὅσα ἐκ πλειόνων συνέστηκε καὶ γίνεται ἕν τι κοινόν*, and PLATO, too, viewed the individual person as a "community", in which the soul ought to rule the body, and within the soul reason ought to rule the passions[2].

Ep. XIV. He conceived of this natural state as a society under the leadership of the best and not as an aggregate of a-social individuals.

This does not mean, however, as SCHILLING (*Naturrecht und Staat nach der Lehre der alten Kirche*, 1914, p. 22/3) affirms, that a real authoritative structure or State is recognized in this natural society. SCHILLING arrives at this conclusion by eliminating the typical structure of the State as a compulsory organization. Leading of the best can also occur in coordinated inter-individual societal relations without any implication of authority and subordination. According to the Stoics, the State is not grounded in nature, but it is only a remedy for the restraint of the evil inclinations of human nature.

[1] PLATO even called the hierarchical structure of the three parts of the soul, the "State in man".

[2] *Pol.* 1254b. Compare also Dr W. ANDREAE, *Staatssozialismus und Stän-*

The metaphysically founded societal theory of these thinkers was not cosmopolitan; it viewed the Greek city State as the only all-inclusive community necessary for the rational and moral perfection of man.

The uniting of the theory of the social instinct in human nature with the construction of a social contract.

In Stoicism, on the contrary, the relation of subordinate to ruler can have no other basis than a functional juridical one [1]. This explains the particular emphasis in CICERO's definition of the State, that the tie binding the multiplicity of individuals into a unity is in essence the legal order.

To CICERO and all antiquity the positive legal order is the same as that sanctioned by the State. And to the Stoics it is precisely the positive laws which serve to restrain human dissoluteness, while natural law does not permit essential subordination.

This Stoical theory of organized communities is easily joined with the later nominalistic notion of a contract as the only natural-law ground for authority in the State and in general for the inequality in human society.

The nominalistic trend of late scholasticism prepared the way for a fusion of the theory of the social impulse of human nature with the individualistic construction of a contract, as the only basis of the civil State.

This conventional construction, however, was to some degree already present in Roman Stoicism [2], influenced by the republican theory of Roman jurists, who sought the origin of the

---

destaat (1931) p. 17 *ff.* In their psychology the Stoics also speak of reason as ἡγεμονικόν, but their psychology is not, as in PLATO, oriented to the idea of the State. The late Stoic theory of organized communities shows no special relation to this psychology.

[1] POLYBIUS, who had a great influence on MACCHIAVELLI, defended the thesis that all authority rests upon the right of the strongest; this was doubtless the view of the radical Sophists, and not that of the Stoics.

Cf. HIRZEL *Ἄγραφος νόμος* in *Abh. der philolog. hist. Klasse der Kgl. Sächs. Ges. der Wissensch.* XX, Leipzig (1903), 91, Anm. 4.

[2] Cf. CICERO, *De Rep.* 111, 13: "Sed cum alius alium timet, et homo hominem et ordo ordinem, tum quia nemo sibi confidit, quasi pactio fit inter populum et potentes, ex quo existit id quod Scipio laudabat, conjunctum civitatis genus".

authority of the State in the *consensus populi*[1], on which they also based the validity of positive law.

In Greek philosophy the contract theory was only developed by the nominalistic-individualistic school of Epicureanism. According to PLATO, however, its germ can already be found in the Sophists[2]. In contrast to the Stoics, the Epicureans had an atomistic and mechanistic view of the cosmos. They denied the *appetitus socialis,* even in the Stoical sense, and held that a community of men does not exist by nature but arises out of a voluntary association of individuals[3]. The State arises, according to this view, through a contract made by individuals in order to protect themselves against common dangers.

Under the influence of the mathematical science-ideal, which intended to construct the State *more geometrico* out of its simplest elements, this contract theory became the only possible juridical basis for organized communities in the Humanist theory of natural law. It was able to join forces with the Stoical theory of the social instinct in human nature, as in HUGO DE GROOT, and with a modern mechanistic and a-social view of human nature, as in THOMAS HOBBES.

In this way developed the theory of positive law as the general will. No citizen can reproach the latter as unjust, because everyone gave his assent in the social contract. This intrinsically nominalist view was already defended by MARSILIUS of Padua in the XIV century, though he did not yet work it out consistently; it reached its pinnacle in the Humanistic theory of natural law, especially in HOBBES. It continued to play an essential role in KANT's political philosophy in the well-known adage: *volenti non fit iniuria.*

The contract-theory must result in the complete eradication of the inner structural differences in the relationships of human society. As early as the late Middle Ages, it was gradually applied both to the Church and to the State[4].

As I have amply treated this development in my *In den Strijd om een Christelijke Staatkunde,* I need not go into more detail here.

---

[1] CARLYLE, *A History of Medieval Political Theory in the West,* Vol. I (1930), pp. 63 ff. Cf. also CICERO, *De Rep.* I, 32, 49.

[2] Polit. II, 358, 359.

[3] EPICTETUS, *Diss.* II, 20, 6, informs us that EPICURUS defends the thesis: *οὐκ ἔστι φυσικὴ κοινωνία τοῖς λογικοῖς πρὸς ἀλλήλους.*

[4] Cf. GIERKE, *Joh. Althusius* (3th ed.), pp. 127 ff.

The influence of the juridical fiction theory of the canonists on the view of organized communities.

In the present context we need only notice the influence of the canonist conception of organized communities, as *personae fictae*.

GIERKE has investigated the development of this fiction theory in detail in his standard work on German corporation law [1]. He points out that the canonists were the first to conceive of organized communities in the *concept of a person* [2]. The Roman jurists, who viewed corporations, as well as collectivities of objects, from the neutral point of view of the *universitas*, restricted the concept "person" to the individual subject of private law.

The canonistic theory of corporations was solely based on the individual human personality and ascribed an actual will to the individual man alone. Therefore it considered an organized community a *persona ficta*. INNOCENTIUS IV, the most prominent defender of this fiction theory, expressly declared that the *universitas ("sicut est capitulum, populus, gens et hujusmodi")* as a unity, is a "*nomen iuris et non personarum*", a "*nomen intellectuale et res incorporalis*". It is in other words merely a juridical construction since in reality only "natural persons" exist.

This theory might seem to be under the influence of nominalism. The fictional character of a collective person is proved by appealing to the abstract conceptual character of *universalia*. PETRUCCIUS SENENSIS, for example, writes: "*Universitas ut universitas, prout est nomen juris, est in abstracto, sicut et "homo in communi*", and JOHANNES ANDREAE (1270—1348) observes that the unity of the *universitas* is not real but only pertains to an "aggregation".

Nevertheless, it would be premature to explain these theses in a really nominalist sense [3]. That the *universalia*, as such, only exist *in abstracto* was also the opinion of ARISTOTLE and THOMAS. Even the conception of the *persona ficta* as a *nomen juris* does not prove that these canonists were nominalists. We can only say that their juridical theory of the corporations was of an individualistic character and does not reveal any connection with

---

[1] Cf. *Deutsches Genossenschaftsrecht* III, pp. 245 ff.

[2] *Op. cit.*, p. 278.

[3] In the Dutch edition of this work I did so.

the general idea of *taxis* in the realist-metaphysical conception of ARISTOTLE and THOMAS. This is why their doctrine concerning the *persona ficta* could readily be accepted in the nominalist theory of natural law.

The Christian conception of the (so-called invisibe) Church, as the *corpus mysticum,* whose head is Christ and whose members are all the faithful, was fundamentally transformed in this canonist theory. It was made to conform to the notion of a hierarchical institute of authority, in which the laity were not considered active members.

As "*persona ficta*", the hierarchical Church institute was supposed to receive its unity from above, through the will of Christ and His representative on earth, the Pope, under whom the entire clerical hierarchy is arranged. It is well-known, however, how in the late Middle Ages, nominalism rejected the canonic-legal theory and viewed the Church as a *congregatio fidelium* (the "democratic" contra the hierarchical trend in scholasticism).

The canonist theory of organized communities, in keeping with the tradition of Roman law, sharply separated the collective unity of persons, as *universitas,* from the *societas,* as a social contract. Nevertheless, apart from its maintaining the supranatural character of the Church with respect to the State, it fell into the absolutistic conception of Roman law, which could not allow any internal structural diversity in the *universitates.* In Roman law, from its very origin, the *universitas personarum* was a concept derived from public law, essentially identical with the concept of the State as a legal person. All other *universitates* could — at least in the imperial period — be constituted, as recognized corporations, only by a *lex specialis.* The latter fitted their organization entirely into the mould of the Roman State [1].

Although the theory of canon law recognized the limited autonomy of the separate corporations, it shared the opinion that there could not be a free formation of the latter in the State or in the Church. The faithful disciple of INNOCENTIUS IV, HOSTIENSIS, taught that the freedom to form corporations is character-

---

[1] Cf. COHN, *Vereinsrecht*, p. 27 ff. and GIERKE, *Genossenschaftsrecht* III, pp. 80 ff. Since MOMMSEN the romanists have disputed that the situation was the same during the republic. It is at present an open question whether or not corporations could be formed freely at least before the time of the emperors.

istic of more or less anarchical situations like those in the Lombardian cities. And JOHANNES ANDREAE viewed independent corporations as being highly dangerous and opposed them by the monarchical principle: *hoc enim expedit reipublicae, quod unus dominus sit et non plures* [1].

The union of the fiction theory and the individualistic contract theory in Humanistic natural law.

In a considerably modified form, the fiction theory was taken over into the Humanistic doctrine of natural law.

The canonists accommodated the Roman legal concept of a universitas to the Roman Church and its sub-divisions. The concept of the corporative *universitas* was, however, completely unsuited for this function. Thus, they essentially transformed this concept into that of a foundation. A foundation has no members and acquires its charter externally. The ecclesiastical institution, as *persona ficta,* is therefore conceived of as an *individuum,* a fictitious personified *unity without internal multiplicity* [2]. As representatives of the "*persona ficta*", the bearers of ecclesiastical authority are juridically conceived of as standing outside of the organized institution. According to the canonists, they function even in the internal affairs of the Church only as *external representatives* exercizing the rights and performing the duties of the "fictitious person" which, as such, lacks legal capacity of acting. The internal side of the institutional Church is thus fitted into the mould of an individualistic representational theory [3].

The Humanistic theory of natural law, which again placed the State in the centre, as a corporative unity, now took over the theory of "*persona ficta*". But it accommodated the fiction-theory in such a way that the individuals, entering into the social contract *(societas)* were supposed to be united by the institution of an organ of authority into an artifical body as "*persona ficta*". The canonical concept of foundation is again superseded by that of the individualistically conceived corporation. This construction was especially worked out in an ingenious manner by HOBBES. The fiction theory henceforth was to domi-

---

[1] GIERKE, *Op. cit.*, p. 290.

[2] ROFFREDUS of BENEVENT, *Quaest. Sabbathinae* 27, calls the universitas: *quoddam individuum.*

[3] Cf. GIERKE, *op. cit.*, pp. 291 ff., pp. 309 ff.

nate the various nuances of the nominalistic conception of organized communities.

It resulted in the denial of any real unity of the organized whole and conceived of a corporative unity as a mere juridical construction.

Wherever Humanistic natural law resulted in State absolutism, the mathematical science-ideal construed the State as a juridical totality whose sovereign authority embraces all other social relationships.

The transition from the individualistic state of nature to the civil State was construed in terms of a social contract, which may or may not be accompanied by an agreement of subjection to constituted rulers and (as in PUFENDORF) by an agreement concerning the form of government. In order to guarantee a really sovereign power to the body politic represented by its head, this contract was so conceived that individuals not only abandoned their original freedom, but the very notion of societal relationships whose internal nature guarantees their inner independence from the State, was excluded. Even the temporal Church-institution must be resolved into the State-Leviathan (*e.g.*, in HOBBES and ROUSSEAU and in the late Middle Ages, though in a more implicit mode of argument, in MARSILUS OF PADUA and JOHN OF JANDUN) [1].

Some Humanistic exponents of natural law, inspired by the Humanist freedom-motive, were favourably inclined to grant freedom to non-political associations. They had a restricted view of the social contract and of contractual submission to political authority. Nevertheless, they continued to consider the State, as well as all other organized communities, to be based upon a social contract between individuals. They were able, at the very most, to recognize a formal juridical autonomy, belonging to associations other than the State, because of a sphere of freedom, outside of the latter's jurisdiction, guaranteed by natural law, and retained by every individual in the body politic.

---

[1] By appealing to the idea of an organism, MARSILIUS of Padua and JOHN OF JANDUN still took into account the medieval Germanic legal situation, in order to champion the desirability of autonomous intermediary corporations between the citizen and the State.

The external and individualistic conception of the difference between the organized communities according to the subjective goals of association implied in the social contract.

Contemplated from the individualistic point of view of the *societas,* contractual consensus was considered the only foundation of the internal authoritative structure of every organized community.

And whenever the different character of "free associations" was considered, it was viewed exclusively from an external point of view in terms of the subjective goals of association. Individuals can unite for an infinite number of reasons. The character of free associations is therefore unrestricted in its potential diversity.

The State alone is distinguished in principle from the non-political associations; it is conceived of as a *societas inaequalis,* in contradistinction to the *societates aequales.* State absolutists employed this distinction to guarantee to the State absolute sovereignty over all the other communities. The liberalist trend in the Humanist doctrine of natural law, on the contrary, construed the State as a political association whose sovereign authority is bound to the exclusive aim of an organized protection of the innate natural rights of man to life, freedom and property. This old liberal idea of the body politic was defended by LOCKE and his followers. Nevertheless, LOCKE accepted, without reserve, the old idea of the *salus publica,* the "public interest", as the "highest law of the State". It was the *salus publica* conceived in the absolutist sense of Roman public law, and it was penetrated by the utilitarian idea of the "*Staatsräson*".

Strongly antagonistic to the freedom of the individual, this idea formed an almost unrestrained threat to individual freedom. Especially in CHR. WOLFF's theory of the police- and welfare State (although it was also based on the Lockian idea of innate rights and devoted much attention to the non-political forms of association), individual freedom in the last instance completely fell a victim to the *salus publica* in this absolutist and utilitarian sense.

§ 7 - THE PROBLEM OF THE UNITY OF AN ORGANIZED COMMUNITY IN MODERN SOCIOLOGY AND PHILOSOPHY OF SOCIETY.

Individualism versus universalism in the modern view of human society from the immanence-standpoint.

Our previous examination has shown that from the times of ancient Greco-Roman philosophy the problem of the identical unity of organized communities fascinated philosophic thought. The attempt was made to approach this unity by means of a realist metaphysical concept of form or order *(taxis)*, or by means of a nominalistic concept of function. Both ways led to a *misconception of the typical internal structures which determine* the inner nature of the different types of societal relationships.

On the immanence standpoint, especially the following problems are permanent subjects of controversy: What is the relation between the total being of a human person and the temporal bonds of society? Is only the individual human being real or also the organized community? And if this question is solved in terms of the latter alternative, is the reality of an organized community equivalent to that of the individual man? If, on the contrary, human society is to be viewed as a functional interaction between elementary components, is it permitted to view human individuals as the true elements? Or are also these individuals to be resolved into functional interactions between more elementary components? Is a temporal communal whole the basis of the perfect individual existence of an individual person? Or is a human being a self-contained individual, whereas *an organized community is merely a functional utilitarian* union of the exclusively real individual human existences?

In all these fundamental questions earlier immanence-philosophy appeared to be driven into the dilemma of a universalist or an individualist conception of human society. But the same dilemma is met with in modern sociology and philosophy of human society.

Behind this alternative is hidden a common lack of insight into the different levels of our experiential horizon in its relation to human society.

In his *Gesellschaftslehre* OTHMAR SPANN believes universalism is generally misinterpreted as the opposite of individualism. "Though the essential characteristic of individualism consists in the autarchy of individual man, so that the individual is everything and society is nothing, the fundamental trait in universalism is not the nullity of the individual, so that society is everything and the individual is nothing; society is not the exclusively real... we repeat that universalism is by no means the theory according to which the totality (especially the State) is everything. This is rather a mechanical (atomistic) conception of universalism which really deprives it of all meaning. Only extreme and misconceived forms of universalism can lead to such conclusions. At bottom the individual person must retain his inalienable inner value to universalistic thought, his own life, his moral freedom" [1].

With respect to this defence of universalism our first remark is that SPANN on his part fails to do justice to individualism by qualifying it in all of its trends as the absolutization of the individual man to a self-contained substance. We shall see presently that in modern sociology there are other trends of individualism which have abandoned any substantialist conception of the individual man. They do not try to construe the organized communities out of autarchical individuals; much rather they seek to resolve every societal whole into a complex of elementary forms of social interaction, synthesized by human consciousness to a unity. And they recognize that these social interactions are constituents of the individual psychical life of man.

This undoubtedly modern functionalist individualism is, for example, found in the so-called formal school of sociology, especially in the German sociologists SIMMEL and v. WIESE; in the general theory of the State it is encountered for instance in GEORG JELLINEK; in the juridical theory of corporations, in JULIUS BINDER in his earlier neo-Kantian phase of thought. And it strikes us that this form of sociological individualism is of the opinion that it has conquered the tradional dilemma of individualism and universalism. The very reason is that individualism was usually identified with the absolutization of the individual man, viewed as the atomistic element of society. That the conception of the individual man as a metaphysical substance has nothing to do with sociological individualism clearly appears from the fact that ARISTOTLE held to this conception although his view of society is doubtless universalistic. Therefore, the usual characterization of sociological individualism sought the essential trait of the latter in the ascription of "autarchy" to the individual substan-

---

[1] *Gesellschaftslehre* (3th ed.) p. 99: "Wenn das Wesentliche des Individualismus in der Autarkie des Einzelnen besteht, wonach der Einzelne alles, die Gesellschaft nichts ist; besteht es für den Universalismus nicht in der Nichtigkeit des Einzelnen, wonach die Gesellschaft alles und der Einzelne nichts wäre, besteht es nicht in der alleinigen Wirklichkeit der Gesellschaft... der Universalismus ist also, wir wiederholen es, keineswegs jene Theorie, für welche der Einzelne nichts, die Gesamtheit (insbesondere der Staat) alles ist. Das ist vielmehr gerade eine mechanische (atomistische) Auffassung vom Universalismus, die ihn eigentlich sinnlos macht. Nur äuszerste und miszverständliche Formen des Universalismus können zu solchen Folgerungen kommen; grundsätzlich aber musz der Einzelne auch für das universalistische Denken seinen unverlierbaren inneren Wert, sein Eigenleben, seine sittliche Freiheit behalten."

tial being of man. But also with this addition the current characterization is insufficient.

In a general sense it can only be said that individualism seeks to construct organized communities out of their "elementary constituents". What these elements are must be left out of account in a general characterization.

Even according to SPANN's own view, we do no violence to universalism, if we view it as the opposite of individualism, in the sense *that it does not try to construe the societal whole analytically out of its elementary constituents, but rather seeks to derive the "parts" from the coherence of the whole.*

SPANN's observation concerning the "moral freedom" and value of the individual in the universalistic view, is correct only in its medieval and modern idealistic-Humanistic trends. It does not concern *sociological* universalism as such, but rather the *axiological* viewpoint.

The Christian conception of human personality, in the Middle Ages, and the transpersonalistic Humanistic ideal of personality of post-Kantian idealism, kept universalism from completely sacrificing the "individual" to the absolute value of a temporal community. Instead, the attempt was made to make the value of the individual personality even more intensive and rich than is possible in individualism. The transpersonalistic point of view ascribes to every individual, as "a part of the whole", the tremendous value of the *"Überperson"*, identified with the totality of the highest community in society.

Nevertheless, even in this trans-personalist view universalism continues to absolutize temporal society at the expense of the radical religious unity of human personality.

We can agree with SPANN's observation that universalism does not necessarily deify the State and that such a deification can only be a rudiment of individualism in an inconsistent universalism. The universalism of the Middle Ages, for example, did not absolutize a particular State; it identified the institutional Church with the supra-temporal kingdom of God, in the idea of the "Corpus Christianum" [1].

SPANN himself sees in the State only a *"Teilganzes"*, which he qualifies as: "a partial whole, — a member of the total whole (*i.e.* Society) — in its function as "total organization of social life", and as "manifestation of the unity of all organizations", so that the remaining partial whole of Society is contrasted to it as the unorganized part" [2].

According to him, the State is thus an organic part of the total society, which includes universalistically conceived natural communities together with inter-individual and inter-communal societal re-

---

[1] In his *De Organische Idee in de Gedachtenwereld van Calvijn* (A.R. Staatk., 2e Jrg. 1926, p. 35) Jos. BOHATEC demonstrated that this term, at least insofar as it signifies both the "spiritual" and secular organism, is not of medieval origin.

[2] *Gesellschaftslehre* (3th ed. 1930, p. 566, cf. pp. 510 ff.).

lations in our sense. Nevertheless, the State is indeed conceived of as the *organized* whole encompassing all other organized communities [1]. Universalism is always characterized by the absolutization of one community to the highest, inclusive of all others as its parts. What is viewed as the total community is a matter of choice.

The individualistic nominalistic trends in modern sociology in their confrontation with the problem of the unity of an organized community.

In its conception of empirical reality, the modern individualist and nominalist view of organized communities is *ex origine* oriented to the classical Humanist science-ideal and its motive of the control of nature [2].

It reduces empirical reality to the "physico-psychical" aspects and speaks of the real man as of a sensorily perceptible "individual", or a natural scientific system of functional relations. All the normative aspects of reality are conceived of as subjective psychological modes of experience. As empirical phenomena, the different modalities of social norms are supposed to be nothing but causal emotional motives of an axiological feeling-character. They may or may not be supposed to refer to a supra-empirical sphere of Ideas, or values; but in any case a scientific view of societal reality should eliminate any idea of a divine world-order containing normative principles of social structures.

The unity and identical continuity of organized communities is here necessarily conceived of functionalistically. It may be explained in terms of an organized causal psychical interaction of individuals (as is done by the entire naturalistic psychological school of sociology), and eventually interpreted as a formal sociological category of consciousness, by which the infinite diversity of relations between individuals is synthesized to an ideal unity (SIMMEL, v. WIESE, JELLINEK, and others). Or it may also be conceived of in a functional juridical sense, as in a particular trend of the Neo-Kantian theory of law (KELSEN), which identifies the unity of an organized community with the functional-

---

[1] SPANN speaks nevertheless of *"arteigene Souveranität"* of the non-political communities. We shall subsequently see that this is not to be confused with sphere-sovereignty in our sense.

[2] This is not only true of the Humanistic theory based on natural law insofar as it holds to the primacy of the mechanistic science-ideal; it is equally applicable to Kantian and Neo-Kantian rationalistic critical theories of empirical reality, and to the positivistic trends in modern sociology.

logical unity in a system of legal norms, derived from a so-called original norm (*"Ursprungsnorm"*) [1].

None of these points of view recognizes any real unity in an organized social whole.

Both the naturalist-psychological and the formalistic schools in modern sociology and jurisprudence are thus rooted in a naturalistic and individualistic conception of empirical reality.

Here follow some utterances of prominent representatives of these schools, which may illustrate the above characterization of their view. SIMMEL, the father of formalistic sociology, held the reality of human society to be only a complex interwovenness of psychical interactions between individuals.

In his *Über soziale Differenzierung* he expressly states: "Ist die Gesellschaft nur eine in unserer Betrachtungsweise vor sich gehende Zusammenfassung von einzelnen... die die eigentlichen Realitäten sind, so bilden diese und ihre Inhalte auch das eigentliche Objekt der Wissenschaft, und der Begriff der Gesellschaft verflüchtigt sich" [2]. [If society is nothing but a merely intra-mental synthesis of separate individuals... who are the true realities, they and their contents form the true object of science; then the concept of society vanishes.] And in his *Soziologie*: "Einheit im empirischen Sinne ist nichts anderes als Wechselwirkung von Elementen: ein organischer Körper ist eine Einheit, weil seine Organe in engerem Wechseltausch ihrer Energien stehen, als mit irgendeinem "äuszeren Sein" [3]. [In an empirical sense, unity is merely interaction between elements; an organism is a unity because of the interaction between energies of its organs being more intense than that with any exterior being.]

Essentially the same point of view is found in LEOPOLD V. WIESE, who in his *Allgemeine Soziologie* I (1924) conceives of sociology as the theory of social relations and *"Beziehungsgebilde"* (relational forms).

It is true that in the first chapter (p. 24) he tries to discard the antithesis between individualism and universalism as a false alternative and writes: "Es gibt nichts, das nur Individuum und nichts das nur Gesellschaft wäre; ebenso wie es nichts gibt, das nur Teil oder nur Ganzes wäre" [4]. But, he is actually only rejecting the older form of

---

[1] For the development of this functionalistic conception in modern sociology and political sciences, cf. the first chapter of my *Crisis in de Hum. Staatsleer* (Amsterdam, 1931).

[2] *Über soziale Differenzierung*, p. 10 (Leipzig 1906, 2e anast. Neudr., 1890). The concept *"Gesellschaft"* as "the totality of human society" is indeed universalistic and unacceptable also to us. SIMMEL's utterance, however, relates to any conception of a social whole as a unity.

[3] *Soziologie*, pp. 5 ff.

[4] "There exists nothing that is a mere individual, and nothing that is merely a society; in the same way there is nothing that is only a part or only a whole."

individualism which conceives of the individual as a static autarchical substance[1]. The modern theoretical concept of function is opposed to this substantial view. But in the last analysis the concept of function resolves both the individual and any kind of social whole into a complex of elementary functional relations, in which the bond of unity is exclusively sought in the categories of human thought. The latter is clearly evident in the following pronouncement concerning the various "group-formations" in society: "Diese sozialen (zwischenmenschlichen) Gebilde bestehen nur in den Vorstellungen der Menschen. Sie setzen aber stets eine Mehrzahl von Menschen voraus, und ihre konkreteren Arten sind, abgesehen von ihren Symbolen, dadurch auch wahrnehmbar, dasz sie in Zusammenhang mit einer Mehrzahl von Menschen stehen." [These social (inter-human) formations exist only in the minds of men. But they always pre-suppose a plurality of men and, apart from their symbols, their more concrete species are also perceptible owing to the fact that they are connected with a plurality of men].

And on this basis v. WIESE arrives at the well-known individualistic misinterpretation of our naïve experience of these communal formations: "Für das naieve Auge ist ein soziales Gebilde nichts anderes als zwei, drei, mehrere, viele, sehr viele Menschen"[2]. [To the naïve eye a social formation is merely two, three, more, very many people.]

Any attempt to construe a real social whole in terms of its elementary constituents is a form of individualism.

It really makes no difference whether the social element is sought in an individual as a "Ding an sich", or in an elementary functional relation. In both instances the internal unity of a societal whole is relegated to the subjective human consciousness and its reality is denied.

The revival of the concept of substance in modern universalistic theories. The idealistic irrationalistic conception of the State as *"Überperson"*, in contrast to the ancient impersonal and the modern naturalistic-biological conceptions.

At least in some metaphysical trends of modern universalism, the concept of substance was revived to comprehend the spiritual reality of organized communities. It is always a metaphysical concept of a *totality* that affords universalism its *basis;* the whole is never construed in terms of *elementary constituents.*

There is, however, a sharp distinction between the older

---

[1] Since in his *Gesellschaftslehre* (3e Aufl., 1930), p. 38, SPANN does not distinguish functionalistic individualism from the older substantial individualism, his critique of v. WIESE's individualism is not entirely to the point.

[2] *Allgemeine Soziologie* I (1924) p. 24. VIERKANDT rightly opposes this view in his *Gesellschaftslehre* (2e Aufl. 1928), p. 323.

(Greek and scholastic) and the modern forms of social universalism. We have seen that the former, as found in PLATO and ARISTOTLE, adopted a realistic metaphysical standpoint. They viewed an organized societal whole as a composite "*corpus*", organic in structure, and rooted in a metaphysical form or *eidos*. Its inner unity was sought in the arrangement indicating the ruling or controlling part.

Modern metaphysical universalism, in contrast, chiefly arose out of irrationalistic, post-Kantian idealism. It broke radically with the objective realistic notion of ideas. We have shown in Volume I, part II [1], that this trend is essentially rooted in a transpersonalistic conception of the Humanist ideal of personality, which conceived of the individual personality as a dialectical moment in the totality of an (individual) higher collective person. An organized community is qualified as a "*Gesammtperson*" and the State as an "*Überperson*".

This signified a definitive break with the impersonal conception of older universalism and with the modern naturalistic-biological conception of a societal whole, as a living natural thing.

In the varied tissue of human society, universalism always seeks a higher self-sufficient whole, of which all others are merely organic "*Gliedkörper*" (constituent bodies). But post-Kantian, transpersonalistic idealism hypostatizes temporal organized communities to *supra-individual personalities* and no longer views them as impersonal bodies or natural things.

The general will or the will of an organized social whole as the latter's substantial unity. HEGEL's idea of the State.

The substantial bond of unity was now sought in a transpersonal communal will, capable of forming itself and operating through organs.

In HEGEL the State becomes a *person* only in the monarch. In its ideal sense, as the ultimate synthesis of the dialectical antithesis revealing itself in civil society, the body politic is the highest realization of the "objective Spirit", the reality of the ethical Idea, "*der gegenwärtige göttliche Wille*" (the present divine will). As the dialectical realization of the Idea in history, this absolute State breaks through the boundaries of particular-

---

[1] Cf. Volume I, pp. 473 and 474.

ity in the family and civil society. The State's will is the real "communal will". Through the latter the State proves its "objectivity", its universal validity [1] and its absoluteness, that is, its real existence as a unity independent of the changing subjectivity of its individual members.

GIERKE's theory of the *"Gesammtperson"*.

The Historical school, which viewed the State only as the political form of organization of a national community, did certainly not accept HEGEL's absolutization of the ideal body politic. Especially in its Germanistic adherents the transpersonalistic view of the organized community acquired a pluralistic elaboration. With his teacher BESELER, GIERKE became the enthusiastic advocate of a recognition of the autonomy of non-political and lower political associations. Nevertheless, he remained entrenched philosophically in a metaphysical universalistic theory of organized communities, which seeks the "substance" of the latter in a *"Gemeinwille"* or *"allgemeiner Wille"* (a common or a general will).

GIERKE also conceived of the different types of an organized social whole as full *"organisch-gegliederte"* personalities, *i.e.* as persons with a "spiritual" organic articulation [2], to which he ascribed a separate soul or spirit, in the will of the corporation, and a separate spiritual body, in the organization. Thus, he coordinated the corporate persons with natural persons, as living beings [3]. GIERKE's interesting theory concerning the essence of human organized communities could not discover the inner structural principles of the latter, exactly because of the *metaphysical* character of his view. The most he could attain to on the ground of this theory was a *formal juridical autonomy* for the internal law of the *"Verbände"*. There could be no room

[1] Recall what we have already said concerning the idealistic concept of objectivity as universal validity.

[2] The concept "spiritual organism" with its own corporative personality, originates in the philosophy of SCHELLING, which had a great influence on the Historical School.

[3] The same idea is expressed by many others. Cf. TÖNNIES' *Einführung in die Soziologie* (1931) p. 19: *"Körperschaften,* d.i. Verbände, die für das Bewusztsein ihrer eigenen Mitglieder eine willens- und handlungsfähige Einheit, also insoweit eine dem einzelnen Menschen gleichartige Person darstellen." But in TÖNNIES this conception is only meant in a fictitious sense.

for a real *juridical sphere-sovereignty*[1]. We shall revert to this important point.

Why also in its modern sense the dilemma of individualism and universalism is impossible on a radical Christian standpoint.

In an earlier context we have established that the dilemma occurring on the immanence-standpoint between social universalism and individualism is meaningless and impossible on a radical Christian standpoint. This general thesis also pertains to the modern forms in which this alternative presents itself.

Man's personality transcends the temporal horizon of reality and thereby all temporal things and relationships.

Anyone who ascribes a full real, supra-individual personality to temporal organized communities, forgets that the personality, insofar as it is not conceived of functionally, as in the concept of a legal person, but is conceived of in the full sense of the ego or self-hood, is not to be found in the temporal horizon of our cosmos, but only in the central religious sphere.

Trans-personalism essentially rests on an irrationalistic hypostatization of temporal communal relationships.

Modern individualism, on the other hand, even more radically misinterprets the full being of man and denaturalizes human personality. In its empiricistic trends it reduces man either to an atomistic self-contained natural thing, or to a functional system of elementary interactions operating according to natural laws; in its metaphysical trends, either to an autarchical metaphysical combination of matter-monads and a central soul-monad (as in LEIBNITZ), or to the idea of a self-sufficient moral *individuum,* which in its "pure will" is considered to be identical with the general form of the ethical law (KANT), or to the idea of a self-sufficient moral ego (FICHTE in his first period), *etc.*

In all of its nuances modern sociological individualism results in the denial of the inner communal structures of temporal society. Without reserve we can concede to the modern universalist OTHMAR SPANN that on the basis of an isolated and self-enclosed individual we cannot arrive at a veritable inner coherence in a communal whole[2].

---

[1] See the extensive critique of GIERKE in my *De Crisis in de Humanistische Staatsleer,* pp. 114 ff.

[2] *Gesellschaftslehre* (3th ed. 1930, pp. 87 ff.).

As long as sociological and social philosophic thought remain entangled in the dilemma of universalism and individualism, the structural correlativity of communal and inter-communal or inter-individual relationships is lost to sight. This is even the case with GIERKE, who was fully aware of the fundamental difference between these two kinds of social relations. The coordination of individual persons and collective persons led him to a sharp division between *"Individualrecht"* and *"Sozialrecht"*. But when we detach this coordination from its speculative metaphysical foundation and reduce it to a separation of external inter-individual and internal communal relations, it appears to be in conflict with the structural coherence between them. We shall revert to this question in detail.

The imputation of the dilemma: individualism or universalism, to the Christian religion by WEBER and TROELTSCH.

It is very regrettable that, especially since WEBER and TROELTSCH, the so-called sociology of religion has tried to introduce the dilemma of individualism or universalism into the Christian religion. According to TROELTSCH [1], individualism and universalism lie hidden in an inner tension in the basic religious idea of Christianity.

Calvinism, in connection with its doctrine of election [2], is qualified, for example, as a form of religious individualism [3]. In modern sociology WEBER's and TROELTSCH's views are as a rule faithfully adhered to on this point (cf. SCHMALENBACH).

The intrinsic error of this view will be shown in detail in a later context [4].

---

[1] *Die Soziallehren der Christl. Kirchen und Gruppen* (1919), pp. 39 ff.

[2] Cf. MAX WEBER, *Die Prot. Ethik und der Geist des Kap.* (Tübingen, Mohr. 1934), pp. 93 ff., concerning the *"innere Vereinsamung des einzelnen Individuums"* in Calvinism. TROELTSCH, *op. cit.*, pp. 623 ff.

[3] Even the idea of the Covenant in the Old and New Testament is individualistically interpreted. This was influenced no doubt by the introduction of the idea of an individualistic contract in the protestant theological exposition of the doctrine of the Covenant. Cf. N. DIEMER, *Het Scheppingsverbond met Adam* (Kok, 1935).

[4] Provisionally let me point to Dr KUYPER's excellent observation in his *Encycl. der Heilige Godgeleerdheid* III, p. 190: "Reformed people have (therefore) always made confession of election as election in Christ, and Christ is confessed to be the head of the reborn humanity. Naturally the operation of the spiritual-real factor is also individual, but individual

Observation: WEBER has pointed out the very heterogeneous meanings of the word individualism (*op. cit.* p. 95, note 3). By arranging the various conceptions of *individuality* under these heterogeneous meanings, however, he causes a great terminological confusion. The concepts individualism and individuality, as such, have nothing in common. There is a "quantitative individualistic" conception of individuality; but being rationalistic, this conception was essentially hostile to the inner appreciation of individuality.

In any case both WEBER and TROELTSCH, in speaking of Calvinism as "religious individualism", intend the term "individualism" to be understood in the sociological sense that the individual, in inner solitude and isolation, is placed completely on his own.

Compare, for instance WEBER's statement (*op. cit.* p. 101): "The conflict between the "individual" and "ethics" (in the sense of SÖREN KIERKEGAARD) did not exist in Calvinism, though in religious matters it placed the individual completely on his own."

The term "Calvinistic individualism" is thus not in any way intended to signify a particular emphasizing of the individual *value* of the personality in Calvinism. This would mean the imputation of an axiological individualistic view to Calvinism.

The relation between the individual and *Gemeinschaft* (community) in dialectical-phenomenological sociology.

In recent times a dialectical-phenomenological school of sociology has developed which believes it has overcome the dilemma of individualism and universalism, by breaking with "objectifying" (*i.e.* natural scientific) thought, as its supposed basis.

THEODOR LITT, in his remarkable book *Individuum und Gemeinschaft,* is one of the most prominent representatives of this modern sociological trend. LITT conceives of sociology as a philosophy of culture, which has to furnish the methodical and metaphysical foundations of the "*Geisteswissenschaften*" [1].

I am here exclusively concerned with LITT's treatment of the relation between human personality and the communal relationships of society. LITT's pretended solution of the dilemma between individualism and universalism, and his influence in modern sociology warrant a detailed treatment of his theory.

---

in connection with and as a result of the operation on the whole. Individuals do not exist in themselves; there only exist *membra corporis generis humani.*" Are we to understand this statement in a universalistic sense? Certainly not. The term "universalism" is an absolutization excluded by the Christian position.

[1] Cf. my *Crisis in de Humanistische Staatsleer* I, p. 48 ff., for a general critical treatment of this movement. "*Geisteswissenschaft*" is also called "socio-cultural science".

LITT contends that the basic error of individualism and of universalism is that they absolutize one of the aspects of the spiritual world. They either hypostatize the individual experiencing ego, as a spiritual centre, or the sphere of objective *social meaning (Sinn)*, through which the ego, in its intentional psychical acts, lives in a communal bond with other egos. The problem concerning the relation between the individual and society is insolvable as long as, in the manner of spatial objectifying thought, the ego and the "social world" are opposed to each other as impenetrable substances.

As an alternative LITT proposes the adoption of dialectical reflexive thought[1]. LITT combines the dialectical method with HUSSERL's method of phenomenological analysis of the "essences".

According to LITT, sociology (as the fundamental *Geisteswissenschaft)* cannot proceed in the same way as does natural science. It cannot eliminate the spiritual structure of the ego and objectifyingly examine things by opposing them to thought as if they were alien to the knowing subject. Sociology must investigate the spiritual world in which the I-hood lives. In this world subject and object[2] are identical. In contrast to natural scientific thought, therefore, sociology may not first dissect spiritual reality into isolated *elements* and then seek to discover the coherence between them. Rather it must start with the totality, the coherence of spiritual reality, necessary for the understanding of the relative proper significance of these "moments".

In scientific thought pertaining to the *Geisteswissenschaften,* which is nothing else but *"die Selbstdurchleuchtung des Geistes"* (self-transillumination of the mind), a provisionally attained conceptual limit may never be viewed as definitive. The limits must continually be broken throu dialectically, not in order to permit the discovered moments to flow into each other without distinction, but only so that the limits are only dialectical moments in the spiritual totality. The "moments" must be conceived of in a "spiritual structural unity", connecting everything with everything not by exterior combination, but by an interlacement full of dialectical tensions; by an interpenetration of the relations of for and against one another[3].

What is this "spiritual reality" of which this dialectical-phenomenological sociology wants to explain the inner structure?

---

[1] Cf. Volume I part 1, pp. 138 ff.

[2] "Object" is used here in the sense of theoretical "*Gegenstand*".

[3] *Op. cit.* pp. 21, 22: "die alles mit allem nicht durch äuszerliche Zusammenfügung, sondern durch ein an Spannungen reiches Ineinandergreifen, durch eine Durchdringung von Füreinander und Gegeneinander verbindet."

It consists, first of all, of the dialectical union of the psychical experience centered in actual egos and actualized in the temporal stream of consciousness, with the intended *timeless social meaning*, signified in the sensory symbolism of social forms of expression; in its "timeless objectivity" this meaning actually possesses a trans-personal character.

The dialectical-monadic structure of the "ego", as act-centre, is misinterpreted, according to LITT, both in the functionalistic and the substantialistic view. The "reciprocity of perspectives".

According tot LITT, the "ego", as a personal centre of experience, is a psychical totality; it is not to be resolved into its transcendental logical function, as is done by the critical school (*i.e.* in its conception of the theoretical knowing subject); nor to be hypostatized into a substance underlying psychical relations, as in realistic metaphysics.

The ego rather displays the dialectical structure of a monad living solely in its psychical acts; it is not to be understood as a self-contained "autarchical substance". In this actual ego-centre, past experiences appear in perspective interwovenness with present experiences; the present is permeated with the past and is not mechanically separated from it. The situation in social reality is analogous; the ego is intertwined in a real *reciprocity of perspectives* with the other ego, the "thou".

In this "*Reziprozität der Perspektiven*", the experience of the ego is embedded in the "experience of the thou", and *vice versa*: "These perspectives are not similar and comparable, they are correspondent; they determine and delimit one another reciprocally, they are interlaced with one another and they live in me and in you; and my immediate awareness of them, as well as yours, is at the same time an awareness of this interlacement" [1].

This interwovenness of I and thou in both of these experiences would not be possible if both did not possess an absolute individuality. Every "ego" is individual and centred in its psychico-

---

[1] *Op. cit.* p. 109/110: "Es sind nicht gleichartige, nicht vergleichbare, es sind zusammengehörige, sich wechselseitig bestimmende, miteinander verschränkte Perspektiven, die in mir und in dir leben; und mein, dein unmittelbares Wissen um sie ist zugleich ein Wissen um dieses Ineinandergreifen".

physical existence; at the same time, it is interwoven with other egos in its experiences.

This reciprocity of perspectives realizes itself in the symbolical expressive movement in which "I" and "thou" spiritually unite and understand each other in the world of timeless meaning, signified by the sensory figure of the form of expression.

This entire structure of the ego can only be comprehended in a phenomenological analysis of "essences". This analysis, as a dialectical method of the "sciences of the human mind", penetrates through the individual moments of spiritual life to the essential structural totality by which these moments are unbreakably interwoven, according to the intrinsic structure of their essence.

In keeping with this conception of the dialectical monadic structure of the "ego", LITT must in principle reject the view of SIMMEL, V. WIESE and MAX WEBER, who seek to resolve the social "*Gemeinschaft*" into a formal system of relations or interactions. For this view is individualistic insofar as it seeks to construe the societal whole of a community, in a natural scientific manner, out of elementary relations, synthesized into a mere idea of formal unity.

The dialectical structural totality of "spiritual reality" can never be understood in this way.

The entire schema of form and content is, according to LITT, only applicable to natural scientific thought, which in its categories must construct an ordered objective reality out of confused sensory impressions.

In the spiritual world, in contrast, the ego itself has an actual existence only in a structural totality not produced by its own thinking. This totality, intelligible only in a reflexive analysis of "essences", is rather a necessary condition for the ego.

The social interwovenness of the ego in the "*Gemeinschaft*" (community) of a "closed sphere".

The real relation between the "ego" and the social "*Gemeinschaft*" is, according to LITT, only to be comprehended in the dialectical concept of a social interwovenness ("*soziale Verschränkung*").

This social interwovenness of the actual ego-centres is given in the essential *Gemeinschaft* relationship, comprehended by LITT in the concept of the "closed sphere" and sharply distinguished by him from all arbitrary forms of organization, in which the

Gemeinschaft actively functions as a volitional unity[1]. His phenomenological analysis is not concerned with organizations; it is solely concerned with the supra-individual "*Gemeinschäfte*" in which the individual ego is interwoven according to its essential structure.

The influence of TÖNNIES' distinction between *Gemeinschaft* and *Gesellschaft*, summarized in the first paragraph of this chapter, is clearly in evidence here.

According to LITT, the elementary structure of a closed sphere (the so-called "closed sphere of the first degree") is present 'wherever in a multiplicity of vital centres (egos), — no matter how many more than two,—each stands in an essential, constitutive correlation and coherence with the others; consequently, each rounds off its relief against the others, just as all the others undergo its formative influences[2].

The "closed sphere" in this sense stands in a dialectical essential coherence with the total system of symbolical expressive forms, necessary in the spiritual meaningful reality for mutual comprehension. As long as the "ego" is in spiritual contact with the "thou", with the *one* "thou", by means of the sensory-symbolical expressive movements of the body, the ideal signified meaning-content is unbreakably bound to the unabbreviated living content of this one momentary vital relation.

It cannot possibly separate itself objectively from the complex of this particular physico-psychical total event.

In the social "*Gemeinschaft*" (community) of a "closed sphere" the symbolical signifying form for the first time acquires a sharp objective character, elevated above the momentary subjective expressive movement. Here, for the first time, the spiritual objectification in meaning and symbolical form becomes *transpersonal,* insofar as the expressive forms no longer change from person to person and from moment to moment. As objective symbols of a social totality, they remain constant in a fixed objective coherence, and acquire a clear distance with respect to subjective experiences.

Thereby it is also possible for a closed sphere to expand to

---

[1] *Op. cit.* p. 392.

[2] *Ibid.*, p. 239: "wo von einer Vielheit von Lebenszentren (egos), gleichviel welcher Zahl oberhalb von zwei, jedes mit jedem in wesengestaltendem Zusammenhang steht, mithin ein jedes sein Relief nach der Seite aller übrigen hin rundet, wie umgekehrt alle übrigen seine formgebenden Einwirkungen erfahren."

an unlimited number of persons, in the successive sequence of generations and in the simultaneous expansion of its scope. It can thus become "a closed sphere of the second degree". In this case it is no longer possible for every member to be in direct spiritual contact with every other. Neither can every member subjectively possess the full content of the spiritual treasures of the *"Gemeinschaft"*. Direct spiritual contact is limited to very narrow spheres ("spheres of the first degree"). By far the greater part of the mutual social interwovenness between the individual personalities is now achieved indirectly through *"soziale Vermittlung"* (social mediation), brought about both in a subjective personal way, and through objective symbolism (communication, *etc.)*.

Subjective-personal social mediation is possible, because in every member of a closed sphere the totality of the social interwovenness with the other members, with whom he has been in direct contact, has acquired an individual form that determines the essence of this person. Consequently, through this mediation, new members are brought into indirect social interwovenness with the personality of these other members. In this manner every member incorporates into his personality something of the other persons with whom he is in direct contact.

The objective-symbolical "social mediation by means of communication of the information", transmits in a very abbreviated form, and with a broad or narrow selection, only the important moments out of the social totality of the spiritual communal life, which moments every member must individually make his own.

The inner unity and continuity of the essential community is guaranteed with LITT by the *"soziale Vermittlung"*.

This *"soziale Vermittlung"* is, therefore, the only real and proper means to realize the possibility of a spiritually filled supra-personal life of the social whole. Through it alone, the latter possesses an inner unity and continuity independent of the perishability and discontinuity of individual bodily existences [1].

This inner unity and continuity of a true communal relationship (a closed sphere) is not a subjective construction of thought, but a spiritual reality. Every ego of a closed sphere has a real share in the total experience, the *"Gesamterlebnis"* of

---

[1] *Op. cit.* p. 274.

that sphere. This supra-personal life of the social whole cannot be individualistically constructed out of isolated elements.

Here the experience and actions of all the members are incorporated in the indivisible unity of a social totality. This totality does not allow of an absolute opposition of an ego's own experience and action to that of the others. Phenomenological analysis can show this structure of the total experience in an elementary form in every common activity of a "closed sphere" (*e.g.*, a consultation, a pronouncement, the making of a decision, and so on).

Critique of LITT's theory. A new type of universalism.

A critical comparison of LITT's viewpoint with earlier universalistic theories, developed in Romanticism and post-Kantian idealism, reveals that LITT unjustly reproaches the latter for employing the method of natural science. LITT himself by no means rises above the dilemma of individualism versus universalism. Notwithstanding his own assertions to the contrary, he holds a decidedly *universalistic* view.

At least in the theories of human society, proposed by Romanticism and the Hegelian school, the important dynamic dialectical motive of the essential social interwovenness in individual personalities was just as strongly developed as in LITT [1].

The dialectical method of the "*Geisteswissenschaften*" [2] was first applied to sociology in this circle; LITT is very decidedly dependent upon their method and way of thinking. He differs from the universalism of the Romanticists and Hegelians in that he no longer holds to the metaphysics of the Idea based upon the Humanist ideal of personality in its trans-personal conception.

For this reason LITT cannot conceive the continuous unity of a "*Gemeinschaft*" metaphysically as an organically articulated "*Gesamtperson*" or "*Überperson*", but only as a structural unity of social interwovenness, guaranteed by the "*soziale Vermittlung*", and centered nevertheless in individual physico-psychical personalities. So the unity of a veritable "*Gemeinschaft*" is conceived of as a real structural totality without an I-hood, without a personality of its own.

---

[1] Cf. my remarks concerning GIERKE in my *Crisis in de Hum. Staatsleer*, p. 117.

[2] The humanities, *i.e.* literature, philosophy, history, *etc.*, as distinguished from natural science.

In this way LITT does not break with the universalistic point of view but merely with its idealistic-transpersonalistic type. The individual personality is supposed to be only constituted in the social totality of a temporal *"Gemeinschaft"*, and — as we shall see — LITT also seeks to find a final or highest temporal community encompassing within itself all other relationships as subordinate parts.

LITT's disciple SIEGFRIED MARCK correctly remarks that LITT has produced "a new type of social universalism in contrast to the old dogmatic and ontological version" [1].

In its conception of the mutual relation between the various types of societal relationships, universalism always appeared to operate with the schema: whole and parts. It seeks an ultimate communal whole which includes all others as its members. Such a method appeared to be possible only if the internal structures of individuality, which determine the inner nature of the various societal relationships, are fundamentally eradicated.

In his analysis of the "essence" of *"Gemeinschaft"* LITT never goes beyond a dialectical general concept of a "closed sphere". He never tries to give a theoretical explanation of the plastic structural principles of the different typical societal relationships. He is prevented from doing so by his universalistic position, upon which his dialectical phenomenological method is based.

The elimination of the normative aspects in LITT's phenomenological analysis of the essence of a *"Gemeinschaft"*.

His conception of a "closed sphere" does not disclose a veritable structure of authority inherent in every organized community and to most of the natural communities *as such*.

Apart from his elimination of the organization, this is understandable if we remember that an authoritative structure displays a normative character and LITT's method of phenomenological analysis begins with an explicit elimination of all normative distinctions. LITT defends this elimination on the ground that distinctions which from a normative point of view have a

---

1 *Substanzbegriff und Funktionsbegriff in der Rechtsphil.* (Tübingen, Mohr 125), pp. 95 ff. Cf. also ALFRED VIERKANDT, who in the 2nd ed. of his *Gesellschaftslehre* (p. 334) calls LITT's standpoint an "immanent universalism".

final and determining significance, are completely indifferent to a phenomenological structural analysis. They are indifferent because, with respect to its essential character, as a structural element of the totality of spiritual reality, what is of the most normative value is in no wise preferable to what is most reprehensible. A structural theory recognizes only one distinction which delimits the sphere of its judgments: that of the *meaningful* and the *meaningless.* The "meaningless" (the natural aspects of reality as the *Gegenstand* of natural science) lies as such outside of the spiritual world which is to be examined by structural analysis [1].

This means that in its search for the spiritual structure of human society, this phenomenology begins by methodically eliminating the modal horizon of reality, a necessary condition for the plastic horizon of structures of individuality.

If the normative modalities are eliminated, the cosmic coherence of meaning cannot provide the basis for theoretical investigation. And it is this coherence which intertwines the law-spheres and alone makes the structures of individuality possible.

The phenomenological theory of structure wishes to discover real structural coherences in a sphere of meaning and of being which precedes all normative distinctions. It intends to leave the investigation of these distinctions to the normative special sciences, which must seek their foundation in this theory of structure (this is perfectly in keeping with the standpoint of HUSSERL!).

But LITT's argument that the normative and anti-normative are mutually *exclusive,* and yet pre-suppose the sphere of meaning in which they are enclosed, appears to be fallacious if we remember that the normative aspects of meaning have their law- and subject-sides, so that an anti-normative subjective behaviour can only occur within a normative law-sphere. What LITT calls "spiritual reality" only functions in spheres of meaning of an essential normative nature and structure. An elimination of this normative structure results in the abolishment of any real sphere of meaning in the post-psychical aspects and the retention of an arbitrary cogitative construction, supposedly elevated above the cosmic order.

The entire conception that "spiritual reality" is a dialectical structural union between psychical experiences, concentrated in

---

[1] *Op. cit.* p. 29.

physico-psychical egos, and a timeless objective coherence of meaning, is rooted in an *a priori* vision of reality. This view does not recognize cosmic time in its universal permeation of the aspects of meaning interwoven by it in an unbreakable meaning-coherence. Instead, it seeks the root of individual temporal existence, *viz.* the self-hood, in time.

Because LITT's basic concepts of social interwovenness and social "*Vermittlung*" are not based on the essential internal structural principles of societal relationships, they cannot furnish any insight into the inner structural differences of the latter.

Even the concept "closed sphere" cannot rightly be maintained in LITT's system if we remember that "*Soziale Vermittlung*" and social interwovenness, as they are understood by him, cannot in principle be shut off within the inner boundaries of a particular "*Gemeinschaft*".

Recall only the "*soziale Vermittlung*" by means of the press or by leading politicians who stand in a narrow international spiritual contact with politicians of other countries and with leading personalities of quite different societal spheres. If the State did not possess its own typical structural principle of individuality, which qualifies and intrinsically limits the principle of social interwovenness, then the "*soziale Vermittlung*" could certainly not guarantee the inner unity of a political community as a "closed sphere".

LITT unintentionally admits this in the fifth chapter of his book when he treats "the system of closed spheres". He recognizes that the "*soziale Vermittlung*", guaranteeing the unity and continuity of the "closed spheres of the second degree" [1], causes the "closed spheres of the first degree" (*e.g.*, the families), which they include as parts, to overlap partially, that is to let their boundaries flow into each other.

But the same must be applicable to the mutual relation of "closed spheres of the second degree", as the city and the nation. As soon as LITT considers the difference between these spheres, the only means of distinction he has at his disposal is the quantitative criterion of their scope.

---

[1] That is every sphere in which the great number of members makes direct social interwovenness between all of its members impossible.

The universalistic-historical conception of the "final or highest social unity" in LITT's theory.

Dialectical thought must recognize that each smaller closed sphere is only a transitional stage leading to the larger sphere which contains a multiplicity of smaller spheres as its parts: 'When we follow the successive stages of the more and more comprehensive social formations, our view must at last reach a vital unity whose spiritual movement nowhere exceeds its own boundaries. It cannot do so, for the simple reason that in the cultural process there does not exist a wider totality encircling this supreme, last sphere' [1].

The answer to the question what will function in this way as the "final societal unity" is entirely dependent upon historical development: 'If in the future historical evolution all nations and tribes of this earth should be united into one single complex unity, the whole of civilized humanity would constitute the one all-inclusive vital cultural totality' [2].

Even enmity or conflict between the component groups of the "highest social unity" does not abolish this inner unity. Conflict merely demonstrates that such groups are socially interwoven. Otherwise they would be completely indifferent to each other's spiritual life.

It is true that LITT denies that this dialectical relation between the highest social totality and its component parts abolishes the inner seclusion and individuality of the latter. *He means, however, that this relation is the same as that between the individual ego and the "closed sphere of the first degree"*.

But if this were really the case, the closed spheres must be recognized as supra-individual ego-centra, as *"Gesamtpersonen"*. As we saw, this is contrary to LITT's intention. The life of a closed sphere is centred in individual persons, who retain their individuality bound to individual physico-psychical existence. But the "closed sphere" of the second degree owes its inner con-

---

[1] *Ibid.*, p. 396: 'Durch die Stufenfolge immer umfänglicherer Sozialgebilde aufwärts steigend gelangt die Betrachtung schlieszlich notwendig zu einer Lebenseinheit, deren geistige Bewegung an keiner Stelle über ihre "Grenzen" hinausführt, hinausführen kann, einfach weil es keine sie umfangende weitere Ganzheit des Kulturprozesses mehr gibt.'

[2] *Ibid.*: 'Sollte einmal der Fortgang der Geschichte alle Völker und Stämme dieser Erde in einem einzigen Zusammenhang verflochten haben, so würde die Kulturmenschheit das *eine* abschlieszende Lebensganze der Kultur darstellen'.

tinuous unity only to the *"soziale Vermittlung"*, which does not imply any fundamental inner limitation, since it reaches beyond the limits of radically heterogeneous types of societal relationships.

Thus LITT's phenomenological sociology ends in a functionalistic universalism of a historicist type. In the final analysis, the inner limits between communal and inter-communal or inter-individual relationships, in our sense of the terms, are completely obliterated.

LITT's final social unity, in the sense of an historical cultural community, is in essence indifferent with respect to the internal limits of the various types of relationships. Much rather it is constituted solely in terms of inter-communal cultural relations between component groups.

The application of LITT's theory to jurisprudence and the theory of the State. SIEGFRIED MARCK and RUDOLPH SMEND.

LITT's disciple SIEGFRIED MARCK, in applying LITT's sociological theory to the field of law, was only consistent when he rejected GIERKE's sharply formulated distinction between the inner corporative law and the inter-individual law (*"Sozialrecht"* and *"Individualrecht"*) [1].

And when SMEND [2] in his work *Der Staat als Integration* tried to apply LITT's theory of *"Gemeinschaft"* to the body politic, the dialectical concept of a closed sphere was only of *seeming* service. The State was viewed as a universal integrational system, brought into a unity and coherence through the various subjective and objective integrational factors (LITT's *"soziale Vermittlung")* [3].

When, however, the question arose how to understand this institution in its typical internal structure, SMEND had to appeal to the historicist view of the State as a functional territorial organization of power. And it now appeared that he was unable to comprehend the internal juridical structural aspect of this or-

---

[1] *Substanzbegriff und Funktionsbegriff in der Rechtsphil.* p. 137. Behind this, there also lurks a lack of insight into the coherence of meaning between the structural modal functions of a communal whole.

[2] Formerly professor at the University of Berlin, later on in Göttingen, now emeritus.

[3] Cf. my *De Crisis in de Hum. Staatsleer*, pp. 70 ff. for SMEND's further distinction between personal, functional and real integrational factors.

ganized community in the structural unity of its individual totality [1]. I shall revert to this point in a subsequent chapter when we engage in analyzing the structural functions of the State.

LITT's conception of a "*Gemeinschaft*" as a closed sphere could not account for the typical internal unity and continuity of the latter. The integrational factors of the "*soziale Vermittlung*" [2], if they are to reveal themselves as internal integrational factors of a communal whole, must themselves receive their inner delimitation from the typical structural principle of the latter. By eliminating this structural principle, however, the concept of "*soziale Vermittlung*", with respect to its personal subjective and objective non-personal side, can only lead to the eradication of all typical structural limits between the societal relationships [3].

Summary

Our critical survey of the various attempts to explain the structure of a communal whole is now complete. The theories examined appeared to be unable to solve the fundamental problem of the structure of a community in accordance with the data of naïve experience.

The realistic metaphysical concepts of order and substance, the individualistic and universalist nominalistic concepts of function, the irrationalistic concept of an organic collective person or "*Überperson*", and that of the dialectical structural unity of a "*closed sphere*" were, each of them in turn, employed to explain the internal unity of an organized community theoretically. LITT in principle excluded the organization from his concept "*Gemeinschaft*". In every case, however, the immanence-standpoint necessarily eliminated the modal structures of the different aspects of social experience and the plastic structures of individuality, thereby causing these theories to hover between the poles of *individualism* and *universalism*.

Immanence-philosophy cannot recognize the real religious transcendence of the human I-ness above all temporal societal

---

[1] Cf. my cited work, pp. 77 ff.

[2] Social mediation.

[3] KELSEN, on the basis of his functionalistic juridical standpoint has also criticitzed SMEND's integration theory on this point. Cf. his *Der Staat als Integration* (1930), p. 40.

relationships. Both universalism and individualism appeared to be irreconcilably opposed to such a view.

Naturally, our rejection of the above theories does not imply a denial of the elements of truth which they contain.

Especially LITT's theory of the social interwovenness in temporal individual human existence (partially oriented to Romanticism and German idealism) contains an important moment of truth that we have already recognized. But, this moment is distorted in the a-normative phenomenological context in which LITT has formulated it.

The situation is similar in the case of PLATO and ARISTOTLE. Their idea of the internal unity of order of an organized community was undoubtedly an improvement when compared with individualism. The older individualism, on the other hand, was relatively justified in its opposition to any radical universalism, sacrificing the independent centre of the individual personality to a temporal community.

But all such partial elements of truth cannot make true the theories in which they appear.

The immanence-standpoint prevented even the most productive and acute thinkers from correctly solving the basic question concerning the societal whole of a community: *What guarantees the latter its inner unity and continuity amidst the change in its individual membership?*

To solve this problem, insight must be gained into the inner structural principles of the communal relationships. Such principles are not arbitrary constructions; they are inherent in the plastic horizon of experience.

CHAPTER II

THE TYPICAL STRUCTURAL PRINCIPLES OF THE NATURAL AND THOSE OF THE ORGANIZED AND UNDIFFERENTIATED INSTITUTIONAL COMMUNITIES

§ 1 - *INTRODUCTION.* THE RELATION BETWEEN POSITIVE SOCIOLOGY AND THE PHILOSOPHY OF HUMAN SOCIETY.

After having explained the typical transcendental problems of a theoretical total view of human society we shall now engage in a detailed inquiry into the typical structural principles of the natural and those of the organized institutional communities.

Subsequently we will devote a general consideration to the typical structures of the inter-communal and inter-individual relationships and to those of the free associations which arise out of the latter.

The method of treatment is insofar the same as that followed in the analysis of the structures of individuality of things, as we begin with an abstraction of the enkaptic interlacements between the different structures. The latter will be examined after our having gained a sufficient insight into the internal structural principles of the different types of societal relationships. This is by no means a concession to the "spatial mode of thought" in natural science, as supposed by THEODOR LITT. We have shown that his dialectical phenomenological method of enquiry, which gives precedence to the intricate interwovenness of all societal relations, before having examined the internal nature of the interlaced relationships, resulted in a universalist levelling of the structural differences. This is not the way to acquire a satisfactory insight into the societal structures. However, we have stressed that social reality does not reveal itself apart from these interlacements.

The relation between our social philosophy and positive sociology.

There is, however, a primordial question which demands our attention in the present context. If a theoretic total view of human society both with respect to its different modal aspects and its structures of individuality is by nature of a philosophical character, how can there be any room for a so-called empirical sociology, in contradistinction to a social philosophy?

We have seen that many sociologists (not oriented to the formal school) have sought in vain for a specific scientific viewpoint by which they could delimit their field of research from that of special "socio-cultural" sciences. The only result was that they appealed to the *total* or *integral* character of this viewpoint, which appeared to be exactly the transcendental basic problem of a philosophy of human society.

Every attempt to delimit this total viewpoint from the philosophic point of view by an elimination of the normative aspects of social experience turned out to block the theoretical approach to this experience and to eradicate the very structures of individuality which lie at its foundation. On the other hand the attempt of the school of SIMMEL to find a specific formal scientific viewpoint for sociology in the elementary forms of social interaction equally appeared to fail.

Does this mean that an "empirical" sociology is impossible? This conclusion would certainly be premature. The only conclusion justified by our critical examination is that such a sociology is not possible without its foundation in a philosophy of human society, which gives a solution to its transcendental basic problems. And we have tried to prove that a really critical solution of these problems is not possible so long as the philosophic immanence-standpoint is maintained.

It is the task of our philosophic examinations to lay the necessary foundation for a scientific sociology which no longer neglects the basic problems mentioned. Our social philosophy does so by engaging in a critical analysis of the structures of individuality of the different societal relationships and the different types of their mutual interlacements. Its task is not to examine the variable societal phenomena, presenting themselves within these foundational structures, in the changing societal forms in which the latter are realized. Such investigations must be reserved to a sociological science which we would prefer to call "positive sociology", since the term "empirical" is inadequate to distinguish it from social philosophy. So we must conclude that, as a science of human society in its total structures, positive sociology has no specific scientific but only a social philosophic viewpoint. But, although determined by the latter, its field of research is different from that of social philosophy. The structures of individuality and the different types of their mutual intertwinements, which are the proper subject of philosophical inquiry, have only the character of necessary *pre-suppositions,* as far as positive sociology is concerned.

One should, however, guard against the conclusion that positive sociology may leave alone the difficult philosophic problems concerning the social structures of individuality and their interrelation, and follow its own course. What course could this be? All the methods of enquiry employed by sociologists appear to be determined by philosophic pre-suppositions. Both a critical scientific description and a causal explanation of societal reality are dependent on the latter, notwithstanding the fact that here, too, there are undeniable states of affairs urging themselves upon every one when they have been laid bare.

A historicist or a pseudo-natural scientific view of this social reality is not independent of philosophic pre-suppositions. Such a view leads positive sociology astray all the more since it pretends to be philosophically unprejudiced. This will appear from our further examinations.

On the other hand our philosophic examinations cannot be independent of a positive sociology guided by our basic cosmonomic Idea. The reason is that the social structures of individuality and the types of their intertwinements cannot be detected in an *a priori* way. Rather they must be traced in a continuous confrontation with empirical social reality. However much the structural principles are the *a priori* cadre of the latter, our *knowledge* of these principles is always *implied* in our experience of concrete variable societal phenomena.

Theoretical analysis can only make this knowledge *explicit.* But it cannot do so apart from empirical reality, no more than we can detect the pattern of an embroidery apart from its objective realization in a material tissue.

Every attempt at a theoretical abstraction of the foundational patterns of the typical structural principles from their interlacements in the positive societal forms in which they are realized, pre-supposes a pre-theoretic experience of the concrete social phenomena in which they are implied. In addition it pre-supposes the theoretical attitude of thought with respect to these phenomena, which is proper to a positive sociological enquiry. This is the inter-relation between philosophy and positive science already explained in the third part of the first Volume.

A. THE STRUCTURAL PRINCIPLES OF THE NATURAL INSTITUTIONAL COMMUNITIES.

The internal structures of the institutional natural communities, *viz.* the matrimonial bond, the family in its most narrow sense as the natural community of parents and their minor children [1], and the family-bond in its broader natural sense, may be treated in one systematic coherence. It will appear that all of them show a typical biotic foundation and a typical moral leading function. From the outset the insight into this state of affairs has been impeded in the philosophy of society and in positive sociology by neglecting the investigation of the internal structural principles of these natural types of community. Instead, all attention was concentrated on the genetical and existential forms in which they are realized, and on the enkaptic interlacements with other types of societal relationships implied therein.

In particular we must repeat our warning against any attempt to seek the inner essence of these primordial natural communities in the aims to which they are serviceable according to a natural teleological order, or to seek for a so-called empirical definition apart from the normative structural principles determining their inner nature. Secondly, the reader should guard against any confusion of the natural family-bonds here intended with the undifferentiated organized communities which are also designated by the terms "family" or kinship.

Neither the ancient Roman and medieval *familia,* as a domestic community with an undifferentiated structure of authority, nor the primitive sib or clan are as such natural communities in the sense here intended. As we shall show in our later investigations, all such primitive communal relationships are typically founded in an historical organization of power of an undifferentiated character. This is clearly proved by the fact that they only appear in a primitive condition of human society which

---

[1] The Dutch term *"gezin"* clearly delimits this narrow family-bond from the family or kinship in its broader sense.

shows a more complicated structure; they are doomed to disappear in the course of the process of differentiation, whereas the really natural communities are independent of a typical power-organization and, according to their inner nature, are found at every stage of human societal life.

This is a fact established by all ethnological investigations since the *a priori* constructions of the development of human society, according to the evolutionist dogma, have been replaced by a really critical method of research. We shall recur to this point in a later context.

§ 2 - THE STRUCTURAL PRINCIPLE OF THE NATURAL FAMILY IN ITS STRICT SENSE.

That the view of human society according to which the latter exclusively belongs to a so-called "spiritual" or "cultural" reality must be wrong, is nowhere more evident than in the case of the natural institutional communities. It is indeed impossible to understand the inner nature of a natural family in its most narrow sense without taking into account its typical foundation in the biotic aspect of empirical reality, which as such pre-supposes the pre-biotic modalities.

The natural derivation and consanguinity of children under age, issuing from the same parents, is the necessary structural foundation upon which such a family is built. This state of affairs cannot be denied by any theory. The typical communal tie between parents and children is genetic; it is grounded in a blood relation of the most immediate character.

The extremely rich structure of procreation by which a human pair bring forth children in the closest possible interconnection of two temporal existences, is certainly not to be understood entirely in terms of biology, and not at all in functional terms.

Nevertheless, the structural typicalness of human reproduction is undoubtedly biotically founded; its functions in post-biotic modalities rest upon a typical biotic substratum. Inter-sexual procreation and descent reveal an original modal-type of individuality only in the biotic law-sphere.

But it is clear that blood-relation in its typical biotic sense is not able to *qualify* the human family-bond between parents and children.

The biotic function cannot be considered to be the "leading" function of this community. Only the radical type plant is qualified as a typical biotic subject. Even the bond between animals and their young is directed in its inner structure by a later leading function, namely, by the sensory instinctive impulse of care and protection founded in the biotic blood-relationship.

The typical leading function of the immediate family-relationship. Refutation of the opinion that the latter does not have a typical leading function which qualifies its inner destination.

What then is the typical leading or qualifying function in the inner structure of the immediate family-bond?

We have seen that the universalist Aristotelian-Thomistic conception has in fact eliminated this structural problem by conceiving the relationship between parents and their children under age as a part of the domestic community. The latter was viewed as an economic unity, embracing primarily the relation between the domestic chief and his servants, and in addition that between husband and wife. The relation between parents and children was then conceived under the general teleological viewpoint of a rational and moral perfection of the undeveloped human nature of the children resulting in their education to good citizens. In the Thomistic theory this natural education requires its supranatural completion by forming the children into good sons and daughters of the Church, as the institution of grace.

This entire view is not concerned with the *inner* nature of the immediate family-bond. Much rather it is directed to the natural and supra-natural aims to which this relationship is serviceable.

But does the latter actuality have a typical qualifying function which determines its *inner* destination? Is it not exactly the rich and universal character both of the matrimonial and the family bond that they are all-inclusive or "supra-functional" vital communities, in contradistinction to the arbitrary associations formed for specific purposes?

This question ought to be examined closely. It originates in a very generally held notion of the universality of the natural family, as the primal cell of society. The word "universality" carries with it a particular temptation, which becomes dangerous if one loses sight of the inner structural delimitations which the temporal world-order places in the way of all universalist constructions.

The absolutization of a specific modal aspect of our experiential horizon appeared also to be defended by an appeal to its universality. It was, therefore, necessary, in our analysis of the modal structures in Volume II, to show how this universality is limited by the cosmic temporal order. The universality of every modal sphere turned out to be bound to its inner specific structure, which excludes every attempt at its elevation to a whole encompassing all the other modalities.

The tempting appeal to the all-inclusiveness or universality of the intimate bonds encountered in marriage and the family ought not to distract us from our aim to discover their intrinsic structural laws.

Insofar as this appeal to universality is intended to arrest our search for the typical qualifying function of the family, it contains a two-fold misunderstanding. It is consciously or unconsciously affected by the undifferentiated Aristotelian conception of a household with its threefold authoritarian relation. And it is guilty of a confusion repeatedly mentioned between the internal destination and the external functional objectives of a community. The inner structural limitation displayed by a communal relationship because of its typical leading or qualifying function, is in no way opposed to the universality of the internal societal bonds, in the sense of all-sidedness. But through its leading function all relations within a community receive their typical qualification and inner direction. The latter is in no way related to the external "ends" of a communal whole.

We admit that the separation of the inner structure of a family from the organized communities with an undifferentiated inner destination, pre-supposes the differentiating process in the development of civilization. This differentiating process, however, concerns only the *positive forms of actual transitory societal relationships.* Their inner structural principles cannot be a product of this historical process, because structural differentiation pre-supposes the constant validity of these principles.

Even when on a lower cultural level a natural family relationship is enkaptically bound in a primitive undifferentiated organized community like the sib or the domestic community, its *inner structural principle* is the same as that of a modern family that has been emancipated from this enkaptic interlacement.

Undoubtedly it makes a great difference for the concrete positive form of the family whether or not the differentiating process has taken place. Nevertheless, even in Greek and Roman antiquity the undifferentiated household was never identical with the actual natural family relationship, even though the positive forms of Greek and Roman family life were closely connected with the former.

Returning to our question we must answer that the denial of a typical leading and qualifying function in the natural immediate family relationship is identical with the denial of its entire typical structural principle, established by the order of creation.

The natural community between a couple of parents and their children under age is not a relationship with an undifferentiated inner destination. If it were, it would disappear in the advance of the differentiating process in historical development. It would then be a rudiment of a former historical phase. But this view is refuted by the facts.

Holy Scripture throws a quite different light on the natural communal bond of the family in its most narrow sense, even though it does not give us a theoretical analysis of its typical inner structure. It presents the family as a typical normative bond of love, based upon the natural ties of blood between parents and their immediate off-spring. This is a reflection of the bond of love between the Heavenly Father and His human children, unbreakably bound to the tie between Christ and his Church [1].

In this temporal natural community, the normative tie of love between the members of a family cannot be identified with the religious meaningfulness of love in the *corpus Christi*, notwithstanding its ultimate reference to the latter in the anticipatory direction of cosmic time. The bond of love is here rather of a temporal modality of meaning, because it is founded in the biotic modality. As the structural leading or qualifying function of the family, it is of a modal character. According to the normative structural law of the natural community in question, this typical moral function ought to give all earlier structural functions their internal *direction and leading*.

According to its inner structure of individuality, the natural immediate family is thus an institutional moral community of love between parents and their children under age, structurally based upon biotic ties of blood relationship.

The leading structural function of the family is consequently not to be found in the abstract modal moral sense of love. The

---

[1] Cf. for instance *Gen.* 2 : 24; *Proverbs* 3 : 12; *Ps.* 103 : 13; *Luke* 15.

family is a typical bond of love between parents and children. Its moral normative typicalness of meaning is not to be understood apart from its typical biotic foundation.

The intrinsically moral character of the bond of love between parents and children is not affected by its typical biotic foundation.

According to the abstract idealistic view of morality, the bond of love between parents and children lacks moral purity because of its very foundation in natural biotic ties of blood.

This view is grounded in a religious absolutization of the ethical aspect already discussed in the second Volume. It is true that love in its central religious sense is independent of all temporal societal relationships, even of the most intimate bonds in the matrimonial and family communities. But in its temporal moral sense love becomes meaningless apart from its individualization and differentiation by the typical structures of society, without which it cannot be realized in human behaviour.

The abstract idealist view of moral relations is destructive to the insight into the inner nature of the natural communities in discussion.

The inner moral character of the bond of love between parents and their children is not affected by its typical foundation in the bonds of blood. On the contrary, this foundation gives it a degree of moral intensity which cannot be matched by any other moral relation except by that between husband and wife in the marriage bond.

It is not true that genuine morality is characterized by an objectivity which does not take into consideration any difference between the societal relationships in which it should be realized. Such an "objectivity", as defended by the Dutch philosopher HEIJMANS, can only exist in an abstract idealist kind of ethical theory which deprives morality of its very meaning by isolating it from the typical structures of individuality of societal life. We have shown in the general theory of the modal spheres that, even in its general modal sense, the moral aspect appeals to the intermodal coherence with all the other modalities, inclusive of the biotical.

If, according to its structural principle, the bond of love between parents and children in the family is of a typical moral character, it cannot be reduced to an instinctive feeling of sympathy. Much rather it is a communal relation implying mutual duties and moral responsibility of a specific character. This does not detract from the fact that it appeals to a feeling of love which is quite natural because of its very foundation in the biotic bonds of blood. But it is not this natural feeling with its emotional fluctuation and polarity which has the leading and qualifying rôle in the inner structure of the family. As a structural function of this natural community, it must itself be opened in the anticipatory direction to the guiding moral bond of love.

The structural principle and the internal unity of the family. The effect of sin.

So the inner structural principle of the family discloses itself in the unbreakable temporal coherence of its leading and foundational function. It has to determine all expressions, within the different modal spheres, of the family's internal unity. As a typical normative principle, it has not been affected by sin. Sin solely affects its human formation and positivization in accordance with the historical situation of a society and the entire subjective side of family life. There could even be no question of a sinful factual family life, if the structural principle of this natural community were itself affected by sin; *a sinful family life* pre-supposes a violation of the structural law of the family. God's law, as manifested in the structural principles of social relationships, is holy and good, untainted by evil [1]. This implies that the internal unity of a family, in its most restricted sense, is a *normative* unity, and that to a large degree it is defectively realized because of sin.

This is entirely lost sight of both in TÖNNIES' irrationalist romantic conception of "*Gemeinschaft*" and in LITT's dialectical-phenomenological idea of the "closed communal sphere". It is true that at least TÖNNIES viewed the "*Gemeinschaft*" in a normative sense insofar as he conceived it as the right condition of human society which is destroyed by the antagonistic factor of "*Gesellschaft*". But he assumed that in the undifferentiated medieval society true "*Gemeinschaft*" in his sense was indeed completely *realized* in a natural organic way.

This was an irrationalist idealistic view of societal reality which is contradicted by the facts. And it is exactly this idealist conception of the realization of a normative Idea that makes the

---

[1] *Romans* 7 : 12.

latter unserviceable to a positive sociology, let alone the fact that this Idea lacked any orientation to the structural differences between the various types of community.

In LITT the normative viewpoint appeared to be intentionally eliminated. The only result is that his phenomenological analysis of the "essence" of a "closed communal sphere" is nothing but a crypto-normative construction which cannot account for the factual side of the societal relationships. His dialectial idea of "social interlacement" between the "psychical experiences" of individual ego-centres, by means of a system of objective symbols, as bearers of time-less meaning, cannot guarantee the inner unity of a communal sphere. It is applicable to the non-communal relationships as well. By ascribing to his idea of "*soziale Verschränkung*" a really unifying function, LITT gives the latter a crypto-normative sense which neither corresponds to the structural principles of the different societal relationships, nor to the sinful factual side of human society, in which they are defectively realized.

If anywhere TÖNNIES' idea of a true "*Gemeinschaft*" should correspond to the factual side of an internal communal life, it must be in the natural family bond in its most narrow sense. The latter seems to be at the same time a standard example of a "closed communal sphere", in the sense intended by LITT. Nevertheless, at any stage of historical development factual family-life shows more or less serious defects, which can manifest them selves to such a degree that we must speak of a destruction of its real communal unity.

And yet, positive sociology cannot eliminate the normative structural principle of this natural community, nor the normative distinction between communal and inter-communal or inter-individual relationships, without losing sight of the social facts themselves.

For, apart from this structural principle, and apart from the distinction mentioned, there cannot exist any factual human family life. We cannot distinguish factual family relations from other kinds of societal relationships without appealing to their inner nature. And the latter is only determined by the normative principle of their communal structure, which also lies at the foundation of all the changing social forms in which it is realized.

If these variable social forms did not pre-suppose this constant structural principle, they could not refer to the same social institution and we had better abandon every historical inquiry into its development in these changing formations.

It is true that in the family bond the social life of parents and children is mutually interlaced in all of its modal aspects. But that this inner interwovenness, as an inner communal unity, clearly delineates itself from all other kinds of social intertwinement cannot be established from the factual side of family life alone. Here we must appeal to its inner nature determined by its normative structural principle.

We shall now examine the manner in which the latter expresses itself in all its modal aspects, thereby maintaining the relative inner seclusion of the family bond.

The destructive character of the Kantian principle of autonomy with respect to the internal moral communal relations of the family. The authoritative nature of the latter.

As to the moral aspect we have already seen how the bond of love unifying parents and children in the family relationship is distinguished from all other kinds of moral relations by its typical biotic foundation. We have now to devote special attention to the typical authoritative character of this moral bond.

According to the Kantian principle of ethical autonomy, true morality is incompatible with any relation of authority and subordination. If this were true, the immediate family relationship would in principle lack any moral character. For, according to its inner structure, it does imply that very heteronomy which KANT considers to be opposed to real morality. And we must add to this that almost all types of communities imply a typical structure of authority; so that we must conclude that Kantian ethics has no room for a moral community. For, the broader kinship bond, which indeed lacks a natural authoritative structure, can no more have a moral character in the Kantian sense than the narrower family, since its typical biotic foundation contradicts the principle of autonomy as well.

But the truth is that this Kantian principle is incompatible with the very nature of the moral law-sphere, as we have shown in detail in the general theory of the modal spheres. By its absolutization the moral aspect has lost any modal meaning in the Kantian system. Even its inner coherence with all the other modal aspects of the temporal horizon, guaranteed by the divine world-order, is incompatible with the principle of ethical autonomy and purity in the Kantian sense. This appeared also to be the reason why KANT rejected the very meaning-nucleus of every moral relation, *viz.* the bond of love, and replaced it by the legalistic motive of respect for the autonomous ethical law.

In sharp contrast to this principle of autonomy we must emphasize the typical *moral qualification* of parental authority. The latter is not restricted to the legal relations in the sense of a typical juridical power or competence. As the communal relation of authority and subordination is inherent in the immediate family bond, according to its structural principle, the typical inner nature of this authoritative relation must be determined by this structural principle. Notwithstanding their intimacy the ties of love between parents and children do not lack the distinction between the authoritative position of the former and the subordinate position of the latter. On the contrary, if the parents abandon their moral authority and factually behave as the older comrades of their children, the typical bond of love which qualifies the family relationship is violated. For this bond implies a typical authoritative character because of the immaturity of the children. And exactly by its natural biotic foundation the paternal authority partakes of the intimacy of the bond of love, characteristic of the family in its most narrow sense.

It is for this reason that God gave the norm of love for the family, "Honour Thy father and Thy mother". This respect for the parents is in no way in conflict with the intimacy of family love, but is rather an essential factor in it.

A levelling democratic idealism may hold up as an ideal a so-called comradeship between parents and children, a relationship which scorns obedience and authority, and implies equality of the individuals related. But such an ideal entirely lacks the tender tone which the divine order gives to love between parents and children. Respect for the divine office of parents plays an essential rôle in the latter, it can never be disregarded with impunity.

This is also the reason why the education of the children in the family sphere shows an irreducible inner nature and cannot be really replaced by any form of education which lacks this character. We shall recur to this point.

The expression of the structural principle in the internal legal relations of the family in its narrowest sense.

Our analysis of the modal structure of the moral aspect in the second volume has shown that this modality contains juridical retrocipations. This implies that the internal ethical relations which qualify a natural community cannot exist without the foundation of internal legal relations, even though the former do not have their original *typical* foundation in the latter.

And these internal legal relations are not, as such, of a civil law character. They can only be juridical communal relations in which the structural principle of the family is expressed.

The authoritative structure of this bond also has its internal juridical aspect in the legal authority that parents have over their children. This competence is not derived from civil law, as dogmatic legalistic positivism teaches.

It is, nevertheless, an authoritive function in the modal sense of *retribution,* an authoritative function, which, on account of the formal interwovenness of all typical legal spheres, also has an external function in civil law. But through its internal structure it is fundamentally different both from a civil legal competence and from a public legal authority, as held by the magistrates.

This structural difference is pregnantly revealed by a comparison between parental disciplinary authority and the competence of the bearers of public authority to punish the subjects who have violated the public order of the State.

The current opinion in jurisprudence is not inclined to ascribe a penal law character to the parental disciplinary competence; it recognizes only the penal law of the State. The latter is opposed to the disciplinary law of specific societal "groups" in general, without any inquiry into the inner nature of the different types of disciplinary law. The general difference between penal law and disciplinary law is then sought in the fact that the latter is restricted to the members of the "groups". This is only a formal distinction, which lacks any reference to the inner nature of the different typical spheres of law. The competence to punish is not a monopoly of the State. The inner character of this competence is, however, completely dependent upon the nature of the relationship in which it occurs.

There is consequently no reason to deny a penal character to the parental disciplinary competence. Nevertheless, a competence to punish is bound to certain conditions. Real punishment pre-supposes legal authority and subordination. It can consequently only occur in communal, not in inter-communal or inter-individual relationships. It implies an infliction of a deserved pain in a retributive sense to restore the respect for the violated communal order, irrespective of the personal interests of the authoritative organ which has to impose the penalty. These general requirements hold good with respect to every penal competence. But they assume a different typical legal character in accordance with the structural principles of the various communities.

In keeping with the inner structural law of the family in its narrowest sense, parental discipline has an exclusively pedagogical character bound to the special guidance of parental love. The exercise of this disciplinary competence ought to be accommodated to the stage of development of the children.

It is true that in modern civil penal law the pedagogical factor in the treatment of children and juvenile persons has also come to the fore; even judicature has been specialized for this purpose. But the pedagogical task of the parents in the internal family sphere is fundamentally different from that of the judge in the public sphere of the State, or from that of a probation officer.

The internal legal sphere of the family, to which the disciplinary competence of the parents is restricted, is in every respect irreducible to any other type. All the rights and legal duties of the members of this natural community show a typical moral qualification and biotic foundation which reflect the inner unity of the structural principle of the family bond.

In this internal communal sphere the children have an essential *right* to receive their livelihood from their parents as a *proof of parental love.* If in the factual family relations love is lacking, the internal juridical sphere is also affected, just like the internal sphere of social intercourse and the other structural modal spheres of this community. The entire inner structural norm of the family is then violated. The reason is that in all of its modal aspects this normative structural principle is an unbreakable unity.

This state of affairs is hardly understandable to jurists who are accustomed to thinking exclusively in the typical categories of civil private law and public law. They are inclined *a priori* to deny a juridical character to the internal morally qualified communal law of the family and to reduce it to morality. But this dogmatical prejudice is not in accordance with the real states of affairs. For, in spite of its unbreakable coherence with, and qualification by the moral requirement of love proper to the family bond, the internal legal sphere of the latter retains its juridical character. And the jurists are confronted with this state of affairs, since in their enkaptical interlacement with the civil sphere of private law, the typically morally qualified legal duties of the parents reappear as so-called *natural obligations.* These natural obligations have civil legal consequences insofar as in modern jurisprudence [1] their performance is not considered to be a donation but the fulfilment of a natural legal duty.

In the general theory of the modal spheres we have shown that this state of affairs cannot be understood apart from the anticipatory structure of the juridical aspect. The realization of the moral anticipations in the retributive modality, however, is in principle bound to the typical structures of the differentiated societal relationships.

It stands to reason that in the internal legal sphere of the family, there can be no question of the formation of general positive legal norms, let alone the presence of an eventual domestic order regulating the affairs of every day. Such general legal rules would lack any sense, since the number of the members of this community is very small. In addition such a generalization would hardly be compatible with the inner nature of the family as a typical love-bond.

It is, however, a pure *petitio principii* to assume that positive law is only to be found in a system of general legal norms.

Even in those juridical spheres which by their typical nature are capable of forming such systems of law, law making has never begun in this abstract way, but rather in the way of case law. In Anglo-Saxon countries this manner of law formation has been maintained in the common law sphere up to the present day.

In the small sphere of the family the internal process of "law finding" is by nature bound to concrete decisions from case to case. Nevertheless, the *legal principle* which ought to lie at the foundation of these legal decisions must be of a general character determined by the internal structure of this community. Otherwise the exercise of parental authority in the legal

---

[1] See Volume II, pp. 407 ff.

sphere of the family would degenerate into arbitrariness. This is sufficient to justify the assumption of an internal legal sphere of the family. The disciplinary power of parents, whose juridical character is generally acknowledged, is only a particular manifestation of the legal sphere proper to this natural community.

The inner structural relations in legal subjectivity.

The inner interwovenness of the temporal existences of parents and children in the family is also disclosed in the juridical structural aspects of this relationship.

The view of legal personality in the older individualist fiction-theory starts from the individual man as a "natural person". The proper legal subject is the *individual,* who is the point of reference of various legal relations. From this point of view the legal personality, *i.e.* the legal subjectivity of a collective unit *qua talis,* becomes an insoluble problem, which is evaded by a technical *"as-if"* construction. The "legal person" is viewed as an "economical" fiction, a mere construction of thought; only a natural person, conceived of as an individual, is supposed to be really a subject in law!

It is undeniable that the legal subjectivity of a child is closely bound up with that of his parents, and that to a certain extent this connection has also juridical consequences in external civil legal relations. But this does not prevent individualism from treating the legal subjectivity of a child as that of an *individual.* A child lacks competence to act in civil law. According to the individualist view, the father appears, therefore, as the *natural (legal) representative of the incompetent "individual".* The truth of the matter is, however, that in addition to inter-individual relations, the legal subjectivity of a child displays a number of communal juridical relations, which are simply unintelligible to an individualistic theory.

The representational function of the father is valid solely in the external inter-individual legal relations, which as such do not pertain to the nature of the internal law of a family. Nevertheless, in civil private law we can ascertain the existence of a *partial intertwinement between the legal subjectivity of the natural representative and that of the represented.* The competence to act which is lacking in the civil legal function of the legal subjectivity of a child is supplemented by that of the father.

This is a (biotic) *organic analogy* in the modal sense of law, by which a partial unity is guaranteed in the duality of the two civil subjects. Juridical imputation here joins the legal actions of the one with the rights and duties of the other.

The consistent individualistic conception of legal subjectivity, (as developed by HÖLDER and by BINDER in his earlier formalistic neo-Kantian period [1]) must misinterpret this organic analogy in the legal relations. The numerical analogy implied in the partial juridical two-unity relation between the representative and the represented is in fact interpreted in an original arithmetical sense. There is a well-known French joke which to the question: how can husband and wife be one? replies: if one of both is zero. A necessary result indeed, if the question is solved in terms of an algebraic equation of the first degree: $x + 1 = 1$. But what is done here by way of a joke, occurs in earnest in the individualist theory of legal representation, defended by the German scholars mentioned. Thus they arrive at their well-known conception that legal representation excludes a juridical personality of the represented child and only implies that of the representative [2].

According to this theory the pupil does not obtain rights and duties through the acts of his representative. Such acts only give rise to *official rights and duties of the latter.*

This doctrine has been rightly opposed in many quarters. Not only is it in conflict with positive civil law, which acknowledges the rights of a child and does not recognize the figure of "official rights" in the sense intended by HÖLDER and BINDER; rather it is also *incompatible with the modal meaning of law,* as such. It denies a state of affairs, implied in the afore-mentioned organic analogy in the modal structure of the juridical aspect and without which legal life is impossible. The partial intertwinement and unity in the civil legal subjectivity of father and child is not to be denied. An individualistic theory here leaves us in the lurch.

And yet the civil legal representational relation between the father and his child under age does not reveal the inner structure of the family relationship. The same partial two-unity is found in the relation between a curator and a curandus, or in that of non-parental guardianship.

The real internal communal relations in legal subjectivity

---

[1] BINDER, in contrast to HÖLDER, does not base his view upon a "natural person" as an individual, but on the functional concept of a legal subject.

[2] HÖLDER, *Natürliche und Juristische Personen,* p. 120; J. BINDER, *Das Problem der Juristischen Persönlichkeit* (1907), pp. 63, 64.

are *a fortiori* not to be comprehended in an individualistic theory.

A child is normally born in a family relationship, and in modern society in a State. If its parents have not completely broken with the Church, a child in a Christian country is usually a member by baptism of a Church community. To a child's legal subjectivity all this is of *constitutive, internal-structural significance.* Insofar as the child does not have any property or capital of its own, the significance of the private civil law side of his legal subjectivity is pushed into the background in his early years.

In these internal communal relations the juridical function of the individual human personality is interwoven in a typical inner manner with that of the other members of the community. And this interwovenness is indeed *constitutive* in the legal subjectivity of the individual person.

As a member of a family, a child in his legal subjectivity is subject to parental legal authority. This is not a legal relation between individuals. Such a relation lacks authority. It is rather a relation between unequal members of a communal whole.

In undeveloped societies the internal relations within the undifferentiated communities are of an all controlling significance for the entire personal legal status.

The recognition of the legal subjectivity of every man as such, apart from his specific communal bonds, does not occur outside of the typical inter-individual sphere of modern civil private law. And this recognition is the result of a long process of development culminating in the legal abolition of slavery. When individualism takes this final result as its starting-point, it forgets that the civil legal personality is only a specific component of the full legal subjectivity. The latter is equally constituted by the internal legal relations implied in the memberships of various communities.

The internal juridical relations within the family and the individualistic way in which law and morality are opposed to each other.

In the internal structure of the family, legal subjectivity assumes an entirely different character from that in civil law. This is at once evident when we compare the internal competences, rights and duties of the individual members of this natural community with their external civil legal function.

Parental authority finds explicit recognition in most systems of civil law, but here its functions are merely inter-individual. These law-systems only require a warrant of attorney for civil actions of minors (we do not mean those who are "factually incapable of legal action"). In the case of a civil marriage, the requirement of parental consent is often extended to majors up to a certain age. In both cases, however, the paternal warrant of attorney or the parental consent may be replaced by those of other persons if the parents are lacking or are unable to act. In the same way parental authority only functions externally in the civil legal administration of any property belonging to the children, *etc.*

By the mere *declaratory* recognition of the parental educational and disciplinary competence, the formal lawfulness of the use of this competence is guaranteed in civil law within the limits inherent in the civil legal protection of the children against any abuse of parental authority. In the same way civil law recognizes the children's right to the sustenance of life by their parents. But civil law cannot give positive rules for the internal family structure of these competences and duties, which we have explained above. This internal structure also supplies the norms for the scope of the internal rights and duties, and for the way in which the members of the family have to actualize them. Civil justice has to be content with external, abstract standards in this case. That is why a man who carries out his civil legal duty of providing sustenance of life, has not yet really fulfilled these obligations in the sense of the internal family law. At this point it is evident that considering the distinction between law and morality as the contrast between an external, merely legal order, and the norms of an inner disposition, originates from an absolutization of civil inter-individual law [1].

This distinction has really been derived from the rationalistic Humanist doctrine of natural law with its tendency to ignore fundamental differences in the societal relationships. In the internal family relations, with their close intertwinements of all

---

1 This also applies to EMIL BRUNNER's rigid, formalistic view of justice in his book *Das Gebot und die Ordnungen* (1932 p. 435 ff.). In a positivistic way he knows of no other positive law besides *State-law*. And he considers this to be the necessary conclusion from the anti-"natural-law" attitude of the Reformed view of life! But he did not see that thus he had become the victim of the individualistic "natural-law" conception to which the positivistic theory of law essentially owes its view of positive law.

its members in all the aspects of their temporal existence, juridical relations cannot be conceived in the external pattern derived from abstract civil law. They cannot be detached from the indissoluble internal structural coherence of this temporal societal relationship. In the juridical structure of a family itself is expressed the intimacy of the subjective intertwinements of its members.

The insufficiency of the juridical concept of function. The individualistic construction (based on the theory of "natural law") of the internal juridical relations within the family.

This proves that the juridical concept of function leaves us in the lurch here. In a notion of function [1] we have to eliminate the structural types of individuality in a law-sphere theoretically, in order to grasp all the modal relations in a functional coherence guaranteed by the modal structure of that law-sphere.

The Humanistic natural law doctrine of the Enlightenment also based the internal juridical relations in the family on a social contract *(societas)*. CHRISTIAN WOLFF includes the *patria potestas* among the *jura ex contractu*, which he opposes, as a general category of acquired subjective rights *(jura acquisita)*, to the innate natural subjective rights of man *(jura connata)* [2].

The result was the theoretical eradication of the typical structural character proper to the internal juridical power of parents. Juridical theory cannot do without an insight into the different typical structures of societal relationships, if it is to be able to account for the rich variations in which the modal meaning of law is individualized in temporal reality.

Juridical sphere-sovereignty as the ultimate inner limitation of the original competence of the different law-makers, according to the structural principles of the societal relationships concerned.

This insight will also give us the clue to a solution of the age-old problem concerning the fundamental limits inherent in every original competence of law-making in a differentiated society.

The recognition of the absolute sovereignty of a particular

---

[1] Cf. volume I, pp. 552 ff.

[2] *Jus naturae* I cap. 1. 35: 'Ita jus parentum in liberos oritur ex obligatione cos educandi quae connata non est, sed contracta... Est igitur jus acquisitum.'

legislator would irrevocably deprive his power of any juridical meaning. Our analysis of the modal structure of the juridical aspect of experience has shown that the nuclear moment of its general meaning is retribution [1], which is incompatible with any absolute (and consequently juridically unlimited) power of a legislator. Even the general juridical concept of competence appeared to include the numerical analogy of a plurality of original spheres of competence, which require a mutual balance and delimitation in juridical harmony, excluding any excess of power[2]. The abstract modal juridical meaning of this concept is individualized by the different structures of individuality of societal relationships.

The insight into the structural principles of natural and organized communities and inter-communal or inter-individual relationships necessarily leads to the recognition of their inner sphere-sovereignty also within the modal juridical aspect. This does not mean a relapse into a rationalistic metaphysical theory of natural law. It is simply the necessary conclusion from the biblical Christian view of the sovereignty of God, Whose order of creation also embraces the structural principles of the different societal relationships, guaranteeing the inner proper nature of each of them. The Christian view of law has found its most pregnant expression in the recognition of this juridical sphere-sovereignty. But the concrete significance of this fundamental legal principle can only be discussed in connection with the investigation of the enkaptic intertwinements between the different types of societal relationships.

Here we can only point out the essential connection between the fundamental juridical principle mentioned and the internal structural principles of human society.

The expression of the structural principle in the aesthetic aspect of the internal family relations.

The internal moral and juridical structural functions of the family relationship refer back to the structural function of the family in the aesthetic law-sphere. The analogical moment of harmony in the juridical sphere is modally founded in the original meaning of harmony which qualifies the aesthetic law-sphere [3].

---

[1] Cf. volume II, pp. 129 ff.

[2] Cf. *ibidem*, pp. 165 ff.

[3] Cf. *ibidem*, pp. 135 ff.

In the internal structure of the family, the aesthetic function retains this necessary meaning-coherence with the juridical and the moral aspects, and the structural principle also expresses itself in this aspect of the family relationships. Family relations show their typical internal beautiful harmony, in accordance with their normative structural law, given by the divine order of creation.

True, this harmony has been subjectively affected by the effects of sin. It may even be completely broken, but this does not abolish the aesthetic aspect of the inner family structure. Even disharmony and ugliness as such, exciting our displeasure, remain enclosed within the aesthetic law-sphere, so that they could not exist without the aesthetic norm. Only those who in a rationalistic-idealistic attitude deny the factual subject-side of the aesthetic aspect of temporal reality will also deny this state of affairs. They will only recognize beautiful harmony as an "ideal norm" or "value".

The family, as a natural communal whole, has its aesthetic structural aspect. If this were not so, it could never inspire fine art. Then we could no longer speak of the beauty of the love between parents and children, and yet in our naïve attitude we feel no hesitation to do so, not merely by way of a metaphor, but in an original aesthetic sense.

This internal beautiful harmony is not itself of an *artistic nature.* It is perfectly qualified by the structural principle of the family. As a result the aesthetic aspect of the latter displays a typical meaning-individuality, based on the original biotic bond of blood, and qualified by the normative communion of love between parents and children and between children mutually.

In this meaning-aspect, too, the structure of authority in the family relationship is and remains an essential characteristic. If authority is eliminated from the family, its internal relations will all go awry. The result will be disharmony, which also excites an aesthetic kind of displeasure. No "modern democratic" theory can reason this unpleasant experience away.

The internal structural principle of the family also expresses itself in its aspects of social intercourse and language.

In all the remaining meaning-aspects of this natural community its internal structural principle is equally in evidence:

in its internal economic function of the household, in the internal relations of social intercourse, in the internal culture, the internal communal feeling of the members of the family, *etc.* In all these modal meaning-aspects the structure of its internal authoritative relation is also maintained, and the internal interweavings are revealed among the relevant subject-functions of the individual persons functioning in this communal relationship. Thus, *e.g.*, the prevailing tone in family-intercourse should be consonant with the typical communal love between parents and children, and brothers and sisters. And notwithstanding the close interweavings of the members of a family in their intercourse with each other, the authoritative structure of this relationship should find expression in the *social respect* shown by the children for their parents.

In social intercourse between human beings and their betters, who are invested with the authority of their office, the inferiors should be polite and obliging[1]. In the family, however, this respect retains its tenderness of tone so essential to the typical structure of family relations.

The same thing holds for the objective internal forms of language and the subjective way of symbolical expression. As a substratum they are immediately connected with the function of social intercourse.

Children should not speak to their parents in a respectless familiar way, but when the language used in a family has the exterior formality of the ordinary social intercourse with strangers, the family tone is somehow wrong.

In a Christian family there should prevail a tenderness of tone whose primordial character can never be taken over by any other societal relationship without "striking a false note". For each human societal relationship has its own inner nature, its own structural principle. In this multiformity and originality, temporal human society unfolds its richness in accordance with the divine ordinances. And even in the corruptive state of society caused by sin, God's common grace has maintained these typical structures of individuality.

---

[1] This "social respect" functions in the modal aspect of social intercourse. It should not be confounded with respect in its moral meaning, intended in the commandment "Honour thy father and thy mother". In reality the two kinds of respect are inextricably interwoven.

The expression of the structural principle in the cultural aspect of the family.

The inner structure of the cultural aspect of the natural family demands special attention insofar as here the particular character of the pedagogical and educational sphere of this community is most clearly revealed.

The formative power of the parents with respect to the cultural development of their children is, of course, dependent upon the historical developmental stage of the society in which a family functions. In an undifferentiated society, the inner cultural family sphere cannot clearly be distinguished from the undifferentiated cultural sphere of the domestic community, and eventually from that of the sib and the tribe. Especially in such primitive societies which lack a strong political tribal organization the spirit of the natural family appears to penetrate societal life in all of its communal relationships.

In this case the cultural aspect of the parental educational task will embrace the whole of the undifferentiated cultural formation which is proper to the folk community.

If, on the other hand, the political tribal organization is strengthened and the natural family is pushed back from its prevalent position, there will be found a beginning of differentiation between the educational sphere of the former and that of the latter. We shall recur to this interesting state of affairs in a later context.

In a differentiated modern society, the cultural education of the children is as a rule completely concentrated in the inner family sphere only in the first years of life of the infants. This is in accordance with the natural development of the psychical and post-psychical functions of the child, which only gradually arrive at a certain stage of differentiation. The intimate family-sphere is the only natural community able to give the first and foundational cultural moulding to the disposition and character of the infant. Both its biotical foundation, and its typical moral qualification as a bond of love between parents and children, provide the formative power of parental education with a particular intimate character not found in any other communal sphere.

It is doubtless true that modern psychology and pedagogy to a considerable degree may help the parents in the fulfilment of their task when they meet with particular difficulties due to an insufficient knowledge of the psychical and mental condition of the infant. But it would be a dangerous overestimation of science if it should be supposed that the formative educational task of the parents had better be taken over by a skilled psychologist or pedagogue. The integral character of the education in the family sphere is irreplaceable and in many respects decisive for the whole further life of the children. The children belong to their parents in a personal sense as long as they have not reached the stage of maturity necessary for them to be considered as responsible persons in human society.

This is also the reason why, according to the structural principle of the family, the determination of the spiritual direction of education continues to belong to the parental competence, even when the process of cultural moulding of the children has reached the phase of modern differentiation which exceeds the boundaries of the intimate family sphere.

School and family.

If the parents are lacking or unable to fulfil their particular educational task, in accordance with the structural principle of the family, it is necessary to make a provision to supply this defect. This provision should as much as possible approach the parental type of education. The general cultural moulding provided by the elementary, secondary and other kinds of schools in the later developmental phases of the children, is of a quite different nature from that of parental education.

A school is a differentiated organized community of a typical tuitionary character. It may be that school tuition in its typical historical foundation is qualified by a typical ethical function; but the latter is certainly not that of the family bond in its natural sense. According to its inner structural principle the moral bond of a school community is that between pupils and their teachers, founded in the cultural formative power of the latter. It can only reveal itself as a bond of mutual comradeship between the pupils with different degrees of intensity, and a bond of mutual attachment between the pupils and their teachers.

Within the internal sphere of a school it is the instructional community which determines the typical character of these moral bonds. But in their factual realization the latter are interlaced with moral relations of several other structural types.

The modern differentiation of education is to a high degree determined by its preparatory task with respect to the later functions of the human person both in free society and in the State and the Church. But in this entire differentiation the parental cultural shaping of the child in the inner family sphere retains its irreducible and irreplaceable nature. This is why the ancient and modern totalitarian ideas of State education of the children contradict the divine world-order and are indeed inhuman and destructive to human society.

In the intimate family sphere the children are culturally formed in a spirit of communal solidarity which cannot be equalled by any other temporal community, except the matrimonial bond. The communal sense here acquired is to be considered as the deepest temporal sounding-board to which any other education to a communal sense has to appeal. A decline or inner denaturing of intimate family life is therefore disastrous to human society in all of its communal relationships.

The typical structure of internal communal thought within the family; the sociology of thought.

In its logical aspect the internal structural principle expresses itself in a communal notion of the internal family relations which determines the typical logical mode of thought of the members. This notion, as such, is absolutely of a pre-theoretical nature, immediately founded in emotional feeling relations between the members of a family; it interweaves their mode of thought indissolubly into these internal relationships, notwithstanding all the individual differences in talents, disposition, and development. The notion of paternal authority is essentially implied in it.

An individualistic autonomy of thought is in conflict with the whole internal structure of that typical communal thought which is embedded in the internal life of a family. This thought is under the typical guidance of the love between parents and children in the distinction of persons in authority and those subject to this authority, and has its own logical structural type.

Before the age of puberty the children generally lack independent logical judgment. The authority of the parental judgment has a typical logical function in the mode of thought of the children in the phase of pre-puberty. During the transitional period parental judgment begins to lose its decisive logical authority and ought to justify itself by sufficient arguments. Nevertheless, even in this critical phase of development of the children, the *internal* communal sphere of thought within the family ought to be maintained in accommodation to the psychical and logical development of the adolescents.

The structural principle of this communal thought immediately loses its validity outside of the sphere of the internal family relations. But within this sphere the peculiar logical structure of this mode of thinking is the indispensable basis for all the functions of the family in the later normative law-spheres.

It stands to reason that in its factual realization this logical structure is closely bound to the stage of historical development of family life and of society in general. Such community of thought as is found in the family may show typical social prejudices of rank, class, ecclesiastical and political groupage, *etc.*, due to the enkaptic interlacements of the family with other types of societal relationships.

The recently developed sociology of thought [1] as a special branch of study is especially concerned with a more profound investigation of such social prejudices of logical thinking. It is, however, of primordial importance for this study not to neglect the typical structural differences between the various communities of thought. It should especially guard against a confusion of the necessary structural conditions and presuppositions of communal thought with illegitimate social prejudices which impede correct judgment and are to be unmasked by sociological science.

§ 3 - AN ANALYSIS OF THE PRE-LOGICAL STRUCTURAL ASPECTS OF THE FAMILY RELATIONSHIP.

The structural principle expresses itself also in the pre-logical aspects of the family relationship. The trap hidden in a purely naturalistic view of these meaning-functions.

The specific structural principle of a family does not only find its typical expression in the normative aspects but also in the pre-logical functions of this natural community. The latter assume their typical direction towards the leading moral function of a family in the opening of their modal anticipatory spheres. For it would be a fundamental error to conceive the biotic and psychic structural relations in the family in the

---

[1] Cf. especially the collective work *Versuche zu einer Soziologie des Wissens* (hrsg. im Auftrage des Forschungsinstituts für Sozialwissensch. in Köln, 1924) with an elaborate introduction by SCHELER; and the important publications of KARL MANNHEIM concerning this subject.

restrictive animal function detached from the relations enclosed in the various normative law-spheres. The naturalist trends in sociology even tried to explain the normative relations as a mere reflex of the biotic relations, in an epiphenomenalistic manner. It must be evident that this attempt at explanation contains a vicious circle. For it no longer conceives of the biotic aspect of the natural family in its "restrictive function", but really in its expanded anticipatory meaning, in which the normative leading function has already been pre-supposed. From the naturalistic utilitarian viewpoint the principle of reciprocity in the morality of a group is strongly emphasized as a biological necessity.

Even ALFRED VIERKANDT is apparently under the influence of this mode of thought, notwithstanding his universalistic-phenomenological attitude. 'Reciprocity', he observes in his *Gesellschaftslehre*, 'is generally of fundamental importance in the morality of a group... It is a biological necessity, because without it anyone who would follow its command one-sidedly, would run the risk of starvation or ruin. When the group requires of every individual a certain amount of considerateness and recognition of the claims of others, it also undertakes in his behalf to guarantee that the others shall reciprocate this considerateness accordingly. It says to every one of the group: Thou shalt not kill, but I shall also take care that nobody kills thee. Wherever in the long run one party is confronted with a complete lack of reciprocity or with purely egotistical aims, he will finally relinquish the communal attitude and change over to an entirely different tactics'[1]. This reasoning is a near approach

[1] *Gesellschaftslehre* (2nd ed. 1928), p. 396: 'Die Gegenseitigkeit ist überhaupt in der Gruppenmoral... von grundlegender Bedeutung. Sie ist biologisch notwendig, weil ohne sie derjenige, der ihrem Gebote einseitig folgen würde, in die Gefahr der Verkümmerung oder des Unterganges geraten würde. Wenn die Gruppe ein bestimmtes Masz von Rücksichtnahme und Anerkennung fremder Ansprüche von jedem Einzelnen fordert, so übernimmt sie dementsprechend ihm gegenüber auch die Gewähr, dasz der andere diese Rücksichtnahme erwidern wird. Sie sagt zu jedem: Du sollst nicht töten; aber ich werde auch dafür sorgen, dasz dich niemand tötet. Wo also der eine Teil auf die Dauer auf einen völligen Mangel an Gegenseitigkeit oder die Absicht eines rein selbstsüchtigen Verhaltens stöszt, da wird er schlieszlich die Gemeinschaftshaltung aufgeben und zu einem anderen Verhalten übergehen'. For the rest this work again and again shows naturalistic-evolutionistic traits. Cf. page 225, where, in the discussion of the "various kinds of community", VIERKANDT writes: 'The

to HOBBES' naturalistic theory about the instinct of self-preservation necessarily urging men to found a State-relationship, as soon as it is viewed in the light of a utilitarian thought. HOBBES embodied the idea of reciprocity in the contractual principle. But one fundamental point is overlooked in VIERKANDT's biologistic explanation of communal morality. The intrinsical interwovenness of the members of the community in the internal relations of law and morality was to be reduced to the biological necessity of the preservation of life. But in this attempt *it was taken for granted,* that the vital conditions for a member of the group are *not* guaranteed by natural, pre-logical factors. In the social group-life of animals, *e.g.* in a "state" of bees or ants, there is no normative moral leading. And yet in such an "animal-society" the principle of reciprocity is absolutely maintained by a restrictive group-instinct. In a human community, on the contrary, the biotic and psychic functions appear to be insufficient to keep the members united. Such a relationship may indeed be destroyed by mutual strife among its members.

These facts make it quite evident that the biotic and psychic aspects of a human community must display a fundamentally different structure from that of the group-life of animals.

The idea of temporal human society having developed from animal groupings is thus merely a piece of naturalistic mythology, from which VIERKANDT apparently also starts [1].

On the other hand it is curious to see that VIERKANDT denies the function of the tie of blood as the biotic foundation ("*Grundlage*") of parental love. He does not admit that this "physiological coherence" has that "mystical causal power". He refers to the "undeniable fact" of "the indifference of the unmarried father to his offspring" and also to the fact that the relation of foster-parents towards their adopted child has the same effects, without any physiological basis [2].

---

oldest of these forms is the community of personal groups *(persönliche Gruppengemeinschaft)*. It had already its precursor in the animal herd, from which we can imagine(!) the human horde to have descended as the primal form of human societal life'. Cf. also p. 183. This is no doubt the reason why THEODOR LITT cannot acknowledge VIERKANDT as a congenial mind.

[1] Cf. the previous note. On the other hand VIERKANDT explicitly admits (cf. p. 387 *op. cit.*) that "the *form* of the norm and of the "Thou shalt" cannot be phylogenetically derived from anything else. This renders the naturalistic motives in his book all the more contradictory.

[2] *Op. cit.* p. 449.

This reasoning proves that VIERKANDT is not able to conceive the moral bond of love between parents and their children in its typical total structure of individuality.

Essentially his view of the structural coherence between the *different aspects of this societal relationship* remains of a (pseudo-) natural scientific causal character. He reproaches the "usual, popular view of the mystical power of blood-relationship as the basis of parental love for the logical error of reducing a great complexity of facts to one single cause". As if naïve experience, which really conceives parental love in its typical coherence with the bonds of blood, were starting from a naturalistic-causal theory!

VIERKANDT makes the old naturalistic mistake of thinking that societal facts can be established apart from their normative structural principle. He does not see that it is impossible to conceive of the biotic bonds of blood between parents and children separate from their typical moral qualification, without denaturing their meaning theoretically.

Of course, a biotic complex of factors as such can have no moral effects. Parental love can never be the "natural product" of the "ties of blood". But as to its inner meaning-structure parental love is originally so certainly founded biotically that it would cease to be the love of parents if it were detached from this foundation [1].

---

[1] This does not contradict the fact that a certain "motherly" love may arise towards other people's children that are continuously *in one's* vicinity, *e.g.* as foster-children. But also in this case this love is really founded in the biotic disposition towards maternity. However else could we speak of motherly love? What would distinguish this love from the general love of one's neighbour, the love of country, friendship, *etc.*? But a foster-child can never belong to the community of the family proper, according to the internal structural principle of the latter. He will never be one of the parents' own children. Although he is treated with ever so much genuine tenderness by his foster parents, he is not interwoven with the latter by means of the immediate bonds of blood. His love-relations with them cannot display the same internal structure.

Rather we are confronted here with an essentially transferred kind of parental love, which treats the foster-child *as if* it were a child of their own. The normative standard of this love is not a natural one, in the proper sense of the word, but is transferred from the genuine parental love to that of foster-parents. We had better speak here of "motherly" and "fatherly love" instead of "maternal" and "paternal" love. Naïve linguistic usage is capable of very fine distinctions in this respect.

According to VIERKANDT, the decisive factor calling forth parental love is "the fact of communal life as a system of continual interactions (in which of course the physiological relations of sexuality and reproduction create a particularly favourable resonance)." From this it would follow that natural parentship is only an accessory "favourable condition" for parental love. Why does not VIERKANDT take the next step then by calling the biotic-organic aspect of the difference in sex only an accessory „favourable condition" for marital love?[1] There are indeed sexual abnormalities to be adduced in favour of the thesis that marital love is not necessarily "founded" in the sexual bond between husband and wife. But since a structural foundation has nothing to do with a naturalist causal explanation of conjugal love, this thesis lacks any meaning.

The psychic structural aspect of the family.

In the typical internal relations of feeling between its members the family has its psychic structural aspect. This can never be conceived in itself as something *purely* psychic (*"rein-psychisches"*), but only in its indissoluble internal meaning-coherence with its typical leading function as well as with its typical foundational aspect. The psychic function proved to be pre-supposed in the internal-logical structural aspect, as the latter evidently contains a retrocipation of the former. The internal communal feeling of the members of a family may no doubt show great defects when considered from its subject-side. But naïve experience rightly looks upon a weakening, or even a total lack of this communal feeling, as something "contrary to nature", something that is flagrantly in conflict with the inner vital law of the family. According to the internal structural principle of this societal relationship, the feeling of most intimate solidarity of parents and children in this communal function should be opened to the moral leading by the love of parents and children in mutual tender affection and devotion. Every injury done to this feeling must evoke an instinctive reaction of pain and indignation.

[1] VIERKANDT does not venture to go so far. He does deny, however, that the sexual instinct is the only or the most important foundation of marriage. Here, too, VIERKANDT conceives of the term "foundation" in a natural-causal sense.

The internal subject-object relation in the psychic and the later structural aspects of the family.

Each of the members of the family feels inclined to try and obtain a permanent "souvenir" of the others, in other words the internal communal feeling expresses itself in an internal structural subject-object relation. Portraits, locks of hair, letters, personal ornaments of the body, in short anything in which the temporal existence of the other members expressed itself, or that was closely connected with their individual existence, becomes the object of the typical communal feeling of a family, the feeling of love, devoted tenderness, and strong solidarity.

This subject-object relation, of course, is also found in the normative aspects of the family relationship. Things that serve as a "permanent souvenir" become objective cultural possessions of the family in its historical structural function. They also function as symbolic objects, as objects of intimate social intercourse, and as typical economic objects. Their economic value as such remains restricted to the family circle, or to the wider circle of relatives. These things only possess a *"pretium affectionis"* in which the typical moral qualification of their economic function is clearly expressed. In addition they have a typical juridical object function, a moral object function, *etc.*

These objective things are consequently interwoven with the internal communal life of the family, they have internal objective structural functions in this relationship.

The internal psychic interlacements between the members of a family cannot be mechanically isolated from the feelings of the individuals.

The authoritative structure inherent in a family is also expressed in the psychic structural aspect of this communal relationship. On the one hand there is the feeling of authority on the part of the parents, on the other hand the feeling of respect on the part of the children. If these feelings are lacking, the tenderness of the mutual emotional relations is not strengthened but rather weakened and falsified. This is not merely a question of a universal *"Unterordnungstrieb"* [1] in the sense intended by the sociological studies of MAC DOUGALL, VIERKANDT and others; but these feelings of authority and respect have a typical internal structure, not found in any other societal relationship.

---

[1] An instinct of subordination, a submissive tendency.

The internal psychic interlacements between the individual members of the family are, however, not a separate department by the side of other "groupal" and inter-individual emotional relations [1]. Nor can we make such an exterior mechanical separation among the different social subject-functions of *human personality* in the case of its normative aspects.

In the legal subjectivity of an individual person the internal structural functions of the latter in the different communal relationships appeared to be an internal constituent. The same thing applies to his emotional life. The internal affective relations between parents and children are actually interwoven with a great many other feelings: national feeling, the feeling of social standing, ecclesiastical communal feeling, *etc.* But in the enkaptic interlacements the internal structural principles of individuality are kept intact, and this is also true in the feeling aspect of temporal society.

Does a communal whole as such have its own life of feeling and thought, distinct from that of its members?

The analysis of the typical logical and psychic structures of a family in its narrowest sense raises a question of general importance with respect to every kind of communal whole. It may be asked whether a community as such has a life of feeling and thought of its own, distinct from that of its individual members.

This is one of the crucial points at issue in the controversy between modern "universalists" and "individualists". The idea of a "*Volksgeist*", a "*Verbandsseele*", a "*conscience collective*", *etc.* (*i.e.* the spirit of a people, the soul of an organized community) was always rejected on the part of the individualists as metaphysical speculation. They tried to construe the typical thought of a community, its communal feeling and communal will by means of a functional conception of the social interactions between individuals.

LITT on his anti-metaphysical universalistic standpoint proved also to reject the hypostatization of a community to a "spiritual organism" or "*Ueberperson*" (super-personality), as an independent centre of "psychic acts" of consciousness. He inferred the "social acts" from the social interweavings among the individual egos.

---

[1] This point has rightly been insisted upon by LITT in his *Individuum und Gemeinschaft*.

This question can only be rightly posed and solved in the light of our previous expositions. We have definitely and clearly rejected the metaphysical universalistic and individualistic conceptions, and are not going to be caught in the dilemma of their mutual struggle. LITT's "monadological universalism" proved no more to be compatible with the Christian conception of the religious transcendence of human personality than any other form of sociological universalism. We have found that every temporal community has a subjective continuity and identity regulated by its structural principle. This continuity and identity as such is to a greater or lesser degree independent of the variations in the number of its individual members unless the community is by nature a two-oneness relationship. But this conception can never result in a metaphysical separation between the communal whole and its members.

A communal relationship is a typical structure of man's own temporal social existence. Therefore the internal continuity of such a particular communal whole, both as to its psychic and all its other aspects, can be actualized only in the communal structure of the relevant functions of its members.

Notwithstanding the variations in the number of its members the internal structure of the whole continues to actualize itself in the feelings and thoughts of the existing members in an individual way. To this fact the communal relationship owes its continuous identity, also in its logical and psychic structural aspects. Especially in the case of an *organized* community this continuous identity extends beyond the individual temporal existences of the members. But this state of affairs does not justify the assumption of a metaphysical "collective soul" of the community. The continual existence of the latter is dependent on the inner act-life and the social activity of human beings by which the communal relationships must be realized. A temporal community lacks a supra-individual consciousness, it has no I-ness as the centre of a collective act-life.

The organological conception of the communal whole.

Admitting the fundamental and unbridgeable difference between a biotically qualified organism and a human community, yet we seem to be confronted with an almost undeniable point of agreement between them.

The life of a plant, too, possesses a continuity extending beyond the span of the always changing individual cells. Nevertheless this continuity can only be actualized in the coherence of the ever changing individual cells themselves. Outside of the structural relationship of the cells themselves, a plant possesses no more life of its own than a human community does outside of the structural relation between its individual members. This was the *tertium comparationis* that always made the organological theories of the structure of temporal human communities sound so convincing.

LITT tried to refute these theories with the argument that the natural organism is bound to an individual spatial-bodily existence, whereas a human communal whole in principle lacks such a vital bond. A "closed circle" of human communal relationships presupposes in his opinion that the living human beings, incorporated in it, are not interwoven into vital coherences as regards their bodily existence [1]. This argument is only to the point in the case of the naturalistic organological view; it is irrelevant with regard to the conception of a community as a "spiritual organism". Besides, it will appear presently that in the case of typically biotically founded communities, such as the family, there are very close vital interlacements between the members with respect to their bodily existence. Especially these types of societal relationships were considered as the prototypes of a truly organical community in the organological theories.

However, if we look at these theories more closely, their naturalistic and idealistic main types appear to force a dilemma on us that must be radically rejected on our Christian standpoint.

The naturalistic types were compelled to consider a temporal human community as an organic natural being. The idealistic views, however, had to conceive of it according to the metaphysical concept of an "organically articulated super-person" *(organisch gegliederte Ueberperson).*

But we have shown in an earlier context that a temporal human communal whole has neither the structure of an organic natural thing, nor as such a spiritual centre above or in coordination with the individual human personality. Nor can it interweave the individual central I-nesses of its members, as THEODOR LITT thought in his "monadological universalism". The reason is that the human selfhood transcends all the temporal structures of societal relationships, and is not to be considered as a temporal *psychical* centre of acts, as LITT supposes.

---

[1] *Op. cit.* pp. 282/3.

> Does the community feel, think, *etc.* in its members, or do the latter think, feel, *etc.* in the communal relationship?

But on our standpoint there now seems to arise an extremely difficult problem, which requires our fullest attention.

The typical structures of human communities have proved to be secondary structures of man's own temporal existence. Neither natural nor organized communities can be considered as independent personalities; they depend on human activity for their actualization. If this is true, we may ask whether it is possible for us to continue calling them *subjective* identical unities. Does not this view imply that a communal whole is again looked upon as a thinking, feeling, willing and acting being, and as such must have an independent personal centre of consciousness? In other words, does not our previously explained conception imply an internal contradiction? Which is correct? Does a communal whole feel, think, *etc.* in its members, or do the latter think, feel, *etc.* in a communal relationship? And if the second alternative is right, can we then still say that a *community as such* has subject-functions in all the modal spheres? Do not the separate human personalities have these functions? If, in opposition to LITT, we are to say that the central egos of these human personalities are not themselves interwoven by the temporal communal relations, what possibility is left for us to view a community as a subjective real unity?

The questions asked here, however suggestively they are formulated, continue to start from a dilemma which we have rejected as false, as our expositions have proved. In a temporal community the individual I-ness *expresses* itself in its supra-temporal religious communion with other human egos. This excludes the possibility that any temporal community has a personal centre of its own coordinated with or transcending the individual human personality. When we say that a community has its own sphere of feeling, thought, *etc.*, its own temporal internal sphere of action, we cannot mean anything else than the life of feeling, thought, *etc.*, and the sphere of action of human beings, in a particular temporal unity of societal relationships. This statement is no relapse into an individualistic or a monadological universalistic conception. For we have discovered the internal structural principle guaranteeing the internal unity of a communal relationship on its law-side, which should be realized in a variable societal form. Owing to their lack of insight into these structural principles the prevailing theories were obliged to accept the dilemma mentioned above, which is meaningless from our point of view. The subjective structural unity of a temporal communal whole is realized through the individual temporal existences of its human members, without the latter being absorbed by the former.

When compared with the personal human ego, in its supra-temporal religious bonds with other human selfhoods, temporal communities cannot be isolated as beings with a "substance" or an "I-ness" of their own. But this fact does not exclude that *in comparison with one another,* they have an inner subjective structural unity. On the individualistic, and on the universalistic standpoint these states of affairs cannot be understood in their true nature.

There is consequently no internal contradiction in the statement that a temporal community functions subjectively in all the law-spheres and as such possesses a structural subjective unity, while at the same time we maintain that only its human members can think, feel, act, *etc.* For a temporal societal relationship as such cannot be personal, but derives from human personality itself, whose supra-temporal spiritual ego, in its religious communion with the other human egos, is the very root of any temporal societal relationship whatsoever.

How the family relationship expresses its structural principle in the biotic, the spatial and the numerical aspects.

After this digression we will proceed with our analysis of the different structural functions of the family relationship.

The immediate substratum of its psychic sphere is its biotic structural function. This function appeared to play a typical foundational rôle in the entire inner structure of the family. No wonder that the latter's internal structural principle cannot fail to express itself in its biotic aspect.

Parents and children are inextricably interwoven by the ties of blood in their temporal existence, although their bodies exist separately. A family relationship, of course, does not itself have a mystical biotic-corporeal organism apart from that of its members. Nevertheless, in the biotic aspect of their individual existences, there are found structural communal relations closely interweaving the members of a family as such in this law-sphere as well. Biology also must recognize these typical relations, which are expressed in the phenomena of heredity.

However, within the structure of the family in its narrowest sense, this "bond of blood" cannot manifest itself solely in a merely restrictive biotic function, or only in a biotic function opened by instinctive animal affective impulses.

And *in itself* the immediate blood-tie can never guarantee the internal unity of the family community. It can only be the foundational function of the latter under the normative leading of the love between parents and children, and that among the latter mutually. This is to say that these biotic relations within the family structure only function in a structural moral anticipation, precluding any identification with the societal relationship between a couple of animals and their young ones.

The blood-bond is not merely a typical foundation of the family-relationship in the narrow sense of the word, but also of the more extensive natural communities of kinship. In its narrowest sense, however, as the genetic biotic relation between the parents and their offspring of the first degree, the blood-bond is only the typical foundation of the family community in the restricted sense here intended. The latter displays closer interweavings of the temporal existences of its members than the larger communities of the same secondary radical type.

*

Our elaborate structural analysis may at first sight seem unusual and strange, but we cannot halt at the psychic and biotic aspects in our examination of the manner in which the structural principle of the family expresses itself in the pre-logical functions.

The integral character of the societal structures of individuality, in the intermodal coherence of all their different aspects, is at issue here. Both the naturalist and the so-called cultural scientific trends in sociology have failed to do justice to these integral structures. This is the reason why we must continue our analysis of the pre-logical aspects of the latter.

The family in its typical total structure displays even physico-chemical and spatial structural aspects as well as a necessary function in the numerical sphere of empirical reality.

If this were not true, the family-structure could never be the structure of an integral unit of societal *reality*; it would be a theoretic abstraction. Temporal reality is only given in the indissoluble coherence of all its modal aspects, and cannot be arrested arbitrarily in a select complex of law-spheres.

We should only bear in mind that even the pre-logical aspects of a societal relationship cannot be realized without human acts and that, insofar as the human body is conditioned by such relationships, it is the body in its qualifying act-structure, which itself embraces all modal aspects of our experiential horizon.

The family community cannot function in the biotic law-sphere unless as such it expresses itself also in those spheres in which, according to the general temporal order of the modal aspects, the biotic law-sphere itself is founded. The whole of the energy aspect of the human body, its "matter" in its opened and enkaptically functioning physico-chemical structural constellation, owes its origin to the female ovarian cell fecundated by the male sperm. This means that even the structural physico-chemical *constellation of our body in its qualifying act-structure* originated from a complete union of a maternal and a paternal component which as such can never be conceived in terms of "pure" physics and chemistry. And yet there can be no doubt that this genetic process in its human communal character has an essential physico-chemical aspect. But the latter displays the typical communal structure of the family-relationship in its process of becoming.

Even the metabolic processes in the human body have a structural function in this communal relationship. Normally it is the duty of a well-ordered family-relationship, especially in childhood, to take care of the bio-physical aspects of our body. This task is to be performed under the normative guidance of the love between parents and children. The care of the bio-physical aspects of our human body is not a restrictive "natural process", but it occurs in the normatively qualified structures of temporal human society.

Left to instinctive natural impulses a human being would die, as the entire complicated enkaptic structure of his bodily existence requires a normative leading of its bio-physical processes by the logical and post-logical functions.

In the spatial aspect of reality the structural principle of a family relationship also finds expression. The intimate interlacement in the temporal existences of the members requires the normative character of this relationship to express itself in a *spatial centre,* where they live closely together. This is not a "natural datum" of human social life in a family-community, but something that requires normative freedom for its realization.

In the psychic structural aspect there is a strong appeal to the spatial function of the family in the universally known "*Heimatgefühl*" conceived in its most intimate structure of the feeling of being *at home* in one's own family community, as well as in the longing for home in case of temporal absence.

We have already referred to the fact that, when family-relations are what they should be, the members of a family appreciate taking some souvenir with them in case of a rather prolonged absence from home. Such souvenirs suggest, as it were, the spatial nearness of the other members of the family [1].

Finally the structure of the family relationship expresses itself in that typical unity in a multiplicity in which every child owes its origin to the sexual intercourse of one father and one mother. No human licentiousness in sexual matters can undo this state of affairs, that there exists a wonderful numerical relation between parents and children. For from the bi-unity of the parents there comes into existence a third human being, a fourth, *etc.*, who all remain indissolubly bound to the parental bi-unity. This numerical relation cannot, of course, be understood in *purely* arithmetical terms. It refers to the normative structural principle of the family community, which finds its quantitative expression in this numerical function. This unity in multiplicity, deriving from a bi-unity, is in other words not a datum which is to be understood apart from its typical moral qualification, nor is it merely the result of mating led by the restrictive sexual instinct, as it is in animal life. But it is to be actualized in normative freedom (in the right or in the wrong way), according to the internal structural law of the conjugal and the family bond. And it is no idle speculation when in his book *Das Gebot und die Ordnungen* EMIL BRUNNER looks upon these numerical structures as an indication that monogamy is the basis of the family bond in the order of creation [2].

[1] This is really an essential emotional factor in such a "souvenir". When the photos of "acquaintances" are given a place in the house, *this "Heimatsgefühl"*, of course, does not play a part.

[2] *Das Gebot und die Ordnungen*, pp. 329 ff.

The expression of the family structure in the faith aspect.

If the reality of the family-relationship cannot be arrested in any modal law-sphere, its typical qualifying function as a particular love bond cannot be its *last* modal function. In the temporal law-sphere of faith the family must also have a function, and in the Christian view of the Reformation this truth finds full recognition. The father of a family should at the same time be the priest of the family in the full sense of the word, according to the priesthood of all believers. Yet a family is not *qualified* as a typical faith communion, but the internal family structure, as a communion of love between parents and children, ought to express itself also in its modal aspect of faith.

According to its internal structural law, the family is not a little Church-community, neither is it a State on a small scale or an economically qualified organization.

In the temporal delimitation of its structure both by its typical biotic foundation and its typical leading function which qualifies its internal destination, this relationship displays its temporal, transitory nature. Even in the purity of its structure according to the divine will, the family is only a *temporal expression* of the religious meaningfulness of human communion in Christ, in His relation to the Divine Father as the Son.

At this point we are confronted with an extremely important state of affairs which is valid for all human societal relationships.

The structural opening-process in the modal functions of a family cannot be arrested by its typical moral qualifying function.

The qualifying structural function cannot bring the opening-process in the internal functions of a family to a functional close. If it could do so, the family-relationship in its internal structure would be independent of the religious root of temporal reality.

Then it could not be the individual sfructural expression in time of the religious fulness of meaning of the communion of men in Christ, including the relationship between man and God as that of a child to the Heavenly Father. In its subjective temporal reality, affected by sin, a family relationship is indeed often a caricature of what it ought to be. But according to the divine world-order, the anticipatory spheres of the structural qualifying function of a family keep waiting for their disclosure in the transcendental direction. They refer forward to the meaningfulness of love in Christ, in Whom God is our Father, and we are His children. In other words, the typical leading function of a human societal relationship can only *qualify* the openingprocess of this individual relationship. But *according to the divine world-order* this structure cannot be deprived of its direction to the fulness of meaning by arresting it in time. If, nevertheless, in a *subjective sense* this is taking place, the family remains caught in the *civitas terrena,* the kingdom of darkness, and even family life becomes a judgment to man.

§ 4 - THE STRUCTURE OF THE BI-UNITARY MARRIAGE-BOND AND ITS CONNECTION WITH THE FAMILY.

The changes in the number of the family members are restricted within narrow limits, in accordance with the structural principle of this relationship.

The natural family relationship in its narrowest sense is only to a very small degree independent of the changes in the number of its members. Membership is absolutely restricted to the parents and their offspring in the first degree. This restriction is implied in the structural principle itself, and excludes the possibility of a total change of all the individual family members.

A family is not a whole in the same sense as a genealogical bond, whose unity is realized in a succession of generations. But a family implies a certain simultaneity in the internal interweavings of its members. There is no doubt that the continuous identity of the family as such is independent of the changes in the number of its children so long as at least one child is left alive. But when both parents have died, the family-tie as such is broken, although the bond of blood-relationship between the surviving children remains intact. Their factual living together in the same house after the death of their parents, possibly under the leading of the eldest, or of another relative, who as their guardian is in charge of the internal authority, cannot be considered to be a continuation of the family relationship.

It is a new formation, a relationship of a different internal structure.

When the children leave home for good because they marry, or because they have grown up, or in case all the children die, the family relationship proper also ceases to exist, although the marriage-bond between the parents remains. The latter communal bond is the presupposition of the family, and is in an enkaptic way intimatety and closely interwoven with the latter during the time of its existence without being absorbed by it.

The typical inner conjugal relations, especially the sexual intercourse between husband and wife, remain strictly separate from the family community.

Marriage is a necessarily bi-unitary bond. Even in polygamy the marriage bond does not itself assume a multiple character.

The marriage bond is by nature incapable of any change in its individual members; it is essentially a bi-unity of husband and wife entirely dependent on the individuality of the persons united in this communal bond.

In polygamy these things are essentially unaltered. The husband is not united with more wives in one marriage bond, but in as many marriage bonds as he has wives. This is striking evidence of the fact that polygamy is against nature. The harem is indeed an authoritative organized community, in which there exists a difference in social position between the wives. As such a harem forms part of a domestic and labour community and is only included in an enkaptic interweaving with the marriage bond. It has so little of a natural community that the relations which necessarily occur in it have a destructive effect on the natural marriage bond and the natural family relationship. Marriage, as such, does not allow of such a social form as that of an authoritative organization in which there would be a unity in a multiplicity of more than two marriage partners. Human arbitrariness cannot alter this. Where polygamy obtains, the separate families originating from the various marriage bonds of the husband [1] necessarily become interwoven in the relationship of a "joint, or extended family" [2]. This is a strongly patriarchial-agnatic kinship, because the children issued from the various marriages are only related through the father [3]. This

---

[1] In Africa as a rule each of these families lives in a separate hut; their households are scrupulously kept apart. Cf. R. H. LOWIE, *Primitive Society* (1921), p. 44.

[2] We borrow this term from the Encyclopaedia Brittannica, 1947 edition, sub.-voce: Family. Cf. W. F. OGBURN and MEYER F. MIMKOFF, *A Handbook of Sociology,* 2nd edition, pp. 460 ff. Cf. also: SOROKIN, *Society, Culture and Personality,* New York 1947, pp. 195 ff., who speaks of "kinship groups" and disagrees with OGBURN and MIMKOFF's nomenclature.

[3] Cf. W. KOPPERS, *Ehe und Familie* (Handwörterbuch der Soziologie

does not mean that the patriarchal extended family can only derive from polygamy. The Roman family, for instance, in its extended patriarchal character excluded any polygamy. But we can establish that, generally speaking, this type of family does not belong to the natural communities because it usually displays the structure of an organized undifferentiated whole. We shall recur to these artificial family types in a later context.

That which occurs simultaneously in polygamy (*i.e.* the simultaneous formation of more than one natural family from different marriages contracted by one man) is only possible in succession in the case of monogamy, if one of the surviving partners re-marries after the death of the other.

It may be asked whether the original family relationship is continued in its subjective identity when one of the parents dies, especially when the surviving marriage-partner remarries. The Dutch Code of Civil Law does not in these cases recognize any continuation of legal *parental* authority over the children born of the marriage concerned, but only the guardianship of the surviving parent. If the mother survives and remarries, her guardianship is shared by her new marriage partner (art. 400 ff. civil Code).

According to the structural principle of the family it cannot be doubtful that in both cases the original family bond no longer exists. For the inner unity and identity of this community is typically founded in the conjugal bi-unity. The dissolution of the latter necessarily implies the dissolution of the family which originated from it. This is an essential difference between a natural family and any other bond of kinship.

The marriage and family bond have individuality structures of the same radical type.

The identity of a family relationship in its natural sense remains thus strictly bound to the identity of the marriage bond. Between these two societal structures there exists an intense enkaptic interlacement of an irreversible foundational type. Such enkaptic foundational relations have also been found in our examination of objective normatively qualified thing-structures and they will appear to occur in nature in a rich variety. But in the case of marriage and family this foundational

hrg. v. ALFRED VIERKANDT, 1931), pp. 117 ff; compare what is said there about polygamy in patriarchal families.

relation is discovered between two individuality structures of the *same radical type*. Both are of a typical biotic foundation and both are qualified as typical moral bonds of love. They are only of a different *geno-type,* in the earlier defined sense of the term.

The marriage bond, as such, is typically founded in the *institutional* (and not in an incidental) sexual union of husband and wife, which is undoubtedly made serviceable for the propagation of the human race. It is according to the order of the creation that normally marriage leads to the formation of a family. In other words, the typical foundational relation between the family and the conjugal bond implies the natural disposition of the latter to procreation. In this sense marriage may be called the "germ-cell" of the family-relationship. Both communities remain most intensely interwoven during the time of their actual existence.

Yet marriage, as a love-communion, maintains its own structure notwithstanding its interwovenness with the family.

Is the conception of marriage as a legal institution contradictory to the view that marriage is qualified as a bond of love?

In our view marriage is *qualified* as the permanent typical bond of love between husband and wife. But does not this conception contradict the traditional view very generally accepted both in Christian and Humanist circles, which in the marriage-bond assigns only a subordinate place to love?[1] And does not it rashly encourage the modern irrationalistic conception, already occurring in FICHTE's actualism, in which the bond of marriage is made dependent on the *actual subjective continuance* of love between the marriage-partners? If in this sense love is considered to be the real meaning of the marriage-bond, does it not follow that the entire institutional legal aspect of this community is ignored?

We might have discussed this question implicitly when we examined the structural principle of the family relationship, which we also qualified, in accordance with its internal structure, as a typical bond of love. It is true, we sharply opposed

---

[1] That this is also done by positivist sociologists is not to the point here, since they intentionally eliminate the normative structural principles of societal relationships.

the naturalistic misconception of the normative meaning of love, but we did not yet consider the objections raised by the traditional view against giving "primacy" to the love bond as the essential factor both in the family and in marriage. This had a good reason. For it is the *connection* between marriage and family that has always been the basis of the traditional objections to the primacy of love in these communities. And it is this connection which is at issue in the present context of our inquiry.

The traditional scholastical conception called marriage an essentially legal institution whose "essence" is determined by its natural aim, *viz.* the propagation of the human race. The natural law order — and in the Roman Catholic view also the divine supra-natural legal order of the Church — seemed to offer a firm foot-hold for this opinion to oppose the theory of the *"primatus amoris"*. Conjugal love was thought of only as a variable and subjective feeling, unsuitable as a "basis" for a permanent life-companionship. Married affection was sometimes considered to be a mere "instrument" for propagation, as the essential aim of the conjugal bond.

But the internal structural principle of the bi-unitary bond of marriage cannot be grasped with a juridical concept oriented to the natural (and eventually supra-natural) aim of this institution. If the marital community has also an internal juridical aspect, the typical character of the latter is certainly not determined by the natural aim of propagation as assumed by the scholastic natural law conception. Civil and canon law contain marital regulations that are far from being a positive juridical expression of the essential inner nature of the institution of marriage. On the contrary, in comparison with the proper internal structural principle of the conjugal bond they only have a formal and external character. The internal legal sphere of marriage, just like the internal law of the family, owes its qualification exclusively to the internal structural principle as a whole. The idea that the juridical function is the "leading" or "qualifying function" of this internal structure is untenable and in open conflict with the Biblical view [1].

---

[1] Cf., for instance, *Ephes.* 5 : 31, where the bond of married love is clearly conceived as qualifying the "being one flesh". This bond of love has its religious consummation in Christ's love of His Bride, the Church, which in the supra-temporal fulness of meaning is also *one body with*

As soon as the juridical viewpoint acquires the leading rôle in the conjugal relationship, it is by nature an *external* legal viewpoint. And if the marriage-partners give to an external legal order the leading rôle in their communal relationship, this is a clear evidence of the complete ruin of their inner bond. Nor can a civil or canon legal order be the *foundation* of marriage in its inner structure. This foundation is of a biotic, not of a juridical character.

No doubt the juridical structural aspect of the marriage-institution cannot be eliminated, but this holds good for all its other structural functions.

Is the continuity of the marriage bond to be guaranteed exclusively by civil law or canon law?

If conjugal love is the qualification of the marriage bond, can the latter then be continued when subjectively this love has vanished? And if the answer is in the negative, does not this prove that only as a legal institution marriage can continue to exist, either regulated by civil or by canon law? Our answer is that the marriage institution as such is identical with the structural principle of this community. We know that according to this structural principle its juridical aspect cannot be independent and self-contained. The inner nature of a marriage bond is not determined by a consensual agreement between two persons of different sex which satisfies the conditions determined by civil or canon law. Those who unite as husband and wife enter into an institutional community whose structure is no way dependent on their subjective arbitrary discretion.

From the outset they are *subjected to* its institutional law.

The normative character of the institution of marriage implies that its continuous identity cannot be dependent on the arbitrary way in which from moment to moment the subjects behave in this structural bond. But this does not mean that the continuous identity of the bi-unitary bond of marriage is to be found only on its law-side. There cannot exist any individual community if its structural principle is not subjectively realized to some degree. The unity in duality existing between husband and wife

---

our Saviour: *ὅτι μέλη ἐσμὲν τοῦ σώματος αὐτοῦ, ἐκ τῆς σαρκὸς αὐτοῦ, καὶ ἐκ τῶν ὀστεῶν αὐτοὺ.*

Thomas Aquinas also recognized that only as a love-bond marriage is a temporal expression of Christ's relation to His Church. Cf. 4 *Sent.* dist. 26q. 2, a.l. ad 3.

should be realized subjectively, be it in an imperfect way, in a constant subjective vital union of the above-mentioned structure. In this sinful world the marriage-partners by no means always behave conformably to this structural law.

But may we yet speak of a marriage bond if the partners *constantly* adopt an anti-normative attitude with reference to the internal structural principle of their union and continually live together like strangers, or even enemies? In such a case there is no denying that the *internal* bond of marriage is not subjectively realized, not even in a very imperfect way. Unfortunately this is the state of affairs in many a marriage contracted rashly or from utilitarian motives. Then sin mercilessly puts to shame the tenderest and most intense temporal bond that God in His order of creation has given to man as a task.

The true sense of the civil law (or, at a more primitive stage of society, the tribal law) and the canon law regulations of marriage. Their relation to the internal structural principle of the marriage bond.

But though as to its internal side a marriage is not subjectively realized, or ruined hopelessly, with regard to its *external* relations in human society it is not thereby *ipso jure* dissolved.

The marriage bond functions in numerous enkaptic interweavings, and as such it is never a matter that concerns husband and wife only in their relation to each other and to God. It is, just as the family, a pillar of human society. According to the divine order of creation it is a union for life. For these reasons the formal dissolution of the marriage bond may not be left to the sinful arbitrariness of the marriage-partners, especially not in times when public opinion no longer respects the institutional character of this bi-unitary community.

If marriage can be formally undone so easily, it spells ruin for human society. In its external enkaptic interweavings the conjugal bond comes especially to the fore in its external function as a civil or (at a more primitive stage of society) a tribal law institution. Human licentiousness in this field meets with an external constraint. In case the internal marriage bond has been definitively broken, only the civil or tribal law order is able either to keep an external frame of the bond intact with the constraining power of the State or the tribe, or to give a binding regulation of its formal dissolution. This is important for the external relations of this institution. Canon law on this point has no other primary function insofar as it is intended as an authentic explanation of the so-called law of nature. Only in the Roman Catholic view of marriage as a sacrament are we confronted with the enkaptic interweavings of marriage with the *internal* sphere of the Roman Catholic Church.

Civil law or tribal law respectively, regulate the general conditions for contracting or dissolving marriage, together with other points that are of general importance for the civil law relations or the tribal relations respectively, in which the marital bond functions. Canon law does the same from the Roman Catholic ecclesiastical viewpoint. The "lawfulness" of a marriage depends on its satisfying the general conditions of contracting it established by these legal orders. And it may occur that on that issue civil law and canon law are in conflict with one another, though we shall show in our analysis of the inner nature of ecclesiastic law that this can only be caused by disregarding the inner boundaries of the State's or the Church's competence to law making. In other words, in the regulation of these enkaptic interweavings of marriage with other societal relationships it is really the civil, or tribal, or canon law function of marriage that takes the lead.

Under this leading the external framework of the marriage institution, *i.e.* its *social form,* is maintained also in its other modal functions. (Witness, for instance, the external forms of social intercourse in which the formal appearance of marriage is maintained even though the true internal bi-unitary bond has been broken). But this external legal framework of marriage should not be confounded with the internal structural principle of this bi-unitary community. The proper internal stability of the latter must never be founded in its supposed essence as a civil, or an ecclesiastical institution. This internal unity cannot at all be maintained by any external legal order, as it can only be realized under the leading of faithful married love.

The false legalistic view of the question concerning divorce.

Christ's pronouncement in the question of divorce was in particular directed against the confusion of the inner institutional structure of marriage, in its reference to the Kingdom of God, with its external institutional aspect. The whole problem of divorce had been obscured by rabbinical legal formalism. *And it is nothing but a relapse into this legalistic view of the matrimonial bond if one tries to derive from the New Testament legal principles for a civil law regulation of the grounds of divorce.* These grounds can only refer to the external legal frame of marriage. They can never replace the personal responsibility of the partners in their internal relation to one another under the structural norm of the institution and the central commandment of love. From the internal moral point of view it is not possible to indicate general grounds of divorce. And the civil legislator should be aware that the legal determination of such grounds will always remain defective and liable to evasion. The fact that Christians have come to look upon the marriage bond as essentially a juridical institution must be denounced as a fundamental deformation of the Biblical view of this natural community.

The Thomistic view of the natural essential character of marriage in connection with the theory of the *bona matrimonii.* Marriage as an institution of natural law.

In his later systematic elaboration of the theory of the *bona matrimonii* THOMAS AQUINAS related the marriage institution *primarily* to its cosmic purpose of propagating the human race. To him this purpose was the *real natural essence* of the marital bond. This theory, already mentioned in an earlier context, was bound to favour a universalistic view of marriage which seeks to understand the essence of this institution from its enkaptic interweavings in the family, the State and the Church [1].

We have established that it is exactly the civil and (with respect to the R.C. Church) the canon law regulations of marriage which in modern Western society play a central and leading rôle in these enkaptic interweavings. That is why the traditional theory of the *bona matrimonii* could not but strongly favour the idea of primacy of the legal institution in the marriage bond. Thus to canonists as well as to Roman Catholic moral philosophers marriage remained both *a divine and a natural law institution,* which Christ had elevated to a "sacrament". In a purely Thomistic-Aristotelian way this conception of marriage as an institution of natural law has been elaborated

[1] In HOEGEN's very able thesis, cited in a later context, we find the following statement, on page 52: "The essence of marriage is determined by its purpose." This is an orthodox piece of Thomism.

in our days, *e.g.* in CATHREIN's ethical philosophy [1]. Typical of the universalistic attitude in this view is CATHREIN's pronouncement: 'Therefore, according to its nature, marriage is an institution whose principal aim is not the *personal* welfare of the marriage-partners, but that of the human species, the honourable maintenance and propagation of the human race' [2].

The traditional scholastic view of marriage as primarily a civil or canon law institution on the basis of the law of nature has especially retained its influence among the modern Roman Catholic canonists. One of the most prominent figures among them, R. VON SCHERER, writes: 'The decision to contract a marriage is eminently a matter of private law *(juris privati)*, but the content and the stability of marriage is rooted in the public law of the legal community, either of the State or of the Church, entirely apart from the creed, the opinion and the will of the contracting parties' [3].

A Roman Catholic reviewer of the Dutch edition of my work has observed that this emphasizing of the legal aspect of marriage finds its explanation in the fact that this bond is treated here only from the viewpoint of canon law. This remark, however, is not to the point. SCHERER's pronouncement that both the content and the stability of marriage are rooted in the public law either of the State or of the Church clearly concerns the essence of the marriage institution as such, and not simply its *external* legal relations. It is true that the essential legal character of this institution is viewed especially from the viewpoint of *positive* civil and canon law and that its foundation in *natural* law is presupposed. But this is indifferent to the conception of the marital community as an institution whose essence is deter-

---

1 *Moralphil.* II (6th ed. 1924) § 3: *Die Ehe als naturrechtliche Institution.*

2 *Op. cit.* p. 412. 'Die Ehe ist also ihrer Natur nach eine Institution, deren Hauptzweck nicht das *persönliche* Wohl der Ehegatten, sondern das Wohl der menschlichen Art (Gattung), die würdige Erhaltung und Fortpflanzung des Menschengeschlechts ist'.

3 R. VON SCHERER, *Handbuch des Kirchenrechtes, Bnd. II,* p. 108, quoted by A. W. HOEGEN, *Over den zin van het huwelijk* (Nijmegen, 1935), p. 84:

'Der Entschluss, eine Ehe einzugehen, ist eminent juris privati, Inhalt und Bestand der Ehe aber wurzelt, ganz abgesehen vom Glauben, Befinden und Wollen der Contrahenten, im öffentlichen Recht der Rechtsgemeinschaft, sei es der Kirche, sei es des Staates'. I quote the first edition of HOEGEN's work, which has been followed by a second edition.

mined by law in accordance with its natural aim, the propagation of the human race.

Agapè, eros and orginal sin in LUTHER. The influence of the Thomistic natural-law conception in scholastic Protestant ethics.

In the Reformation there did not provisionally come a permanent fundamental breach with the traditional view of the essence of marriage as a natural law institution.

At first LUTHER made an important attempt to arrive at a better conception. He was the great antagonist of celibacy and to the vow of chastity on the part of priests and was fully alive to the unsatisfactory character of the theories of marriage propagated by medieval Scholasticism. It is true that his definition of the marriage bond as *"conjunctio unius maris et unius feminae inseparabilis, non tantum juris naturae, sed etiam voluntatis et voluptatis, ut ita dicam, divinae"* [1] did not contain a clear characterization of the inner nature of this community. Nevertheless, in the explanation of the sixth commandment of the decalogue in his great Catechism LUTHER emphatically established that in the inner sphère of marriage the bond of conjugal love takes the lead [2]. But the dualistic scheme of nature and grace, in its Lutheran conception, in addition burdened with the traditional Augustinian view of sexual pleasure as an effect of original sin, made it impossible for him to gain a pure insight into the marriage-structure as a whole. The sexual *eros*, as such, was ascribed to the corruption of human nature.

The result was that the internal structural unity of sexual and love union was split up in an irreconcilable dualism. The pre-Thomistic Roman Catholic view of marriage as a "sacrament" was meant

---

[1] Cf. J. KÖSTLIN, *Luthers Theologie* (2nd ed. 1883), p. 482.

[2] 'Ubi enim volumus conjugali castitati locum esse, ibi necesse est ante omnia, ut vir et mulier in amore concordes conversentur, ut alter alterum ex animo mutua quadam benevolentia et fide complectatur. Quod si praesto fuerit, ipsa quoque castitas sua sponte sine mandato consequetur'.

This statement testifies to a conception of married love which is quite different from the purely instrumental view of this love-bond as a necessary means serviceable to the realization of the natural aim of marriage, the procreation. The latter view was for instance defended in the Spanish scholasticism of the 16th century by FRANCISCUS DE VITORIA in his *Reflectiones Theologicae*, where he observes that the natural aim of marriage is not to be realized *"sine mutuo amore et animorum concordia"*. Cf. HANS THIEME, *Natürliches Privatrecht und Spätscholastik* (Zeitschrift der Savignystiftung, Germ. Abt. Vol. 67 (1953) p. 477). Cf. also: WALD. KAWERAU, *Die Reformation und die Ehe* (in Schriften des Vereins f. Reformationsgesch. IX, 1892) and MARIANNE WEBER: *Ehefrau und Mutter in der Rechtsentwicklung* (1907), pp. 282—285.

to sanctify the supposed sinful sexual erotic basis of the conjugal union through the "means of grace of the Church".

This view was rejected by the Reformation, it is true, but in the Lutheran conception the dualism of nature and grace and the relation of sexual pleasure *qua talis* to original sin retained its influence[1].

By appealing to the Thomistic theory of the cosmic purposes of the marriage-institution it seemed to be possible to find a compromise between "sinful nature" and the order of creation. Sexual pleasure was justified in it in a rational "natural" way by an appeal to its procreative purpose. This explains why in the later Lutheran ethics of marriage great emphasis was laid on the divine and relatively natural law character of the marriage institution. It was considered a basic legal ordering of sexual intercourse including the duty of procreation. Nevertheless the reference of marriage to the union of Christ and His Bride, the Church, was not denied[2].

In this way the real marriage-problems were almost entirely relegated to the domain of civil law, or that of consistorial law, and consequently externalized.

Reformed ethics, too, as far as it was affected by Scholasticism, could not get free from the influence of this view[3].

In later times, under the influence of the Enlightenment, the

---

[1] In spite of his fundamental rejection of celibacy and the vow of chastity of monks and nuns, LUTHER thereby remains very much dependent on the Roman Catholic view of marriage as a "less perfect state". This forms a striking contrast with CALVIN's conception. Cf. MARIANNE WEBER, *op. cit.* p. 284.

[2] Cf. TROELTSCH, *Die Soziallehren der Christl. Kirchen und Gruppen* (1919), p. 558.

[3] G. VOETIUS devoted a very elaborate consideration to marriage in his *Politica Ecclesiastica* I, III tract. I. As to the "essentia" and the "properties" of marriage he simply refers to what philosophers wrote about these things (Tract. I, cap. I, 1, the beginning). His own tract is entirely based on the law of nature and on ecclesiastical and civil law. CORNELIS VAN VELZEN in his *Institutiones theologiae practicae,* pars II (Groningen, 1749) sect. II, lib. I, cap. XLVI (p. 654) defines marriage as "*maris et feminae unius voluntariam et indissolubilem conjunctionem, procreationis, castitatis et mutui auxilii gratia institutam.*" And then he continues: "Est haec *conjunctio* juris quadruplicis; Divini nempe vel revelati, cum a Deo sit instituta; *Naturalis* ob animorum et corporum unionem in ea; *Gentium,* quia requirit *consensum* maris et feminae; atque *Civilis* per formam et solennitates, quibus consummatur". It is then explicitly stated that the essential nature of marriage must be inferred from its *purpose,* which is to be found in the procreation of mankind: "Conjugii *Finem,* ex quo illius natura pressius intelligitur, dicimus esse *procreationem* sobolis, adeoque propagationem *generis* humani, quae ex maris et feminae coitu oritur". This is called the chief end of marriage, to which "mutual aid and assistence" and the "*remedium concupiscentiae*" are *subordinated* as less essential purposes!

rationalistic conception of married love as essentially a "blind passion" was especially prejudicial to a correct insight. When this individualistic rationalism found its way in Protestant ethics there was of course no longer any possibility of a really Christian notion of married love as the most intense moral bi-unity. Symptomatic is the utterance recorded by P. KLUCKHOHN [1] of the methodist preacher WILLIAM WHITEFIELD (1714—1770), who boasted that in his proposal of marriage there had been no question of love: "God be praised, if I know my own heart a little I am free of that foolish passion which the world calls love". This shows how far the rationalistic utilitarian spirit of the Enlightenment had penetrated under the guise of Puritan piety [2].

The conception of the marital relationship under the contractual viewpoint in canon law and in the Humanistic doctrine of natural law.

In the individualistic Humanistic doctrine of natural law the genetic juridical form of the marriage bond was absolutized. This resulted in a denaturation of this natural community to a contractual relationship giving rise to mutual *iura in rē, viz.* the right of using one another's body [3]. On the other hand, the contractual viewpoint was not consistently applied as long as one held to the traditional conception of marriage as a permanent union which cannot be dissolved by mutual agreement. This conception was not seriously attacked before the time of the Enlightenment.

The juridical view of the matrimonial bond as a contract giving rise to *iura in rē* was already developed in detail in canon law. But here the contractual viewpoint was not related to the

---

1 *Die Auffassung der Liebe in der Literatur des 18. Jahrh. und in der deutschen Romantik* (Halle, 1922) p. 12.

2 There is no doubt that at first the idea of the sinfulness of sexual love *as such* prevailed in Puritanism and that its connection with a rationalistic utilitarianism was due to the influence of the Enlightenment. However, MARIANNE WEBER is right in saying (*op. cit.* p. 289) that Puritanism did not stop at a utilitarian view of marriage. On the contrary, it was, as she shows, precisely in these circles that the Biblical conception of the internal nature of marriage as a love-union between husband and wife came strongly to the fore.

3 Cf., *e.g.* HUGO DE GROOT, *Inl. H. Rechtsgel.* I, 5, § 1. HEINECCIUS, *El. jur. civ.* tit. *Inst. de Nuptiis,* § 146, GRONOVIUS, *Ad Grotium de Jure Belli ac Pacis* II, 5, 8.

essence of this institution, but only to marriage "*in the state of becoming*". In this restricted sense, as the "*matrimonium in fieri*" (not in *esse*), the marriage contract was viewed as the source of a real right of husband and wife to each other's body and the mutual tradition and acceptance of this right was related to the purpose of procreation as its "*causa*" [1]. Apart from its contractual source the right mentioned was considered to be essential to the matrimonial bond.

Thus the Spanish canonist THOMAS SANCHEZ explicitly taught that the *essence* of marriage is found in the "*traditio corporum*", by means of which each of the partners obtains the ownership of the other's body [2]. KANT, too, was unable to free himself of this view. This is all the more remarkable because in his conception the Humanistic *law of nature* ("*Naturrecht*"), developed under the primacy of the science-ideal, was turned into *a law of reason* ("*Vernunftrecht*"), in which the personality-ideal is given priority. He even detaches the marital relationship from the procreative purpose and exclusively relates it to *mutual subjective sexual enjoyment*. Hence his crude definition of the marriage bond as "the union of two persons of different sexes for the life-long mutual possession of each other's sexual qualities" [3].

Reaction in post-Kantian German Idealism in favour of the conception that marriage is a love-union between husband and wife. The Romantic ideal of "free love" versus the institutional character of marriage.

Not before post-Kantian German Idealism did the immoral character of this conception become apparent under the influence of the ascription of absolute supremacy to the Humanistic personality-ideal. And immediately the love-relation be-

---

[1] Can. 1081 2: 'Consensus matrimonialis est actus voluntatis quo utraque pars tradit et acceptat ius in corpus, perpetuum et exclusivum, in ordine ad actus aptos ad prolis generationem'.

Can. 1111: 'Utrique coniugi ab ipso matrimonii initio aequum ius et officium est quod attinet ad actus proprios coniugalis vitae'.

[2] SANCHEZ, *Disp. de sancto matrimonii sacramento libri decem* (Venet. 1612) 1. 5 disp. 10 nr. 2: 'Matrimonium enim essentialiter consistit in mutua corporum traditione, qua uterque constituitur dominus alterius corporis, ad quod dominium intrinsece consequitur ius et potestas utendi illo corpore'.

[3] *Metaphysik der Sitten, Rechtslehre,* § 24: 'Die Verbindung zweier Personen verschiedenen Geschlechts zum lebenswierigen wechselseitigen Besitz ihrer Geschlechtseigenschaften.

tween the conjugal partners found recognition as the essence of the marriage bond, in direct contrast with the earlier one-sided juridical view.

But now the institutional character of marriage was seriously in danger of being overlooked. For, in an irrationalist-dialectical way, married "love" was considered as a free, subjective higher feeling in which "nature" and "freedom" are dialectically united without any binding to a general norm. Especially in Romanticism this view resulted in the glorification of the ideal of a love that should enjoy life in absolute freedom. This conception implied an explicit opposition to the structural principle of the conjugal bond, to marriage as an institution. The strongly aestheticistic character of the morality of men of genius current among the younger Romantics [1] did not belie its irrationalistic nature, although its protest against the traditional civil-juridical conception of marriage was partly justified.

In FRIEDRICH SCHLEGEL's novel "*Lucinde*" (1799) this Romantic ideal of free love, realizing itself in an high-minded harmony of sexual sensuality and spiritual surrender, found its most prominent literary expression. FICHTE, too, though by no means a Romantic, arrived on account of his actualistic view of sexual love at a conception of marriage which was incompatible with the institutional character of this bi-unitary bond. In a typical functionalistic manner he thought he could deduct the entire essence of marriage from the bare moral notion of love: "If a woman surrenders to a man out of love, the necessary result in a moral sense will be a marriage... The mere concept of love implies that of marriage in the sense indicated" [2]. This not only means ignoring the entire external *civil* juridical aspect of the marriage-bond, but essentially also its *internal* juridical side. In his "*Grundlinien der Philosophie des Rechts*" HEGEL tried to remove this error by considering a *juridical-moral* kind of love as the essence of marriage. Thus the "transitory, capricious and merely subjective" nature inherent in love as "*Empfindung*" (= sensation) should give way to an ideal restriction [3].

---

[1] Cf. volume I, 2, p. 462 ff.

[2] W.W. IV, 330: 'Ergibt sich das Weib aus Liebe einem Manne, so entsteht dadurch moralisch notwendig eine Ehe... Im bloszen Begriff der Liebe ist der der Ehe, in der soeben angegebenen Bedeutung enthalten'.

[3] W.W. VIII (Berlin 1833), 116, 223.

HEGEL must be credited with again emphasizing the normative determination of married love, not only in opposition to the rationalistic-Humanistic conception, which was chiefly naturalistic-psychologistic, but also in contrast with the Romantic ideal of free love.

However, he no more grasped the internal structural principle of the marriage union than did those thinkers whose conception he tried to correct. His view of this bond remains dialectical-functionalistic, *misinterpreting the supra-modal character of its structural law* founded in the plastic horizon of our experience.

The recent reaction in Roman Catholic circles in favour of the recognition of the "primacy of love". The "new tendency" and the encyclical "*Casti connubii*" (1930).

In Roman Catholic circles the earlier scholastic conception of marriage has never been explicitly abandoned. It is, however, highly interesting to find that here, too, an at least implicit reaction has set in which starts from the *primacy of love* in this community. At the same time it sharply opposes the misinterpretation of married love as a transient sensual-erotic inclination.

This "new tendency", whose most gifted representative is DIETRICH VON HILDEBRAND [1] is important also because it runs counter to the older universalistic trends. It emphasizes the *absolutely peculiar* internal character of the marriage bond as the constant love-union between husband and wife.

In his *Die Ehe* (published in 1929) HLDEBRAND writes as follows: 'Love is the *primary meaning* of marriage *according to the creation*, just as its *primary purpose according to the creation* is to produce new human beings. When compared with this primary meaning its function for human society, and certainly its importance for the State, is entirely subordinate. This will become particularly clear to us if we call to mind the peculiar nature of married love...' [2].

I do not overlook the fact that HILDEBRAND's view of the essence of married love as an I-thou-union, (as such far superior to a mere

[1] Cf. A. W. HOEGEN, *Over den zin van het huwelijk* (diss. Nijmegen 1935), pp. 209 ff.

[2] D. von HILDEBRAND, *Die Ehe* (München, 1929), p. 7: 'Die Liebe ist der primäre Schöpfungssinn der Ehe, wie die Entstehung neuer Menschen ihr primärer Schöpfungszweck. Ihre Funktion für die menschliche Gesellschaft, gar nicht zu reden von ihrer Bedeutung für den Staat, sind demgegenüber ganz untergeordnet. Dies wird uns insbesondere deutlich werden, wenn wir uns die Eigenart der ehelichen Liebe ins Bewusztsein rufen...'.

"We-ommunity as the State or the nation) betrays a strong influence of modern personalist and existentialistic tendencies in immanence-philosophy.

On the other hand, from a radical-Christian standpoint, we must raise serious objections to many essential parts of his views.

Let me mention only some critical points. HILDEBRAND hypostatizes the masculine and the feminine principle in creation to a metaphysical difference of essence. This leads him to detaching the inner meaning-structure of married love from its temporal biotic foundation in the organic difference between the sexes. This is a metaphysical speculation, which, of course, does not become more acceptible by a typically Roman-Catholic concentration of the metaphysical feminine principle in the Holy Virgin [1]. His conception that the individual persons in marriage have been interwoven by the conjugal bond into an actual "I-thou" union is essentially dependent on BUBER's personalism. It results in the view that this union transcends all other temporal societal relationships since it implies a *central* contact between husband and wife, a real *meeting* in the central sphere of existence. This means an absolutization of the marriage bond which in my opinion is incompatible with the Biblical standpoint.

We have had to reject the Thomistic teleological-metaphysical axiology, but we can no more accept its modern irrationalistic- romanizing modification in HILDEBRAND's thesis: 'A community ranks higher in proportion to the good which determines the scope of its meaning, or closely connected with this, in proportion to the depth of its point of unity in the human personality, and to the extent to which love plays an essential part in it, and finally in proportion to the directness with which the unifying principle is concerned with our supra-natural destination [2]. There is also the specifically Roman Catholic distinction between marriage as a "natural union" and as a "sacrament of grace" which is unacceptable from the Reformatory Christian standpoint.

But in spite of all these serious objections it may be gratefully acknowledged that on many points the writer voices the Biblical-Christian conception of the conjugal bond as a typical and incomparable institutional love-union between husband and wife, as the expression of the eternal love of Christ towards the Church as His Bride.

In this respect he implicitly contradicts the traditional scholastic theory. This attitude also enables him to oppose the subjectivistic romantic view of married love with its revolutionary consequences.

---

[1] Op. cit. p. 11 ff.

[2] Op. cit. p. 42: 'Eine Gemeinschaft steht um so höher, je gröszer das Gut ist, das ihren Sinnbereich bildet oder was damit eng zusammenhängt, je tiefer die Stelle in der Person ist, an der der Einheitspunkt liegt, je gröszer und wesenhafter die Rolle ist, die die Liebe in ihr spielt und endlich je unmittelbarer das einigende Prinzip mit unserer übernatürlichen Bestimmung zu tun hat'.

HILDEBRAND lays due emphasis on the fact that the *tendency to be indissoluble* as long as life lasts is naturally implied in the very meaning of marriage as the closest love-union [1]. The traditional scholastic theory had lost sight of this, through seeking the only guarantee for the institutional character of this bond in the legal sphere. HILDEBRAND has also sharply realized that the "institution" as such retains its character *as a law*.

Real married love indeed postulates a union *for life* in which the temporal existences of the partners are interwoven into the closest possible temporal unity, which is not possible without conjugal *fidelity*.

In virtue of the divine world-order this love necessarily appeals to an internal juridical relation. But the latter is placed under the leading of love and not *vice versa*. If this love is lacking, the internal conjugal union is really absent. In the second volume we have shown in detail the modal difference and inter-modal meaning-coherence between the sexual *eros*, as a biotic drive and psychical feeling, and the moral *agapè*, as normative married love. Of course it is the latter which is meant by the apostle Paul when he stresses the duty of the marriage-partners to love each other[2]. In fact this was not denied by the older Roman Catholic moral philosophers [3]. But under the influence of the Aristotelian psychology, love was here primarily conceived of as an affect of pleasure in a corresponding good, originating in a sensory knowledge of this good, which rouses the sensual appetitive power.

"Spiritual love" — subject to norms — was held to derive from "spiritual knowledge" *through the effect of reason* (νοῦς) *on the* appetitive faculty. This resulted in an elimination of the modal sphere-sovereignty of love, as the nuclear meaning of morality. Love was levelled down to a general analogical concept comprehending every natural appetitive tendency to realize a good [4]. THOMAS' conception of "spiritual" love was no more modally defined in its meaning than his view of sexual *eros* and his concept of the good.

In opposition to this, the modern trend has maintained the specific meaning of love in contradistinction to sensual passion.

---

[1] *Op. cit.* p. 36: 'Welche Oberflächlichkeit nicht zu verstehen, dass die Tendenz auf Unauflöslichkeit aus dem Sinn der Ehe als engster Liebesgemeinschaft von selbst hervorgeht, sondern sie aus Nützlichkeitsgründen ableiten zu wollen'. [How superficial to infer this tendency of marriage towards indissolubility from utility-grounds and not to understand that it is a consequence of the meaning of marriage as the closest love-union.]

[2] Cf. *Ephesians* 5 : 25—33.

[3] Cf. CATHREIN, *Moralphilosophie* II (6e Aufl. 1924), p. 428.

[4] Cf. THOMAS AQUINAS, *Summa Theologiae* I, 2 ae, q, 26—28. In its widest sense THOMAS defines love as: *'aliquid ad appetitum pertinens, cum utriusque objectum sit bonum'* (q. 26 art. 1). This definition explicitly comprises even the natural "appetite" (taken in the Aristotelian sense) of a heavy object *"ad locum medium"*, as *"amor naturalis"*!

In a short time the new tendency gained ground in Roman Catholic circles, so that, to a certain extent at least, it found official recognition in the well-known encyclical *Casti Connubii,* issued by pope Pius XI on the 31st of December 1930. This encyclical frankly assigned "primacy of honour" *(principatus nobilitatis)* to married love in a Christian marriage. All this was in striking contrast with what happened in Protestant circles two years later, when the moral theologian EMIL BRUNNER, published his book *Das Gebot und die Ordnungen,* in which love, if viewed as the basis of marriage, was called a "sandy ground" and marital love was identified with erotic inclination!

The internal deepening of the marriage bond by the formation of a family.

After having gained a sufficient insight into the inner structure of the marriage-bond we shall now try to deepen our insight into its inner coherence with the family. According to the divine order of creation marriage is intentionally adapted to the family relationship. In the light of our previous explanation this means that marriage is enriched and deepened by its natural interweaving with the family relationship, and conjugal love is deepened and enriched in parental love. How is this to be understood?

We have rejected the opinion that in conjugal and family relationships the central I-ness of human personality is interwoven with that of the other members of these communities, and is only thereby formed and deepened.

The central religious interweaving of the human egos is independent of temporal bonds, although the converse is not true.

There is no doubt that the selfhoods of the conjugal partners are for all eternity interwoven in the new root of life, Christ Jesus, if they are really united in Him. This is the religious fulness of meaning of marriage. But in this religious interwovenness Christian marriage partners become aware of belonging to one another, not as husband and wife in the temporal marriage bond [1], but as children of one Father in Christ Jesus. Here on earth they may only belong to each other "as though they did not" [2]. For temporal ties, even the most intense in this life, are perishable; the invisible union with Christ is eternal.

[1] Cf. *Matth.* 22 : 30; *Mark.* 12 : 25.
[2] Cf. 1 *Corinth* 7 : 29—31.

But this religious union should find its typical expression in the temporal bond of the marriage-partners.

When the marriage bond has expanded into a family relationship the former is enriched and deepened in its meaning by its close interweaving with the latter, because its bi-unity in conjugal love has produced a unity in plurality.

In the conjugal union, as such, the expression of the personality in the temporal existence of each of the married persons is enriched, enlarged and completed by that of the other. A woman becomes "wife" in the full sense of the word only in the conjugal union with her husband, and *vice versa*. And the expression of the personality in the bi-unitary bond assumes a wider and deeper perspective in the multi-unitary bond of the family.

Yet it is not possible to deduce the essential internal structure of the marriage-bond from the "cosmic purpose of propagation", as was done by THOMAS AQUINAS. This traditional universalistic construction, amply discussed above, necessarily results in an eradication of the boundaries between the marriage union and the family relationship. This is evident from THOMAS' statement that posterity is essential to the marital bond [1]. Such a construction must naturally restrict itself to a deduction of the general *institution* of marriage from the purpose of procreation. For it cannot be denied that individual marriages that remain childless still retain their character as conjugal bonds. But the structural law and the subjective marital bond subjected to it can never be separated from each other, so that in its application to the factual relationships THOMAS' view leads to constructions of a very artificial and internally contradictory character. We need only mention his explanations of the relation between the individual act of sexual uniting and the "objective procreative purpose". THOMAS concedes that sexual intercourse in a barren marriage, or in general such which is not carried on with a concrete procreative intention, is morally permissible. But then it will not do to seek the inner essence of the conjugal institution in the aim of propagation [2].

Then the internal structure of the marriage bond, in its difference from the family relationship, irresistibly forces itself upon us.

---

[1] "Constat quod proles est essentialissimum in matrimonio" (4 *Sent.* dist. 31, q. I, a. 3, c).

[2] THOMAS AQUINAS conceives the procreative purpose only as the essential purpose of marriage in an "objective" institutional sense.

The fundamental difference between animal mating and the human marital bond is that the former does not occur within a communal relationship which in its inner nature is independent of propagation. As soon as the animal offspring is no longer in need of the parental care, or the mating lacks a procreative effect, the couple separates.

The marriage bond on the contrary, normally embraces husband and wife for life, independent of the natural procreative end.

No "rational procreative purpose" can justify the sexual consummation of marriage in an ethical sense, but only married love sanctified in Christ. This love (and not a utilitarian kind of thought) is the true regulator and educator of married sexual life towards temperance and chastity.

In the divine order of creation, marriage is the only ordered *way* to form a family; marriage and family are mutually adapted to each other. But they retain their own peculiar internal structure and value. If this is ignored or misinterpreted, our marital morality will result in a labyrinth of contradictions of our own creating, and the lucid simplicity of the divine ordinance [1] will be obscured.

The internal structure of marital authority.

Only the insight into the structural principle of the marriage bond as a whole enables us to understand the internal nature of marital authority. The traditional defenders as well as the individualistic opponents of the latter have so very often fundamentally misinterpreted it. This authority is not at all qualified by its external civil juridical function. In this latter function *e.g.*, the husband's authorization is required for the validity of legal acts of the wife, and the husband has the management of his wife's separate property, as long as civil law does not recognize the wife's complete competence to perform legal acts [2].

No doubt this civil juridical function is not completely separate from the internal structure of marital authority, but it remains something formal and external with respect to the latter. *A fortiori* this internal structure, as such, has nothing to

[1] This word is taken in the Biblical sense, cf. *Psalm* 119 : 91, of the Authorized (King James) Version.

[2] In English law all the wife's property is separate, but "restrained from anticipation", so that she cannot alienate it, nor anticipate the income of it.

do with the historically founded form of the *manus mariti* in old Roman *jus civile,* which individualistic opponents of marital authority often consider as its objectionable prototype.

The Roman legal concept of *agnatic patrician "familia"*, in which the wife was included only by passing into *manum mariti,* merely comprised the juridical aspect of an as yet undifferentiated societal relationship. This was the domestic community of the *pater familias,* into which the marital and family bonds proper were only enkaptically interwoven. The "family" itself was part of the patrician gentilicial community, which, as we shall see, was not founded "in nature" either. In the later juridical development the union of the conjugal bond and the agnatic domestic community as represented by the "*manus*" marriage, was gradually broken. As a consequence the old "*manus*" entirely disappeared from the civil juridical aspect of the Roman marriage.

The "*manus mariti*" in its autocratic semi-political, semi-proprietary structure, in which the husband even had a *jus vitae ac necis* assigned to him with respect to his wife, cannot be inferred from the internal structural principle of the marriage bond. This authority was only connected with natural marriage in an *external enkapsis.* The internal structure of marital authority can only be understood from the typical love-union between the conjugal partners in which, according to the divine order of creation, the husband is "the head of the wife". He has to *lead* her, but by no means to *dominate* her, because the female part in the bi-unitary bond is perfectly equivalent (though not *equal)* to the male element and ought to be fully recognized as such. The authoritative relation in its normative internal structure does not in any way detract from the intensity and closeness of the love-relations between husband and wife. On the contrary, marital authority plays an essential rôle in them [1].

Marital authority and the normal emotional aspect of matrimony. Can psychology speak of "normal"? Cultural influences on female emotional life.

It cannot be denied that normal female emotional life in the marital bond wants to find support and guidance in the husband, and is disappointed if they are lacking. Also in a man's normal

---

[1] Cf. *Ephesians* V, where Saint Paul strongly emphasizes this rôle of marital authority in the love relationship.

affective life the instinctive impulse to support and lead corresponds to these female needs.

On a functionalistic standpoint the question may of course be asked: what is a normal male and female life of feeling? Then the deviations from what we have explained above are treated as phenomena of perfectly the same value as those corresponding to this standard.

But then it should be remembered that it is no longer possible to speak of the structure of *male* and *female* feeling; for these structures in the psychical aspect of human existence cannot be approached apart from the normative structural functions. They are included in the act-structure of a human body though, in a restrictive or closed sense, they also function in its lower animal structure qualified by instinctive psychical impulses. No doubt there occur female feelings in men, and male feelings in women. But this cannot be established without a standard for male and female feeling. If we eliminate the coherence between the psychical and the later normative structural functions, all the human individuality structures in the feeling-modus are levelled out. Then we are only left with the modal-functional coherence between the most heterogeneous psychic phenomena.

It is no doubt correct to say that in the transcendental direction feeling in man and woman is indissolubly bound up with its *historical formation* in the different cultural periods. A number of psychical differences between the sexes depend on the cultural influences of many successive generations. Modern psychology has rightly set these facts in the light. *But this state of affairs is exactly an indication of the indissoluble coherence between the psychic function of feeling and the normative structural functions in human existence.* These facts can never be argued against the constancy of the internal-structural principle in the emotional relations between husband and wife. For this principle is already pre-supposed in the historical formation of male and female feeling in marriage.

Cultural education cannot change the male structure into a female one, nor the other way round. Only a fundamental encroachment upon the biotic structure of the human body would be able to accomplish such a structural alteration because sex difference has a typical biotic foundation. As long as psychology continues to speak of a male and a female feeling-structure, it will be in need of a normative structural principle which itself is independent of the concrete historical development.

To point out effeminacy in a man's emotional life, implies a normative structural principle lying at the foundation of this statement.

The structural authoritative moment in the internal juridical, aesthetic, and social (intercourse) functions of the conjugal bond.

The structure of authority in the marital community also has its internal juridical aspect. Even in the best of marital relationships there may occur a difference of opinion about certain matters. Yet the partners will have to come to a decision if their union is to remain intact. According to the internal structural principle, the juridical competence to make a decision belongs to the husband as the head of the conjugal bond.

But the very structure of marital authority does not permit its autocratic exercise. Marriage is a bi-unitary community under the typical leading of conjugal love; it is not a "State in miniature". That is why political forms of government such as monarchy and democracy cannot be transplanted in the internal domain of matrimony. A wife ought to be co-responsible for such decisions. In internal domestic affairs she is entrusted with the daily management of the household, and not her husband. But also outside of the narrow circle of household affairs the internal structure of the marriage bond requires a loving consultation between the marriage partners with full respect for the internal competence and responsibility of the husband as the "head".

Civil law, though fundamentally different in character from the internal matrimonial law, should, nevertheless, respect this internal structure of marital authority insofar as the latter also functions "enkaptically" in the civil juridical relations.

From this point of view it is not recommendable, in case a married couple differ in opinion, to give the civil judge an unrestricted competence to decide.

In this way, the civil legislator would elevate the internal disturbance of the matrimonial union to a *civil juridical rule.* Even from a pedagogical point of view this is a dangerous attitude. Of course, when the internal bi-unitary bond in marriage has been subjectively realized, be it in an imperfect and sinful way, the introduction of the civil judge as the supreme power of decision above the marriage partners will not have any practical sense. But this bond may be disturbed to such a degree that with regard to internal marital affairs the marriage partners are opposed to each other as parties in a civil law-suit. Only in such cases may the view arise that an impartial judge must be entrusted with the decision. The question in how far a task is to be ascribed to the civil judge in this situation will be discussed in a later context. We shall then try to find the internal boundaries set to civil law in the enkaptic structural interlacements within the juridical law-sphere.

*

The internal structure of marital authority is also expressed in the aesthetical law-sphere. The original matrimonial harmony presupposes the complete concord of the male and female elements in the conjugal relations, in accordance with their own structural character. The wife should not play the typical leading part of the husband. If she does take the lead in a general sense, the situation will excite our aesthetic displeasure. The consideration that perhaps the husband is a weakling and that this fact necessitated the wife to take the lead, cannot obviate our impression of disharmony.

The structure of authority also expresses itself in the social and in the lingual aspect. The positive, historically founded social and lingual forms of intercourse between husband and wife differ, of course, according to place and time. The forms used at the time of the patriarch Abraham cannot do duty in our days. The utterance of St. Peter about this question in his first epistle[1] does not mean to contradict this state of affairs. But the *structural principle* of marriage, which is not dependent on the historical development, should find expression also in the internal social[2] and lingual relations. These relations ought to be very tender and close, but the leading position of the husband should constantly be given expression in them, which is something different from the required mutual respect for each other's person. As soon as in the internal marital union the social and the symbolic respect for the husband as the *head* of the community has been lost, we are confronted with a subjective infringement of the internal vital law of marriage.

---

[1] Ch. 3 : 6.

[2] This term is meant here in the sense of the modal aspect of social intercourse.

The original biotic foundation of marital authority, which cannot be interpreted as its ground of justification.

In the last instance marital authority has its typical foundation in the aspect in which marriage itself is originally founded, *viz.* the biotic sphere. The leading rôle of the husband in sexual intercourse, and the passive receptive part of the wife form the original basis of the meaning-individuality of marital authority in the retrocipatory direction of cosmic time. In the Middle Ages this functional-biotic basis of marital authority was misconceived in many respects. This was due to the influence of primitive biological notions derived from ARISTOTLE about the genesis of the female offspring in consequence of a defeciency in the natural process. Nature was supposed to show an androcratic tendency in the procreative process. As a consequence the wife was thought to be essentially imperfect and by nature subjected to the husband. For this reason THOMAS AQUINAS calls woman *"mas occasionatus"* according to her genesis, which is in perfect agreement with ARISTOTLE's views. As a marriage partner she was supposed to be only *"aliquid viri"* and not *"civis simpliciter"* [1]. Apart from these Aristotelian and medieval misconceptions, it stands to reason that in the light of our cosmonomic Idea the "*justification*" of marital authority cannot be found in its original biotic foundation as such. Marital authority has no other justification than the divine ordinance revealed in the normative structural principle of this community as a whole. On the Christian standpoint there can be no question of a "rational justification" in the Platonic and Aristotelian sense, or in that of the Humanistic theory of natural law.

The divine order of creation is not grounded in "reason", but inversely human "reason" is grounded in the divine order. Theoretic "reason" can only try to trace the structural principles that God has ordained for human society in His temporal world-order and which alone enable us to experience the factual societal relationships *in their different inner nature.* Apart from the structural principle of the marital bond, philosophy will seek in vain for a tenable justification of the husband's authority in its typical character.

---

[1] Cf. A. W. HOEGEN, *op. cit.,* p. 131, with the literature and sources mentioned there.

The structural principle should also be the ὑπόθεσις of ethnological researches after marital relations. The interpretation of the facts in accordance with their meaning-structure and the positivistic attitude in science.

This structure cannot be ignored with impunity neither in practical social life nor in social science and philosophy.

Ethnological research after the internal marital conditions in different primitive societies should also be based on this structure as its ὑπόθεσις. Then we shall avoid the error of confounding the genuine marital relations with societal relationships of an entirely different structure and we shall no longer run the risk of repeatedly misinterpreting the facts.

At this point the supposedly neutral positivistic conception of science will accuse our standpoint of intruding "metaphysically founded evaluations" into the investigations of the "facts". At a deeper level this fundamental contrast hides a basically different view of experiential reality. "Facts" can only be conceived in their *structural meaning*. If the attempt is made to examine the facts of societal relations apart from their normative structural principles on account of a naturalistic or positivistic historicist prejudice, the result will be a falsification of the data.

Ethnological research after conjugal and family relations is concerned with subjective phenomena within realized supra-arbitrary institutions, which cannot be understood apart from their internal structural principle. Neither the contradictory notion of merely arbitrary ("empirical") norms, nor that of constructive "ideal types" as applied by MAX WEBER, can replace the genuine structural principles of matrimonial and family relationships. The nominalistic prejudice in positivistic science inevitably leads to a complete eradication of the fundamental boundaries between the various structures of human society.

The misinterpretation of the so-called matriarchal phenomena in the older evolutionist ethnology.

The older naturalistic evolutionist tendency made the most consistent attempt to eliminate the structural principles of marriage and family as the *hypothesis* of ethnological research. But it was exactly this trend which indulged in the most phantastic interpretations of the facts. Its evolutionistic construction of the development of marriage and family life was presently popularized by the social democratic theorists ENGELS and BEBEL. It was founded on a complete misunderstanding of the so-called *matriarchal phenomena.*

This misconception had been introduced into ethnology by LEWIS H. MORGAN, who was strongly influenced by the Swiss law-historian J. J. BACHOFEN, though the latter was a romantic thinker rather than a Darwinian evolutionist. MORGAN's evolutionistic theory has by now been generally rejected as unscientific. But we may establish that he would never have construed such erroneous conceptions from a defective material of ethnological facts, if he had not first purposely eliminated the basic structural principles of marriage and family.

The theory of matriarchy was propounded by BACHOFEN in his famous work *Das Mutterrecht, eine Untersuchung über die Gynäkokratie der alten Welt nach ihrer religiösen und rechtlichen Natur* (Stuttgart, 1861). He tried to prove that human sexual intercourse had started with an initial stage of absolute promiscuity. For this thesis he adduced the "matriarchal phenomena", already found among various peoples of antiquity (*e.g.*, the Lycians). These peoples computed kinship, and often the right of inheritance, from the mother and not from the father. BACHOFEN explained this by assuming that originally sexual relations were so irregular that the family was formed with the mother for its centre and not with the unknown father.

From such conditions original matriarchy or gynarchy developed since the invention of agriculture, which must be ascribed to women, so that the original family was not patriarchal but matriarchal. Patriarchy was the next stage in the development of human family life.

BACHOFEN set forth this view in the mythological symbolic forms of late Romanticism. His theory was completely rationalized and systematically elaborated in a Darwinist sense by the American ethnologist LEWIS MORGAN.

According to the latter the human family passed through the following stages of development: 1) unlimited promiscuity of sexual intercourse; 2) the kinship family (in which only sexual intercourse between ascendants and descendants is prohibited); 3) the "punalua family" (sexual intercourse is forbidden between brothers and sisters as well; the women of one half of the tribe are accessible to the men of the other and vice versa; group-marriage); 4) matriarchal "syndasmic" family (the initial stage of individual marriages, polygamy, uncertainty about the father); 5) patriarchy, a polygamous family; 6) a monogamous individual marriage.

This constructive evolutionist theory (criticized already in its palmy days by distinguished ethnologists like C. N. STÄRKE, E. WESTERMARCK and E. GROSSE) has been completely refuted by the ethnological researches of Father W. SCHMIDT, R. J. SWANTON, X. R. H. LOWIE and others, so that it can no longer be taken seriously. In his book *Die Stellung der Pygmäenvölker in der Entwicklungs-*

geschichte der Menschheit (Stuttgart, 1910), which should be consulted with a critical mind, SCHMIDT shows that with the pygmean peoples monogamous marriage is predominant. This is all the more important as the pygmies are among the comparatively oldest extant representatives of the human race [1]. This fact has at any rate been established, however much opinions may differ with regard to the "problem of the pygmies". As for North-America, the territory which was supposed chiefly to supply the material for MORGAN's theory, R. J. SWANTON showed the absolute untenability of the matriarchy and promiscuity theory as early as the year 1905 [2]. And the well-known American ethnologist R. H. LOWIE in his book *Primitive Society* explicitly states: 'Sexual communism (after the manner of the "group-marriage") as a condition replacing individual marriage, is nowhere to be found at present. And the evidence of its earlier occurrence must be rejected as insufficient' [3].

With reference to the bilateral family the same author remarks: 'In a word, the bilateral family (*i.e.* the family consisting of husband and wife and their children) is an absolutely universal unit of human societal life'.

It was particularly the introduction of the "culture-historical" method in genetic ethnological research which caused the complete defeat of the older constructive evolutionist theory. For it put an end to the arbitrary grouping of facts and their interpretation according to an *a priori* evolutionist scheme.

The "*Kulturkreislehre*" [4] and the normative evaluations of married and family life among primitive peoples.

The culture-historical trend in modern ethnology is represented by two schools, *viz.* the so-called "*Kulturkreislehre*" and the so-called critical school of the American scholar FRANZ BOAS.

The point of difference between these schools concerns an old question in ethnology, namely whether or not the occurrence of similar cultural elements with different primitive peoples is to be ascribed to derivation. BASTIAN and his followers answered this question in the negative. According to him the different peoples have produced the "elementary principle" of their culture, for instance of their technical level of development, their armament, their cult

[1] Cf. W. KOPPERS, *Ehe und Familie* in Handwörterbuch der Soziologie, hrg. v. A. Vierkandt (Stuttgart, 1931) p. 112. Compare also the critical remarks made by F. GRAEBNER in his *Methode der Ethnologie* (Heidelberg, 1911) p. 39 note 1 and p. 124 on SCHMIDT's book.

[2] *The Social Organisation of American Tribes* in American Anthropologist, N.S. VII, 663—673.

[3] R. H. LOWIE, *Primitive Society* (1st ed. New York 1920; 2nd ed. 1929, pp. 58—59).

[4] *I.e.* the doctrine of "cultural circles".

etc., independent of one another. RATZEL, on the other hand, tried to prove that the propagation of similar elements of culture is to be explained from emigration of peoples and from derivation. He set ethnology the task to trace the origin of the different primitive cultures. RATZEL himself, however, remained entangled in a naturalist milieu-theory which tried to understand the cultures in the first place as products of geographical factors.

This naturalist viewpoint was broken through when the famous investigator of Africa, LEO FROBENIUS, in his book *Ursprung der Afrikanischen Kultur* (1898) applied RATZEL's idea of derivation to entire cultures and began to avail himself of a culture-historical method. Thus he became the founder of the so-called "*Kulturkreislehre*" as it is adhered to by students like ANKERMANN, FR. GRAEBNER, EDUARD HAHN, W. FOY, Father WILHELM SCHMIDT, W. KOPPERS and others. The centre of this school is Vienna, but it also has its adherents in France. The "*Kulturkreislehre*" wants to trace the genealogical coherence between the so-called "cultural circles" which it supposes it has established. According to its adherents ethnology belongs to the science of history. Together with the science of primeval history, it should contribute to the description of world-history by providing a scientific picture of the earlier developmental phases of humanity.

The followers of BOAS (LOWIE, MARETT, SWANTON, GOLDENWEISER and others) agree with the "*Kulturkreislehre*" in the acceptance of historical coherences on the ground of the occurrence of similar cultural elements with different primitive peoples. But they reject the method of so-called complex formation which results in the construction of cultural orbits embracing even peoples that are completely separated geographically. This is the point where doubtless BASTIAN's view of the independent origin of the "elementary principle" of the different cultures shows its influence.

The "*Kulturkreislehre*" has undubitably devised an impressive conception of the developmental coherences of primitive cultures, although there are many hypothetical elements in its genealogical construction, especially with respect to the delimitation of the "cultural circles". SCHMIDT's view according to which the pygmaean peoples are to be considered as the original representatives of the human race, remains highly problematical. In addition, in a later phase of the development of his doctrine he was obliged to abandon certain fundamental theses, as, for instance, that concerning the complete lack of totemistic organization with the pygmaean peoples.

Besides it must be observed that, notwithstanding the acceptance of the culture-historical method, the one-sided method of causal explanation of whole societal institutions has continued to play a considerable rôle in this doctrine. Thus, in a rationalist way, KOPPERS tried to explain matriarchal law and totem belief from merely economic factors.

From our own standpoint the main objection to this genealogical doctrine of the cultural orbits concerns its tendency to level out the fundamental difference between "closed" and "opened" cultures insofar as it also includes the latter in the programme of its ethnological researches. For its method of defining the "cultural orbits" ("*Kulturkreise*") according to their spatial areas of validity and their order of succession in the historical order of time remains entirely oriented to the primitive circles of culture.

According to its temporal criterion "mixed and contact cultures" are invariably of a secondary nature everywhere, and therefore of a later date than their two cultural components which are supposed to be of a "primary character" [1]. This thesis implies that the "cultural circles" first developed in complete isolation before getting into historical contact [2].

This may be true for primitive closed cultures whose mutual contact and fusion generally does not elevate them above a "closed cultural level" although they show different stages of development and a relative advance in technical industry, in societal forms, *etc.* But if the same method were applied to cultures that have been taken up by the trend of expanded and deepened cultural development, this view would be false and unhistorical. Not any of these cultures have been able to develop from within the seclusion of their isolation before they came into contact with the others. In other words, only in the mutual contact with the others could the peculiar character of each culture be developed [3]. Here lies the fundamental difference between historical science proper and a genetic ethnology which follows cultural scientific methods: the former can do nothing with "cultural orbits" defined according to the ethnological viewpoint, because they are essentially of an isolated and static character (even the so-called secondary types).

These "*Kulturkreise*" lack the typical deepened individuality revealed only in disclosed cultural development. The seven great "cultural orbits", analysed by W. Schmidt and W. Koppers in their standard work *Völker und Kulturen* [4], are irrelevant and useless from a really *historical* scientific viewpoint.

The ethnological conception of time entirely lacks the deepened meaning of the time of disclosed historical development. In the latter the succession of cultures can never be an exterior order of *prior*

---

[1] Cf. Graebner, *op. cit.* p. 127, and p. 140 (cf. Ratzel, *Anthropogeographie* II, p. 651 ff) and W. Schmidt in *Völker und Kulturen* I (1924) p. 69.

[2] Cf. Schmidt, *op. cit.* p. 72 ff. Compare, however, Graebner, *op. cit.* p. 159.

[3] Cf. Volume II, part 1, Ch. III § 5, pp. 273 ff. In the "*Kulturkreislehre*" the influence of Frobenius' biologistic conception of development is undeniable to my mind.

[4] *viz.* 1) the exogamous-monogamous orbits; 2) those characterized by exogamy and totemistic sib-organization; 3) those characterized by exogamy together with the equality of husband and wife; 4) the exogamous patriarchal and 5) the exogamous matriarchal orbits; 6) those characterized by free matriarchal legal relations; 7) those characterized by free patriarchal legal relations.

and *posterior*, or an exterior mingling of elementary cultural complexes. It always shows *interpenetration, overlapping* and *mutual formation*.

Especially SCHMIDT shows a lack of insight into the fundamental difference between historical and ethnological thought.

This defeciency appears from his rejection of the criterion that historical science proper only has to examine those cultures of which written documents or inscriptions in stone have come down to us [1].

In our second volume we have explained that the historical law-sphere discloses its symbolical anticipatory sphere only in deepened historical development [2]. When the objective symbolical signifying of a cultural development is lacking, there is no certainty at all that the lingual anticipatory sphere in the historical aspect has really been opened, and that in the bearers of this culture the historical consciousness has awakened [3]. We leave aside the possibility that there may be a reliable (non-mythological) oral historical tradition. But when all these things are absent, even the restrictive development of technical skill [4] and a more complicated formation of human society [5] cannot raise cultural life above the rigid restrictive level of civilization.

It is an undoubted fact that the introduction of a cultural scientific method in ethnology has meant a great gain. Once for all the

---

[1] Cf. W. SCHMIDT, *op. cit.* p. 40, where he quotes with complete agreement the utterance of RATZEL: "Die Zeit ist nicht mehr fern, wo man keine Weltgeschichte mehr schreiben wird, ohne die Völker zu berühren, die man bisher als ungeschichtliche betrachtete, weil sie keine geschriebenen oder in Stein gemeiszelten Nachrichten hinterlassen haben. Geschichte ist " Handlung"! Wie wenig bedeutet daneben Schreiben oder Nichtschreiben, wie ganz nebensächlich ist neben der Tat des Wirkens und Schaffens das Wort ihrer Beschreibung". [The time is not far when no history of the world will be written without referring to the peoples that up to now have been treated as non-historical, because they have not left any written documents or inscriptions in stone. History is action! How unimportant are writings or the absence of writings in comparison with this essential characteristic. In comparison with action and production, how insignificant is the word that describes them].

GRAEBNER's viewpoint is more critical in this respect. He nowhere denies the difference between ethnology and historical science. Cf. his *op. cit.* pp. 163 ff.

[2] Cf. Volume II, part I, pp. 284 ff.

[3] This is not saying that the historian should restrict his researches to the written records, as FUSTEL DE COULANGES did in his *Histoire des institutions politiques de l'ancienne France*. The results of excavations, *etc.*, may shed a surprising light on the written sources.

Cf. E. FUETER, *Geschichte der neueren Historiographie* (3rd ed. 1936) p. 564 and 602 ff.

[4] *E.g.*, in agriculture, in the construction of tools and arms, *etc.*

[5] *E.g.*, in totem-clans, and in a greater measure of differentiation of the tribal organs.

idea has been given up that "primitive" peoples ("*Naturvölker*") have no history at all. It is also a gain that this method broke with the constructive evolutionist manner of thought. Quite a different point is the question as to whether different adherents of the "*Kulturkreislehre*" have sufficiently freed themselves from this evolutionism, and if especially the economic factors are not too much treated as if they influenced societal relations in a natural-causal way. In this connection the very just remarks of the North-American ethnologist R. H. LOWIE in his book *Primitive Society* with respect to such economic explanations are worth listening to [1].

Our objections raised against the "*Kulturkreislehre*" chiefly referred to the eradication of the boundaries between ethnology and history proper. But we want especially to emphasize the great merits of various adherents of this view (W. SCHMIDT, KOPPERS, and others) in their researches after the marriage, family and kinship relations among primitive peoples. These Roman-Catholic scholars seriously tried to base their investigations on the structural principle of these communities as given in the order of the creation [2]. It is true that their characterization of these relationships as "*Sympathieverbände*" (bonds of sympathy) is still too vague. Perhaps as a consequence of the influence of the traditional scholastic view they approach the internal marriage and family relations among primitive races still *too* much from their external popular juridical regulations. Nevertheless, these authors have penetrated to the insight that, according to their internal structure, these relationships cannot be conceived apart from their normative structural law but must be qualified as typical love-bonds. And this again and again causes them involuntarily to distinguish between the external and the internal functions of these communities. For a correct interpretation of the facts this is methodologically very important [3].

As SCHMIDT and KOPPERS maintain the supra-arbitrary structural principles of marriage and family relations, they also point to the fatal influence of some external forms within which these relations have to be realized among the different primitive peoples of the

---

[1] R. H. LOWIE, *Primitive Society* (1929), pp. 184 ff.

[2] On the other hand these investigators handle an extremely undefined conception of the State. W. SCHMIDT, *op. cit.* 1. 147, simply identifies the State with the "totality of all the purposive organizations" (*die Gesamtheit aller Zweckverbände*), in contrast to the "sympathetic relationships" *(Sympathieverbände)* such as marriage, family and kinship.

[3] This does not detract from the fact that in the work of SCHMIDT we are also confronted with constructive interpretations of the facts, against which GRAEBNER has already warned.

[4] According to the "*Kulturkreislehre*", the temporal order of succession of these cultures is as follows: 1) original primitive cultures (of the simplest and comparatively oldest race); 2) the primary cultures; 3) mixed or secondary cultures. In this ethnological time-schema the seven great "*Kulturkreise*" are arranged.

so-called primary and secondary cultures[1]. These influences are fatal to the internal solidarity, purity and intimacy of these communal bonds. Of course, from the "anti-axiological" point of view in ethnology this is only an objectionable confusion of science and a world- and life-view.

The truth is, however, that the supposedly unbiased scientific view starts from a *nominalistic a priori, viz.* that the subjective human societal relations can be grasped apart from their supra-arbitrary structures of individuality.

Even on the biological natural scientific standpoint it is unavoidable to state that certain external environmental factors are destructive to a living organism. How then should it be contrary to the scientific standpoint when the Christian ethnologist establishes that certain external factors (often of a typical historical foundation and economic qualification), like matriarchy and polyandry, have a disturbing influence upon the internal marital and family relations? Could the reason be that such axiological statements presuppose the handling of normative structural principles in ethnological research, which should be eliminated in order to conceive the social facts in an unbiased way? But we have seen that apart from these normative structural principles the facts do not reveal their true societal meaning.

The total elimination of these principles which only enable us to speak of marriage and family in a univocal scientific sense, makes any exact ethnological investigation of the factual marital and family relations impossible. The nominalistic prejudice which lies at the foundation of this elimination is not warranted by science, and is bound to result in a continual misinterpretation of the facts.

The matriarchal phenomena in the light of the cultural-scientific method of investigation and of the theory of the individuality structures.

The modern cultural scientific school in ethnology has brought to light that among the comparatively oldest extant primitive peoples marriage and family are carrying on a very vigorous actual existence in their internal structure of typical biotically founded love-unions. This is quite contrary to the teachings of the evolutionist theory. Among the pygmies, and pigmoids in Central Africa, Southern Asia, and in the Pacific Ocean, certain tribes in South-Eastern Australia, the old Californians, the Ges-tribes in South-East Brazil, the Fuegians, and others, monogamy, matrimonial fidelity, mutual freedom in the choice of the

[1] According to the "*Kulturkreislehre*", the temporal order of succession of these cultures is as follows: 1) original primitive cultures (of the simplest and comparatively oldest races); 2) the primary cultures; 3) mixed or secondary cultures. In this ethnological time-schema the seven great "*Kulturkreise*" are arranged.

marriage-partner, parental love, love on the part of children and married love are of normal occurrence.

Among these races the natural family is still the centre of the simple societal relations. As a rule the sib and the clan are lacking here[1]. The popular or tribal organization is still of an extremely simple type, and of slight stability.

In their presumably original form (not yet mixed with the totemistic clan-organization) the so-called "matriarchal" phenomena do not enter into the cultural evolution until the rise of the tillage of the soil with the help of mattock-like implements. This tillage was the wife's achievement in the development of civilization. When marrying she did not want to leave the spot where the field lay that she had tilled. BACHOFEN has already pointed out this connection between matriarchy and agriculture. It is probable that where these conditions arose, man and wife at first lived apart from each other[2].

In the second stage of development the husband found himself compelled to reside at the house of his wife's relatives, temporarily or for good (bina-marriage). In his wife's kinship he was more or less considered a *stranger*. All this must lead to the effect that the internal marriage- and family-bond were forced into the background.

This is the origin of the *avuncular* relationship, *i.e.* the remarkable juridical kinship relationship (not that of the family proper) in which the children born of a marriage are at least also[3] placed under the authority of their mother's eldest brother and are his heirs. The father's heirs are his brothers' and sisters' children[4].

[1] LOWIE, who does not start from the "*Kulturkreislehre*", says (*op. cit.* p. 144) about the least complicated cultures in general: 'In short, with the one notable exception of the Australians, the simplest cultures lack the sib and possess the family, and even in Australia there is no evidence that the sib is more ancient than its invariable concomitant'.

[2] W. SCHMIDT, *Völker und Kulturen* (p. 267) says that this is the first stage in the development of matriarchy and that it can still be found among the Synteng-Khasi (Further India) the Menangkabau Malay, the North American Hurons and Iroquois, *etc.*

[3] Among the matriarchal Pueblo Indians the wife is the owner of the house, and the father's authority over the children is only *shared* by the men belonging to the house in which the father lives merely as a guest. Cf. LOWIE, *op. cit.* p. 68.

[4] Various investigators have noticed that in the case of a formal matriarchal system of inheritance the father tries to do justice to the natural family relations as much as possible by donations to his children. Here it appears once again that it is necessary to distinguish the internal and the external relationships in family life.

Thus arises the computation of the children's descent from the mother's and not from the father's lineage. Not the wife herself, but her kinship acquires a position of authority over the children here.

It must at once be clear that these so-called matriarchal phenomena do not belong to the internal domain of the marriage bond and family community. As typical positive forms of the relations in marriage and family they cannot be adduced to prove the absolute variability of what we have called the internal structural principles of these communities.

They cannot at all be understood from the internal positive structure of the marital and family community among the primitive peoples; rather they are exclusively connected with the *external enkaptic interweavings* in which at most the *variability-types* of these societal relationships can be founded.

Levirate, sororate, brother polyandry and the so-called "pirra-ura", as abnormal external forms in which marital and family relations have been interwoven.

What has been said about the original matriarchal forms in their relation to the structure of marriage and family life also applies to other abnormal external forms of these institutional and natural communities among primitive races, and even among peoples taken up in the expanded cultural development. We are thinking of the institution of *levirate,* which in its stringent form was an *obligation* on the part of the husband's brother to marry his brother's widow. Then there are the so-called *sororate,* and *brother-polyandry,* and the *"pirra-ura-relation"* (among the Urabunna- and Dieri-Australians).

The misinterpretation of these external forms as structural relations of marriage proper still played an important rôle in FRAZER's attempt to prove the evolutionist hypothesis of a so-called "group-marriage", as the first phase in the development of real married life [1].

As is generally known, MORGAN's hypothesis of the "consanguineous family" was based on a misconception of the so-called *classificatory system of kinship* in which father and uncle were indicated by means of the same name. His hypothesis of "group-marriage" was also chiefly based on this terminology. Later on it was conclusively proved that this name does not denote any blood-relationship at all.

---

[1] *Totemism and Exogamy* IV, 151 ff.

Then the attention of the investigators was turned to certain data about some forms of marriage among different primitive peoples of which it was supposed that they were either remnants of an earlier, or indications of a still extant group-marriage.

FRAZER, for instance, appealed to the following data: 1) to the levirate marriage, 2) to the husband's right of sexual intercourse with his wife's sisters while she lived, 3) to the husband's right to his wife's sisters after her death. Both rights (intended sub 2 and 3) are found among various peoples, and, according to FRAZER, the latter is nothing but a later modification of the sororate in its original sense, which finds expression in the husband's right mentioned sub 2.

FRAZER thought he could explain the levirate as a weakened form of an original polyandry. Finally the adherents of the group-marriage theory emphatically pointed to what was later on found among two tribes of the central part of South Australia, *viz.* the *Dieri* and the *Urabunna.* They were supposed to have a real group-marriage even at the present day.

But what are the real facts? Levirate and sororate are extremely differentiated forms of so-called "preferential marriages", whose hypothetical connection with an original "group-marriage" (whose occurrence has never been proved) is absolutely speculative (cf. LOWIE, *op. cit.* p. 58).

Really authentic cases of polyandry are very thinly scattered over an extremely restricted area, and found among some Eskimo groups and especially in Ceylon; in India chiefly among the Dravidas, but also among some Munda and Tibetan-Birmese tribes in Bhutia (Nepal); and, in connection with these, in Southern Arabia (Mot'a marriage) and among some Hamitic tribes [1].

By far the greater part of these cases are only concerned with *brother* polyandry. Only the first born son marries *one woman.* His younger brothers theoretically have a share in his whole fortune and also in the possession of the wife. Immediately the problem crops up, whether there is here question of a real conjugal relation between the wife and the husband's brothers, or if it is only a question of a sexual pleasure outside of wedlock, legalized by popular customary law. It is very remarkable that nearly always the phenomenon of polyandry only occurs among peoples that lived or are still living in matriarchal conditions. According to the *"Kulturkreislehre"*, the phenomenon originated from the mixing of matriarchal with patriarchal peoples that recognized the right of primogeniture. THURSTON [2] already observed that the practice of polyandry was intended to prevent the splitting up of the family property. Though theoretically all the sons have a share in the father's

---

[1] Polyandry seems to have existed also in the old Babylon. At least Urucagina of Lagasch (about 2800 B.C.) boasted that his reforms had also abolished the earlier existing custom of one woman belonging to more than one man.

[2] *Castes and Tribes of Southern India* VII, 98.

property, it is really the eldest son on whom the possession and administration of the *tarwad*-property devolves. The others only have a right to sustenance as long as they remain in the same *tarwad*-house.

That is why exclusively the eldest son *marries*, the others only getting a share in the *enjoyment* of the wife, *just as in that of the other possessions.*

In its original form this polyandry did not allow the taking of more than one wife. This can be explained by referring to the strict form of the older matriarchy, which made the wife the owner of the house and fields, and permitted the husband only to come and live in her house. A very strict kind of monogamy prevailed here.

Therefore we can say that this polyandry has nothing to do with MORGAN's hypothetical group-marriage. In our opinion it is even no matrimonial form at all. In the absolutely preponderant form of brother-polyandry it seems much rather to be a kind of legalized sexual relationship outside of marriage, sanctioned merely as a juridical proprietary share in the wife. Only by way of exception polyandry is found outside of the brothers, for instance among the matriarchal Nayar-caste in India. According to W. SCHMIDT, these sexual relationships clearly originated in an irregular concubinage between Nayar-girls and the rigidly patriarchal Rambutiri-Brahmans, and in a brother polyandry derived from it[1]. This is also the key to understand the "classical" example of polyandry among the Todas. Their best informed investigator, W. H. R. RIVERS[2], showed that they originated very probably from the mixing of the Nayar-Dravidas with the Rambutiri-Brahmans.

As regards the pirra-ura-relations among the Dieri and Urabunna the facts that have been established are the following: In addition to his real wife, a man later on has one or more other women assigned to him. They must invariably be married themselves, however, and their own husbands must give them permission to the so-called *pirra-ura (pira-ungaru), i.e.* to an essential concubinage with the other man outside of marriage.

This abnormal sexual relation is only interwoven with the marriage bond proper in an external *enkapsis*, and has nothing whatever to do with a group-marriage[3].

In an earlier context we have seen that the external enkaptic interweavings of marriage and family play a leading part in the popular and tribal regulations of these institutions.

If this is true, it is methodically unsound to deduce the internal positive structural relations of marriage and family among a

---

[1] Cf. W. SCHMIDT, *op. cit.* pp. 313/4.

[2] W. H. R. RIVERS, *The Todas* (London, 1906).

[3] Cf. LOWIE, *op. cit.* pp. 49 ff. He clearly shows that this is a question of concubinage which already in popular law is sharply distinguished from the strictly monogamous marriage relations.

certain people from what is found about these institutions in customary popular or tribal law[1]. LOWIE, too, emphatically warns against the overestimation of the traditional popular juridical conceptions of marriage in a particular tribe if one wants to gain an insight into the real position of a married woman[2]: 'The conditions involved in the relations of men and women are many-sided, and it is dangerous to overweight one particular phase of them'[3], he observes. But we must immediately add that for a proper distinction between the different sides of these relations it is necessary to have an insight into their *individuality structure.* The *facts* require an *interpretation* if they are to be understood in their proper meaning-structure. Any one who *a priori* eliminates the structural principles from his investigations continually runs the risk of misinterpreting *the facts.* For the latter are always essentially related to these principles, irrespective whether they satisfy their structural norms or contradict them. Apart from them nobody can succeed in finding a sufficient criterion for the distinction between marital and family relationships proper, and sexual and kinship relations of a different character.

§ 5 - THE STRUCTURE OF THE NATURAL FAMILY- OR KINSHIP COMMUNITY IN ITS BROADER SENSE.

Why the natural family or kinship-community in its broader sense cannot be an organized community.

Together with the marriage bond and the family in its narrowest sense the kinship community or bilateral family in its broader extent belongs to the radical type of the biotically founded communities with a moral qualification. By *kinship* or *cognate family* in this broader natural sense I exclusively understand the circle of the living blood-relatives, both in the paternal

[1] This also applies to popular legal conceptions about the position of wives in marriage and the family prevalent, for example, among the Kirghizes of Central Asia, or among the Bantu tribes of Africa. That according to these conceptions the wife is nothing but a piece of the husband's property just like his cattle, is not yet decisive for its internal position in these communities.

[2] *Op. cit.* p. 179: 'In other words, it is important to ascertain what customary or written law and philosophic theory have to say on feminine rights and obligations. But it is more important to know whether social practice conforms to theory or leaves the latter halting in the rear, as it so frequently does'.

[3] *Ibidem.*

and the maternal lines, forming a *cognate* community, from which must be excluded those distant relationships that can no longer be realized in the actual communal conscience of the members.

The so-called agnatic patriarchal or matriarchal types of "*joint family*" show the character of an authoritative organized relationship. As such they are not among the typically biotically founded communities. We shall return to this important point. The *kinship community* or cognate family in its broader natural sense is not an *authoritative* organized community in the sense defined in an earlier context, no more than marriage and the family bond in its strictest sense show this character. It is true that in this "cognate family" the internal unity according to its structural principle is even more independent of the changes in the number of its members than it is in the narrower circle of the family, as a bond between parents and their children under age. But — unlike an organized community — a "cognate family" or kinship community lacks an authority-structure. This community, though only existing between living relatives, is necessarily founded in the genealogical bond, which is realized in the coexistence as well as in the temporal succession of its members.

A kinship community in its broader natural sense is differentiated into wider and narrower circles.

Though the "cognate family" or kinship community in its broader natural sense as such lacks historically founded forms of organization, it necessarily includes smaller groups of nearer relatives which are clearly distinguished from the others. The communal relations with more distant relatives have a tendency to slacken, especially in times and conditions that are unfavourable to the maintenance of an active kinship life [1].

On the substratum of the degrees of closeness of the biotic blood relationship the internal love-relations among the members of a cognate community thus display a great variety. No doubt this fact induced LITT to distinguish between "closed cir-

---

[1] In various *leges barbarorum* of the Germanic tribes these wider or narrower circles of kinship found recognition, *e.g.* in the distinction between the "*vierendelen*" and the "*achtendelen*", *i.e.* the kinship groups constituted by the four grandparents, or the eight great-grandparents of one individual person.

cles" of the first and of the second degree. However, he took no account of the internal structural principles of these circles.

The narrowest circle of blood relationship is formed by the ascendants and descendants of the first degree, at one time united in one conjugal family, which was dissolved when the children became of age and left the paternal home. For the biotic foundation of the family in its narrowest sense differs from that of the kinship community in its broader natural extent insofar as the former is bound to the condition that the children have not yet reached the age of maturity [1].

Even if the grown-up sons or daughters remain in the same house with the parents, the natural family community in its strict sense cannot continue to exist after its typical biotic foundation has fallen away. The natural paternal authority in its typical structure ceases to function, as it is founded in the natural dependence of a child on its parents, who have brought him into the world.

The parents remain the natural advisers of those adult children who have left their parental home for good. As the former bearers of authority the father and mother remain entitled to the honour due to the office held by them in the conjugal family, because *they are integrated with their grown-up sons and daughters into the structure of the narrowest circle within the kinship community.* But the authority of their parental office is at an end, just as their children's duty to obey after the latter have reached the state of maturity. Any positive authoritative functions on the part of the parents after their sons and daughters have arrived at this state cannot be deduced from the paternal office as such, but at most from their leading position in an eventually continued domestic community with their children.

The expression of the structural principle of the kinship community or cognate community in their different modal aspects.

The cognate community in its central and more peripheral circles of kinship possesses its own internal structural principle expressing itself in all the modal aspects of the communal relation. In the *numerical aspect* it is a unity in the multiplicity of relatives under the guidance of the relations of love and sym-

[1] The primitive method of establishing puberty and maturity is based on the examination of the body of the individual. Later on general popular law regulations are made concerning majority.

pathy founded in the bonds of blood. If there is no spatial centre of the community, such as is found in the case of the conjugal family, there exist special communal relations between the spatial centres of the separate families expressing the spatial *aspect* of the cognate community.

The organic-genetic kinship relations, opened by the structural principle, express the latter in the physically founded *biotic aspect* of the cognate family. In the *psychical aspect* this typical structure finds expression in the disclosed typical feeling of solidarity on the part of the relatives, varied according to the wider and narrower kinship circles. In the *historical* function of the cognate community the structural principle expresses itself in the typical cultural circle of this community with its tradition and cultural objects of its own. In the typical internal forms of social intercourse among the relatives, which centres in family parties and family honour, *etc.* we find the structural principle expressed in its *social* aspect. In the *economic aspect* this structure expresses itself in the saving of typical family property which is evaluated economically as very closely connected with beloved members of the family and consequently having an "affective value" in this kinship community (recall family-portraits, old souvenirs of deceased relatives, *etc.*). The *juridical* aspect of the cognate kinship structure is expressed in the internal mutual duty of sustenance of the relatives (which is recognized in civil law only to a very limited degree); in the internal communal sphere of guardianship exercized by the next of kin, and of the natural hereditary right of the kinsmen, *etc.* All these are internal communal juridical relations that cannot be grasped apart from the typical biotically founded moral qualification of the kinship community in its natural sense.

In its normative meaning-structure the family bond points above time to the religious community of mankind in Christ. In Him all reborn human beings find the religious fulfilment of their temporal kinship ties as members of the human race on the basis of *palingenesis* [1].

---

[1] Cf. *Mark.* 3 : 34, 35.

B. THE UNDIFFERENTIATED ORGANIZED COMMUNITIES

§ 6 - DIFFERENT TYPES OF UNDIFFERENTIATED ORGANIZED COMMUNITIES.

The general character of undifferentiated organized communities.

In our previous inquiry into the structural principles of the natural communities we have repeatedly established that, on a cultural level showing only a slight degree of differentiation, these communities are often intersected by undifferentiated social units which show a deceptive resemblance to them.

It was therefore all the more necessary to give precedence to a detailed analysis of the structural principles of the real natural communities before engaging in an investigation of the main types of undifferentiated communal relationships. For we have seen that the latter are repeatedly bracketed with the former.

This misconception appeared to a high degree to be influenced by TÖNNIES' distinction between "*Gemeinschaft*" and "*Gesellschaft*", in the particular meaning ascribed by him to these terms. As soon as this distinction is conceived of in a *structural typical* sense, the confusion mentioned is unavoidable.

TÖNNIES himself calls this contrast "*ideal-typical*", somewhat in the sense intended by MAX WEBER, *i.e.* the concepts "*Gemeinschaft*" and "*Gesellschaft*" are understood as "normal concepts", or as "standard types". They serve to grasp societal reality in its *subjective meaning,* without having a *normative* sense [1]. Nevertheless, our earlier analysis of these concepts, in the typical sense which TÖNNIES has ascribed to them, has shown that they do include an axiological standard to judge the historical development of human society. TÖNNIES holds that a "*Gemeinschaft*" is ruled by a "natural will" resting on an instinctive basis. He mentions the immediate family and the extended kinship community as its prototypes. But we saw in an earlier context that his standard-type "*Gemeinschaft*" also includes the domestic community or "household" and the mark-community, the village community, the medieval city-community with its guilds, *etc.* If this concept of community is consequently conceived to be *structural typical,* we run the risk of eradicating the internal fundamental structural differences between all those communities in which we can find, as a standard of behaviour, the "natural

[1] Cf. TÖNNIES' *Gemeinschaft und Gesellschaft,* and his smaller treatise *Gemeinschaft und Gesellschaft* in Handwörterbuch der Soziologie hrg. v. A. Vierkandt, p. 186.

communal mind" in the sense intended by Tönnies. For in the "organized communities with an undifferentiated qualification", which we now have to examine in more detail, there is indeed evidence of a strongly developed communal mind, prescribed by their inner structural law, *i.e.* a "natural will" (versus an arbitrary will) in Tönnies' terminology. At least insofar as the kinship mind prevails in them, their members are obliged to consider one another as genuine blood relatives, even when real kinship is completely lacking among them.

It is consequently quite natural on Tönnies' standpoint to reckon these societal forms among the "organic" relationships with a natural communal mind. For in his structural investigations he has no criterion but the subjective conceptions obtaining in a particular group of people concerning the character of these societal relationships. But these societal forms are not at all included in the radical type of the biotically founded and morally qualified communities. Rather they belong to the typical historically founded societal relationships. Nevertheless, there is a good reason for treating them immediately after the natural communities. This reason is that in fact the most intensive types among these undifferentiated social units preferably seek to strenghten their communal bond by conceiving it after the pattern of a natural kinship.

What do we understand by "organized communities with an undifferentiated qualification"? In general they are those institutional societal units which to a greater or lesser degree perform all those typical structural functions for which on a more differentiated cultural level separate organized communities are formed, with typical structures of their own, showing both a differentiated foundational and a differentiated leading function.

In this sense we might call them "supra-functional". Nevertheless, they are not really *all-inclusive* in the sense meant by Gurvitch, since they do not really include the natural communities, but rather intersect them in an artificial way.

The organized communities with an undifferentiated qualification are historically founded forms of interlacement of social structures.

This state of affairs indeed requires a more detailed investigation. Our previous expositions have made it clear that without any exception the societal relationships function in all the modal aspects of reality. From this it follows that the difference between undifferentiated and differentiated communities cannot be *solely* found in the modal dimension of our experiential horizon. It can only be completely understood in a structural typical and not in a modal-functional way.

This means that, *e.g.*, such a primitive organized community as the *sib* does not function merely in a *modal*-economic way, but that it may have such structural economic functions as, on a differentiated cultural level, are exclusively found in an *economically qualified agricultural or cattle rearing* undertaking.

In the same way it has not merely a *modal* function of social intercourse, but acts as a kind of club, which on a differentiated cultural level is typically *qualified* by its aspect of intercourse; it has not only a *modal* juridical function, but performs typical *juridical functions* which in a differentiated society exclusively belong to a political community; it has not only a modal function in the aspect of faith, but it really performs the task of a cult-community, which on a differentiated cultural level is typically qualified by its aspect of belief.

Of course, also a modern differentiated organized community may take over typical structural functions of other societal relationships. Thus a modern State may run a State-owned industry or a public school, *etc.* The medieval Roman Catholic institutional Church assumed many functions proper to the body politic, and in different periods of history the State performed ecclesiastical functions. But, notwithstanding all this, truly differentiated communities retain their own internal structure, in which a differentiated leading function can be distinguished. They have to call into existence organizations with a specific typical leading function for the non-typical structural functions they perform. A State-run industry after all remains an *industry* according to its internal structure, and its close connection with the State is not proper to its radical and geno-type. The fact that a particular industry acts as a State-run concern is only related to the *pheno-type* (or variability-type) of the former. In an "undifferentiated organized community" the state of affairs is entirely different. Here it is useless to look for such a simple structural principle in which the foundational and the leading function are both geno-typically differentiated within a comprehensive radical type of societal structures. In principle such a societal unit may combine the most heterogeneous structures in accordance with the needs of a society at a particular primitive cultural level. These various structural principles are realized in *one and the same form of organization.*

When in the development of civilization a culture is disclosed, such primitive social units are ultimately resolved into differentiated societal relationships. In other words, these primitive communities are really the result of a close interweaving of heterogeneous structural principles, whose interlacement is *essential* to them, but displays an *intra*-communal and not an *inter*-communal character. They are historically founded in a particular *formation of power,* but the latter appears to have an undifferentiated character which is closely bound to the vital conditions of primitive social life.

The structural principle of a natural community may play a dominant and leading part in the as yet undifferentiated societal units. This is very clearly seen in the patriarchal, so-called "joint family" [1], in the sib, and in many a tribal organization of the comparatively oldest extant primitive peoples. The structural principle of the family or the kinship community in its broader sense may also have been pushed into the background, however, by accentuating other structures that are interwoven in the undifferentiated social whole. Thus *political* structures are very markedly operative as dominant factors, *e.g.,* in the secret men's associations ("*Männerbünde*"), explained by W. SCHMIDT as a reaction against matriarchal forms of primitive organization.

In consequence of these facts a proper analysis of the essential structure of such undifferentiated societal units is extremely difficult. Do they actually posses internal structural unity, or are they after all no more than an agglomeration of different structures? But if the latter is the case, how can they function as real social units?

These problems are not even *raised* in the prevailing tendencies in sociology, because the individuality structures of human society are not paid proper attention to. Instead, "general concepts" such as "group", "class", *etc.,* are handled, which are only differentiated according to functional view-points. And insofar as any attention is devoted to "supra-functional" or to "multi-bonded" groups, their structural *unity* is supposed rather than explained.

---

[1] German: "*Grossfamilie*", *i.e.* great family, larger family or extended family. *Transl. H. d. J.*

In any case it is an established fact that the undifferentiated communities cannot have a simple structure. We must try to gain an insight into their structural unity, which in consequence cannot be of the same character as that of natural communal bonds or of differentiated organized communities.

But we must do so in close contact with the social facts, in order to avoid any *a priori* construction.

The structural interweaving in the patriarchal "joint family".

Our first example is the patriarchal "joint family" which by the "*Kulturkreislehre*" is classed with the "family form" of the pastoral nomadic peoples. This societal relationship seems indeed to display a natural kinship structure, since it comprehends parents, children and grandchildren in one societal whole and it is characterized by a strong patriarchal mind in its members. On closer examination, however, it appears that this community does not display the simple structural principle of the natural kinship bond. I refer to the following traits of the patriarchal "joint family": The married sons with their newly formed families remain included in the domestic community of the father, even when they settle in their own tents (*e.g.*, with the Minussinsk Tartars). The patriarch exercises real authority over the totality of the separate family communities which are integrated into the "joint family". In the latter there develops an exceedingly important right of primogeniture of the eldest son. All these traits are by no means natural consequences of the internal structure of the kinship community formed by the narrow circle of grandparents, parents and grandchildren. Neither the patriarch's authority, nor the special position of the eldest son in this patriarchal relationship, are of a *typical biotic* foundation. Only the historical formation of power on the part of the patriarch can be the typical substratum of his authority in this typical kind of community.

And the entire patriarchal relationship, as such, cannot be biotically founded, but can only have its typical foundational function in an historical form of organization.

When we try to trace the real structural principle of this historical power-formation on the part of the patriarch, we must first pay attention to the undeniable connection of this patriarchal authority with economic factors.

We should especially note what the ethnologist RADLOFF tells us about the origin of the "joint family" (the "aul") among the Kirghiz[1]: 'The interests of the nearest relatives among the members of the "joint family" were very much interdependent on account of their indivisible common property, which is an absolute vital requirement of the existence of smaller herds. Then individual more distant relatives joined them, as also did families connected with them on other grounds. Together they formed the smallest societal unit, the "aul". It remained intact winter and summer and was composed of from six to ten separate families. The leader of the "aul" is the oldest member of the family with the largest property and the greatest number of relatives in the "aul"'[2]. Such an historical economic foundation[3] of patriarchal authority and (in close connection with the latter) of the right of primogeniture of the eldest son is, indeed, a mere external factor as regards the natural internal kinship bond; but certainly not as far as the patriarchal community is concerned.

Is then the patriarchal "joint family" to be considered an economically qualified pastoral undertaking as regards its internal structure? There is no doubt that it performs the structural functions of an organized industrial community, but it is by no means qualified as such. In the first place the industrial relationship remains structurally interwoven with a particular narrow kinship circle. This interweaving cannot be dispensed with without disrupting the patriarchal societal relationship

---

[1] A Mongolian race living on the Caspian, N.E. of the Kalmucks.

[2] *Aus Siberien* (Leipzig, 2e Aufl., 1839). 'Die Familienglieder, welche in nächster Verwandschaft standen, waren durch einen gemeinschaftlichen unteilbaren Besitz, der für kleinere Herden eine Existenzbedingung ist, in ihren Interessen eng an einander gekettet; an sie schlossen sich einzelne fernere Verwandte und durch andere Verhältnisse nahestehende Familien an und so bildete sich die kleinste soziale Einheit, das "Aul". Dieses bleibt Winter und Sommer zusammen, es besteht in sechs bis zehn Einzelfamilien. Der Leiter des Auls ist das älteste Familienglied derjenigen Familie, die den grössten Besitzstand und die meisten Verwandten im Aul besitzt'.

[3] In the last instance this is a question of a *historical foundation*, in which the basis of power and tradition are decisive. This is evident from the fact that patriarchy, when proper to a conquering people, is usually maintained even when such patriarchal peoples mix with those living in matriarchy in connection with agriculture (which was a female task). The continuation of patriarchy then appears to be independent of its former economical basis.

proper. And in the second place the interweaving of a particular kinship- and business structure with other societal structures is equally essential to this patriarchal "joint family". The latter also implies an obvious *political* structure, typically founded in *armed power* and asserting itself in keeping up the internal peace, in the vendetta and in the defence of the small community against external enemies. This structure can certainly no more be derived from the internal structural principle of the natural kinship community than the industrial relationship, but in the patriarchal societal unit it is essentially interwoven with a partial kinship community.

What then gives this societal whole its inner structural unity in this complex intertwinement of radically different structures? This cannot be its organization alone. For the latter itself displays the variety of structures whose mutual interlacement is essential to this undifferentiated whole. A true structural unity in this divergence can only be maintained *if one of the interlaced structures has the leading rôle in the multi-bonded totality.* It is indeed the internal structural principle of the family bond that plays a dominant part in the patriarchal "joint family", *i.e.* the family mind entirely permeates the complicated structure of this societal relationship.

This is most evident in those cases where within it a cult develops in the form of ancestor worship. Such a cult community embraces all the members of the patriarchal "joint family", irrespective of the question whether or not they belong to the natural kinship of the patriarchal chief.

FUSTEL DE COULANGE's book *La cité antique* gives an elaborate description of this ancestor worship in its more developed form among the Indo European peoples, especially among the Greeks and the Romans. He shows that in this cult there was a continual exchange of acts of love between the living and the dead members of the family. The ancestor received the series of meals for the dead from his offspring, which was the only pleasure he could have in his second life. The descendant, on the other hand, received from his ancestors the support and the power that he needed in this life.

Thus a strong tie connected all the generations of one and the same gens, creating an "eternal" unbreakable totality.

The deification of the ancestors in the community of cult and faith of the patriarchal "joint family" clearly proves that under the leading of the function of faith all the internal relations in this societal unit are permeated by the family mind. The agnatic kinship community in this undifferentiated societal relationship is thus indeed the *leading* and *central structure*, although this kinship bond as such does not display a real authoritative and organizational structure [1].

The structural interweaving within the sib or clan.

The primitive *sib* or *clan* is another example of an organized community with an undifferentiated qualification. This societal unit is usually characterized as a wider group of relatives, often organized as an association [2], in which kinship is only taken in a unilateral sense, either in the paternal or in the maternal line [3]. Even such a keen observer as LOWIE writes that the "sib" is a primitive type of social unit "that resembles the family in being based on kinship, but otherwise differs fundamentally from it" [4].

If this were true, the sib would have to be reckoned among the typical biotically founded societal relationships.

Just like the marital bond, the natural family in its narrowest sense and the natural kinship bond in its greater extent, the clan

---

[1] Cf. A. VIERKANDT, *Gesellschaftslehre* (2nd ed. 1928) p. 445, on the initial stage of the ancestor cult (*"Ahnenkultus"*) among the Battaks, the Dschagga negroes and other still less civilized primitive races: 'Wenn die Quellen in derartigen Fällen vielfach die Auffassung vertreten, dass das Verhalten des Menschen bei dem hier gemeinten Typus lediglich durch Furcht und den sogenannten Egoismus bestimmt werde, von einer Liebe und Verehrung aber keine Spur in sich trage, so darf diese Auffassung hier so wenig wie sonst im religiösen Leben als richtig gelten: sie verwechselt die reine Selbstfürsorge mit dem Solidaritätsverhalten innerhalb der Gemeinschaft. Es ist klar, dass hier eine Gemeinschaft besteht, die diejenige der Familie über das Grab fortsetzt. Eigenfürsorge mag sich gelegentlich einmischen, ist jedoch dann nur eine Oberflachenkraft'. [When in such cases the sources often maintain that in the type meant here the attitude of man is only determined by fear and so-called egoism, and that there is no trace of love and adoration, this opinion can be as little correct here as with regard to other manifestations of religious life: it confounds pure self care with the attitude of solidarity within the community. It is clear that there is a community which continues that of the family beyond the grave. The care of oneself may now and then be mingled with it, but is then only a peripheral motive.]

[2] This is contrasted with the patriarchal joint family. We shall, however, see that the sib, too, may have a chief, whose authority only lacks patriarchal traits.

[3] The patrilineal sib is called *gens* among the Romans.

[4] *Primitive Society*, p. 105.

would be "of all times", *i.e.* its actual occurrence in temporal human society would not depend on a definite historical level of culture. Lowie himself, however, has clearly shown that this is not the case. The older evolutionistic view held that in the development of human societal life among primitive peoples the sib preceded the family and the bi-lateral kinship community proper. In an earlier context we have seen that Lowie has energetically contributed to the refutation of this conception. He demonstrated that precisely the least developed primitive peoples (*i.e.* the peoples of the so-called "primary cultures" according to the "*Kulturkreislehre*") do not know the sib and that the latter disappears in the long run when civilization is expanded and "opened" (in our sense). But the conjugal family and the bi-lateral kindred communities are absolutely universal institutions at all times. Lowie also proved that among primitive peoples as a rule the sib or clan relationship appears only when agriculture or cattle-breeding have wholly or partly replaced hunting as the basis of economic life [1]. Lowie has even admitted that the common descent claimed by the sib-mates, as the foundation of this societal relationship, is for a large part only a fiction [2].

The supposed descent from a common ancestral father or mother is indeed sometimes entirely mythological, *e.g.*, with the totem-clans, and therefore it is no real *typical biotic* substratum of the societal *relationship as such*. Even animals and plants, or dead objects are often worshipped as ancestors [3].

Also outside of the typical totem cultures the idea of a common descent as the basis of the sib relationship is very often merely a mythological motif. This idea can then only be kept alive in the minds of the members of the sib or the tribe by means of a

---

[1] *Op. cit.* p. 141.

[2] *Op. cit.* p. 109: 'When we investigate by genealogical methods the average sib, we generally find it impossible to derive all the members from a single ancestor. What we discover is a series of independent lines of descent merely theoretically united by a common ancestry... Thus, in taking a census of the Hopi I found that several very small mother-sibs were not composed wholly of individuals related to one another by blood but could be separated into two or three distinct matrilineal groups which regarded themselves as related only by a legal fiction'.

[3] Totem clans do not always worship the totem animal or totem plant itself as ancestor. They sometimes imagine to have only a common ancestress married to a particular animal and giving birth to the clan's totem animal.

symbol or a myth. This does not alter the fact that in the sib, which is often of a fairly great extent[1], different unilateral kinship bonds are actually included, although they are not connected with each other in one single *real* family community. The sib relationship cannot exist without at least comprising a considerable part of the natural kinship community in the paternal or in the maternal line. As a rule membership depends on the natural basis of birth. Apart from cases of adoption, everyone of the members belongs to the sib through birth. This proves the institutional character of this undifferentiated community.

Just as in the case of the patriarchal joint family, the internal structural principle of the natural family plays a central, leading rôle in this form of interwovenness of societal structures which is the sib. The natural communal mind of the family also here dominates the entire societal relationship.

Because of the usually fictitious or mythological basis of common descent this fact is more striking in the sib than it is in the patriarchal joint family. For the latter is connected with the natural family community much more closely and really than the former.

The sib draws a line of demarcation across the conjugal and the family community, in accordance with the rule: "Once a sibmate, always a sibmate". Consequently the married woman is never admitted to the husband's sib, nor *vice versa.* But, no matter how remote their real blood relationship may be, and though this relationship does not really exist between *all* the members of the same sib, they consider one another as *members* of the same kinship. This is clearly brought out by the rule of *clan-exogamy,* in virtue of which the members of a sib are not allowed to marry with each other. Among the different primitive peoples the penalty for an infringement of this societal norm may vary, but the offence is always considered to be incest[2].

---

[1] How large the number of the members of a sib may be is seen in the Ostiaks, a tribe living in Western Siberia, where the exogamous paternal sibs often number thousands of members. Cf. LOWIE, *op. cit.* p. 113.

[2] Cf. LOWIE, *op. cit.* p. 107: 'With us a third or fourth cousin hardly ever functions as a member of the family at all; but by the fixity of the sib bond even the most remote kinsman is still known as a member of the same unit, which is most commonly designated by a name borne by all the members, thus leaving no doubt as to sib affiliation. The feeling of community thus established is reflected in the terminology of kinship: sib mates of the same generation usually call one another siblings, and

Besides the structure of a partial blood relationship there are, just as in the patriarchal joint family, entirely different structures interwoven in the sib, in accordance with the needs of primitive societal life. This fact again is a clear evidence of the undifferentiated character of this primitive kind of organized community.

The sib, *e.g.*, functions as a *peace-relationship* between the sib-mates, which testifies to its undoubted typical structural rôle as a political organization. Just like the patriarchal joint family, the sib is charged with the execution of the *vendetta.* All this proves that at least in this respect its structure is typically founded in the *historical* figure of *armed power* [1].

To this political structure also belongs the internal-juridical position of a special sib-chieftain, found in particular among the totemistic clans. He is at the same time the leader of the rites and as a magician he possesses great power in the cult-community.

The sib may also have the structure of a quite different societal unit, *viz.* that of an economically qualified *business organization,* either in the domain of agriculture or in that of the hunt. Then it regulates the distribution of the work and the use of the soil by the sib-mates and often functions as the owner of the soil concerned [2].

In the interwoven whole of the sib the primitive structure of a cult community also plays an important rôle. In particular the totemistic clans are centres both of a common mana-belief [3] and of common rites and magical actions.

---

from this, given the primitive attitude towards names, it is but a step to the feeling that marriage between sib-mates would be incestuous. Hence we find as one of the most common traits of the sib the law of exogamy'.

[1] Cf. a.o. HOSE's and MC.DOUGALL's statements on the *military* position of a sib in: *The Pagan Tribes of Borneo I,* 158.

[2] For the importance of the old-Germanic sib as an agrarian-economic unit see CAESAR's description in his *De Bello Gallico* VI, 22.

[3] In keeping with my expositions on the theme "magic and faith" in volume II, part I, pp. 316 ff., I still hold that in the belief in mana the cult-element of worship of the mysterious divine is essential, however much it may be permeated by magical motives. Mana belief is really a phenomenon of a faith-cult in the sense explained in an earlier context, and cannot be reduced to mere "magic" This view is not invalidated by the motive of control in this primitive belief. This motive is even more pregnantly in evidence in the Humanistic science-ideal with its deification

In this cult-community the sib-chieftain is the typical leader and possesses strongly "charismatic" authority (in MAX WEBER's sense), because he is believed to embody the magic power of the whole clan [1]. The totemistic ancestor-cult, in which the structural principle of the family-community clearly takes the lead, reveals the strongly mythological nature of the family-conception in the clan-relationship. The leading function of the structural principle of the family community in the sib is especially accentuated among some primitive peoples when the whole clan occupies a common long house, as one single household-community.

The leading rôle of the family bond (and not of the political structure, *e.g.*) is very obvious also in totemistic clans if, owing to special outside influences (perhaps matriarchal factors in particular), the tribal organization cuts across the sib, so that members of the same clan belong to different tribes. With many peoples [2] the members of the same clan remain solidary when the tribes concerned get into a conflict, and the clan mates refuse to take up arms against one another. If this is impossible, they spare each other wherever they can.

In the undifferentiated organized communities one of the interwoven structures assumes the rôle of the leading structural principle.

From the above we may conclude that as to its structural unity the sib exhibits the same state of affairs as we could establish with respect to the patriarchal joint family. Whatever different *societal structures may be interwoven in a sib, in accordance* with the primitive social needs [3], these structures are not realized

---

and worship of the thought of natural science. And yet this "ideal" has the *meaning of a faith* in its cult of the deified ratio.

In my opinion the question is not whether the mythic motive of a magical operational coherence is necessarily connected with mana-faith, but if the latter contains the characteristically pisteutic moment of deification and worship. To my mind the latter traits are undeniable in this primitive experience of the "supra-natural".

[1] Cf. W. SCHMIDT, *op. cit.* p. 236, and A. VIERKANDT, *op. cit.* p. 451.

[2] For instance, the Iroquois in North America, the Kima, the Nassim in British New Guinea, and different other tribal groups. Cf. SCHMIDT, *op. cit.* p. 237.

[3] The question *which* structures are really interlaced in a sib completely depends on the societal conditions. LOWIE rightly observes (*op. cit.* p. 115): 'The sib thus appears as an extraordinarily changeable unit.'

in a mere agglomeration of different societal units. On the contrary, they are interlaced in the form of one single organized community, which is often extremely close-knit, and has an undifferentiated qualification.

Such a "multibonded" undifferentiated community can only attain to real internal unity (on the law-side), if one particular structure in this form of interweaving assumes the leading rôle among the other structures. Instead of the leading function qualifying the differentiated natural and organized communities, we find here a leading structural principle in the form of interweaving of different structures.

But for the leading of the structural principle of the family, the sib could not realize its structure as a defensive and peace organization, and as an industrial and cult-community.

In this connection special attention should be paid to what A. VIERKANDT remarks on the collective responsibility of the sib in case of blood-guilt: 'To modern moral feelings', he observes, 'the collective requital of a blood-guilt, in which a sibmate of the guilty person can be made to undergo the punishment, seems a callous act, or frankly immoral. However, we should remember the strong solidarity obtaining among the sibmates. The result is that each of them is continuously under the sib's control and made responsible by the group for his entire behaviour. And conversely, the group is to a much higher degree actually responsible for the individual member on account of his greater dependence on the sib' [1].

Indeed, but this strong internal and external solidarity in the sib relationship in its turn can only be understood from the leading rôle of the structural principle of the (unilateral) family-bond in this form of interweaving. And yet we could establish that the undifferentiated sib-organization, as such, is not really founded biotically in the "bonds of blood". The unilateral family community is only a partial structure in this form of inter-

---

[1] *Op. cit.* p. 452: "Dem sittlichen Gefühl unserer Zeit erscheint die kollektive Ahndung einer Blutschuld, bei der statt der schuldigen Person irgend ein anderer Sippengenosse herausgegriffen werden kann, als eine Härte oder geradezu als eine Unsittlichtkeit. Man muss aber an die starke Solidarität der Sippengenossen dabei denken. Sie hat zur Folge, dass jeder in seinem ganzen Verhalten fortgesetzt von der Gruppe kontrolliert und verantwortlich gemacht wird, wie umgekehrt auch für den Einzelnen wegen dieser gesteigerten Abhängigkeit die Gruppe in viel höherem Masse tatsächlich verantwortlich ist'.

weaving which does not at all comprise all the members of the societal unit. The societal relationship *as such* usually appeared to rest on a *fictitious* or *mythical* affiliation. Does not this prove the structural principles as such to be dependent on human arbitrariness to a certain extent? Our answer is: Not at all. The state of affairs we are confronted with in this case is a perfect parallel of the relation between foster-parents and their foster-child, examined in an earlier context [1]. As a rule adoption is a very important feature of the sib. When a man adopts a child, it automatically becomes a member of this man's sib, insofar as the latter reckons affiliation only in the paternal line. If the sib was matrilineal, the child would automatically be adopted by his wife's sib [2]. Relations of love and sympathy among sib-mates not *really* affiliated can only analogically display the internal structure of the unilaterally limited family bond, because this blood-relationship is only a fiction.

The fiction of common descent itself proves that the structural principle is supra-arbitrary. It would be perfectly superfluous, if the qualifying structural principle of the family-bond were really independent of its typical biotic foundation.

The undifferentiated character of the typical foundational function of the primitive forms of interweaving.

The essential typical foundation of the sib or clan-relationship appeared to be *the historical form of a more or less many-sided organization of power* (just as in the case of the undifferentiated societal relationship of the patriarchal joint family). The latter, of course, is restricted within modest limits. The sib's foundational function, however, proves to be as much undifferentiated as the inner qualification of the whole. It appears to be nothing but the typical foundation of a primitive form of interweaving of societal structures. Since Ernst Grosse [3], modern ethnology has paid special attention to the influence of economic factors on the formation of patriarchal joint-families and sib-relationships. Koppers even attempted to explain the rise of the totemistic clan-organization exclusively in terms of economic

---

[1] Cf. p. 292, note.
[2] Cf. Lowie, *op. cit.* p. 109.
[3] Ernst Grosse, *Die Formen der Familie und die Formen der Wirtschaft* (Freiburg-Leipzig, 1886).

causes[1] — which to my mind is an evident overstraining of the latter. KOPPERS does not even exclude the faith aspect of this organization from his economic interpretation, though he admits that all the details can by no means be accounted for in this way.

It is undoubtedly true that both in the formation of the patriarchal joint family and in that of the sib (even apart from the latter's typical totemistic forms) *economic motives* play an important part. Our remarks on the patriarchal family in this respect are equally valid for the formation of the sib. But we can certainly not speak of a *typical economic foundation* of the latter[2].

Its essential typical foundation is only found in the historical form of a more or less many-sided concentration of power.

The different structures of this power (*e.g.*, the power of the sword, the power of faith, economic power, *etc.)* are again united in one single form of interweaving.

The individual family bond is no longer able to fulfil all of its earlier functions in the more complicated societal relations occurring among more developed primitive tribes. Therefore an undifferentiated organization is formed on the typical basis of the above-mentioned *historical* concentration of power, which itself has an as yet undifferentiated character.

Neither the natural family in its narrowest sense, nor the

---

[1] KOPPERS, in volume III *(Die Menschliche Wirtschaft)* of the standard work *Völker und Kulturen*, pp. 479 ff.

KOPPERS summarizes his conclusions (p. 482) as follows: 'Auf jeden Fall erfliesst als klarstes Ergebnis aus unseren Darlegungen, dass der Totemismus als solcher im letzten Grunde in bestimmten wirtschaftlichen Verhältnissen wurzelt und daher aus diesen Verhältnissen heraus seine erste und beste Erklärung schöpfen muss.' [In any case it follows from our expositions as their clearest result that in the last instance totemism as such is rooted in particular economic conditions, and that consequently its first and best explanation must be derived from these conditions.]

[2] The confusion of the *subjective motives* with the *foundational relationship according* to the *structural* principle of a community is very obvious in the case of A. VIERKANDT, in his cited work, where he says (p. 450): 'Der Sexualtrieb bildet nicht die einzige, auch nicht die vorwiegende *Grundlage* der Ehe, ebensowenig wie etwa das wirtschaftliche Interesse, vielmehr kommt beides und noch anderes zusammen. Die Ehe bildet eine Lebensgemeinschaft, bei der ein ganzer Komplex von *Motiven verschmolzen ist*'. [The sexual drive does not constitute the sole or the most important *basis* of marriage, no more than economic interest. But both motives and also others cooperate. Marriage is a vital bond in which an entire complex of *motives are merged together.*] (Italics are mine).

natural marriage- and broader kinship community are as such founded in a typical historical substratum of power.

The undifferentiated primitive societal units, on the contrary, stand and fall with this typical foundation.

Primitive forms of structural interwovenness under the guidance of the political structure. The more strongly organized tribal community.

This statement is *a fortiori* true for undifferentiated communities like the more developed and more strongly organized tribe, which has a much larger number of members than the sibs of which it is composed. In the least complicated primitive societal relations, *e.g.*, among the pygmies and the pigmoid peoples, the undifferentiated concentration of power which forms the typical foundation of the small popular community is only slight. But the coherence of this community is for this very reason extremely weak and loose, as is generally admitted in modern ethnology. The folk unit is no more than a very primitive form of interweaving constituted by a comparatively small number of individual families for those societal needs that cannot be satisfied by these families separately. As observed, on this historical level the natural family and the broader kinship bond are the undisputed centre of the societal relations. This is why the structure of the natural kinship plays the leading rôle also in the folk community. This is proved by the fact that *exogamy* here assumes a *local* character, showing that all the members of the small people consider each other as blood-relatives. Fairly general are the reports about the spirit of mutual helpfulness, participation in the spoils of the chase, the care of the infirm, *etc.*, found in such communities.

No trace is found here of a constant monopolization of armed power by the popular community as a whole. When there is a conflict between particular members of the latter, the tribal chief or influential elders act at the utmost as mediators [1].

When the disputants want to settle their quarrel with the arms, they are at most bound by the general norms of the tribe. If one of them is killed, the other has to fear only the vendetta of the slain man's relatives, but no punishment on the part of the tribal community. The structure of a primitive industrial

---

[1] Among the Andamanese the weapons of excited men are sometimes taken away. Cf. W. SCHMIDT, *op. cit.* p. 179.

community interwoven with this weak organization of the folk community is closely adapted to the economic division of labour between husbands and wives in the several families [1].

The male members of the folk community go hunting together, the females collect fruits, roots, leaves. In the distribution of the spoils of the chase and of the collected fruits universal societal norms have to be observed [2]. In most cases the whole people, not the individual families, are the owners of the soil. Also the structure of the cult-community, interwoven in this primitive society and playing an important rôle in *the rites of initiation,* is clearly directed and guided by the structure of the natural family [3].

The political organization is still very weak at this stage of historical development of the small tribal or folk community. A stronger form of political organization in the tribal community is incompatible with the leading part played by the structural principle of the natural family and kinship bonds in these societies.

Neither the patriarchal joint family, nor the individual natural family and the kinship community allow of a strong tribal organization so long as they play a central and dominating rôle in the societal relations.

On the other hand the patriarchal totemistic peoples have a rather complicated tribal organization resting on a much more intensive basis of power. There the structure of the natural family no longer has a leading function; the *political structure* has taken over this leading rôle and even shows a distinct anta-

---

[1] W. SCHMIDT, *op. cit.* p. 149: '*Die ersten Ansätze zu wirtschaftlichen Verbänden* sind in der deutlichen Arbeitsteilung gelegen, die gerade bei den Stämmen der Urzeit zwischen den beiden ersten Konstituenten der Familie, zwischen Mann und Frau, sich einrichtete'. [The first beginnings of organized industrial relationships are to be seen in the evident division of labour which exactly among the earliest primitive tribes was adapted to the difference between man and woman, as the first constituents of the family].

[2] Cf. W. SCHMIDT, *op. cit.*, p. 185 ff.: "*Soziale Fürsorge im Urstaat*".

[3] Cf. HOWITT's description of these rites among the Kurnai in *The Native Tribes of South-East Australia* (London, 1904). Among the primary norms solemnly promulgated on this occasion for the initiated youths to observe, the first commandment is: listening to their parents and obeying them; the second commandment is: sharing their goods with their fellow-tribesmen, *etc.*

gonism with the natural structures of the family, and the marriage- and broader kinship community. When the totem-clans are subdivided into originally matriarchal phratries, the tribal form becomes even more complicated.

In his book on the age-groups and men's associations [1] H. SCHURTZ has already pointed out how the strengthening of the political structure in the primitive tribal organization is always brought about by depriving the family and marriage bonds of the central leading position they had when societal relations were less complicated.

The introduction of age-groups already emancipates boys from the family community since the moment of their initiation. Among many totemistic tribes we meet with separate young men's houses, which means that the young men are no longer allowed to live in the paternal home after their initiation. They often have to live as young bachelors up to their thirtieth year, either or not strictly separated from the female members of the tribe. They are only connected by their membership of the tribe, and the community of their house and their sex. Among various more strongly organized tribes the boys, on the occasion of their promotion to the rank of tribal membership by initiation, are explicitly forbidden any longer to obey their mother [2]. This forms a striking contrast to the primitive phase of tribal development in which the structure of the natural community has a leading rôle.

The structural interwovenness implied in the secret *"men's societies"*.

In this context we must also refer to the "secret men's societies", which are of very general occurrence among the more developed primitive peoples. In these associations the structure of the natural family bond can no longer have a leading part, because practically every internal tie with the structure of the immediate family and the more extensive kinship community has been broken.

W. SCHMIDT is of the opinion that the original structure of these unions was that of aristocratically organized associations. They keep their internal regulations a close secret from women and outsiders. Members intimidate the latter by means of the terrifying

---

[1] H. SCHURTZ, *Alterklassen und Männerbünde* (Berlin, 1902).

[2] W. SCHMIDT, *op. cit.* pp. 278 ff; cf. our remarks on p. 362, note 3.

secrecy of the organization, by all kinds of violent and frightening devices, and even by capital punishment.

Executions partly take place in "*Vehmgerichte*" and are applied both to members who have betrayed club-secrets to women, and to women who have succeeded in finding these secrets out or who have overheard them.

At first these clubs only accepted men who had stood the severest tests of eligibility in a series of ceremonies, sometimes even including the killing of a near relative. Membership is classified in a vertical order of gradation. After passing a test and initiation it is possible for a man to rise to a higher grade. But admission and promotion always depend on the payment of a certain sum in real values, such as pigs, fruits, *etc.* The proceedings of these meetings are for the greater part unknown to us, because their secret is jealously kept, especially from Europeans.

Yet it has been established that ancestor worship (often connected with a skull-cult) plays an important part in them. Large feasts are organized, for which the village-women are compelled to make preparations and to procure the necessary foodstuffs. For that purpose they are terrified by men wearing ghost-masks.

Nowadays there are various secret societies accessible both to men and to women among primitive peoples. Sometimes they do not have different grades, — *e.g.*, in New Guinea. The Dukduk society in New Mecklenburg and Eastern New Pommerania also includes children, and especially performs the typical political part of legislator, judge, police, and executioner in the primitive society of these islanders. In the Banks' Islands the men's clubs with their strong graduated hierarchy are also characterized by a political structure, which appears from their public and secret administration of justice and their terrorism over outsiders. But the West-African Butwa union in the Congo admits men as well as women. In this latter type of union the political and the social[1] structures have not been erased, *but the whole relationship is here under the leading of the* structure of a faith- and cult-community. The club especially provides protection from evil spirits and at the same time promotes unbridled sexual intercourse. In North America the structure of a faith- and cult community generally comes to the fore in these secret societies, including ancestor-worship as well as magic in the most different forms. But here we also encounter a beginning differentiation and consequently a dissolution of the ancient clubs as undifferentiated organizations, as in the case of the prairie Indians who form special dancing clubs, military associations, tobacco unions (embracing both men and women), *etc.*[2].

W. SCHMIDT explains the original meaning of these secret

[1] *i.e.* the structure of a community qualified by its function of social intercourse, as found in a modern "club".

[2] G. HOLTKER, *Männerbünde.* (Handwörterbuch der Soziologie, hrg. v. VIERKANDT, 1931) p. 352.

men's societies as an organized resistance to the dominant position of women in the old matriarchal cultures[1]. If he is right, the leading rôle of the political structure in this particular type of interwoven societal relationship is implicitly explained.

True, his view is oriented to the "*Kulturkreislehre*", but even if it should appear to be incorrect, it cannot be denied that at least in the aristocratically organized form of these undifferentiated associations the political structural principle plays the leading part. According to SCHMIDT this aristocratic form is the original one.

The origin of the "men's societies"[2].

H. SCHURTZ introduced the name "*Männerbünde*" (men's societies) into ethnological writings and sought the origin of these primitive associations in the "dichotomy of the sexes"[3]. His argument is based upon the following considerations. A woman's nature possesses a preponderant sexual drive towards a man and shows an interest in family and kindred which surpasses all other instincts and interests. In the male sex the psychical disposition is quite different. In a man sexual love is only strong intermittently. His interest is consequently not entirely occupied by family and kinship relations, but may be strongly directed towards social life in general and towards his intercourse with his own sex. This would explain the origin of age-groups, clubs and secret societies in a genetic order. This psychological attempt at explanation, however, is already refuted by the occurrence of "secret women's unions" among primitive peoples.

Moreover, "secret societies" cannot at all be a further development of age-groups, because their organizational form proves to be independent of age. Therefore, we cannot accept WEBSTER's view either that "secret societies" developed from initiation rites and age-groups on account of the men's desire to establish an aristocracy via a democracy and a plutocracy[4]. There is no demonstrable connection between age-groups and secret societies.

Practically there remain two important interpretations which really take account of all the available ethnological material. They are LOEB's theory and that of W. SCHMIDT. LOEB[5] holds that the secret societies in all their various forms can indeed be traced back to one common root, *viz.* the initiation rites of boys. But for the rest these societies arose independently of each other in

---

[1] Cf. his treatise *Initiations tribales et sociétés secrètes* (Sem. d'Ethn. Rel. III, 329—340), and especially *Völker und Kulturen* I, pp. 281 ff.

[2] Cf. HOLTKER, *op. cit.*

[3] Cf. his work *Alterklassen und Männerbünde.*

[4] *Primitive Secret Societies* (New York, 1908).

[5] *Tribal Initiations and Secret Societies* (Univ. of California Publ. in Am. Arch. and Ethn. 25 (1929), 249—288).

different areas as mere parallel phenomena (owing to a kind of convergence). SCHMIDT's theory, already mentioned in our text, starts from an original structure of men's unions as a political reaction in the old *matriarchal cultural circle*. He considers the divergent forms of development to result from a later denaturation. To the adherents of the *"Kulturkreislehre"* SCHMIDT's theory must seem the most satisfactory of the two.

SCHMIDT describes these aristocratic secret men's unions at the culmination of their power as a kind of "State within the State" [1]. The union opposes a secret power to the legal authority of the tribal chief and his council, and in course of time succeeds in acquiring the political control over the whole tribe.

In different places, *e.g.*, in New Pommerania, on the Solomons isles, *etc.*, the tribal chiefs made formal agreements with these secret societies. Or by causing themselves to be incorporated and reaching the highest rank in them, these chiefs tried to make the union's political power subservient to their own ends. In other parts of the world, *e.g.*, in West-Africa, the unions openly defied the authority of the tribal chief and made his power illusionary.

SCHMIDT further points to the fact that these societies show a peculiar tendency to extend their propaganda to various tribal territories, thus exceeding the narrow limits of their own people. On the other hand, they remained the powerful guardians of their rigid tradition against European influence and showed themselves to be the bitterest enemies of the latter. Thus it appears that at least in the golden age of these aristocratic secret men's societies the political structure no doubt played a leading part in this primitive interwoven whole comprising the structures of faith- and cult communities, as well as those of another nature. In various parts of the world these societies lose their political power partly or wholly. Then the faith- and cult- structure (in ancestor worship, masked dances, *etc.*), implied in their interweaving forms from the outset, takes the lead. Or, as in the case of the prairie Indians of North America, the originally undifferentiated secret associations are affected by the process of differentiation. This means that these societies have undergone an essential structural change and have lost their former central significance within the tribal community. All this holds good only, if SCHMIDT's theory of the common origin of these men's societies is correct.

---

[1] Naturally this characterization is terminologically inadequate.

In any case the name "men's society" introduced by SCHURTZ does not cover a real structural identity in the various types of associations indicated by it, insofar as they occur among primitive peoples at the present day. This is not merely a question of different varieties of the same basic structure of primitive associations, but the complicated structure of these different types is really *different in principle.*

Other types of undifferentiated communities.

There are other typical forms of undifferentiated communities which have not yet been discussed in this section, for instance *the guilds, the primitive vicinages, the pre-feudal and feudal* manorial communities *(villae, domaines)* and seigniories, *etc.* The guilds, in the sense of brotherhoods (fraternities), are primitive associations which imitate the sibs without including any bond of real or fictitious common descent. Nevertheless, the institutional trait of the sib is present insofar as the guilds generally embrace also the children under age of the guild-brothers as passive members. So the structural principle of the kinship community also here plays the leading rôle. Such guilds may include different kinds of trade-unions (of craftsmen, merchants, farmers, *etc.*), cult-communities, political organizations, *etc.* Especially in the Germanic peoples during the Middle Ages they have displayed a rich variety of possibilities. The medieval towns[1], as well as the medieval vicinages in the country were to a large extent organized as guilds. But these undifferentiated organizations are also to be found in extant primitive peoples. Among the Cheyenne of North America we even meet with female craftguilds. As to the medieval manorial communities *(villae, domaines)* we may observe that they are often indicated in the latin sources as "*familiae*", after the pattern of the old undifferentiated Roman domestic community *(familia),* which also included the structure of an agricultural organization. The feudal vassal-relation was, just as the Germanic *trustis,* originally also closely connected with the domestic community of the seigneur, as is shown by the *formula Turonensis 43,* which is the oldest source of our knowledge of the vassal's original condition. In its later development the feudal bond was gradually emancipated from the domestic power of the seigneur without losing its undifferentiated structure. During the period of its military

[1] We shall show in a later context that in the towns the guild-system was soon involved in a process of differentiation.

significance a political principle took the lead in this structure. But we shall see later on that no single feudal seigniory can be viewed as a real State because of its pluri-structural character impeding any realization of the differentiated structure of a body politic.

§ 7 - THE UNDIFFERENTIATED ORGANIZED COMMUNITIES AND THE SCHEMA OF THE WHOLE AND ITS PARTS IN THE UNIVERSALISTIC THEORIES WHICH CONSIDER THE FAMILY AS THE GERM-CELL OF THE STATE. THE PROBLEM OF THE SO-CALLED "PRIMITIVE PRIMARY NORM".

The Aristotelian theory of organized communities and the undifferentiated structure of the Greek *phylae* and phratries.

Our analysis of the complicated structure of undifferentiated organized communities can only strengthen our former hypothesis about the historical background of the so-called "organic" universalistic views of human society, which are based on the Aristotelian conception of the social nature of man. They look upon the family as the "germ-cell" of all authorative societal relations. They state that the "social impulse" is realized in a gradual process of extension to ever more inclusive communities, culminating in an all-inclusive societal whole of which all the others are the *"parts"*.

In an earlier context we have seen that when ARISTOTLE discusses the family he does not mean the differentiated structure of the natural family as such; rather he had in view the undifferentiated societal relationship of the ancient Greek "household" (*οἰκία*), including the conjugal and family community as well as the industrial community of the Greek land-owner and his slaves subject to his domestic authority. And it appeared to be the economically qualified structure of the latter relationship which in his view characterized the household as a whole.

The "village community" (*κώμη* among the Dorians, *δῆμος* among the Ionians) he conceived of as a union of different "households", based on neighbourship. His conception of the *polis* (the city-State) appeared in no way to correspond to our modern idea of a State. It is really the whole organized Greek society within the territory of the city-State under the political supremacy of the *polis*. ARISTOTLE's metaphysically founded conception of the natural development of the *polis* as the societal totality, originating in the "household" as its political germ-cell, was no doubt adapted to the undifferentiated societal relationships preceding the rise of the democratic republic.

Ancient Greek society had known these relationships, and the Greek "household" in the golden age of Greek culture had retained most of its original features[1]. The ancient Attic and Dorian "*phylae*" were originally parts of the tribal organization and real organized communities with chiefs of their own (φυλοβασιλεῖς), chosen from the domestic chiefs belonging to the patrician sibs. They were divided into *phratries* (called ὠβαί by the Dorians), which consisted of the patriarchal gentes (γένη) enkaptically including the separate domestic communities. Up to the time of SOLON's political reforms the real pillars of the entire structure of the Athenian *polis* were the four Attic *phylae* and their subdivisions, the twelve *phratries*, in their indissoluble coherence with the *gentes*.

SOLON introduced the four property classes (τιμήματα, τέλη) and deprived the *phylae* and phratries of their political significance, except for the control of a citizen's claim to noble descent as an essential requirement for constitutional citizenship. The newly married female citizen was incorporated in her husband's *phratry*, every new-born child in its father's *phratry* and *gens*. The old Ionian *phylae* were not abolished before the democratic reform of SOLON's constitution, accomplished by KLEISTHENES after the expulsion of the Pisistratidae. Every connection between the ancient γένη *(gentes)* and the constitution was broken. The *phratries* were continued solely as cult-communities without any political structure. Or, in case new ones were formed, they lacked any connection with the ancient gentilitial structure.

Also the ancient Roman city had a political structure which was originally wholly interwoven with the undifferentiated structure of the *gentes*. Each of the ten ancient *curiae* of the city community contained a number of *gentes*, which were at first undifferentiated social units and functioned as cult communities and closed agrarian organizations as well[2]. This

[1] ARISTOTLE himself points this out in his *Pol.* 1280*b*, 35; 1264*a*, 8; 1319*b*, 18; and in other places.

[2] Cf. THEODOR MOMMSEN, *Abriss des römischen Staatsrechts* (2nd ed. 1907) p. 11.

According to NIEBUHR *(Röm. Geschichte)*, the old curia was identical with the *gens*, which was not at all founded in blood-relation but was originally a constitutional legal relationship of ten families with a common name, common *sacra* and closed landed property. For this statement he

probably explains the local character of the old *curiae*, which as "gentilitial societies" were also agrarian landed-property communities. Roman citizenship was at first closely interwoven with the patrician gentilitial structure. This is clearly evident from the oldest designation of Roman citizens as *quirites*, which name, according to MOMMSEN, is connected with the *curia* as a *gentilitial society* [1]. Every *gentilis* as such was a *quiris*, and those who did not belong to a patrician gens at first lacked political rights.

It must be clear, however, that the reference to the ancient undifferentiated structure of Greek and Roman society cannot justify the Aristotelian universalistic view of human social life. Apart from the fact that even in an undifferentiated society the really natural communities do not permit themselves to be conceived as parts of the sibs, this universalism, because of its metaphysical foundation, must lay claim to its application to every possible human society, irrespective of its historical level of development. In ARISTOTLE's days the Greek *polis* was certainly not to be viewed as a social whole composed of primitive vicinages and households. It was a real city-State, though in a condition of decline. A universalistic theory of society based on its archaic condition is reactionary from a political point of view.

Such a theory can never be "historically" justified, as it misconceives a structural state of affairs which as such is *the foundation* of the historical development of human social life.

The problem of the "primitive primary norm" and the functionalistic conception of it. SOMLÓ's view.

Our insight into the interwoven structures of the undifferentiated societal relationships also sheds light on the problem of the so-called "primitive primary norm".

The term "primitive primary norm" *(primitive Urnorm)* has been introduced by the late professor FELIX SOMLÓ of the University of Budapest in his book *Juristische Grundlehre* (1st ed. 1917; 2nd ed. 1927) [2]. By this term he meant to signify that primitive

---

quotes CICERO, *Topica 6* (where the gentiles are defined as follows: "qui inter se eodem nomine sunt, ab ingenuis oriundi, quorum maiorum nemo servitutem servivit et qui capite non sunt deminuti"). However this may be, the name *gens* also means *sib*, in which at any rate the family structure *played a leading part*, however slight the affiliation among the members might be, especially in later times.

[1] Cf. THEODOR MOMMSEN, *op. cit.* pp. 5 and 11.

[2] *Juristische Grundlehre* (2nd ed. 1927), § 27.

peoples do not have differentiated modal systems of norms. Their legal, moral, social and faith rules are still interwoven into an undifferentiated unity. This state of affairs was already generally known among modern ethnologists, although MALINOWSKI has denied it on grounds which in my opinion are not convincing [1]. It was interpreted in different ways.

But it was not realized that the "primitive primary norm" can only be explained by means of the *structures of individuality of undifferentiated societal relations, and never by means of a modal concept of function.*

Thus it was often asserted that primitive societies do possess an idea of "*Sitte*" (*i.e.* propriety, morals) but not our notion of "law". Law was supposed to be a late product of differentiation derived from the undifferentiated "*Sitte*" [2].

In contrast with this, FELIX SOMLÓ holds that the "primitive primary norm" must be considered as primitive "law", and that there is not yet any question here of "*Sitte*". 'It is even clearer', so he observes, 'when we say that in primitive societies there exists no real "*Sitte*" at all in the technical sense of the word. Such undeveloped societies lack the differentiation which shows us norms of a character different from the traditions that constitute the "law" of these societies ("law" because backed by their supreme authority) and corresponding to our notion of "*Sitte*" since they do not originate from such a supreme authority' [3].

According to SOMLÓ a primitive society, therefore, only knows law, as an undifferentiated complex of norms, to be traced back

---

[1] Cf. his *Crime and Custom in Savage Society* (2rd ed. 1940). Notwithstanding many important observations and an interesting criticism of the current view of modern ethnologists concerning the undifferentiated character of primitive customs, MALINOWSKI goes doubtless too far by ascribing modern differentiated categories of norms to primitive peoples. Apart from the fact that his criterion of law is unsatisfactory, he neglects the structural problem implied in an analysis of primitive societies.

[2] It is especially this current opinion which is criticized by MALINOWSKI.

[3] *Op. cit.* pp. 88 and 89: "Noch deutlicher ist es, zu sagen, dass es in den primitiven Gesellschaften gar keine eigentliche "Sitte" im technischen Sinne des Wortes gibt. Es fehlt in solchen unentwickelten Gesellschaften die Differenziertheit, die uns neben den Ueberlieferungen, die das Recht jener Gemeinschaft bedeuten, weil hinter ihnen deren "höchste Macht" steht, auch noch anderweitige von altesher überlieferte Normen erkennen liesse hinter denen jene höchste Macht nicht steht und die unserem Begriff der Sitte entsprächen".

to the "supreme authority" in the tribal community. From this common root the other modal complexes of norms are supposed to be differentiated in the course of time. According to the other opinion the very reverse should be assumed. Both views fundamentally fail to interpret the phenomenon of the "primitive primary norm".

SOMLÓ's conception is entirely dependent on his genetic-positivistic view of law, which has been strongly influenced by AUSTIN's concept of sovereignty. SOMLÓ delimits legal rules from all other classes of norms as the sum-total of all the "norms originating from a permanent, supreme, extensive power [1] that is usually followed". If this definition is accepted, the conclusion is inevitable that all the rules that are valid within a primitive tribal community must be conceived as *juridical* norms. At least if it is also assumed that they all originate from the bearer of the supreme tribal authority, a supposition which does not at all correspond to the facts. But apart from this untenable supposition SOMLÓ's conclusion only proves that his positivistic conception of law is based on an eradication of the modal structure of meaning proper to legal norms. Any attempt to gain an insight into the structure of the "primitive primary norm" in this way is bound to fail. It starts from an absolutely arbitrary thesis which in every respect is contrary to the primitive consciousness of norms. This modern positivistic thesis seeks the only origin of a legal order in the arbitrary power of a supreme human authority. But primitive conciousness does not recognize any human arbitrariness in the norms of a time-honoured tribal order. It does not at all understand SOMLÓ's conception that juridical rules belong to the category of "merely empirical" or arbitrary norms.

The view of FRITZ MÜNCH.

More important is FRITZ MÜNCH's conception of the "primitive primary norm" which he explained in his treatise *Kultur und Recht* [2]. MÜNCH starts from the thesis that primitive peoples as such are entirely outside of history [3]. They have a social, but not

---

[1] *Op. cit.* p. 105.

[2] FRITZ MÜNCH is a neo-Kantian of the South Western German school. His article was published in *Zeitschrift für Rechtsphilosophie in Lehre und Praxis.* Bnd I (Leipzig 1914) pp. 345 ff.

[3] This thesis has been rejected by us. Cf. Vol. II, pp. 259 ff.

an historical life. "Social" in this context is to be taken in the usual sense of "concerning human society". In the primitive "pre-historical state" the needs and interests of humanity are supposed to be exclusively concerned with the maintenance of the life of the individual and that of the species. The latter was the starting-point for the development of the "social moment", the formation of a community, and for communal life. Tribes are formed whose individual members have a feeling of solidarity. Thus a common "popular consciousness" or a "tribal consciousness" arises. The individual tribesman feels embedded in it and derives the rules for all his vital relations from it. This "social consciousness" at first embraces an undivided unity of norms for all possible spheres of life: *i.e.*, for all those fields of action that are later on distinguished as "religious", scientific, aesthetic, moral, juridical, economic, technical, hygienic, gymnastic-pedagogic spheres [1].

At a particular moment in this development the original unity is replaced by differentiation when the authority of the tribal consciousness is undermined. The blind faith in the authorities that up till then had been unconditionally recognized becomes shaken. The individual member emancipates himself from the power of the tribal community, and considers himself as the "measure of all things". This is the breaking up of the old traditional unity of the normative consciousness. The different "cultural spheres" begin to assume some measure of independence, and at first each of them strives after absolutizing its own specific leading idea. Only then does primitive *social* life become truly *historical*. The *given* unity of the normative spheres in the tribal consciousness gets lost. The unity of the differentiated normative spheres becomes a *task*, an *"Aufgabe"*, only realizable in a freely planned *system of Ideas*. This is a system "which combines all particular ideas (and the cultural spheres constituted by them) into a synthetic harmony, in accordance with the specific significance each single meaning-realm has for the totality of culture [2].

I am not going to discuss MÜNCH's conception of history. Naturally I agree with his thesis that the process of differentiation does not start before a people has outgrown the primitive stage

---

[1] *Op. cit.* p. 348.

[2] *Op. cit.* p. 348: "das in Harmonie alle Einzelideen und die von ihnen konstituierten Kultursphären synthetisch zusammenfügt gemäss der spezifischen Bedeutung jedes einzelnen Sinngebietes für das Ganze der Kultur".

of its culture. But it is an untenable view that this moment is only there when the individual is considered to be "the measure of all things"[1]. The chief point is that MÜNCH's view of the "primitive primary norm" cannot give us an insight into the real *structure* of this phenomenon, because he tries to approach it psychologically, from the undifferentiated feeling of norms within a primitive society. But the undifferentiated communal feeling about what ought to be and what ought not to be can only be understood from the inner structure of the undifferentiated community itself, and not *vice versa*. For we cannot be satisfied here with tracing the merely *modal* structure of this collective feeling[2]. *The problem of a primitive primary norm is really that of its individuality-structure.*

Primitive primary norms should not be identified with the internal structural norms of a differentiated societal relationship. A revision of my former view of this question.

In the first draft of my *Encyclopedia of Jurisprudence* I was of opinion that this structure could also be illustrated by means of a natural community such as the family in its narrowest sense. Our elaborate analysis of the structural aspects of the natural family will immediately explain how I could arrive at such an opinion. For in the internal relations of this simple societal relationship all its modal aspects are indeed interlaced into the indissoluble unity of its basic individuality structure. The internal norms of the family present themselves to the members as a structural unity in which the separate modalities cannot be grasped in isolation. When a child is continually rude to its parents it does not only transgress a separate complex of norms relating to social intercourse, but it also violates parental rights;

[1] *Op. cit.* p. 352.

In a note MÜNCH writes: 'Für das Typische dieses kulturhistorischen Vorgangs ist es irrelevant ob man ihn sich an der Sophistik oder am Aufklärungszeitalter, oder an den modernen Relativismus, Historismus, Pragmatismus veranschaulicht'. [*It is irrelevant to the typical characteristic of this cultural historical process whether the Sophistic period or the time of the Enlightenment, or modern Relativism, Historicism or Pragmatism is taken as an illustration.*] These examples themselves prove MÜNCH's criterion to be insufficient. For nobody will be able to maintain that before the occurrence of these movements human society was at a primitive stage of culture, without any differentiation of its structural norms.

[2] Cf. Vol. II, part. I, pp. 111 ff.

it shows a lack of love of its parents; it assails the aesthetic harmony within the family; it is guilty of a contempt of the norm of faith implying that its parents have received their authority from God and are invested by Him with an office, *etc.* In other words, the internal norms of the family are really structural norms of this community, which can never be resolved into their separate modal aspects.

The prevailing conception holds that this peculiarity can only be found in the case of "primitive primary norms". I at one time identified the "primitive primary norms" with the internal structural norms of a natural community. But it will be clear now that this view is equal to a denial of the primitive character of the phenomenon in question.

My old view provisionally had an advantage over the prevailing functionalistic conception. For it shed a sharp light on the fact that the internal norms of a natural community cannot be grasped with a modal concept of function.

But the identification of the so-called "primitive primary norms" with the internal structural norms of a natural community gives no satisfaction. It is undeniable that truly primitive societal norms of an undifferentiated character are much more complicated than those of a simple family structure.

Primitive primary norms are essentially interweavings of various structural norms.

"Primitive primary norms" are forms of interweaving of various structural norms. A sib, *e.g.*, not only forms internal norms of brotherhood within its undifferentiated structure, but also internal industrial norms, internal political norms, internal norms of a cult community and those of a "club", in accordance with the variable social needs of a primitive society.

These complexes of internal norms have not been differentiated according to separate societal relationships, but are positivized in an undivided and undifferentiated form of social organization. We have shown, however, that in this societal form one particular structural principle plays the leading part. This is the reason why in a primitive societal relationship its members are unaware of the structural differentiation among these societal norms. Norms of social intercourse, legal norms, those of morality and faith, *etc.*, are never realized by the primitive consciousness in their abstract modality, but exclusively in the *concrete structure of one and the same primitive community.*

This implies that there can *a fortiori* be no question of a differentiated legal, or moral consciousness or one of social intercourse as such. The undifferentiated structure of the primitive societal unit also covers up the *modal aspects* of these complicated primitive norms in the communal consciousness.

This phenomenon of the primitive primary norm is something quite different from that of a complex of norms containing rules of different structures but destined for *various differentiated societal relationships.*

If, for instance, a modern State has adopted the principle of a State Church (in England the Established Church) the government as "*praecipuum membrum ecclesiae*" may, *e.g.*, enact certain ecclesiastical norms. The same statute may also contain truly internal constitutional norms of the body politic. But the fact remains that in this case Church and State each possess a differentiated societal structure. Nobody who has not got entangled in a historicistic positivism will deny that the structural norms concerned also have a differentiated character.

In the case of "primitive primary norms" things are entirely different. The various individuality structures of human society have not yet been formed into differentiated communities. Only one undifferentiated form of organization interweaves them all to the unity of its primitive structure.

PART II
(CONTINUATION)

THE STRUCTURES OF THE DIFFERENTIATED INSTITUTIONAL COMMUNITIES WITH A TYPICAL HISTORICAL FOUNDATION

CHAPTER III

THE STRUCTURAL PRINCIPLE OF THE STATE

§ 1 - INTRODUCTION TO THE INQUIRY INTO THE STRUCTURE OF THE STATE INSTITUTION. THE CRISIS IN THE THEORY OF THE STATE AND THE DIALECTICAL PROCESS IN THE DEVELOPMENT OF THE VARIOUS THEORIES.

In the last chapter we first discussed the structures of natural institutional communities embraced by the radical type of the biotically founded and morally qualified societal units.

To this we added an inquiry into the historically founded main types of primitive undifferentiated and organized units, whose structure is often erroneously confounded with that of the natural communities. We shall now investigate the structural principles of the historically founded communities of a *differentiated* character which exhibit an institutional nature in the sense defined earlier [1].

Among the primitive organized communities we have also met with societal units which may be called institutional insofar as their members belong to them by birth or at least are not free to leave them. But not all types of these undifferentiated organizations appeared to exhibit this institutional trait. The men's and women's societies, for instance, discussed in the 5th section of the preceding chapter, can certainly not be considered as institutional communities. They are to be sharply distinguished in this respect from the patriarchal joint families, the sibs and the primitive domestic communities, which do display this character, just like the tribal organizations, and to some degree the medieval guilds, insofar as they imitate the sib-structure.

Among the differentiated organized communities only the State and the Church appeared to be of an institutional nature. The present chapter will be devoted to an ample analysis of the inner structural principle of the State. That of the Church-institution will demand our attention in the next chapter.

---

[1] See p. 187 of this volume.

The chaotic confusion in the conception of the nature of the State.

Perhaps there is no other organized human community whose character has given rise to such a chaotic diversity of opinions in modern social philosophy and social science as the State. And the neglect of the study of the internal structural principles of human societal relationships has nowhere been more disastrous than in the general theory of the body politic. In recent times this theory has come to a crisis that the Humanistic views were unable to overcome. But the neglect of the transcendental internal individuality structure of the State in political and social theory is not a recent evil. Already in ancient philosophical political theories the conceptions of the State appeared to be so vague and undefined as to the inner nature of this institution that they were bound to vitiate the entire view of human society.

In an earlier context we have seen that the Platonic and Aristotelian conceptions of the *polis* operated with the metaphysical scheme of the whole and its parts, and conceived of the State simply as the totality of human society. The Aristotelian view of the *polis* as *"societas perfecta"*, as a self-sufficient, "autarchic" community whose aim is the "good life", really lacked any internal structural limitation [1].

Besides, there was no insight here into the typical historical foundation of the State as a *non-natural* institution. On the other hand this view remained free from the prejudice of a modern historicistic positivism that looks upon the body politic as a variable historical phenomenon, apart from any normative principle.

In PLATO and ARISTOTLE a normative idea of the State of a supposed supra-temporal, metaphysical character is recognized as *the normative essence* of this community, and laid at the foundation of any empirical enquiry into its factual manifestations. PLATO's ideal State is partly oriented to a constructive idealistic metaphysics, and partly historically bound to the formal patterns of the Doric and Cretan States.

[1] This is erroneously denied by A. MENZEL, *Griechische Staatssoziologie* (Z.f. öff.R.XVI, 1936) pp. 24 ff. The fact that ARISTOTLE treats of territory, nation, and magistrate, and recognizes the important position of the military factor in the State, does not mean that his view is oriented to the real structural principle of this institutional community. Cf. *Pol.* I, 1280 b, where the only *essential* characteristic of the State is called: *κοινωνία τοῦ εὖ ζῆν* (community of good life).

Nevertheless it is remarkable that notwithstanding the universalistic identification of the ideal *polis* with the whole of societal life, the inner structural principle of the State proper urges itself upon PLATO, at least in his project of the organization of the typical political functions.

There are two genuinely *political* classes in this polis, *viz.* that of the philosophers, who rule according to the *idea of justice,* and that of the warriors, in which the State's *monopoly of the sword-power* is represented. This division implicitly recognizes the two peculiar structural functions that will appear to be radical-typical for the State institution. In itself this fact is important, especially in its contrast with the modern historicist conception, which denies the State an invariable structural principle and considers it to be an absolutely variable historical phenomenon.

The character and the different meanings of a crisis in the theory of the State. The Greek Sophists and the Renaissance figure of MACCHIAVELLI.

Every time the belief in an invariable structural principle of the body politic has been sapped — in whatever sense this principle is conceived of — there arises *a crisis in the theory of the State.* A relativistic attitude then gains the upperhand.

Such a crisis may be the result of a really critical-theoretical attitude with regard to traditional political theories which in an uncritical way hold an existing historical form to be the unchangeable model for every kind of political life. Then the crisis is a necessary transitional stage in the theoretical reflection on the problem of the State, and it may be called useful at least in this respect.

Such a theoretical crisis has no doubt been prepared for in the course of time by an internal process of decline in the traditional life of the body politic. This process may simply be a symptom of decadence, but it may also be an unavoidable transition to a new concentration of public life. The first theoretical crisis in the Greek view of the State was started by the radical left wing sophists. It was the result of a decay of the foundations of Athenian democracy after the death of PERICLES. Then the entiry Greek city-State passed through a fatal "twilight of the gods" and the once so proud *polis* was never to see another dawn.

The naturalistic theory of the absolutist power-State, on the contrary, directed by the Renaissance statesman MACCHIAVELLI against the traditional medieval view, announced a real renaissance of political thought. It was the theoretical precipitation of a crisis which had already found expression in the individualist-nominalistic theory of the later Middle Ages. It announced the transition from an internally decaying medieval idea of the Holy Roman empire to the modern bureaucratically organized and strongly centralized national State. In the hopelessly divided Italian city-States of the Renaissance period the necessity of a powerful national body politic was sharply felt. The modern State-idea was a subject of lively discussion. Here the name "*stato*" was first used to indicate the body politic as a whole.

The recent crisis in the Humanistic theory of the State.

The most recent crisis in political theory, culminating in the "theories of the State without a State-idea", has been prepared for by quite a complex of factors to which I have devoted an elaborate analysis in my *De Crisis in de Humanistische Staatsleer.*

In it the decline of the normative Humanist idea of the civic law-State plays a dominant part. This idea was based on the Humanistic science- and personality-ideal, whose metaphysics has been worn away by relativism and historicism. Western man had become aware of a fundamental historical relativity of the supposed self-subsisting ideas of natural and rational law. In the crisis of a regular "*Götterdämmerung*" [1] of all "absolute" standards, the world of ideas of post-Kantian freedom-idealism had also been unmasked as historically conditioned. Then in political theory, too, relativistic positivism and historicism came to the fore. There was no longer room for an invariable normative structural principle of the State. RICHARD SCHMIDT merely formulated the prevailing relativistic conception in his *Allgemeine Staatslehre* when he wrote: 'Modern political theory emancipates itself from the speculative view, it leaves alone the metaphysical question about the idea of the State and restricts itself to the empirical world' [2].

---

[1] *i.e.* twilight of the Gods.

[2] RICHARD SCHMIDT, *Allgemeine Staatslehre* (Leipzig, 1901). Bnd. I, p. 117: 'Die neuere Staatslehre macht sich von der spekulativen Betrachtungsweise los, lässt die metaphysische Frage nach der Staatsidee bei Seite und beschränkt sich auf die Erfahrungswelt'.

CARL SCHMITT also gave expression to the relativistic destruction of the entire ideology of the State founded in the Humanistic faith in reason. About the modern "material" concept of statute law (which nowadays contains no other criterion for its distinction from the statute in a formal sense than its pertaining to a general rule) he says: 'All other properties of the statute law as a substantial-rational, just and reasonable arrangement have become relativized and problematical. The faith in natural law, implying the belief in the law of reason and in reason in the law, has disappeared to a considerable degree. The civic law-State is only saved from completely merging into the absolutism of changing Parliamentary majorities by the still factually existing respect for this universal character of the statute law' [1].

A metaphysically conceived normative idea of the State is no longer recognized in modern scientific thought insofar as it has been infected by Historicism [2]. Neither can this thought

---

[1] CARL SCHMITT, *Verfassungslehre* (1928), p. 156: 'Alle andern Eigenschaften des Gesetzes als einer substanziell-rationalen, gerechten und vernüftigen Anordnung sind heute relativiert und problematisch geworden; der naturrechtliche Glaube an das Gesetz der Vernunft und die Vernunft im Gesetz ist im weiten Masze entfallen. Was den bürgerlichen Rechtsstaat vor völliger Auflösung in den Absolutismus wechselnder Parlementsmehrheiten bewahrt ist nur der tatsächlich noch vorhandene Respect vor diesem generellen Character des Gesetzes'.

Cf. also HERMANN HELLER, *Der Begriff des Gesetzes in der Rechtsverfassung*, Veröffentlichungen der Vereinigung der Deutschen Staatsrechtlehrer, Heft 4 (1928) p. 115: 'Einer klaren Erkenntnis von der Bedeutung des Gesetzesbegriffs im Rechtsstaate steht heute die politische Degeneration des Rechtsstaatsgedankens im Wege'. [A clear knowledge of what the concept of law means in a law-State is made impossible nowadays by the political degeneration of the idea of the law-State].

A critic of my book *De Crisis in de Human. Staatsleer* has argued against it that such pronouncements were only to be found in *German* writings on the State. But this is hardly tenable for anyone who has been acquainted with recent political literature. Not only German but also the French political literature after the first world-war was penetrated by this crisis of the law-State idea. In the Netherlands this crisis found its most striking expression after the second world-war in the remarkable book of H. W. SCHELTEMA, entitled *Beschouwingen over de Vooronderstellingen van ons Denken over Recht en Staat* (1948). In consequence of the appearance of this work I wrote an article entitled *De Vooronderstellingen van ons Denken over Recht en Samenleving in de Crisis van het moderne Historisme* (in the juridical quarterly Themis-Rechtsgeleerd Magazijn 1949, pp. 193—249).

[2] Of late in Roman Catholic circles an *institutional theory* has been

accept the idea of an immutable structural principle of the body politic in our sense. The shibboleth of a scientific political theory was declared to be the elimination of all normative evaluations. Thus the attempt was made to form an a-normative notion of the State on a merely historical and positivist sociological basis.

The supra-historical societal structures of "historical phenomena".

But in what way could such an a-normative conception be formed on the basis of the infinite multiplicity of "historical forms" of political life? Evidently any historical inquiry into the development of the State-institution must be based on a structural idea of the latter, if we are to be scientifically justified in speaking univocally of a *State.*

Is a State an absolutely transient historical occurrence, like *e.g.*, "the battle of Waterloo"? Evidently not. On second thought "the battle of Waterloo" itself cannot be grasped in an *exclusively* modal-historical sense. *It is related to the structure of the State* insofar as it occurred in a war between the Napoleonic French State and the allied States which had united to put an end to the Napoleonic empire. Outside this relation it cannot be understood in its historical structural meaning. All individual historical phenomena manifest themselves in social individuality structures which *as such* are not of *a modal historical* nature, let alone of an absolutely transient individual historical character. The variable social forms in which the State-institution is realized in the course of time should never be confounded with its structural principle, founded in the plastic horizon of experience and reality, which alone makes possible our ex-

---

gaining ground, which tries to give the historical sociological conception of the State a metaphysical foundation. It has been founded by the late French professor of constitutional law, M. HAURIOU, who in his earlier sociological works was strongly under the influence of Comtian positivism but later on underwent the influence of the philosophy of life and ultimately founded his institutional conception of the State in a metaphysical State-idea, conceived of in a neo-Platonic sense. His colleague at the Nancy University, G. RENARD *(La théorie de l'institution, Essai d'ontologie juridique* 1930), tried to accommodate the institutional theory of HAURIOU to the traditional Thomistic-Aristotelian view. HAURIOU himself, however, was much more oriented to the Augustinian-Platonic metaphysics. The institutional theory lies outside of the cadre of the "crisis in the Humanistic doctrine of the State" and, therefore, we need not enter into it in the present context.

perience of the transient State formations. This fundamental truth must again and again be imprinted in our readers' minds, in opposition to the prevailing relativistic tendencies of thought.

The representatives of modern political theory who tried to give a critical account of the structure of the State and did not content themselves with a kind of naïve empirical positivism, were often oriented to a merely methodological neo-Kantianism. The leading part in their epistemological reflection was given to the dualistic separation between *sein* and *sollen*[1] as methodological viewpoints. Accordingly the general theory of the State was divided into an "empirical" sociological, and a normative juridical part. From this dualistic methodological viewpoint, which in the last analysis was ruled by the Humanist basic motive of nature and freedom, any attempt at a synthesis of the juridical and the sociological conceptions was excluded in principle. The German scholar GEORG JELLINEK, who nevertheless tried to combine these antithetic conceptions, could not indicate any starting-point from which such a synthesis would be made possible. We shall presently return to this dualism in the general theory of the State.

A result of so-called critical epistemological reflection in the general sociological theory of the body politic was the reduction of this organized community to a subjective synthesis of a multiplicity of socio-psychical relations into a teleological unity ("*Zweckverband*"), which was supposed to function only in human consciousness, without any correspondence to reality. The so-called pure legal theory of the State, on the other hand, even resolved the body politic as an organized community into a logical system of legal norms, which should be conceived apart from any causal sociological viewpoint. This entire epistemological reflection remained oriented to a naturalistic, merely *functionalistic* and individualistic conception of reality. All individuality structures in human society were in principle levelled down, and the organized communities were resolved into a formal synthesis of elementary relations. The material content of this formal synthesis was completely abandoned to the historicistic view.

---

[1] Between what *is* and what *ought to be.*

The levelling of the individuality structure of the State in the overstraining of functionalistic thought.

In my book *De Crisis in de Humanistische Staatsleer* I have shown in great detail what modern nominalistic sociological and "normological" theories of the State have left of the body politic, as a result of this overstrained functionalistic mode of thought. To give only some examples: To LUDWIG WALDECKER the unity of an organized community, as such, is merely a synthetical category of thought. By its means an incalculable multitude of socio-psychical interactions between individuals cooperating in the social process are made accessible to thought in their totality[1].

From this nominalistic viewpoint there is not any qualitative essential difference between *the State* and *"all other organizations"*. 'Neither the organizations with a particular purpose, (such as, *e.g.*, a limited liability company), nor the autonomous political communities which are components of the State (*e.g.*, *municipality*, *district*, *and province*), are different from the State in a qualitative sense, but only quantitatively and functionally"[2]. From this viewpoint it is not surprising that the writer does not mind qualifying also the territorial national evangelical Churches as *States*. He justifies this view by the argument that however much nowadays we associate the idea of "spiritual interactions" with the notion "Church", this association is only *historically* determined[3].

A similar mentality is evident in MAX WEBER's pronouncement that sociologically speaking a modern State can only be considered as a "large-scale economic business" and that there is not any essential difference between a private economic enterprise, *e.g.*, a large factory, and a present-day State[4]. KELSEN could readily subscribe to this statement on his "normological standpoint", and remarked that for this very reason the organizational problem in both cases is identical[5].

The same tendency is seen in the guild socialist view, which

---

[1] WALDECKER: *Allgemeine Staatslehre* (1927) pp. 81—82 and 214—215.

[2] "Weder die Organisationen für bestimmte Zwecke, sagen wir etwa vom Typus einer Aktiengesellschaft, noch die Kommunalverbände (Gemeinde, Kreis, und Provinz), unterscheiden sich qualitativ, sondern stets nur quantitativ und funktional vom Staate".

[3] *Op. cit.* p. 217.

[4] MAX WEBER, *Parlement und Regierung im neu geordneten Deutschland* (1918) p. 15.

[5] *Vom Wesen und Wert der Demokratie*, p. 17.

HAROLD LASKI has characterized as the opinion that the State is "a body on the same footing as the Miners' Federation"[1]. In opposition to the levelling sociological conceptions of the body politic which eliminate its normative structure, the "normological" theory of KELSEN handled only a "purely juridical" viewpoint, which was found in the "*Sollensebene*"[2]. His overstraining of the juridical concept of function, denatured in a logicistic way, assumed grotesque proportions in the "normological" identification of the State with a logical system of legal norms deduced in his so-called "pure legal theory".

The dialectical "cultural-scientific" ("*geisteswissenschaftliche*") method applied to the general theory of the State. RUDOLF SMEND and the former "Berlin School".

The introduction of the dialectical cultural scientific (or "*geisteswissenschaftliche*") method into the general theory of the State, oriented to LITT's earlier discussed phenomenological sociology, could not show a way out of the crisis. It did not rest on a normative structural idea of the State in which the historicistic relativizing of all normative standards is to be overcome. In my *De Crisis in de Humanistische Staatsleer* I criticized the application of this method of thought to political theory in an analysis of the "*Integrationslehre*" of the founder of the former "Berlin School", RUDOLPH SMEND. In the meantime this school was definitively dispersed by the national socialist revolution in Germany.

HELLER's dialectical structural concept of the State, and the historicist view of reality.

There is, however, one work on the general theory of the State which, at least partly inspired by LITT's dialectical formal sociology, deserves our special attention in this context. I mean that of the German scholar HERMANN HELLER.

HELLER's methodological starting-point and his actualistic view of the unity of the State as always involved in a process of becoming, as "*plébiscite de tous les jours*"[3], were the reason why I formerly classed him with the "Berlin School". His conception

---

[1] LASKI, *A Grammar of Politics*, p. 73.

[2] The realm of what *should* be.

[3] He borrowed this word for the State from RENAN. Cf. his book *Die Souveränität* (Berlin und Leipzig, 1927, p. 82).

of the State, however, deviated already from the outset from that of SMEND. And HELLER's *Staatslehre* (1934), published posthumously and edited by GERHART NIEMEYER, cut through nearly every connection with SMEND's *"Integrationstheorie"*. In spite of his formal maintenance of LITT's dialectical-sociological method, he also relinquished some basic thoughts of LITT's sociology. As a matter of fact he seems never to have quite understood them [1]. He broke with the anti-axiological conception of sociology [2] and recognized the real State-institution as a subjective *"Aktzentrum"* [3]. His standpoint as to these two points thus became the direct opposite to LITT's, though HELLER did not realize this [4]. But this renders his posthumous work all the more important as a serious attempt to overcome the theoretical crisis in the general theory of the State. By means of a dialectical structural concept of the body politic he at least *means* to do full justice to the all-sided structural reality of this institutional organized community, and to bridge the neo-Kantian dualism of "*sein*" and "*sollen*" dialectically.

It seems to be promising that the normative functions of the State-institution are recognized and that the functionalistic conception of the latter is rejected. HELLER even seems to make room for a normative idea of the State in his theory. We will, therefore, examine HELLER's dialectical structural concept a little more in detail, in order to give account of its relation to the invariable normative structural principle of every real State-institution, we are seeking for.

HELLER's fundamental thesis is: 'The theory of the State is a *structural, not a historical science*'. This thesis seems indeed to have risen above the historicistic standpoint. Explicitly HELLER opposes a general political theory like R. SCHMIDT's, which exhausts its resources in giving a survey of the "development" of the "State" in the course of the history of the world. For lack of any well-defined concept of the body politic such an historical

---

[1] Cf. my *Crisis in de Hum. Staatsleer*, p. 50/1, note 3.

[2] *Staatslehre* (Leiden, 1934), pp. 51 ff.

[3] *Op. cit.*: "Unsere Aufgabe ist es, den Staat nachzuweisen als ein wirkliches einheitliches Aktzentrum innerhalb der Vielheit wirklicher und selbständiger, sei es einzelmenschlicher oder kollektiver Akzentren'. [Our task is to show that the State is a real unitary act-centre within the multiplicity of real and independent, either individual or collective act-centres.]

[4] Compare p. 254 and pp. 255 ff. of this volume.

survey applied the term "State" to intrinsically heterogeneous societal relationships that display some trait of a political organization of power. HELLER is also opposed to SMEND's integration theory which at bottom is equally historicistic and irrationalistic. This theory considers "integration" as the State's essential characteristic, conceiving this process as a perpetual renewal of the unity of the body politic [1]. But this viewpoint cannot be suited to a general theory of the State: 'For in the multiplicity of succeeding processes of integration', says HELLER, 'exactly that which alone can be the object of political theory must be eradicated and vanish, *viz.* the unity of the State which maintains itself in all changes" [2]. On a higher theoretical level HELLER even wants to do justice in a certain sense to the naïve conception of the "political status" as a relatively constant and real social unit.

On closer examination, however, he appears to give up the historicist view of reality only seemingly. His structural theoretical view of the State is meant to overcome the functionalistic historicist theory, but it is not oriented to an invariable, supramodal structural principle. HELLER only tries to conceive the "historical reality of the State" in all its incessant changes and dynamics according to a viewpoint other than that of the historian. In his opinion the "historical forms of human activity", among which he explicitly mentions the State, the Church and industrial life, cannot be understood, let alone explained, with the logical means of historical science, *i.e.* with the category of "temporal succession". They can only be understood from the simultaneity of coordinated human activity guaranteed by its social structure, so to say from the cross-section of the stream of history [3].

This vertical section through the horizontal functional stream of development of history does not display a chaos of separate facts and occurrences, but an ordered coherence of actions with a certain measure of stability and durability, in which the separate

---

[1] SMEND, *Verfassung und Verfassungsrecht* (1928), pp. 18 ff.

[2] HELLER, *Staatslehre* (Leiden, 1934) p. 49: 'Denn in der Vielheit einander ablösender Integrationsprozesse muss gerade das ausgelöst werden und verschwinden, was allein Gegenstand der Staatslehre sein kann: die in allem Wechsel sich behauptende Einheit des Staates'.

[3] *Op. cit.* p. 50: 'Nur aus dem gleichzeitigen Miteinander der gesellschaftlichen Wirkungsstruktur, sozusagen aus dem Querschnitt des Geschichtsstromes sind sie zu begreifen'.

structural forms function in mutual interdependence. 'Only because we distinguish different functions and structures within the totality of historical reality, do we become aware of the ordered picture of the stream. In this way alone are we capable of making a meaningful selection from the infinite multiplicity of (historical) facts' [1].

This means a complete acceptance of the historicistic view of reality which conceives all the normative aspects of the State under a historic basic denominator. The concept of function and that of structure, too, are historicized. HELLER does not want his structural concept to be conceived as a concept of the essential nature of the *State as such,* but only of the modern West-European State as it has developed since the Renaissance [2].

This historicistic attitude is also very clear from the following quotation from HELLER'S *Staatslehre,* which we insert here on account of its importance for our insight into his dialectical structural concept of the State:

'This only enables us to point out *within historical reality* [3] the starting-point for the theory of the State as a structural science. Not for a moment do we forget the genetic historical character of the State; neither, however, do we forget the political form of this process. We do not forget that the very theory of the State has to bring about that which historical science is unable to produce with its historical means: *to recognize the State as an historical structure, as a function within the totality of the concrete socio-historical constellation.* (Italics are mine). Under the aspect of historical science, speaking with HEGEL, *becoming* manifests itself as the truth of being. But in no way does *being* appear as the truth of becoming under the aspect of the structural theory of the body politic. With such a judgment we would be sanctioning that which political theory and juridical science have always done and especially again in our generation, *viz.* the absolutization of the momentary State.

'All political categories, however, are historically changeable, even the functions and certainly the structure of the present State. They in no way transcend history. All history is of unique occurrence in the irreversible direction of the stream. The structure of a body politic which is real within a particular basic structure of society, is therefore to be considered fundamentally impossible within another historical total situation' [4]. (Italics are mine).

---

[1] *Op. cit.* p. 50.

[2] *Op. cit.* pp. 3 ff.

[3] I italicize.

[4] *Op. cit.* p. 50/1: 'Damit haben wir erst die Möglichkeit innerhalb der geschichtlichen Wirklichkeit den Ansatzpunkt der Staatslehre als Strukturwissenschaft aufzuweisen. Sie vergisst zwar keinen Augenblick den Werdecharakter des Staates, sie vergisst aber ebensowenig die staatliche

This quotation makes it clear that HELLER considers the internal structural principle of the State to be a "merely empirical" historical phenomenon.

He did see that the historian must base his description of the history of a body politic on a structural concept of the latter. He also saw that only by means of a particular structure the multiplicity of human actions in particular situations are ordered into the peculiar unity of the totality of action of a *State*.

But he only conceives of this totality of actions in a *positivistic* sense as an "empirical form" or "pattern" of merely comparative stability, which is uninterruptedly carried along in the stream of history. He did not see that the *positivized and realized structure of the State* is only possible as a formation according to a *supra-positive structural principle*. Compare the following statement he makes: 'Insofar as this structure has a certain duration, political theory has been given its "*Gegenstand*"; insofar as this structure or configuration of the State is uninterruptedly carried along in the stream of history and permanently, though hardly perceptibly, included in a process of change, this configuration cannot be thought as closed, but only as open. History flows through it. Therefore it is absolutely necessary for political theory to know the process of becoming in what has come about, the developmental tendencies of the structure of the State' [1].

Geformtheit dieses politischen Werdens; sie vergisst nicht, das gerade sie das zu leisten hat, was die Geschichtwissenschaft mit ihren Mitteln nicht zu leisten im Stande ist: den Staat als geschichtliche Struktur und zwar als Funktion innerhalb der Totalität des konkreten geschichtlich-gesellschaftlichen Gefüges zu erkennen. Unter dem Aspekt der Geschichtswissenschaft erscheint, um mit HEGEL zu reden, das Werden als die Wahrheit des Seins. Unter dem Aspekt der struktur-theoretischen Staatslehre aber erscheint das Sein keineswegs etwa als die Wahrheit des Werdens. Mit einem solchen Urteil würden wir das sanktionieren, was die Staatslehre und Rechtswissenschaft von jeher und ganz besonders wieder in der letzten Generation getan hat: die Verabsolutierung des augenblicklichen Staates. Alle politischen Kategorien sind aber historisch wandelbar, selbst die Funktionen und erst recht die Struktur des gegenwärtigen Staates sind nichts weniger als geschichtstranszendent. Alle Geschichte ist ein einmaliges Geschehen in unumkehrbarer Stromrichtung und eine Staatsstruktur, die innerhalb einer bestimmten gesellschaftlichen Grundstruktur wirklich ist, muss eben deshalb prinzipiell als unmöglich angenommen werden innerhalb einer andern geschichtlichen Gesamtsituation".

[1] *Op. cit.* p. 51: 'Indem diese Struktur eine Dauer hat, ist der Staatslehre allererst ihr Gegenstand gegeben; sofern aber auch diese Staatsstruktur oder Gestalt des Staates ununterbrochen im Fluss der Geschichte steht und in dauernder, wenn auch oft kaum merklicher Wandlung begriffen ist, kann diese Gestalt nicht geschlossen gedacht werden, sondern nur offen; die Geschichte geht durch sie hindurch. Deshalb ist es unumgänglich, dass die Staatslehre das Werdende im Gewordenen, die Entwicklungstendenzen der Staatsstruktur erkennt'.

In perfect agreement with this historicistic structural concept is the moderately historicist normative idea of the State, without which in HELLER's opinion a genuine theory of the body politic cannot be set forth.

The following quotation shows the moderately historicistic character of this idea [1]:

'Theory no more than practice should deduce its leading ideas from the pure mind, both should derive them from the psychological-pragmatic motivations of living men. It is of little importance in this connection whether one believes one can "calculate" the future tendencies of politics from the dialectical tensions of the present — as Marxists do — or whether one holds up a future ideal to the present, as an imperative demand which is more or less in agreement with particular tendencies. For in either case the dialectician's view of the future is an evaluating orientation (transcending reality and consequently the present) in the sense intended by MANNHEIM; hence a Utopia [2], which he cannot give up... *Only by assuming that particular developmental tendencies are valid, does he find a leading idea enabling him to orient himself, to make a selection, and to give an interpretation...These political decisions do certainly not imply that the formative will of the political present is morally right, aesthetically beautiful, or valuable from the viewpoint of some general system of values.* What they do imply is, that they consider these tendencies to be "the next stage in the history of the world"' [3].

In my book *De Crisis in de Humanistische Staatsleer*, p. 83 ff., I showed that even the "moral-juridical principles", which according to HELLER alone can justify the State [4], are not considered

---

[1] A radically historicist view leaves no room for normative ideas.

[2] Cf. KARL MANNHEIM, *Ideologie und Utopie* (1929), p. 169.

[3] *Op. cit.* p. 56/7: 'Die Theorie darf ihre leitenden Ideen ebensowenig wie die Praxis aus dem reinen Geist deduzieren; beide müssen sie den psychologisch-pragmatischen Motivationen lebendiger Menschen entnehmen. Ob man dabei des Glaubens ist die Zukunftstendenzen der Politik liessen sich — wie die Marxisten meinen — aus den dialektischen Spannungen der Gegenwart "berechnen", oder ob man der Gegenwart in mehr oder weniger starker Uebereinstimmung mit bestimmten Tendenzen ein forderndes Zukunftsideal entgegenhält, macht in diesem Zusammenhang wenig aus, denn in jedem Fall ist auch die Zukunftsschau des theoretischen Dialektikers eine wertende, wirklichkeits-, also gegenwartstranszendente Orientierung, im Sinne Mannheims also eine "Utopie", auf die er nicht verzichten kan... Nur dadurch, dass er bestimmte Entwicklungstendenzen als gültig setzt, findet er eine Leitidee, die ihm Orientierung, Auswahl und Interpretation ermöglicht... Dass das gestaltende Wollen der politischen Gegenwart moralisch gut, aesthetisch schön oder von einem sonstigen allgemeinen Werstsystem her wertvol erscheine, besagen diese politische Entscheidungen gewiss nicht; wohl aber, dass sie in diesen Tendenzen die nächtste Stufe der Weltgeschichte sehen."

[4] *Op. cit.* p. 216 ff.

by him to be "supra-historical". He is strongly influenced by the modern irrationalistic philosophy of life. In his opinion the *"Entscheidung des Augenblicks"* (the decision of the moment) is superior to any principle, and he therefore rejects the idea of a supra-historical *"ordre naturel"* [1].

The distinction between the State and the other organized communities according to the scholastic method of the search for a *genus proximum* and *differentia specifica.*

That HELLER's dialectical structural concept of the State-institution is not really oriented to the internal structural principle of the latter, is at once evident when the distinction of the body politic from other human communities is at issue. This problem is crucial in every theory of societal relationships that starts with eliminating the structural principles given in the divine world-order.

For lack of an internal structural criterion HELLER again has recourse to the external method of classification found in ARISTOTLE's logic, *viz.* the method of determining the *genus proximum* and the *differentia specifica.* In our general theory of the modal law-spheres this method has been found to be insufficient, even to give account of the *modal* structures of reality [2].

'*Genus proximum* of the State', HELLER writes, 'is consequently the organization, the organized pattern of behaviour planned for the unity of decision and action. Its *specific difference* from all other organizations is the property of its sovereign command over a territory. This sovereignty and this relation to a territory, inherent in the State's power, give all the elements of its organization their specific character' [3].

---

[1] *Die Souveränität,* p. 176/7; these pages might just as well have been written by EMIL BRUNNER.

[2] HELLER indeed applies this method also to delimit his concept of law. Cf. *op. cit.* p. 183.

[3] *Op. cit.* p. 237: 'Genus proximum des Staates ist somit die Organisation, das zur Einheit der Entscheidung und Wirkung planmässig organisierte Handlungsgefüge. Differentia specifica allen andern Organisationen gegenüber ist seine Eigenschaft der souveränen Gebietsherrschaft. Durch die Souveränität und Gebietsbezogenheit der Staatsgewalt empfangen alle Elemente der Staatsorganisation ihren spezifischen Charakter'. In his book *Die Souveränität,* p. 81, the *"genus proximum"* and *"differentia specifica"* were slightly differently formulated: 'Der Staat, nach einem Worte F. J. STAHL's die "realisierte Rechtsordnung", ist das einheitliche Zusammenwirken von bestimmten menschlichen Akten, darin allen ande-

This was the "specific characteristic" by means of which already GIERKE tried to distinguish the body politic from other societal relationships[1]. Its vagueness is at once evident when we recall that the concepts "organization" and "sovereign territorial power" must exactly receive their internal delimitation of meaning from the eliminated structural principle of the State. Apart from this principle these notions remain perfectly multivocal "analogical concepts", which cannot enrich our insight; let alone that the concept of sovereignty is heavily burdened by a State absolutist tradition.

The problem of the relation between State and law in HELLER's dialectical structural theory.

The fundamental insufficiency of HELLER's structural concept is also evident in his attempt to conceive the relation between State and "law" dialectically.

All individuality structures in the juridical relations are levelled by purposely (*"zweckmässigerweise"*) reserving the term "law" only for the order of such norms which have been formed and sanctioned by special organs of the State-organization[2]. This makes it impossible for him to grasp the individuality structure of the internal constitutional law of the body politic. For modern times HELLER does not recognize any other positive law except State-law. Explicitly he calls the State "the formal source of validity of all legal rules" (p. 187). As regards modern Western society he denies the original competence of organized communities of a non-political nature to make their internal

---

ren menschlichen Verbänden gleich, von ihnen aber dadurch grundsätzlich geschieden, dass die ihn realisierenden Akten die Garantie des gesammten Zusammenwirkens auf diesem Gebiete darstellen'. [The State, according to a statement made by F. J. STAHL, the "realized legal order", is the unified cooperation of definite human actions, and in this respect similar to all other human organized communities. But fundamentally dissimilar to all of them is that the actions realized in the State are the guarantee of the total cooperation in this domain.]. The purport of this formulation is the same, which, moreover, appears from the identification of "universality" and "sovereignty", *op. cit.* p. 110: 'Staat heisst die auf einem bestimmten Gebiet universale, deshalb notwendig einzigartige und souveräne Entscheidungseinheit'. [State is the universal and, therefore, the necessarily unique and sovereign unity of decision in a certain territory.]

[1] Cf. GIERKE, *Die Grundbegriffe des Staatsrechts* (1915) pp. 99 ff. and my *Crisis in de Hum. Staatsleer*, pp. 119 ff. on this point.

[2] *Op. cit.* p. 186/7.

legal order, independent of the agreement of the State. He considers the relation between State and law only as an *historical problem*[1], quite in accordance with the historicistic viewpoint.

Neither the modal meaning-structure of law, nor the transcendental individuality-structure of the State are in the least taken into account. Positive law is supposed to develop "historically" from an undifferentiated "convention" because of the organization of legislative and administrative juridical organs for the formation of the legal order. In the period of developed economic social life with its increasing division of labour he holds the hierarchical State alone competent to organize a positive legal system[2]. This view is entirely in accordance with BODIN's absolutistic theory of sovereignty, which HELLER had already rehabilitated in his book *Die Souveränität*[3].

---

[1] *Op. cit.* p. 186: 'Auch das Verhältnis von Staat und Recht lässt sich nur historisch begreifen und allen Behauptungen über dieses Verhältnis, welche mit dem Anspruch geschichtstranszendenter Allgemeingültigkeit auftreten, muss *von vornherein* (italics are mine) mit Misstrauen begegnet werden'. [The relation of the State to law, too, can only be understood historically, and we must in advance suspect any views of this relation which claim a universal validity transcending history.] This is a clear and unmistakable formulation of HELLER's historicistic prejudice.

[2] *Op. cit.* p. 186: 'Im Zeitalter der entwickelten Verkehrswirtschaft hat nur die staatliche Hierarchie die Möglichkeit, eine entsprechend funktionierende Normordnung zu organisieren. Bis dahin war sicherlich jede organisierte Gemeinschaft mehr oder weniger zur Rechtserzeugung befähigt, wie kraft des Faust- und Fehderechts fast jeder zur Rechtsdurchsetzung berufen war. Wollten wir uns zum Zwecke der Bestimmung des Rechtsbegriffs nicht daran orientieren was ist, sondern daran, "was einstens war und was vielleicht wieder einmal sein wird", so müssen wir allerdings erklären, dass nicht nur der Staat, sondern auch die Kirchen, Territorien, Geburtsstände, Städte, Zünfte und Berüfsstände, kurz alle organisierten Verbänden Recht zu erzeugen und zu sichern im Stande sind'. [In the age of developed social economy only the hierarchy of the State is able to organize a correspondingly functioning normative order. Up till then certainly every organized community was more or less competent to create law, just as in virtue of club law and the law of the vendetta almost everybody was called upon to enforce the law. If for the purpose of determining the concept of law we do not want to orient ourselves to that which is, but to that which "was once and may be again", then we must at all events declare that not only the State but also the Churches, territorial units, nobility, cities, guilds and vocational classes, in a word all organized communities are able to create and to guarantee law.]

[3] Cf. *Die Souveränität*, p. 57, where we read: 'dass für die juristische Betrachtung des heutigen Staates die Positivität der ihm eingeordneten

Thus the problem of the relation between State and law is posited in a levelling way as that of the relation between State and positive law *in general ("überhaupt")*. Its solution is found by applying the dialectical method in an extremely simple manner, so that the juridical norm (*"das rechtliche Sollen"*) is considered to be indissolubly bound up with the human volition (*"das menschliche Wollen"*) of the legislator. HELLER conceives the will of the State explicitly as a subjective psychical act (p.189), which gives rise to a dialectical, *i.e.* an *intrinsically antinomic* concept of law. For here the modal boundaries between the juridical and the psychical aspect are theoretically eradicated [1]. It is simply impossible to reduce the law-forming will of the legislator to a complex of psychical act-functions.

The concept of law here is used in the sense of a *pseudo-concept* of function [2], without in the least taking into account the internal structural diversity within the juridical law-sphere as a modal aspect of reality. As HELLER's concept of "structure" of the State does not really approach its individuality structure, it cannot give us an insight into the internal expression of the latter in the different modal aspects of this societal institution. Modern historicism undermines HELLER's entire conception of the body politic, and prevents him from liberating himself from the relativistic view of the latter's structure. For all these reasons the conclusion is inevitable that in principle HELLER's interesting theory has not at all overcome the crisis in modern theory of the State.

The crisis in the practical political life of modern parliamentary democracies and the new irrationalistic and universalistic idea of the totalitarian State.

The entire crisis in the *theory* of the State, culminating in a "*political theory without a State*-idea", was closely connected with the crisis in the practice of western political life and the terrible economical crisis between the two world-wars. It was connected with the symptoms of dissolution that had assumed

Verbandssatzungen abgeleitet erscheint von der Positivität der staatlichen Rechtsordnung'. [for the juridical view of the present State the positivity of the legal rules of organized communities integrated into the body politic proves to be derived from the positivity of the legal order of the State.]

[1] Cf. Vol. II, part I, pp. 37 ff.

[2] *Pseudo-*, because the modal, *really* functional concept of law cannot be oriented to the State as an individuality structure of human societal life.

such alarming proportions in several parliamentary democracies; with the corruption and the subjection of politics to the interests of particular groups and classes. These facts hardly need separate mention. The recent fascist and national socialist reaction, however, which turned against these symptoms of dissolution in politics, and transformed the central and southern European States into authoritarian *"Führerstaaten"*, meant indeed a barbarian "subversion of all values" implied in the Christian and Humanist traditions of Western culture. This reaction found its philosophical background in the modern irrationalistic philosophy of life, which substituted for the ideology of natural law, founded in the Humanistic personality ideal, the vital *political mythology* and the *technical means of mass-psychology*. The new idea of the totalitarian or integral State was no longer rooted in the belief in an idealistic metaphysical rational order, but appealed to the vital instincts of the masses. It really aimed at subjecting all the internal spheres of the non-political societal relationships to the "totalitarian State". Such an attempt was not new in the history of the world. But it acquired a really demonic character by its refined methods of mass suggestion, its unscrupulous sacrificing of the individual personality, and its appeal to the spiritually uprooted mass-man.

The dialectical basic problem in the development of the political theories oriented to the immanence-standpoint.

Since the rise of theoretical reflection on the "problem of the State" in Greek philosophy the development of the seemingly diametrically opposed political theories, oriented to the immanence-standpoint, has always centred around one dialectical basic problem. This problem may have been posited from different religious starting-points and in different historical situations, but in the foreground has always been the question about the relation between "right and might" in the structure of the State institution. And on the immanence-standpoint this problem necessarily assumes the form of a dialectical tension between these two factors, because this standpoint makes the insight into the plastic horizon of the individuality-structures impossible.

This dialectical tension on the one hand manifests itself in the sharp mutual antagonism between the various theories, in the fundamental contrast between the idea of the law-State and that of the absolutist power-State. On the other hand, if the attempt was made to reconcile the two factors in one and the same theory, the dialectical tension became evident within such a theory itself.

As early as in ancient Greece the Sophist KALLIKLES, starting from the Greek matter-motive, defended a naturalistic individualistic idea of the political ruler which might be called a prelude to NIETZSCHE's idea of the "*Herrenmensch*" (super-man). In essence this was the justification of subjecting the weak to a despot, who is bound neither to justice nor to morality. With almost prophetic indignation PLATO opposed to this his idea of the State ruled by justice, in which reigns the idea of *τά ἑαυτοῦ πράττειν*, in its concentric direction to the divine Idea of the Good. Nevertheless, PLATO has never overcome the totalitarian view of the body politic: no more has ARISTOTLE. This was due to the fact that their idea of political justice was oriented to the Greek form-motive, which implied a religious absolutization of the cultural aspect. For the modal meaning-nucleus of the latter is *power*. The result was that the idea of political justice oriented to this form-motive lacked any material limitation of the *competence* of the city-State in its relation to the non-political societal spheres. In this way there remained a dialectical tension between the idea of justice and the totalitarian State idea, which in principle conceives the body politic as a power-State.

The polar contrast between might and right in the State has also dominated the entire Humanistic political theory from the times of the conflict between the abstract normative law of nature and reason, and the naturalist theory of "*Staatsräson*" [1], until the most recent antithesis between the individualistic, democratic law-State, and the universalistic authoritarian power-State. This conflict was ruled by the dialectical basic motive of nature and freedom, opposing the mathematical or the cultural science-ideal respectively to the personality-ideal of Humanism.

As long as the classical Humanistic science-ideal prevailed, the theory of natural law accepted BODIN's notion of sovereignty, which was devised to construe the State as the supreme power-organization ruling human society in its totality. As soon as, on the other hand, the personality-ideal with its Humanist freedom-

---

[1] Compare the ample explanation of the tension between the idea of "*Staatsräson*" and that of natural law in my *In den Strijd om een Christelijke Staatkunde*, I, XV (in the quarterly *Antirevolutionaire Staatkunde*, Year I, 127, pp. 142 ff.).

motive acquired the precedence, the conception of inalienable human rights was opposed to the sovereign power of the State, without the latter being denied. Generally speaking, the adherents of the idea of the power-State tried to save the appearance of the law-State, although the Macchiavellian theory of the *raison d'état* was openly explained in different realistic reflections on the "necessities of politics". Even the fascist and national socialist theories did not wish to give up the ideology of the law-State but tried to adapt it to their totalitarian conception of the power-State. They introduced a deceitful "idea of the material law-State", which was opposed to the 'demo-liberal ideology of the rule of law'.

The absolutist idea of the power-State may then be conceived in a naturalistic positivistic and individualistic way, as well as in an idealistic and universalistic sense (HEGEL, and his adherents). And the idea of the law-State also allows of various conceptions.

Even GIERKE has not overcome this internal dialectical tension between "might and right" in his theory of the body politic, although in other respects he has done great service to the theory of the organized communities. Though being an adherent of the historical school that originated from German romantic idealism, he later on also fully appreciated what the theories of natural and rational law had really done for the development of the legal aspect of Western societal life. He was on principle an opponent of the formalistic positivism in constitutional legal theory that came to the fore in the German school of LABAND and GERBER. And he was unwilling to sacrifice the idea of the law-State, in its material sense, to the "historical reality" of the State as a "sovereign territorial organization of power". Nevertheless, he *shut off* the reality of body politic in its historical function of "organized power". After having delimited these two from each other antithetically, he had then only an external dialectical connection left between the reality of the State and the legal order. Thus, like RUDOLPH SMEND of late, he viewed the life of the body politic and that of law as "two independent specifically different aspects of communal life" [1]. He circumscribed this contrast as follows: "The former manifests itself in the sovereign power to realize the desired common purposes, and culminates

---

[1] "zwei selbständige und spezifisch verschiedene Seiten des Gemeinlebens".

in political *action*. The latter reveals itself in the marking out of spheres of action for the volitions bound by it, and culminates in legal knowledge (knowledge of what is in accordance with the requirements of law)' [1].

True, he says that State and law are interdependent, although they are entirely different "aspects of community life". They can find their real fulness of life only if they mutually support one another. But State and law are contrasted here as equivalent and comparable "aspects" of human cultural society. This is due to the view of the Historical School that the State is nothing but the historical form of political organization of a national community. Nevertheless this historical-political "aspect" is identified with the full reality of the organized community which is called a State! This shows that even such a profound thinker as OTTO GIERKE lacked the insight into the individuality structures of human society, and that into the relation of these structures to the modal aspects of reality. And this in spite of the fact that it was especially *he* who had laid full emphasis on the significance of the structures of the societal organizations.

The dialectical tension between the juridical and the sociological conception of the State. The dualistic theory of the body politic.

Since the rise of a formalistic juridical method in the science of constitutional law (the School of LABAND and GERBER, represented in the Netherlands by BUYS), the internally contradictory dualism of "right and might" also led to a dualistic theory of the State, *viz.* a sociological so-called "empirical", and a normative juridical theory, as they were set forth in JELLINEK's *Allgemeine Staatslehre* (1st ed. 1900), without any successful attempt at an internal reconciliation.

And finally it led to a fierce antagonism between these two,

[1] *Grundbegriffe des Staatsrechts* (1915) p. 105: 'Jenes manifestiert sich in der machtvollen Durchführung gewollter Gemeinzwecke und kulminiert in der politischen That, dieses offenbart sich in der Absteckung von Handlungssphären für die von ihm gebundenen Willen und gipfelt im rechtlichen Erkennen ("für Recht erkennen")'.

In the same way SMEND *(Verfassung und Verfassungsrecht,* 1928, p. 98), characterizes State and law as two "indissolubly cohering, but nevertheless self-contained provinces of spiritual life, serving to realize two different particular values". ['zwar untrennbar verbundenen, aber doch je in sich geschlossenen, der Verwirklichung je einer besonderen Wertidee dienende Provinzen des geistigen Lebens'].

when the naturalistically minded sociology began to deride the "scholasticism of the jurists" and, conversely, the "normological" school of KELSEN caricaturized the efforts of the naturalistic sociologists to conceive the State in a manner different from the "purely juridical" way. Even SIEGFRIED MARCK, though oriented to LITT's dialectical sociology, frankly capitulated to this dualism. According to him, political theory as "an empirical science" *(Wirklichkeitswissenschaft)*, as a "sociology" dealing with "the totality of the State in its empirical configuration", always remains caught in the dualism of "*sollen*" and "*sein*". Only a Hegelian dialectical metaphysics would be able to develop a normative idea of the body politic which would be able to give a supposed synthesis transcending the fundamental antithesis between a juridical and a sociological conception of the State [1]. But MARCK explicitly rejects this metaphysics.

In contrast to this view we have established that outside of its supra-modal individuality structure the empirical State cannot exist at all. There can simply be no question of juridical and other *aspects of the body politic*, if we do not relate them consciously or unconsciously to this normative structural principle. But MARCK could not accept this state of affairs on his dialectical phenomenological standpoint. Consequently, like other dualists, he could find no way out of the crisis in the theory of the State.

The primary task of a Christian theory of the State. Rejection of the dialectical view of EMIL BRUNNER.

In contrast with the entire dialectical development of the theories of the State rooted in the immanence-standpoint, Christian theory has to disclose the internal structural principle of the body politic as it is found in the divine world-order. In itself this task is of a theoretical philosophical character, and seems to have no bearing on the burning questions of our time about the State and "society". The elaborate and penetrating analysis of the transcendental structures of reality demanded by the philosophy of the cosmonomic Idea does not belong to the kind of literature that is in vogue among present-day politicians and sociologists.

But I venture the statement that there is nothing of which our

---

[1] *Substanzbegriff und Funktionsbegriff in der Rechtsphilosophie* (1925) pp. 150 ff.

time is so much in need with respect to the State and society as an insight into the constant transcendental structural principles of societal relationships. They have not been devised by man's reason, but are anchored in the divine wisdom exhibited in the world order. The Christian theory of the State has up to now been unable to undertake its task with all its powers. Again and again it has formed a synthesis with immanence philosophy and thereby blunted the point of its Christian basic thoughts, so that after their elaboration the result was often their very opposite.

In advance we must warn against the recent error propagated under the influence of the "dialectical theology" to the effect that a Christian theory of the State is impossible on a Reformed Christian standpoint. In the structure of the State the factor of constraining power is held to be an intrinsically demonic and radically sinful element. As such it is supposed to remain necessarily caught in a dialectical tension with the Christian commandment of love and the idea of true communion.

Especially EMIL BRUNNER in his repeatedly quoted book *Das Gebot und die Ordnungen* (1932) defends this view. He considers it to be a necessary consequence of the essential difference between Roman Catholicism and Protestantism that there is a Roman Catholic but not a really Protestant philosophy of law and of the State. Wherever Protestantism tries to project such a philosophy it has already been affected internally by the Roman Catholic leaven [1].

Roman Catholicism bases its philosophy of the State on the Aristotelian natural law which is not of Christian but of pagan origin. Reformed Christianity cannot recognize any form of natural law and has to accept the State in the latter's peculiar dialectical structure. In it there is an irreconcilable tension between three factors, *viz.* an element of the order of creation in the moment of communion, a constraining legal order related to sin, and an in no way justifiable system of power which is "merely factual, unjust, hungry for power, and half demonic" [2]. The fundamental nature ("*Grundwesen*") of the State is considered not to be *justice,* but *power* [3].

---

[1] *Das Gebot und die Ordnungen* (1932) pp. 647 ff.

[2] *Op. cit.* p. 432 "schlechthin faktisches, ungerechtes, machtshungriges, halbdämonisches *Machtswesen*".

[3] *Op. cit.* p. 433.

This dialectical enigmatic formation ("*Rätselgebilde*") is supposed to escape any univocal and finished theory, and "Christian theology" does not have the task to propound a Christian theory of the State [1]. For such a theory could not reconcile these dialectical contrasts in the structure of the body politic. Christian theology only has to call attention to the fact that the "riddle of the State" points back to another "riddle", which is as little to be solved in theory, *viz.* the riddle of creation and the fall into sin within man [2].

It is remarkable here that on his Christian standpoint BRUNNER necessarily relapses into a synthesis with the State-theories of the immanence standpoint by in principle accepting the dialectical basic problem of the latter.

Erroneously he thinks he can reduce this basic problem to the "basic antithesis" in the Christian view between creation and fall.

At the back of this synthetic standpoint emerges the false contrast between nature and grace which already at an early period infected Christian thought. In BRUNNER this contrast assumes the irrationalistic form of a dialectical tension between the "commandment of love of the moment" and the „law as such" [3].

We must observe here that a really Christian view of the State, because of its very starting from the Biblical basic motive of creation, fall into sin and redemption, should radically reject BRUNNER's "dialectical basic problem" derived from the immanence-standpoint. The internal structural principle of the State as a supra-arbitrary institution can never be internally antinomic; neither can the function of power in this structure be called "semi-demonic" and "unjustifiable in any sense" on our standpoint. BRUNNER commits the serious error of confusing the factor of power in the *structure* of the body politic with the *subjective way* in which States in the sinful world can abuse their power. But when BRUNNER writes: "There has never been and there will never be a Christian State" [4], the question must be asked: Is the word "Christian" intended here in the sense

---

[1] But nobody who is aware of the limits of "theology" will entrust this task to it.

[2] *Op. cit.* p. 430.

[3] Cf. my study *De Wetsbeschouwing in Brunner's Boek "Das Gebot und die Ordnungen"* (A.R. Staatkunde, quaterly review, 1935).

[4] *Op. cit.* p. 449.

of "without sin"? If so, can this statement then not be applied with equal justice to all the other types of societal relationships, inclusive of the Church, in their subjective manifestations? Then the thesis loses any *special* meaning. BRUNNER on the one hand derives the power of the body politic from the divine will. But on the other hand he writes: 'The State is a secular ordering; it is not sacred'. This statement shows a serious lack of distinction between the divine structural law and the subjective manifestation of the State (which is subjected to this law) in sinful reality. BRUNNER characterizes the supposed essence of the body politic as *power,* as an "irrational product of history", which can only be "understood" by faith (not "comprehended" by the intellect) by thinking of the "hidden God" in all history. This merely proves how much this author's conception of power has been infected by modern irrationalism. His conception of law has chiefly been derived from neo-Kantian positivism, and his "idea of community" from irrationalistic phenomenology [1].

It is a matter of serious doubt if the task of the Christian should be to lend the Biblical Christian background of creation and sin to this *dialectical "mixtum compositum"* of Humanistic conceptions.

That the State-institution cannot be understood from creation without taking account of the fall into sin, must immediately be granted to BRUNNER. We shall return to this point in our analysis of the structural principle of this institution. But when BRUNNER tries to combine this really Biblical-Christian insight with a Humanistic-irrationalistic view of reality, the result must be a complete confusion. This should be clear from all that we have said about such attempts at synthesis.

§ 2 - ORGANIZATION AS THE "FORM" OF ALL HISTORICALLY FOUNDED COMMUNITIES AND THE TYPICAL FOUNDATIONAL FUNCTION OF THE STATE.

If the State, as a differentiated societal institution, really has a typical *historical* foundation, its *historical "form"* as such must play a special foundational rôle in its radical type.

Naturally "form" is to be understood here in an internal structural-typical sense, not in the sense of a variable, only

[1] Cf. my above mentioned treatise on BRUNNER's view of the *"Ordnungen"*.

more of less durable *result* of human formation. In our discussion of the "social forms" we have seen that the latter, as forms of realization of the societal structural principles, are necessarily of a phenotypical character and are real nodal points of enkaptic interlacements. In the present context, however, we consider the typical *internal historical* form of the State, and such only in its *pre-positive,* internal structural function, as the foundational structural *aspect* of the State's *radical type.* As such it does not have any factual duration but is a structural condition of any possible body politic, irrespective of its variable societal form. A typically historically founded community like the State implies such a typical historical form as its internal structural basis. And this same statement must be valid for all radical types of historically founded communities. This explains the special importance of "organization" as the form of their unity of will and action. Their internal unity in multiplicity is not typically founded in a pre-logical aspect of reality. Therefore their structural principle requires an *historical organization,* a *formation,* as the *original foundation* of the internal unity of the societal relationship.

For this reason it is incorrect to conceive "organization" as a "universal property" of all temporal communities. In a family we have also discovered the essential structure of a community. But the latter here lacks a form of organization as its typical foundation. The relation between parents and children is that of the bearers of authority to those who are subjected to this authoritative office. This relation is "founded in nature" and as such is not in need of organization.

In itself the concept "organization" is not at all a real structural concept of individuality. In HELLER it becomes a vague, undefined, "general concept", a *"genus proximum"* in the traditional sense. Before HELLER it had been deprived of all internal structural meaning in PLENGE's theory of organization [1], which HELLER himself admitted to be "much too general" (*"all zu allgemein"*).

Organization and Organism.

The origin of the term in its prevailing, structurally undefined sense betrays a certain polemical commitment in the conflict between two tendencies in the Humanistic theories of human

[1] Cf. PLENGE's book *Drei Vorlesungen über Organisationslehre* (1919).

communities. For this word assumed a certain polemical connotation in its contrast with the term "organism", by means of which the romantic organological philosophy of human society had signified its peculiar irrationalistic metaphysical conception of community [1].

In the second part of his *Naturrecht* (1798) FICHTE on purpose replaced the Schellingian term "organism" by "organization". Thus he opposed the entire organological view of the State as a supra-individual being which historically develops from a natural community after the pattern of the growth of a natural organism *(naturwüchsig)*, in contradistinction to all revolutionary artificial work.

After this, under the influence of MARX, the concept organization was taken in the sense of an artificial, so-called "mechanistic" social whole. This was a conception which in the nature of the case could not contribute anything to clarifying our insight into the structure of the organized societal relationships. Nevertheless, the sharp distinction between "organization" and "organism" was a gain, insofar as the fundamental difference was realized between the so-called "natural" and the historically founded communities.

For even GIERKE conceived all organized communities indiscriminately as "personal spiritual organisms". Under the influence of SCHELLING's organology he wrote: 'The individual State is not the free creation of individual men but the necessary product of the social powers working in the individuals. Originally States arise and grow without any cooperation of a conscious creative will, as a natural product of the unconscious social impulse' [2].

Organization and ordering.

In "organization" the present-day positivistic sociology generally seeks the unifying principle of an organized community. This concept is fairly generally identified with that of "social ordering" by the positivistic tendencies. They mean a certain

---

1 Cf. WALDECKER, *Allgemeine Staatslehre* (1927) p. 86.

2 *Die Grundbegriffe des Staatsrechts*, p. 97: 'Der einzelne Staat ist keine freie Schöpfung des Individuums,, sondern das notwendige Produkt der in den Individuen sich bethätigenden gesellschaftlichen Kräfte. Ursprünglich werden und wachsen die Staaten ohne jede Mitwirkung eines bewusst schaffenden Willens, ein naturwüchsiges Erzeugnis des unbewussten(!) Gesellschaftstriebes'.

regularity in social behaviour brought about by particular psychical representations of convention or norms. Jurists preferably understand the term in a functional juridical sense [1]. There is a necessary correspondence between this functional psychological or juridical conception of "organization" and the individualistic and naturalist view of reality which is considered to be the only empirical basis of the supposedly *fictitious* unity of an organized community.

HELLER considers "organization" to be the *real* structural unity of the State and in principle rejects the individualistic view of societal relations. It is therefore understandable that he sharply opposes the identification of *organization* and *ordering*. Starting from the socio-psychological concept of "ordering", as the factual regularity of social behaviour [2], he observes that in this sense every human societal relationship is "ordered". But such an "ordering" in itself implies no more than the possibility of "unified" (*"einheitliche"*) collective cooperation. 'However, from ordering to organization, from the unity of social behaviour to the comparative durable unity of action it is still a far cry' [3].

Organization is a collective unity of action to him and is only constituted by the "category of collective ability to decide and to act" (*"Kategorie der kollektiven Entscheidungs- und Aktionsfähigkeit"*). A unity of collective activity in the multiplicity of individual centres of activity is only possible when the actions of the many have been caused to cooperate by the "organ" (or "the organs") of the organization according to a conscious, carefully considered plan. Every organization, therefore, needs at least one "organ" and when it has assumed certain proportions it also requires a rationally formed "ordering".

---

[1] Cf. among many others AFFOLTER Arch. f. öffentl. R. 20, 374 ff., CARRÉ DE MALBERG, *Contribution à la théorie générale de l'Etat* II nr. 373, KELSEN, *Allgemeine Staatslehre* (1925) p. 268; H. J. WOLFF, *Organschaft und Juristische Person Vol. I, Juristische Person und Staatsperson* (1933) pp. 164 ff.

[2] *Allgemeine Staatslehre* (1934) p. 86: 'Sowohl die bloss tatsächlich regelmässigen wie die auch regelgeforderten" (*i.e.* those that have been caused by the feeling or the representation of what ought to be) "Regelmässigkeiten des gesellschaftlichen Verhaltens fassen wir also zusammen unter dem Begriff der gesellschaftlichen Ordnung". [Both the merely factual regularity in social behaviour and the regularities which are demanded by norms we include in the concept of social ordering.]

[3] *Op. cit.* p. 88: 'Von der Ordnung zur Organisation, von der Einheitlichkeit des gesellschaftlichen Verhaltens bis zur relativ dauernden Einheit der Aktion ist aber noch ein grosser Schritt zu tun'.

On account of its members and organs cooperating according to an "ordering" and arriving at a "unitary result", the real unity of the organization is brought about as the "unity of action" ("*Wirkungseinheit*")[1].

The antithesis between "organization" and "organism" in SIEGFRIED MARCK and FR. DARMSTAEDTER.

Of late the concept "organization" has assumed a special meaning in connection with TÖNNIES' distinction beween "*Gesellschaft*" and "*Gemeinschaft*"[2]. In this connection "organization" is deemed to be characteristic of the associations formed by "*Kürwille*" (arbitrary volition)), whereas a "*Gemeinschaft*" is considered as a social "organism", in which a "*Wesenswille*" (natural volition) reveals itself. An organization is characterized by its rational aims, which are to be realized by organizational cooperation ("*Zweckrationalität*" in MAX WEBER's sense). An organism, on the other hand, is characterized by the irrational consciousness of a member's having grown into the whole[3].

FR. DARMSTAEDTER gives a peculiar turn to this modern conception by relating the contrast between "organization" and "organism" to KANT's distinction between *autonomy* and *heteronomy*. He says: 'An individual person joins an organization as something existing outside of himself, as an apparatus or an heteronomous mechanism imposed on him from outside, laying hold of the individual by means of duties imposed on him from outside and secured by force. An organism, on the other hand, has grown in the individual himself. It confronts him as a duty from outside only because he accepts it autonomically, because he knows he is a member of the organism, because he consciously becomes integrated into the organism'[4].

---

[1] *Op. cit.* p. 231.

[2] Cf. Vol. III pp. 184 ff.

[3] Cf. SIEGRIED MARCK, *Substanzbegriff und Funktionsbegriff in der Rechtsphil.* (Tübingen 1925, p. 99 ff.). More or less in the same sense: STANISLAUS DNISTRYANSKI, *Zur Grundlegung des modernen Privatrechts* in Jherings Jahrbücher f. d. Dogmatik des bürgerl. Rechts, Bnd. 43, Jena 1928 p. 1 ff.

[4] *Die Grenzen der Wirksamkeit des Rechtsstaates*, Heidelberg, 1930), pp. 139 ff.: 'In die Organisation fügt sich das Individuum ein als in einen ausserhalb seiner selbst vorhandenen, von aussen her ihm heteronom auferlegten Apparat oder Mechanismus, der das Individuum in Form von äusserlich auferlegten, durch Zwang gesicherten Pflichten ergreift. Der Organismus dagegen ist gleichermassen im Individuum selbst gewachsen,

This distinction is then applied to the contrast between the law-State and the power-State. The former is considered to be preponderantly supported by "the willingness of the individual to be integrated into the whole" whereby it is characterized as an organism, whereas the "power-State" is nothing but a "mechanical organization". This conception is very characteristic of the lack of insight into the internal structure of the State. It again rests on the fallacious way in which the problem of the relation between State and law has been posited. The State is considered as a *self-contained* "organization of power" and dialectically brought into an external relation with an individualistically conceived legal order. This view has very little to do with TÖNNIES' conception of a *"Gemeinschaft"* since it has been inspired by a liberalistic idea of liberty.

DARMSTAEDTER considers both State and law to be a piece of "natural reality" which must be related to the "values" *regulation of a community* and *governmental power*, in order to become the *"cultural objects(!) State and law"*. This view is oriented to the South Western German school of neo-Kantians (WINDELBAND, RICKERT, LASK). The "natural reality" that State and law are supposed to have in common is that they are "a multitude of people"(!): 'This multitude of people is the only available reality for the State as well as for law, the total available reality to which the appropriate moment of value can be attached' [1]. In other words, State and law only differ according to the "specific values" that can be attached to a "multitude of people" (as a "natural reality").

Law in the sense of "value" is then defined as a "regulation for a community by which certain behaviours of one individual towards another are commanded or prohibited".

According to its "validity as a value" the State, on the other hand, is characterized in such a way that it brings man into relation with the original power of the supreme magistrate, who 'takes up his position outside of and beyond the human individual' [2].

Thus also DARMSTAEDTER arrives at *a sharp formulation of the dialectical basic antithesis* operative in the entire Humanistic theory of the State, as an internal antinomy between "right and might": 'Behaviour corresponding with the axiological validity of law,

---

er tritt dem Individuum nur darum von aussen als Pflicht entgegen, weil dieses ihn autonom billigt, weil es sich als Glied des Organismus weiss, weil es sich wissend dem Organismus eingliedert'.

[1] *Op. cit.* p. 119: 'Diese Menschenmenge ist sowohl für das Recht wie für den Staat die einzige verfügbare Wirklichkeit, die gesamte, zu Gebote stehende Wirklichkeit, an welche sich das ihnen zugehörende Wertmoment knüpfen kann."

[2] *Op. cit.* p. 120: "ausserhalb und jenseits der einzelnen Menschen ihre Stelle hat."

and such that satisfies the axiological validity of the State, are mutually exclusive. The axiological validity of law demands from men a behaviour that excludes the axiological validity of the State, and *vice versa*. The value law and the value State are opposed as mutually exclusive and contradictory, as opposite values with regard to the same reality'[1]. Both are reconciled when the State relinquishes its claim to its own absolute value and is prepared to do duty as a "*Mittelwert*" (instrumental value) with regard to law as a "*Selbstwert*" (value in itself)'.

I only mention this development of the concept "organization" to show how little in itself it is able to account for the internal unity of the historically founded organized communities. The functionalistic attitude is in evidence wherever this notion is handled as a levelling "general concept", apart from the internal individuality structures. HELLER's "dialectical structural idea" proved to labour under the same defect.

The relation between organization and the structural principle.

The truth is that the word "organization" must derive all its structural determination of meaning from the individuality-structure of an organized community.

This relation is reversed in the prevailing functionalistic tendencies, and the attempt is made to derive the internal unity of the State from the general concept "organization". But this levelling way of thought makes it impossible to gain an insight into the internal structural principle of the body politic.

An *organization of power* as the *foundational historical form* of a radical type of communal structures only acquires its internal determination from its structural coherence with the typical leading function. For this reason we must emphatically reject the view that the internal structure of an organization can be conceived according to one and the same functional or dialectical "specific" schema for all types of organized communities. It is immaterial whether this schema is functional-juridical, or socio-psychological or a dialectical synthesis of these two. The

[1] *Op. cit.* p. 121: 'Das der Wertgeltung Recht entsprechende Verhalten und das der Wertgeltung Staat genügende Verhalten schliessen derart einander aus. Die Wertgeltung Recht fordert von dem Menschen ein die Geltung des Wertes Staat ausschliessendes Verhalten und umgekehrt. Der Wert Recht und der Wert Staat stehen als gegenseitig sich ausschliessende und verneinende, als Gegenwerte an der nämlichen Wirklichkeit einander gegenüber."

internal organization of a Church is not merely *specifically* but *radically* different from that of a State or that of a modern industrial enterprise. The insight into the internal structural principles is made impossible beforehand, if one tries to approach *e.g.*, the "Church-organization" from a functional juridical, or a psycho-sociological viewpoint, or from HELLER's dialectical point of view.

If "organization" is really related to the internal structure of an historically founded community, it can only be seemingly a *genus proximum.* As a "general concept" which is supposed to refer to a *genus proximum* it is nothing but a multivocal *word.* When in our preliminary distinctions we introduced the term "organized communities", we did not use it in this undefined sense. Rather we intended to indicate by it only a transcendental difference between the natural and the historically founded communities *as to their typical structural foundation,* a difference whose transcendental significance as a "social category" will be explained later on. But since the term implies nothing with respect to the typical qualification of the organized communities, it can never signify an ultimate *genus* of the latter, which indeed is not to be found in the structural temporal horizon of our experience. For there are different (secondary) radical types of such communities notwithstanding the fact that all of them prove to be typically founded in the historical aspect. And we have seen that the radical types are the *ultimate genera* of the structures of individuality.

In order to find the radical type of the State, the obvious method is for us to concentrate on those two functions in the structure of the body politic whose mutual relation proved to be the dialectical basic problem in the theories rooted in the immanence-standpoint. We cannot possibly believe that in this dialectical basic problem the historical function of power and the juridical function would have been so constantly emphasized, if they did not really have the meaning of radical typical functions of the State-structure. And this supposition appears to be confirmed by the empirical data concerning the realization of the latter.

The empirical data concerning the State's character.

The radical typical and geno-typical structural principle of the body politic cannot be traced apart from its realization in the development of human society.

In this respect we must establish that a real State-institution does not appear before the destruction of the political power concentrated in the primitive undifferentiated tribal and gentilitial organizations. There is a radical difference between the latter and a real body politic appearing from the undeniable fact that they are incompatible with one another. Wherever a real State arose, its first concern was the destruction of the tribal and gentilitial political power or, if the latter had already disappeared, the struggle against the undifferentiated political power-formations in which authoritative, and private proprietary relations were mixed with each other. Irrespective of its particular governmental form, the State-institution has always presented itself as a *res publica,* an institution of the public interest, in which political authority is considered a public office, not a private property.

In this respect there appears to be a fundamental and radical difference between a real body politic, and the ancient Asiatic empires, the Merovingian kingdom and the medieval feudal kingdoms, which lacked the republican character.

It is extremely confusing that the term republic is used to indicate a non-monarchical form of government. In common speech it is unavoidable that the same words have very different meanings. But in the general theory of the State this is indefensible. The erroneous opposition between republics and monarchies is here only caused by the fact that the rise of a real State-institution in Greece and Rome occurred in a non-monarchical form and our political terminology is of a Greco-Roman origin. In addition, the undifferentiated conception of political authority, as the personal property of the rulers, mostly maintained itself in monarchies. But these historical facts cannot justify a scientific use of the term republic in a sense which has nothing to do with its proper meaning. A real State with a monarchical form of government is by nature a monarchical republic. A kingdom like the Merovingian empire which was nothing but a *res regia* lacks the character of a real State-institution. The historicistic view, which levels out these radical differences and speaks of gentilitial, tribal and feudal "States", may not be called "empirical" since it ignores undeniable empirical states of affairs in order to carry through its historicist prejudice.

Even from a logical point of view this use of the concept State is indefensible since it is contradictory to subsume under one and the same notion characteristics which exclude one another in an analytical sense. It is true that the State belongs to a particular *radical type* of societal relationships which may also include organized communities of a different geno-type. But in this case the term State may not be applied to this radical type but only to a specific geno-type of the former.

The adherents of MAX WEBER's ideal-typical method will readily agree that their ideal-typical concept of the State is only applicable to the modern bodies politic. But this by no means implies an abandonment of the historicist prejudice concerning the changeable character of the State's inner nature. The geno-type State cannot be defined from an historical point of view only, since it is a real structure of individuality, which, as such, embraces the integral horizon of modal experiential aspects.

The typical foundational function of the State.

If we now try to trace the structural principle of individuality of the State from the empirical data mentioned above, it is in the first place necessary to devote our attention to the typical foundational function in this structure.

That this foundational function must be of a typical historical character cannot be doubted. For it appeared that the State-institution is based upon a typical concentration of power which has its historical condition in the destruction of the independent political power formations inherent in undifferentiated social organizations. But what type of individuality is revealed in this political organization of power proper to the State?

From our ample analysis of the modal structure of the historical aspect in the second Volume we know that power, in its nuclear modal sense, allows of widely different individuality types [1]. The historical power of the Christian Church has an entirely different individuality structure from that of a modern or an ancient State, and the power of each of them is structurally entirely different from that of a modern large-scale industrial undertaking, or that of a scientific or of an aesthetic "school", *etc.*

In an undifferentiated organized community different individuality-structures of historical power may be interlaced in one and the same organizational form, but the *State,* as such, has a differentiated structure. Therefore its internal power-formation can no longer display an undifferentiated structure. We must keep in mind that we are looking for the typical foundational

[1] Cf. Vol. II, part I, pp. 196 ff.

function of this societal institution which is the original substratum for the type of individuality of its leading or qualifying function. In whatever way we consider the matter, this foundational function of the geno-type "State" can nowhere else be found but in an *internal monopolistic organization of the power of the sword over a particular cultural area within territorial boundaries.*

The reader should remember that this typical historical structural function may in no way be naturalistically misinterpreted. According to its *modal* meaning it is a normative structural function implying a *task,* a *vocation* which can be realized in a better or a worse way. There has never existed any State whose internal structure in the last instance was not based on organized armed power, at least claiming the ability to break any armed resistance on the part of private persons or organizations within its territory.

The myth of blood-relationship in the German national-socialistic ideology of the "third Empire", and the typical foundational function in the structure of the State.

In the political mythology of German national-socialism it was suggested that the community of blood and soil was the real foundation of "the third Empire". But even in this case the internal structure of the State was not supposed to have a typical biotic foundation in a common descent. The starting point of this view was the community of the German people as including the entire individual personality, all the special structural communities and relationships such as the State, the Church, industry, political party, youth organization, *etc.* These societal units were viewed as differentiations of the primary community of the people, although the State was finally considered to be its totalitarian *political form of organization.* Only for this "community of the people" was postulated a "community of blood" in the myth of the race.

This myth was not to be understood in the sense of a naturalistic racial theory. This must be evident to anyone who has realized that the background of this racial ideology was found in the irrationalist-historistic view of life and the world[1] entertained by German

---

[1] A view of life and the world as such is not a theory. This is an important point in this context. Cf. Vol. I Prolegomena, pp. 156 ff. In his famous article in the *Enciclopedia Italiana* on the *Dottrina fascista* (1932), MUSSOLINI made the following observation as to fascism as a view of life and the world: 'To fascism the cosmos is not that material world in which man is led by a law of nature', and: 'Fascism is a mental attitude born out of the general reaction of our century to the superficial and

national socialism [1]. There was a reminiscense of irrationalistic Romanticism in the German national socialist ideology of the "pure racial community of blood of the German people", though it was deprived of any Romantic idealism. It was connected with the old Germanic myth of a common descent claimed for all Germanic peoples. The mythology of Italian fascism, on the other hand, consciously fell back on the old idea of the eternal Roman empire [2]. Therefore Italian fascism was *State-minded* [3], whereas German national-socialism was *folk-minded*, an ideological difference on which the German nazists laid strong emphasis [4].

If full justice to such myths is to be done, they should be interpreted from the irrationalist-historicistic spirit of the view of life and the world in the background. Their essential aim was to elevate the historically developed nationality (the "cultural race", or the "national State" respectively) to a "spiritual power". This power should be actual and always again be actualized and assume all-absorbing validity in the conviction of the people [5]. The political myths also aimed at exorcizing powers that were alleged to be a menace to the deified nationality.

In the German national socialist *theory* of the State it was realized that the structure of the State, as such, cannot be derived from a national community as a "community of blood". This is evident, for instance, from WALTER HAMEL's book *Das Wesen des Staatsgebietes* (1933), in which the State and the people are explicitly conceived to be connected in a dialectical tension. The State, as such, is *historically*

---

materialistic positivism of the 19th century'. This could be taken over literally by German national socialism.

[1] Thus WALTER HAMEL in his treatise cited below.

[2] Cf. MUSSOLINI's statement in his quoted article on the *Dottrina fascista* II, 13: 'The fascist State is a will to power and dominion' (una voluntà di potenza e d'emperio). It is the tradition of ancient Rome which is appealed to here. Cf. A. MENZEL, *Der Staatsgedanke des Faschismus* (Leipzig und Wien, 1935) p. 61. Cf. also pp. 83 ff. *op. cit.*

[3] Compare MUSSOLINI's statement in the article quoted from the *Enciclopedia Italiana:* 'It is not the nation that creates the State, as was asserted in the naturalistic doctrine of the 19th century. But the nation is created by the State which only gives the people the consciousness of its own moral unity, a will, and therefore its real existence'. The German national-socialist doctrine of the nation as "a community of blood", as a "racial community" was unconditionally rejected by MUSSOLINI. Cf. MENZEL *op. cit.* p. 74/5.

[4] Cf., *e.g.*, WALTER HAMEL: *Volkseinheit und Nationalitätenstaat*, in Zeitschr. f. d. ges. Staatswissenschaft, Bnd. 95, 4e Heft, (1935), p. 587.

[5] Cf. MUSSOLINI's pronouncement at Naples in October 1922: 'We have created a myth; a myth is a belief, a noble enthusiasm; it need not be a reality; it is an impulse and a hope, faith and courage. Our myth is the nation, the great nation, which we want to make into a concrete reality." Cf. A. MENZEL, *op. cit.* p. 15/6. Cf. also GIULIANO BALBINO: *L'idea etica del fascismo* (in *Gerarchia* 1932, XI, p. 949).

founded in the sovereign control of a "political territory" (*"politischen Raum"*). This *"Bodemgemeinschaft"* (community of territory) is explicitly qualified as the adversary of the people (*"Widersacher des Volkes"*), which, however, always strives after a dialectical connection with the "community of blood" [1].

Of course, it is perfectly true that a State cannot maintain itself long if it is not rooted in the moral "conviction of the people", at least of the ruling groups of such a people. The State will be short-lived if it is divided and torn by internal strife, or if it lacks sufficient economical means to assert its power. But all this only proves what we have pointed out from the beginning, *viz.* that the typical foundational function in the structure of the State is not self-sufficient. It does not imply that the State is not typically *founded* in the monopolistic organization of the power of the sword over a territorial cultural sphere.

The fundamental error of considering all different forms of power intrinsically equivalent components of the power of the State.

For a real insight into the individuality structure of the State it is essential to guard against the view which emphasizes the all-sidedness of political power and treats all its components alike. The fallacy of this opinion does not lie in the recognition that in a way State-power is all-sided. For as regards *its historical aspect,* the State is not *merely* the organized power of the sword over a particular territory. If the State did not have at its disposal typical economical, moral, pisteutic and other forms of power[2], it would even be *impossible* to form a military organization. But this is not the point at issue. None of the other forms of power is in itself typical of *the State*. The monopolistic organization of the power of the sword is the only typical form which *is not found as a foundational function* in any of the other differentiated societal structures. The other forms of power, insofar as they are really *internal* forms of State-power, are themselves only intelligible from the structural principle of the body politic, which implies a monopolistic military organization as

---

[1] *Wesen des Staatsgebietes* (1933) p. 231 ff. Cf. also his treatise cited above.

[2] These other forms of power are anticipatory forms of historical power, enclosed by the modal structure of the historical law-sphere, and having no original economic, moral, or faith modality. Cf. Vol. II, pp. 70—71.

its typical foundational function. They may also belong to the *variability-types* of the State, which originate from enkaptic interweavings with other societal structures.

To give an example: if there are powerful industries, large-scale agricultural undertakings, world-wide shipping organizations, *etc.*, within its territory, the power of the State is closely bound up with the prosperity of these non-political organizations. But this does not mean that the economic forms of power of these organizations, which in modern times are for a good deal of an *international* character, are internal constituents of the power of the State.

There may be an open antagonism between the power of the State and that of industry or commerce, if the latter abuse their means for political aims contrary to "national interests". A State whose organized military power is weak will never be a *powerful State,* though having large economic means of power, a very rich soil, a flourishing science and art within its territory. If the levelling schema of the whole and its parts is applied to the relation between the power of the State and the other structures of power within its territory, the resulting conclusions will always be in conflict with reality. They misinterpret the individuality-structures of reality. On this error is based the mythological character of the idea of the totalitarian State. No matter how this idea is elaborated, it always implies that all the other individuality-structures of this power will retain their own essential character when they are made into internal constituents of the State's power. But all forms of power that really become internal elements of the power of the body politic must necessarily assume the internal individuality-structure of the latter. We have discovered that all mythology is a false interpretation of God's revelation in creaturely meaning. So also this political mythology rests on a false deification of the creaturely expression of God's omnipotence in the meaning-structure of the State's power.

The original character of the individuality type of the foundational function. The seeming antinomy in the relation between foundational and leading function of the State.

As the foundational function of the body politic is not merely modal, but really an internal structural function, it must be studied in its indissoluble coherence with the leading function of this societal institution.

The structural principle of the whole must express itself in each of its modal aspects. The circumscription of the foundational function of the State as the organized monopolistic power of the sword over a certain territorial cultural area, is consequently not wholly satisfactory, because the full structural principle of the institution is not yet expressed in it. But theoretical analysis must necessarily proceed in a successive meaning-synthesis in order to elucidate the internal structure of a societal relationship. The initial theoretic separation of the two radical functions which internally hang indissolubly together, is inescapable in this procedure.

It will be useful once again to give an account of the exact relation between the individuality type of the leading and the foundational function in the structure of an organized community. Our thesis is that the monopolistic organization of military power within a particular territorial cultural area is the foundation of the individuality type of the leading function of the body politic. At the same time, however, we state that this foundational function can only be conceived in its indissoluble coherence with the leading function, *i.e.* that the historical function is apparently only a real structural one insofar as its meaning is opened and anticipatory. At first sight these two statements seem to be contradictory. There seems to be an inevitable antinomy in the fact that the differentiated, historically founded communities have a foundational structural function whose type of individuality must necessarily be of an anticipatory character. For the latter state of affairs apparently excludes the original or nuclear character of this type of individuality. But if the foundational structural function has no original type of individuality, its foundational character is thereby annihilated. And then the internal contradiction would have been admitted. This antinomy seems to be inevitable especially in the case of the differentiated societal relationships with a typical historical foundation. The reason is that the entire process of differentiation in the societal structures can only be brought about in the anticipatory direction of time.

*

The solution of this seeming antinomy. The anticipatory character of the foundational function does not affect its original type of individuality.

The solution of this seeming antinomy was already found in an earlier context of our enquiry when we investigated the structural relation between the foundational and the leading function of a geno-typical individuality-structure in general[1]. It appeared that this relation is founded in the necessary correlation between the foundational and the anticipatory direction of the universal order of time in the opening-process of the foundational function.

The anticipatory character of the foundational function does not affect its original or nuclear type of individuality. For the latter is only to be found in the foundational direction of time. The disclosure of its anticipatory moments by its structural subordination to the leading function can only deepen the individuality type of the foundational function, it cannot abolish its foundational character. In other words, this individuality-type as such does not belong to the anticipatory types which we have formerly distinguished from the nuclear and the retrocipatory types. The differentiated monopolistic organization of military power within a territorial cultural area can indeed only be brought about in the anticipatory direction of time. The historical vocational power acquired in such an organization points beyond itself to the leading function of the structural principle of the State. But we shall show that this leading function lacks a nuclear type of individuality. In this respect there is consequently no difference between the State and the natural communities. In both cases the structural disclosure of the foundational function in the anticipatory direction of time *presupposes* the original type of individuality of this function. *Anticipatory types, on the other hand, which lack this original character are only constituted in the anticipatory direction of time.* It is therefore essential to distinguish between the anticipatory individuality-types of an *un-original* character and the *original* individuality-types with an anticipatory opened meaning-structure.

The invariable character of the foundational function in the structure of the State.

The *original* character of the individuality-type implied in the

[1] Cf. Vol. III, pp. 91 ff.

foundational function of the State has thus been established. We will nog engage in a more detailed analysis of the monopolistic organization of the power of the sword over a territorial cultural area, as the typical foundational function in the structure of the body politic. In its transcendental character this foundational function cannot be eliminated from the structural principle which makes all variable real life of the State only[1] possible and is itself invariable, constant, in the cosmic order of time. No "idealistic" theory has been able to reason away this structural foundation of every real State. The "metaphysical essence" of the body politic could be sought in the "idea of justice", or in the idea of a perfect community, but the basic function of the historical power of the body politic could not be ignored consistently.

This structural foundation is essential in every positive historical form in which the State has manifested itself in the course of time: in the Greek *polis* and in the Roman world-empire, as well as in the Carolingian State and the Italian city-States of Renaissance times; in the absolute French monarchy that developed under the "*ançien régime*" after the annihilation of the political power of the "estates", as well as in the constitutional State after the French Revolution; in the modern parliamentary democracies, as well as in the recent form of the totalitarian dictatorial States. It is quite true that the foundational military organization of power may have been weakened and endangered by military organizations of certain groups or parties within the State's territory. This may even justify the question whether in such a condition we had not better speak of a revolutionary chaos instead of a real body politic. It is also possible that a young State has not yet completely succeeded in monopolizing the organized power of the sword within its territory, without giving up its claim to this monopoly. But, as we have repeatedly emphasized, our discussion is concerned with a *normative structural function* implying a *task*, a *vocation* for the internal organization of the State's power. This vocation can be fulfilled in a better or a worse way. It may be that in a certain part of its territory the body politic has actually monopolized the organized military power, and that outside of this area the State is only "a name". But all these really variable situations do not detract from the universal validity of the normative struc-

---

[1] Cf. Vol. II, p. 246 ff.

tural principle of the State, which implies the territorial monopolistic organization of military power as its typical foundational function. If in a well-ordered body politic a revolution breaks out, this state of affairs is put to the test; and it is proved that the structural relation mentioned cannot at all be altered by human arbitrariness. Such a revolution may be prepared by theoretical and practical political propaganda, by exerting a systematic influence on "national conviction". But as soon as the revolutionary leaders want to take the government in their own hands, they must start with mastering the organized military apparatus either with sanguinary or with bloodless means.

In his famous article in the *Enciclopedia Italiana* on the *Dottrina fascista* MUSSOLINI seemed to represent the fascist idea of State-power as an idea of *moral* authority, in which the territorial military organization would not at all have a typical foundational position [1]. But this statement was concerned with international relations of power. Contrary to it there are many others in which the peculiar position of organized military power in the structure of the State is fully recognized, and even absolutized [2]. The fascist revolution culminated in the historical march on Rome. This was an illustration of our exposition of the foundational place which the monopolistic organization of military power over a territory occupies in the structure of the State.

A truly political revolution which pulls down the existent government of a body politic, is radically different from a revolution which is typically founded in other historical structures of power and typically guided and directed by another leading function than that of the body politic. There are revolutions in science, in art, in the Church, *etc.*, which as such do not have any *political* character.

---

[1] *Dottrina II,* 13: 'According to fascist theory, power is not a territorial, military or mercantile concept, but a moral and spiritual idea. It is quite well possible to imagine the working of a power exercized by one nation over another without the necessity of conquering even a quarter of a square mile of foreign territory' (quoted by A. MENZEL, *Der Staatsgedanke des Faschismus,* 1935, p. 61). Indeed, such "influence of power" can be imagined. Recall, *e.g.*, the influence of cultural power that vanquished Hellas had on Rome! It may be doubted if MUSSOLINI would have been satisfied with such a *typically non-political* power for the "Italian nation". In addition it can be imagined that a mighty State controls its weak neighbours simply by the dread of its military power. But this possibility does not fit to the intention of MUSSOLINI's statement.

[2] Cf. the Duce's essay: *My Thought on Militarism* (1934, quoted by MENZEL, *op. cit.* p. 62): 'The doom of a nation lacking a military spirit is sealed. For in the last instance it is war that is decisive in the relations between States. In my definition war is the supreme court of justice of the nations'. Cf. also MENZEL, p. 70.

The structural subject-object relation in the monopolistic organization of military power over a territorial cultural area.

According to its individuality structure this monopolistic organization of the power of the sword is not merely a *technical apparatus*. The foundational structural function of the State displays that typical subject-object relation which we already discovered when discussing the thing-structure of reality. It is true, the structural foundation of the State comprises an *objective* apparatus of military arms, buildings, aircrafts, airports, *etc.* But this military apparatus, as an historical object, is only meaningful in connection with an organized army or police force. Only subjective military bearers of power can actualize this objective apparatus: without them it remains "dead material". As soon as we consider the organized military power of the State according to this subjective point of view, it is immediately evident how insufficient is a merely functionalistic technical conception. And also, how little this organized power can be *shut up* in the historical law-sphere. Military rules of discipline, rigid military forms of organization appear to be powerless in an army or police-force in which a revolutionary mentality has undermined the sense that the authority of the present government is *legitimate* [1].

It is evident here that the military organization of State power displays an opened, *anticipatory structure* that cannot be explained in terms of *merely* armed control.

All the same, this organization appeared to be an *original* historical type of individuality. The structural subject-object relation in the foundational function of the State is indeed very complicated. It also comprises the relation between the organized military power and the territorial cultural area of the body politic. From a modal historical standpoint this cultural area is to be viewed only as an object of the formative power of the State. From a structural viewpoint this historical aspect of the State-territory can never be conceived apart from the leading juridical function of this societal institution. But this necessary structural relation between the foundational and the leading function is no reason to ignore the peculiar modal meaning of the foundational function. *Military* organization of power in its historical modality is not of a *juridical* character. For this reason

[1] There are good observations on this point in E. Brunner, *Das Gebot und die Ordnungen* (1932), pp. 433 ff.

the area of the State's military power, as the object of the subjective formation of military control, cannot be grasped in a *modal juridical* sense.

The typical foundational function of the State-institution marks the latter as an institution because of sin. The attempt to accommodate this Biblical conception to the *Aristotelian philosophy of the State.*

In Holy Scripture, both in the Old and the New Testament, the organized power of the sword, which we have found to be the typical structural foundation of the State, is emphatically related to man's fall[1]. Theologians have defended the view that in the Divine Covenant with Noah[2] the magistrate's power of the sword was called into existence. I will express no opinion on this point.

At an undifferentiated stage of culture there did not yet appear to be any question of a real body politic. The power of the sword is still enclosed in undifferentiated forms of interweaving. But from the Biblical point of view it cannot be seriously doubted that the power of the sword inherent in the office of the government, in its structural coherence with the leading function of the State-institution, has been incorporated into the temporal world-order by God because of sin. We have already observed that it would be fundamentally wrong to confuse the fact of this "because of sin", referring to the institutional office of the military power, with the sinful subjective way in which the power of the sword is handled in a particular State.

We must first of all conceive of this power of the sword in its institutional structure. Then only can we judge of the actual handling of it, so that our judgment remains free from the naturalistic, or idealistic, rationalistic or irrationalistic conceptions, set forth in immanence-philosophy, as if the State were a "demonical" or a "divine formation of power".

Christian synthesis-philosophy, especially since THOMAS AQUINAS, has made the attempt to accommodate the Biblical view of the sword of the magistrate to the Aristotelian idea of the State, as a perfect natural community[3]. The State, as such, was considered to be founded in the (metaphysical essential) nature of man; only the power of the sword was supposed to be given to the

---

[1] Cf. *Rom.* 13 : 1—5; 1 *Peter* 2 : 13; *Revel.* 13 : 10.

[2] *Genesis* 9 : 6.

[3] Cf. Vol. III, p. 219.

government because of sin [1]. This coercive power was considered to belong to relative natural law, *i.e.* natural law as it is modified by sin, in accordance with the Christian-Stoical terminology. But this attempt at accommodation entailed the metaphysical levelling of the societal individuality-structures criticized in an earlier context.

The levelling constructive schema of the whole and its parts confronted with the fourfold use of a fruitful idea of totality.

Once the typical foundational function of the State has been theoretically pushed into the background, the entire individuality structure of this societal institution will be eliminated. Then there seems to be no alternative for an "organic theory" but to construe the relationship between the body politic and the other societal structures according to the metaphysical schema of the whole and its parts. The remarkable and dangerous feature of an idea of totality, oriented to a constructive metaphysical principle of a perfect community like that found in ARISTOTLE, is the indeterminateness of its meaning [2]. For it has not been oriented to the individuality-structures of human societal life.

Up to now we have found three different kinds of correct and fruitful use of the Idea of totality: [3]

1. in the Prolegomena, as the transcendental Idea of meaning-totality;
2. in the general theory of the modal spheres, as the Idea of the totality of structural moments in a meaning-modus.
3. in the theory of the individuality-structures of reality, as the idea of the whole of a thing or occurrence, or that of the whole of a particular relationship of human social life.

In this threefold use the Idea always remained oriented to a divine world-order which did not originate in "reason", but limited and determined reason itself. In the constructive level-

---

[1] On this conception of the body politic SCHILLING (*Naturrecht nach der Lehre der alten Kirche*, 1914) bases his interpretation of the Stoic and patristic theories of the State and of absolute natural law.

[2] Vol. III, pp. 201 ff.

[3] The reader should remember that the *Idea* of totality is to be sharply distinguished from the modal *concept* of totality. The latter is merely a provisional resting-point for thought and only embraces the *restrictive* structure of a meaning-modus; it is transcendentally dependent on the *Idea* of totality.

ling abuse of this Idea, it loses its essential structural character and the delimitation of its meaning.

Later on we shall discover a fourth use of the totality-Idea, *viz.* as *the Idea of the integration of human societal relations.* Then we can do justice to the moment of truth in the totality-Idea of the universalistic theories. At the same time, however, we shall find that the Idea of totality in this fourth application remains absolutely bound to that in the first, second and third uses. Apart from these three it must lead to a fundamentally false construction of the mutual relations between the societal structures.

§ 3 - THE TYPICAL LEADING FUNCTION OF THE STATE AND THE THEORY OF THE SO-CALLED 'PURPOSES' OF THE BODY POLITIC.

We will now examine the typical leading function of the State's structure in its indissoluble coherence with the foundational function analyzed above.

At the outset we warned against identifying the leading or qualifying structural function of a thing with the purposes it is to serve. We have repeated this warning with reference to the inner structure of natural communities. Similarly, the leading or qualifying function of an organized human community should not be misinterpreted as the end or ends that human beings try to reach in this relationship by means of their organized endeavours. This warning is especially to the point in the case of the typical leading function in the structure of the State.

The theories of the "purposes of the State" bear no reference to the internal structural principle of the body politic.

The theory of the purpose of the State is as old as political philosophy. It is burdened with the great diversity of meanings implied in the word "purpose", which is used now in a metaphysical-realistic, now in a subjectivistic-nominalistic sense, now in an absolute, then in a relative way. In immanence-philosophy the theory of the purpose of the body politic sometimes contained an *a priori* rational construction, serving to justify the State, and thus assumed an explicit *axiological* character.

Realistic scholasticism used this theory to prove that the institutional Church is of a higher value than the State. The

Humanistic doctrine of natural law and that of "*Vernunftrecht*", in their subjectivistic-teleological constructions of the body politic, made the latter into a mere instrument in the service of the individual or into that of a national cultural community. Then the "purpose of the State" was conceived in the sense of the classical liberal idea of the law-State[1] (LOCKE, KANT, V. HUMBOLDT) or in the eudaemonistic sense of the "welfare State" (the police-State of CHR. WOLFF and his pupil JUSTI). Or again in the idealistic sense of a culture-State (FICHTE is his last phase)[2]. But this teleology never had any inner relation to the real *structural principle* of this societal institution. From an historical standpoint the different theories of the subjective "purpose of the State" propounded in the Humanistic doctrines of natural law prove to be only the expression of a political tendency at the time of their inception. This explains why they became untenable as soon as the historical situation changed. Hence the futility of every attempt to grasp the intrinsic structural limits to the task of the State in such a teleological way.

The old liberal theory of the law-State as a theory of the purpose of the body politic.

We shall once more consider the Humanistic theory of the law-State[3].

In its first stage, *viz.* the classical natural-law stage (LOCKE, KANT, VON HUMBOLDT), this theory aimed at limiting the "purpose of the body politic" construed in the social contract. The State was supposed to have no other aim than the organized protection of the "innate absolute human rights" of all its citizens to freedom, property and life. It should not interfere with the non-political society which by the liberal economic theory was viewed under an exclusively economical aspect and sharply distinguished from the body politic. Thus this theory was the expression of the old-liberal programme of non-interference ("*laisser faire, laisser passer*"). But its starting-point was an individualist-nominalistic view of reality and could not but

---

[1] The term law-State is used here in the sense of the German term "*Rechtsstaat*", which is not to be adequately rendered by "rule of law".

[2] FICHTE defended his idea of a culture-State in his *Staatslehre* (1813).

[3] My view of the development of this theory has been amply elaborated in the standard work of Prof. Dr. J. P. A. MEKKES, *Proeve eener critische Beschouwing der Humanistische Rechtsstaatstheorieën* (Utrecht-Rotterdam, 1940), 752 pp.

eliminate the structural leading function of the State-institution. "Law" itself was conceived in the individualistic natural-law sense of "innate subjective rights" and supposed to be a "purpose" lying outside of the State. In an earlier context we called LOCKE's "law-State" a limited liability company continuing the "state of nature" under the protection of governmental authority [1].

In KANT's idea of the law-State, public law and civil law are materially identified. Civil law "guarantees the external 'mine' and 'thine' by means of State-laws" [2]. KANT's "concept of law" (in his way of thought it should be called his normative *Idea* of law) is nothing but an *a priori* idea of civil private law, the principle of civil-legal co-existence: 'Law is the totality of the conditions under which the arbitrary will of one individual with the arbitrary will of another can be united according to a general law of freedom' [3].

This idea was further defined, by applying THOMASIUS' criterion of law as a *coercive* regulation, as "the possibility of a mutual universal constraint which is in agreement with everybody's freedom according to general rules" [4].

The classical liberalistic idea of the law-State finds its pregnant expression in KANT's pronouncement on the contents of public law: 'The latter does not contain any more or any other duties of men to one another than can be thought of in the former (*i.e.* in the natural state of private law); the matter of private law is exactly the same in both. The rules of the latter are therefore only concerned with the legal form of its union (constitution), with respect to which these rules must necessarily be considered as public' [5].

---

[1] Vol. I, part. II, p. 318.

[2] *Metaphysik der Sitten, 1er Teil* (W.W. Grosh. Wilhelm Ernst Ausg. V), p. 425.

[3] *Op. cit.* p. 335: "Recht ist der Inbegriff der Bedingungen, unter welchen die Willkür des Einen mit der Willkür des Andern nach einem allgemeinen Gesetze der Freiheit zusammen vereinigt werden kann."

[4] *Op. cit.* p. 337: ..."die Möglichkeit eines mit jedermans Freiheit nach allgemeinen Gesetzen zusammenstimmenden durchgängigen wechselseitigen Zwanges."

[5] *Op. cit.* p. 425/6: "Dieses enthält nicht mehr, oder andere Pflichten der Menschen unter sich als in jenem (*i.e.* in dem Zustand des Privatrechts) gedacht werden können; die Materie des Privatrechts ist eben dieselve in beiden. Die Gesetze des letzteren betreffen also nur die rechtliche Form ihres Beisammenseins (Verfassung), in Ansehung deren diese Gesetze notwendig als öffentliche gedacht werden müssen." Compare also

In the *"trias politica"* [1] postulated by this idea of the State, in which according to MONTESQUIEU's prescription, the legislative, the executive, and the judiciary powers ought to be kept strictly apart and equilibrated, the "executive authority" is merely an alien element (*"Fremdkörper"*). There is no room for an "administrative authority" with an independent positive task in this civil-law idea of the body politic. The State has become a *form* (*"Verfassung"*) for private juridical life.

The only thing in this idea of the law-State reminiscent of the internal structure of the body politic is the *coercive* character of the legal order. It has been conceived in an undefined "general concept" of "coercion", and is connected with the idea of freedom, as the supposed normative *essence* of justice, in a characteristic logicistic-dialectical way: Legal *coercion* is the negation of a negation of freedom (injustice), according to general rules, and according to KANT it is thus consonant with freedom.

It is important to note that KANT thinks he must restrict this civil law idea of the law-State to the *internal* relations of the latter. In the *external* relations to other States he conceives of the body politic only as a "power", as a "potentate" [2]. In KANT's definition of the State, as the "union of a multitude of people under legal rules" [3], the foundational function has been ignored, almost on purpose. He appa-

---

the extremely vague definition of public law in § 43 (p. 431) *op. cit.*: 'Der Inbegriff der Gesetze, die einer allgemeinen Bekantmachung bedürfen um einen rechtlichen Zustand hervorzubringen, ist das *öffentliche Recht*. Dieses ist also ein System vom Gesetzen für ein Volk, d.i. eine Menge von Menschen, oder für eine Menge von Völkern, die im wechselseitigen Einflusse gegen einander stehend, des rechtlichen Zustandes unter einem sie vereinigenden Willen, einer *Verfassung* (constitutio) bedürfen, um dessen, was Rechtens ist, teilhaftig zu werden.' [The totality of the rules that require general publication in order to create a legal order, is *public law*. This is, therefore, a system of rules for a nation, *i.e.* a multitude of people, or for a multitude of nations who mutually influence each other and are in need of an organization (constitution) under one will that unites them, if they are to obtain that which is law.]

[1] *Op. cit.* pp. 433 ff.

[2] *Metaph. der Sitten* (the edition cited), p. 431. Cf. also FR. DARMSTAEDTER: *Die Grenzen der Wirksamkeit des Rechtsstaates* (Heidelberg, 1930), p. 2. HEINRICH RICKERT's pronouncement in his *Kant als Philosoph der modernen Kultur* (Tübingen 1924), p. 113, that KANT would have held the view "the State is power", is to be restricted to the international relationships as long as no international jurisdiction has been instituted. Besides, KANT could only conceive of power in an *empirical naturalistic* sense.

[3] *Metaph. d. S.* (the edition cited), p. 433.

rently derived this definition from CICERO. But even KANT's critical freedom-idealism could not carry this disregard through consistently.

The theory of the law-State in its second phase as the theory of the merely formal limitation of the purposes of the State. The formalistic conception of administrative jurisdiction.

In its second phase (STAHL, OTTO BÄHR, RUDOLPH GNEIST) the theory of the law-State was not really a theory of the purpose of the body politic any longer. It assumed a formalistic character: the old liberal idea of the law-State was transformed into that of the rule of statute law. Law, in the sense of a civil legal order protecting the subjective innate rights of man, was no longer considered to be the *purpose* of the body politic. Instead, the idea of the law-State was now related to a public administrative legal order as a *formal limit* to which the magistrature would have to be bound in its administrative activities, when promoting cultural and welfare purposes. This formal legal limitation was required in the interest of the legal security of the citizens. This "legal restriction" of the "executive authority" was found by subordinating the administrative organs to legislation. The statute law was to protect the citizens from administrative arbitrariness. In this sense the modern idea of the law-State was formulated by FR. JULIUS STAHL in his statement: 'The State should be a law-State... It should accurately determine the roads and boundaries of its activity as well as the free spheres of its citizens in a legal way... and it should not realize the ethical ideas any further than insofar as they belong to the legal sphere. The concept of the law-State is not that the body politic only maintains the legal order without any administrative purposes, or accords only complete protection to the rights of individuals; it does not mean the aim of the State but only the mode and character of realizing its political ends' [1]. In itself this utterance

---

[1] FR. JULIUS STAHL, *Philosophie des Rechts nach geschichtlicher Ansicht* (3e Aufl.) Bnd. II, I, pp. 137—138: "Der Staat soll Rechtsstaat sein... Er soll die Bahnen und Grenzen seiner Wirksamkeit wie die freie Sphäre seiner Bürger in der Weise des Rechts genau bestimmen... und soll die sittlichen Ideen von staatswegen nicht weiter verwirklichen als es der Rechtsphäre angehört. Dies ist der Begriff des Rechtsstaates, nicht etwa dass der Staat bloss die Rechtsordnung handhabe ohne administrative Zwecke, oder vollends bloss die Rechte der Einzelnen schütze, er bedeutet nicht Ziel des Staates sondern nur Art und Charakter, dieselben zu verwirklichen."

seems to be quite acceptable. But in the context of STAHL's view of law it implied that public administrative law was depreciated to a merely formal law and opposed to (civil) *material* law in a dualistic way. According to STAHL the principles of *material law* are to be found in the Decalogue, and the subjective private rights are in principle grounded in the latter.

It is evident that in this conception of the law-State the legal order is connected with the power of the body politic only in an *external, formal* way. STAHL, and all the adherents of this idea of the law-State, look upon administrative law only as a formal limitation ("*Schranke*") within which the government can operate free of material legal principles when pursuing the "cultural and welfare purposes".

The non-juridical "purposes of the State" are not given any internal structural delimitation, if their administrative realization is only bound to the formal limits of legislation. This formalistic conception of public law is closely connected with the equally formalistic, and essentially civil juridical view of *administrative judicature,* represented as a requirement of the modern constitutional State by the Hessian jurist OTTO BÄHR[1] and RUDOLPH GNEIST[2].

Even at the present time it is customary to distinguish between *legal questions* and *utility questions* in the theory of administrative judicature. The *merely formally conceived legal questions* are subjected to the decision of the administrative judge; but the material, internal legal questions are not, because the latter are qualified as "questions of utility". This is really a consequence of the formal idea of the law-State, and shows a lack of a really structural conception of the internal law of the body politic. We shall recur to this point in a later context.

In its second phase the theory of the law-State is the expression of a political tendency that has radically broken with the old-liberal programme of political non-interference with the free (non-political) society. The "executive" is here subjected to the formal limits set by the legislature as far as the State's administrative task is concerned. This task is supposed to be the pecu-

---

[1] O. BÄHR, *Der Rechtsstaat,* p. 134, explicitly demands that "the power of the government... in its application..., just like private rights, shall be subordinate to the law" (die Regierungsgewalt... in ihrer Betätigung... *gleich den Privatrechten unter* dem Rechte" stehen soll).

[2] R. GNEIST, *Der Rechtsstaat.*

liar domain in which the body politic has to promote the prosperity and the "culture" of the national community.

The third phase in the development of the theory of the law-State. The uselessness of any attempt to indicate fundamental external limits to the State's task by the construction of limited subjective purposes of the body politic.

The extreme denaturing of the idea of the law-State is seen in its *third stage of development*. Then it no longer purports to be a political idea of the legal delimitation of the State's task but is viewed to be nothing but a logical consequence of methodical purity in the general theory of the body politic. This conception has found expression in the theory of KELSEN and his school. In this theory State and law are identified at the expense of the entire content of both the idea of the State and that of law.

In the logicist formalism of this school even the "dictatorial absolutist State" formally becomes a "law-State", in which the executive has only gained absolute priority over the legislature. For, according to KELSEN, every State must be "logically" conceived as "law" [1]. Thus this concept of the law-State also embraces the totalitarian absolutist State and thereby loses any material normative meaning.

Indeed, even the national socialist and fascist power-States laid claim to the qualification of true or *material law-States*. Yet their ideology did not recognize any material juridical limits to the competence of the authority of the body politic [2].

This fact in itself is important insofar as it shows that these political ideologies could not completely ignore the structural principle of the body politic, notwithstanding their overstraining the idea of power. For in this structural principle the juridical function has indeed the typical leading rôle.

Another fact, too, is evident, *viz.* how little the traditional idea of the law-State was oriented to the invariable internal structure of the latter. The classical individualistic liberal idea of the body politic

---

[1] Cf. my *De Crisis in de Hum. Staatsleer*, p. 45 and KELSEN's statement quoted there.

[2] Cf. for the fascist ideology of the *stato giuridico* (law-State) MENZEL, pp. 73 ff., GIUSEPPE LO VERDE, *Die Lehre vom Staat im neuen Italien* (Berlin, 1934) pp. 54 ff. and S. PANUNZIO, *Allgemeine Theorie des fascistischen Staates* (Berlin und Leipzig, 1934) pp. 78 ff. For the German national-socialist ideology of the law-State cf. KOELLREUTER, *Deutsches Verfassungsrecht*, p. 12, CARL SCHMITT, *Nationalsozialismus und Rechtsstaat* (J.W. 1934, 63 Jg., Heft 12/13) and G. HAVESTADT, *Der Staat und die nationale Gesamtordnung* (Arch. d. öff. R., N.F. 27 Bnd., I Heft, 1936, pp. 76 ff.

ignored the typical public communal law of the State in the sphere of public administration, but claimed the monopoly of being "an idea of the law-State". The same privilege was claimed by the formal *idea of the law-State with its formalistic conception of* public law. But we fail to see what entitled these views to such an exclusive claim. Also the Italian fascist State formally bound its organs to the prevailing legal norms and allowed for a certain administrative judicature. This State, just like the German "third Empire" *(Dritte Reich)*, pretended to realize a *material, universalistic conception of* law, in contradistinction to the formalistic and individualistic legal idea.

From the outset the old liberal theory of the law-State lacked the insight into the typical internal structure of the legal function as the leading function of the body politic. This explains why it could not really stem the rising tide of the idea of the totalitarian State. For the historical development made fresh demands on public life incompatible with the earlier political conceptions of the State's purposes.

The attempt to curtail political absolutism by means of the construction of restricted "purposes of the State" was doomed to failure. The political ideas about the external extent of the State's task are necessarily dependent on historical development. They should not be confounded with the invariable normative structural principle of the body politic [1].

Kelsen must undeniably be credited with having detected this weak spot in the anti-absolutist theory of the restricted "purposes of the State". He opposed the introduction of "political postulates" in the general theory of the State. But his own "normo-

---

[1] This confusion also occurs in G. Jellinek, *Allgemeine Staatslehre* (3e Aufl. 1919), pp. 235 ff. He posits that only such a definition which takes the State's purposes into account, can offer a well-defined criterion to distinguish the body politic from other societal structures (*e.g.*, the Church). This thesis is closely connected with his subjectivistic individualistic conception of an organized community as a "purposive unity" *(Zweckeinheit)* in a socio-psychological sense. Cf. *op. cit.* p. 179: 'Eine Vielheit von Menschen wird für unser Bewusstsein geeinigt wenn sie durch konstante, innerlich kohärente Zwecke mit einander vereinigt sind'. [To our consciousness a plurality of people are united when they are combined by constant, internally cohering purposes]. Therefore in his opinion the sociological theory of the State should point out 'those purposes by means of which the multiplicity of people united in the State appear to us as a unity' (*op. cit.* p. 234). Meanwhile Jellinek has not succeeded in showing an inner coherence between the different political aims of the modern State so that they are to be conceived as a unity.

logical" theory resulted in the theoretical negation of both State and law.

The question what concrete subjective purposes a body politic has to realize at different times and in different places, presupposes the internal structure of the State as such. This is the first insight to be gained if we want to grasp the internal leading function of this societal institution. A State cannot serve any "purposes" if it does not *exist as such.* And it can have no real existence except within the cadre of its *internal structural principle* determining its essential character.

The objective -metaphysical ideology of the State, and the theory of the State as an absolute "*Selbstzweck*" are equally objectionable.

But this insight implies a fundamental rejection of any attempt to derive the essential nature of the State from an "objective" cosmic purpose the latter is supposed to serve. What we have remarked with respect to such a metaphysical teleological view of the institutions of marriage and family, is equally valid for the body politic. Of course, this does not imply that we reject the inquiry after an essential purpose of the State on positivistic grounds. Neither do we make any concession to HEGEL's political philosophy which rejects the idea of an essential purpose of the State because the body politic is supposed to be an absolute end in itself ("*Selbstzweck*"). In his view, just as in the organological theory of the State of Romanticism, this societal institution is the highest revelation of the "objective Spirit", the totality of morality ("*Sittlichkeit*"), "the absolute unmoved end in itself", in which freedom attains to its highest rights. This final purpose has in its turn the highest claim on the individual whose highest duty is being a member of the body politic [1].

No Christian conception of the State can deify this institution to a self-contained "absolute end in itself", if it wants to grasp the typical meaning-structure of the body politic.

The typical leading function of the State in its indissoluble coherence with its foundational function.

As soon as the confusing totalitarian identification of the State and the whole of human society is abandoned and the nature of the body politic as a *differentiated republic* is acknowledged, the tracing of its typical leading function becomes indispensable.

[1] Cf. on this KARL LARENZ, *Staatsphilosophie* (München und Berlin, 1933), p. 177.

This typical leading function as a structural qualification of the State-institution is only to be found in the juridical law-sphere.

It is in vain to seek for another qualifying aspect. That a real body politic cannot be *qualified* by its territorial military power-formation must be evident as soon as we consider that, as a *res publica,* it is always in need of the subordination of its armed force to the civil government in order to guarantee that *stability* of its public legal order which is characteristic of a State. A temporary delegation of the governmental authority to a military commander has in the nature of the case an exceptional character. It is an emergency measure to which a body politic has only recourse in times of war or revolutionary disorder. But in its internal structure the monopolistic military organization is always subservient to a stable territorial public legal order, which also in international law is the ultimate criterion of the existence of a State. This order is only *founded* in a monopolistic organization of armed force.

KELSEN has convincingly shown that every attempt of a naturalist or cultural-scientific sociology to gain a concept of the State apart from the normative legal viewpoint, is doomed to fail. His erroneous identification of the body politic with a system of legal norms can only be explained by the fact that the juridical aspect has indeed a qualifying position in the structural principle of this organized community. This is precisely the difference between the State and all differentiated communities of a non-political character. It is true that the latter also have an internal legal sphere. But they are never *qualified* by this internal juridical function.

A real State cannot find its qualifying function in any other than the juridical aspect, and without this leading function it would degenerate into an organized military gang of robbers, because of its very foundation in armed force.

This is not merely a *specific* difference, but it distinguishes the body politic *radically* from the non-juridically qualified organized communities, such as a Church, an industrial community, a family, a school, a club, *etc.* But the State's qualifying function can only be grasped in its structural coherence with its typical foundational function. The indissoluble, typical-internal structural coherence between "right and might" in the State-relationship is first of all expressed in the *structure of its authority.*

In contradistinction to this structure in all non-political communal relationships, authority in the State, according to its inner nature, is *governmental authority* over subjects *enforced by the strong arm* [1].

The government does not carry the sword in vain. It has been invested with the power of the sword, and as soon as the sword slips out of its hands, it is no longer a government. But according to the structure of its divine office this power is internally directed to the structural guidance by that typical legal communal function whose type of individuality is *founded* in this sword-control. All internal communal law of the State-institution in a structural sense is public territorial law imposing itself with governmental legal authority and maintained with the strong arm. Its sphere of competence will appear to find its internal limits in this structure itself.

That is why GIERKE's elaborate discussion [2] of the "*Obrigkeitsstaat*" in contrast with the "*Volksstaat*", oriented to the "Germanic associational mind", is misleading, at least *terminologically*, and also *historically*. Every true State is essentially an "*Obrigkeitsstaat*", according to the internal structure of its authority. But governmental authority is certainly not identical with some bureaucratic, centralistic and absolutist form of organization, excluding any active participation of popular organs in governmental affairs. MAURICE HAURIOU has rightly observed that the State-idea, which initially only influences a small elite undertaking its realization, has the natural tendency to *incorporate* itself in the whole of a people. What is really meant in GIERKE's contradistinction between "*Obrigkeitsstaat*" and "*Volksstaat*" is the contrast between the autocratic Roman imperium-idea and the democratic form of government. But the latter should not be brought in connection with the old Germanic and medieval Germanic associations which in their undifferentiated character were rather opposed to the State-idea.

All the pre-legal internal modal functions of the State should be guided by and directed to the territorial *public legal community* qualifying the body politic. A military usurper who does

---

[1] Cf. on this KARL LARENZ, *Staatsphilosophie* (München und Berlin, 1933), p. 177.

[2] The Dutch text has "*overheidsgezag over onderdanen*" (German: "*Obrigkeitsgewalt über Untertäne*"). These pregnant terms are not to be rendered by adequate English words.

not perform the typical duties of the public legal office of the government can never be an organ of the *State,* but remains the leader of an organized gang of robbers. But on the other hand it must be emphatically repeated that the legal organization of the body politic, in its typical authoritative character, remains indissolubly founded in the historical organization of territorial military power. Apart from the latter, the internal public legal order of the State cannot display that *typical* juridical character which distinguishes it from all kinds of private law. It would be erroneous to suppose that this internal public law order lacks an inner *juridical* type of individuality and is only characterized by its external connection with the coercive apparatus of military power. We shall show in the sequel that it is rather characterized by typical legal principles. It was the disregard of the latter that led to the formalistic view of administrative jurisdiction mentioned above.

Only within the framework of its invariable structure can a *real* State-community be formed with an organized communal will. The "will of the State" is by no means a fictitious legal abstraction, but the real organized will of a communal whole. It is true that this will is *qualified* by the juridical relation between the government and its subjects, and *founded* in historical territorial military power. But it asserts itself in all the aspects of our social experience as an organized unity of volitional direction, realized in the *organized* actions of a societal whole. And it is fundamentally wrong to oppose this typical organization as a one-sided "mechanical" organization of governmental functions, to the people, as if the latter had an independent existence opposite to that of the government. After the definitive dissolution of the primitive popular and tribal organizations, no people of a differentiated cultural level exists otherwise than in a *public community,* by which it is indissolubly united with a government, as the bearer of authority. In the national State there does not exist *a people* apart from a government; and there is no *government* apart from a people. The people become a political unity only in the territorial organization of government and subjects. This truth must be strongly upheld against the romantic theory of the "people" as a mystic "natural organism".

The difficult question concerning the relation between a State, and a national community which is not identical with the political unity of a State's people, will demand our attention in a later context.

The typical integrating character of the leading legal function in the structure of the State. The State's people as an integrated whole.

We have now arrived at the most critical point of our inquiry. The leading function in the structure of the State has proved to be a public legal relationship uniting government, people and territory into a politico-juridical whole. As the structural whole has priority to its constituents, it makes no sense to speak of the latter in terms of separate "elements" of the body politic. This is also to be kept in mind with respect to the leading juridical aspect of the State-institution. That the latter has nothing to do with a *particular aim* of the State has been shown above in our critical analysis of the old liberal idea of the law-State. A body politic cannot realize specific purposes unless it *exists as such*. And it cannot exist apart from its structural principle qualified by its leading function. This leading function lacks a *typical non-juridical qualification,* since the foundational function of power cannot supply this. In principle this implies the unique *universality* and *totality* of the internal legal community of the State, which is not found in any other societal structure.

The traditional universalistic theory of the State as the integral totality of all the other societal structures seems thus to be justified at least with regard to the *legal* organization of the body politic. In the internal structure of the State the *modal* juridical sphere-sovereignty does not seem to be individualized as a typical *structural juridical* sphere-sovereignty. But is the State, in its internal juridical sphere, really a juridical community with an unqualified coercive legal power, absorbing all the internal juridical relationships of a different radical and geno-type, as its component parts? This is impossible, since the individuality-structures of the non-juridically *qualified* legal relationships can never assume the structural character of public legal relationships inherent in the State. The relation between the typical universality of the internal public legal sphere of the State, and the qualified juridical spheres in non-political societal structures, cannot be conceived of in the schema of the whole and its parts.

The problem raised by the leading function of the State will perhaps be brought nearer to its solution if we remember that every body politic organizes a *people* within a territory into a typical, legally qualified, public community. The State's people is indeed the typical totality of all the citizens irrespective of their family-relations, their Church-membership or their philosophical convictions, their trades or professions, class-distinctions, or their social standing. The State constitutes a typical *integrating* political unity in spite of any differences or divisions which its people display in other societal relationships.

How is this integration possible? The State cannot integrate these differences in profession or trade, ecclesiastical or philosophical trends, social classes, *etc.*, into the structure of a totalitarian professional or industrial organization, a totalitarian philosophical or Church community, or in the social structure of a totalitarian class. Nor can the State become an undifferentiated totality of all the "special" societal relationships within its territory. The integration of the citizens into the political unity of a people is in principle bound to the typical structure of the body politic, in which the leading function is that of a public legal community. This is an unparalleled, unique structural principle enabling the State to organize within its territory a truly universal legal communal bond transcending all non-juridically qualified legal societal relations. Neither internal ecclesiastical law, nor internal industrial law can have this typical *public juridical* integrating function, however large the number of the members of a Church or an industrial community may be. These legal spheres are limited by the typical particularity of their non-juridical qualification and lack the universally integrating character inherent in the internal public legal sphere of the State. In the territorial legal community of the body politic all the specifically qualified juridical interests should be harmonized in the sense of a truly public legal retribution, and integrated into "the public interest".

This implies that the principle of public interest must itself have a typical *juridical qualification which delimits its supra-arbitrary structural meaning.* It can never warrant an encroachment upon the internal sphere-sovereignty of non-political societal relationships. For the idea of an absolute competence of the State contradicts the modal meaning of the juridical aspect and is incompatible with the typical structural principle of the body politic. We shall recur to this point presently.

The real structure of the internal public law. In the monistic legal theories this structure is ignored and an unjustified appeal is made to legal history.

It is the principle of public interest which in its leading juridical aspect also gives a typical material legal meaning to the internal public law of the State. Wherever the State-structure, as such, expresses itself as a differentiated *res publica,* within the juridical aspect of human society, this public law appears. In unbreakable mutual coherence it embraces legal *organizational* and *behaviour* norms. The former regulate the organization and competences of the different authoritative organs of the body politic; the latter regulate the public legal relations between the authoritative organs and the subjects. In spite of any enkaptic structural interlacements with civil private law, and with the non-political communal or inter-individual legal spheres, this public law retains its internal structure. True public communal law is never non-juridically *qualified,* although under the lead of the principle of public interest the legislator may pursue different political aims. Besides, the general principle of public interest will be differentiated in its material content by the different branches of the State's task, which varies with the historical development of a differentiated society.

The functionalistic juridical theories do not know what to do with the concept of "public law" in its classical contradistinction to private law. This is not surprizing since they do not take into consideration the internal structure of the State.

The view implied in these theories must result in the levelling of the individuality-structures. Such may be due to a formalist (logicistic) conception of law (KELSEN) or to a historicist-psychological view of the latter (KRABBE, V. IDSINGA). Insofar as such monistic theories make an appeal to medieval legal conditions[1], to prove that the distinction between public and private law cannot be fundamental, we should be on our guard. It is necessary then to lay bare the structural-theoretical conditions of a really scientific historical inquiry into the human societal relationships, to unmask the *petitio principii* in this supposed "objective" historical demonstration. If the feudal medieval society lacked a fundamental distinction between public and private law, this can only be due to the fact that the undifferentiated condition of this society had not yet room for a real State. It can never prove that the distinction mentioned is not essential to the State as such.

It is not critical to seek for a fundamental distinction between public and private law in the Middle-Ages without considering the preliminary question whether medieval society, as long as the feudal system prevailed, had any room for a real republican idea of governmental authority. In this connection we mention V. BELOW's studies of the "medieval German State". They are of special methodological

[1] In addition an appeal is often made to the modern British legal system, which is supposed to lack a distinction between public and

importance, in as much as he has pointed out the erroneous absolutization of the economic-historical viewpoint in various monistic interpretations of the legal historical material. He has tried to deprive the monistic theory of one of its most cherished arguments, *viz.* the lack of a fundamental difference between public and private law in the Middle-Ages[1]. Other German legal historians have followed him in this attempt.

But to my mind VON BELOW has not been able to free himself from the prejudice that the question as to whether we can speak of a real *State* in the Middle-Ages, can be answered in a purely historical way. He also holds that we must not base our inquiry on structural theoretical insights into the essential character of the body politic[2]. This shows a lack of critical insight. Moreover, this historian has most certainly based his investigations on some structural theoretical insight into the nature of the State. This appears from the emphasis he has laid on the necessity of a juridical training of historians who want to examine the medieval political conditions[3]. In this context

---

private law. But this is simply a misinterpretation of the "rule of (common) law" which could maintain itself in England almost until the end of the XIXth century. This "rule of law" had nothing to do with an elimination of the classical distinction between public and private law as such, which is as old as the State itself. It only meant that since the glorious Revolution there was no longer a specific royal administrative jurisdiction exempt from the courts of common law. DICEY praised this system and erroneously supposed that the French system of administrative jurisdiction had no other aim than to provide the organs of public administration with a privileged position. The truth was that in the long run the common law jurisdiction could not provide the citizens with a sufficient legal protection against administrative acts implying an undue encroachment upon their legal interests. The French *Conseil d'Etat* gave this protection in an exemplary way by applying typical public legal principles to the State's responsibility even when the latter might not be grounded on civil law rules which before 1912 were applied to unlawful acts of public administration by the *Cour de Cassation* (Cf. PAUL DUEZ, *La Responsabilité de la Puissance Publique*). And the British system of the "rule of common law" has since long been broken through by the introduction of a continually increasing administrative jurisdiction.

[1] Cf. v. BELOW, *Der deutsche Staat des Mittelalters*, Bnd. I (2e Aufl. 1925). We would especially refer to the critical methodological remarks against straining the economical viewpoint: pp. 75 ff. Cf. also his: *Die Entstehung der deutschen Stadtgemeinde* (1889); *Der Ursprung der deutschen Stadtverfassung* (1892) and *Territorium und Stadt* (1900), especially pp. 303 ff. Cf. also H. MITTEIS, *Lehnrecht und Staatsgewalt* (Weimar, 1933) pp. 198 ff., pp. 300, 321, 406, 516, 520, 575, etc.

[2] Cf. *Der deutsche Staat des Mittelalters* (2e Aufl. 1925) p. XXV.

[3] Cf. especially *op. cit.* p. 84. Here v. BELOW blames NITSZCH for a fundamental lack of insight into the medieval political conditions on account of the fact that "notwithstanding his absorbing interest in the

he could only mean that the legal historian should have an insight into the fundamental difference between public and private law inherent in the structure of the State. But this insight is not sufficient. The legal historian should also be aware of the danger of interpreting the medieval feudal system in terms of legal structural distinctions which only fit to a differentiated condition of human society. He should have a theoretical insight into the fundamental difference between undifferentiated and differentiated societal structures. How is the historian to gain such an insight from the changing historical facts if the latter are not included in supra-historical structures? These structures must first be clearly seen if the historian wants to interpret his legal material correctly.

From the historical viewpoint one should fight shy of a generalizing conception of the medieval political conditions. The political conditions of the late Middle-Ages were very different from those of early and High medieval feudalism. And as to the Frankish kingdom there is a fundamental difference between the Merovingian *patrimonial regnum* and the Karolingian *State*, founded on the idea of the *res publica*. These differences are not duly considered by VON BELOW. Compare, for instance, his generalizing characterization of the public legal foundation of the Frankish empire (*Der deutsche Staat des Mittelalters*, pp. 210 ff. with an appeal to WAITZ, ROTH and SOHM).

The real meaning of the absolutist idea of the State and the true idea of the law-State.

A real public legal integration of a country and people is, therefore, only possible within the internal limits set by the structural principle of the State-institution itself. This integration can only be accomplished within the juridical limits set by this structural principle to the competence of the body politic, and with due regard to the internal sphere-sovereignty of the other societal structures. Every political theory denying these limits is in principle a theory of the "power-State", even though it masks its absolutization of the State's power by a law-State ideology.

In whatever shape the absolutist idea of the body politic is set forth, it does not recognize any intrinsic legal limits to the authority of the State. This idea implies an absorption of the entire juridical position of man by his position as citizen or as subject of the government.

---

enquiry into the facts NITSZCH lacked that juridical intuition or training without which a description of constitutional history is simply unthinkable." ["dass ihm bei all seinem verzehrenden Interesse für die Erforschung der Realien die juristische Beanlagung oder Schulung gefehlt hat, ohne die nun einmal die Darstellung der Verfassungsgeschichte... undenkbar ist."

If we cannot appeal to any law outside of the State, if the body politic has a so-called *"Kompetenz-Kompetenz"*, *i.e.* a pseudo-juridical omnipotence, then the authority of the State has been theoretically deprived of any legal meaning and has in principle been turned into juridically *unlimited political power.* Neither a theoretical subjection of this power to some general principles of natural law, nor a theoretical construction of a so-called legal self-restriction of the State-power, can undo the harm implied in the initial absolutization inherent in the idea of sovereignty of the body politic, current since BODIN. But in the true idea of the law-State, the divine structural principle of the body politic limits the peculiar universality of the internal public law to a universality and sovereignty within its own sphere of competence. Every attempt on the part of an absolutist government to exceed the intrinsic boundaries of its legal power results in a despotism which undermines the very fundamentals of its authority. But even such a despotism can only occur within the structural principle of the body politic, which is beyond any human arbitrariness.

The idea of "the public interest" and the internal limits set to it by the structural principle of the State.

When we have gained an insight into the inner nature of the public legal communal sphere of the State, we can also find the *internal limits* to the idea of the "public interest" *as a guiding principle for the internal State-policy.* In the nature of the case this principle cannot be identical with its *leading juridical aspect.* But it is only the latter which can give to it its inner limitation as the material principle of public communal law.

The idea of the *"salus publica"* displays a genuine Protean character in political theory. It was made subservient to the ancient universalistic-organic theory of the State, to the doctrine of the "reasons of State", to WOLFF's natural law theory of the police-State, to HOBBES' and ROUSSEAU's natural law construction of the Leviathan-State, but also to the classical liberal doctrine of the constitutional State (LOCKE and KANT), and to the modern totalitarian political theories.

For the sake of the public interest PLATO and FICHTE defended the withdrawal of the children from their parents and wanted their education to be entrusted to the body politic. With an appeal to the public interest PLATO wanted to abolish marriage and private property as far as the ruling classes of his ideal

State were concerned. ARISTOTLE wanted education to be made uniform in "the public interest"; on the same ground ROUSSEAU wished to destroy all the particular associations intervening between the State and the individual citizen. WOLFF desired the body politic to meddle with everything human and, at least for the Protestant Churches, he wanted the government to fix the confession. The idea of the "*salus publica*" was the hidden dynamite under the Humanistic natural law theories of HUGO GROTIUS and S. PUFENDORFF [1]. In CHR. WOLFF's doctrine of natural law this idea resulted in a frankly admitted antinomy with his theory of innate natural rights [2]. The slogan of the public interest was the instrument for the destruction of the most firmly established liberties because it lacked any juridical delimitation.

The terrible threat of Leviathan is audible in this word as long as it is used in a juridically unlimited sense. The universalistic political theories could conceive of the relation between the State and the non-political societal structures only in the schema of the whole and its parts. This is why they could not delimit the idea of "the public interest".

According to ARISTOTLE the State, as the autarchical "perfect community", has to supply its citizens any good they cannot obtain either individually or in the "lower communities". This is not an inner structural criterion of the legal limits of the public interest but only one for the external extent of the State's task. It is oriented to a metaphysical theory of the *purpose* of the State, and is entirely in accordance with the ancient totalitarian idea of the body politic. In this conception there is in principle no possibility of freedom outside of the State.

ROUSSEAU's idea of the "public interest" was only limited by the natural law principle of the equality of all the citizens before the statute law and consequently by the exclusion of any private privileges of individuals. This idea was to be expressed in the "general will" (la '*volonté générale*'); it did not imply any material legal restriction of competence of the legislator; it sanctioned the absolutist power of the State over all spheres of life, even over public worship.

CHR. WOLFF's criterion of the *salus publica* is based on his eudaemonist theory of natural law, and is identical with his conception

---

[1] Cf. my *In den Strijd om een Christelijke Staatkunde,* I, XV (A.R. Staatk. driemaand. orgaan, 1e jg.) pp. 142 ff.

[2] CHR. WOLFF, *Jus Naturae* VIII, 1, § 117; here he speaks of a real "*collisio legum*" between his principles of natural law and the basic principle of his theory of the State: "*Salus publica suprema lex esto*". He cuts the Gordian knot with his construction of an emergency law of the State: "*Necessitas non subditur legi*".

of the purpose of the State embodied in the social contract. In his opinion the public interest consists in the *vitae sufficientia, tranquillitas et securitas*[1]. This view was oriented to the absolutist idea of the police-State that the "enlightened despots" in Prussia and Austria tried to realize.

As far as I know, KANT was the first Humanist philosopher who tried to give the idea of the *salus publica* an entirely new meaning, which was anti-absolutist and non-eudaemonistic. The eudaemonistic conception of the public interest was in conflict with KANT's practical idea of autonomy.

According to WOLFF, who is here in line with ARISTOTLE, the State should procure all the commodities its citizens need for their temporal well-being and perfection, insofar as the smaller communities of family and kinship cannot provide them. This was the only conception of the adage *"Salus publica suprema lex esto"* which was supposed to guarantee a rationally justified constitution. But KANT breaks with this eudaemonist conception. According to him the idea of the *salus publica* can have no other meaning than that of a constitutional principle containing the *a priori* juridical norms which *ought to be realized as a duty prescribed by a categorical imperative*. The contents of these juridical principles are found in KANT's conception of the law-State and its idea of the *trias politica*[2]. We saw, however, that this idea of the law-State does not approach the internal structural limits to public law but is essentially an individualistic civil law idea. In KANT's conception the internal structure of the State is reduced to a mere organizational form for the creation, the maintenance, and the judicial application of private civil law (the organized form of the legislature, the police and the administration of justice)[2].

The idea of *salus publica* should be oriented to the structural principle of the State, else it will become the instrument of an unbridled State-absolutism, or the embodiment of an arbitrary conception of the external content of the State's task. In spite of all theoretical misconceptions of this principle it has a universally valid meaning, internally delimiting all real political activity of the State.

The *positive* contents of this principle, however, are dependent on an intricate complex of variable socio-cultural conditions.

The *salus publica* and distributive justice.

In its qualifying juridical aspect the *public interest* implies the typical public legal measure of distributive justice which requires a proportional distribution of public communal charges

---

[1] *Jus Naturae* VIII, 1, § 2.

[2] *Met. Anfangsgründe der Rechtslehre* 2er Teil, 1er Abschnitt § 49 *in fine* (Grossh. Wilhelm Ernst Ausg. V, p. 439).

and public communal benefits in accordance with the bearing power and the merits of the subjects[1]. In his book *La Responsabilité de la Puissance Publique,* the French professor of constitutional law PAUL DUEZ has especially pointed to the significance of this public legal standard in the administrative jurisdiction of the French *Conseil d'État.* But it is of a universal import with respect to the whole internal public administration and administrative legislation. And as a legal principle of the public interest it clearly contradicts the erroneous opinion that administrative law is only a formal juridical frame-work for the pursuing of communal aims.

The *salus publica,* thus conceived, is a political integrating principle binding all the variable political maxims to a supra-arbitrary standard. It binds the entire activity of the State to the typical leading idea of public social justice in the territorial relations between government and subjects. Externally the task of the State cannot be delimited in a universally valid way, because the body politic, as a real organized community, functions in all the aspects of temporal reality. In principle, it is impossible even to exclude the State from the spheres of morality and faith. The State may promote the interests of science and the fine arts[2], education, public health, trade, agriculture and industry, popular morality, and so on. But every governmental interference with the life of the nation is subject to the inner vital law of the body politic, implied in its structural principle. This vital law delimits the State's task of integration according to the political criterion of the "public interest", bound to the principle of

---

[1] KANT, and the Humanistic teachers of natural law before him, did not understand the original Aristotelian sense of the idea of distributive justice. This idea originally bore on the internal communal law of the State, and not on private civil juridical relations as intended in KANT's idea of law as a normative principle of juridical coexistence. We have shown in an earlier context that even the Aristotelian conception of commutative justice is not to be understood in an individualistic sense. KANT, however, understands by *iustitia distributiva* or *"austeilende Gerechtigkeit"* only such justice as is administered by a civil judge, as an impartial instance created by the "general will" for deciding private legal disputes. Cf. *Met. Anfangsgründe,* I §§ 39 and 41.

[2] Remember that in case the modern State gives financial support, this is done with revenues from taxation levied from its citizens by means of governmental coercion. State-support is therefore something quite different from that given by a private association for the promotion of sciences or the fine arts, because in associations the members give support out of their own free will.

sphere-sovereignty of the individuality structures of human society.

The internal political activity of the State should always be guided by the idea of public social justice. It requires the harmonizing of all the interests obtaining within a national territory, insofar as they are enkaptically interwoven with the requirements of the body politic as a whole. This harmonizing process should consist in weighing all the interests against each other in a retributive sense, based on a recognition of the sphere-sovereignty of the various societal relationships.

To give a concrete example, we will consider the administrative juridical regulation of the many-sided concern of public health. This is a real concern of the public legal sphere of the State which, as such, is not qualified by a non-juridical aspect. The particularity of the subject matter of this administrative legal regulation is its concern with the bio-social structural aspect of the national community. Nevertheless, the regulation itself ought to be guided by the public legal principle inherent in the "public interest".

No doubt such a positive regulation is intended to serve a particular political purpose, *viz.* the improvement of public health. This purpose in itself does not differ from the aims of private societies for the improvement of national health. But this part of administrative law, as well as all the relevant executive measures taken by the organs of the State, has an internal, public juridical qualification. The internal structure of administrative law makes it obligatory on the government always to weigh the various private legal interests carefully against each other, and against the "public interest", in a retributive sense. These private interests must be harmonized and integrated in the public juridical interest. This is not required in the case of private societies for the promotion of public health, whose structure has a non-juridical qualification, and which are not founded in military power.

The civil law-sphere of the State.

The internal public law-sphere of the State has its typical correlate in the sphere of civil law as a private *common law (jus commune).* Every communal legal sphere is correlated with inter-individual legal relationships. But in addition to its correlation with the typical international relations of a public law character, the public communal law-sphere of the State has a *typical* correlate in an inter-individual legal sphere which is unbreakably bound to the structure of the body politic.

It is true that private common law does not immediately develop within the framework of the State so long as the undifferentiated societal relationships have not yet been completely conquered. The Carlovingian State did not succeed in replacing the ancient barbarian tribal laws by a common private legal order. This body politic lacked stability, and before Charlemagne's organization of the public administration could be followed by the development of a private common civil law, the republican empire collapsed.

The Roman republic started with an elevation of the primitive ancient inter-gentilitial law of the Quiritian tribes to a civil law bound to Roman citizenship. The *lex duodecim tabularum* was nothing but a description of old customary rules and was on the same primitive level as the barbarian *lex Salica* described under the reign of the Merovingian king CHLODOVECH.

It was only under the influence of the *ius gentium* that the idea of a *common private law* developed. Initially this *ius gentium* did not exceed the boundaries of a law containing the common ingredients in the legal customs of the old Italian tribes. But gradually it emancipated itself from the primitive tribal inter-gentilitial law. In keeping with the expansion of the Roman city-State into a world-empire, the *ius gentium* assumed the characteristic of an integrating world-law founded on the principle of the legal equality of all free men, as legal subjects in the inter-individual legal relationships. It was this private world-law which the classical Roman jurisconsults connected with the Stoic conception of the *ius naturale*.

The Stoic idea of natural law in principle broke through the classical Greek idea of the city-State as the perfect natural community. It proclaimed the natural freedom and equality of all men as such. It is true that the Roman *ius gentium* did not entirely satisfy these principles of freedom and equality, insofar as it maintained slavery; nevertheless, it constituted an inter-individual legal sphere in which every free man was equally recognized as a legal subject independent of all specific communal bonds, even independent of Roman citizenship. This was the fundamental difference between the undifferentiated Quiritian tribal law and the private common law.

It was within this legal sphere that the undifferentiated authoritative proprietorial right, contained in the *dominium ex iure Quiritium*, was dissolved into a "*bonitary*" ownership lacking any authoritative character. Under the influence of the *ius gentium* the term *pater familias*, which in the ancient Quiritian tribal law meant the quality of domestic chief, was in its civil legal use transformed into a simple *nomen iuris* designating nothing but the abstract quality of a legal subject, belonging to every free man as such.

If we consider only the fact that the *ius gentium* even emancipated the function of legal subject from Roman citizenship, the question may arise as to whether this common law had anything to do with the structural principle of the State. One might suppose it was much more related to the Stoic idea of a temporal community of the whole of mankind. But we have seen in an earlier context that this universalist idea did not correspond to any structure of individuality in which a temporal community can only be realized.

To answer the question asked above, we should consider that the *ius gentium* could only become a real common private law by abstracting the legal relationships regulated by it from any specific non-juridical qualification. It may be that the Roman *societas,* as a contract of common law, took its origin in the Roman *familia,* later on oriented itself to occassional contractual cooperations for the purpose of economic profit or speculation, and finally to durable economically qualified undertakings. Nevertheless, its common law rules neither interfered with the internal sphere of the family, nor with that of industrial or commercial life. The same thing can be observed with respect to the other contracts regulated by the *ius gentium,* to the *jura in re* of the latter, to the common law rules concerning family law and hereditary right, *etc.*

The inner nature of the Roman *ius gentium.*

The common private law was only led by natural law principles of justice, the "nature of the matter", legal security, and equity, in their application to the inter-individual legal relationships of men as such. In this respect it was indeed the typical private legal correlate of the public communal law, which equally lacks a specific non-juridical qualification and is ruled by the principle of public interest. In addition, the *ius gentium* was a typical system of legal rules destined for the decision of lawsuits by the common courts of the State. As to its formal juridical source it was praetorial law during the classical era of Roman jurisprudence. In its typical character as an integrating private common law it could not develop outside of the frame-work of the *res publica,* which was only able to *realize* the typical principles of the *ius gentium.* This realization was doubtless a matter of public interest, although the Roman lawyers emphatically established that, as to its inner nature, the common private law did not pertain to the *res publica* but to the interest of the individual legal subjects in their inter-individual relationships. The public interest was concerned with the private common law insofar as the *res publica*, by means of an impartial common jurisdiction, could prevent a complete desintegration of private law and a revival of the ancient undifferentiated legal spheres; for the latter were incompatible with the State's monopolistic organization of the sword-power and the public legal authority.

In this respect the sharp distinction between public and private law was a vital concern of the *res publica*. By controlling the jurisdiction over all private law-suits, in as much as they pertained to the sphere of common private law, the State was able to prohibit any attempt on the part of private power-formations to usurp an exclusive authority over the subjects of the body politic. Since the common private law was also sharply distinguished from all internal private legal spheres of a typical non-juridical qualification, its formation was by the nature of the case *bound to* the *res publica*. Outside of the latter there was not any room for an inter-individual common legal sphere based upon the natural law principle of equality of all free individuals as such. As to their inner nature the non-political societal relationships nowhere corresponded to this principle. But with respect to the State this principle was the natural correlate of the principle of the public legal equality of its subjects as to their common subjection to the public authority.

The distinction between *jus civile* and *jus gentium* was doomed to disappear, since under the influence of the praetorial law the former lost its material coherence with the archaic Roman tribal law and was almost completely accommodated to the *jus gentium*. In addition, Roman citizenship was to an ever increasing degree attributed to peregrines. In the classical period of Roman jurisprudence the victory of the *jus gentium* over the *jus civile* was already decided. JUSTINIAN's codification abolished the last remnants of the ancient civil law, which had long lost any practical significance.

It is true that, as to its material content, the formation of the private common law, at least in the classical period of Roman jurisprudence, was not due to the legislator but to the Roman lawyers. In this sense it was doubtless "*Juristenrecht*". But the work of the jurisconsults was bound to the system of actions formed by the praetor. And it was by means of these actions that the State retained the legal control over the private common law-sphere, which apart from the *res publica* was doomed to disappear.

Legal history shows that this bond between the idea of a private common law, in the sense of the *jus gentium*, and that of the *res publica* is not an exclusive peculiarity of the Roman legal system. There is not any instance to be found of a private common law, in the sense defined above, which has developed outside of the State.

It may be that the Roman legal tradition has exercised a considerable influence upon the development of private common law in the modern continental States of Europe where the legislator has codified its rules. But in England the influence of Roman law was only small. Nevertheless here, too, a civil law-system has developed based on the essential principles of juridical equality and freedom of all individuals in their inter-personal civil legal relations. Here this development took place by means of a material transformation of the feudal law into a common private law. And it was brought about by the formative activity of judicial organs of the State, *viz.* the common law courts and the supplementary equity jurisdiction of the chancellor. The classical English jurists considered this common civil law as the expression of natural justice, just as the Roman lawyers had looked upon the *jus gentium* as the expression of the *jus naturale*.

We could also point to the Scandinavian States whose common civil law has not undergone the influence of the Roman *ius gentium*.

The radical difference between common private law and the undifferentiated popular or tribal law.

Under the influence of the Historical School the erroneous conception arose that common civil law was nothing but the ancient folk- or tribal law, developed in a technical sense by the jurists. This view was opposed to BODIN's idea of the sovereignty of the legislator with respect to the formation of civil law. The truth is that there is a radical difference in nature between primitive folk-law and the highly differentiated common private law; the latter could only develop after the material destruction of the undifferentiated primitive society of which the popular or tribal law was a juridical expression.

And this destruction was due to the rise of the State as a real *res publica.*

Irrespective of the question as to whether the common private law has been codified by the legislator or has been preponderantly formed by the courts of the State, it is by its inner nature a legal sphere bound to the body politic. And the original competence to its formation cannot belong to any other organized community but the State. By means of this common private law the body politic can bind in an enkaptical way any specific (non-juridically qualified) private law to the principles of inter-individual justice, legal security and equity. But the internal spheres of these specific kinds of private law, qualified by the non-juridical leading function of the societal relationships to which they belong, remain exempt from the competence of the State. In the introduction to the general theory of the enkaptic structural interlacements we shall show that this thesis is not an arbitrary assumption due to a subjective political conviction. It will appear that it is rather founded in the structural conditions of every differentiated human society, which cannot be disregarded with impunity.

The State as an instrument used by the ruling class in human society to oppress the other classes. The depreciation of the classical idea of public interest and the civil legal principles of freedom and equality in positivistic sociology.

That the classical conception of the private common law was dependent on the classical idea of the State as a *res publica,* is also indicated by the fact that a denial of the latter was always accompanied by a denial of the former.

The Humanist natural law doctrine of the XVIIth century, insofar as it was oriented to the Roman legal tradition, absolutized the State's common private and public legal sphere. Starting from BODIN's concept of sovereignty, the adherents of this doctrine strove after a new legal order in which no law should be recognized that was not to be subsumed under one of these two legal orbits. The result was that this view of law lost contact with social reality. As soon as it is forgotten that the civil legal principles of freedom and equality make sense only in that relatively small sector of the private legal relationships which lacks a specific non-juridical qualification, these principles seem to be nothing but the result of metaphysical speculation. And as soon as it is forgotten that the principle of public interest has a typical juridical qualification bound to the inner structure of the State institution, it seems to be nothing but a mask for the interests of a ruling social class.

This may appear from the view of the French founders of positivistic sociology. Radically breaking with the natural law doctrine, they at the same time abandoned both the classical conception of the State as a *res publica* and the classical conception of the *ius gentium*. How did they arrive at this negative conclusion?

We have seen that the classical Greek and Roman view of the *res publica* identified the latter with the whole of human society, as it presents itself within the territorial boundaries of the State. This was the reason why all sociological problems were treated in the framework of political theory. This tradition was continued in the political works of BODIN and MONTESQUIEU.

It was the liberal economical theory which, allied with the Lockean natural law doctrine, broke with this traditional conception, and made a sharp distinction between the State and the non-political civil society. The latter was exclusively considered from the economical viewpoint as a system of free market relations. But its foundation was the private civil property, whose organized maintenance and protection was viewed as the chief aim of the political association of individuals. The State should not interfere with this "civil society", unless to prevent the formation of monopolist market positions, which disturb the natural operation of economic laws.

It was this "civil society" which drew the special attention of ST. SIMON and AUGUSTE COMTE. But they fully realized that the economical viewpoint embraces only an abstract aspect of human society. The latter does not only display economically qualified relationships but also such of a so-called "ideal" character, as science and philosophy, the fine arts, "religious" communities, *etc.*, and its foundation is the family. What is the place of the political organization in this society as a whole? This was the first question that intrigued the French founders of positivist sociology.

ST. SIMON was struck by the fact that since the beginning of the French revolution until 1815, France had been provided with ten different constitutions, whereas society cannot change so rapidly. From this he concluded that the constitution, which regulates the political form of government, cannot have the essential and central position in human society assumed by the natural law doctrine. In his opinion the real political changes are much rather dependent on the economical factors in "civil society", which are the real foundation of the political relation of authority and subordination, and on a change of the ideas, to which perhaps St. Simon (and in any case Comte) ascribed a leading and integrating rôle in human society.

This meant a complete reversion of the classical view about the relation between the State and human society. According to St. Simon and Comte, the body politic is only a secondary product of "civil society" in its economically qualified relationships. The "leading ideas" of societal life are by no means the natural law ideas of the classical and modern political theories, which had no inner coherence with the factual condition of society. The latter does not exhibit that natural freedom and equality of all men which the speculative jurists supposed to lie at the foundation of the civil legal order. Nor can there be any truth in the classical conception of the State, with its military foundation, as an institution of the public interest. The truth is that civil property gives rise to class differences and class contrasts and that political authority always belongs to the ruling class.

In order to give politics a scientific foundation, it was deemed necessary to extend the natural scientific method (so successfully applied by Galileo and Newton to the natural phenomena), also to the investigation of the societal relationships. The latter should, therefore, be taken in their rude factuality, apart from any normative viewpoint. Only by tracing the general natural laws to which society is subject, both in its relatively static condition and in its dynamical process, can sociology provide politics with a scientific basis. In itself this was completely in keeping with the science-ideal of the Enlightenment in the so-called empiricistic trend.

But the new sociology (this name was introduced by Comte) intended to synthesize the natural scientific method with the universalist historical mode of thought of the Restoration. Society should be viewed as an organic whole, all of whose parts are interrelated, in contradistinction to the individualistic conception of societal relationships. According to Comte, the historical method is the specific sociological method; but it is not to be conceived in the irrationalist sense of Romanticism. It is much rather the highest specification of the general natural-scientific mode of thought. Its aim is the discovery of the general empirical law of societal development. And this law was supposed to be that of the three stages, viewed as a law of continuous social progress. From a military type ruled by "theological" ideas, human society proceeds to an industrial type whose truly leading ideas will be developed by positivist sociology. The intermediate stage is that of the dissolution of the theological ideas by metaphysical concepts which lack any coherence with the beginning industrial development and its intrinsically positivist mind. As during this metaphysical stage society is deprived of integrating leading ideas, there arise revolutionary tensions culminating in the bloody French revolution.

According to COMTE, States arise during the theological stage when the theological ideas have assumed a polytheistic character. They display a strongly organized military type. Especially the Roman State was an organization of conquerors. The prisoners of war are no longer killed since the economical interest of the conquerors is better served by making them slaves. Thus the legal order of the military State sanctions the distinction between rulers and slaves, which is also the foundation of the economic process of production. The relative significance of the military State is that it accustoms its subjects to discipline and division of labour.

Christian monotheism brought about the medieval separation between the priestly and the secular power, which in classical Greco-Roman antiquity had been united. So the spiritual power of Christianity could penetrate the whole of medieval society. It restricted war to a defensive function, whose social organisational form was the rule of the knight over the domain he could protect, *i.e.* feudalism. At the same time the spirit of Christianity succeeded in bringing about a gradual transformation of slavery into a colonate, and finally its influence led to the complete abolition of the latter in the medieval towns.

The personal freedom guaranteed by the towns gave rise to industrialism, *i.e.* a system of free production of commodities, which in the metaphysical stage initially developed independently of and in opposition to the military State, until since the latter part of the 17th century the latter begins to favour industry as well as the fine arts and science. The condition of society during this metaphysical period is "inorganic", for lack of a central spiritual power and truly integrating leading ideas. It is, however, the positivistic stage which will bring about a new organic condition of society. Positivistic philosophy will become the new spiritual power which will lead society by its integrating ideas. The political power will lose its military character and be transferred to the industrial entrepreneurs. St. Simon had already predicted that in this third stage of societal development politics *would completely turn into economics: government, i.e.* the rule over men, will be replaced by an "administration of the common interests", *i.e.* a conscious direction of the economic process of production according to an organisational plan [1]. This is to say that the State in its proper sense will disappear.

But together with the State the civil legal order, as a private common law, will lose its proper meaning. Comte emphatically argues that positivistic philosophy will introduce moral principles into the relations between labourers and employers which have until now been lacking. Social duties will take precedence of private rights [2]. Though Comte rejects communism, he conceives private property exclusively as a *social function* bound to the aim of an organized and directed economic production [3]. In the positivistic stage the capitalists will consider themselves exclusively as administrators of the social capital [4]. The political organization corresponding to the industrial type of society in the positivistic stage will be no longer a national State but a universal European political community [5], whose "political" character will gradually be replaced by a moral bond of solidarity [6].

There is not any room in the future industrial society for a civil law order in its classical sense, because there is no room for the State with its intrinsically public legal relation between government and subjects. The disappearance of the latter necessarily implies that of the former.

The Marxian view of the State and of civil law.

From a *dialectical historic-materialist* standpoint *orthodox* Marxism arrived at the same conclusion. The State, viewed as

---

[1] *Oeuvres de St. Simon et d'Enfantin* (Paris, 1865—1876). Vol. XXI

[2] *Cours de phil. pos.* (3th ed. E. Littré, Paris 1869) t. VI pp. 268 ff., pp.

p. 151; Vol. XXXIX pp. 129 ff., 136 ff., 143, 154.

511, 515, 520, 522.

[3] *Discours préliminaire,* p. 147.

[4] *Cours* VI, p. 511.

[5] *Cours* V, p. 446; VI, p. 169.

[6] *ib.* V, pp. 304 ff.; VI, p. 446.

an instrument of the struggle between the classes, will disappear in the future communistic phase of social development, when all class-distinctions have been abolished. Society will arrive at this ultimate condition after a transitional phase of socialism in which, by means of the power apparatus of the body politic, the united world-proletariat will destroy the capitalist class and enforce the socialization of the means of production. And the expiration of the State will imply the expiration of the legal order of the body politic, both of its public law order and of its private civil law, which are nothing but the precipitation of the economic class-interests of the bourgeoisie.

MARX was completely aware of the essential rôle which the idea of the "public interest" plays in the classical conception of the State. He was strongly influenced by Hegelian philosophy whose dialectical-idealist view of the relation between the "civil society" and the State he only reversed in a so-called historic-materialist sense. In his *Philosophy of History,* HEGEL had already shown a deep insight into the inner tensions of "civil society" in its economically qualified relationships.

In this society the antithesis between the particular economic interests of the classes cannot be reconciled into an ultimate synthesis. It is only the State, as the highest revelation of the "objective spirit", in which all particular interests can be integrated into the real communal interest of the societal whole as "ethical substance".

In MARX the State, in the sense of *res publica,* becomes an ideological supra-structure of the only real, economically qualified "society". In his work on *Historical Materialism* he parallels the State with religion. The latter devises a kingdom of heaven to escape from the misery of earthly life. Similarly the State, as an institution of the public interest, is an ideological escape from "civil society" torn by its class struggle [1]. ENGELS argues that when in primitive society a conflict between classes presents itself for the first time, it becomes necessary to separate a sphere

[1] *Der Historische Materialismus* I, p. 244. (Die Frühschriften hrg. von S. Landshut und J. P. Maijer, Leipzig 1932): 'Religiös sind die Glieder des politischen Staates durch den Dualismus zwischen dem Leben der bürgerlichen Gesellschaft und dem politischen Leben; religiös indem der Mensch sich zu dem seiner wirklichen Individualität jenseitigen Staatsleben als seinem wahren Leben verhält, religiös, insofern die Religion hier der Geist der bürgerlichen Gesellschaft, der Ausdruck der Trennung und der Entfernung des Menschen vom Menschen ist.'

of the general interest, distinguished from that of the particular concerns. This separate sphere is the State. But since in the economic struggle of the classes the idea of a common interest is illusory, the State is necessarily an ideological whole. Seemingly concerned with assuring equal rights to its subjects, it can in fact only be serviceable to the particular interests of the ruling class [1].

It is true that neither MARX nor ENGELS have denied that the State, as an ideological supra-structure, can to some degree influence the historical-economic process of society. Dialectical Historical Materialism does not reduce the State to a mechanical product of the economically qualified societal relationships. It leaves some scope to ideological factors. But this does not detract from the Marxian view that the State, as a *res publica*, and its civil legal order, with its principles of freedom and equality, are mere ideologies. The real social infra-structure of the latter is nothing but an organization of coercive power serviceable to the ruling class and the private property of the bourgeoisie. From this historic-materialistic viewpoint ENGELS, too, announced the inevitable extinction of the State in the communist society of the future: 'The management of things and the direction of the processes of production will replace the government of men. The State will not be abolished, but it will die out' [2].

That according to the orthodox Marxian view the disappearance of the body politic necessarily implies the disappearance of any civil legal order cannot be doubted. Civil law was generally considered to be unbreakably bound to the capitalistic system of production and the economic interests of the bourgeoisie. It was based on private property. And Marxism completely accepted the doctrine of LOCKE that the State was founded for the purpose of an organized protection of this "innate human right" [3].

---

[1] F. ENGELS, *Ludwig Feuerbach* (Stuttgart 1903), p. 51.

[2] F. ENGELS, *Herrn Eugen Dühring's Umwälzung der Wissenschaft* (1878), p. 302/3: 'An die Stelle der Regierung über Personen tritt die Verwaltung von Sachen und die Leitung von Produktionsprozessen. Der Staat wird nicht "abgeschafft", *er stirbt ab*'.

[3] BEBEL, *Die Frau und der Sozialismus*, p. 340. Here it is argued that the State only came into existence with the rise of private property and its concomitant, the contrast beween social classes. The State is the organization and power for the protection and maintenance of private property ("*das Eigenthum schützende und aufrecht erhaltende Organisation und Gewalt*"). When distinctions of class and relations of power have vanished, the State will disappear as a matter of course.

LOCKE ascribed to this right such a central position that he even subsumed under it the other innate rights to freedom and life. In his earlier period ROUSSEAU, too, defended the opinion that the body politic was only founded for the sake of protecting private property, although his appreciation of the latter was quite different from LOCKE's. In his *Discourse on Inequality* (1754), he argued that the right of property arises from a sanctioning of the crime of forceful seizure, and that therefore the State is the source of the increasing inequality of men and of the class-contest between the poor and the rich. This thesis reappeared in PROUDHON's initial qualification of property as "theft". It was due to the liberalist economic theory that the common private legal order of the State was considered to be unbreakably bound to the economically qualified relationships of civil society. This meant a complete denaturation of this legal sphere, which, as such, appeared to be characterized by its very lack of a specific non-juridical qualification.

And the French, Dutch and other codes of civil law had indeed initially deviated from the essential legal principles of this private common law by an extremely poor regulation of the labour contract which gave the employers a privileged position and sanctioned the economic exploitation of the labourers.

No wonder, therefore, that Marxian sociology considered the private and the public legal sphere of the State as an ideological supra-structure of the economically qualified infrastructure of "civil society".

The dispute about the possibility of a socialist civil law in the Bolshevist legal theory.

In the Bolshevist legal literature the question has been amply discussed as to whether civil and public law is in the nature of the case of a bourgeois character, or if a socialist civil and public law is possible. In truth this discussion concerned law as such because law and State-law were identified. The question had become acute since the N.E.P., which temporarily again allowed private commerce, had given rise to the civil law code of 1923 and other codes. The older Bolshevist legal school denied the possibility of a really socialist law. Its most prominent representative, PASJOEKANIS, had emphatically argued that law, and especially civil and penal law, is unbreakably bound to commodity exchange from which it derives its determining principle of equivalency. This implied that the transition from the equivalent distribution (everybody receives the equivalent of his labour) to the communist distribution (everybody receives what he needs) necessarily leads to the expiration of law.

The State arises when the class-organization of power embraces a market community of sufficient extent. As protector of the exchange relations it becomes public power. State and law are consequently forms of "civil society". The proletariat is urged to use them as long as there is not yet one single planned economy. As long as there exist market-relations between the State industries, civil law and public law cannot disappear. But they can never be transformed into a socialist law. The technical rules for the coordination of the Soviet-economy which will replace them are sometimes called "economic law". But when they lose any public coercive character it makes no sense to retain this name. This view of PASJOEKANIS' was indeed in accordance with the "Leading Principles" of the Penal Law of the R.S.F.S.R. of 1919, which emphatically declared that law, as a function of the State, will in the last instance be destroyed by the proletariat.

Nevertheless, the conception of this prominent Soviet-jurist and his adherents was fundamentally rejected in the standard-work *The Law of the Soviet State* (1938), written under the guidance of WYSJINSKIJ, and apparently inspired by STALIN's policy of intensification of the Soviet State and its law. WYSJINSKIJ argues that all Soviet law is ruled by the same socialist principle, and that it is perfidious to divide it into a bourgeois sector of civil law and a socialist sector of economic ordering law. The civil law which protects the property of the toiling labourers is as much socialist as the economic law. This meant a decisive turning point in the bolshevist theory of civil law, and the adherents of the old theory were urged to revoke their theses [1].

The Soviet civil code of 1923 and its ruling principle. The influence of DUGUIT.

This dispute is very interesting from the viewpoint of the inner nature of civil law and its intrinsical relation to the State as *res publica*.

The first article of the civil code of 1923 contains the fun-

---

[1] Cf. the interesting thesis of G. KUIJPERS, *De Russische Problematiek in het Sowjet-Staatsbeleid* (1954), pp. 135 ff.

damental principle which rules this Soviet code. It establishes that civil rights are protected by the State insofar as they are exercized in conformity to the socio-economic aim for which they have been granted by society. This introductory article betrays the indirect influence of the famous French jurist, Léon Duguit, whose sociological theory of law and of the State was strongly dependent on Emile Durkheim's positivist view of social development explained in his work *De la Division du Travail Social.*

Duguit vehemently attacked both the classical conception of the sovereign State and the "individualistic" classical idea of civil law as a private common law founded on the natural legal principles of the freedom and equality of men. In keeping with Saint Simon and Comte, he denies the human rights of the natural law doctrine. The entire idea of subjective rights is, according to him, of a metaphysical origin. It should be replaced by the positivist sociological concept of "social function". There exists only "objective law" which is not the creation of the State, but has its real origin in the laws of solidarity which rule human society.

Durkheim was of the opinion that in primitive societies this solidarity is of a mechanical character and reveals itself as a *solidarité par similitude, i.e.* a uniform pattern of socio-psychical feelings, representations and social behaviour urging itself upon the individuals by the mechanical pressure of the "collective consciousness". In differentiated societies, on the other hand, this solidarity assumes an "organic" character as a solidarity caused by division of labour (*"solidarité par division du travail"*). The "solidarity by uniformity" finds expression in a so-called "segmentary" pattern of societal organization whose articulation displays similar parts. The "solidarity by division of labour" gives rise to an "organic" pattern of differentiated societal organization according to different industrial and occupational syndicates, each of which fulfils a particular social task or function. Whereas the legal order of a primitive society displays a preponderantly penal type, that of a differentiated society assumes a preponderantly contractual and restitutional type. The process of social development is realized along lines of differentiation. The territorial division of the State is nothing but a residue of the primitive segmentary type of social organization. It will be replaced to an increasing degree by a functional division according to the different branches of socio-economic service.

On the basis of this view of societal development which he accepts without taking over DURKHEIM's idea of a collective consciousness, DUGUIT developed his theory concerning the transformation of the State and of civil law. According to him the State is not a *res publica,* in the sense of an organized sovereign community endowed with a legal personality. It is nothing but a factual relation of force between stronger and weaker individuals. The former impose their will on the latter by means of mechanical coercion. As such they have no single legal authority or competence nor can they lay claim to obedience in a normative sense. Rulers and subjects are equally subject to the objective law, which is exclusively social law ("*droit social*") originating from the solidarity of societal life, independently of their will. In a society whose solidarity is dependent on division of labour this law is composed of socio-economic rules, and customs of propriety *(moeurs)* or "moral" norms of human behaviour. Because of their preponderant import for the maintenance of social solidarity, such rules may be elevated to the "highest" level of social norms, *viz.* to *legal* norms. It is the feeling of justice which gives them this legal normative character. This axiological feeling, though subjectively expressing the individual's autonomy, is nothing but the psychical reflex of objective laws of solidarity deserving sanction. The legislator cannot create any legal norm. He can only establish existing standards of objective law.

Thus DUGUIT proclaims the "sovereignty of law" from a naturalistic sociological viewpoint, just as the Dutch jurist KRABBE had done from an ethico-psychological, and KELSEN from a normological point of view.

The juridical problem of competence seemed to have been completely eliminated. If law is a spontaneous reflex of the societal relations of solidarity, it does not need human formation by competent organs. Then there can no longer be a fundamental problem concerning the mutual relation between the original spheres of competency that the traditional legal theory had eliminated by attributing sovereignty to the legislator.

The Historical School had already taught that law is not made by men after a rational pattern of natural law but that it is an organic product of historical development, having its original source in the national mind and the people's conviction of juridical propriety. But it had restricted its romantic doctrine concerning the spontaneous growth of law to the primitive stage of folk-law ("*Volksrecht*"). As to the further phases of development it recognized the necessity of formative organs, *viz.* the jurisconsults and the legislator. The Germanist wing of this school (BESELER and GIERKE) added to this the organs of the free corporations, which form an "autonomous social law" distinct from traditional private civil law and from public law.

In fact the conception concerning the spontaneous growth of law is a romantic or (in its positivistic turn) a naturalistic misinterpretation of the nature of legal norms. We have shown in the general theory of the modal spheres that the necessity of human formation by competent organs is already implied in the modal structure of the legal norms. And the fundamental problem concerning the mutual relation between the original spheres of competence to law making, urges itself upon a correct observation of the legal phenomena by the structural diversity displayed by any differentiated society. In his voluminous work *Traité de droit constitutionel,* DUGUIT was obliged to recognize the formative factor in law. He did so by distinguishing between *normative* and *constructive* legal rules: 'Legislation', so he observes, '...does not create objective law, but it is doubtless an important factor in its formation' [1]. And the problem of the relation between the civil legal sphere and the non-civil legal sphere of industrial life reappears in its full importance when DUGUIT, in line with his program of law reformation, engages in outlining the necessary transformation of the traditional civil private law and public law, resulting from his view of the sovereignty of "social law". He does so in the deceptive form of a simple description of the factual tendencies which are to be observed in the legal development since the latter half of the XIXth century. Then it appears that, notwithstanding DUGUIT's view concerning the merely metaphysical character of the classical ideas of the *jus naturae et gentium* and the State, there did exist an individualistic civil law and a public law, based upon the "metaphysical" principle of human rights and upon the classical idea of the State as an authoritative *res publica,* respectively. Then the collective contracts, the customary stipulations, and the standard agreements in industrial law are alleged to prove that the private autonomy in contractual legal intercourse, which was a basic principle of the French *code civil,* has been gradually transformed by the factual evolution of human society.

Thus DUGUIT's view of the "sovereignty of law" turns out to mean nothing but the sovereignty of the typical industrial legal sphere which should *replace* the genuine civil legal sphere of the State. And the "transformation" of the State, which he conceives in accordance with the view of DURKHEIM, is tantamount to the abolition of the body politic in its proper sense.

DUGUIT's idea concerning the social function of law implying the denial of subjective civil rights of men was not generally accepted by the sociologically oriented students of civil law without reserve. They realized that the abandonment of the concept subjective right would mean a frank abandonment of civil law itself. Thus they strove after a compromise. The egoistic civil rights should be viewed as private rights granted by society on the condition of their being exercized in accordance with the socio-economic function to which they were considered to be subservient. This conception was amply elaborated by the famous French jurist LOUIS JOSSERAND in his work *De l'Esprit des Lois et de leur Relativité* (1924), and laid at the foundation of his theory concerning the abuse of rights [1].

It is this conception which had already found expression in the first article of the Russian civil code of 1923 before JOSSERAND published his book. Is it compatible with the essential fundamentals of civil law as a common law? Certainly not. We have seen that the latter does not permit itself to be bound to a specific non-juridical purpose which is supposed to *qualify* its inner character.

In this respect it is important to note that the Dutch Supreme Court *(Hoge Raad der Nederlanden)* in a constant judicial view has rejected the criterion of abuse of civil rights assumed by JOSSERAND. The negative criterion handled by this Court, according to which an abuse is present when a civil right is exercized without any reasonable interest only with the intention to hurt another person, is the only criterion compatible with the inner nature of civil law, as an inter-individual *jus commune*.

The first article of the Russian civil law code indeed binds private rights to the socialistic economic politics of the State. Insofar it is really a socialist code, which has transformed civil law into a social law with a specific economic qualification. The inner nature and structure of a typical legal sphere

---

[1] It is true that he accepted a small category of rights *(les droits non causes)* which were supposed to have no social function. But this is not relevant in this context, because this category does not pertain to real subjective rights. The same holds good as to his third category of "*droits à esprit altruiste*".

is beyond human disposal. Meanwhile the Soviet State continues to exist. It has neither been transformed into a communist society nor into a syndicalistic organization in the sense of DUGUIT. The State industries are real industrial organizations enkaptically bound by the body politic in the most narrow way, since it is the State itself which is the proprietor of the means of production and which has assumed the function of *entrepreneur*. But they are no more intrinsical parts of the State than the private enterprises whose existence the N.E.P. has allowed. We can only say that this State follows a totalitarian policy which has no room for civil freedom as supposed by a private common law.

The socialist State, however, can only exist so long as it remains bound to the structural principle of every body politic, *i.e.* as long as it is qualified as an authoritative public legal community typically founded in a monopolistic organization of the power of the sword. A public legal order remains essential to it even when a private common law with its fundamental principles of civil freedom and equality is lacking.

For this very reason both LENIN and STALIN fully realized that a really communistic community in the orthodox Marxian sense is incompatible with the State institution. In this future community, in which indeed the economical function of a planned production will replace the public legal function, in its typical leading and qualifying rôle, the State is necessarily doomed to disappear. When by a perfect plan of coordination of all its branches the process of economic production will have reached such a level of intensity that everybody can gratuitiously get what he needs and the bourgeois mind will be completely replaced by a real communist spirit, there will be no need at all of a coercive State apparatus.

This is Utopia; it is alien to reality, because it does not know the real root of all evil. But it is at least a consistent Utopia.

The so-called political pluralism.

On this point orthodox Marxism is theoretically much more distinctly alive to its consequences than "political pluralism". The latter wants to dissolve the State into a federation of mutually independent syndicates or corporations, each administrating a particular branch (function) of public services according to an economical viewpoint. These corporations are to stand up for the particular interests of their own separate services. The "political function" proper which has to weigh the interests of the whole against each other, would have to be organized separately[1]. This pluralism keeps talking of a "State"[2], although in principle it wants to eliminate the structure of the latter from the internal administrative activity of the projected syndicalist federation.

There is no awareness of the inevitable "economic monism"[3] that will result from its principles which leave no room for a real State. The opinion of the French syndicalist EDOUARD BERTH: "*l'Etat est mort*"[4] is the inescapable consequence for every "political pluralism" in the sense meant here.

The fundamental importance of our structural theory for the theory of constitutional law, the general theory of the State, and practical politics.
The structural idea of the State cannot be used in a rationalistic deductive way.

We cannot use the theoretical idea of the structural principle of the State, as it has been explained above, in a rationalistic deductive way. Neither can we do so with that of the structural principles of the other societal relationships. For in an actually existing body politic the invariable structural principle assumes

---

[1] Cf. my *Crisis in de Humanistische Staatsleer*, p. 155, and the literature quoted there.

[2] Cf. LASKI, *A Grammar of Politics* (1925), pp. 72 ff. This writer criticizes the political pluralism of guild-socialism. His critique is, however, not fundamental since, from his socialist point of view, he also strains the economical aspect in the structure of the body politic. He defines the State as "the body which seeks so to organize the interests of consumers that they obtain the commodities of which they are in need" (p. 69). The State is distinguished from other "associations" only by the coercive nature of its membership, and by its territorial character. Notwithstanding the addition of these specific characteristics, this view continues to seek the typical leading function of the body politic in the economical aspect. This fact appears from the argument adduced for the territorial criterion: "The interests of men as consumers are largely neighbourhood interests; they require satisfaction for the most part in a given place(!)".

[3] This term is from Prof. KUNG CHUAN HSIAO in his excellent book: *Political Pluralism. A Study in Contemporary Political Theory* (1927), pp. 122 ff.

[4] *i.e.* "The State is dead". Cf. LÉON DUGUIT, *Le droit social, le droit individuel et la transformation de l'Etat* (Paris, 1908), p. 38/9. DUGUIT is also an adherent of "political pluralism".

a relatively variable positive shape. We can understand the positive realization of the structure of the State only in its coherence with the variable historical-political situation, and never apart from its enkaptic structural interweavings.

It is only in the latter respect that the relative truth of the view can be recognized that the body politic is always liable to the influence of class interests. But it is certainly incorrect to reduce the State to an instrument of these particular interests. The truth is that no real body politic can exist if it would indeed completely set aside its inner nature as a *res publica*. The famous German sociologist LORENZ VON STEIN, who was at first strongly influenced by the theory of ST. SIMON and the French socialists, realized this when he remarked later on that by its inner nature the State will always try to elevate itself above class interests. If not, it would dissolve itself into the economically qualified societal relationships of "civil society".

The insight into its invariable structural principle is therefore fundamental both for the special sciences investigating the body politic in its different modal aspects, and for the general theory of the State; it is also of fundamental importance for practical politics.

In my book *De Crisis in de Humanistische Staatsleer* I have shown that the theory of constitutional law was led astray by eliminating the structural principle of the State-institution. The introduction of the formal-juridical method into this theory was bound to result in an empty juridical scholasticism.

A large number of fundamental problems can only be theoretically elucidated with the help of a real structural theory of the State, *e.g.*, the problem of sovereignty; that of the juridical sense of the parliamentary system; the theory of the basic rights; the juridical conception of administrative law; the difference between administrative and civil jurisdiction, *etc.*

I pointed out that the "sociological political theory", insofar as it tries to study the real life of the State with the aid of naturalistic methods, eliminates the real structure of the body politic. This "sociology of the State" is therefore no theory of the *State*. As to practical politics I tried to show that the influence of a wrong view of the body politic is evident in many a conception of "organic representation" and of "organic suffrage". In a separate treatise devoted to the latter subject I examined the appeal to the political position of the medieval craft-guilds as an example of "organic representation" [1]. Then it appeared that any such appeal to these

[1] *Het Vraagstuk van het organisch Kiesrecht in een nieuw Stadium*. (Almanak van het studentencorps N.D.D.D. aan de Vrije Universiteit, 1935, pp. 105—122).

guilds is based on a lack of insight into their fundamentally different internal structures as *industrial* organizations, and as *political* components of a medieval town. In the latter capacity the guilds had political domination founded in military power. This fundamental structural difference was in most cases apparent in the distinction between industrial members and political members. Different categories of the latter had nothing to do with the industrial community of the craft-guilds. We shall revert to this subject.

§ 4 - THE STRUCTURAL PRINCIPLE AS IT EXPRESSES ITSELF IN THE DIFFERENT ASPECTS OF THE STATE-INSTITUTION, AND THE CHRISTIAN IDEA OF THE BODY POLITIC.

The structural principle of the State necessarily expresses itself in all the aspects in which this societal institution functions as a real unity. Our analysis will start with the moral function. The qualifying juridical function has already been amply discussed, and we will postpone the discussion of the function of faith to the end of this section. The reason is that this latter function presents particular difficulties connected with the idea of a Christian State, which we had better treat as a separate theme.

The expression of the structure of the State in the moral societal function of the love of one's country. State and nation.

Does the State *as such* function in the moral law-sphere? No doubt the (moral) *love of country* displays an internal societal structure not reducible to the inter-individual relationships in the moral meaning of love. There are, however, two different objections to be made against the statement that the structure of the State expresses itself in this typical bond of love.

First of all it may be argued that love of country may assert itself *in opposition* to the State. We may refer to the re-awakening of patriotism in the nations incorporated into the French empire by Napoleon I. The oppressed nationalities at last rose on the oppressor. Their struggle for freedom was a strong stimulus to the Romantic conception of the "national spirit", as a primary datum of nature, of which the national State is merely an outward manifestation.

In this context we should also pay special attention to the first occasion of HERDER's discovery of national individuality. During the important years of his stay in he town of Riga, HERDER came into contact with the Lettish folk character ("*Volks-*

tum"), which made a deep impression on him and suggested his idea of nationality. In the case of the Letts, the people's individuality had no political structure, for there was no Lettish State. As HERDER remarks in his essay on Ossian, he had first noticed the expressions of the indestructible peculiarity of this folk in its language, songs, popular dances and customs, *notwithstanding* its tyrannical oppression in a cultural and political respect [1].

He was the first to consider the nation as a "natural organism" with an entelechy of its own, a vital purposive force, in sharp contrast with the artificial organization of the State. It was this conception which inspired the doctrine of the Historical School concerning the "national spirit" as the real source of culture. This irrationalistic Romantic view found its antipode in the rationalistic political conception of nationality prevailing in the natural-law ideas of ROUSSEAU and the French Revolution.

Although the former was doubtless right insofar as it rejected a simple identification of a national unit with a State, it has not really increased the insight into the nature of a national community.

The latter cannot be approached with the aid of a biological analogy. In the second Volume we have elaborately explained *that there is an intrinsic difference between a primitive folk* community and a nationality, whose historical aspect of individuality can only develop in the anticipatory direction of time. This implies that a nationality cannot be of an undifferentiated character. It is not folklore which can lay bare its characteristic traits, since this specific branch of ethnology is unable to explain the real integrating potency of a nation. In the last instance the ethnical particularities may strongly differ within one and the same nation.

The so-called supra-functional view of a national community, as it is defended by GURVITCH and other modern sociologists, is not able to clarify our insight. It is strongly influenced by the irrationalist and universalistic conception of the Historical

---

[1] HERMANN ONCKEN, *Nationalitätenbewegung des 19. Jahrhunderts*, in his *Nation und Geschichte* (Reden und Aufsätze 1919—1935, Berlin 1935), p. 308/9 — quotes HERDER's words: "Lebendige Reste dieses alten wilden Gesanges, Rhythmus, Tanzes unter lebenden Völkern...denen unsre Sitten noch nicht völlig Sprache und Lieder und Gebräuche haben nehmen können." [Living remains of these old wild songs, rhythms, dances in living nations... whom our manners and customs have not yet entirely been able to deprive of language, songs and customs.]

School, which impedes a critical structural analysis. In what sense can we speak of a national science, national fine art, a national industrial life, a national Church, *etc.*? Does this really mean that there exists an all-inclusive national community, which as such is independent of any organization? If so, why has nobody succeeded in discovering any tenable criterion of such an all-embracing national whole?

The reason is that an unorganized all-inclusive community cannot exist within the structural horizon of time, because in the nature of the case it would lack any structure of individuality which alone makes a temporal individual whole possible. An irrationalist universalism cannot uphold the illusion of an all inclusive national community without levelling out the fundamental difference between the geno-typical structure of a nation and its enkaptic interlacements with other societal structures of individuality. In addition it does not sufficiently distinguish a nation from an ethnical unit. The term "national" in its geno-typical sense refers to the inner nature of a national community. But it may also mean a particular variability type which other societal relationships assume in their enkaptical function within a national unit. It is therefore necessary to account for the geno-typical characteristics of a nation.

Community of language or religion [1] or natural descent are certainly no inner geno-typical characteristics. They are only of an occasional pheno-typical character, and for this very reason they have always proved to be insufficient to define the inner nature of a national unit. A nation is not a natural community in the sense defined earlier. It is the result of a political formation which presupposes the differentiation and integration of human society. The typical character of a nationality has always been formed in a struggle for its internal political integration and for its international legal acknowledgement as an independent political unity. Well, nobody has succeeded in describing the individuality of a national character in an adequate way. The reason is perhaps that this individuality can only be approached in a pheno-typical way because it does not display itself but in the full complexity of the enkaptic intertwinements between a nation and the other societal relationships.

Are the individual traits of a nation indeed the same in its

---

[1] The term religion is of course not used here in its central religious sense, but in the current sense of a system of faith and worship.

individual political life, in its relation to fine arts, science, ecclesiastic life, industry and commerce, *etc.*? This must be true if the irrationalist and universalist view of a nation as a supra-functional and all-inclusive community is right. But at this point we should remember that such irrationalism elevated the subjective individuality of a national character to a norm of its historical development. As this is not really possible it replaced the individual traits of a nationality by an ideal normative image of its "true" individuality. And the unity of this image was only an idealistic construction, especially because no single effort was undertaken to give a precise description of this ideal image. The famous German lawyer, RUDOLPH v. JHERING, who in his work *Geist des römischen Rechtes* indeed tried to give a description of the individuality of the Roman national character without any idealization, defined it as "the mind of disciplined egoism". But in fact he took into account only what he supposed to be the national spirit of Roman law since the time that it was no more than a primitive folk law. And even in this restricted sense his conception of the Roman national mind was untenable since he interpreted the primitive Roman tribal law from an individualist point of view, which is incompatible with the very structure of a primitive society.

As to the geno-typical characteristics of a nation the state of affairs is quite different. Here we have to do with a differentiated structural type which lacks the complexity of a pheno-type. In this sense a nation is a people (and not merely a group of persons of the same nationality within a foreign country) which has become conscious of its internal political solidarity irrespective of its eventual ethnical differences. The present Dutch nation was not born before the common political trial of the Napoleonic rule melted together the different provinces, which formerly could never conquer their particularism.

A real nation never lacks a political organization, but it may be that the latter has not yet attained to the position of an independent State, or that it has lost this position. Nevertheless, State and nation have the same radical type, and every national community has the potency to become a real State. This explains why, at least in a democratic constitution, the so-called "*pouvoir constituant*", *i.e.* the original political competence, can only belong to the nation. But this is not to be understood in the sense of the people's sovereignty as it was conceived by the Humanist natural law doctrine. For this supposed sovereign people was nothing but a mass of individuals united only by the construction of a so-called social compact. It was nothing but a speculative ideology lacking any contact with political reality.

It is possible that initially a State embraces different nations. But if it does not succeed in integrating this difference into a higher national unity, it contains in itself the germ of political dissolution. The former Danube-monarchy is a striking instance of the inner weakness of a pluri-national State.

It is not necessary to go further into the relation between State and nation to get an insight into the structure of individuality of the moral figure of "love of country". In the present context it will suffice to say that in any case "love of country" is entirely dependent on the political structure into which country and nation have been organized. Love of country is not identical with love of an ethnical group of people, nor with the biotically founded love of the land of one's birth alone. The strong manifestation of patriotism in a struggle for freedom (like the Dutch eighty years' war with Spain, or the American war of independence against the British mother-country) is for the benefit of a rising State which has been given a provisional organization.

Exclusively as a political organized unity under a provisionally constituted or still existing government can a nation turn on a foreign usurper, either manifestly or underground. Genuine love of country always displays an internal political structure, especially when it opposes domination by a foreign State. A would-be patriotism does not know the subject of its love when it ignores the internal structure of the life of a body politic and a nation. This patriotism pictures its beloved as a chiliastic ideal of gentleness, but as soon as the State (the existing or the rising State) demands from its subjects their sacrifice of life and property, there is no longer any room for idealistic dreamers. Stern reality will show which love of country is genuine, and which is internally false. True love of country knows that its way may lead through blood and tears, and in its Christian manifestation it implies the painful consciousness that the State is instituted "on account of sin".

The light-hearted, but in reality demonic joy in "the strong State" with its powerful army is entirely in conflict with a Christian love of country.

Is the State the subject or the object of love of country? The objective conception is impossible.

The second objection to the view that in love of country the State structure is *subjectively* manifest, is that the "native country" can never be the *subject*, but only the *object* of this love. When I made my first attempt to investigate the individuality structures of human societal life, I thought that the qualifying function of an organized community must always be its last subject-function in reality, and that such a community can only have object-functions in the later law-spheres. I drew this conclusion from the example of subjectively qualified natural things. But I very soon had to give up this view as contrary to the entire structure of human societal relationships.

If this view were true, a community for social intercourse (*e.g.*, a club) or an economic-industrial community could never function as a *juridical subject*. This consequence conclusively proves the untenability of the hypothesis.

In love of country we may consider the country (in the sense of a political territory) as *the object*; but the national community of the State as such cannot be an object. The members of the nation can only be bound together by love of country in the *subjective* structure of the State's people. The second objection to the view that in love of country the structure of the body politic finds its subjective expression thus proves no more to be founded than the first.

The internal limits to love of country, and the *principium exclusae collisionis officiorum.*

Its internal structural principle delimits love of country so that this love can never become an unqualified totality of love relations revealing themselves within other individuality structures. State worship is utterly un-Christian also in its unbounded exaggeration of love of country. This love is *limited* by its own internal structure in all of the extremely intricate interlacements with the love-relations in marriage, family, kinship, Church, local, and occupational communities, international relationships, *etc.* If these internal limits are ignored, love of country will become intrinsically false.

The Aristotelian view that love of country is a "higher" form of love ("friendship", as it is called by ARISTOTLE) than that in family and kinship cannot be true. An argument for this view seems to be that, when the members of the same family or kinship have a different nationality, the duty towards the State should prevail over the natural bonds of blood. But this does not at all prove that love of country is higher than the other forms of love. It only proves that within its own internal structural limits love of country does not recognize any rival. But exactly the same thing applies to other societal structures of love. The love among the members of the same Church, *e.g.*, does not allow of competition on the part of love of country. The latter should never divide the members of the same Christian Church within the internal love-relations implied in the community of faith. Similarly the mutual love among the members of a family must never be dominated in the internal family relations by love of country. The typical political relations are not included in the internal family relations. There can be no question of a real *collisio officiorum* in the normative relations of love. Such a conflict is precluded by the cosmic principle of sphere-sovereignty within the individuality-structures, just as much as cosmological antinomies are precluded by the *principium exclusae antinomiae*.

But this does certainly not mean that a confrontation with the different duties of love may not give rise to extremely painful tensions in our subjective feelings. Nor does it exclude real conflicts caused by an excessive expansion of the moral claims of the love of country, or of those of other societal structures of love-relations.

The principium exclusae collisionis officiorum, just as the *principium exclusae antinomiae,* does not imply a denial of conflicts on the subject-side of societal life and temporal reality in general. It only excludes a subjectivist denial of the cosmic temporal order, and the elevation of antinomies to the rank of a dialectical law of reality itself.

Love of country and the problem of the international public relations.

The structural principle ultimately limits the internal integration on the part of the State to its own country and people. At this point the vast problem of the relations among the different States forces itself on our attention. The international political relations in which the State is involved are quite different from those between the State and non-political societal relationships, or from the function of the State in private inter-individual relations.

We have rejected the dialectical basic motives in the prevailing political theories concerning the internal structure of the State, but we thereby did not mean to deny the possibility of a seemingly unavoidable conflict between "might and right" in international politics. The internal structural principle of the State cannot offer a solution of such a conflict. For in this case the different States have external inter-communal societal relations to each other of a very special kind, which display neither the internal communal structure of the State, nor that of *private* inter-individual relations. Foreign policy remains bound to the internal structure of the State, but it has an international character and, therefore, it cannot be carried on according to the standards of internal policy. This was what JOHN LOCKE had in view when he made a distinction between the executive and the federative power and subsumed foreign policy under the latter. The rules of private inter-individual legal intercourse do not suffice here. For in the first place the different States occupy very unequal positions of power in international life. And in the second place the chief interests involved in international relations are of a characteristically public societal nature.

This is why international conflicts involving the danger of war cannot be judged of according to a civil juridical standard, as KANT proposed in his individualistic project of a league of nations. KANT's idea of law, which lay at the foundation of this project, was exclusively oriented to civil legal intercourse. It had no room for the recognition of the essential nature of international relations which do not belong to this private civil sphere [1]. There is no denying that there are international private relations for which the various States must devise international arrangements. But the dangerous conflicts in the international intercourse between States are always concerned with the essentially public interests of the latter, each of them vital to their own internal structure. Here the principle of the "reasons of State", in the sense of an unbridled and egotistic pursuit of their own interests by the bodies politic involved in such a conflict, displays its most dangerous and alluring aspect. This is all the

---

[1] Cf. my treatise *Norm en Feit. Een critische beschouwing naar aanleiding van het geschrift van Mr Rozemond over Kant en de Volkenbond* (in the review *Themis, 1932*, no. 2, pp. 1—60).

more serious since this problem takes account of the individuality-structure of the body politic much more according to its *foundation* than does the individualistic natural-law view of the international relations.

During the whole history of the modern system of States since the Westphalian Peace until the second world-war no great power has been prepared to have questions of really vital interest withdrawn from its own sovereign final decision. The famous third chapter of the *"Acte général"* of 1928 of the former League of Nations provided for obligatory arbitration in disputes about interests. But this provision did not materially alter the situation. Owing to the reference to the 38th Article of the Statute of the Permanent Court of International Justice, the arbitration mentioned above could only result in the maintenance of the formal *"status quo"*, in so far as no compromise was made. It was this international situation before world-war II which I had in view when in the first (Dutch) edition of this work I wrote: 'So long as the pluralistic modern system of States continues to exist, there is no other peaceful settlement of disputes about the interests of the States than mutual consultation under the guidance of an international public juridical idea of inter-communal relationship. Conflicting interests should be harmonized on the basis of a mutual insight into, and at least partial recognition of each other's vital interests as each State's well-understood own interests. Added to this the members of the League of Nations should take effective action to prevent or stop wars as means of settling disputes. Recent experience, however, has been deeply disappointing, as far as the application of Art. 16 of the Covenant of the League of Nations is concerned. It has become clear how precarious is the international juridical position of weak States, if the old imperialistic spirit is allowed to persist in the international policy of the Big Powers.'

Meanwhile the post-war experience has opened some new perspectives at least for the democratic States of the West European continent. I do not mean that the Charter of San Francisco has really strenghtened the international position of the small States, as members of the new organisation of the United Nations, in comparison with their position under the Covenant of the former League of Nations. But I have especially in view the growing insight into the common military and economic interests of the West European States, which gradually pushes back the old individualist dogma of sovereignty and tends to a gradual realization of the federative idea.

I cannot think of submitting this extremely important and complicated question to a more thorough investigation in the present context. Besides, it falls entirely outside of the subject under consideration and would require a separate study. I could not omit to refer to it in passing, however, because I wanted to avoid the misunderstanding that I am absolutizing the internal structural principle of the individual body politic at the expense of the international public relations between the various States. The Christian view of the State must never capitulate to a naturalistic theory of the "*raison d'État*" elevating the "sacred egotism" of the States to a kind of natural law in international relations. Such a theory is intrinsically false and contrary to the individuality-structure of the States as well as to the basic structure of the international order.

The internal vital law of the body politic is not a law of nature but bears a normative character. A State can never justify an absolutely selfish international policy of the strong hand with an appeal to its vital interests. God has not given the States such a structure that, with a kind of natural necessity, they are compelled to carry on a Kain's policy for the sake of self-preservation. Only a blind man does not see that the vital interests of the nations are in a great many ways mutually interwoven. It is not the political structure of national life but the sins of the nations that have caused the individualistic selfish power of the States to dominate international politics.

In international legal relations the internal public juridical structure of an individual body politic is necessarily correlated with that of the other States in public juridical, inter-communal relations. Similarly the love of a particular country cannot fulfil the moral commandment in the international moral relations between the States without its counter-weight in international love of one's neighbour among the nations. Any absolutization of patriotism leads to a blind chauvinism, which lacks the true moral sense of love. It is an absolutely un-Christian thought that the commandment of temporal societal love of one's fellow-men is not valid in international intercourse between the nations organized in States. International relations are also subject to the moral law; they cannot be ruled by a purely egotistic principle. But the structure of the international norm of love is not identical with that of private moral intercourse between individual men. The moral relations between the States remain bound to the structural principle of international political relationships, which presupposes that of the body politic itself.

The norm of love can never require a State to resign itself to a foreign attack on its independence and to deliver its own subjects to the violence of a usurper. The moral duties of a body politic cannot be measured according to private standards.

The expression of the structural principle in the juridical forms of organization of governmental authority. The typical foundation of the different constitutional forms.

As to the expression of the structural principle in the juridical aspect of the State we have to add some remarks with respect to the typical juridical forms of the organization of governmental authority. The different constitutional forms depend on the latter. The distinction between autocracy and democracy is the most fundamental of all. These forms have a typical historical basis, and their character is determined by the manner in which the political power is organized; *viz.* either by the free initiative of the nation itself, which by suffrage and political representation (or eventually in a direct way) retains a continuous control over the government, or by an authority which has imposed a certain governmental form upon the people [1]. But the variable positive juridical forms of organization of governmental authority remain absolutely determined by the internal structural principle of the State. This means that, *e.g.*, an economic form of power as such can never be the typical foundation of the juridical form of organization of a government's authority. Only in the pheno-type of a constitution can a government's authority be typically interwoven in an *enkapsis* with types of authority founded in economic types of power. The insight into this state of affairs is also of fundamental importance for an enquiry into constitutional history, as well as for the theory of constitutional law, and for the general theory of the State.

In v. HALLER's patrimonial theory of the State, *e.g.*, monarchy was viewed as the normal and the oldest form of political organization, which was supposed to be always exclusively founded in large-scale land-ownership [2]. This view has had a great influence

[1] Cf. HELLER, *Staatslehre* (1934), p. 246.

[2] Cf. *Restauration der Staatswissenschaft* (2e Aufl.) Bnd. 3, p. 157: "Die ganze Geschichte bestätigt unwidersprechlich, was sich schon durch die blosse Vernunft beweisen lässt, dass nicht nur die Monarchien

on the interpretation of the facts of medieval legal history, as v. BELOW has convincingly proved. V. HALLER's patrimonial view of the State has also penetrated into the famous work *Ongeloof en Revolutie* of the Dutch Christian historian and statesman GROEN VAN PRINSTERER. In his description of the patrimonial conception of a kingdom under the feudal regime, and of the foundation of the political rights of the old estates on landed property, he thought he had detected the real historical fundamentals of the "Christian-Germanic State-idea". And he opposed the latter to the classical republican idea of the body politic defended by the *a priori* natural law doctrine. Fortunately he abondoned this erroneous and reactionary view when he became acquainted with the writings of F. J. STAHL.

We have already remarked that the so-called democratic form of government of a "medieval town" [1], in its later stage of development, and the dominant position often occupied in it by the craft-guilds, was not typically founded in economical forms of power. When these guilds acquired political power, the latter was indeed founded in their military organization; their political structure was merely enkaptically interwoven with their structure as industrial organizations.

Their temporary dominating influence in the city-government was the result of political action, often of an actual revolution directed against an existing aristocratic régime, from which they extorted the control of the town. During the period of their greatest power, the Utrecht guilds acted as independent potentates, and entered into negotiations with foreign sovereigns. But the political and the industrial structures of these guilds were kept distinctly apart, notwithstanding their mutual interweavings: all the citizens of a town had to join one of the guilds, no matter what was their occupation or trade. They thus became "political members" for the sake of their political rights [2].

---

die ersten, ältesten und häufigsten Staaten waren, sondern dass die meisten Fürstentümer ursprünglich auf dem haus- oder grundherrlichen Verband oder dem sog. Patriarchat beruhen, alle anderen aber sich in der Folge nur durch dieses Verhältnis befestigen konnten". [All history confirms beyond contradiction what can already be proved by mere reason, *viz.* that monarchies are not only the first, the oldest and the most frequent forms of the State, but that most principalities were originally based on the domestic community or on the seignorial relationship of an estate, a so-called patriarchy. All the others could only establish themselves later on by means of this relationship.]

[1] Of course this terminology is not quite justified historically; we cannot really speak of "the medieval town" in a general way. But we are discussing the general phenomenon of the *guild-movement* and its political importance for the city governments. This revolutionary movement displays, at least in its main traits, a fairly common character and is everywhere characterized by the same anti-aristocratic tendency.

[2] Cf. J. C. OVERVOORDE en J. G. CH. JOOSTING, *De gilden van Utrecht tot*

Naturally it cannot be denied that, irrespective of the specific form of constitution, particular economically qualified classes may gain a temporary hegemony in the government of the State. In the same way the franchise may be dependent on a property qualification. But these political privileges are never of a typically economical *foundation*, as was erroneously assumed by ARISTOTLE when he characterized democracy as the rule of the poor. Economic types of power are never *qua talis* really political in character; they are at most *interwoven* with types of political power. The modern view of a social democracy, as it was especially propagated after the first world-war, uncritically assumed that we can apply the political forms of government to the family, the Church, the school or to an industry. But it levelled all the differences of the internal structures of human societal relationships[1].

The expression of the structural principle in the aesthetic aspect of the State.

The typical harmonious integration of the interests of nation and country, manifest in the leading public juridical function of the State's structural principle, refers back to the aesthetic function of the latter.

In antiquity Greek political philosophy paid special attention to this aesthetic structural aspect. The idea of public justice was mostly conceived aesthetically. In PLATO's ideal State the idea of the τὰ ἑαυτοῦ πράττειν was aesthetical rather than juridical. According to this idea every citizen had to remain in his own social class in order to cooperate in his own sphere to the harmony of the whole.

In the second book of his *Politica* ARISTOTLE requires politics to be a "symphony". It is an art, and, as such, it must not contain any dissonance and should continue in the same key which produces harmony. In the time of the Romantics the exaggeration of the aesthetic motif reappears. This aestheticist view of the body politic would never have arisen, if the structure of

---

1528, 1e deel (1897) in the collection *"Oud-Vaderlandsche Rechtsbronnen"*. An excellent description of the Italian and German medieval guild-movement is to be found in H. LENTZE, *Der Kaiser und die Zunftverfassung in den Reichsstädten* (1933).

[1] This has been vividly described by G. GUY GRAND in his book *La démocratie de l'après-guerre*, published after the first world-war.

the body politic did not have an aesthetic aspect making disharmony possible as well.

CALVIN has also emphatically pointed out this aesthetic structural aspect. He calls the societal relationship of the State a "well-ordered condition" and opposes it to the anarchical ἀταξία a "*confusum et dissipatum chaos*". The State is a "*pulcherrimus ordo*", in which prevails "*symmetria, proportia*"[1]. Anarchy is not only objectionable in an ethico-political sense, as disturbing the community, it is also unaesthetical, because it is offensive to our aesthetic sense[2]. But the State is not a work of fine art, it is not qualified by its aesthetic aspect. The typical foundation of its structure betrays its institution on account of sin. And this tragic trait is also inherent in the aesthetic aspect of the State.

The expression of the structural principle of the State in the internal sphere of political economy.

The aesthetic structural aspect of the body politic necessarily refers back in the foundational direction of the temporal order to the *economic* modality. The problem of "the relation between the State and economy" has been posited on the immanence standpoint in as confusing a manner as that of "the relation between the State and law". The confusion was due to a lack of insight into the relation between the modal and the individuality structures of reality. Even those writers who emphasize the plurisidedness of the State as a real "social organism", in opposition to the individualistic theories, go astray as soon as they want theoretically to conceive of the relation between the body politic and the economic law-sphere.

As examples of such a confused and erroneous way of positing the problem I mention that of OTTMAR SPANN and HERMANN HELLER. In his interesting book *Fundament der Volkswirtschaftslehre* SPANN summarizes his view of the relation between the "State" and "economy" as follows: 'As an active part of economic life the State has meanwhile become a real element of economy and is within the latter no longer a "State", but a capital of a higher order, the support of all economic activity, the instrument of all instruments — and therefore itself "economy". With this social genus of "economy" a social genus like the body politic can as little mix, as food mixes

---

[1] C.R. 49, 503.

[2] Cf. BOHATEC, *Calvin und das Recht* (1934, Teudingen in Westphalia), p. 64.

with blood: the food must first change into "blood", if it is to work like blood; else food remains an inactive foreign body in it" [1].

Here the entire economic structural aspect of the State is fundamentally denied. The State as such is only conceived of in an external teleogical relation to "economy", and this latter is merely considered a means for the attainment of non-economic purposes, in this case for political aims [2].

HELLER's way of positing the problem is equally wrong. Besides, he restricts it to the relation between the State and the typical capitalistic "*Marktwirtschaft*" [3]. He, too, conceives the "State" and "economy" as self-contained and equivalent functions of human society, each of them with *relative autonomy*. The State can only affect economic life *from the outside*. But HELLER lacks the insight that the body politic has an internal economic aspect, in which its individuality structure finds expression, just as in its internal juridical and moral spheres. This internal economic sphere of the State is quite different from the free economic market relations in which the former is only enkaptically bound.

The structural principle of the State necessarily expresses itself in its internal economic aspect. This really *political* economic sphere can never be understood in terms of private inter-individual economic intercourse. The internal political economy is a territorial "*Zwangswirtschaft*" [4], in which the economic function has been structurally opened in a typical direction to the public juridical leading function of the State. The system of taxation, as a typical political manner of economical provision of income and capital, forms the basis of the whole of the State's internal economy, and unmistakably displays a political individuality-

---

[1] O. SPANN, *Fundament der Volkswirtschaftslehre* (3e Aufl. 1923) p. 184; cf. also p. 28, 103 ff. The German text of the quotation reads as follows: 'als wirksamer Teil der Wirtschaft ist er (*i.e.* the State) indessen wirklich Bestandteil derselben geworden und in dieser nicht mehr "Staat", sondern Kapital höherer Ordnung, Beistand alles Wirtschaftens, Werkzeug aller Werkzeuge, also selber "Wirtschaft". In die Gesellschaftsart "Wirtschaft" kann sich eine Gesellschaftsart "Staat" ebensowenig einmischen wie sich Speise mit Blut mischt: sie muss erst zu "Blut" werden um in diesem als Blut zu wirken oder sie bleibt wirkungsloser Fremdkörper darin'.

[2] *Op. cit.*, p. 60. SPANN's definition of economy is: "Wirtschaft ist die rangordnungsgemässe Widmung von Mitteln für Ziele durch ausgleichendes und sparendes Abwägen... bei Knappheit an Mitteln". [Economy is the devotion of means to ends according to a scale of needs ordered in conformity to a balancing and sparing mode of estimation... when there is a scarcety of means.]

[3] *Staatslehre* (1924) pp. 211 ff.

[4] Compulsory economy.

structure. In this typical economic structure the system of taxation is subject to politico-economic norms of a communal character. In it the modal economic principle of a frugal administration of scanty means, in the alternative choice of their destination, according to a well balanced scale of needs, has been typically individualized and opened under the leading of the juridical idea of public interest.

The modal economic principles are not at all eliminated from the internal political economy: but here the question as to *what* (not *how*) is economic, is entirely dependent on the individuality structure of this typical economic sphere. The internal economic value of the material apparatus of a military and a police organization, of a network of roads, *etc.*, for the political economy of the State cannot be measured according to the market value of the required goods and services, nor according to a certain marginal utility.

In the internal economy of the State it *may* be justifiable in an economic sense to deviate from the prices in the free market and from the principles of efficiency prevailing in a free economic enterprise, if such deviations are required by the politico-economic structural relations [1].

From the teleological viewpoint the entire economic sphere is considered to be merely a means for the attainment of non-economic purposes. But this view is subjective, and destructive to a correct insight into the internal structural relations in economy; for it excludes the question as to *what* is economic, from the "*Wirtschaftstheorie*" [2]. SPANN also does so.

The integrating function of the State in the internal political economy and the exaggeration and denaturing of this function in the modern absolutist idea of the State's economic autarchy.

In an internal economic sense the State also performs a political integrating function, which is fundamentally different from that of economically qualified societal relationships, such as international trusts, cartels and the like. The positive contents of this task cannot be defined in a universally valid way be-

---

[1] Remember the expensive administrative services required by the juridically qualified "public interest". These services must not be judged according to the profit earning efficiency-principles in a free enterprise.

[2] Economic theory. The *economic* needs of the State are in principle dependent on its individuality-structure.

cause of their variable character. There is a tendency in modern times to a large-scale "ordering" of the whole of "national economy" within the territory of the State. The idea of economical ordering and planning reveals a radical reaction to the old liberal idea of the free play of social forces in economic life ruled by a "natural order", in which the State should not interfere. The entire development of modern Western political and economic life has resulted in abandoning the old liberal policy of "*laissez faire, laissez passer*".

In itself this thought of ordering is congenial. But it may bring on all the dangers of the totalitarian idea of the absolutist State, if it is not subject to the control of the structural principle of the body politic. The economic integration of the State's population within its territory by means of a political ordering of non-political economic industrial life should remain under the leading of the juridical idea of public interest. The structure of the State necessarily requires this typical leading so that the internal sphere-sovereignty of the economically qualified societal structures will be safeguarded.

The tendency towards planning may be the result of a totalitarian policy, aiming at economic "autarchy", the selfsufficiency of the national production with a view to increase the power of the State as an end in itself. In this case the State's task of economic integration will be fundamentally falsified because the typical leading function of the body politic is lost sight of. Naturally a complete economic autarchy of a State, however large it may be, is impossible, since it is excluded by the increasing economic interdependency of all parts of the world. But, as a politico-economic maxim of the totalitarian State, the principle of autarchy means that, within the territory of the body politic, the whole process of economic production is to be made serviceable to the policy of power. Then there is not any respect for the justified economic interests of other nations, nor for the internal sphere-sóvereignty of the non-political societal relationships.

This autarchical principle was already defended by FICHTE in his project of the *closed commercial State*. Its tyranny over economic life has been painfully brought home to various countries in the last economic world-crisis. Even its partial realization accelerated the dislocation of economic relations before the second world-war enormously. It is easy to see what dangerous effects it must have on States that are poor in raw-materials. The counterpart to the principle of autarchy, as the characteristic consequence of the modern idea of the national power-State, is an *imperialistic foreign policy.* It is, therefore, misleading when RUDOLF KJELLÈN defends the autarchical principle on the ground of his vitalistic-organic idea of the body politic by identifying it with the principle of the "individuality of the State in the economic sphere". He puts it on an equal footing with the *geographic* individuality of the State's territory and with nationality revealing the *demic* individuality of the State [1].

In this sense the autarchical principle is intended as a general individualistic principle of economic policy valid for all nations; but as such it does not at all take their *individuality* into account. If carried through consistently, it means the dissolution of the whole intricate complex of international interlacements and mutual relations of dependence in economic life. But then it appears to be nothing but a fantastic dream of power in the modern nationalistic political mythology [2].

Only as an example I mention the leading ideas of economic planning according to which the Italian fascist State intended to carry out its programme of economic integration. They have been summarized by WOLDEMAR KOCH in his book *Die Staatswirtschaft des Faschismus* [3] as follows:

1. The idea of the maximum area for the production of foodstuffs for the growing population;
2. The idea of economic independence;
3. The idea of ruralization;
4. The idea of an equal economic development of the separate parts of the country.

The author does not omit to point out that these four ideas were directly or collaterally dependent on the idea of the *"Potenza della*

---

[1] RUDOLF KJELLÈN, *Der Staat als Lebensform* (2e Aufl. 1917) p. 162.

[2] KJELLÈN shrinks back from this consequence. He writes: "Auch das autarchische Prinzip darf nicht zum Fetisch werden, dessen Anbetung gegen die Bedeutung und das Bedürfnis eines wirtschaftlichen Verkehrs zwischen den Völkern blind macht" (*op. cit.* p. 166/7). [The autarchical principle should not be made into a fetish whose worship would blind us to the importance and the need of economic intercourse between the nations.]

But the real issue is whether or not the principle as such implies the individualistic exaggeration that in principle does not allow of any restriction. The entire notion that according to its internal economic structure the State is a "closed and self-sufficient organism" has originated from an absolutization.

[3] *Die Staatswirtschaft des Faschismus* (1935) p. 14/5 (Finanz. Forsch. hrg. v. Fritz Karl Mann).

Nazione" (the power of the nation). He rightly adds that Italy's practical policy could not strive after a complete autarchy but only after a restricted economic independence of foreign countries, and that even such a restricted autarchy was extremely difficult to realize: 'For the one-sided dependence on foreign countries is founded in the natural basic conditions of the Italian national economy' (p. 17). This is true, for Italy is poor in raw-materials, and as far as agriculture is concerned, the comparative costs assign to Italy the place of "a garden of Europe". The developmental tendencies of Italian agriculture not affected by the State, favour exactly those branches of industry in which that country can boast of an advantage over other countries. This would entail a considerable amount of interweaving of Italian economy with the international effort to supply economic needs.

The carrying through of the German national-socialistic "*völkische*" idea of autarchy in agriculture was to be accomplished by means of a compulsory organization of the farmers in a "*Reichsnährstand*" and by the "*Erbhofrecht*". Cf. Dr. HEINRICH STOLL: *Deutsches Bauernrecht*, Mohr, Tübingen 1935.

The expression of the State's structural principle in the internal aspect of social intercourse.

In the social law-sphere of human intercourse, which is the immediate basis of the economic aspect, the internal structure of the State expresses itself in the whole system of typical forms of intercourse between government and subjects, in public ceremonies, in the special honours paid to national symbols, in the celebration of national festivals and days of commemoration, *etc.* The structural coherence between the internal function of social intercourse and the leading public juridical function, as well as with the typical function of power of the State, is manifest in the typical figure of *national honour*. An offence to the national honour is an offence to the individual State as a whole. It affects government, country and nation together as an integral unity, and can in no way be understood individualistically.

The meaning of such an offence cannot possibly be *restricted* to the aspect of social intercourse, but, as an infringement of the norms of this intercourse, it can only be understood from the point of view of the typical political structural principle as a whole. In this principle the public juridical community plays the *leading* part. In the internal life of the State the government must not allow such an offence to be committed with impunity. The entire structure of the individual body politic is concerned in such an offence, which in the last instance affects the honour of God as the Sovereign.

But the national honour displays its most important implications in international relations. From antiquity down to the present day this honour has been recognized as a valuable matter in which the requirements of courtesy are interwoven with those of international law and with the prestige of the nation's power.

A violation of the typical norms of courtesy committed at a foreign court with respect to the State's ambassadors was already considered as one of the four *casus belli* in ancient Rome [1]. The affront offered to Israel's ambassadors, sent by David to condole with the Ammonite king HANUN on the death of HANUN's father NAHAS, was answered by David with a declaration of war and the annihilation of the united armies of the Ammonites and their allies, the Syrians [2]. In modern times international courtesy in the refined manners of diplomacy is generally considered as an essential element in the international relations between the States. The slightest violation of these rules of courtesy are implicitly recognized as an embarrassing incident of international juridical and moral significance [3].

From what we have said it appears once again that any effort to delimit the juridical and moral norms from each other by means of external criteria is doomed to failure. In the individuality-structure of human society the modal norms form an unbreakable coherence and are indissolubly interwoven. We cannot eliminate their internal irreducible modality, if we wish to have a universally valid criterion to distinguish the normative law-spheres.

Remember the internal disciplinary rules in the army with respect to uniforms, to saluting, *etc.* The individuality-structure of these internal political societal norms makes it impossible to understand their modal aspect of social intercourse *apart* from the internal public juridical disciplinary aspect qualifying these norms. But in a *modal* sense these aspects retain their sphere-sovereignty also in their individuality-structure. If we have not acquired an insight into their modal sovereignty within their own sphere, we cannot gain an insight into their individuality-structure.

From this it appears that in its internal aspect of social intercourse the State is also a typical integrating whole uniting a plurality into a unity. But in this structural function the State's

---

[1] TITUS LIVIUS, *Rerum Rom. ab urbe condita*, libri IV, 19.

[2] 2 *Sam.* 10.

[3] Cf. V. N. DNIMITSCH, *La courtoisie internationale et le droit des gens* (1930), on the "incidents Tisza" (26 May 1888) and "Philip Snowden" (10 Aug. 1929), when the disregard of international courtesy threatened to disturb international relations seriously.

integrating function remains as much typically limited by the structural principle as in its other structural aspects. This means that internal norms of human intercourse in other communal relationships, or those of private inter-individual relations, can never become component elements of the internal social norms concerning the body politic.

The State cannot abolish class-distinctions in the social relations of intercourse in modern society. These distinctions can only be *integrated* in the structure of political intercourse in a better or a worse way. The State cannot give a political structure to private social relations of intercourse. A compulsory political uniform manner of saluting, imposed on non-political social intercourse, cannot really be conducive to the unity of the nation. It can only rouse the aversion of free-minded people and has a ridiculous effect in the social intercourse with foreigners. The universalistic totalitarian idea of the State shows its mythological character also in the modal aspect of social intercourse.

The expression of the structural principle in the internal linguistic aspect of the body politic.

In the foundational direction the modal aspect of social intercourse refers back to the internal linguistic aspect of the structure of the State. The latter expresses itself here in a very elaborate system of objective symbols (standards, the national ensign, the national coulours, badges and insignia, the national arms, fixed formulae introducing official governmental documents, titles, *etc.*), realized in an objective thing-structure (symbolically-politically qualified), and depending on continual actualization by the government and its subjects. Smend called these things symbolical summaries of "material integrating factors". The typical structure of the State's authority expresses itself symbolically in the titles and the badges of office of the bearers of authority.

The State may also have an integrating function with regard to verbal languages ("*Volkssprachen*"), when more than one language is spoken by the nation. In the war of languages in Belgium the government had to take sides in an integrating manner, because the State also functions in the law-sphere of symbolic signification. But here, too, the governmental task of integration remains bound to the structural principle of the body politic, *i.e.* it remains bound to the leading of the juridical idea of public justice.

When the nation has more than one language spoken within its territory, public justice requires the government to strive after peace between these languages. When in its internal policy a government tries to enforce a lingual integration by oppressing one of the competing languages, a particular national group will be *tyrannized*. Then the government exceeds the limits of its office and is guilty of *détournement de pouvoir*. Experience has shown that such a high-handed policy has always been powerless when a linguistic group puts up a strong resistance. The history of the Low Countries at the time when Holland and Belgium were united after the fall of Napoleon furnishes a striking example of a government's political failure in linguistic matters.

The expression of the structural principle in the historical function of the State.

The State's typical structural foundation is found in the historical aspect, in which the structural principle of the body politic expresses itself in the political cultural unity of the nation. In this cultural aspect of the body politic the entire all-sided concentration of the State's power remains typically based on the monopolistic organization of military power over a territorially limited cultural area, in the way explained earlier. The political cultural unity of the nation is indissolubly bound to the leading function of the State and can only in this way perform its individual historical task. Within this cultural aspect of its structure the integrating function of the body politic is directed to the national-political unity of culture. This unity should be realized and rank in priority to any possible group cultures within the national territory. For this purpose national museums are built and properly attended to; monuments are erected on the occasion of important national events; national festivals and anniversaries are kept; national history is made an obligatory educational subject for schools, measures are taken to promote art and science, insofar as the latter have a national pheno-type.

But the task of political integration remains bound to the structural principle of the State also in this case. Only in a political sense can the State realize the historical cultural unity of nation and country under the leading of the juridical idea of public interest, and while respecting the sphere-sovereignty of the non-political cultural circles. The non-political cultural communities cannot be shut up within the boundaries of the State; they have to perform an integrating task of their own of a non-political character.

The modern totalitarian idea prompted some States to make the historical formation of power in the non-political cultural circles subservient to the State's political striving after power. But we have shown in an earlier context that if science, Church, art, *etc.* are made into permanent *component elements* of a State's political concentration of power, the internal life of these cultural circles will be destroyed. The sphere-sovereignty of the non-political individuality structures cannot be tampered with, because it is founded in the divine world-order.

The logical structure of political communion of thought, and the integrating function of "public opinion".

All the integrating functions of the State we have examined pre-suppose a political function of communal thought whose internal structure expresses the structural principle of this institution. In all the types of communities investigated hitherto we have discovered a specific logical structure of communal thought. This structure appeared to be incompatible with an individualistic autonomy of thought, and to be typically guided by the qualifying function of the societal relationship concerned. The internal family community, the internal marital community, *etc.*, cannot be actualized without their typical communal structure in the thought of their members. This especially holds good for the primitive undifferentiated sibs and tribes with their rigid tradition.

Of course, the typical logical structure in the body politic does not actualize itself from moment to moment. But whenever government and nation manifest their internal societal unity, the peculiar logical structure of their typical political thought becomes at once evident. This does not mean that in this case all and each of the citizens reveal this structure in their political thought. In a modern State whose population has been rent with economic class-warfare, a degenerated party-system, strife between different national groups, these disintegrating factors can never be completely neutralized, not even at moments when the national political community of thought is most strongly concentrated.

But the central importance of "public opinion" reveals itself in the structure of the national political community of thought. We should be mistaken if we identified the structural figure of "public opinion" with the variable historical forms of its expression. Public opinion is not only of fundamental importance for the logical aspect of political thought, but for the whole organization of the political will of a nation. We cannot characterize "public opinion" as a mere historical-political phenomenon revealing itself only in modern political life, and absolutely unknown in former times.

No doubt the influence of the press as an "organ of public opinion" and, more generally, all kinds of technical means to guide public opinion, such as radio, motion picture and television[1], are modern. But the typical structure of a political communion of thought is constant and positivizes itself in variable forms wherever there is really a question of the political life of a State. Nor is it correct to say that "public opinion" asserts itself only in a *democracy* and not in an *autocracy*. Never perhaps has "public opinion" been considered so important as in the modern dictatorships with their autocratic leader-principle and their ceaseless propaganda to regulate and control public opinion. Public opinion does not one-sidedly arise from a politically amorphous mass with the government standing by as an interested spectator. On the contrary, it interweaves government and nation into an internal political coherence of thought. It cannot be understood individualistically, as if its bearer were an unorganized "public", *i.e.* the total number of those who back this opinion and are willing and able to judge of it[2]. It is formed under the guidance of prominent politicians who know the art of rousing the national conscience. Basing themselves on the national tradition they succeed in winning the leading national circles' acceptance of simply formulated political slogans.

In a parliamentary democracy the political parties are indeed also concerned with the organization of "public opinion". But to my mind it is an error to conceive of public opinion as composed

---

[1] Compare on this subject W. ALBIG, *Modern Public Opinion* (2nd rev. ed. New York, 1956).

[2] Cf. TÖNNIES, *Kritik der öffentlichen Meinung* (1922), pp. 84 ff. TÖNNIES cannot appreciate "public opinion" because he considers it exclusively in the light of his individualistic and rationalistic view of the "*Gesellschaft*".

of a number of opposing "public opinions" formed and politically crystallized in the separate classes and parties [1].

A particular party-cry as such can never lay claim to the title of "public opinion". The leading groups of the nation are the bearers of the national conviction, and only if they accept a certain political view can we speak of a genuine "public opinion". In other words "public opinion" has a necessary integrating function in political thought in so far as it transcends differences of party and of interests, and to a certain extent embodies the national political unity of thought [2]. It is essential that such an integrating political thought has attained to a certain national political position of power. Then groups or individuals with views that deviate from those of the leading circles will feel their separateness as an isolation from the prevailing national mood. In the logical individuality-structure of public opinion this indissoluble coherence with its historical-political hegemony is expressed in the authority with which it imposes itself on political thought as a true *national* opinion. But the political function of power can only play a foundational rôle in this logical structure. The communal structure of an integrating mode of political thought assigns the leading rôle to the idea of public societal justice [3].

From a metaphysical idealistic standpoint especially HEGEL has stressed this fact, but we do not accept his speculative-dialectical conception. He holds that "public opinion" contains the eternal essential principles of justice, the true contents and the result of the entire constitution, legislation and public condition in general, in the form of common sense (as the moral basis pervading everybody in the shape of prejudices), as well as the real needs and right tendences of reality [4].

---

[1] Cf. HELLER, *Staatslehre* (1934) p. 181, who, however, also makes very good remarks on this subject.

[2] A public opinion may of course be expressed as the popular conviction of some particular districts of the State (*e.g.*, a borough, or a province). I am only discussing the structure of the national opinion of the State as a whole.

[3] This is really a question of the *idea* as a subjective guiding principle in political *thought*.

[4] HEGEL, *Rechtsphilosophie*, p. 317: "die ewigen substantiellen Prinzipien der Gerechtigkeit, den wahrhaften Inhalt und das Resultat der ganzen Verfassung, Gesetzgebung und des allgemeinen Zustandes überhaupt, in Form des gesunden Menschenverstandes als der durch Alle in

But "public opinion" in its logical individuality, as a subjective integrating political mode of thought within the structure of the State, is by no means the infallible interpreter of the supra-subjective normative principles of justice. Public opinion is a plastic figure requiring formation and may be led astray by the responsible political leaders. Nevertheless, the latter cannot act arbitrarily by merely bringing suggestive emotionality to bear on the "masses"[1]. The "thought of the day" should not at all be identified with "public opinion", which remains bound to the historical tradition of a nation and has a normative character insofar as it is subject to the structural principle of the body politic.

The government has it own formative task with respect to "public opinion", because it cannot govern *in opposition to* a truly national conviction. Every government needs the support of the latter to justify its policy in the national mind. Public opinion does not really govern, as the demo-liberal ideology tried to suggest[2]; but in its logical societal structure the *national opinion has an integrating function in every State-relationship.* Without public opinion the unity of the body politic cannot be realized.

The logical structure of public opinion is that of a strongly emotionally bound communal thought. Its internal logic remains immediately founded in the political structure of feeling and can never be understood in a merely functional sense.

§ 5 - THE EXPRESSION OF THE STRUCTURAL PRINCIPLE IN THE PRE-LOGICAL FUNCTIONS OF THE STATE-INSTITUTION. THE IDEA OF A CHRISTIAN STATE.

The naturalistic sociological theories conceive of the State as a system of intensive psychological interactions; or as the

Gestalt von Vorurteile hindurchgehenden sittlichen Grundlage, sowie die wahrhaften Bedürfnisse und richtigen Tendenzen der Wirklichkeit".

[1] Therefore every naturalistic-psychological "explanation" of public opinion as a case of psychical mass-suggestion or slavish imitation, as RATZENHOFER has tried to give, is fundamentally erroneous; cf. his *Wesen und Zweck der Politik* (1893), I, pp. 188 ff.

[2] This ideology was first formulated by the physiocratic school (cf. HELLER, *op. cit.*, p. 173). MERCIER DE LA RIVIÈRE was the first to give expression to the doctrine of popular government in the "*opinion publique*", in opposition to the doctrine of absolutist monarchy. In this respect his ideology was a direct outcome of the natural law theory of the people's sovereignty.

"chance" of a unified ("*einheitliche*") physico-psychical process of human cooperation, oriented to the subjective idea of a normative coercive juridical order; or as a biotic organism; or as the product of a struggle of races or of social classes, explicable in terms of natural causes.

The criticism passed on these theories by KELSEN and his school from the standpoint of their formalistic juridical normological view of the State, is irrefutable to a certain extent. None of the pre-logical "natural aspects" of the body politic can be understood without an appeal to its structural juridical organization. All these naturalistic theories show the same basic error of trying to approach the natural aspects of the State by means of a naturalistic *conception of function.* They are oblivious of the fact that even in the pre-logical aspects of experience the State presents itself as an internal unity whose political natural functions can only exist in a *normative, juridically qualified individuality-structure.* None of these pre-logical functions are a *natural datum.* They are all the product of a *formative political activity,* which of course is something quite different from an objective technical *artifact* made to order. KELSEN must be especially credited with having unmasked the naturalistic theories of the State as *crypto-ethical political* theories that have not at all been composed according to the method of natural science.

The psychical structural aspect of the State: the typical societal feeling of political solidarity.

The psychical structure of the State cannot really be conceived as a system of merely gradually stronger psychical interactions between individuals. If we leave the typical individuality-structure of the political feeling of national solidarity out of account, we can only agree with KELSEN's remark that "psychical interactions between individuals" do not stop at the territorial boundaries of the State. These interactions, as such, can never give expression to the unity of the body politic. But the State cannot exist as a real unity without the modal aspect of feeling having realized itself in its individuality-structure. The political feeling of national solidarity is a social feeling that has been given a definite *form* in an opened meaning-structure. It binds government, country and nation together.

The structural principle of the body politic expresses itself in the internal sphere of political feeling in such a way that the foundational rôle is assigned to the societal feeling of national military power, and the leading rôle to the feeling of public justice with its implied feeling of authority and submission. This individuality-structure can only reveal itself *in the opened historical and juridical anticipatory spheres of the psychical law-sphere.* The modal feeling of power and that of justice here assume their typical individuality-structures. In the logical law-sphere the expression of the political structure also constitutes itself in the anticipatory spheres. Only a careful analysis of the modal meaning-structures enables us to understand the expression of the individuality-structures within a law-sphere. In a modal psychical sense the subjective feeling of political solidarity remains indissolubly related to the expression of the State's structure in sensory objectivity, *i.e.* to the objective sensorily perceptible aspect of the political organization.

The structural subject-object relation is also essential to the psychical societal function of the State; and the psychical interwovenness of government, country and nation remains bound to this subject-object relation.

The political feeling of national solidarity, as it is briefly analysed here, can no longer be grasped in a general (non-structural) psychological concept of *function.* It implies the feeling of solidarity of government, nation and country, and as such it cannot comprise foreign countries with their foreign governments and their foreign nations. Enkaptically, however, it remains interwoven with political feelings of international relations. Here the State also performs an integrating task under the leading of its qualifying public juridical function. But this integration, too, remains limited by the body politic's inner nature and cannot affect the non-political individuality-structures in the modal sphere of feeling.

The expression of the structural principle in the biotic aspect of the State. The political problem of races.

In the foundational direction the psychical structural function immediately refers back to the biotic aspect of the State-structure. The error of a biologistic conception of the body politic would never have arisen if the latter did not really function as a vital community of government, country and nation. As such it is, however, not a natural *datum,* but a structural aspect of political formation, which can never be conceived apart from the leading and the foundational function of the State. The State's territory also functions as an objective vital space of nation and government, but only as a politically organized and opened vital area. In this space the foundational and the leading functions of this societal institution express themselves in an anticipatory direction. According to this aspect the State really functions as a political form of life (KJELLÈN) which, however, is not at all qualified as a *natural* macro-organism.

In the biotic space of the State we do not find an unbridled interplay of natural forces, or a biotic "struggle for life" which does not observe any norms, but life displays a politically ordered structure here. The State's population is internally interwoven with the national soil, and in the long run a bio-psychic type may be formed. This type is not a mere product of nature but the result of formation in a particular political vital area.

Again the racial problem claims our attention here. I cannot enter into the different biologistic political racial theories in this book. Suffice it to refer to ERICH VOEGELIN, *Rasse und Staat* (Tübingen, 1933) [1], to GOLDSTEIN, *Rasse und Politik* (4e Aufl. 1925) and to the excellent criticism of these theories made by HELLER and SOROKIN [2].

Recent political racial theories are inspired by the work of the Frenchman Count GOBINEAU, *Sur l'inégalité des races humaines* (1853), and are based on the thesis that there are three original main races (the white, yellow and black races) with different ramifications in constant primary or natural races (*e.g.*, the Nordic, the Caucasian, the Alpine, the Mediterranian, the Mongoloid, the Proto-negroid races, *etc.*). These races are grounded in the biotic blood relationship and possess fundamentally different mental, political, and cultural dispositions and potentialities [3]. The constant biotic race is supposed to be endowed with a constant "racial soul" and "racial mind", identifiable by means of objective physiological and anatomical criteria (the colour of hair and eyes, face, and skin, cranial index, *etc.*). And these

---

[1] Ch. 2, p. 36 ff.

[2] HELLER, *Staatslehre*, pp. 148 ff. SOROKIN, *Théories Sociologiques Contemporaines* (1938), pp. 172 ff.

[3] The existence of "primary races" should not be *a priori* rejected for political reasons, as is done, *e.g.*, by BOAS, *Kultur und Rasse* and LUSCHAU, *Völker, Sprachen, Rassen.* Only the political myth of the race is unscientific, especially in its anti-semitism. Another question is whether the hypothesis of the polygenetic origin of the human races is acceptable from the Christian standpoint.

criteria were also used to distinguish the superior from the inferior races. ALFRED ROSENBERG based his entire "cultural philosophy" on this racial theory in his book *Der Mythus des XX Jahrhunderts* (25 and 26th ed. 1934), with its glorification of the Nordic, or "Aryan" race. This book was soon considered to be the "philosophical justification" of HITLER's inhuman anti-semitic policy.

It is evident that this criminal political application of the biologist sociological race-theories fell completely outside of the boundaries of science. Nevertheless, CHAMBERLAIN's work *Grundlagen des Neunzehnten Jahrhunderts* (1899) was already permeated by a mystic pan-Germanism and a vehement anti-semitism, and KARL PEARSON frankly defended the right of the "Aryan race" to a complete expulsion of the "inferior races".

But when we leave alone these political excesses and consider these theories from a scientific point of view, we must establish that any attempt to base the supposed superior mental, cultural or political qualities of a "Nordic" race on criteria like colour and cranial index has proved to fail. In addition, the hypothesis of a polygenetic origin of the human races lying at the foundation of different theories of this kind, is a gratuitous assumption; and the assumption of an Aryan or Nordic race rests upon a fallacious ethnological conclusion drawn from a purely linguistic theory concerning Sanskrit as the common origin of the European languages. The chief point, however, is that the positivist biologistic foundation of the racial theories is incompatible with any axiological view of a "superior race". Leading political theorists, such as GÜNTHER[1] and WOLFF[2], implicitly admitted this.

They reversed their initial (biotically founded) racial concept with the assertion: "It is the mind which builds the body", and with pathos they turned on materialism, naturalism and vitalism. The fashionable philosopher, H. ST. CHAMBERLAIN, deemed every scientific definition of race to be superfluous in comparison with the feeling of "race in his own heart".

This does not detract from the fact that there are considerable differences between the human races which have been estab-

---

[1] GÜNTHER, *Rassenkunde des deutschen Volkes* (15e Aufl. 1930), pp. 426 ff.

[2] WOLFF, *Angewandte Rassenkunde* (1927), pp. 27 ff.

lished in a scientific way[1]. It is undeniable that *up till now* the cultural and political abilities of the negro have proved to be relatively small in comparison with those of the white and yellow races, though there are remarkable individual exceptions, and though we must not forget that hereditary dispositions are flexible and capable of disclosure by a good education.

This may give rise to very difficult political problems in States like the South-African Union where the *ruling white race is* confronted with a majority of primitive ethnical groups of black race, of mixed breed, *etc.* It is difficult to see how in the near future a real national political unity could arise in which all of these different racial groups are integrated. And here again it appears that the natural law ideas of the freedom and equality of men cannot be legally realized without an adequate historical political basis. Such a basis is certainly not present so long as a majority *of black people are still in a condition of primitive* culture. At the same time it must be established that the condition of such a body politic in which the majority of the people are placed under the guardianship of a white minority and are *not* really *integrated* with *the* latter into a national unity, is extremely precarious.

We have already observed that within the State's territory a particular national political bio-type may be formed in the long run on account of the biotic coherence of the successive generations. Then also foreign elements may be assimilated, if this type becomes strong enough in its development. This state of affairs is something quite different from what the naturalistic theories try to suggest. For here it is not the "blood" that creates the nation and the State, but the very opposite happens[2].

However, this process is by no means a structural necessity in the biotic aspect of the State; it is only a variable phenomenon within the structure of the latter and does not occur at all times and in all countries. For the formation of secondary or cultural races, the political factor is only one of the many that are essential.

The typical biotic integrating function of the State consists in a political formation of the vital conditions for the totality of

[1] Cf. R. B. DIXON, *The Racial History of Man*, N.Y. (1923) p. 518 and SOROKIN, *op. cit.*, pp. 223 *ff.*

[2] HELLER, *op. cit.*, p. 159. Cf. also LIERMANN, *Das deutsche Volk* (1927), p. 28.

the nation within the political living-space. This integration is to be brought about under the typical leading of the public legal principle of the "public interest" (the domain of bio-politics).

As observed above, a real political racial problem can only arise when in the same State there exist more or less sharply isolated racial types that have not been assimilated in a bio-cultural respect. This is especially the case when they organize themselves as mutually enimical and isolated parts of the population (recall the racial problem in South Africa, or the negro problem in the southern States of the U.S.A.). This example clearly shows the close connection between the political integrating function of the State in the biotic sphere and the structural principle of this societal relationship. It also shows that the body politic is unable to bring about an *absolute* vital integration within the national territory. We also learn from this example how essential is the dependence of the political integrating activity on the normative leading function of the State. Owing to this dependence every policy of oppression directed to a particular part of the population is qualified as a tyrannical excess of power.

The various contrasting interests of the mutually hostile groups of subjects must be carefully balanced against each other according to the criterion of the public juridical interest. And this implies that also the different cultural positions of the ethnical groups within the political totality should be considered, though at the same time the cultural level of under-developed groups should be elevated as much as possible. By means of levelling individualistic-Humanistic standards of justice we can never solve a political racial problem.

*

In this way we might continue our analysis of the pre-logical structural functions of the State: the physical (the compulsory organization of energy), the phoronomic, the spatial and the numerical functions. However, our aim is not to give a complete theory of the body politic, but we want to explain the expression of the structural principle in the various modal aspects of the State-institution. Therefore we shall restrict ourselves to a general remark on these last four structural functions. The distinction between them may at first sight strike the reader as a little artificial, but it is none the less necessary. In these aspects the State has also subject-functions as well as in the psychical and the biotic aspects. But in the later law-spheres they are only to be referred to in an objective retrocipatory way. This insight is of importance to the general theory of the State, which we will demonstrate with the doctrine of the *State's territory.*

The theories about the State's territory and the methodical necessity to distinguish the modal aspects in the structure of the body politic.

There are principally three theories on this subject: 1. the object-theory which considers the territory merely as the object of a subjective right of the State; 2. the subject-theory defended by the organic doctrine of the State, which conceives the territory as an essential subjective component of the organism of the body politic, and holds that it can never be objectified. The territory is the "body" of the State and the latter is hypostatized to a collective person; 3. the competence-theory identifying the State's territory with a territorial sphere of competence.

Each of these theories contains an element of truth, but by ignoring the structural coherence in the different modal aspects of the State's territory they are in principle incorrect.

The first of them considers the territory of the body politic one-sidedly according to the juridical subject-object relation. In this relation the territory can only be the object of a public subjective right of the State as a "legal person". But it is a fundamental error to *merge* the structure of the State's territory entirely into this modal subject-object relation.

The second theory considers the territory as a subjective component of the personality of the State, and is right insofar as the State's territory in its original spatial structural aspect does function subjectively. This aspect is really interwoven in an essential structural coherence with the entire subjective unity of the body politic. Apart from the untenable metaphysical hypostatization of the State, this theory forgets, however, that the State's territory can function subjectively only in a single modal aspect. In the total structure of the State the territory has an undoubted *objective* juridical *qualifying* function and an objective historical foundation. In a modal juridical respect as well as in a structural theoretical sense the subject-theory is false, although it is perfectly correct to say that the State cannot be conceived individualistically *apart* from its territory.

The third theory ignores the whole of the structural subject-object relation in the State's territory, conceiving it exclusively in an abstract juridical way from its law-side. This theory is right insofar as in the juridical norm-side the State's territory only functions in the spatial analogy of a juridical sphere of validity, of a territorial legal sphere of competence. But this theory forgets that the juridical law-side of the territory is only meaningful in its coherence with the juridical subject-side. In the latter the State's territory functions only objectively. Here the juridical subject-object relation has an internal structural character which can only be understood from the supra-modal structural principle of the body politic.

Political geography and the structure of the State's territory.

From a structural theoretical standpoint the territory of the State is a totality which in the first place has an objective public juridical qualification. As soon as special sciences, such as political geography (RATZEL and his school use the term "*geopolitics*"), political history, or the science of constitutional law, institute an enquiry into the territory of the State, we are urged to ask according to which of the modal aspects they intend to consider its structure. In the political geometrical structure we find the figure of the boundaries, the extent, and generally the subjective spatial form of the national territory with its political central and its peripheral parts. They all occur in their disclosed political form and cannot be grasped apart from the objective physical, biotic, sensuous and later structural functions. In a *modal* sense the political geometrical structure remains distinct from all these functions. If this structure is ignored, all the modal structural aspects founded in it will lose their basis.

The prevailing tendencies in political geography do not theoretically take account of the structural principle of the body politic, but proceed along naturalistic paths. This science will have to orient itself to the structural principle of the State and to distinguish the modal structural functions of the State's territory in their sphere-sovereignty.

The expression of the structural principle of the State in the transcendental limiting aspect of the temporal order. The political function of faith.

We have now reached the most central point of our investigations, *viz.* the expression of the political structural principle in the last modal limiting aspect of the temporal order, that of faith. In faith this structural principle points to the religious root of the State-institution. At this point the problem of the "Christian State" claims our attention. We can only discuss it here in a very concise and summary way, for an elaborate treatment belongs to the *special* philosophy of the State. We shall restrict ourselves to the structural problem.

The reality of a societal relationship cannot be shut off in the leading function of its social structure. In its full all-sided reality the body politic must also have a societal function in the law-sphere of faith.

Doubtless, the State is no more *qualified* as a community of faith than the marriage-bond or the family-relationship. But as little as the latter does the State permit itself to be shut off from the transcendental limiting function of the whole of our temporal reality. The character of all created being as *meaning* prevents such a seclusion, and in particular the fact that the societal relationships are structures of man's own temporal existence. The primary question is not how in the course of history the actual States have behaved in their function of faith, but how the divine structural law of their existence *enables* them to function *as such* in the modal law-sphere of belief. This is a question of the *structural principle* of the State expressing itself within the modal aspect of faith. We are not examining the influence of faith on the individual political lives of the separate human beings in the series of generations that have been united or will be united in a body politic. But we want to find out whether the State *as such* displays its *structure as an organized community* in the modal sphere of belief and how this structure *can* express itself in this modal aspect.

Is a Christian State possible? A false way of positing the problem.

Can the State only express itself in the aspect of faith in the sense of a "natural" political belief in God? Can the State only live by the light of God's common revelation in created "nature"? Or should not the State rather imply a faith community which, in accordance with its divine calling, has to subject itself to the divine Word Revelation? In other words, should it not be a really *Christian* community within the limits of its political structure?

It is fundamentally wrong to identify this basic problem of every Christian theory of the body politic with the question about the relation between the State and a temporal institutional Church. Such an identification usually implies that the only possible manifestation of the Christian State is its subservience to the Church as an institution. Then the body politic has to use its power of the sword to suppress the promulgation of doctrines rejected by the Church as heretical. And, in addition, the State has to follow the leading of the institutional Church in all matters concerning the salvation of the souls of its citizens. But we have seen that this view is certainly not the outcome of a Christian way of positing the problem which starts from the radical Biblical basic motive. In this conception it is taken for granted that the State as such, *i.e.* in its internal essential structure, cannot have a Christian character. This latter must be imparted to it from outside by means of a teleological attitude of subservience towards another temporal societal structure, *viz.* the Church as an institution.

Such a conception is only compatible with the scholastic basic motive of nature and grace. The question about the relation between Church and State can only be correctly posited after one has gained an insight into the internal structural principles of these two temporal types of societal institutions. If it should appear that the structure of the State as such cannot express itself in a Christian faith-community, then a Christian State is impossible, because it is pre-cluded by the structural principle. In this case not any structural interweaving with an institutional Church can impart the internal stamp of Christianity to the body politic.

The primary character of the structural theoretical problem in the discussion about the Christian Idea of the State.

Any inquiry into a possible manifestation of the Christian belief in the historical development of sinful subjective life of the body politic is of a secondary character compared with the structural theoretical basic question. The answer to this basic question is also decisive for the answer to the question whether a truly Christian politics is possible. Also in this case the primary question is not whether in a particular country and in a particular constellation of national conviction a Christian policy can be carried out, but if such a policy is possible according to the internal structure of the State as such.

It is, therefore, also irrelevant to argue that the State has to comprise both Christians and non-Christians, or that on account of the splitting up of Churches it is impossible to decide which Church-creed would have to be adopted by the Christian State. In fact the latter argument again owes its origin to the objectionable idea that the Christian State ought to have an ecclesiastical character. We have already established that the State as such necessarily functions in the modal law-sphere of faith. In its public communal manifestations the body politic may recognize a God above it and above the entire world-order; or it may deify itself or human reason; or again openly declare itself a self-sufficient "*état-athée*" which only appeals to the belief in a social ideal and in man's autarchical power to realize it. But never can the State as a temporal societal relationship struggle free from the grasp of the sphere of faith, within which a higher will than its own has assigned a structural function to it. This is the astounding truth which must at least arouse every wavering mind from his dreams of political neutrality with respect to the life of faith.

The State can no more be neutral in this respect than science. The political slogan of neutrality is as much under the leading of an attitude of faith and as certainly originates from a basic religious commitment as any other political conviction.

The Revelation of God in the political structure of the State-institution.

According to the structural principle of the body politic the modal revelational principle as it presents itself in the aspect of faith[1] assumes a political type of individuality. In the State, as such, God reveals Himself as the Sovereign Origin of all governmental authority, as the Holy omnipotent avenger of all iniquity. In His will the two radical functions of the State's structure, *might* and *right*, find their unity of origin and their self-sufficient fulness of being. Not any body politic is able to obliterate this structural Revelation of God from its essential nature. In its function of belief every State remains subject to this politico-pisteutic revelational principle as to an unbreakable *political norm of faith*.

But this revelational principle in the "nature", *i.e.* in the internal structure of the State-institution, cannot be detached from the Word-Revelation. The latter reveals the State as an institution "ordained on account of sin" and thus connects it in the faith-aspect of experience with the fall into sin of the whole of mankind and the redemption in Christ Jesus. Without this Word-Revelation the political revelational principle becomes a "law of the flesh", a law of the sinful idolatry either of ARES or of DIKÈ, or in whatever form the two radical functions of the State may be absolutized. And always this political apostasy is included in a process of opening and deepening of the modal function of faith, because the structure of the State can only realize itself at a *disclosed* level of culture. The political confes-

[1] Cf. Volume II, part I, pp. 302 ff., pp. 314 ff.

sion of faith in God's sovereignty over the life of the body politic has from the start been typical of a Christian view of the State[1].

This confession would be deprived of its Christian sense if it were taken to mean nothing but the expression of a merely "natural" belief", *i.e. apostatized* from the Word-Revelation. God's sovereignty over the State can only be accepted by us in its true sense if we recognize the "*regnum Christi*". Only in Christ as the Incarnate Word can we truly know and worship God as our Sovereign in the life of the State. Without the political confession of our faith in the "*regnum Christi*" our recognition of God's sovereignty will become idolatrous.

Christ as the Prince of all the State-governments. The testimony of Holy Scripture.

If all this is true, we can no longer deny that according to its faith-aspect the State is subject to Christ's kingship, which ought to find its own typical expression in the internal life of the State[2]. Holy Scripture is too explicit on this subject for a Christian to be permitted to think that the structure of the State as such falls outside the Kingdom of Christ. According to the Scriptures Christ is the "Prince of the kings of the earth". David's hundred and tenth Psalm, cited by Christ against the pharisees, calls on all earthly kings and rulers to bow down under the Son's sceptre. All Messianic prophecy is unanimous on this point though with increasing emphasis it points to the suffering and death of the Messiah as the road to the establishment of His Kingdom[3]. The New Testament maintains this thought to the end of the Apocalypse, where the Incarnate Word appears as the King of kings and the Lord of Lords[4]. He is the Judge pronouncing

---

[1] Cf. GISBERT BEYERHAUS, *Studien zur Staatsanschauung Calvins mit besonderer Berücksichtigung seines Souveränitätsbegriffs* (Berlin, 1910), § 10—§ 16.

[2] CALVIN remarks (C.R. 66, 635): *'Hodie non habemus terrenum regem, qui sit Christi imago: sed Christus per se ecclesiam vivicat.*" In these words CALVIN only refers to the special typological meaning of the Israelitic kingship in David's line for the Messianic future. After the Incarnation of the Logos the office of the government can no longer have *this* typological meaning.

[3] The well known Rabbinical exegesis of the texts which speak of "the suffering servant of the Lord", according to which this refers to the Israelitic people, breaks down in the face of Daniel 9 : 26 where it is expressely stated that the Messiah (the promised Prince) will be killed.

[4] *Revelation* 19 : 11—17.

the last judgment on the world, Who will beat down the heathens with the sword of His mouth and rule them with an iron rod [1].

The Scriptural data exclude the view that according to its essential character the State, as an institution of common grace, has to live by the light of "natural" revelation only. This conception, moreover, essentially implies the acceptance of the dualistic basic motive of "nature" and "grace". A State that does not bow before Christ's sceptre and excludes Him from all political activities, although living in the light of the revealed Word, remains irrevocably lost in the *civitas terrena,* the kingdom of darkness. But God maintains the divine office and the divine structural law of the body politic also in this state.

Why the internal structure of the State does not allow it to have a Church confession. The integrating function of the State as a political community of faith.

But this does not mean that in any of its manifestations the "Christian State" as such should have an ecclesiastical confession, or that the State ought to assign a public juridical position in political life to the institutional Church. Such a view is incompatible with the structural principle of the body politic. The Christian State is not qualified as a Church community, but ought to respect sphere-sovereignty also in its function of faith.

This is even the first fruit of a truly Christian policy: that the sphere-sovereignty of the different societal structures ordained by God in His holy world-order is recognized and respected in all the spheres of life. The State should not strain its power to dominate the internal societal relations that have received their own specific vital law from God. The very lack of a particular ecclesiastic confession of a binding character, which is incompatible with the internal structural law of a Christian Church, should be accepted with respect to the political faith community of a Christian State. This latter has to perform a Christian political integrating function in the national life of faith. In the confession of God's sovereignty in Christ Jesus, the Incarnate Word, the Victor over sin and death, as the Sovereign of all earthly sovereigns, the State has to unite the whole nation into a Christian political community of faith, so long as the public national opinion shows a Christian stamp.

---

[1] *Revel.* 2 : 27.

The political integration remains bound to the structural principle of the State, the public juridical societal function should take the leading rôle of the State's typical qualifying function, and not an ecclesiastic confession of faith. As a typical institution ordained on account of sin, the State can only be a temporal expression of the supra-temporal radical unity of governmental power and governmental justice in Christ Jesus. Christ is the King and Ruler of the State and the Redeemer from the disintegrating effect of sin in the life of the nations, *i.e.* He is the King of common grace.

The relation between common and particular grace. Rejection of the theory of the two realms.

We have now to answer the question: what is the relation between common grace and particular grace? In contradistinction to the institutional Church, the State is not a *separate institution* of special grace but belongs to the general temporal life of the world, just like the family and the other non-ecclesiastical societal structures [1]. The Dutch Christian thinker and statesman Dr A. Kuyper Sr has laid full emphasis on this point in accordance with the evangelic viewpoint of the New Testament. The State is not the direct product of the original order of the creation, but owes its existence to common grace as "an institution ordained on account of sin". In its typical structure, the body politic has a general soteriological vocation for the preservation of temporal society in its differentiated condition. This means that a pagan State does not cease to be a State, just as a pagan marriage and family life, pagan art and science, *etc.* remain possible as temporal life in apostasy.

On the other hand, the special structure of the temporal institution of the Church is only possible as a *Christian* institution. Common grace in the first place consists in the maintenance of the temporal world-order in all its structures against the disintegration by sin. In this sense common grace embraces "the evil and the good together" and is restricted to temporal life. Special grace, however, is concerned with the renewal of the religious root of the creation in Christ Jesus as the Head of the regenerated human race and must not be considered in an individualistic soteriological sense. From this it follows that par-

---

[1] Cf. Dr A. Kuyper Sr, *De Gemeene Gratie,* and *Encyclopaedie der H. Godgeleerdheid* (2e druk 1909) vol. III, pp. 328 ff.

ticular grace is the real root and foundation of common grace. It is therefore absolutely contrary to the Biblical standpoint when a distinction is made between two independent realms or spheres of grace.

As the Redeemer, Christ is the Regenerator of the entire fallen cosmos. As the Mediator of the Covenant of grace in its religious fullness, He is the Root of common grace, the King whose kingship embraces the whole of temporal life. The *civitas terrena,* as the world in apostasy, cannot claim any sphere of life as its own in opposition to Christ. A State divorced from the new root of life does not owe its manifestation of apostasy to Christ but to the *civitas terrena.* In such a State the structural office is maintained and thereby God bestows his temporal blessings on mankind [1]. Both this office and its blessings belong to the Kingdom of Christ, Who is the king of common grace, because He is the Head of regenerated mankind. We must therefore undertake the struggle for the Christian State. In its actual societal life, notwithstanding the effects of sin, the Christian State expresses the structural principle of the body politic in its opened and expanded meaning directed to Christ.

True humanity is rooted in Christ and in Him the whole temporal world in its true meaning-structure is saved. That which remains alien to Him is doomed to eternal death and will find Him to be the judge, who will come to pass judgment on the kingdom of darkness. He has already judged the world, but up to the last Judgment the *civitas Dei* and the *civitas terrena* will remain in conflict.

Therefore we cannot find a pure and untainted manifestation of the "body of Christ" under the rule of common grace in the temporal life on earth. The antithesis reveals itself in the direction of life towards Christ or away from Him. In the principle of the Christian State political life in its internal structure is directed towards Christ. The positive formation of the typical leading public juridical principles of the body politic is opened to give expression to Christ's kingship over the whole of the internal political life of this societal relationship. But this is only possible on the basis of the historical power that the Christian conception of the State has been able to secure in the national conscience. This should be the first goal of any political struggle for the Christian State.

---

[1] Cf. 1 *Tim.* 2 : 1—7.

The "Christian State" is certainly not a system of external formulas. If there is no Christian political community of faith uniting government and people, it is impossible for an official prayer[1], or the formula "by the grace of God" to impart a Christian character to the State. But the Christian character of public life in the body politic does not depend on the individual attitude of faith of each of the subjects. Everything in the State depends on the character of this institution as a public community, on the spirit pervading all its communal activities.

If the life of Christian faith is considered to be only an *individual* concern, it is not possible for us to conceive a political Christian community of faith. Then the idea of a Christian State is a *contradictio in terminis.* But if we take this individualistic view seriously and do not shrink from thinking it out consistently, it is equally impossible for us to speak of a Christian community of faith in the *temporal institutional Church.*

---

[1] After the above expositions I need not elaborate my view here that an official prayer intended for the use of the various public boards is to be rejected in principle if any Christian character has been purposely kept out of it.

CHAPTER IV

THE STRUCTURAL PRINCIPLE OF THE TEMPORAL CHURCH-INSTITUTION

§ 1 - INTRODUCTION. THE BASIC PROBLEM OF THE RELATION BETWEEN THE "ECCLESIA INVISIBILIS" AND THE "ECCLESIA VISIBILIS"[1] IN ROMAN-CATHOLICISM AND IN THE REFORMERS.

From the outset Christian thought related the idea of the Christian State to the idea of the "*una sancta ecclesia*". So long as the Church was conceived in its supra-temporal religious fulness of meaning as the body of Christ, this conception was the only one possible.

---

[1] I adopt the traditional indication of the transcendent *corpus Christi* and its immanent temporal manifestation as *ecclesia invisibilis* and *ecclesia visibilis* respectively, because I want to restrict my deviations from the prevailing terminology to what is strictly necessary. But I cannot say that I think this terminology particularly felicitous. It has been derived from the metaphysical antithesis between *noumenon* and *phenomenon* (even Dr A. KUYPER, *Encycl. der H. Godgeleerdheid* III, p. 191 uses these terms). However, we need not at all interpret these terms in a speculative sense. CALVIN did not do so, nor does KUYPER use the terms *noumenon* and *phenomenon* in this connection in a speculative sense. In any case the terms "*ecclesia visibilis*" and "*invisibilis*" are to be preferred to the new terminology proposed by KATTENBUSCH in his work *Doppelschichtigkeit in Luthers Kirchenbegriff* and by BRUNNER in *Das Gebot und die Ordnungen, viz. "Kirche des Glaubens" (Kirche im Grundsinn)* and "*Kultgemeinde*". The conception implied by this terminology unambiguously absolutizes the temporal community of faith to the *transcendent root* of the Church. The "cult community" as an "empirical community" is not conceived of in its only possible sense of a temporal *community of faith* in its common cult but is *opposed* to the community of faith as the empirical versus the transcendent, hidden Church (cf. BRUNNER, *op. cit.*, p. 521). This fideistic standpoint falsifies the structure of the temporal Church-institution. Its consequences are apparent in the entire view these writers take of the conception that the Reformers had concerning the relation between the *ecclesia visibilis* and the *ecclesia invisibilis*.

There should not remain any doubt about this in the mind of those who place themselves on the Biblical standpoint [1].

St. Augustine was not wrong when he held the State which had been separated from the body of Christ, to be part of the *civitas terrena.* Neither was he wrong when he considered the body *politic as a divine institution and not sinful* as such, although human apostasy is apparent in the historical realization of its structural principle.

The reason is that this sinful human formative activity cannot affect the inner nature of the State as a divine institution. In line with Reuter and Gierke, St. Augustine's basic thought has often been fundamentally misrepresented, because the internal structural principle of the State, and human positivation and actualization of this structural principle, as a subjective activity, were not properly distinguished. Moreover, Augustine himself has given occasion to misunderstanding since he did not properly distinguish the Church, as the kingdom of Christ in the hearts of men, from the temporal Church institution. This was why he held to the erroneous opinion that the State can only become Christian by subjecting itself to the guidance of the institutional Catholic Church. In this respect his famous work *De Civitate Dei* laid the foundation for the medieval view of the Holy Roman Empire, with its secular and spiritual sword, under the supremacy of the latter.

The deviation from the Christian view of the State and the Church starts with the universalistic absolutizing of the temporal Church-institution. The Roman-Catholic conception of the Church.

In this medieval view the "*ecclesia visibilis*", as the temporal manifestation of the "*ecclesia invisibilis*" (*i.e.* the supra-temporal body of Christ), was already identified with the temporal Church institution. The latter was assumed to have the transcendent fulness of power and the all-embracing scope of the "*ecclesia invisibilis*". This was at the same time the beginning of a deviation from the Christian conception of the State.

This universalistic conception of the Church institution was the erroneous starting-point of the scholastic theory of human so-

---

[1] It was also Calvin's view; this has been elaborately demonstrated by Bohatec in his *Die organische Idee in der Gedankenwelt Calvins*, translated under my supervision and published in the periodical *A.R. Staatkunde*, 2e jrg. 1926, pp. 362 ff.

cietal structures. In an earlier context we have shown that it involved a compromise with the classical Greco-Roman view of the State as the perfect whole of human society inclusive of the public religion [1]. Fundamentally it was a manifestation of the "carnal desire" to deify the temporal Church-institution, to give the temporal authority of the Church dominion over the souls of the believers, and to guarantee the temporal Church the supremacy over the whole of societal life, including the secular government. Of course the universalistic conception of the Roman Catholic Church developed since GREGORIUS VII recognised that the hierarchical ecclesiastical institution is only the temporal manifestation of the "*ecclesia invisibilis*". But the "*ecclesia visibilis*", viewed as the hierarchy of a sacramental institution of grace, with its monarchical culmination in the papacy, was as such supposed to transcend all the "secular" societal relationships, and to embrace the whole of Christian life. In this universalistic conception the Church-institution is absolutized to the perfect Christian society.

THOMAS AQUINAS only gave this medieval view a new foundation in the scholastic basic motive of nature and grace and adapted the former to the Aristotelian metaphysics and politics. The dogma of papal infallibility, promulgated in 1870 (by the Vatican Council), transfers Christ's absolute authority to the temporal institution as a hierarchical official organization. The conception of the seven sacraments, as the supra-natural means of grace of the Church-institution, is essentially connected with the Roman-Catholic view of the supra-natural power of the hierarchically organized clergy. The indispensable requirement for carrying through this conception was the assignment of a real sovereign governmental character (not derived from the State) to the official hierarchy.

At the same time the ecclesiastical juridical community had to be modelled on the public juridical organization of the State [2], an imitation strongly favoured by the medieval conception of the Holy Roman Empire. And finally it was necessary to subordinate all secular authority to that of the pope. The universalistic curial conception of the institutional Church obtained its sharpest

---

[1] Cf. Vol. III, pp. 150 ff.

[2] Accordingly the pope has legislative authority, the highest judicial authority, the supreme administrative authority, the competence to impose taxes and to appoint ambassadors to foreign secular courts.

formulation in the famous bull *Unam Sanctam* (1302) of BONIFACE VIII, which summarized the theory of the two swords as follows: "The one Church has only one head. One flock, one shepherd. This shepherd has two swords, the spiritual and the secular sword (*Luke* 22 : 38). The secular sword must be maintained for the benefit of the Church; the spiritual sword must be maintained by the Church; the spiritual sword by the priesthood, the secular sword by kings and soldiers, but in accordance with the will of the priest and as long as he allows it. The secular authority is subject to the spiritual. For Divine Truth teaches us that the spiritual power must institute the secular and pass judgment on it, if it is not right..." [1].

The relation between the *ecclesia visibilis* and *ecclesia invisibilis* according to LUTHER.
The influence of the nominalist-dualistic separation between "nature" and "grace".

Against this absolutization of the Church-institution, the Reformation engaged in a fundamental struggle. But the relation between the "*una sancta ecclesia*" and the internal individuality-structure of the temporal institutional Church remained a problem which could not be solved in a really Biblical sense so long as the scholastical basic motive of nature and grace was not abandoned in principle. LUTHER's view of the Church started from the supra-temporal "invisible" Church, whose only Head is Christ. This was the Biblical conception of the Reformers generally. The "invisible Church" is the true body of Christ but, as such, it has no temporal organization. Therefore it can never coalesce with the temporal institution. The important question was: what is the true relation and connection between the "*ecclesia invisibilis*", and the institutional "*ecclesia visibilis*" as an organized community? The point at issue was the temporal organization of the institutional Church and its individuality structure. LUTHER held that the Church is at once visible and invisible. He thus related the "*ecclesia visibilis*" to the "*ecclesia invisibilis*". The Augsburg Confession says that the Church is "the congregation of saints and true believers, in which the Gospel is rightly taught and the sacraments are rightly administered" [2].

In its "essence" the Church is invisible. In its temporal manifestation as a "congregation", it has its "visible marks" as the true

[1] HEFELE, *Conciliengeschichte* VI, 346.
[2] *Conf. Aug.* VII, R. 11.

Church in the pure preaching of the Word, in the just and Scriptural administration of the Sacraments, and in the fruits of faith. But only the faith aspect of the temporal Church has been considered here. The historically founded internal organization of the institution has not yet had due attention, so that the structural principle of the Church-institution remains unexplained. From the outset LUTHER was caught in a dualistic scheme when he had to conceive the relation between the Church, in its qualifying aspect of a community of faith, and its internal institutional organization.

His difficulty originated from the nominalistic dualistic separation between "nature" and "grace". The temporal Christian community of faith is unexpectedly lifted out of the temporal world-order and hypostatized to the "supra-natural", which has no internal connection with the "natural" order. The "*essence*" of the Church as a Christian community of faith, with its visible signs of a right administration of the Word and the Sacraments, is contrasted with its internal institutional organization. The latter is said to belong to the merely natural earthly forms of life. On the other hand the hypostatizing of the faith aspect of the institutional Church as "*congregatio fidelium*" threatened to weaken the organized institution by favouring the formation of sectarian conventicles. These consequences can be clearly demonstrated in the evolution of LUTHER's views on this subject. But we cannot enter here into a detailed analysis of the latter [1].

The great Reformer remained fully aware of the fact that the institutional Church embraces both true believers and hypocrites, who cannot be distinguished by means of external criteria. Yet after his breach with Rome he inclined to favour the formation of conventicles, to constitute an "*ecclesiola in ecclesia*" that was to contain "true Christians" only. The idea of the "*congregatio fidelium*", originating from the nominalistic trend in the Conciliar Movement of the XVth century, assumed an unmistakable individualistic character here. The institutional communal

---

[1] Cf. the summary of this development in Dr. H. BOUWMAN, *Ger. Kerkrecht* (1928) I, p. 199. Recent investigations in the domain of Church history, instituted by HOLL and others, have brought to light so many facts about LUTHER's development that TROELTSCH's exposition, of LUTHER's standpoint in his famous work *Die Soziallehren der Christl. Kirchen und Gruppen*, must be considered obsolete. This does not mean that we agree with recent attempts to accommodate the opinions of LUTHER and CALVIN by eradicating their differences.

operation of the Word and the Sacraments recedes into the background for the sake of group-formation based on personal rebirth and conversion [1].

These ideas really tended to sectarianism, and very soon LUTHER had to give them up. His experiences in the peasant revolt made it clear to him that it was necessary for the "*ecclesia visibilis*" to have a strong order and organization. But now it appeared that his dualistic starting-point did not enable him to conceive the internal structure of the organized Church institution in its unbreakable coherence with the Church in its central religious sense. He looked upon the temporal arrangement of the Church, the "*äusserliche Gemeinde*", as a merely external juridical organization. In his opinion this temporal order is not internally connected with the spiritual *essence* of the Church, and Holy Scripture gives no binding norms for it [2].

Therefore he could provisionally leave the church organization to the sovereign without any fundamental objection. The secular government, the Protestant lord of the country, was appealed to — though from necessity [3] — to give the Church its organization.

The secular authorities had to establish and to maintain the legal order; this was their task and office. The lord of the country, as "*praecipuum membrum ecclesiae*", had thus to supplement the purely internal spiritual order of the Church with a compulsory secular legal order. This "external" authority was, however, to be exercised in accordance with the ministry of the Church [4].

---

[1] His attitude is characteristically revealed in his motivation why he could not yet realize his plan: 'Aber ich kann und mag noch nicht eine solche Gemeinde oder Versammlung ordnen oder ausrichten. Denn ich habe noch nicht Leute und Personen dazu; so sehe ich auch nicht viele, die dazu dringen.' [But I cannot and must not yet order or establish such a congregation or assembly. For I do not yet have the people for it; nor do I see many who urge me to do so.]. (*Luthers Werke*, Braunschweig, 1892, VII, p. 168).

[2] LUTHER explicitly declared this in his *Vom Papstum zu Rom wider den hochgerühmten Romanisten zu Leipzig* (June 1520).

[3] Cf. BOUWMAN, *op. cit.* I (1928) p. 205; compare also the view of KARL HOLL, *Ges. Aufsätze* I, 349. A different opinion is held by KATTENBUSCH, *Die Doppelschichtigkeit in Luther Kirchenbegriff*, pp. 94 & 101.

[4] LUTHER turned to the Elector of Saxony with the request to institute visitation. The Elector then established a "*kurfürstliche Visitation*" and composed an instruction. The visitors became *his* officers and were only responsible to *him*. Thus the territorial Church government was intro-

In the Lutheran territorial Churches consistories were introduced, which were ecclesiastic organs instituted by the lord of the country. They had the power of imposing secular public juridical penalties, which was no doubt contrary to LUTHER's own views [1]. But the difference was not fundamental when considered from the standpoint of the *juridical organization of the Church* [2]. LUTHER looked upon ecclesiastical law as the external work of man that was unconnected with the internal essence of the Church [3]. His only concern was that the legal rules and the form of government should not affect the pure doctrine and the right administration of the sacraments. But he did not see that there is an internal sphere of ecclesiastical law in which the inner nature of the Church institution itself finds a typical expression. In this way it was of course impossible to conceive the internal structural principle of this institution.

The episcopal system.

Meanwhile the older Lutheran conception of Church government, prevailing until the end of the seventeenth century, was still based on a sharp distinction between *jurisdictio ecclesiastica* and *jurisdictio saecularis*. The former chiefly consisted in maintaining the purity of the ecclesiastic doctrine and should be executed by the protestant lord of the country only in accordance with the wishes of the ministers as the real office bearers (the *ministerium*). Theologically the external authority of the secular sovereign within the Church was justified by an appeal to the position of the Christian sovereign as the guardian of the two tables of the decalogue. In this capacity the magistrate was the "*praecipuum membrum ecclesiae*" [4].

The first jurists who specialized in the scientific study of Protestant ecclesiastical law were the brothers JOACHIM [5] and MATTHAEUS STEPHANI [6]. They ignored the theological arguments for the secular Church government and tried to find a positive juridical justification. In a modified form this construction was connected with the older

---

duced, although it was certainly not in line with LUTHER that the Elector exercised this government as a sovereign chief of the Church.

[1] Cf. SOHM, *Kirchenrecht* I, pp. 542—633 and K. MÜLLER, *Ueber die Anfänge der Konsistorialverfassung*, Hist. Zeitschr. B. 102, pp. 1 ff.

[2] Cf. TROELTSCH, *Die Soziallehren der Christl. Kirchen und Gruppen* (1919), p. 517/8 note 235.

[3] Therefore LUTHER's ideas about the possibility of giving the congregation the right to elect the Church officers and the task of maintaining doctrinal discipline are not of fundamental importance. (Cf. *Luther's Werke*, Braunschw. VII, 139).

[4] Cf. MELANCHTON, *Loci (Corpus doctrinae Lips.*, 1561), p. 640.

[5] *Institutiones juris canonici* (1604).

[6] *Tractatus de jurisdictione* (1611).

theological view since REINGKINK. Owing to the peace of Augsburg (1555), episcopal Church government in Protestant countries had been delayed until the religious struggle had been settled. According to the brothers STEPHANI this Church government *ad interim* had devolved upon the Protestant sovereigns as an extension of the *jus advocatiae*, introduced at the time of the Frankish monarchy. Already before the brothers STEPHANI, jurists had followed this construction [1]. The STEPHANI's, however, drew certain conclusions from this: they distinguished two different persons in the sovereign, *viz.* the sovereign *qua talis*, and the sovereign as the representative of the bishops *ad interim*. The sovereign has secular authority *jure proprio*, but he has episcopal or ecclesiastical authority only on account of a special imperial concession (*concessione imperatoris*), as a merely provisional authority lodged with him only *instar depositi* until the settlement of the religious differences.

This juridical construction is at present called the "episcopal system" [2] and in line with THEODORUS REINGKINK it was henceforth connected with the older dogmatic theological construction of the sovereign as "*praecipuum membrum ecclesiae*" and "*custos utriusque tabulae*". This view was then justified by an appeal to the "nature" of the matter and to Holy Scripture. As a result the juridical construction of the STEPHANI's was considerably changed.

The episcopal authority was now considered to be an illegal usurpation. The arrangement of the religious peace was not thought to be a *provisional* concession (devolution), but a final *restitution* to the sovereign of his natural rights within the Church.

This theologically and juridically founded episcopal theory was elaborated by GERHARD, CARPZOVIUS, and others, to the famous doctrine of the three "estates", clearly oriented to a universalistic conception of the temporal Church relationship. The Church consists of the civil magistrate (the "*status politicus*" or governing class), the class of the fathers of a family ("*status oeconomicus*") and the ministry ("*status ecclesiasticus*"). Only the last of these three possess internal Church authority proper, because they only have to judge of questions of doctrine according to the Scriptures. The secular government only possesses a *potestas externa* in the Church. This external power consists of the maintenance of public worship, the institution of the ministry, the convocation of synods, the suppression of idolatry and heresy, the punishment of unchristian conduct and the enforcement of decisions concerning doctrine and liturgy. The class of the family fathers have *potestas communis* and are to form their own opinion by means of independent study of the Scriptures. Without their consent the government or the ministers could not impose any *iudicium* on the family fathers [3].

---

[1] Sf. STAHL, *Die Kirchenverfassung nach Lehre und Recht der Protestanten* (2e Aufl. 1862), p. 5 note 4.

[2] STAHL, too, is in favour of this system in his book cited above.

[3] This theory has been elaborated in the clearest and completest way by CARPZOVIUS in his *Diss. de jure decid. theol. controv.* (1695).

The attempt made in this theory to distinguish the internal Church authority from the secular, and to bind the former to Holy Scripture was doubtless praiseworthy. Nevertheless, the *juridical* aspect of the Church as an institutional community continued to be viewed as external political. And the doctrine about the three "estates" clearly betrays its origin from the late medieval nationalist view of the Church.

The distinction between internal and external jurisdiction lacked a sharp juridical signification, at least insofar as this theory did not recognize that the internal church authority has an original legal competence independent of the secular government.

The territorial system.

This was the *vitium originis* of the Lutheran episcopal theory which made it an easy prey to the Humanistic natural law theories of the *territorial system* and the *collegial system.*

The territorial system ousted the episcopal system chiefly under the influence of THOMASIUS, and was inspired by the desire to guarantee ecclesiastical tolerance to pietists by the sovereign power of the State [1]. Thus the contrast between internal and external official authority in the temporal institution of the Church was radically abolished. All organizational authority in the latter was merged into that of the territorial sovereign and the ministry were denied any influence on Church government. The secular government has this power in its own right, and according to THOMASIUS' natural law conception, the secular authority in ecclesiastic affairs has the exclusive task to maintain the external peace in the Church. The maintenance of doctrinal discipline in the latter was in principle made impossible. It is true, J. H. BÖHMER, the most important defender of this system, made room in the government of the Church for the settlement of controversial doctrinal questions. But, entirely in accordance with THOMASIUS, this establishment of the *doctrina publica* was only intended as a means to safeguard the external peace within the Church in the interest of the State. This was the reason why that task was solely entrusted to the secular governors *"sine concursu necessario Theologorum* [2].

The collegial system.

Finally the *collegial theory* destroyed the last remnants of the insight into the specific structural character of the Church-institution. This theory had been founded by CHRISTOPH MATTHAEUS PFAFF, and was carried through in the German territorial Churches in the second half of the eighteenth century. It seemed to favour the liberty

---

[1] Cf. STAHL's elaborate discussion, *op. cit.*, pp. 15 ff. THOMASIUS' Humanistic idea of tolerance was in no way in accordance with the views of SPENER *c.s.*

[2] *Jus ecclesiast. prot.* lib. I. lit. 1 § 32 sqq; quoted by STAHL, *op. cit.*, p. 21.

of the Church, but conceived of this institution as a mere "*societas*", a "social contract" in accordance with the individualistic natural law scheme. The Church was construed as a free private association or society composed of individuals having the same religious faith. In this association every norm and authority was founded in an agreement made by the members. The relation between the Church and the State was defined in the same way as that between the State and all other free private associations. The State has the sovereign authority over the Church, the *jura majestatica* including the competence of reformation, the supreme control and the protection of the ecclesiastical community. The Church possesses the *jura collegialia* including the contractual establishment of dogma, the regulation of the liturgy, the ordaining of the ministry, the contractual enactment of ecclesiastic regulations, and the maintenance of discipline.

The *majority* has the power to decide upon everything. There is no longer any question of the believers as such having any authority, let alone of Christ's kingship in the institution.

ZWINGLI'S conception of the institutional Church. BULLINGER and ERASTUS.

The Lutheran view of the Church could not do justice to the internal structure of the latter as an institution. ZWINGLI [1] finally also delivered the organization of the ecclesiastical institution to the State, because he had an insufficient insight into the internal structural principle of the temporal organization. In line with LUTHER, the Zürich Reformer started from the *ecclesia invisibilis,* and later on characterized it as the community of the elect. This conception, however, became blurred through the influence of a Humanist "universal theism". Only the "visible Church" has an organization. This organization was considered as an essential characteristic of the "*ecclesia visibilis*". Here ZWINGLI differed from LUTHER and opposed the sects. The visible Church consists of the assemblies of local congregations (the "*Kilchhören*") [2].

Only the institutionally organized local Church is to be viewed as a Church assembly invested with authority. But the actual organization and the whole of the internal ecclesiastic government were left to the reformed lord of the country to be exercised in

[1] Cf. SCHULTHESS-RECHBERG: *Luther, Zwingli und Calvin in ihren Ansichten über das Verhältnis von Staat und Kirche* (1909); and GOTTSCHICK: Zeitschr. f. Kirchengeschichte, Bd. VIII, pp. 590 ff.

[2] In a great many places the "*Kilchhören*" are called members of the universal *ecclesia invisibilis* because they take the Word of God as the standard of their ecclesiastical actions. Cf. GOTTSCHICK, *op. cit.*

accordance with the congregation, not "*jure suo*", but "*in Namen der Kirche*" (in the name of the Church). This is why ZWINGLI and the adherents of his ecclesiastic juridical views like BULLINGER and THOMAS ERASTUS, were sharply opposed to the Calvinistic conception of church discipline.

According to the latter, ecclesiastic discipline is the peculiar competence of the Church as an institution. According to the Zwinglian view the ministers have no other duty than that of exhortation and admonition, but the power of the keys of the Church lacks any internal juridical sense.

CALVIN'S conception of the Church institution.

CALVIN was indeed the first to conceive the *ecclesia invisibilis* (as the "mystic body of Christ", the assembly of the elect) in close connection with the internal structure of the Church institution as a temporal societal relationship. It is true that the Genevan reformer could not struggle free from the traditional conception of the Christian State in which only the "organic" bond with the Church could give the political community its Christian character. But in his conception of the Church this view does not play a part. He was the first to infer the nature of the temporal Church institution, as a real organized community, from its internal structural law, revealed in the New Testament. He does not only distinguish the institution from the "*ecclesia invisibilis*" but conceives it as essentially connected with the invisible Church. On the one hand his conception of the institutional Church is purified from the Roman Catholic idea of hierarchy, which concentrated all ecclesiastic power in the clergy. This is done by the principle of Christ's absolute authority, exercized through Christ's Word and Spirit, a principle already clearly explained by LUTHER. On the other hand CALVIN lays full emphasis on the essential importance of the internal Church organization, in its unbreakable relation to Holy Scripture and the confession of faith.

Precisely because CALVIN had in principle broken with the dualistic basic motive of "nature" and "grace", he could no longer leave the internal organization of the institution to the secular power as an indifferent, worldly concern. He is keenly alive to the fact that the internal communal law of the Church is essentially dependent on the exceptional structure of this institution. From the basic thought of Christocracy in its application to the structural principle it necessarily follows that the

Church also has sovereignty within its own sphere in a *juridical sense.* As the institution is a real organized community, its internal structure must express itself in all the aspects of its actual existence. The structure of authority in this societal institution cannot be conceived exclusively in its qualifying aspect of faith, with the abstraction of all its other modalities, as LUTHER did. This authority also has its juridical, moral, economic, aesthetic, historical, psychical aspects, *etc.*

As CALVIN takes full account of the structural principle of the Church institution, as a *real organized community,* his view is not one-sidedly spiritualistic. This is the reason why, unlike LUTHER, he does not look upon the Church institution exclusively as a "*Heilsanstalt*" (an institution of salvation), but recognizes its functions belonging to its specific communal structure in all the spheres of human societal life [1]. It also explains why CALVIN, like JOHANNES À LASCO, could justify his plea for the necessity of the internal organization of the Church by an appeal to every other organized community [2]. But with respect to the disposition of the four offices as well as to the manner in which he wanted to let the congregation share in the election of Church officers, he was exclusively guided by the structural law of the Church institution, as he found it described in the New Testament. This is the fundamental difference between CALVIN's view and that of the secularizing nominalistic trends in the period of the Renaissance.

Needless to say that authors like KAMPSCHULTE, MARCKS, DILTHEY, SOHM and THOMPSON have fundamentally misunderstood CALVIN's view by interpreting it as a theory of people's sovereignty, a political democracy and a modern system of representation [3]. This is perfectly clear from a study of the basic

---

[1] This peculiarity has been emphasized by HUNDESHAGEN (Zeitschr. f. Kirchenrecht, Bnd. 1, p. 455) and K. RIEKER, *Grundsätze reformierter Kirchenverfassung* (1899), p. 68.

[2] Cf. *Institutio religionis Chr.* IV, 11, 1: "Quemadmodum nulla urbs nullusve pagus sine magistratu et politia stare potest: sic ecclesia Dei... sua quadam spirituali politia indiget." In the same spirit JOHANNES À LASCO expresses himself in the first part of his *Forma ac ratio tota ecclesiastici ministerii* (ed. Kuyper II, p. 45).

[3] KAMPSCHULTE, *Joh. Calvin* I, p. 269/270: 'Das vornehmste Recht der kirchlichen Gewalt, die Excommunication, dürfen die Geistlichen nicht ausüben ohne Hinzuziehung der Vertreter der Gemeinde: noch viel weniger darf diese Strafe von einem Einzelnen verhängt werden. Es war nur consequent, dass die *Souveränität der Gemeinde* in der Ausübung

principles of CALVIN's conception of ecclesiastic organization explained in the fourth book of his *Institutio.*

§ 2 - THE TRANSCENDENTAL LIMITING CHARACTER OF THE INDIVIDUALITY STRUCTURE OF THE CHURCH INSTITUTION. THE CHURCH AS AN INSTRUMENTAL INSTITUTION OF REGENERATING GRACE, AND THE PROBLEM OF CHURCH AND SECT.

The radical type of the temporal Church institution.

Already in its radical type the internal structure of the Church institution assigns a unique and exceptional position to this community. There is no doubt that it has its qualifying function in the aspect of faith (*i.e.* it can only find its leading function in a temporal community of belief subject to the Divine revelational norms), and that it must display a typical historical foundation. But this merely radical typical qualification is not a sufficient definition of the essential *Christian* character of the Church institution [1]. Every differentiated religious community necessa-

---

dieses wichtigsten kirchlichen Rechtes auch in besonderer Weise äusserlich zum Ausdruck gelangte." [The clergy are not allowed to exercise the principal right of ecclesiastical authority, *viz.* excommunication, without consulting the representatives of the congregation. Still less may this punishment be inflicted by one single individual. It is only consistent that the *sovereignty of the congregation* should find special external expression in the exercise of this most important ecclesiastical right.] The view of this Roman Catholic writer that CALVIN seeks the sovereignty over the Church in the collective will of the Church members is shared by ERICH MARCKS, *Gaspard von Coligny* I, 1, p. 296 ff; also by DILTHEY in the essay *Die Glaubenslehren der Reformatoren* (Preuss. Jahrbücher, Bnd. LXXV, p. 79) and by SOHM, *Kirchenrecht* I, p. 649 Anm. and pp. 653 ff.; STAHL is also inclined to this view when he says that in CALVIN the general priesthood of the believers is the *constitutive* element of the church ordinance, in contrast with LUTHER's conception. RIEKER rightly contradicts this, *op. cit.*, p. 141.

R. E. THOMPSON, *A History of the Presbyterian Churches in the United States*, p. 286 and SOHM, *op. cit.*, pp. 653 ff. assert that in the presbyterial organization of the Church the elders are the representatives of the congregation, in the modern sense of the political representative system in the State. But RIEKER, *op. cit.*, pp. 141 ff. has conclusively refuted these views.

[1] This theoretical definition of the radical type of the institutional Church is not meant by us as an attempt to subsume this relationship under a higher logical genus as a pseudo-general-concept. In his *Enc. der H. Godgel.* III, p. 191 KUYPER makes some excellent remarks against such an attempt, which are entirely in agreement with our own conception. But

rily has it qualifying radical function in the modal law sphere of faith. But even the merely modal circumscription of this leading function suffices to show that the domain of the structures embraced by this radical type, occupies a unique position in temporal human society.

In the general theory of the modal law-spheres the function of faith has been proved to possess a transcendental limiting character. Even in its apostate closed condition, this function necessarily refers to a revelation of the divine Origin of the creation. And we have seen that even in its modal meaning-kernel it points to the central religious sphere of human existence, which transcends the temporal order. Therefore, every societal structure qualified by the modal aspect of belief must display this transcendental limiting character, which does not belong to any other type of organized community. It is true that other types of societal relationship also function in the second limiting aspect of the temporal order, but none of them is *qualified* by the function of faith. Also in the modal sphere of belief their own structural principle is maintained, and in this principle their typical leading function as such lacks the transcendental limiting character.

The individuality-structure of the *Church-type* is thus found within the radical type of historically founded societal structures with a pisteutic qualification. When we examine this Church-type, we at once understand why it is only possible as a temporal manifestation of the *ecclesia invisibilis.* Every attempt to approach the structure of the ecclesiastic institution theoretically has, therefore, to *start* from the Christian confession of the *una sancta ecclesia in Jesu Christo.* The transcendental *Christian* limiting character of this institution dominates its structure.

It is impossible to speak of a real *Church* if it lacks the temporal institutional (though defective) manifestation of the supra-temporal body of Christ [1].

---

that the temporal Church-institution must have a radical type founded in the temporal order of creation cannot be doubted from the Biblical standpoint. It is only the scholastic basic motive of nature and supra-natural grace which led to the denial of this truth.

[1] EMIL BRUNNER has an excellent remark on this point, *op. cit.,* p. 521: "Sie" (*i.e.* the institutional Church-community) "muss sich der Welt gegenüber wenigstens als Erscheinungsform der Kirche dokumentieren..." [The organized institution must at least document itself before the world as manifestation of the Church...].

A non-Christian State, a non-Christian marriage and family community, *etc.* may retain their original character as a State, a marriage and family community, *etc.*, although they do not manifest any Christian faith. A non-Christian Church, however, is a *contradictio in terminis*, as surely as a non-Christian Christian community of faith is self-contradictory. We do not mean a merely logical self-contradiction, but one that is precluded by the internal structural principle. The temporal Church institution may degenerate and fall a victim to all kinds of sin and error. But the structural principle of a Church makes it impossible for us any longer to recognize as a *Church* any so called "religious" [1] community that has really *completely fallen away from* the Divine Word-revelation in Christ. For this structural principle characterizes the temporal Church institution as a manifestation of the supra-temporal *corpus Christi*. If this internal vital law is set aside, the internal unifying bond of this institution cannot be realized. Then the term "Church", if it is maintained, does not correspond in any way to the inner nature of the community to which it is applied. A State, a family relationship, *etc.* remain within the boundaries of their structural principle, in spite of their subjective apostasy from the Christian root of life. But the individuality-structure of the temporal Church has a *transcendental limiting character* which does not allow of an apostate isolation from its Head, Jesus Christ.

According to its internal structural law, the Church institution is an institutional manifestation of the "*gratia particularis*".

The relation between "particular" and "common grace" reconsidered.

Again we are confronted with the problem concerning the relation between "particular grace" and "common grace".

In an earlier context we have defined this relation as follows: particular grace directly concerns the supra-temporal root of mankind, whereas common grace remains restricted to temporal life. But we stressed the Christo-centric standpoint that common grace has its root and centre only in Christ as the incarnate Word. We opposed any kind of dualistic theory of specific "*spheres of grace*", which is essentially nothing but an after effect of the dualistic basic motive of "nature" and "grace". But

---

[1] The term "religious" is here meant in the sense of "qualified by the modal function of faith".

now it might be asked: "If the Church, as a temporal organized community, is recognized as an institution of particular grace, do not we then run the risk of identifying this temporal institution with the supra-temporal "*corpus Christi*"? And on the other hand, is there not a risk of eradicating the difference between common grace and particular grace, if, in line with Dr. A. KUYPER, we make a sharp distinction between the "Church as an institution" and the non-institutional manifestations of the *corpus Christi* in temporal life, which KUYPER, in a really confusing terminological way, styled "the Church as an organism"? [1]

These questions are of a fundamental character and may not be considered as merely theological problems. For the Biblical basic motive of Christian philosophy is at issue here. The terms "special" and "common" grace have been introduced into Reformed theology. But this terminology is a little scholastic and must lead us astray as soon as it is interpreted in the sense of the scholastic basic motive of nature and grace, which has retained a great influence in protestant theology. It may easily induce us to think of "*gratia specialis*" as concerned with a "special supra-natural sphere" of an inner spiritual life of grace, and of "*gratia communis*" as embracing the "general sphere" of "natural human life" *qua talis*. But such a view would contradict the radical and integral meaning of the Biblical basic motive of creation, fall into sin, and redemption.

"*Gratia specialis*" or "*gratia particularis*" really refer to the radical change brought about by Christ Jesus in the apostate root of the whole temporal cosmos, which is concentrated in mankind; therefore this "particular" grace bears a *radical-universal* character. Already in the *present* dispensation this radical change of direction in the root of life must necessarily reveal itself in temporal reality, in its conserving effect as well as in its regenerative operation. Its conserving effect is primarily manifest in the preservation of the temporal world-order by God in Christ Jesus, as the Head of the Covenant [2], so that the disintegrating effect of the fall into sin in temporal life is checked.

God does not renounce His creation, not even in its subjective apostasy. He maintains the temporal structures, which cannot find their creaturely root, their religious centre, in the spirit of

[1] Cf. A. KUYPER, *Enc. der H. Godgeleerdheid* (2e druk 1909) III, p. 204.

[2] Christ is the Head of the Covenant also before the Incarnation, *viz.* as the promised Mediator.

darkness, the spirit of apostasy [1]. It is true that the temporal world-order with all its diversity of structures belongs as such only to the law-side of creation, and is related to the central commandment of love as its religious radical unity. But this divine order both in its temporal diversity and radical religious unity would be meaningless if it were not *realized.* Therefore it necessarily refers to Jesus Christ, who has come to fulfil it in its religious fulness of meaning. In the full Scriptural sense of the word Christ Jesus is the "second Adam", in Whom nothing of God's creation can be lost. Only in Him all the nations of the earth are blessed according to the testimony of the Scriptures. Only in Him is God willing to have mercy on his fallen creation, and only in Him can the conserving effect of common grace have its creaturely root. Outside of Him there is no Divine grace, no "common grace" either, but only the manifestation of God's wrath on account of sin. This conserving common grace also embraces the apostate, dead members of mankind for the sake of the full and true human race, included in the "*corpus Christi*", in the "*ecclesia invisibilis*" [2].

"Special grace", which we had better call "*renewing*" or "*regenerating grace*", only embraces the "*ecclesia invisibilis*", *i.e.* reborn mankind. This renewing of meaning of God's creation in Christ, cannot remain hidden *in time,* but necessarily reveals itself as the root of the temporal conserving grace as well. The temporal manifestation of the "*ecclesia invisibilis*" pervades temporal society in all its structures. It is found wherever the Christian attitude to life expresses itself in a temporal form. Thus the deeper unity between conserving and regenerating grace finds expression in every sphere of human society, insofar as it reveals the influence of the Christian spirit, and not merely in the Church institution. This is what Dr. KUYPER meant by his view of the "Church as an organism", in which he clearly and fundamentally opposed the dualistic separation between "special" and "common grace". The term "Church as an organism" had better be replaced by the expression "temporal manifesta-

---

[1] Therefore, it is not sufficient to relate "common grace" only to the Triune God as its Origin. For then the question about the creaturely religious *centre* of this grace remains unanswered.

[2] Cf. Jesus' parable of the tares and the wheat which must grow up together till Judgment Day, that the wheat may not be pulled out together with the tares.

tion of the body of Christ in all societal relationships", but *in this broad sense it also embraces the temporal institution.*

It is evident that the "*ecclesia visibilis*" in this universal sense cannot be identical with the temporal Church institution. This institution remains bound to its specific structural principle and could only make its appearance after Christ's coming into the flesh. The temporal revelation of the "*corpus Christi*", in its broadest sense, on the other hand, embraces all the societal structures of our temporal human existence, and made its entry into the world at the first manifestation of the antithesis between the *civitas Dei* and the *civitas terrena.*

The temporal Church institution as the instrument of renewing or regenerating grace.

We shall now try to answer the question how we can recognize the temporal Church institution as the institution of "*gratia regenerativa*" without identifying it with the supra-temporal body of Christ. The institutional Church, as a temporal organization, has been instituted by Christ within the modal and radical typical structures of temporal reality given already at the creation [1].

By conserving temporal grace (the so called "common grace"), these structures are preserved from the disintegrating operation of sin. But unlike the State, the institutional Church is not a special institution of conserving grace, because by virtue of its leading function, as the institutional community of believers in Christ, it has not been ordained to embrace believers and unbelievers alike in one temporal community. Naturally, every institutional Church community can have many members who only formally belong to it and do not belong to the *ecclesia invisibilis.* It is beyond human power to establish which of the members of a Church are really Christians and which are so only in name. Nevertheless, as to its inner nature the Church institution embraces only those who have been included in the New Testament Covenant by baptism and (when they are adults) by their confession of faith. And in comparison with the other temporal societal relationships revealing the *ecclesia invisibilis,* the institutional Church insofar occupies an exceptional position as it is *qualified* as a *Christian community of faith.*

---

[1] Cf. also Dr. KUYPER's excellent exposition in his *Enc. der H. Godgel.* III, p. 211.

In this sense the Church institution is really a particular institution of renewing or regenerating grace. The offices and functions instituted in this Church are typically qualified according to their internal structure as instruments of the working of the Word of God and that of the sacraments in the community of the Christian believers. But regenerating grace also reveals itself in the institutional Church *as the true root of temporal conserving common grace.* For in this *institution* the structure of the function of faith, implanted in the human race already at the creation, is again opened to the Divine Word-revelation in Christ Jesus, disclosing the true meaning of the belief-aspect. as the second terminal aspect of human experience. This function of faith belongs to temporal human existence as such, and its structure remains intact through conserving grace, notwithstanding apostasy.

The institutional Church-type and the sect-type. TROELTSCH's view of both.

Meanwhile, the very fact that the Church institution can only exist as a temporal community of Christian believers raises a new fundamental problem.

This problem may be formulated as that of the relation between a Church and a sect. Already at an early date this problem disturbed the Christian Church in its institutional manifestation. In the modern "*religions-soziologische*" studies of MAX WEBER [1] and ERNST TROELTSCH [2] this question has again been discussed from a viewpoint which was supposed to be dogmatically unprejudiced. TROELTSCH explicitly declares that his theoretical inquiry into the structure of churches and sects is oriented to the "formal tendency" in sociology introduced by SIMMEL [3].

WEBER's special standpoint and his own methodology cannot be discussed here in more detail since it would demand an ample critical treatise. In the present context I shall restrict myself to TROELTSCH's view of the relation between church- and sect-types, as it is explained in his book *Die Soziallehren der Christlichen Kirchen und Gruppen.* Here he calls Church and sect two independent sociological types, implied in what he styles the "reli-

---

[1] Cf. especially MAX WEBER's treatise: *Kirchen und Sekten in Nord-Amerika* (Christl. Welt, 1906, pp. 558 ff. and 577 ff.), which had a great influence on TROELTSCH's view.

[2] *Die Sociallehren der Chr. Kirchen und Gruppen* (1919), pp. 358 ff.

[3] *Op. cit.,* p. 364 note 164.

gious sociological basic scheme of Christianity", with its radical tension between individualism and universalism. In this way the "sect" loses all trace of being inferior to the Church and becomes a sociological type perfectly equivalent to the church type. Important moments of the oldest stage of Christianity, pushed in the background within the church-type, find renewed expression in the sect-type, albeit in a one-sided way.

As an organized community the Church is a supra-individual institution (*"Anstalt"),* an organized permanent institution of saving grace. One becomes a member of this community at birth, and is immediately included in its "*Wunderkreis*" (supra-natural circle) at baptism. The official organization remains the bearer of the treasure of grace, independently of accidental personal unworthiness on the part of the office-bearers. These institutional traits make it possible to compromise with the existing "worldly ordinances"; for notwithstanding all the faults and defects of the persons, the sacred character and the divine nature of the institution remain unaltered. Through its inherent miracle-working power the Church will conquer the world according to the divine promise.

The Roman Catholic hierarchical institution is the purest embodiment of this type, which naturally implies the universalistic ideal to subject all existing secular temporal societal relationships to its own authority. These relationships are incorporated into the Church as a lower, previous stage of the Christian community of grace.

But now it is necessary to relativize the absolute evangelical standards. For this purpose the latter are combined with the Stoic and Aristotelian conceptions of the *lex naturalis.* So TROELTSCH's theoretical church-type is the incarnation of the universalistic synthesis between the "supra-natural Christian religion of grace" and the "natural" societal order. Such a compromise can only be philosophically justified by means of a synthesis-philosophy like that of THOMAS AQUINAS. Sociologically the church-type in some form or other always aims at an "ecclesiastical-civil organization of human society, and at an "ecclesiastical cultural unity". In this culture the institutional Church takes charge of the whole of "natural" society, both in its political and non-political structures. This sociological type is considered to be the necessary consequence of the universalistic factor in the sociological basic scheme of Christianity, which aims at conquering and renewing the world.

The sect-type explicitly relinquishes the idea of the Church as an institution of saving grace independent of the personal qualities of its officers; consequently it also abandons the universalistic social ideal of world government by the spiritual authority of a hierarchically organized clergy.

A sect prefers a voluntary community to an institution, because it is a condition of a real communion of believers that the latter join deliberately of their own free will. Such is compatible only with an associational form of organization. This implies that everything depends on the personal dignity of the cooperating individuals. The sect community does not incorporate any one at his birth but exclusively on account of his personal conversion. This community is not Christian or sacred because of the objective guarantee of an institution, with its sacraments of grace, but because of the personal Christian attitude of life of the individual members. Consequently the sect-type can only form small groups. Such a small community wants to derive its social ideal exclusively and purely from the Gospel and Christ's commandment of love, without stooping to any compromise with existing secular ordinances. Those secular societal ordinances that are incompatible with the evangelical societal ideal are not recognized, but either avoided in Christian patience, or openly opposed in an enthusiastic eschatological attack, launched to replace them by a purely Christian order [1].

TROELTSCH considers this sect-type as the sociological consequence of the second or individualistic factor in the religious sociological basic scheme of Christianity.

One aspect of Jesus' teaching is this radical individualism which emphasizes the eternal and infinite value of the individual personality as a child of God.

All differences in social position lose their meaning in comparison with this value of the individual person, who has direct communion with God without the intermediary of any institution.

Critique of TROELTSCH' conception of the church- and sect-types.

TROELTSCH' conception of the relation between the church- and sect-types briefly summarized above stands and falls with his

---

[1] *Die Soziallehren der Chr. Kirchen und Gruppen* (1919), p. 362, 372 ff; pp. 427 ff.

view concerning the "religious sociological basic schema of Christianity", which itself is dependent on the starting-point of his "*Religionssoziologie*". The latter is rooted in the historicistic immanence standpoint, according to which theoretic thought has to view the Christian religion, and all the temporal manifestations of the "*corpus Christi*" in societal life, merely as historical sociological phenomena. Their subjective meaning-content has to be approached according to a supposedly dogmatically unbiassed scientific method [1]. This method uses such "formal sociological ideal types" as "church" and "sect", which are mere subjective schemes of thought and have not been based on the internal individuality-structures of the communities concerned. These schemes are supposed to be deducible from the subjective historical phenomena, whose rational tendencies are purposely overstrained and idealized in order to understand their subjective meaning-content "*zweck- und wertrational*" [2].

Thus the inner nature of the temporal Church-institution is replaced by a schematic subjective "ideal type". Such a type is thought to be derivable from a particular moment of the "religious-sociological basic scheme" of the historical phenomenon "Christianity", and its rational subjective effects in historical development.. The "ideal type" is then imposed on the phenomena as *the* church-type and used to interpret all real church-formations as historically determined nuances of one and the same basic sociological schema.

It stands to reason that in such a scientific attitude a truly normative structural idea of the institutional Church, ruled by the Biblical basic motive itself, cannot play any rôle. Instead, the kingdom of Jesus Christ in the hearts of men is interpreted in the sense of a universalistic sociological conception of the temporal Church-institution, inspired by the dialectical scholastic basic motive of nature and supra-natural grace.

In this way TROELTSCH' ideal type church is completely oriented to the medieval Roman Catholic view of the Holy Roman Empire under the papal supremacy. The primordial question as to whether this conception of the ecclesiastic institution is compatible with the Biblical meaning of the religious kingdom of Christ is not seriously taken into consideration. Nor is the

---

[1] Cf. also E. BRUNNER's criticism in *Das Gebot und die Ordnungen*, p. 673/4.

[2] According to the rational consequences of their purpose and value.

fundamental question raised as to whether the structural principles of the temporal societal order really contradict the central commandment of love, so that from the evangelical point of view they can only be accepted by means of a compromise, philosophically justified by the Thomistic system.

The result is that TROELTSCH's church-type is nothing but a scientifically untenable generalization of a typical Roman Catholic social form in which the structural principle of the institutional Church has been realized. It is impossible that such an ideal type can do justice to the different Church-formations issued from the Reformation, let alone that it should be able to account for all facets of the modern Roman Catholic view of the Church. Rather it prevents the investigator from gaining an insight into the inner nature of the Church-institution *as such*, guaranteed by its normative structural principle.

And without this insight the different social forms in which this structure has been realized cannot be related to one and the same structural type.

TROELTSCH starts with assuming a polar tension in the "religious basic idea" of the Gospel between religious individualism and religious universalism. He has wrenched the Gospel from its context in the whole of the Divine Word-revelation [1]. Consequently the relation between the Christian religion and the temporal-worldly ordinances must be described in terms of a dilemma, *viz.* that of ascetic avoidance, versus a compromise and synthesis with an inferior "nature". The "church-type" must necessarily have "universalistic tendencies", and strive after "ecclesiastical unity of culture", under the leadership of the institution of grace. The idea of a "free Church" must necessarily belong to the sectarian type. Even such an eminent scholar as ERNST TROELTSCH could not help going astray, when he tried to interpret the phenomena of Church and sect from these *a priori* basic tenets.

He forced CALVIN's conception of the Church into his own scheme of "church- and sect-type", but gave a fundamentally wrong interpretation of the Reformer's views. This has been convincingly proved by Dr SEVERIJN in his essay: *Ernst Troeltsch over de Betekenis van het Calvinisme voor de Cultuurgeschiede-*

---

[1] Cf. Dr A. KUYPER, *Enc. d. H. Godgel.* III, p. 186 — against isolating the "doctrine of Jesus".

nis.[1] and in a broader context bij BOHATEC in his great work *Calvin's Lehre vom Staat und Kirche* (Breslau 1937).

We have shown in the first section of this chapter that the universalistic conception of the institutional Church is to be considered as an apostasy from the Biblical Christian standpoint. In its classical form it embodied the medieval synthesis with the pagan Greek view of the "perfect society". If we are called upon to interpret the social facts, we are *forced* to a religious commitment with respect to this fundamental point. There is no possibility here of a truly scientific neutrality because it is not possible to conceive the temporal Church institution apart from the true religious sense of the Kingdom of Christ. TROELTSCH, too, could not help committing himself to a religious standpoint. In fact he approached the structure of the Church from a Humanistic religious point of view, with its dilemma: the motive of domination or that of personal freedom.

TROELTSCH's church- and sect-types are both in conflict with the Christian transcendence-standpoint, on which a sect cannot be equal to the Church institution.

Church- and sect-types, as conceived by TROELTSCH, are both in conflict with the Christian transcendence-standpoint. The sect-type is of an individualistic-nominalistic origin and serves to construe the temporal Church-community from the "converted individuals". Insofar as its starts from the dialectical basic motive of nature and grace, it holds to the dualistic nominalist conception of the latter. Therefore *it cannot be equivalent to the idea of the institutional Church* when viewed from the Biblical standpoint. But we must immediately admit without any reserve that the rise of sects is often an indication of a process of decay in the Church institution[2].

As soon as the temporal Church-community is based on the personal qualities of converted individuals, it ceases to be a *Church*. According to the Biblical view of the latter the foundation *of our salvation is solely to be sought in Christ Jesus* and not in ourselves. *He* is the firm ground on Whom the temporal Church relationship is built. Apart from the fact that it is beyond

[1] Cf. *Antirevol. Staatk.* (driem. org., 1e jrg., 1927) pp. 1—72.

[2] Dr A. KUYPER in his "*Tractaat van de Reformatie der Kerken*" (1884) p.110, says: "Sects nearly always arise through the fault of the Church..." The same view is found in E. BRUNNER, *op. cit.*, p. 527.

human power to judge the hearts of our fellow men, the qualities of the individual Christians are a treacherous kind of quicksand for a church-formation. This is why the concept "association" does not suit the institutional Church. The true Christian Church, in its institutional manifestation, is not built by men. Christ builds His Church by His Word and His Spirit, and not out of "converted individuals" but in the line of the Covenant. The Church members are members of one body sanctified in Christ alone [1].

If we believe Christ is to rule the temporal Church-institution, we must acknowledge that He alone is the judge of the regeneration of the individual members. Such judgment cannot be entrusted to men. Any attempt to base the temporal Church community on personal regeneration is an act of interference with the authority of the King of the Church, a fundamentally revolutionary thought, inverting the relation between the *ecclesia visibilis* and the *ecclesia invisibilis*.

The temporal Church community can only be an *instrument* of the Divine grace in Christ Jesus through the administration of the Divine Word and the sacraments. In virtue of its internal structural law this community must have an institutional character, which should express itself in the form of its organization [2]. The institutional administration of the Word and the sacraments is the constitutive centre of the Church-institution, in its corporative structure as a temporal *congregatio fidelium*. But this corporative structure should be conceived in accordance with the norm of faith, *i.e.* the divine Word-revelation. This "*congregatio*" is an outcome of the divine Covenant and not an assembly of mere individual believers. The Covenant embraces the believers with their children [3], although the latter may later on prove to be unbelievers who do not wish to belong to the *ecclesia visibilis* in its institutional sense. If we break with the thought of the Covenant in the temporal organization of the Church, we open the door to the individualistic sect-type.

---

[1] Cf. *Matth.* 13 : 18, 19.

[2] Cf. CALVIN, *Inst.* IV, 8, 2: "id dotum non proprie hominibus ipsis, sed ministerio, cui praefecti sunt, dari; vel (ut expeditius loquamur) verbo cuius ministerium illis est commissum." [This authority has not been given these men themselves but to the office of which they are the bearers; or (to say it more clearly) it has been given to the Word whose ministry has been entrusted to them.]

[3] Cf. *Gen.* 17 : 7; *Matth.* 19 : 14; *Luc.* 22 : 11; *Acts* 2 : 39; and 10 : 47; *Col.* 2 : 11, 12, 13 and other passages of Scripture.

The sect considers the visible Church, in the sense of *congregatio fidelium*, as a group of converted individuals and thereby misinterprets the divine structural law of the institutional Church[1]. Although this institution cannot be built on the personal regeneration of its members, it remains qualified as a Christian faith-community in the organized administration of the Word and the sacraments, and as such it is necessarily an institutional manifestation of the *ecclesia invisibilis electorum*[2]. The spiritually dead members are not really included in the invisible Church, although outwardly they behave like believers. They cannot be outwardly distinguished from the true believers by us, but they are left to the judgment of the King of the Church.

TROELTSCH says that these facts prove the unavoidable compromise embodied in the Church as an institution. But in the sect-type we find in fact the same state of affairs, which is based on man's absolute incompetence to judge the heart of his fellow-men[3]. The subjective intention to build the Church community from regenerated individuals alone cannot alter this fact.

Does the temporal Church-institution have a higher value than the other societal structures?

Our remarks on the only possible guarantee of the Christian character of the temporal Church-institution holds indeed for the whole of the *ecclesia visibilis*, within its institutional manifestation as well as outside of the latter.

This guarantee can nowhere be found in "converted individuals" but only in the authority and power of the Word of God in the different spheres of life, each according to its own structure. This raises the question whether from the religious point of view the special institution of regenerating grace is superior to all the other societal relationships. The answer must be negative, for it should always be remembered that the *ecclesia visibilis* is not limited to the institutional Church, but in principle

---

[1] Cf. CALVIN, *Instit.* IV, c. 1, §§ 13, 14, 18, 19, 24.

[2] CALVIN, *op. cit.*, expecially stresses St. Paul's attitude to the Corinthian Church into which so many horrible sins had crept. The apostle keeps recognizing this congregation as a Church.

[3] In this connection E. BRUNNER (*op. cit.*, p. 527) makes a striking remark: 'In der Regel aber wird in der zweiten oder dritten Generation die Sekte sich innerlich mehr und mehr der Kirche' (*i.e.* as an institution) 'annähern...'. [As a rule the sect will internally approach the Church-institution more and more in the second or the third generation...].

embraces all the structures of human society. The only Christian starting-point remains the supra-temporal "*ecclesia invisibilis*". In this religious radical community in Christ all temporal societal structures are equivalent to one another, just as all the different law-spheres are irreplaceable refractions of the fulness of meaning in Christ, each in its own modal structure.

Naturally, this does not mean that from the viewpoint of temporal life all societal structures are of the same importance. It is quite evident that in this respect the institutional structures are much more fundamental than the structures of free associations. But an axiological arrangement of the structures of human society assigning the "highest religious value" to the Church-institution takes its origin in a universalistic scholastic view of the temporal societal relationships and is incompatible with the Christian transcendence-standpoint. Insofar as the other societal relationships, in their actual reality, are *subjectively* withdrawn from the "*Corpus Christi*", they fall outside of the "*ecclesia visibilis*". Only in this respect do they remain enclosed within the *civitas terrena, viz.* in a *subjective sense.* But the conserving grace in Christ preserves and maintains the structural offices of the institutional organizations and communities, and liberates them, at least in principle, from the *civitas terrena.* And the typical structures of the inter-individual and the non-institutional communal relationships can no more belong to the *civitas terrena* than those of the institutional communities. The relation between the *civitas Dei* and the *civitas terrena* cannot be conceived as an "*axiological hierarchy*", but only as an irreconcilable antithesis.

Consequently, the radically Christian idea of societal relationship can only consider the temporal societal structures as equal in rank *in their common root*: the *ecclesia invisibilis.* But at the same time we must recognize the fundamental internal diversity in these structures and their mutual irreplaceableness in their own *temporal* value. And this implies the acknowledgment of the completely exceptional position of the institutional Church, as a particular institute of regenerating grace.

In perfect agreement with this view both CALVIN and KUYPER laid full emphasis on the thought that in its institutional manifestation the Church is the *mother* of our faith in Christ Jesus [1].

---

[1] CALVIN, *Instit.* IV, 1, 1. KUYPER, *Encycl. d. H. Godgel.* III, 193; *Tractaat,* p. 178.

In truth: The light of eternity will always glow in the sanctuary of this particular Christian community.

§ 3 - A FURTHER INQUIRY INTO THE STRUCTURAL PRINCIPLE OF THE CHURCH-INSTITUTION IN ITS TWO RADICAL FUNCTIONS.

In the preceding section it appeared that the institutional Church, though only possible as a temporal manifestation of the *ecclesia invisibilis,* is nevertheless integrated into the temporal world-order, as a societal relationship with an individuality structure of its own. There could be no doubt about the two radical functions of this structure. The typical leading function has been found in the sphere of faith and the typical foundational function lies in the historical law-sphere. All historically founded communities possess a typical organization which can only be understood from their structural principle. We will thus try to gain a more detailed insight into the structural principle of the Church-institution to acquire from this a deeper insight into its typical form of organization.

The typical foundational function of the temporal Church institution.

According to its institutional manifestation the Church is founded in an organization of historical power. This statement only determines the typical foundational function in a *modal* sense. We can say the same thing about the State and the undifferentiated societal relationships. And yet the concept "organization of historical power" is not a multivocal "general concept", because in its theoretically analysed *modal* sense it is perfectly defined.

We must, however, give an account of the individuality-type of this organization of power. Then it appears that the Church and the State display a *radical* difference because each of these two societal structures possesses an absolutely different radical type. The foundational function of the State has been described as the monopolistic organization of military power over a territorially limited cultural area. We have shown that the State's organization of historical power can only be grasped as an *opened meaning-structure,* anticipating the typical leading function of the body politic as a public juridical coercive community. Nevertheless, this qualifying function itself appeared to offer to theoretical thought at least a *provisional resting-point* since the juridical aspect in which it presents itself lacks as such the transcendental limiting character inherent in the faith aspect.

However, the organization of historical power on which the Church-institution is based, directly expresses the *transcendental limiting character* of this societal relationship. This character does not even offer a provisional resting-point to thought but directly points beyond time to the transcendent root of the *ecclesia visibilis, i.e.* to Christ's Kingdom in the hearts of men. The whole temporal Church-institution is founded in the historical power of Christ as the incarnate Word. It is the historical power of "the sword of the Divine Word" which by faith is directly grasped as the revelation of Christ's transcendent fulness of power, of His kingship over the whole world. Christ himself gave this historical power its first provisional organization in the institution of the apostolic office and the sacraments: 'Go ye therefore, and teach all nations, baptizing them in the name of the Father, and of the Son and of the Holy Ghost'. By his Word through the mouth of his apostles He has ordained the basic structure of the institutional Church-organization.

According to its transcendental limiting character, the ecclesiastical organization of power does not allow of *territorial* boundaries like that of the State. Its historical task, revealed by Christ himself, is to gain the spiritual dominion over all nations and peoples. As will appear later on, this does not exclude the formation of *local* churches. But through its limiting position between time and eternity the Church's historical world-dominion is radically distinguished from any other meta-historically qualified organization of power. Its sole qualification is the unshakeable power of Christ's Word and Spirit.

In its non-institutional manifestations the *ecclesia visibilis* also has real historical *faith-power*, operating in all societal structures, and in each of them according to their specific nature. This power of faith reveals renewing grace hidden in the "*ecclesia invisibilis*", as the true root of conserving grace. But it is only the institutional organization which enables this historical power to be the typical foundational function of the temporal Church-community, as a societal structure with a character of its own. In this organizational form the institutional ecclesiastical power, as the typical foundation of a real communal whole functioning in all the law-spheres, possesses a certain all-sidedness, just like the State's power organization. Other forms of power are united in it, *e.g.* economic, juridical, moral power, *etc.* But the power of Christian faith is the typical internally qualifying form of organized power of the Church according to the ecclesiastical structural principle. The organization at once reveals the imperfect human factor of this institution as a temporal instrument for the effects of the power of Christ's Word and Spirit. According to its structural principle, the institutional Church is a typical temporal societal relationship whose internal organization can only be actualized by sinful human action.

The institutional offices are holy, and the Word and the sacraments, administered by the office bearers as instruments, are holy. But the Christians who hold these offices are sinful human beings, who are only sanctified in the hidden *ecclesia invisibilis* in Christ Jesus.

According to CALVIN's view, which has broken with the Lutheran dualism between faith-community and organization, the basic rules of the internal Church organization have been ordained in God's Word-revelation. All the communicant members have been invested with the general office (*διακονία*) to cooperate in the work of formation and reformation of the Church-institution, in the election of the special office-bearers, *etc.* By the side of this general office Christ has ordained the special offices of the administration of the Word and the sacraments, of eldership and diaconate. The Church-institution can only function according to its Biblical structure when there is active cooperation between the general office of the believers and the special institutional offices within the congregation. Thus the internal historical power of the institutional Church becomes an institutionally organized power *qualified* by the Christian community of faith. As such this power is entirely derived from Christ, as the true and the only King of the Church [1]. In this organization of faith-power the institutional and the corporative factors have been harmoniously combined, but the power of the institutional administration of the Word and the sacraments is the centre of ecclesiastic organization. In these characteristic traits of its typical organization the structure of the Church-institution re-

---

[1] Therefore, the undefined general concept "order" *(Ordnung)* employed by BRUNNER, *op. cit.*, pp. 517 ff. to approach the internal organization of the congregation is wholly inadequate and unserviceable. Cf. pp. 406 ff. in the present volume.

veals its uniqueness, which can only be understood from its Biblical basic principle [1].

As soon as alien political elements are introduced into this internal organization of power, the institution will be denatured and its sovereignty within its own sphere affected. Such deformations are only *possible within the normative basic structure of the organized Church.* The organization of power in which this institution is founded, is incompatible with political dominion resting on the power of the sword, and also with the vassalage of the secular sword.

The typical historical foundation of the institutional *ecclesia visibilis* explains why it is not *of all times.* Its structural principle is indeed constant and based on the temporal world-order, but as an *actual formation* the Church-institution could only appear after Christ's incarnation, death and resurrection. In the Old Testament there was a people of the Covenant, isolated from the other nations. In this people of the Covenant, kingship, priesthood and the prophet's office were sharply distinguished from each other and foreshadowed Christ's kingship, priesthood and prophetic office. There was already an "*ecclesia visibilis*" as the temporal manifestation of the "*ecclesia invisibilis electorum*", but there was no *institutional Church* as a typical societal institution of regenerating grace in the community of Christian faith [2].

The leading function of the temporal Church-institution. Community of confession is required by the structural principle. The idea of a national Church (above any division of faith) and the confessional Church.

The internal organization of the ecclesiastical institution in its transcendental limiting character is qualified by its leading function as *an institutionally organized community of Christian believers in the administration of the Word and the sacraments.* According to this structural principle its internal unity is exclusi-

---

[1] But it can never be understood apart from the transcendent root of the Church. Therefore TILLICH's view in his *Kirche und Kultur,* and DIBELIUS' conception in his *Das Jahrhundert der Kirche,* are fundamentally wrong. They hold that the Church, as a "sociologically approachable" societal relationship can be explained by means of *general* sociological concepts. Cf. E. BRUNNER, *Das Gebot und die Ordnungen,* p. 517.

[2] Cf. Dr A. KUYPER, *Tractaat van de Reformatie der Kerken* (1884), p. 11/12.

vely possible in a real community of confession. Therefore the institutional Church can only be a *confessional* Church. The idea of a national Church uniting the whole nation, irrespective of fundamental differences in confession, into one and the same ecclesiastical institution, is only a *deformation*, or even a *disintegrating* thought [1].

This is not a matter of an entirely subjective insight on the part of particular "sectarian ecclesiastical groups", but it concerns the essential character of the institutional *ecclesia visibilis*. It is the internal structural principle of the institutional Church itself which does not allow of any other bond of unity than that from within, and not from a *political* organization *alien* to its true nature. The institutional faith-community in the Church-institution is radically different from a political community of faith like that of a Christian State. In such a State the whole nation, insofar as it displays a Christian basic character, should reveal its political unity also in a general political bond of Christian belief, in spite of the differences in confessions of the various Churches [2].

The internal unity of the Church-institution is qualified by the bond of faith and not by a public-legal function. The community of faith in it cannot be truly realized without the unity of confession about the Word and the sacraments. For the internal institutional Church-community is only possible in the administration of the Word and the sacraments.

Among the drawbacks of a *confessional* Church E. BRUNNER [3] mentions the danger of its becoming a "sect" through misunderstanding the central teaching of the Gospel, *viz.* justification by faith alone. The *national* Church may show other serious disadvantages, but by recognizing infant baptism as the basis of Church membership it has the advantage of influencing the nation as a whole, especially youth. But this pronouncement shows the writer's lack of insight into the true nature of a confessional Church. We have seen in an earlier context that a true

[1] Cf. A. KUYPER, *Enc. d. H. Godgel.* III, p. 191 and *Tractaat van de Reformatie der Kerken*, p. 12.

[2] A national Church which denies any binding force to its confessional documents, need not be an established Church; but it seeks its temporal universality in the ecclesiastical union of the nation, as such, without considering that a Church can only maintain its real *Church*-character as a Christian community of *faith*.

[3] *Das Gebot and die Ordnungen*, p. 535/6.

confessional Church is distinguished from the sect-type precisely by recognizing infant-baptism, and accepting the children of the believers as baptismal members. This acceptance is based on the idea of the *Covenant*. BRUNNER overlooks that infant-baptism must lose any meaning as an institutional sacrament, if it is detached from the confession of the Church as a community of Christian faith. Then baptism is degraded into a cultic ceremony about which everybody is free to confess what he likes.

By virtue of the internal structural law of the Church-institution, fundamentally different confessional tendencies will assert themselves within the "national Church" making the essential internal ecclesiastical unity illusory[1]. A confessional Church does not imply a mechanical uniformity in the conception of the confession. It should leave room for differences insofar as they do not affect the fundamentals of the Church doctrine. As to the latter, however, a unity of conception is indispensible, provided that this conception is always subject to the spiritual moving power of the divine Word and does not interpret the Holy Scripture from an unbiblical basic motive. BRUNNER's standpoint with regard to a confessional Church is dependent on his misconception of the essential relation between the internal Church organization and the character of the institution as a temporal Christian community of faith ruled by the living Word of God[2]. We shall return to this point presently. The confession postulated by the internal structural principle of the institutional Church is the confession of a community giving the norm of faith for the congregation a *positive form*. Like every positivization this confession is the *work of man*, and can have no other authority than that founded in the divine Word by which it should always be tested. For this very reason the Church confession should not be

---

[1] The question about political parties in the State is a quite different matter, because these parties have another structural principle than the body politic, as will be shown in a later context.

[2] Cf. *op. cit.*, p. 536: 'The way in which the Church has been organized is not decisive. There is only one thing decisive: the living Word of God'. ["Wie die Kirche organisiert ist, kann nie etwas Entscheidendes sein. Entscheidend in ihr ist nur eins: das lebendige Wort Gottes".] Compare with this KUYPER's sober-minded pronouncement in his *Tractaat van de Reformatie der Kerken*, p. 110: 'You will not save your Church by means of a good Church government if the Spirit of God leaves it; but if your Church government is bad, you cannot prevent your Church from deteriorating, even if you could equip your Church government with a strictly orthodox personnel'.

rigid and static. It requires actual adaptation to the historical development of pisteutical insight into the Word-revelation, under the guidance of the Holy Spirit, and to the development of the way of expressing the essential contents of Christian belief.

The Church confession should not degenerate into theological dogmatics. According to its internal structure it should never be elevated to an infallible authoritative document stifling the Christian freedom of believers [1].

Fundamental differences in confession such as those between Roman Catholics, Lutherans, the Reformed Churches, *etc.* which occasioned different church organizations *opposing one another more or less sharply,* are to be *deplored* as a *disruption* of the institutional *ecclesia visibilis.* To my mind they are to a high degree caused by the influence of the dialectical motive of nature and grace. This regrettable state of things should urge all true Christians to confess their guilt and to repent, because every guilt of the Church is our own guilt. An appeal to the "pluriformity" of the Church cannot heal this deep wound. This pluriformity has doubtless a good sense, but it should not be misinterpreted to mask the fundamental raggedness of the ecclesiastical institution, or to justify fundamental deviations from the integral and radical basic motive of the divine Word-revelation. But every human endeavour to arrive at ecclesiastical unity by obscuring the real basic differences in confession, is in conflict with the inner nature of the institutional Church [2].

---

[1] Compare also what CALVIN remarks in his *Instit.* IV, 1, 12. The confusion between a confession of faith and a theological dogmatics disregards the inner nature of the Church community and must lead to a deformation of the latter. The ecclesiastic confession is no theology, and the ecclesiastical institute has no authority in theoretical theological questions.

[2] E. BRUNNER also recognizes this, *op. cit.*, p. 529. But he goes further, and lapses into relativism with regard to the Church institution. He even unexpectedly eradicates the boundaries between the institutional Church, the sect and the non-institutional manifestations of the Church, which he formerly took into account. He writes: 'also the Quakers and even the individualists who purposely reject any ecclesiastic community have some truth of the Gospel lacking in any of the present-day institutional Churches. Christ's inheritance is divided, who shall investigate who has retained or acquired the biggest part!' ["dass auch die Quäker und selbst die bewusst unkirchlichen Einzelgänger Wahrheit des Evangeliums für sich haben, die jeder der heutigen "verfassten" Kirchen fehlt. Die Erbe Christi ist zerteilt, wer will untersuchen, wer das grösste Stück behalten oder bekommen hat!"] This procouncement can no longer be understood

A quite different question is whether it is not an urgent necessity that the divided Churches seek for an ecumenical basis for cooperation where this is possible. In the face of the increasing dechristianization and spiritual uprooting of modern mankind this necessity is so evident that any further argument is superfluous. The only reserve to be made is that the ecumenical cooperation should be aware of the inner boundaries of the ecclesiastical task and that its starting point should be the pure basic motive of Holy Scripture. For apart from this latter every possibility of an ecumenical basis of cooperation between the Churches is illusory because of the inner nature of the Church-institution.

§ 4 - THE EXPRESSION OF THE STRUCTURAL PRINCIPLE OF THE TEMPORAL INSTITUTIONAL CHURCH IN THE INTERNAL AUTHORITATIVE ORGANIZATION OF ITS OFFICES AND IN ITS DIFFERENT MODAL ASPECTS.

After our detailed structural analysis of the other institutional communities it is not necessary to investigate the expression of the structural principle of the Church in *all* its modal aspects. We shall make a suitable selection and start with an inquiry into the typical structure of authority in the ecclesiastical institution, which radically differs from that in other organized communities.

The typical structure of authority in the temporal Church-institution.

The structure of ecclesiastical authority cannot be restricted to the aspect of faith, but it is doubtless *qualified* by the latter. And so it shows the transcendental limiting character peculiar to the structural principle of the institutional Church. This explains why on the Scriptural standpoint the Church makes confession of its faith in the sole sovereignty of Christ in the ecclesiastical community, and at the same time recognizes that this authority is exercised by means of the offices ordained by the King of the Church. The ecclesiastic offices are *qualified* and *destined* as the instruments of faith for effectuating the absolute authority of the Divine Word and Spirit. They are founded in

---

as a "*cri de coeur*" deserving our sympathy, but it has a deeper background in BRUNNER's conception of the Church. Cf. p. 509, note 1, of this volume.

the organized formative power of the latter in historical development. This view should not be considered as a *merely subjective reformed conception* of the ecclesiastical offices, because it is concerned with a state of affairs implied in the structural principle of the institutional Church as such. If this state of affairs is ignored, we shall form an erroneous subjective idea of the authority of a Church office, assigning alien characteristics to the internal structure of the Church-institution. An ecclesiastical office is qualified as *service* in the community of faith in Christ. This qualification is grounded in the internal structure of the Church-institution, and retains its pregnant sense in the juridical aspect of ecclesiastical authority[1]. Therefore, the structure of ecclesiastical authority is radically different from that of the State's authority. No doubt, from the Christian point of view the office of the secular government is also a *ministerium*, a *service*, under the sovereign authority of God, which finds its religious expression in Christ's kingship. It was the Carolingian monarchy in which this Christian conception found its first recognition.

But, according to its structural principle, authority in the State is not *typically qualified* as *service*, but as *public legal* authority of the *government*, founded in the power of the sword. The government's office can only be seen as *service* from the point of view of the *moral* and *pisteutical*[2] aspect of the body politic. Under the leading of *Christian* legal principles the *juridical* organization of secular governmental authority will be influenced by the Christian conception of office. But this fact does not alter the *governmental* structure of the State's coercive authority.

Ecclesiastic official authority is entirely different. It is *qualified* as a *ministerium* in the community of faith, and therefore it is to be understood as *service* also in its juridical structural aspect, and not as *governmental dominion*. A Church that really displays a legitimate Scriptural constitution, cannot recognize any public legal governmental authority in its internal legal

---

[1] KARL RIEKER observes in his *Grundsätze reformierter Kirchenverfassung*, p. 114, note 2, that the conception of "governmental power" in the Church as *service*, and not as *dominion*, is of Reformed origin. We had better say that this conception is of Biblical origin, because, if the Scriptural structure of this authority is recognized, no other conception is possible.

[2] "Pisteutical" means: "in the meaning-modality of faith".

order[1]. Therefore, the organizational forms of the secular government's political authority cannot be transferred to the internal ecclesiastical order without violating the structure of the latter. The typical political forms of authority, such as *monarchy, democracy* and *aristocracy,* in their different historically founded varieties, *e.g.,* constitutional monarchy, parliamentary democracy, *etc.,* are absolutely incompatible with the structural principle of official ecclesiastic authority.

The supposed "democratic" character of the Reformed principles of ecclesiastic government.

We have seen in an earlier context that CALVIN recognized the indissoluble internal coherence of a legitimate ecclesiastical organization with the basic principle of Christocracy. He was deeply convinced of the fundamental difference between Church government and the government of the State. He did not at all favour the idea of any sovereignty on the part of the congregation in the Church, and made no attempt to introduce a kind of representative system of ecclesiastical government. By interpreting the Reformer's conception in terms of such democratic political ideas its real meaning is completely misunderstood. SOHM summarizes all these misconceptions in his *Kirchenrecht* (I, p. 649, Anm. 37) when making the following remark with respect to CALVIN's conception of the organization of the Church: 'Everywhere there is evidence of the thought that the Church of Christ is organized in a worldly fashion; the constitution of the Church has been conceived in exactly the same manner as that of a town. It is well known that this is the general opinion prevailing at present' [2].

---

[1] RIEKER, *op cit.* refers to KLIEFOTH, *Acht Bücher von der Kirche* I (1854), pp. 435 ff. when he observes: "According to the Lutheran conception Church government is a service in the same sense as the government of the State, *i.e.* in a moral sense; in a juridical sense, however, it is dominion, a government in the proper sense of the word, as well as the exercise of the State power." This remark does not do full justice to the original Lutheran view. In the preface to MELANCHTON's "*Unterricht der Visitatoren*" (1528), LUTHER explicitly states that the various Evangelical princes were not to have dominion in the Church but to render a *service of love.* But LUTHER did not properly understand the juridical aspect of this "*ministerium*", and practice in the Lutheran territorial Churches very soon showed the tendency described by H. LIERMANN in his *Deutsches Evangelisches Kirchenrecht* (1933) p. 152: "But also with the sovereigns... office became right, service turned into dominion." ["Aber auch bei den Landsherren wurde... aus Amt Recht, aus Dienst Herrschaft."]

[2] 'Überall schlägt der Gedanke durch, dasz die Kirche Christi nach weltlicher Art verfaszt ist: wie eine Stadtverfassung gerade so ist die Kirchenverfassung beschaffen. Es ist das bekantlich die heute allgemein herrschende Auffassung'.

The passages quoted from CALVIN's *Institution* by KAMPSCHULTE in his *Joh. Calvin* I (pp. 269 ff.) to prove his view that the Reformer started from the principle of the sovereignty of the congregation, have nothing to do with this question, or they prove the very contrary. The first quotation is from *Inst.* IV 3, 13 and 14. But here CALVIN only remarks that the extraordinary way in which the apostles were elected is not a rule for the election of the "ministers of the Word". In *Inst.* IV, 3, 15, he says indeed that in accordance with the Word of God the call of a minister is lawful '*ubi ex populi consensu et approbatione creantur qui visi fuerint idonei*' [1]. But a moment before it has been made clear what importance CALVIN attaches to this election by the whole congregation: 'Bene ergo CYPRIANUS, dum contendit, *ex divina autoritate descendere,* ut sacerdos plebe praesente sub omnium oculis deligatur, et dignus atque idoneus publico iudicio ac testimonio comprobetur'. (Italics are mine) [2].

So CALVIN does not at all derive the election of office-bearers by the congregation from a kind of "people's sovereignty" in the Church, but from the authority of God's Word; in the latter this manner of election has been ordained that it might be accomplished as purely and as honestly as possible.

This is why CALVIN concludes this 15th paragraph as follows: "Praeesse autem electioni debere alios pastores, ne quid per levitatem, vel per mala studia, vel per tumultum a multitudine peccetur" [3].

In this light we must also view CALVIN's demand (*Instit.* IV, 11, 6 and 12, 7) that no excommunication shall be carried out by the ministers without the cooperation of the representatives of the congregation.

This, too, is not a consequence of some sovereignty of the congregation (which is incompatible with CALVIN's Christocratical thought) but a guarantee ordained by the Word of God against any arbitrary excercise of the "power of the key". The elders in the Reformed Church constitution are not the "representatives" of the congregation in the sense of the modern political system of representation, as is supposed by THOMPSON and SOHM. It is true that CALVIN uses the term "representatives" to qualify the office of the elders. For example he calls the elders and the members of the consistory in general those "*qui totum corpus ecclesiae repraesentant*". But RIEKER correctly observes that the modern concept of representation

---

[1] 'When those who are found suitable are elected with the consent and approval of the people'.

[2] 'Therefore CYPRIANUS rightly says that it was from the Divine authority when a priest was elected in the people's presence and the sight of them all, and considered to be worthy and capable by public opinion and testimony'.

[3] 'The other pastors should preside over this election so that no wrong may be done either through levity, or through partiality, or through the riotous spirit of the multitude'.

was foreign to his days. The elders are called representatives of the congregation insofar as they are *ministering organs* of the congregation according to their office. RIEKER says: 'Calvin is far from looking upon the ecclesiastical office-bearers as representatives of the congregation in the modern sense of "mandataries of a popular will above them". He chooses his position not below but above the congregation when he grasps the idea of Church government' [1]. How averse CALVIN was to a "popular will" in the Church of the Lord is completely clear from the initial paragraph of the third chapter of the fourth book of his *Institution,* where he writes: 'We have now to speak of the manner in which the Lord has wanted his Church to be governed. For He Himself rules and governs His Church and must preside over it and have the highest authority. And although this government and rule must be accomplished by His Word alone, since He does not dwell among us by a visible presence to inform each of us of His will by word of mouth, we have already said that He employs the service of men and appoints them as a kind of vicars. He does not transfer His own right and honour to them but only does His own work through their mouths, just as a workman uses a tool to carry out his work' [2].

These words concisely express the Scriptural view of the authority of an ecclesiastical office.

RIEKER's remark is very much to the point when he says: 'The individual member has the right to examine if their (*i.e.* the Church officers') orders and arrangements are in accordance with the Word of God, and only if, and insofar as this proves to be the case, he is in duty bound to obey. For there is no other authority for a Christian than that of Christ and His Word: only to this authority is the Christian subject' [3]. The exclusive sovereignty of Christ in His Church

---

[1] 'CALVIN ist weit entfernt davon, in den kirchlichen Amtsträgern Vertreter der Gemeinde im modernen Sinne, Mandatare eines über ihnen stehenden Volkswillens zu erblicken. Er nimmt, indem er die Idee eines Kirchenregiments fasst, seinen Standort nicht unten, in der Gemeinde, sondern oben über der Gemeinde'.

[2] 'Iam de ordine dicendum est quo ecclesiam suam gubernari voluit Dominus. Tametsi enim solum ipsum regere ac regnare in ecclesia, in *ea quoque praeesse vel eminere,* et imperium hoc solo eius verbo exerceri atque administrari oportet, quia tamen visibili praesentia inter nos non habitat, ut voluntatem nobis suam ore coram declaret, hominum ministerium in hoc adhibere diximus, et quasi vicariam operam, non ad eos ius suum honoremque transferendo, sed tantum ut per *os ipsum* suum ipse opus agat, qualiter ad opus quoque faciendum instrumento utitur artifex'.

[3] *Op. cit.,* p. 114: 'der Einzelne hat das Recht der Prüfung, ob die Anordnungen jener (*i.e.* der kirchlichen Amtsträger) dem Worte Gottes gemäsz seien, und nur wenn und soweit dies zutrifft, ist er ihnen Gehorsam schuldig. Denn es gibt für den Christen keine andere Autorität als die Christi und seines Wortes: nur ihr ist er Unterthan'. In a note

is also the foundation of the Calvinistic principle of collegial Church government and of the collegial organization of the exercise of ecclesiastical discipline. All important ecclesiastical decisions should not be made by one single office-bearer but collegially: no "individual" shall rule in the Church in the name of Christ. CALVIN formulates this principle sharply and concisely in his pronouncement: 'He (*i.e.* Christ) attributes nothing but a common ministry to men and to each of them a particular part' [1].

In the latter half of the nineteenth century the German evangelical territorial Churches introduced synodal forms and a system of congregational representation into the ecclesiastical organization. This change was the beginning of the "*Synodal-Konsistorialsystem*", which at first sight displays some connection with the old Reformed tradition. But this connection was only *formal* in character. LIERMANN emphatically states that the material origin of these new forms of organization is much rather to be found in modern political constitutional thought asserting itself also in Church government since 1848 [2]. The typical character of the ecclesiastic offices as *service* was more and more ignored. The "synod" was organized like a real "parliament" and a formal kind of "parliamentarism" made its way into the German territorial Churches. Thus the process of deviating from the internal structural principle of ecclesiastical organization continued when it had once started with imposing political forms of organization on the Church. The constitution of the Church fell a victim to the political spirit of the age, and every change in the political regime was bound to reflect itself in the internal Church-organization.

Such forms of organization lack any internal ecclesiastical structure and must be qualified as alien, political forms. It is impossible to "let the facts speak for themselves", if we have no insight into the true nature of this deviation from the structural principle of Church organization. The facts will only speak the language of the positivist after an injection with the positivist's

---

RIEKER points out that "the right of private judgment" is explicitly acknowledged in the ecclesiastic order and government of the Presbyterian Church in Ireland.

[1] *Inst.* IV, 6, 10: 'Hominibus nihil tribuit' (*viz.* Christ) *'nisi commune ministerium,* et unicuique modum particularem'. Compare with this the pronouncements of the *Confessio Helvetica* XVIII, 16 and those of JOHANNES À LASCO quoted by RIEKER, *op. cit.*, p. 122/3.

[2] *Deutsches Evangelisches Kirchenrecht* (1933) p. 172/3.

theory. Then the facts will indeed re-echo the positivist's own prejudice.

The internal structural principle expresses itself in the moral aspect of the Church-institution as a community of love among fellow-believers in Christ.

In the foundational direction of the temporal order the qualifying or leading function of the temporal institutional Church immediately refers back to its moral structural function. According to the latter the Church is a typical community of love among fellow-believers in Christ Jesus, bound together by their common confession of faith.

This community of love cannot be understood in the merely modal moral sense of a general love of one's neighbour, but is rather the typical expression of the entire internal structure of the temporal Church-institution. It shares the transcendental limiting character of this structure by which it is qualified as a community of love guided by the bond of a common Christian faith and confession. Therefore all differences of nationality, family, social class or position, fall away in the internal Church-structure. This internal community of love in the faith in Christ Jesus does not tolerate competition on the part of any love relations of a different internal structure. No love among comrades, or "class" mates, no love of country, not even paternal or filial love, as such, may cause any separation in the internal community of love of the institutional Church, because all these are of an entirely different internal structure. The internal community of love which, according to the ecclesiastical structural principle, should interlace "those who are of the household of faith" in "brotherly" and "sisterly" bonds, can be realized only under the leading of a living community of faith. But in this life such a realization will always be imperfect and defective, especially in the modern conditions of large towns. It is nevertheless, even in this defective form, one of the "fruits of faith" and displays its limiting character in being only possible as a temporal manifestation of the bond of love in Christ Jesus[1]. There is no true community of faith without the bond of love in Christ Jesus.

This internal transcendental structure also explains the character of the particular Church office of *diaconate*. In cooperation with the general priesthood of all the Christian believers the organized office of charity towards the poor members of the

[1] Cf. 1 *John* 3, esp. verse 17.

congregation has been entrusted to the deacons. According to the Scriptural structural principle of the temporal Church-institution, this office is an essential part of the internal ecclesiastical organization[1]. The very structure of the institutional Church demands this special *office*. In the non-institutional manifestations of the Church of Christ on earth charity to one's fellow-man belongs to the general office of the believers.

In its ecclesiastical organizational structure the diaconate is *qualified* as a Christian *institution of faith*, an instrument for the working of Christ's Word and Spirit in the first place among the members of the congregation. Christ's divine priestly office of charity finds its institutional official expression in the diaconate. This characteristic fundamentally distinguishes the diaconal from the civil care of the poor on the part of the State government, as well as from private charity.

In Lutheran countries this church-office could not develop according to its own internal nature. The State interfered with the government of the Church and as a result ecclesiastical and civil charity were mixed. This was doubtless not in accordance with LUTHER's own standpoint. He pointed out the necessity of an ecclesiastical diaconate, though he was not so emphatic and energetic in this respect as CALVIN was.

Civil relief remains qualified by the juridical principle of public interest, and as governmental care of the poor it can never have the character of free Christian charity. Private charity, manifesting itself in a particular, non-ecclesiastical form of a philanthropic organization, remains qualified by the typical moral leading function of this organization. This moral qualification also appears in Christian charitable societies. Only in the diaconal care of the poor is the typical societal organization of charity qualified by the community of Christian faith. As soon as this typical dependence on its leading function is ignored, diaconal charity is denaturalized.

---

[1] BRUNNER (*op. cit.*, p. 542) has a striking remark on this point: 'A Church that does not produce a living congregational diaconate must be seriously suspected of being mortally ill'. But BRUNNER only recognizes the essential character of the *ecclesiastical function* of charity, he denies the necessity of an *institutional office* of charity. This viewpoint is connected with his dualistic separaton between the "*ordinances*" and the "*commandment of love*", and especially with his identification of the "*Glaubenskirche*" with the "*ecclesia invisibilis*", discussed in an earlier context.

The expression of the internal structural principle in the juridical aspect of the Church-institution. SOHM's denial of a true internal ecclesiastic law.

The moral structural function of the temporal Church-institution necessarily refers back to the juridical societal aspect. At this point we are confronted by the question if there is a real internal antinomy, and a dialectical tension, between a Christian faith community and a juridical order. This problem has played a very important part in the history of ecclesiastic law since the Reformation.

SOHM argued that the legal order and the essential nature of the Church are mutually exclusive. And with particular emphasis the question has been discussed ever since in every modern textbook on Protestant Church-law. This is quite understandable. For the issue of the debate is the question whether the Reformation has or has not remained faithful to its basic principles in the development of a Church-law of its own. This debate will always be useless if the problem is posited in a fundamentally wrong way, which so often happens. If the Christian philosophic theory of the modal and the individuality structures of human society is to explain anything, it must shed light on the way this problem should be formulated.

SOHM's thesis is: 'Church-law is contradictory to the essential nature of the Church'. This thesis is rooted in the Lutheran antithesis between the Gospel and the Law, in which we have discovered an after-effect of the dualistic-nominalistic scheme of "grace" and "nature". 'The essence of the Church is spiritual, the essence of law is secular'. This is SOHM's basic tenet. It is the same dualism expressed in E. BRUNNER's antithesis between "the commandment of love" and the "secular ordinances" in recent times. "Law" was not really conceived in its true *modal* sense, but in the formalistic and positivistic sense of a formal order of communal life (thought of in terms of the coercive State law). The binding force of this legal order was derived from the will of the secular legislator.

In his work *Das Gebot und die Ordnungen* E. BRUNNER does not even recognnize any other law than *State* law, and proclaims this positivistic juridical view to be the original typical conception of the Reformers. He contrasts it, as the Protestant view of law, to the Roman conception of natural law [1]. If such a positivistic

---

[1] *Op. cit.* p. 653 note 17 (435). BRUNNER only rejects *naturalistic* positi-

dogma is accepted, the question as to whether a typical internal Church-law with sovereignty in its own sphere can exist, is of course implicitly answered in the negative. SOHM's elaborate investigations of the organization of the Church in early Christianity, Roman Catholicism, and the Reformation, could not really contribute anything to prove the correctness of the negative answer to the above-mentioned question. These investigations started from his *petitio principii*[1]. In his antithesis between the nature of the Church and that of law, SOHM commits a second error by conceiving the "essence of the institutional Church" in the transcendent religious sense of the perfect "Kingdom of God". Thereby the problem of the relation between Church and law has been wrongly posited from the outset.

The antithesis between form and content in Church law in E. BRUNNER's dualistic conception.

BRUNNER posits the problem a little differently from SOHM. He realizes that, as a temporal institutional organization, the Church cannot exist without a legal order. Just like KATTENBUSCH he conceives of the Church as a "*Kultgemeinde*" (cult community) and opposes this to the "*Kirche des Glaubens*" (the Church of faith), which stands for the "*ecclesia invisibilis*" in his view. In the Church as a cult community he admits the necessity of a material Church-order. Such an order is subservient to the "commandment of the moment" ("*Gebot des Augenblicks*") of the "Word of God", and its peculiar legal character is precisely broken through and cancelled by its direct relatedness to this irrationalist view of the central commandement.

---

vism and thinks he has thereby finished with juridical positivism as such. His "critical" positivism, however, is no better than the naturalist kind, since it replaces the modal structure of the juridical aspect by formal categories of thought which may assume any arbitrary content.

[1] K. KAHL correctly remarks in his *Lehrsystem des Kirchenrechts und der Kirchenpolitik* (1e Hälfte p. 73) that SOHM is wrong in principle when he represents his thesis concerning the incompatibility of Church and law as the result of historical research: '*Der Lehrsatz selbst bleibt... falsch.* Was zu bekämpfen ist, sind nicht in erster Linie Geschichts*thatsachen*, sondern Geschichts*reflexionen*, die aus den Thatsachen gezogenen *Schlüsse.* In der Thesis redet nicht die Sprache der Geschichte, sondern SOHM's Sprache *über* die Geschichte'. ['*The thesis itself... is false.* What we have to combat are not in the first place historical *facts* but historical *reflections, conclusions* drawn from the facts. In the thesis we do not hear the language of history, but we hear SOHM speak *about* history'].

As an *order* it retains its secular character and, in this sense, it should keep at a proper distance from the authority of the Word of God. But in matters of faith, in establishing the confession as the norm of "pure doctrine" for instance, the Church-order is closely related to the "*Kirche des Glaubens*", which only lives by God's Word. Although the "cult-community" is merely a "human form" of the divine, in such matters of faith it has some share in the divine authority. Such Church-orders owe their *legal* character exclusively to the State. On this point BRUNNER explicitly agrees with SOHM. Consequently the question about the real nature of Church-law is answered as follows: 'In a material sense, according to the nature of its content, protestant Church-law is ecclesiastical; in a formal sense, however, according to its juridical nature, it is purely secular-political...' [1]. The famous form-matter scheme, in its neo-Kantian sense, is thus called in here to elucidate the problem concerning the essential character of Church-law. This scheme is, however, anything but appropriate to do so [2]. It owes its origin to a misconception and disruption of the divine world-order, and must always end in an internally contradictory dualism. In BRUNNER's solution this dualism is obvious at the first glance: The juridical order proper is a perfectly *alien* political element in the Church-relationship. But according to its content this order is supposed to be essentially related to the Church-institution. The consequence is that the *juridical form* is perfectly alien to the *content* embraced by it! Practically speaking, BRUNNER's unreal and forced construction is as obscure as that of the Lutheran "episcopal" system, and displays the same *vitium originis*.

The background of BRUNNER's dualism between *form* and *content* of Church-law is the deeper dualism between "nature" and "grace", Law and Gospel. So long as this dualism keeps ruling thought, it is impossible to gain an insight into the individuality-structure of the temporal Church-institution. The contrast BRUNNER makes between "*Kirche des Glaubens*" and "*Kultgemeinde*", replacing the distinction between "*ecclesia invisibilis*" and "*ecclesia visibilis*" (the institution), testifies to a lack of insight into the internal structure of the institutional Church.

---

[1] *Op. cit.*, p. 533: 'Materiell also, seiner inhaltlichen Eigenart nach, ist das protestantische Kirchenrecht kirchlich, formal aber, seiner Rechtsnatur nach, ist es rein weltlich-staatlich...'.

[2] Cf. our critical analysis of this neo-Kantian scheme in Vol. II, pp. 12 ff. and pp. 208 ff.

If the modal meaning of law is not from the outset theoretically misinterpreted by including in it the typical political moment of governmental coercion, there is nothing in the juridical aspect as such which is incompatible with the internal structure of the temporal ecclesiastical institution. We must put it even more strongly: we cannot have grasped the individuality-structure of this organized community correctly, if we start denying that it necessarily possesses an *internal-juridical structural* aspect.

The criterion of the internal Church law. Why its formal legal source is no criterion.

This internal juridical structural aspect, however, cannot be grasped in a positivistic (pseudo-)concept of law, oriented exclusively to the State's apparatus of coercion. Nor is it determined by the formal juridical source of Church law. As such, this genetic juridical form of binding legal norms is no more than a human legal declaration of will, made by an organ invested with competence to law formation. The various individuality-structures of law cannot be founded in such formal juridical sources; on the contrary they lie at the foundation of all human law making.

We shall see later on that it is precisely these genetic juridical forms that function as real nodal points of enkaptic structural interlacements within the juridical law-sphere. That is to say, not everything contained in the genetic juridical form of a Church regulation displays the individuality-structure of internal Church-law. Neither are all rules contained in the constitutional form of statute law thereby characterized as internal constitutional law of the State. This observation holds with even greater force when alien legal structures have penetrated an ecclesiastical organization because the Church has become unfaithful to its own nature.

Recall an official church-rate imposed also on the baptismal members[1], and collected after the manner of the State; recall also alien political forms of ecclesiastical organization. Legal rules concerning such points may be Church rules in a *formal* sense, *i.e.* they may have been formed and positivized by ecclesiastical organs. But they have nothing to do with the internal structure of the Church-institution; according to their material sense, they are much rather in open conflict with this structure.

---

[1] *I.e.* members who have not yet been confirmed.

True *internal* Church-law can only be such law that displays the individuality-structure of the ecclesiastical community. Its material meaning is indissolubly connected with the leading function of the Church as a community of faith and confession in the administration of the Word and the sacraments.

We refer to the legal rules concerning the inner constitution of the ecclesiastical community, the competence of the different offices and the conditions to be satisfied with respect to the investiture with these offices, ecclesiastical discipline, the establishment and alteration of the confession, *etc.* All such regulations belong to the internal legal sphere of the Church insofar as they are indissolubly connected with questions of Christion belief and confession, and do not encroach on the public order and the civil law of the State, both conceived according to their own structural principles.

If Church-law is really conceived in this internal sense, it can never be in conflict with the nature of the ecclesiastical institution, and it cannot be involved in any rivalry with the internal public legal order of the State, or with the civil legal order of the latter.

Such rivalry can only arise when either the State or the Church-institution in their law formation exceed the inner boundaries of their competence. A striking example of such a rivalry is to be found in the Roman Catholic conception that the legal regulation of marriage, except that of the purely financial relations, belongs to the exclusive competence of the Church. Even from the Roman Catholic viewpoint that the matrimonial bond has a supra-natural side, as a sacrament, this conception ignores the inner boundaries of ecclesiastical law. For, this viewpoint implies that marriage also has a natural substructure whose legal aspect is as such not of an ecclesiastical character. In its internal sphere the Roman Catholic Church is doubtless competent to establish ecclesiastical legal rules concerning the matrimonial bond, insofar as the latter is viewed as a sacrament. But this can never imply an exclusive competence to regulate this bond as a natural institution, which has so many enkaptic interlacements with the State and other "natural" societal relationships (in the scholastical sense of the term "natural"). The very fact of these interlacements implies the competence of the State to regulate marriage as to its civil legal side, which as such is independent of the Roman Catholic viewpoint of faith that marriage is a sacrament. It is only due to a universalist view of the Church-institution, and to the pretention of the Roman Catholic ecclesiastical authority to give a binding interpretation of the so-called natural ethical law, that this truth has been lost to sight. This is why the traditional Roman Catholic view concerning the relation between Church and State lacked a sharp criterion for the distinction between the spheres of competence of these two institutions.

The internal ecclesiastical legal rules display the general modal meaning of a retributive harmonization of interests, inherent in every juridical norm, irrespective of its typical structure of individuality.

It is consequently not merely a question of terminology, as BRUNNER thinks, when in this modal sense we call the inner Church-order a *legal* order. For the *juridical* sphere-sovereignty of the Church depends on this real juridical character of the ecclesiastic order *in its contradistinction to the legal spheres of the State.* According to its individuality-structure as *Church law,* it is qualified as an instrument of faith for the effectualization of the sole authorithy of Christ Jesus by His Word and Spirit. As such, it does not permit any coercive sanction on the part of the State. The unique and incomparable *principles* of Church-law in this individuality-structure are implied in the Scriptural structural principle of this institution itself.

No *ius divinum positivum.*

But there can be no question of a *ius divinum positivum* in the internal sphere of the Church. The forming, the positivization of the legal principles for the internal structure of the ecclesiastical institution is a human activity, and has been entrusted by Christ to the lawful organs of His Church. As this juridical forming always remains bound to the substratum of historical development, positive Church law cannot have an unchangeable character. Owing to its transcendental limiting character as an instrument of faith, ecclesiastic law does not permit any *formalism* in its application, whereby the abstract legal rule would dominate the activity of faith [1].

---

[1] That the internal juridical principles in the institutional Church have a different character from the civil juridical, or from public legal principles, has been demonstrated in my treatise: *De Structuur der Rechtsbeginselen en de Methode der Rechtswetenschap in het Licht der Wetsidee (Wetensch. Bijdragen door Hoogleraren der V.U. aangeboden ter gelegenheid van haar 50-jarig bestaan,* Amsterdam, 1930).

The internal Church-law is a very sensitive instrument for the working of God's Word and Spirit in the community of Christian believers. Of course, the moment of legal *ordering* remains typical of the organizational norms of this legal sphere. This juridical moment of ordering cannot be dispensed with, because the Church cannot do without an official organization.

But this organization possesses an ecclesiastical individuality-structure, which should be positivized in accordance with the Scriptural indications. Therefore the *ordering moment* in the internal Church-law does not remain alien to the Church as a temporal community of faith in the administration of the Word and the sacraments. It is entirely qualified by this ecclesiastical leading function so long as the order is conceived in the *Scriptural sense.* It is characterized as *service,* and it is never *qualifying.*

So we may conclude that the view according to which the institutional Church has no internal juridical sphere, originates from a lack of insight into the individuality-structure of this community, and from an erroneous view of law, which identifies the latter with a formalistically conceived State-law. Especially in Lutheran circles the relation between Church and law has been conceived in an unscriptural way, as an antithesis between Gospel and Law, "grace" and "nature". This was partly the result of a justifiable opposition to the Romanist deformation of Church-law to a supposed *ius divinum positivum.* This latter was modelled after the juridical organization of the State and dominated the community of faith, since it was supposed to contain true public juridical governmental regulations. On this point too, CALVIN showed the Reformation the true Biblical way.

The expression of the internal structural principle in the other aspects of the temporal Church-institution.

After the detailed analysis of the three last structural functions of the temporal Church-institution only a few remarks will be made on the expression of the structural principle in the other aspects of this community. It is not necessary to prove separately that in the institutional Church there is an internal aesthetical, an internal economic, an internal social [1], an internal linguistic

---

[1] "Social" has here the modal sense of the aspect of human intercourse.

structure[1], *etc.* Our previous investigations have clearly shown that all the modal aspects in the internal structure of a societal relationship are indissolubly interwoven.

Internal Church-law cannot function without the substratum of internal-ecclesiastical harmony, internal ecclesiastical economy, *etc.* In all these structural functions the internal structural subject-object relation presents itself.

In this relation objective thing-structures function enkaptically in the subjective ecclesiastical community, and, as such, are subservient to the subjective leading function of the Church institute. In this light internal ecclesiastical art should be viewed in its objective structures as a *structurally bound* art[2]. According to its internal structural principle it should be permeated by the Christian Spirit to be an instrument of the community of faith in the service of the Word and the sacraments. The structural subject-object relation in which ecclesiastical art functions, is not aesthetically *qualified.* Therefore, the aesthetical function should not *obtrude* at the expense of the transcendental leading function of the institutional Church-community. Such an obtrusion disturbs the *internal* aesthetical harmony in the objective structure of the church-building. And the internal aesthetical harmony is also disturbed when objects of an explicit political structure are placed in the church-building where they do not belong, *e.g.*, coats of arms, flags, standards, *etc.*

The "*Garnisonskirche*" in Potsdam is one of the most horrible examples of disharmony in this respect. Another example is Westminster Abbey in London, which partly functions as a national museum.

When investigating the typical structural functions of the temporal Church institute in the modal law-spheres of social intercourse, language, the historical development of culture, logical thought, feeling, *etc.*, the internal structure of this institution should be sharply distinguished from the external structural interlacements in which it functions enkaptically.

Nationality, the State's order, local customs and manners, *etc.* can only give the positive form of the Church-institution an *external variability type,* but they should never affect the *real internal structure* of the different Church formations. As soon as

---

[1] Recall ecclesiastical symbolism, the ecclesiastical way of linguistic expression, *etc.*

[2] Cf. Vol. III, pp. 139 ff.

such external factors dominate the factual internal relations within the ecclesiastical community, the Church-institution is *radically deformed.*

The "pluriformity of the Church" can only be justified in the sense of external variability types of ecclesiastic forms, but never on the ground of their internal structure.

The spatial structural function of the institutional Church, and the internal sense of local Church formation.

From the point of view of the internal structural principle it is obvious that the connection between the *spatial* boundaries of a Church formation and those of a State (and its component parts) can only have an *external*, variable, but never an *internal, fundamental* character.

The view of the Church-institution prevailing in the Reformation correctly emphasized that the *local congregation* is the *primary* institutional manifestation of the Church of Jesus Christ. In opposition to the Roman Catholic conception, the starting-point for more comprehensive ecclesiastical bonds is to be found in the local congregation. It was pointed out that the apostles recognized every local Church formation as an ἐκκλήσια and always spoke of ἐκκλήσιαι or Churches, but never of a Church in the sense of the fusion of all local congregations into a more comprehensive organization [1]. This primary *local* character of the institutional Church must be explained from the internal structural principle, and not from the external interlacement with the spatial boundaries of the municipal parts of the State-organization. According to its leading function, as a confessional community of faith in the administration of the Word and the sacraments, the institutional Church can only find its spatial centre in *local* congregations. For the service of the Word and the sacraments can only be performed regularly in a local Church. The spatial boundaries of the local Churches are determined from within by the possibility of a real temporal community in the regular divine services. That these boundaries should coalesce with those of the civil municipality [2] is untenable, if the

---

[1] Cf. A. KUYPER, *Tractaat*, p. 35/6.

[2] I do not subscribe to KUYPER's argument on this point, *op. cit.*, p. 16. This does not mean that the congregational thought of the Independents was more consonant with the structural principle of the Church-institution. For in this congregational thought there is a strongly individualistic

individuality-structure of the institutional Church is not to be levelled down. The boundaries of a civil municipality display the individuality structure of the State, and are dependent on all kinds of factors that have no importance for the local Church. Recall the continual modifications of the boundaries of large cities by the annexation of neighbouring municipalities.

When emphasis is laid on the primary local character of the institutional Church, it should be borne in mind that, according to its internal structure, the local boundaries do not possess the character proper to the territorial boundaries of the State and its component parts. The spatial structure of the institutional Church displays that transcendental limiting character in which the universality of the *ecclesia invisibilis* should find its temporal expression. The Church of Christ has no "territory" in the political sense of the word, but the territory in which the Church is established is that of the State. The national frontiers separate the different States because the organized monopolistic military power can only be of a territorial character. That is why no government can exercise its office on its own authority within the territory of a foreign "sovereign" State. But this state of affairs does not apply to the Church.

The idea of the spatial universality of the Church in its static and its dynamic conception.

Insofar as they are one in a confessional sense the local Churches all over the world must be in principle viewed as a unity since they are joined by an intrinsic communal bond. This is in accordance with the idea of the spatial universality of the Church in the omnipresence of its King Christ Jesus. This unity is historically founded and dynamical in character. It expresses itself in the formation of organizational bonds between the local congregations culminating in general synods, whose authority over the separate Churches is recognized as a ministry. There is no single ground to be derived from the inner nature of a synodal organization in favour of the thesis that the authority of a synod should be restricted to the territorial boundaries of a State. The coherence between the inter-congregational organiza-

---

tendency, which is accentuated by the repression of the institutional character of the Church in its official organization. Besides, it is denied that the congregations are bound by the authority of the "larger assemblies" (classes and synods).

tion and a national community can only be of a phenotypical character and is a consequence of enkaptic interlacements between the ecclesiastical and the national unity. The idea of spatial universality of the institutional Church as a whole can be internally determined only by the requirement of a community of confession. The external limitation by the difference in language, the impossibility of actual communication, *etc.*, is only variable in character.

Therefore, *national* groupings of local congregations into a more comprehensive organization can only be conceived as *variability types* of the institutional structural principle of the Church. The Roman Catholic idea of the latter lacks the moment of *dynamic growth from local congregational unities* in its conception of the spatial universality of the ecclesiastic whole; for it holds that from the outset the papal centralized hierarchical institution embodies the all-inclusive unity of all the present and future parts of the Church. From the outset the Roman Church presents itself as an ecumenical world-Church and has no room for the thought that the institutional manifestation of the *ecclesia Christi* must start from the local congregations. This static universalism originates from an absolutization of the ecclesiastical institution. It can be realized only by a centralized bureaucratic organization fashioned on the model of the Roman Empire, and is not really founded in the internal structural principle of the institutional Church.

The full realization of the spatial universality of the body of Christ in its institutional manifestation has not been given in time, but continues to express itself only in the transcendental direction to the eschatological future of the Kingdom of heaven.

PART II

(CONCLUSION)

THE STRUCTURES OF VOLUNTARY ASSOCIATIONS AND THE INTER-INDIVIDUAL AND INTER-COMMUNAL RELATIONSHIPS IN A DIFFERENTIATED SOCIETY

CHAPTER V

THE STRUCTURAL DIVERSITY OF VOLUNTARY ASSOCIATIONS AND THE CHARACTER OF INDIVIDUALIZED INTER-INDIVIDUAL AND INTER-COMMUNAL RELATIONSHIPS

§ 1 - THE TRANSCENDENTAL CHARACTER OF OUR SYSTEMATIC CATEGORIES AND THEIR RELATION TO THE INDIVIDUALITY-STRUCTURES OF THE SOCIETAL RELATIONSHIPS.

Why we were in need of preliminary transcendental distinctions in our systematic inquiry into the societal structures.

In the course of our inquiry into the individuality-structures of human society the broad outlines of a system are beginning to show themselves. We did not start from a pre-conceived elaborate systematic scheme into which all the different types of societal relationships were forced. Only a few preliminary distinctions proved to be indispensable to penetrate to the field of inquiry, because they were supposed to be of a transcendental character, and thus to be the very condition of any well-founded systematic investigation. A further systematic classification of human societal structures is only valuable, if it derives from the theoretical disclosure of these structures themselves, and has not been externally imposed on them in a *subjective a priori way*. This is a methodological postulate discussed in our epistemology [1].

In the first (Dutch) edition of this work I even restricted the preliminary distinctions to those between communal and inter-individual or inter-communal relationships, and between natural and typically historically founded communities. The further foundational systematic categories were not developed before the present chapter, as a *result* of the structural investigations

[1] Vol. II, Part 2, pp. 554 ff.

contained in the previous chapters of the second part of this volume. Now it is doubtless true that all foundational systematic distinctions introduced in my structural examinations are only discovered in confrontation with the societal structures of individuality themselves. Nevertheless, it stands to reason that we could not arrive at any systematic division of our enquiry without laying the really transcendental preliminary distinctions at its foundation. From this methodical point of view the initial restriction of the latter was indeed arbitrary. This is why in the English edition I have abandoned this restriction and introduced all of the preliminary distinctions together in the first chapter.

The transcendental social categories as the points of reference for the individuality structures.

All the same, the question may be asked why in the theory of the societal structures we were in need of such preliminary distinctions, which apparently intersect the radical types of these structures. Have we not established that the radical types are the ultimate *genera* of a well-founded classification of the individuality structures?

The answer must be that our preliminary transcendental distinctions do not pertain to supreme *genera* embracing different radical types of societal relationships. Rather they refer to transcendental societal *categories* which, in the plastic dimension of the temporal order, lie at the foundation of the individuality-structures proper. Transcendental categories are the real points of reference of the latter. Our inquiry into the structures of individuality of things and events was in the last analysis also related to such foundational categories as thing, event, enkaptic intertwinement, internal structural causality and enkaptic causality, and their closer categorial distinctions (natural and cultural, or historically founded things and events, *etc.*).

The only reason why the preliminary categories of human societal relationships required special attention was that they cannot be reduced to those of natural things and events, whereas the latter in structural subject-object relations appeared to function in the former.

The transcendental social categories as the connecting links between the modal and the plastic dimension of the temporal order of creation in its reference to the social human relationships.

One should guard against a confusion of these transcendental categories with those of Aristotelian metaphysics, Kantian epistemology or Husserlian phenomenology. They are neither related to a metaphysical idea of being, nor to a constitutive formative function of a transcendental subject of experience, either in its Kantian or in its Husserlian sense. Apart from the structures of individuality and those of the modal aspects they lose any ontological meaning within our experiential horizon.

In a certain sense we can say that they are the connecting link between the modal and the plastic dimension of the temporal order of creation in its reference to the social human relationships. This is why the most fundamental societal category, *viz.* the correlation between communal and inter-communal or inter-individual relationships already revealed itself in the modal structures of our social experience and appeared to be ultimately founded in the modal aspect of social intercourse. In the same way the contrast between differentiated and undifferentiated societal relationships proved to be founded in the modal structure of the historical aspect. This is to say that these transcendental categories pertain both to the modal and to the plastic horizon of our social experience, and, in the former, refer to social human relations *as such* in their different modal meanings, and in the latter, to their plastic structures of individuality.

The other societal categories, *viz.* those of natural and (historically founded) organized communities, and those of institutional and non-institutional communal relationships, are not found in the modal structures of social experience. They give the primary categories a *typical* direction to the structures of individuality, without themselves being individuality structures in a proper sense. They urge themselves upon any serious analysis of the different societal structures of individuality as necessary typical categories founded in the temporal order of creation. As such they lie implicitly at the foundation of our naïve experience of social relationships.

There cannot exist any ordered human society without the basis of natural and institutional communities, which are sharply distinguished from free associations. This primary state of affairs is even more fundamental than that concerning the typical structures of individuality of the societal relationships. We have seen that neither the undifferentiated nor the differentiated institutional communities which imply a typical historical foundation, are an essential condition of every human society. And as to the natural communities we have established that there may be particular types of a non-institutional character (*e.g.*, such which are founded in a neighbourhood, in a bio-spatial sense).

This is why, when we consider the necessary conditions of human society as such, the categories of natural and institutional communal relationships, in their contrast with non-natural and non-institutional organizations, urge themselves upon our social experience as transcendental conditions of every further determination of the societal relationships. It is true that real natural communities prove to display the same radical type. But it is not their radical type as such, but their common biotic foundation, in contrast to all organized communities, which is implied in the transcendental societal category of natural communal relationships. For in this category is revealed the *temporal order* in the *genesis* of human communal bonds. In the genetical order historically founded communities are always preceded by natural ones, irrespective of the typical individuality structures of the former. And this is also the reason why the transcendental division of the natural communities into institutional and non-institutional is more fundamental than their common radical type. For, as to their genetical order, institutional natural communal relationships precede those of a non-institutional character.

The same state of affairs can be established with respect to the genetic order of institutional organized communities and free associations in a differentiated society. Only the former can give that necessary stability to a differentiated society which is the condition of the genesis of voluntary associations. It may be that the condition of a society which is involved in the process of differentiation does not yet allow the acknowledgment of the freedom to form voluntary associations. But there is no instance of a differentiated society which could exist without the stable foundation of institutional organized communities. And this factual state of affairs has a transcendental basis in the necessary conditions of human society as such, irrespective of the typical structures of individuality realized in it. For the primary condition of a society is its relative stability, and the latter cannot be provided by voluntary associations but only by institutional communities.

The systematic categories of societal form and enkaptic social interlacement.

Thus we may conclude that our preliminary systematical distinctions were not derived from an arbitrary method of logical classification but were indeed *systematic categories of a strictly transcendental character.* It stands to reason that this also holds good with respect to the categories of societal form and social interlacement which — *apart from their typical variable realization* — we have continually applied in our former investigations. Their transcendental character appeared from the explanation of their real meaning. Every societal relationship, irrespective of its typical structural principle, implies a genetic and an existential societal form as the necessary condition of its realization. These forms turned out to be typically founded in the modal structure of the historical aspect and to have an inner connection with the general norm-character of the structural laws of societal relationships. They proved to be the nodal points of enkaptical interlacements between the social relationships which have a different radical typical, or at least a different geno-typical inner structure. And these enkaptical relations themselves appeared to be founded in the plastic dimension of the temporal order, which guarantees the continuous temporal coherence between the societal structures of individuality, notwithstanding their inner sphere-sovereignty. This is sufficient to establish the transcendental relation of the two categories concerned to these individuality structures.

*

The above introductory explanation of the transcendental foundation of our general systematic categories was necessary to justify our systematic division of the societal individuality structures, which intersects the radical types of the latter.

It was especially necessary to justify our subsequent subsumption of all voluntary associations under the same category, notwithstanding the immense diversity of their inner nature. For at first sight it might seem that at least this category is nothing but a "general concept", which lacks any foundation in the transcendental horizon of human experience, and is handled as a kind of logical *genus proximum* to the effect that the inner structural boundaries of the different types are obliterated. This erroneous impression might be strengthened by the fact that the term "voluntary associations" implies indeed a close connection with human purposes. And we have continually emphasized that the internal structural principles of the societal relationships are not to be traced from a teleological point of view. Does this statement lose its validity with respect to voluntary associations? If so, there could not be any question of a transcendental foundation of the category concerned. For we have seen that really transcendental categories of societal relationships are the necessary points of reference for the individuality structures of the latter. If, however, the voluntary associations really belong to a transcendental societal category, we are in need of a more detailed analysis of the transcendental relation between their undeniably purposive character and their internal structural principles.

And since this category evokes all these fundamental questions which could not be answered in the first chapter, we preferred to postpone the transcendental explanation of all our systematic categories in their mutual coherence until the present stage of our inquiry. In the first (Dutch) edition of this work I had not yet arrived at a clear insight into the transcendental foundation of these categories. But the problem concerning this foundation has occupied me from the very outset. For, so long as it lacked a satisfactory solution, there seemed to remain an inner antinomy between the theory of the internal structural principles of the societal relationships and the systematic categories under which they were subsumed.

§ 2 - THE CONSTITUTIVE SIGNIFICANCE OF PURPOSE IN THE GENETIC FORMS OF VOLUNTARY ASSOCIATIONS AND ITS RELATION TO THEIR INTERNAL STRUCTURAL PRINCIPLES. THE GENETIC RELATION BETWEEN THESE ASSOCIATIONS AND THE INDIVIDUALIZED AND DIFFERENTIATED INTER-INDIVIDUAL RELATONSHIPS.

In order to gain a clearer insight into the transcendental character of the societal category which embraces all differentiated voluntary associations, we have first to realize its connection with the category of societal form. For it is evident that the first category solely pertains to the genetic form of organized communities which can only originate in the free individualized and differentiated inter-personal relations. This genetic form, however, must have a *typical* relation to the individuality-structures of these communities, if it is to be considered as a *typical* category on the same footing as that of the institutional organizations. For the category of societal form, as such, lacks this typical character. As soon, however, as it assumes a *typical* transcendental relation to a well defined category of societal structures of individuality, its rôle as a typical connecting link between the modal and the plastic dimension of our social experience is assured. And in this case we can also explain the particular function of purpose in this category.

This consideration gives us an opportunity to revert to TÖNNIES' theory concerning "*Gemeinschaft*" and "*Gesellschaft*", this time to elucidate the kernel of truth in his conception of the voluntary associations.

According to him it is the "*Kürwille*", the arbitrary will, which predominates in these associations. They are the rational products of the "*Gesellschaft*", in contradistinction to the "*Gemeinschaft*", although in some of them (*e.g.*, in trade unions) there are some remnants of "*Gemeinschaft*" to be found [1].

The truth in this view is that they are really the products of an individualizing and rationalizing process in the inter-individual and inter-communal relations of human society.

No longer enclosed in undifferentiated institutional communities with their collective patterns of thinking, volition and belief, the individual man acquires a relative autonomy in the inter-individual relationships with his fellow men; he is thus enabled to seek for free forms of organized cooperation according to a rational plan of means and ends. The purposes pursued in these organizational forms are to be freely chosen and as such display an immense variety, in accordance with the enormous increase and variation of human needs in the process of cultural disclosure. It is, therefore, necessary for the genetic forms consti-

---

[1] *Einfürung in die Soziologie* (1931), p. 108. TÖNNIES adopts WEBER's ideal-typical method of investigation, and consequently he does not sufficiently distinguish the field of these free associations from that of the organized institutional communities. He classes the modern State, for instance, and the institutional Church, with the "normal" or "ideal concept" association, cf. *Einführung in die Soziologie*, pp. 112—132. We find no trace of an inquiry into the internal structures of the societal relationships in his work. As we have repeatedly established, the "ideal typical" method in its subjectivistic levelling character is useless for such an inquiry.

tuting the voluntary associatory communities to display an abstract character. Only the establishment of a specific purpose and of the means to realize it can give them a typical relation to the particular inner nature of the organized community to be constituted.

As to their juridical aspect they imply a social compact or another type of contract, whose abstract figure, viewed apart from its specific ends, functions in the typical sphere of *common* private law. For we have seen that only in this private legal sphere, proper to the body politic, can the juridical relations be abstracted from any non-juridical qualification. This confirms our former statement that in the temporal order the State, as an institutional organized community, has priority over the differentiated voluntary associations, which have lost any foundation in the institutional communities of primitive society.

We have already observed in § 3 of the first chapter that besides the associatory forms of voluntary organization which give rise to communities in which the supreme authority belongs to all members together, there are also authoritarian forms. The latter constitute communities whose members are subject to an authoritative order which does not derive from their united will, but is imposed upon them by the founders. In this case membership originates from a labour contract, a contract of enrolment (as in the case of a private tuitional community), *etc.* and not from an associatory agreement. But, apart from its civil legal aspect, such a labour contract or contract of enrolment is, just as an associatory agreement, only a genetic form constituting a communal relation. Because of this contractual constitution of their membership these communities, too, are in principle to be considered as voluntary associations, though we have observed that they may assume an indirectly compulsory character in their existential forms.

This contractual character of their genetic forms is indeed a transcendental condition of all differentiated voluntary associations, because of their originating in the individualized and differentiated inter-individual relationships. The process of individualization and differentiation in the inter-individual and communal societal relations has proved to be typically founded in the opening or disclosure of the modal meaning of the historical aspect, and as such to have a transcendental basis in the temporal order.

As the inter-individual relationships lack in principle any

communal and authoritative character, they cannot give rise to organized communities but in an inter-individual genetic form. And in the nature of the case this form is a contractual one.

The typical difference between a contract of association and agreements which are not directed to the formation of voluntary organized communities, is to be characterized as follows: the former is a collective inter-individual act of consensus constituting a unified will of a whole, bound to a common purpose, whereas the latter lack this effect.

TÖNNIES has overlooked this difference when he supposed that all associatory bonds originating in the "*Gesellschaft*" are based on the egoistic contractual principle *do ut des*. The German jurists BINDING and TRIEPEL, on the other hand, have denied any contractual character to the genetic form of an association and called it a "*Vereinbarung*", *i.e.* a unifying volitional act. They held to the view that a contract is in the nature of the case restricted to two parties which have opposite interests and aims. They, too, were of the opinion that it is always based on the principle *do ut des*. This is certainly not true since a contract as such is nothing but a form of volitional agreement which is not bound to a specific content and only requires *at least* two parties. A contract may be to the benefit of only one of the parties and have a typically moral qualification as to its contents. There are collective contracts which harmonize opposite interests of the parties, and such which are entered into on account of one and the same interest of all the parties concerned. In addition BINDING and TRIEPEL do not restrict their concept "*Vereinbarung*" to volitional agreements which are directed to the constitution of an organized community. They even extend it to an agreement between two parties involved in a law-suit to finish the latter, because also in this case the will of the parties is directed to the same purpose. Thereby the arbitrary character of their distinction between a "*Vereinbarung*" and a *contract* is only accentuated.

If we restrict the meaning of the first term to the genetic forms of communities (inclusive of some institutional ones), it can only signify a *typical kind* of contractual agreement. But then it lacks a transcendental sense since institutional communities, insofar as they are compatible with such a typical genetic form, are not bound to the latter as their *necessary* genetic condition. Only voluntary associations are strictly bound to the genetic form of a "*Vereinbarung*" in which the above-mentioned establishment of the purpose of the association gives the contractual form its typical relation to the inner nature of the organized community constituted by it. And it is this typical purposive genetic form combined with the principle of free joining and leaving which distinguishes the category of free associations fundamentally from that of the institutional communities.

The Humanist natural law doctrine has thus rightly concluded that any organized community originating in completely individualized inter-individual relationships must have a contractual form of constitution. Its fundamental error was only the assumption that the institutional communities, too, can only arise from such individualized inter-individual relations and that the latter correspond to an original "state of nature".

It is true that in a modern individualized and differentiated society the agreement of the future marriage partners is an essential *condition* for constituting the institutional conjugal bond. But this agreement is in the nature of the case not a contract of free association in which the establishment of a specific purpose is constitutive. And in most countries it is not sufficient to constitute a marriage. As to the State, the natural law doctrine of its contractual genesis has been generally relinquished. With respect to the Church-institution it still plays an important rôle in the civil law doctrine. We shall revert to this question later on.

The internal leading function of the voluntary associations can never be identical with the purpose that its founders had in view.

The purpose that the founders of a voluntary association have established in the articles of the latter does not *coalesce* with the internal leading function of the organized community, originating from the act of foundation. This purpose and the established means to realize it can only mean the free choice of the type of association and give form to its internal structural principle. The latter is not the result of the act of formation but its transcendental condition. The foundation of a modern mining industry, *e.g.*, necessarily establishes an organized community of a supra-arbitrary structure. In this structure the foundational function is an historical (subjective-objective) organization of power comprising capital, management, division and coördination of labour. The economical administration of the organized process of production, in its necessary economically qualified subject-object relations, plays the rôle of the leading function. This structural principle, lying at the foundation of every organized industrial undertaking concerned in the process of production, assumes a particular geno-type by the specific object of production. The genetic and existential forms in which it is realized not only give it a positive shape in the *internal* relations of the organized community, they also embrace the *external* relations of the latter and thus function as true nodal points of enkaptic interlacements.

This is a second reason why the establishment of purpose and means of the voluntary association can never be identical with the internal structure of the community concerned. Its constitutive function in the genetic form of the latter gives the category of free association its typical relation to the internal structure of individuality to be realized *in a necessary correlation of communal and inter-individual relationships.* In addition its formative rôle is to a high degree dependent on the general patterns of genetic and existential societal forms which prevail in a certain developmental phase of human society, and belong to the positive order of the latter.

The subjective purpose of the founders of a modern department store is to buy commodities wholesale and to sell them retail to the public in order to make profits. The foundation of the department store is the established means to realize this purpose as it may be circumscribed in the genetic form of a joint stock company. But the societal relationships between sellers and purchasers are of an inter-individual character and are sharply distinguished from the internal structure of the business as an economically qualified labour community, historically founded in an organization of economic power. The establishment of purpose and means of the association implies a free choice of this type of organized community. But the formation of the latter is bound both to its internal structural principle and to general patterns of societal forms, which are beyond the subjective arbitrariness of the founders. Only within the scope between these supra-arbitrary limits can the subjective purposive plan of the founders play an individual formative rôle.

The interlacement of internal communal and external inter-individual relations in the establishment of purpose and means of a voluntary association. The internal structure of a trade union.

The state of affairs which revealed itself in the two above adduced examples of voluntary associations applies to all types of this societal category. We may formulate it in the general thesis: *The purpose of a voluntary association is not restricted to the internal life of the organized community to which it refers. It is necessarily directed to the correlation of internal communal and external inter-individual relationships.*

Even if the purpose should seem to concern only the inner sphere of the association, as in the case of a closed club, the established means to realize it necessarily imply external inter-individual relations. For the aim of the founders could not be a formative factor if it abstracted the internal leading function of the voluntary community from the inter-structural interlacements in human society. The genetic form itself in which the establishment of aim and means plays a constitutive rôle appeared to be a nodal point of such intertwinements. It is only *within* the latter that the distinction between the internal and the external relations of an association makes sense.

A clear insight into this state of affairs is of fundamental importance for a structural analysis of the voluntary associations. To complete this insight we shall consider the rôle of purpose and means in two other types of this category. This will give us occasion to elucidate the typical relation between the purpose and the leading function of the constituted voluntary community in some other respects, which cause particular difficulty in the case of an exclusively teleological view of the associations.

When the workmen in a particular branch of industry form a trade union primarily for the improvement of the labour conditions in this industrial branch, it is at once clear that their purpose implies both internal communal and external inter-communal relations. The labourers must be organized in a union of a typical internal structure in which their solidarity can only be maintained in relations of authority and subordination. And on the other hand their purpose is necessarily directed to their collective action outside of their organization in the inter-communal negotiations entered into on an equal footing with the organized or unorganized employers. It may be that these inter-communal relationships give rise to more or less permanent organs, composed of representatives of labourers and employers, and instituted by a collective contract. Such an organized cooperation with the employers may from the outset be implied in the purpose of the founders of the trade-union.

Besides, an association of some size like a trade-union will not restrict its efforts to one single purpose. But the qualifying or leading function in its internal structure must display a unitary character.

The internal leading function of a trade-union, in its typical coherence with the foundational function, is to be defined as a *moral bond of solidarity between the labourers typically founded in their organized historical vocational power to elevate labour to an essential and equivalent partner in the process of produc-*

tion. Purposes like the promotion of the intellectual and bodily development of the members, *etc.*, can as such never *qualify* the internal community. They may also be pursued in associations of a quite different structure of individuality. Only the chief aim has a typical relation to the internal leading function of the community, without being identical with the latter. But it will not always be easy to indicate one single chief purpose. As a matter of fact a multiplicity of aims can only get its coherence and inner articulation in chief and secondary ends by its relation to the structural principle of the community to which it gives a first positive form.

The typical relation between purpose and internal structure in a criminal organization. SINZHEIMER's legal sociological and HAURIOU's "institutional" view of a criminal association.

The establishment of the purpose of a voluntary association is a subjective act of the founders, in contradistinction to the structural principle of the organized community, which is a supra-arbitrary structural law. This explains how the subjective purpose may give the internal leading function of the organization a fundamentally illegal and criminal form, and that nevertheless the internal community remains bound to some typical moral, juridical, economical, and social normative principles which are indispensable to maintain the organizational bond between the members.

The German sociologist HUGO SINZHEIMER has overlooked this irrefutable state of affairs. In order to demonstrate that empirical sociology of law can investigate the societal human relationships apart from any normative legal viewpoint, he adduces the figure of a criminal organization. From a sociological point of view, the latter may be no less important than lawful associations [1]. I can agree with this statement. But it does not provide any argument in favour of his basic tenet. In the first place it is not possible to establish the factual existence of a criminal organization without the aid of norms functioning in a societal order.

A sociological positivist would doubtless reply that we may consider these norms only as factual rules of behaviour prevailing in a society which has accepted them. This may be granted. But this positivist viewpoint (which is not SINZHEIMER's)

[1] *De Taak der Rechtssociologie* (Haarlem, Tjeenk Willink & Zn.), p. 21.

cannot explain the undeniable fact that an organized gang of robbers, in its internal communal relations, maintains some fundamental norms of the "normal" society which it does not respect with regard to outsiders. It is in vain to consider this only as a question of utility. There exists a "code of honour" and an internal authoritative order in these organizations which cannot be explained in a utilitarian manner only, for it has a supra-arbitrary foundation in the structural principle of their internal communal sphere. This structural principle is in itself independent of the criminal purpose of the association and is not different from that of a "lawful" industrial labour organization. Just as the latter it has its foundational function in a power-formation of capital and division and coordination of labour by a managing intellect; in the same way it has its leading function in the economic administration of the undertaking; and it embraces relations of authority and subordination inherent in any business organization.

This implies a typical complex of normative (pre-positive) principles in the internal communal sphere, which are not different from those of a lawful industrial labour community and are indispensible to maintain the communal bond. But the criminal purpose of the organization and the maxims established to realize it give to this structural principle and to the different modal normative principles implied in it, an illegitimate *positive form* so that the association assumes the character of an organized community of professional crime, which may even display some traits of a military organization.

Maurice Hauriou, from the viewpoint of his "institutional theory", also stressed the difference between the purpose of the founders of an association and the internal "institutional idea" of the community. But, as we have seen earlier, he does not take into account the internal structural principles but replaces them by speculative neo-Platonic Ideas, which, via their attractive influence upon man in his social milieu, embody themselves in the organized communities as "*idées d'oeuvre*".

From this metaphysical viewpoint the criminal associations cause a particular difficulty. Hauriou finds no other way out to explain their "institutional" nature but the assumption of "bad Ideas" by the side of the "good Ideas", though subordinated to the latter. But, apart from the fact that this assumption contradicts the very fundamentals of the neo-Platonic doctrine of Ideas, it cannot solve the difficulty. For Hauriou overlooks that a "bad

Idea" cannot explain why even an organized gang of robbers in its internal communal sphere maintains some normative principles of behaviour which have a supra-arbitrary foundation in the divine world-order.

Evil does not possess an independent power but can only derive its attractive force from the divine creation. It can only *deform* but not *build* a societal community and even its deforming power is derived from the creation of man in the image of God.

In an organized gang of robbers it is the criminal purpose of the undertaking which deforms the positivation of a structural principle which as such is good. But apart from the latter the gangsters could not realize any communal relationship.

*

If the typical relation between the established purpose of the association and the supra-arbitrary principle of the latter is lost sight of, and the subjective purpose is considered the only factor which determines the typical internal nature of the voluntary association, there is nothing left but an eradication of the boundaries between the internal communal and the external inter-individual relations. Then the latter are also misinterpreted in a subjectivistic sense, as we shall show presently. Such a misconception is implied in the view that the types of organized communities that come into existence in the form of a free association are exclusively to be conceived from the viewpoint of an inter-personal contractual agreement. This view prevails in the nominalistic theory of natural law, as well as in modern juridical positivism.

TÖNNIES also holds this view of the "*Körperschaften*" originating from the free inter-personal relations. In his opinion the contract containing the external rational purpose is the exhaustive explanation of the nature of such associations, at least if they do not contain any remnants of what he calls a "communal mind". This is a second reason why from the outset I objected to adopting his contrast between "*Gemeinschaft*" and "*Gesellschaft*", although I readily admit that it contains an important element of truth. The point is that TÖNNIES ignores the internal structure of voluntary associations. He calls their internal unity a "construction of thought" [1]. The organized whole formed in

[1] *Op. cit.*, p. 98.

this way is in his opinion really the sum of internally unconnected *individuals* who, in spite of all organization, continue to be separate and single. This view cannot be correct. But it must be admitted that the non-institutional societal units meant here have arisen from the free inter-personal relations. And it is true that their internal communal bond may be of a superficial character. They will always betray their inter-individual origin in the form of their organization.

The process of individualization in the inter-personal relations as the emancipation of the individual man from the all-sided temporal embracement by the undifferentiated societal relationships. Once again TÖNNIES' antithesis between "*Gemeinschaft*" and "*Gesellschaft*".

Let us once again consider this genetic coherence between the voluntary associations and the differentiated inter-individual relations in its typical historical foundation. The elements of truth in TÖNNIES' view will thereby come to the fore in their real significance.

We have seen that all voluntary associations, in whose genetic form the establishment of aim and means plays a constitutive rôle, pre-suppose a process of individualization in the inter-personal societal relations. This individualization guarantees the separate individual person, as such, a sphere of private liberty in his temporal life *outside of all institutional communities.*

On a closed level of historical development human society is dominated by the undifferentiated communal relationships, embracing the whole temporal existence of the individuals except their natural communal and inter-communal bonds. Even in their inter-individual relations the individual persons are not present as such, but only in their inclusion by the special institutional organizations as members of different sibs and tribes or of various joint families. The inter-individual relations really function *primarily* between the undifferentiated social units, and *secondarily* between the individual members of the latter.

In the above-mentioned individualizing process of the inter-individual relations a real *emancipation* takes place. The individual spheres of liberty of the separate individual persons are recognized as falling outside of all institutional communal bonds. This individualizing process cannot start before the process of differentiation and integration begins to operate in human society. Then the undifferentiated forms of interlacement of societal structures are gradually dissolved. Under the influence of romanticism TÖNNIES considered the latter as natural communal bonds, in which the true "spirit of community" is operative in an unadulterated and energetic form. He overlooked that these primitive societal forms shut people off in a kind of exclusive "*symbiosis*" within comparatively narrow boundaries. These undifferentiated types of institutional communities are incompatible with the thought that individual men, as such, should have an individual sphere of social liberty withdrawn from any *communal sphere.*

Consequently there is doubtless a close connection between the rise of organizations constituted by an associational agreement or by a one-sided private act of foundation for a special purpose, and the breaking up of the undifferentiated institutional communites. But the result is that the inter-individual relations are no longer enclosed within the narrow limits of the tribe or the primitive ethnic community but, in principle at least, the individual may enter into free relations with other people wherever his new contacts may carry him. And in itself this is not fatal to human society but, on the contrary, it is completely in line with the opening-process of history and the vocation of man. To the latter point we shall revert presently.

The contrast between a large city and the country.

There is no doubt that this individualizing process has been much faster and more intense in the culture of a large city than in the country. In the country all kinds of remnants of undifferentiated societal relations may have been retained in a tenacious tradition connected with a certain dependence on the soil. This is suggestively illustrated by the simple comparison of a more or less patriarchal family of agriculturists with the family relations in a metropolis, where the differentiating and individualizing process has developed to an extreme degree of intensity.

It is true that, in contradistinction to a medieval town, a large modern city is as such not a community. But the medieval town could only be an institutional community by means of its guild-organization, which after all retained a primitive, relatively undifferentiated character. This does not detract from the fact that, as centres of trade and industry, these towns displayed developmental tendencies which in comparison with the medieval country must be called progressive. But these very tendencies necessarily led to the future dissolution of the guild-system and the breaking down of the town as a closed community.

The modern city has not dissolved all communal bonds into inter-individual relationships in which men are reduced to isolated individuals. Rather it shows the picture of a very complicated system of enkaptic interlacements between natural, political and ecclesiastic institutional bonds of community, inter-individual relationships of a cosmopolitan character, an immense variety of voluntary associations that may or may not give rise to differently qualified labour-communities, *etc.* The only really integrating communal bond in this extremely differentiated enkaptic system of societal relationships is the political bond of municipality; but it cannot make the modern metropolis in all of its differentiated communal and inter-individual relationships into a real communal whole.

In this respect the modern large city has a typically different character from a village in the country which has more or less retained the traits of a natural community, founded in biotic neighbourhood. In the metropolis the spirit of the natural communities no longer dominates societal life. The enormous expansion and individualizing of the inter-individual relationships has to a large degree deprived the latter of that intimate character which is characteristic of the inter-individual social life in an out of the way village. This is why, viewed apart from the central commandment of love, the metropolitan inter-individual societal relations display, at least preponderantly, an impersonal trait.

The Christian view versus the individualistic idea of inter-personal relations.

Viewed from its *structural* basis, and not from the sinful subjective way of its realization, this process of expansion and emancipation in the coordinated inter-individual relations does not have an un-christian and dissolving character. On the contrary, the Christian religion has laid the foundation of a world-wide expansion of the individualized inter-individual relations. By laying bare the religious root of mankind in creation, fall and redemption, it has revealed the meaning-fulness of the idea of community, in opposition to all narrow-minded nationalism and to all kinds of deification of particular temporal societal relationships. For the true idea of the free inter-personal relations, as conceived from the Biblical standpoint, does not start from an idea of man as a self-sufficient, autarchical "*individuum*", but from the religious supra-temporal unity of the human race founded in creation. According to its transcendental structure every temporal societal relationship should be an expression of this supra-temporal community, which reveals its full sense in the *corpus Christi*.

In the individualized opened inter-personal relations men are not socially united in a special *temporal* community, but they are nevertheless bound together in the transcendent unity of mankind. There is no question of a depreciation of these inter-individual relationships in the New Testament. In the parable of the merciful Samaritan, Jesus intentionally chooses such an inter-individual relationship to answer the question who is one's neighbour. The Jews and the Samaritans did not entertain any private temporal communal bonds with each other. But Jesus revealed their radical community, which implies that the central commandment of love also has validity outside of the temporal communal relations. Even in the most extreme differentiation and individualization of these free inter-personal relations man is never an autarchical self-contained "individual". The self-insufficiency and fundamental dependence of every single man assumes larger and larger proportions. The reason is that the opening-process in society is accompanied by an *immense increase of the individual man's needs* and thereby of his dependence, his reliance on others. For the means to satisfy these needs can only be produced in a highly differentiated process of division of labour.

HEGEL's dialectical idea of the "*bürgerliche Gesellschaft*".

HEGEL conceived the unbreakable correlation between the individualizing process in the inter-individual relations of "civil society" ("*bürgerliche Gesellschaft*") and the increasing interweaving of the interests of individual persons, as a "strategem of reason" *(List der Vernunft)*.

In his dialectical idealistic conception of "civil society" he tries dialectically to reconcile the naturalistic-individualistic construction of the free inter-personal relations, devised by THOMAS HOBBES, with the Humanistic idea of law and morality in KANT's individualistic conception of the ideal of autonomous personality.

Both conceptions are finally combined into a higher synthesis in HEGEL's own universalistic freedom idealism of the "objective spirit", objectifying itself dialectically in history. Thus he considers the individualizing process in the inter-individual social relations which started in the 16th and 17th centuries in the Western world, primarily to be an inevitable development of the selfishness of the "individual", in the sense of HOBBES' naturalistic view of society. The same natural necessity, however, causes the antagonistic principle of interdependence and solidarity to assert itself. Conceived within the categories of HEGEL's metaphysical logic, the dialectical unity of the "particular" and the "universal" finds its expression in this process. The particular purposes of the egoistic individual must assume the form of universality in order to come to themselves. In the *"beziehungsreiche Bezogenheit"* of all individual interests the welfare of others is promoted together with the selfish purpose of the individual person.

The particular purpose assumes the form of universality, though in "civil society" this universality remains restricted to the external relations [1] (*i.e.* the free inter-personal relations in our sense).

This "civil society" embraces all the individuals in the interwovenness of its totality. Thereby the moral Idea finds its expression in the social movement. This morality is still dominated by the compelling necessity of satisfying economic needs. It is the child of need and merely rational considerations, but it elevates civil society above blind natural necessity into the sphere of freedom. The ethical Idea as the substantial unity of subjectivity and objectivity (the latter intended in the sense of the legal and the moral *norms*), here diverges into these two dialectical moments. Subjectivity strives after the unlimited pursuit of its selfish economic interests, in its "free arbitrariness", not from a blind natural urge only.

This "free arbitrariness" of subjectivity is the sphere of its *abstract subjective right.* But in this it is confronted by the legal and ethical norm of universality, as its dialectical opposite. Thus the *"bürgerliche Gesellschaft"* drives the individual out of family life and raises him to a higher spiritual level of development pointing beyond itself to HEGEL's *"Vernunftstaat"*. In this *"Vernunftstaat"* the moral ideal reveals itself again in its substantial unity, because here the antithesis between subject and norm has been cancelled in the no longer *formal* but *substantial* moral freedom of everybody as a part of the whole. HEGEL's conception of "civil society" does not only embrace the "free inter-personal relations", in our sense, but also the State in the external intellectual conception of the *"Aufklärung"* (as the organized administration of justice and *"Polizei"*), together with all the voluntary associations [2]. In this view three main struc-

[1] Cf. Vol. III of HEGEL's *Encyclopädie der phil. Wissenschaften* (2nd ed.) §§ 523 and 534.

[2] Cf. *ibidem*, § 523: "die in sich entwickelte Totalität dieses Zusammenhanges (*i.e.* of the individuals and their private interests) ist der Staat als bürgerliche Gesellschaft oder als äusserer Staat". [The totality that has developed in this coherence is the State as civil society or the external State.]

tures are distinguishable within the *"bürgerliche Gesellschaft"* [1]:

1. the economic system of needs and their satisfaction in the economic process of labour, in which all the individuals cooperate in mutual dependence;
2. the system of the civil legal order and administration of justice, guaranteeing the work of all the individuals to be bound to those universal civil requirements by which subjectivity is subjected to the norm of universality;
3. the system of *"Polizei"* (police) in the wider sense of *"Verwaltung"* (*i.e.* public administration), as the factor of power suppressing all disturbing moments in the social development that are contrary to the requirements of external universality, and promoting the moments conducive to the private welfare of everybody.

In this conception civil society is from the outset made a preamble to the ideal State, as the "totality of substantial morality" and the final stage in the development of "objective Spirit". The internal structure of this society is conceived as a complex of economic purposes regulated by civil juridical and administrative legal rules.

The family and civil society are dialectically elevated to a higher unity in the totality of the absolute State. HEGEL from the outset conceives of the economic system of the needs of society in the modern form of the capitalistic system. The complete development of individual entrepreneurial dispositions and of private interests are predominant here. And with a keen eye HEGEL sees how the unrestrained development of mechanical production inevitably makes a whole class of the population dependent on the capitalists [2].

HEGEL fully realized that the increasing differentiation in social needs necessarily entails an increasing division of labour. In the latter the individuals form *social classes* according to the kind of work they share of their own free choice in the process of labour. The "reason immanent in society" (*"immanente Vernunft"*) finds expression in this grouping into social classes. For in the infinite variety of individual purposes *general* features appear in a common occupation. Thus the social coherence is differentiated into special systems of needs, the means of their satisfaction, and labour; and the individuals have to integrate themselves into one of these systems. Social class distinctions can be reduced to a logical triad:

1. the substantial or agricultural class;
2. the reflecting or formal class, the class of manual labourers and manufacturers, and

---

[1] Cf. *Enc.* §§ 524, 529 and 533.

[2] Cf. PAUL VOGEL, *Hegel's Gesellschaftsbegriff* (Berlin, 1925).

3. the general class which does not depend on a natural soil like the first, nor, like the second, on the free treatment of a material in adaptation to the variable demand of a market, but looks after all those interests relating to the maintenance and the ordering of civil society as a whole.

HEGEL'S view of the corporative vocational classes.

HEGEL is of the opinion that the formation of voluntary associations in our sense, or "*Korporationen*" (as he styles them), is of a more fundamental importance only for the second social class, that of the manual labourers and manufacturers. The typical productive work of this social class is dependent on the variable demand of a market. Consequently they run the risk of losing themselves in the striving after more or less insignificant private interests, and of entirely failing to see the higher, general concerns.

Corporative joining together is the remedy against this evil. In the social corporation the individual citizen leaves the sphere of his private interest to cooperate in the service of the comparative universality of the organized corporative group interest. This is the highest form of public spirit attainable in civil society. But in principle it remains below the level of the State, in which society, just like the family, can only have the position of a *part* within the *whole*.

HEGEL conceives free associations only in the sense of "corporative occupational classes". The "corporation" is the only seat and guarantee of "vocational class honour". Any one who is no member of any recognized corporation has no such "honour". He is isolated; and to maintain himself he must concentrate all his attention on the selfish aspect of his occupation. His sustenance and enjoyment of life are entirely dependent on the uncertainty of his individual income. His selfish diligence tries to outstrip all others with any means that promise to be successful, without taking account of the interests of the others. He does not feel obliged to live in accordance with his social station because there is no "social station" for him.

The mere fact that his occupational fellows have much in common with him is not sufficient to make him a conscious member of a "class". Only the corporation strives after reconciling the sharp antithesis in civil society between individual interest and the demand of universality in the form of civil law. Each of its members recognizes the private welfare of any other member as a right which he helps to guarantee and to maintain. Just like the sanctity of the marital and the family bond, the corporative class-ethics must be maintained, if civil society is not to be doomed to decay.

Criticism of HEGEL's view of society.

This summary of HEGEL's view of "civil society" has been somewhat elaborate, because all modern theories about the structure of social life, and also TÖNNIES' theory of "*Gesellschaft*", have been more or less influenced by it. This is sufficient to indicate its importance. HEGEL has given a masterly interpretation of the historical development of the modern individualized inter-individual societal relations. He has integrated his insight into some essential features of this development, into his universalistic Humanistic freedom idealism. He has evaluated the influence of the Christian idea of free inter-personal relations on the individualizing process in modern social relations; he has shown that in the ancient Greco-Roman culture such an individualizing process was impossible since the religious value of the individual personality was not yet recognized.

But notwithstanding all these important elements of truth, HEGEL's Humanistic conception of modern society is unacceptable to us. In a universalistic way it is oriented to a deified national State so that it cannot correctly conceive of the peculiar integrational tendencies in the individualized free inter-individual relations. HEGEL's logicistically founded scheme of three social classes has a speculative-constructive character. The economic motives in free society are considered to be the primary forces in individual development though unconsciously directed by the "moral idea". This is an exaggerated conception of the significance of the economic motives oriented to the idea of the *homo economicus.* Historical materialism was to transform this liberalist assumption into the thesis that the foundational rôle belongs *to the technical-economic forms of production* as supra-individual driving forces of society.

Thus the individualizing-process is misrepresented and, as a consequence, HEGEL's account of the internal structural diversity of the voluntary organizations is also defective. The latter are forced into the constructive scheme of the three occupational classes. This scheme from the outset unjustifiably restricts HEGEL's theory and renders it insufficient as a truly philosophical structural theory of the inter-individual relationships, and the voluntary associations arising from them.

Nevertheless, one of the most important elements of truth in this theory is the insight into the peculiar generalizing and integrating tendency in the free societal purposes, which forms the necessary counterpart of the increasing individualizing tendency. Here HEGEL has really discovered a structural law of modern society which (though often misinterpreted in a natural-scientific sense) has found general recognition in sociological theory. It is this law which first demands our attention.

§ 3 - INDIVIDUALITY STRUCTURES IN THE INDIVIDUALIZED FREE INTER-INDIVIDUAL AND INTER-COMMUNAL RELATIONS, AND THE INTEGRATING TENDENCIES IN MODERN SOCIETY.

The structural law HEGEL discovered had best be called the normative law of correlative differentiation and integration in the inter-individual societal relations founded in the opened historical development.

We have already seen that this structural law also holds for the development of the organized communal relationships. For the dissolution of the undifferentiated organized communities proved to be accompanied by the rise of integrating institutional communities, which pull down the partition-walls between different ethnical groups and unite them into a higher differentiated whole. But in the free inter-individual societal relations, as such, this structural law cannot manifest itself in the same way. Integration cannot result here in a transformation of non-communal relations into communal ones. How then does this law operate in the inter-individual spheres of human society?

Individuality-structures in the differentiated inter-individual and inter-communal relationships.

Let us first consider the individuality-structures displayed by the differentiated inter-individual or inter-communal societal relations. For it would be a fundamental misunderstanding to suppose that at least the latter lack such structural types. If this were so, they could not belong to the full temporal reality of societal life. For this reality necessarily reveals itself in individuality-structures in which the modal structures of the law-spheres are only implied or pre-supposed *a priori*.

Free market relations, publicity, the differentiated fashions (in dress, recreation, conversation, *etc.*), sports and competition, the press, the various kinds of traffic, public musical and theatrical performances, private philanthropy, diplomacy, international political relations, electioneering propaganda of political parties, missionary activity, *etc.*, imply a rich variety of structural types in the differentiated inter-individual and inter-communal relationships. That the latter are necessarily correlated with (voluntary or institutional) organized communal relationships does not detract from their own structural typicalness.

Just like those of a differentiated communal character, the individuality-structures of the differentiated inter-individual or inter-communal relationships possess two radical functions of which the leading function has the qualifying rôle. Fashion, *e.g.*, as an inter-individual societal phenomenon, is qualified by a typical function of *social intercourse,* just like "sports". Such phenomena as a free market, publicity, market competition, *etc.* are economically qualified, social philantropy is of a *moral* qualification, missionary activity is qualified as an activity of faith, *etc.* All these structures are of a typical *historical foundation.*

Also individual acts display different individuality-structures according to their inter-individual side. Saluting a friend in the street, *e.g.*, is *qualified* as a typical act of *social intercourse* although, as a concrete act, it functions in all the law-spheres. A purchase agreement or a lease-contract is *economically* qualified [1], a public performance of music is *aesthetically* qualified, giving an alms in public is *morally* qualified, *etc.* In this sense the free inter-individual relations, too, may be said to have an *internal* structure. But this structure does not include people in a solidary internal unit as to their temporal existence, as is done by the structure of a community. The structure of an inter-individual relationship, *as such,* is not based on an organization, but the individuals functioning in it are left to act in essential coordination, although they are dependent on one another. In the inter-individual or inter-communal spheres human actions interlock either in cooperation or in antagonism. They are either pointed in one direction (*e.g.,* in following fashions), or they supplement one another (in the process of the social division of labour), or they are at strife with each other (competition in the

---

[1] Such an agreement is *not juridically* qualified. Only in their enkaptical interlacement with State-positivized "civil law" do social agreements acquire a civil juridical aspect. As explained earlier, civil law is not identical with inter-individual private law, but it is essentially private law, integrated by the State, and leaving the internal structure of economically qualified inter-individual law intact.

market, relations of war, *etc.*). The positivized structural norms act as regulators in this process, and the normative leading functions of the various structures of inter-individual relationships also open the latter's pre-logical functions in an anticipatory direction. Therefore any attempt to explain the inter-individual relations as "natural phenomena", as was done by the older mechanist trend in sociology, rests on a fundamental misconception.

Primitive and opened inter-individual societal structures.

We shall now explain in what way the law of integration reveals itself in the differentiated typical structures of the individualized inter-individual societal relationships. Therefore it is necessary to consider once again the difference between these differentiated structures and those of primitive inter-individual social relations.

We have seen that the latter are as yet undifferentiated and wholly interwoven with the undifferentiated order of the narrow tribal or folk-community. Primitive inter-individual societal relations consequently possess the same *isolating* and *limiting* character as these organized communities themselves. The inter-individual social customs and manners vary from tribe to tribe. Everything outside the primitive folk-relationship is experienced as something *alien* or even *hostile.* Each tribal relationship has its own *vertically individualized,* isolated, miniature "society".

Compare with this state of affairs modern individualized "society" based on Western civilization, and it is at once evident that the modern positive structural norms of inter-individual relationships show an opposite tendency: their sphere of validity tends to *horizontal expansion* all over the civilized world, and not to vertical isolation. Even the modern State is unable to set vertical limits to this horizontal expansion though, as an institutional organized community, the body politic itself exhibits an integrating character. In principle modern inter-individual relations have *international* tendencies.

In the positivizing process of their structural types organized or un-organized "leading groups" generally come to the fore. As such, they do not possess any societal authority implying a claim to obedience, but they take the lead in inter-individual social life, and are generally followed and imitated.

The integrating character of fashion. Fashion and national dress.

"Fashion" is a very interesting example of social imitation. Its proper nature asserts itself quite obviously in the horizontal inter-individual societal relations. Here fashion integrates the way in which people dress, their inter-individual behaviour in general, the choice of their recreations, *etc.*, without uniting the individuals to a temporal societal unity. On the contrary, fashion in this sense is experienced as a dividing factor in human society. Originally it was a means used by the higher classes to distinguish themselves from the lower classes, although the latter are always eager to imitate them. Think of SCHILLER's *Ode an die Freude:*

> *"Deine Zauber bindet wieder*
> *Was die Mode frech geteilt."*

The fashion-norms of dress are very variable, they even vary with the seasons. They are not formed by some casual "individuals", but by the "leading circles" who possess organized power in social intercourse, by the "leading" houses in Paris, London, Vienna, *etc.* These circles cannot *create real norms of fashion* in a perfectly arbitrary way. They remain bound to dynamical principles of social taste, distinction, efficiency, founded in historical development, as well as to the individuality structures of the societal relations in which the various types of dress are worn. These principles leave ample scope to the formative phantasy of these designers of fashion. Models that do not reckon with these principles will not easily find acceptance in society. *Extravagances* of fashion never have a *normative* function.

Norms of fashion in inter-individual societal relations have a patent *expansive, international* character, although their positive forms may display an extraordinary capricious variability. They overstep the boundaries of the national communities and express the idea of modern world citizenship albeit in a very external sense. In a restricted area there may still exist a "national dress", which had better be styled a "folk-dress" since it is characteristic of an ethnical group, rather than of a nation as a whole. But there is no *national fashion* in dress. Modern fashion is intrinsically international and the avowed enemy to "national costumes", making the latter to a kind of atavism in modern society. Fashion is the great cosmopolitan ruler representing a powerful integrating factor in inter-individual social relations, notwithstanding its capriciousness.

It is meaningful to point these things out emphatically, in opposition to v. JHERING, who in his work *Der Zweck im Recht* treats fashion as a social excrescense, in contrast to "folk-dress". Fashion he considers as originating solely in impure motives of class pride and vanity [1]. But he forgets that modern society displays an integrating process in every sphere. This process is incompatible with the preponderance of historical-ethnical peculiarities in social forms of inter-individual intercourse, and is in itself certainly no sign of decadence, but the necessary condition of an expansive development of the inter-individual societal relationships. Nor is it as such a symptom of the impersonal "mass-man", since it leaves scope to the expression of personal individuality.

In the modern reaction of fascism and national socialism an artificial national element — in fact nothing but a device of the ruling totalitarian party — was made to dominate even the inter-individual relations of social intercourse (witness the "German" and "Italian fascist" manner of saluting). This was a foolish set-back of the normal development of modern inter-individual social life, caused by the setting up of national barriers (also in the economically, scientifically, and aesthetically qualified relations).

The *differentiating factors* in the *integrating tendency* of individualized inter-individual relations are the individuality-structures of the latter. Fashion in general, *e.g.*, as an integrating structure, is only radical-typically qualified by its leading function in the social relations of *intercourse*. It is geno-typically and pheno-typically differentiated according to particular subject-object relations and its interweaving with other structural types of inter-individual relations: there is, *e.g.*, a fashion in sporting clothes, in evening dress, in travelling clothes, lounge-suits and street-dresses, *etc.* This differentiation, however, is no longer predominantly dependent on national or local peculiarities [2], but it bears an *expansive cosmopolitan* character.

---

[1] *Op. cit.* II, p. 188.

[2] The climate and other natural factors to some degree continue to cause a separation. In Indonesian society, *e.g.*, even the social forms of intercourse among Europeans are influenced by climatic factors, in the first place with regard to clothing.

This statement holds good for *all* opened individuality structures in the modern inter-individual relations of human society. In the first place in *all* the types of the latter qualified by the function of social intercourse, and not solely in those belonging to fashion, the differentiational process is indissolubly bound up with an international integrating tendency, imparting a cosmopolitan character to the forms of social intercourse. In civilized modern society the national character is becoming less and less decisive for the differentiated forms of inter-individual intercourse; the recent reactionary phenomena, mentioned above, may be left out of account because they have disappeared since the break-down of the totalitarian political systems which gave rise to them. National or local forms of inter-individual intercourse and customs which have no typical foundation in climatic or other natural factors, are increasingly experienced as obsolescent peculiarities that are gradually dying out. Only where modern "civilized" man enters into social contact with people of a more or less isolated culture, the vertical contrast between the different cultural characters is also fully revived within the inter-individual relations of human society.

The correlation between the modern integrating and differentiating tendencies reveals itself perhaps even more strongly in the typical economically qualified inter-individual relationships. Here modern technical development and modern world traffic are the great integrating factors. The differentiation is brought about chiefly according to the international branches of trade, industry, *etc.* The typical integrating tendencies within these economically qualified structures of inter-individual relationships are founded in the economic power of the leading entrepreneurial groups.

The economically qualified integration of contractual law in the different branches of the inter-individual industrial relationships.

This state of affairs is clearly revealed in the inter-individual legal relations of industrial and commercial life. The increasing integrating significance of so-called customary stipulations, standard-contracts, general conditions, *etc.* in the individual economically qualified agreements has left only very little scope to the private autonomy of the contracting parties in this typical sector of inter-individual relationships. In the so-called *contrats d'adhésion* the contents of the agreement are even completely one-sidedly established by the organized industrial groups; those who want to make use of their economic services are obliged to accept their contractual conditions because they have no other choice. It is evident that the organized leading groups have no single legal competence to impose their integrating contractual rules upon the individual parties of an agreement. These rules can only assume the character of customary law because they are usually accepted by the contracting parties themselves. It is only their leading rôle in the inter-individual relationships of industrial and commercial life, based upon their organized economic power, which enables the organized groups to bring about a horizontal integration in the contents of the individual agreements. And this integration is differentiated according to the horizontal branches of industry or trade.

This does not mean an intrinsical transformation of civil law into an economically qualified "social law", as DUGUIT supposed. The integrating process in the economically qualified inter-individual relationships does not pertain to the internal sphere of civil law, but to that of inter-individual industrial and commercial law, which is only enkaptically interwoven with the former. We have already seen that outside of the internal sphere of civil law there is no question of any abstract "equality" of the (coordinated) subjects in the inter-individual societal relations. Everywhere differences in talent, social-economic position, *etc.* assert themselves in the latter.

The rationalizing process in modern society. Technical progress and science as rational integrating factors.

Modern technical progress is one of the most powerful integrating factors in the modern individualized and differentiated inter-individual societal relations. In this process the social rôle of *science* as a necessary integrating factor is implicitly set in the clearest light, together with the enkaptic inter-structural interlacements of the different types of inter-individual societal relationships. As a *concrete* social phenomenon, presenting itself in the correlation of inter-individual and organized communal relationships, *"science"* displays a theoretically-logically qualified (and materially differentiated) individuality-structure *founding* that of modern technical progress.

The opening and individualizing process in the free inter-individual societal relations is at the same time a rationalizing process of human society. As such, the latter is no more a symptom of apostasy and decadence than the process of integration, provided that is is accomplished harmoniously, and not by overstraining theoretical thought. Rather it is destined to disclose and to realize the potentialities and dispositions inherent in the social relations according to the divine world-order.

The individualizing, differentiating and integrating process in the free inter-individual relations as well as in the internal organizational relationships cannot dispense with the support of science in the long run. Even the formation of positive norms in the different normative modal aspects of the inter-individual societal relations needs the aid of science, when the process mentioned above progresses.

As far as the formation of law is concerned, the Historical School had a correct insight into this state of affairs. In the description of the development of law this school set in the light that the class of scientific jurists began to play a necessary part in the formation of law when juridical relations became more and more complicated. But this insight did not warrant the inference that theoretical jurisprudence is a formal source of positive law, as PUCHTA and JHERING (in the second volume of his *Geist der Römischen Rechtes*) supposed. For juridical science as such, lacks the competence to form law. The juridical concept of competence is an essential moment of the concept "*source of law*".

The growing influence of individualistic tendencies in modern society during the first half of the XIXth century and the irreconcilable struggle of the Christian idea of inter-individual relationship against them.

The correlated differentiating and integrating tendencies in the modern inter-individual societal relationships cannot fail to result in an individualistic process of disintegration in modern society, if they are not counter-balanced by a due unfolding of the organized institutional communities and voluntary associations. This disintegration is what actually happened under the leading of the Humanistic science-ideal in the first phase of industrial revolution. The rationalized and absolutized idea of free inter-individual relations dominated the entire industrial sector of Western society and gave it an extremely individualistic and merciless capitalistic form. It is true that the process of differentiation and integration tends to increase the interweaving of individual interests. But in the free inter-individual societal relations the unrestrained striving after separate interests gave rise to fierce antagonism, which even lacked the remedy indicated by HEGEL, *viz.* the formation of organized occupational classes.

The process of unlimited one-sided technical rationalization in economically qualified industrial life sharpened the contrast between the interests of labour and capital to a real class-struggle. Labour was viewed apart from the human personality as market ware, and in the factories the labour-community was to a high degree affected by the individualist, exclusively contractual viewpoint. The unlimited competition on the market made the Hobbesian picture of the state of nature, as a condition of "*homo homini lupus*", into a terrible reality.

As the inter-individual societal structures are indissolubly interwoven with those of the institutional relationships, family and kinship as well as the State were also affected by this morbid process of disease in "free society". Societal groups for the promotion of private interests tried to seize the political power to make the institution of the State subservient to their social ends. The factor of private economical interest and the poisonous ideology of the dogma of class struggle penetrated the political party system. Family- and kinship-life of the labourers were denatured by the encroachment of the impersonally rationalized industrial labour-relations. In international political relations the "sacred egoism" of the separate States was elevated to the highest law.

Such individualistic tendencies in social development form an irreconcilable antithesis with the Christian idea of free inter-individual relations. The *civitas terrena* revealed itself in this individualistic process of distintegration, and Christianity was doomed to decay whenever it thought of making a truce, or concluding a peace-treaty with this kingdom of darkness.

The counter-tendencies in the forms of horizontal organization of modern society. The so-called Christian solidarism and its universalist view of industrial life.

For reasons of self-preservation it is necessary for modern society to develop counter-tendencies against the unbridled operation of individualism. This is what modern society is actually doing in the formation of voluntary associations or unions which direct the typical integrative tendencies in *horizontal forms of organization.*

These organizational forms are to be observed in the most different sectors of free societal life, in science and fine arts, in sports and the different branches of instruction, in journalism, philantropy, *etc.* But the most impressive image of this organizational integrating process is to be found in the economically qualified societal relationships. Both employers and labourers in trade, traffic and industry have organized themselves according to the various branches of the latter, though in all these branches organization has not arrived at an equal level of development.

In addition, trusts, large business concerns, *etc.* have been formed, which often display an international character. And although cartels are not organized communities, they often exercise an international restraining influence on unbridled competition, though they may also imply serious dangers to healthy market relations. The increase of collective bargaining stimulated the idea that employers and labourers should try and find new horizontal forms of organized cooperation. The aim was to give expression to their solidarity in taking to heart the common interests in the different branches of industrial life and to strengthen the communal bonds between employers and labourers in the separate industrial undertakings.

It was especially the Christian conception of social solidarity which inspired this idea, frankly in opposition to the Marxian dogma of class-struggle. In different countries it has exercised a salutory influence upon the integrating tendencies in modern industrial societal relationships. Nevertheless, it must be granted that this movement of Christian solidarism had not completely emancipated itself from the universalist-romantic view of human society, current in the so-called Christian-historical trend of thought in the period of the Restauration. Especially the conception of an entire branch of industry as a "natural community", which was considered as an autonomous and "organical" part of the "national whole", revealed an after-effect of this romantic view, which could eventually be synthesized with the Aristotelian-Thomistic view of society.

It was overlooked that a branch of industry necessarily displays a correlation between organizational-communal and intercommunal or inter-individual relationships, and that the latter can never be transformed into the former. It was further overlooked that a national community can never encompass the internal industrial relationships, notwithstanding their enkaptical intertwinement with national life.

This universalist misconception resulted in the erroneous idea that a public legal organization of industrial life was to be considered as a natural development of the true inner nature of the different branches of industry, as "natural communities". From an "organical" view of human society it was concluded that the horizontal organizations of these industrial branches could lay claim to a public legal competence *on their own account* by virtue of an "historical right", consequently a competence not derived from the legislator. Here we meet with the appeal to the medieval guilds, whose public legal autonomy preceded the rise of the modern State as a *res publica.* Some Christian politicians, influenced by the Germanist wing of the Historical School, had argued that this political autonomy should be attributed also to modern industrial organizations in line with the organic development of history. This original (not derived) public legal competence should only be accommodated to the modern "organic" State-idea by acknowledging the sovereign power of the body politic to test the autonomous compulsory regulations of the industrial associations to the public interest.

This "organical view" was readily accepted by the movement of Christian solidarism both in its Roman Catholic and Protestant trends. In the Netherlands the Protestant Christian league of trade unions interpreted the principle of sphere-sovereignty (Dutch: "*souvereiniteit in eigen kring*") of industrial life in this sense. But in this way this principle was completely misunderstood since it was viewed apart from its structural foundation in the temporal order of reality. It was overlooked that medieval political autonomy, so long as it was viewed as a subjective right of the guilds, only suited to an undifferentiated society and that a public legal authority is never to be derived from the inner nature of a private organization of industrial life in its different branches. Here, too, it appears that a universalist denaturation of the genuine Christian idea of social solidarity necessarily leads to an eradication of the structural principles of the different types of societal relationships.

A public legal organization of industrial life, as it was introduced in the Netherlands by the Public Industrial Organization Act of 1950, can as such never belong to the inner sphere-sovereignty of industry and agriculture as economically qualified sectors of the societal process of production. Within a State's territory any public legal authority exercised by organs composed of representatives of organizations of employers and trade unions, is derived from the legislator. A public legal organization means an organization of the industrial and agricultural branches which is typically qualified by the leading juridical function of the State. The organs of such an organization may have a delegated autonomy, whose limits are completely dependent on the public interest in the previously defined sense. But any confusion of this autonomy with the inner sphere-sovereignty of the economically qualified private industrial and agricultural relations must lead either to a deformation of public legal authority, or to an absorption of free industrial and agricultural life by the political sphere of the State.

The international tendencies in the political integration of modern society.

By means of a public legal industrial organization the State can strengthen the integrating tendencies revealing themselves in the formation of private horizontal organizations in the different branches of industry, agriculture, *etc.* In line with the modern view of public industrial ordering, the State will not be satisfied with such a horizontal public legal integration but combine the latter with a compulsory vertical organization of the processes of national production which intersect the horizontal branches of industry and agriculture. In both respects the integrating function of the body politic continues to be restricted by its own internal structural principle, as we have explained in an earlier context. By means of a public legal industrial organization, the State can only bind the industrial (and agricultural) relationships insofar as the latter are enkaptically interwoven with its own structure.

And the same restriction holds good for its integrating function with respect to the other non-political spheres of societal relationships which lack an institutional character.

Meanwhile, even the typical political integration of these relationships under the leading viewpoint of public interest displays international tendencies which, especially since the second world-war, have assumed a considerable extent. The two terrible world-wars have clearly shown the increasing interdependence of the individual States and the untenability of the dogma of political sovereignty in its earlier sense, based on an individualistic view of the international political relations. The latter display an integrating tendency similar to that of non-political inter-individual relationships. The big powers have the leading rôle in this process, especially in the international military integration of the defensive means of the weaker States. This process is only checked by the recent division of the world into two opposite camps of political ideology. The first principle, formulated in the second article of the Charter of the United Nations, according to which all the members of this international organisation are considered on the footing of sovereign equality, does certainly not pertain to questions of international security. On the contrary, the leading position of the big powers in this international political sector is clearly confirmed in article 23 of the Charter concerning the composition of the Security Council.

In the present context we are, however, not further concerned with questions of international security, but much rather with the integrating function of the U.N.O. in the non-political spheres of human society. The first article of the Charter mentions as one of the purposes of the United Nations: to achieve international co-operation in solving international problems of an economic, social, cultural, or humanitarian character, and in promoting and encouraging respect for human rights and for fundamental freedoms for all, without distinction as to race, sex, language, or religion; and to be a centre for harmonizing the actions of nations in the attainment of these common ends.

The enormous activity developed by the U.N.O. and its subdivisions in the performance of this integrating task is well known. This might raise the question as to whether at least the U.N.O. is not to be viewed as an all-inclusive society embracing all human societal relationships in a supreme unit. So long as the teleological viewpoint supersedes the structural analysis of the different societal relationships the semblance of such a supreme unit of modern society might lead us astray. The truth is, however, that the U.N.O. is nothing but a voluntary association of individual States; its internal structure is qualified by an international public legal function and founded in an historical international organization of power. Though its structural principle is consequently of the same radical type as that of the State, it lacks the institutional character of the latter. In addition it lacks any monopolistic organization of armed force and a territory. And for lack of an independent armed force it cannot exercise real governmental authority over the States which are its members. So it is far from being a *civitas maxima*. And even a *civitas maxima* would lack the character of an all-inclusive societal whole of mankind.

The established purposes and means of this international organization (*viz.* the U.N.O.) cannot define its inner nature, which gives an internal restriction to its integrating task with respect to the international relations in the non-political spheres of human society. It is the juridically qualified principle of international public interest which determines the inner nature of this integrating function. The latter displays a promoting and supporting political character and not the compulsory trait of a governmental State regulation, which eventually can impose an ordering deemed to be necessary from the viewpoint of public interest (though the binding force of such a measure cannot exceed the inner boundaries of the State's competence).

The radical Christian idea of human freedom and the tension between the individualistic and the binding integrating tendencies in modern society.

Against the individualistic tendencies in free society God's conserving grace thus calls into play antagonistic organizational tendencies of an integrating character.

In this way the divine world-order is also maintained in the individualized inter individual societal relations. But if this process develops under the predominant leading of an apostate attitude of faith absolutizing temporal interests, there is no harmonious cooperation between the free development of inter-individual relations and the increasing integrative significance of organizational bonds.

Indeed it appears that modern social development displays the picture of a continuous tension between the two tendencies, alternately overstraining the one or the other at the expense of the sound development of both. After a period of extreme individualism modern society is now threatened by a communistic universalism which seeks to realize a totalitarian community of mankind by means of the State's power, although in its ideology the State is completely depreciated. More than a third part of the human race is delivered to the political power of this totalitarian ideology.

Western democracy is in fear of this tremendous adversary and seeks to defend itself by an international integration of its military forces. Nevertheless, by military means alone the freedom of man is not to be protected. It should not be forgotten that communism in its Marxian and Bolshevist sense is primarily a spiritual power, a secularized eschatological faith in the final liberation of mankind in a future classless society. It should be borne in mind that, viewed from this spiritual background, it has originated in the dialectical process in which Western thought has been involved since the religious Humanist basic motive of nature and freedom began to reveal its driving power in Western history. And the historical rise of Humanism was closely connected with the dialectical process in which Christian thought was involved by the introduction of the dualist scholastic basic motive of nature and grace.

In this entire dialectical process of Western thought the view of human society was continually swayed between the poles of universalism and individualism. All attempts to find a way out of this alternative were doomed to fail so long as the immanence standpoint was maintained, and the radical and integral freedom of the individual or the radical and integral community of mankind were sought in the temporal order of our earthly existence.

It is of no avail to disregard the fact that to a large extent the spiritual basis of the modern Western ideas of freedom and authority has been undermined by Historicism and relativism. The simple fact that the fascist and nazist totalitarian ideologies could be presented as the only real alternative over against the communistic system was a symptom of this process. And that this suggestion could acquire such a tremendous influence in many countries of central and Southern Europe should be a warning against an optimistic judgment of the real state of affairs. The truth is that since the decline of individualism, even in democratic countries new universalist ideas have penetrated the practical and theoretical view of society. They are presented as a mere historical necessity and adapted to the traditional democratic ideas, which have changed their sense, and in the prevailing theories of the State have been emancipated from their former foundation in an eternal natural law order.

This is why the integrating tendencies in the inter-individual or inter-communal relationships and in the voluntary organizations are readily interpreted as a process of socialization in which the idea of community gains the upperhand. Since this view of social development is emancipated from the structural principles of the differentiated societal relationships, it results in an overestimation of the integrating rôle of the national and international political communities.

Even the traditional doctrine of unassailable human rights is not able to check the absolutization of temporal communal relationships, if these rights themselves are interpreted in a universalistic sense. As soon as the inter-individual and inter-communal relationships are viewed as *intra-communal,* and the structural idea of internal sphere-sovereignty of the different orbits of societal life is replaced by those of autonomy or functional decentralization, there is no *fundamental* and *radical* defence against the totalitarian systems.

This radical defence is only found in the Biblical view of human freedom implied in the basic motive of creation, fall into sin and redemption by Jesus Christ. For it converts the whole view of temporal society; it excludes in principle both universalism and individualism, and it enables us to see the structural patterns in the complicated interlacements between inter-individual and communal relationships. The internal sphere-sovereignty of the different temporal structures of societal relationships is the expression of the transcendent destination of mankind. This is the only basis of a harmonious relation of authority and freedom in social development.

§ 4 - A MORE DETAILED EXAMINATION OF SOME TYPES OF FREE ASSOCIATION.

The voluntary associations display an infinite structural variety. Some of them only touch man's temporal existence very superficially, such as "clubs"; others, *e.g.*, the horizontal occupational organizations such as trade unions, *etc.*, occupy a very important and extensive place in modern society and are at least partly animated by a strong spirit of community and solidarity. Here follows a discussion of the structure of two different types, one of which unites people only very superficially, the other more intensively.

The structural principle of the *restricted club.*

The typical foundation of the restricted club is an historical form of organized social [1] power exercised by the higher classes.

---

[1] The adjective "social" is here meant in the sense of "related to the modal aspect of social intercourse".

Its typical leading function is that of social intercourse within a closed communal circle. The special means of promoting this social intercourse in the club relationship are dependent on the special purposes that the founders wanted to realize within the typical structure of their society. The structural principle reveals itself in the typical structural coherence between the foundational and the leading function, and these functions are found in the historical law-sphere and that of social intercourse, respectively. All the really internal communal relations of this type ought to be determined by this structural principle in such a way that the latter finds expression in all the aspects of this societal relationship. Only the internal juridical aspect will be examined here.

The club relationship as such possesses its typical structure of authority which is fundamentally different from that in the organized communities hitherto investigated. The club's authority structure is qualified by its leading function as a communal relationship for select social intercourse. In the internal juridical aspect this structure expresses itself in the juridical authority over the individual members vested in the board and the general assembly. The typical internal juridical competences and duties of the members can never be conceived in their material juridical sense apart from the structural principle.

By suffering a member's mere bodily presence in the club's premises, while deliberately excluding him from any personal social intercourse, the club deprives such a member of his internal societal rights, even though such an internal juridical wrong cannot be redressed in a civil legal way. The provisions concerning the requirements for membership and the grounds of expulsion are of a typical *internal* juridical character, for these provisions cannot be conceived in their material juridical meaning apart from the structural principle of the club-relationship. Recall the ballot in connection with the social position of the applicant for admission, and the expulsion of a member on the ground of actions that are deemed incompatible with the standing of the club. But all this internal societal law has its reverse side in civil legal inter-individual relations. This will appear in the discussion of juridical sphere-sovereignty in the enkaptic interlacements of communal with inter-individual societal relationships.

The structural principle of the political party and some sociological definitions of the latter.

We shall have to devote a more elaborate investigation to the structural principle of a political party, which we have chosen as a second example of the application of our method of analysis to structural types of voluntary associations.

We are not concerned here with the interesting investigations which in recent writings have been instituted into the political party from the viewpoint of positive political sociology [1]. Our only concern is to try and find the transcendental foundation which alone makes the appearance of such a voluntary association possible. This type of association displays a very remarkable close enkaptic interlacement with the State, guaranteed by its primary aim of influencing the policy of the latter. This aim is essential both to the genetic and the existential societal forms of a political party and also gives to the inner structural principle of the latter its first positive shape. This is to say that it is meaningless to extend the concept of political party to primitive undifferentiated unions as is done, for instance, by SOROKIN: 'Under different names', so he observes, 'political parties have existed in practically all historical societies and in less crystallized form in many preliterate populations. As soon as two or more organized factions appear, each endeavors to attain this or that political, economic, or other goal... All such groups have the basic characteristics of a political party as a temporary league with one central goal and program. As soon as such groups are organized and endeavor to realize their purposes, political parties are established and the population differentiates along party lines' [2].

It should be noted that in this circumscription there is question of "the basic characteristics of a political party" without any attempt being made to define these characteristics. On the contrary, by treating political, economic "or other goals" of factions on the same footing, SOROKIN even deprives the term "political party" of its exclusively political sense and the only characteris-

[1] Cf., for instance, M. DUVERGER, *Les parties politiques* (1951); R. MICHELS, *Zur Soziologie des Parteiwesens in der modernen Demokratie* (2nd ed. 1925); R. T. Mc. KENZIE, *British Political Parties* (1956) and the older standard work of M. OSTROGORSKI, *La démocratie et l'organization des parties politiques,* (2nd ed. 1903).

[2] *Society, Culture and Personality. A System of General Sociology* (1947), p. 219.

tic that is left is the undefined term "organized faction". However, there may be "factions" in a Church, in a school, in a trade union, *etc.* They may even organize themselves in separate unions. Are all such "factions" to be viewed as political parties? If so, one had better replace the latter term by the general word "party-formation", used by the social scientists of the formal school to denote a relatively constant general "element" of all societal relationships.

But if an exclusively political purpose is acknowledged as an essential characteristic of a political party, as is done in OSTROGORSKI's definition of the latter as a "grouping of individuals for the attainment of a political goal" [1], we have not yet really advanced in defining this type of associtaion. The adjective "political" is multivocal and the purpose of a political party presupposes the inner nature of the latter, determined by its transcendental inner structural principle. Its primary goal, however, cohering (though not identical) with its inner structure of individuality, binds this structural principle undissolubly to that of the State as a *res publica.* This structural principle cannot be bound to a *particular modern form* of State government, such as the parliamentary system. But it is certainly confusing to speak of political parties in medieval society so long as there did not yet exist a real body politic with its principle of public interest.

A primordial question. Can a political party have a normative structural principle? The political contrast between the parties, and political relativism.

Meanwhile, there is a primordial question to be answered before we engage in an investigation of the inner nature of the political party: Does not the latter imply a division of the State's people into opposite factions? If so, how can such a party have a normative structural principle of a supra-arbitrary transcendental character? This difficulty is indeed insoluble so long as the internal structural principle is not distinguished from the subjective purposes and factual behaviour of the actually existing parties.

In itself the rise of political parties is a manifestation of the interest and the feeling of responsibility of its founders and members with respect to State affairs.

In his famous work *Modern Democracies* JAMES BRYCE has

---

[1] *La démocratie et les parties politiques,* p. 642.

rightly observed that political parties, notwithstanding the justified complaints lodged against them in their factual appearance, are indispensable in any large and free country. No single representative government can do without them. They awaken and maintain the public spirit in the people, they bring about a necessary order in the chaos of the enormous mass of electors. Party discipline, though it should be bound to certain limits, has proved to be a remedy against political egoism and corruption[1]. We may add to BRYCE's observations that the divergence of opinion concerning the principles of policy of the State is a necessary result of the individualizing process of human society, which proved to be implied in the process of disclosure of the latter. There can be nothing wrong in such a divergence so long as it does not concern the supra-arbitrary fundamentals of the State and of the societal order in general. Within this scope no single subjective political opinion of a party can as such lay claim to absolute validity. Therefore, a debate between different parties may contribute to a mutual correction and to finding a common basis of cooperation in practical questions of policy, without eliminating the fundamental divergence of political viewpoints. This is the considerable value of the parliamentary debate in the framework of the modern parliamentary system.

But this state of affairs should not be interpreted in the sense of a universal axiological relativism, which KELSEN has ascribed to democracy as its life- and world-view, in contradistinction to autocracy, which is supposed to be founded in the belief in an absolute verity[2]. The truth is that no single political total view is independent of a religious basic motive, which rules both the practical life- and world-view and the theoretical view of temporal reality. If indeed democracy, or at least modern parliamentary democracy, should be deemed to be incompatible with the belief in an absolute Truth, this would be tantamount to its inner dissolution as a political governmental system. For a consistent axiological relativism cannot allege a single ground for the maintenance of the State and the entire societal order, which impose themselves upon everybody, and are incompatible with anarchism as an axiological view. Such a relativism cannot provide any argument for the superiority of democracy to

[1] *Op. cit.* Vol. I, ch. XI. BRYCE adduces different interesting examples which corroborate the latter thesis.

[2] *Vom Wesen und Wert der Demokratie* (1920), *Allgemeine Staatslehre*, pp. 396 ff.

an autocratic system of government. It cannot even account for the democratic majority principle.

If democracy should imply that, for lack of an absolute standard, no single political belief may lay claim to a higher legal appreciation than the others, it contradicts itself by attributing prevalence to the opinion of a parliamentary majority. For the principle of proportionality to which KELSEN appeals[1] is not warranted from a relativistic point of view. And if the relativist should try to base the rule of majority upon the necessity of binding legal rules and decisions, we must observe that this very necessity is not to be justified from a relativistic standpoint.

If, however, every theoretical and practical political conception concerning the State and the principles of a just government in the last instance is dependent on a religious basic motive, which transcends any *theoretical* axiological relativism, no single political party can start from the latter. For this would be tantamount to a flat abandonment of its claim to superiority in comparison with other parties. Of course, this does not mean that a subjective political aim or program can as such lay claim to absolute validity. It only implies that without the belief in an absolute supra-theoretical Truth and in supra-arbitrary political norms any struggle between political parties becomes meaningless.

It is true that modern Historicism has to a high degree undermined the belief in eternal ideas or values and even has led to the fundamental crisis of Humanism amply described in the first volume of this work. But we have shown that this Historicism itself *did not originate in an independent theoretical thought*, but much rather in the religious dialectic of the Humanist basic motive. Theoretically it may result in a complete relativism and nihilism, but practically it cannot maintain this relativism which even destroys its own foundation, *viz.* the absoluteness of the historical viewpoint as such. A political party is concerned with practical policy though it cannot do without the aid of political theory. Therefore it cannot hold to an axiological relativism in the sense of KELSEN. It must appeal to a supra-relativistic starting-point in the central religious sphere of human existence, irrespective of the question as to whether or not it pretends to be neutral with regard to religion.

This has nothing to do with the untenable assumption that the

---

[1] *Allgemeine Staatslehre*, p. 370.

factual grouping of a population into different political parties coincides with the differentiation into "religious groups"; this assumption is no better than the opposite supposition that party-grouping coincides with the occupational or class-differentiation. Opposite political parties may start from the same religious basic motive and it may be that the same party embraces Christians and atheists. But this does not detract from the fact that the radical antithesis between the Biblical basic motive and the apostate religious starting-points is of decisive importance to the ultimate division of the political views. For it rules the most fundamental divergence in the total view of human society and in the conception of the place of the State within the temporal societal order. It is only the influence of the dualistic scholastic motive of nature and grace which may cause this fundamental line of division to be blurred.

From the above it should not be concluded that it is always and in every condition necessary to form separate Christian parties. It may be that this is factually impossible or undesirable, just as this may be the case with respect to the formation of Christian trade-unions or other Christian associations.

But it is certainly a serious misconception to suppose that the Christian religion has nothing to do with the formation of political parties, or that according to its inner nature a political party is sinful and lacks a structural principle in the temporal world-order. As to its supra-arbitrary inner nature a political party is no more sinful than the State or any other social relationship. It is only the human formative activity and its subjective purpose which can give the structural principle of this type of association a sinful direction.

The typical foundational function in the structural principle of a political party.

How then are we to conceive of this inner structural principle? Its typical foundational function is doubtless of a disclosed historical character. It may be circumscribed as *an organization of the unifying power of a political conviction concerning the principles which have to guide the policy of the State and its administrative parts.*

Let us consider this circumscription somewhat more in detail since it implies some questions we have first to pay attention to.

In the first place we have to observe that, according to its inner structural principle, a political party is not founded in the power of the sword, as is the State-institution, but only in that of a political conviction. As soon as a political party factually relies on military force, it turns into a revolutionary power opposing the power of the State and attempting to overthrow the existing authority of the government. This may be implied in the *subjective purpose* of a party, but it cannot belong to its *inner nature.* Its internal structural principle cannot contradict that of the State, which implies the monopoly of armed power within its territory. In other words, a military organization always exceeds the inner boundaries of a political party. If connected with the latter, it is an association *sui generis,* which is not to be identified with the party, as such, whose revolutionary political purpose gives it an illegitimate character, in a positive legal sense.

Another question is whether it makes sense to speak of an anarchistic political party. Strictly speaking this seems to imply a *contradictio in adjecto* since anarchism means a fundamental rejection of the body politic and of any form of political government. On the other hand, however, it should not be forgotten that the structural principle of an organized community is a structural law which because of its normative character does not exclude a factual behaviour contrary to its normative content. The only restriction to be made with respect to the applicability of the concept political party to a factual voluntary organization, is *that the latter be not withdrawn from the internal sphere of validity of the structural norm concerned, because it displays a different inner nature.*

It certainly makes no sense to include in the concept political party a trade-union or a merely philosophical association, though eventually both may strive after *political purposes apart from their inner structure.* But an anarchistic association whose primary purpose to influence the policy of a State is clearly expressed in its inner organization, falls doubtless within the structural boundaries of the concept concerned. As to its inner foundational function it is an organization of the unifying power of a political conviction concerning the principles of the State's policy, albeit that this conviction implies a fundamental rejection of the State. And since this foundational function is unbreakably bound to the internal leading function of a political party, which we shall investigate presently, the inner nature of such an anarchistic association corresponds to the structural principle of a political party.

*

Secondly we must emphasize that the foundational function of the latter is fundamentally different from that of an occupational organization. An organization of the unifying power of a common economic-occupational interest can, as such, never be the typical historical foundation of the type of voluntary association whose structural principle is at issue in the present context. A farmer party, a labour party, or a middle-class party can never be real geno-types but only variability-types of political parties. This means that an occupational differentiation in the political party-formation can only be enkaptically interwoven with a differentiation according to political views. The danger of such a pheno-type of political party is that the political conviction of the members is easily ruled by the power of particular economic class-interests. Nevertheless, no single political party can function as an economically qualified occupational organization. Its structural principle is out of reach of human arbitrariness.

As a rule the membership of a party which shows a phenotypical interweaving with an occupational class is not restricted to those who factually belong to the latter. The English labour-party, for instance, and the Dutch labour-party which after the second world-war replaced the former social-democratic party, is only bound to social-democratic political principles that may be adhered to by persons of different occupational classes.

The leading function of a political party and the different meanings of the term "political".

The leading or qualifying structural function of a political party organization is not so immediately evident as that of the previously analyzed types of voluntary association. As observed, the adjective "political" is multivocal. It may mean:

1. of or concerned with the State, the State's government or politics;
2. a definite governmental organization;
3. taking sides in politics[1].

The second sense, at least if it is restricted to the governmental organization of a real State, is rendered into Dutch by the word "*statelijk*" *i.e.* displaying the structure of the body politic. The other meanings are ambiguous. They may have a theoretical-scientific meaning as well as a pre-theoretical,

---

[1] Cf. Webster's *New World Dictionary*, College Edition 1953.

practical sense. In the phrase "political party-organization" the adjective "political" cannot mean: "displaying a State's nature or governmental organization", nor can it mean "theoretical political". The leaders of the party are certainly in need of some theoretical political knowledge in order to be able to lead the party. A political party may even join with an institution[1] for scientific political studies in order to deepen the insight into its principles. But the "party bond" cannot be of a theoretical political character, because the party functions as an organized community taking sides in *practical* politics.

This implies a practical view concerning the nature and value of the body politic and its relation to the non-political orbits of human society, the task of the State in a given political situation, its competence and the relation between authority and freedom, the public interest and its relation to particular group-interests, *etc.* Without such a common view, be it expressly formulated or not, the unity of conviction concerning the principles of policy would lack any stable character and the association would not be a real party community, but at the utmost an organization *ad hoc* for the realization of certain special transitory political purposes. As examples we may refer to the Anti-Corn Law League of 1838 and the Eastern Question Association of 1878 in England. So long as the questions concerned caused a crisis in political life, these associations could play an important rôle. But as soon as this crisis was over, they lost their reason of existence and were doomed to disappear.

According to its structural principle any real political party requires some total view of the State and its policy, as a guarantee of its relative stability. It is true that in every political party there may be a divergence of opinions concerning specific points of practical politics. There may be a difference between a more conservative and a more progressive trend, which should be bridged by a kind of compromise. There may even exist some divergence of opinion with respect to the fundamental view concerning the relation of the State to the non-political societal relationships. All such divergences cannot affect the inner unity of political conviction *so long as they are capable of a compromise which can really unite the divergent opinions on a deeper basis of common principles.*

[1] The term "institution" is used here in a general sense current in common speech, not in the transcendental systematic sense defined earlier.

In the latter restriction lies the fundamental difference from a political compromise which opposing political parties, in their inter-communal intercourse, may make in a mutual political agreement *ad hoc*. Such an inter-communal compromise can never concern the established fundamental political principles about which each party must show a unity of conviction. No single party can allow itself to compromise about these principles without abandoning its "*raison d'être*". Within the unity of such a political conviction we have thus to seek the typical leading function of the political party, according to its inner structural principle.

But which of its modal aspects should have the typical lead in this unity of conviction? In the first (Dutch) edition of this work I sought this internal leading function in the modal aspect of belief or faith. I arrived at this conclusion by considering that the fundamental political principles of a party are dependent on a common practical life- and world-view, and that the unity of the latter is in the nature of the case only guaranteed by a unity of belief. I immediately added that there could only be question of a *political* and not of an *ecclesiastical* belief. But on second thought this solution of the problem concerning the internal leading function of the political party's structural principle cannot be deemed satisfactory.

First, the adjective "political" in the formerly defined sense, in which it applies to a party-organization, is not compatible with a pisteutical[1] *qualification*. This is already excluded by its essential relation to the State's policy. Both a voluntary association and an institutional community which are really qualified as a community of faith cannot exist without concentrating their activity in all its aspects upon affairs of belief. This implies that a fundamental divergence of the members in their conviction concerning the central religious questions, necessarily results in a dissolution of the particular communal bond. This certainly does not hold with respect to political parties which have not bound themselves to a particular confession. A common *political* belief which is concentrated upon the ultimate questions concerning the origin and the final aim of the State institution, of the authority of a government and of the freedom of man, is doubtless of great importance to the inner unity of a party. But it cannot be the qualifying function of the latter. And

[1] "Pisteutical" means here: functioning in the modal aspect of faith.

it can only be of a really political character if it is directly or indirectly related to the party's practical political principles.

This does not detract from the fact that the fundamentals of any theoretical and practical view of the State, its place in the societal order, its political task and competence, *etc.* are dependent on a religious basic motive. But this does not imply that such a view is typically qualified by its aspect of belief. If the religious basic motive is of a dialectical character, as in the case of the Humanist motive of nature and freedom, it will tend to disperse the political views in opposite directions, as may appear, for example, from the dialectical contrast between liberalism and socialism.

Similar dialectical contrasts in the political views may occur in Christian parties when the Christian starting-point is affected by the dualist scholastic basic motive of nature and grace. Then it is possible that a Christian liberalism is opposed to a Christian socialism or a universalistic Christian solidarism. Such political divergences may occur between Christians of the same ecclesiastical confession. And this state of affairs can easily lead to the erroneous conclusion that practical policy has nothing to do with the religious starting-points. Nevertheless, it is only the ultimate contest between the religious basic motives which can give the political struggle between the different parties its final meaning and inspiration. For in the central religious sphere alone we are confronted with the absolute standard of Truth and Falsehood apart from which nobody can escape from a fundamental scepticism and relativism. And we have seen that the latter is incompatible with any political conviction.

If, however, it cannot be a common political belief which qualifies the unity of political conviction in the internal communal sphere of a political party, where have we then to seek its leading structural aspect? I think it should be sought in the modal normative sphere of morality. It may be that the inner unity of political belief is lacking in a party, though this is certainly not in accordance with its structural principle. But no political party can exist without a typical moral bond of political conviction. As soon as the latter is broken the inner communal sphere of a party is necessarily dissolved. For a community of political conviction cannot be maintained by the internal legal rules of the party-organization if the leading moral bond is lacking.

From this it appears once again how much SOROKIN has over-estimated the unifying rôle of legal rules by seeking in them the central trait of any organized community [1]. It is true that he adds the condition that these legal norms must be "effective obligatory and, if need be, enforced in the conduct of the interacting persons". But this addition cannot make his view acceptable. The truth is that the internal legal order of a party-community is itself completely dependent upon the internal structural principle of the latter and that, as soon as the juridical viewpoint should take the lead in the inner life of the party, the latter would be doomed to dissolution.

The moral bond of political conviction is a retrocipatory (non-original) individuality-type in the moral aspect of experience. The nuclear or original type of individuality to which it refers is that of formative power in its typical politico-cultural sense, which appeared to be the historical foundational function of the party's structural principle. The term "political" has an original typical historical meaning insofar as it is used in a *modal* sense. Every political party community is historically founded in its formative political power, which implies an historical vocation of a particular degree of responsibility.

The moral bond of political conviction, which in my present opinion is the typical guiding function of the party's inner communal sphere, implies moral duties of a particular political type and content, which are not to be understood apart from the typical formative vocational power of this kind of association. The common love towards the fundamental principles of policy, adhered to by the party, should produce a mind of politico-ethical solidarity among the members and a readiness to strengthen the party's political power by propagating its political views. This can never imply a blind obedience and self-surrender to the party's interests and insights. A totalitarian party discipline contradicts the internal structural law of this type of voluntary association exactly in its guiding moral aspect. It originates in a pseudo-religious commitment to the party's totalitarian political ideology, which includes the belief in its infallibility.

---

[1] *Op. cit.*, p. 70: 'The central trait of an organized interaction (group, institution, social system) is thus the presence in it of law-norms'.

The moral bond of political conviction and the organizational stratification. Pessimist sociological judgments of party-ethics.

Apart from such a totalitarian party ideology the integrity of the moral bond of common political conviction may be threatened by a form of organizational stratification which factually frustrates any influence on the part of the lower strata. Especially very big parties are subject to this danger. SOROKIN is doubtless right when he observes that a stratification is in the nature of the case inherent in any organized "interaction". But it is certainly not necessary that it results in a purely passive rôle of the lower strata of members. The judgment of modern political sociologists concerning the freedom of criticism in political parties is in general extremely pessimistic. OSTROGORSKI observes: 'Life within the party is a long school of servile obedience. The lessons the citizen receives here, are lessons in cowardice and cravenness. The better the party is organized, the more demoralized are its members, and the lower the level of social life" [1]. SOROKIN remarks about the present forms of party organization: 'The party, through suppressing independent thought and permitting little criticism, turns into a sort of fanatical sect in which dead dogmas replace living creative thought'. And a little further he adds the following destructive judgment: 'Face to face with the party the individual is a negligible quantity, bound hand and foot by it. Any criticism of the party is regarded as a breach of party discipline and is followed by expulsion of critical heretics. Instead of educating the individual to liberty, the party trains him to servility' [2].

It is seriously to be doubted whether such generalizing observations are scientifically warranted. They are, for instance, certainly not applicable to all the political parties in the Netherlands. The overstrained party-discipline as it is found among the democratic countries, for example, in the United States of America or in the Australian labour-party, should not be elevated to an "ideal type". No better grounded is in my opinion SOROKIN's generalizing utterance: 'the present form of party organization leads also to the selection of mediocrities and hypocrites as its leaders'. The only argument he adduces for this bold statement is that 'independence of thought not being tolerated, individuals with creative minds, courageous and honest with themselves and

[1] M. OSTROGORSKY, *op. cit.*, p. 642.

[2] SOROKIN, *op. cit.*, p. 224.

others, avoid joining the party'. It is certainly true that political individualists, irrespective of their being "creative minds" or "mediocrities", can hardly accommodate themselves to the moral discipline which is necessary in every party community. But it is certainly not justified to assert that "the present form of party organization" (which of the different forms is meant here?) must lead to the selection of mediocrities and hypocrites as its leaders. Modern political history mentions various first rank politicians among the party-leaders.

Apart from these factual questions we repeat that, especially in very big parties with hundreds of thousands or even millions of members, the integrity of the moral bond of political conviction may be in serious danger of being affected by a dictatorial power-formation of an élite or a leader, in consequence of an overstrained party discipline. If this really occurs, as in the case of the two big American parties, the leading moral political bond degenerates. But if it is factually *broken*, the inner party community is dissolved, since according to its structural principle it is a voluntary community of political conviction whose organized formative political power is dependent on the moral bond of this communal conviction. If the members have lost their moral confidence in the rightness of the party's principles, they will leave the party. Naturally it is possible that there are members who have joined the latter, not on the ground of their political conviction, but because of impure motives of personal interest. But as a rule such motives cannot be decisive for a durable choice of the party which the citizen wants to join. A different situation arises if a party has a revolutionary character, or has acquired a monopolistic position and gives a number of privileges and advantages to its members, as in the case of the Russian Communist party or the former Nazi party in Germany. But in the latter case the membership is bound to such rigorous requirements and the party control with respect to the reliability of the members is so sharp that it is a great risk to join without the real motive of political conviction.

In a country where the formation of parties is free, an abnormal situation with respect to joining may arise in consequence of a large scale immigration and subsequent naturalization of people who lack any knowledge of the political questions of their new country. In this case a strongly organized party may indeed succeed in recruiting a large number of new members who lack a political conviction and join because of personal interests only. A striking example of such a situation was found in the large cities of the U.S.A.[1]. But this can only be a transitory phenomenon, whose abnormal character is evident from the viewpoint of the inner nature of a party community. Exclusively personal interests can never be viewed as a durable basis of a party's membership and they cannot explain the well-known loyalty of the American citizens to the party they have joined. This loyalty presupposes a moral confidence in the political standpoint of this party, albeit perhaps a blind confidence, which lacks the foundation of an independent political judgment.

It is true that in general the membership of a big party may imply the chance of participating in the distribution of positions, sinecures, and "spoils", if the party has been successful in the election struggle. This especially applies to the American "spoil system" in its former extreme shape, which gave rise to a serious corruption of public administration, particularly in the large cities. But it is hardly to be imagined that this system could influence the durable membership of the parties, since the result of the next election is always uncertain.

A more serious danger of corruption of a party's moral bond of political conviction is the external influence of so-called "pressure groups" upon the party programs and the competition for the favour of the voters by deceitful slogans and promises. Especially opportunistic parties which lack a firm basis of political principles are liable to this danger. But a purely opportunistic political standpoint contradicts the inner structural principle of the party, since it cannot lead to the formation of any stable political conviction of its members.

The essential enkaptical interweaving between the political party and the State.

According to its inner nature the political party is a particular type of voluntary association. This implies that as such it can never be a part of the State. Its inner sphere-sovereignty is guaranteed by its structural principle. The moral bond of a common political conviction typically founded in the formative political power of this conviction is, as such, beyond the reach of the State power and the sphere of the State's competence. Naturally the public activity of a party may be prohibited. But

---

[1] Cf. the interesting analysis of this situation in BRYCE's *Modern Democracies* II, Ch. 3.

the effect of such a prohibitive measure is very doubtful, since an underground activity of a formally illegal party may be relatively easily withdrawn from the State's control. It may even become much more dangerous to a government which has enacted the probibition. In any case the party's internal social sphere of life, insofar as it is determined by its structural principle, is withdrawn from the State's original legal power.

Nevertheless, by its primary purpose, which essentially coheres with its inner structure, a political party is very closely enkaptically bound to the State. Especially in parliamentary democracies, by partaking in electioneering and in the negotiations concerning the formation of a new cabinet after the election, it has a typical enkaptic function within the inner constitutional sphere of the body politic. Insofar the political parties also have a function in the constitutional law of the State and are bound to public legal rules. When exercizing their public function as electors, the citizens are bound to the lists of candidates established by the parties. The parliamentary system of government is insolubly bound to the latter and the State government is to a high degree under their control.

It must be clear that this most spectacular side of party life does not belong to the inner sphere-sovereignty of this type of voluntary association. Its public legal functions are derived from the State, and the political power which the party possesses with respect to the State government depends in the last instance upon the nation in its public function as electorate. A very small party which does not yet partake in election, and has no single representative in Parliament, doubtless retains the inner nature of a political party provided that by propagating its political principles it strives after the realization of its primary aim: to influence the State's policy. The fact that, historically viewed, party organization in the modern representative democracies arose from local election commitees or associations is only a question of its *genetic form*. It cannot determine the party's inner nature and structure.

This fundamental difference between the inner nature of a party community and its enkaptical functions in the body politic should especially be borne in mind when we consider the position of a monopolistic party in the modern totalitarian States. At first sight it might seem that such a party is only and exclusively the chief and all-controlling organ of the body politic. But in fact we are confronted here with a form of extremely close enkaptic interlacement similar to that of a Church-State. As the chief organ of the State, the party rules the whole machinery of the body politic. But, as such, it remains bound to the structural principle of the latter. In its inner sphere, as a closed community (the Russian Communist party has limited its membership to 4.200.000 members), the party remains bound to its own structural principle and nature, which is qualified as a moral bond of common political conviction. In its enkaptical function as an organ of the body politic it cannot impose this conviction upon all the citizens of the State. If it wishes to propagate its political views, it is obliged to have recourse to the means of any other political party in a free democratic country, albeit that its political propaganda has acquired a legally sanctioned monopoly and may be supported by the financial means of the State. Even a monopolistic party cannot identify itself with the body politic.

The political party in its relation to so-called "religious groups". The ambiguity of the terms "ecclesiastical" and "confessional" parties.

We have already observed that the differentiation of a population according to political parties may not be identified with that according to so-called "religious groups". It is especially confusing to speak of "ecclesiastical" parties. This term lacks a univocal sense. It may mean: factions which have formed themselves within a Church. It may also denote: political parties which have bound themselves to a particular ecclesiastical confession, or to the guidance of a Church authority, or strive after a privileged position of a particular Church. It is finally also applied to political parties which have expressly bound themselves to a Christian political belief in the formerly defined sense, without accepting any ecclesiastical binding.

As to the first meaning we must observe that the formation of factions within a Church is never to be justified from the viewpoint of the inner nature and structure of this latter. It is a strong indication of an inner schism which excludes a real unity of belief and confession. As to the second meaning we must observe that it may imply a serious confusion between the inner nature of a Church and that of a political party. An ecclesiastic confession does not permit itself to be bound to a particular political party conviction and party program. True, the Church has the indispensable prophetical task to oppose any manifestation of the spirit of apostasy in political life and to remind the State government that its authority derives from God and is subject to Him. But it is certainly beyond the competence of the ecclesiastical institution to establish principles of a Christian policy or to bind its members to a particular Christian party. For the political belief of the latter, as it is formulated in its program or declaration of principles, cannot be separated from the whole of its practical political views, and by giving its adhesion to such a program the Church would exceed the boundaries of its mandate. It is always the universalistic view of the temporal Church-institution rooted in the dialectical scholastic basic motive of nature and grace which is responsible for an eradication of these boundaries.

In its most consistent form an ecclesiastical party in the second sense cannot accept members who do not agree with the confession of the Church to which the party has bound itself. But such a consistent ecclesiastical binding of the membership will be hardly found. As a rule, a Roman Catholic or a specific Protestant ecclesiastic party will only have members who belong to the Church-community concerned. But if the membership is not formally bound to a specific Church confession, such a party will nevertheless reveal its ecclesiastical binding by subjecting itself to the guidance of a Church-authority or by striving after the elevation of a particular Church to "Established Church". As an example we mention the Catholic national party *(Katholieke Volkspartij)* in the Netherlands. In the first article of its "general political program" (established 22 December 1945) the essence and purpose of the party is formulated as follows: 'The *Katholieke Volkspartij* is an association which is open to all Netherlanders. Its purpose is to promote the public interest in the Kingdom of the Netherlands by participating in political life. It is founded in the principles of the natural ethical law and the Divine Revelation, as to which it accepts the rules of the Ecclesiastical Doctrinal Authority"[1]. Here we meet with a close enkaptical binding of the party to the Roman Catholic Church. Nevertheless, the former retains its own inner nature and structure. It

---

1 The Dutch text reads as follows: 'De Katholieke Volkspartij is een vereniging, welke open staat voor alle Nederlanders en ten doel heeft het algemeen welzijn in het Koninkrijk der Nederlanden door deelneming aan het staatkundige leven te bevorderen. Zij staat op de grondslag van de beginselen van de natuurlijke zedewet en de Goddelijke Openbaring, waarbij zij de uitspraken van het Kerkelijk Leergezag aanvaardt'.

cannot be viewed as a part of the R.C. Church. It is only its subjection to the doctrinal authority of this latter which gives it an ecclesiastic binding.

In its third sense the term "ecclesiastical party" is completely misleading, since there is no question here of any binding of the party to a Church. As an example of a Christian party which really maintains its independence of any ecclesiastic authority we may refer to the "Anti-revolutionary Party" in the Netherlands [1], whose political belief is expressed in the third article of its program of principles. This article reads as follows: 'It avows the eternal principles revealed to us in God's Word also in the sphere of politics; in such a way, however, that the State government shall be bound to the divine ordinances neither directly, as in Israël, nor through the judgment of any Church, but in the conscience both of the government and the subject [2].

It is clear that what is said here about the way in which the State government is to be bound to the Word-revelation, similarly applies to the party. The political belief of the latter is related to the political principles contained in its program in the broader context of a life -and world view. This life- and world-view is rooted in the Biblical basic motive of the Reformation without the interference of the dualist scholastic motive of nature and grace. In this way the structural principle of the political party finds its clear expression in the faith aspect, not by means of a particular enkaptical binding of the party to a Church authority, but *according to its own inner nature, i.e.* within its internal sphere-sovereignty. The party is not *qualified* as a community of faith. Nevertheless its leading moral bond of political conviction appeals to a common political belief in a divine order of human society to be known in the light of the Word-revelation. Thereby the fundamental political principles contained in the program of the party, are subjected to the test of a trans-subjective order and the party fundamentally opposes any revolutionary political view which rejects this divine order. In this appeal

---

[1] After the Labour party and the Catholic National party this party has the strongest representation in the Dutch Parliament.

[2] The Dutch text reads: 'Ook op staatkundig terrein belijdt zij de eeuwige beginselen, die ons in Gods Woord geopenbaard zijn: zó evenwel, dat het Staatsgezag ten onzent noch rechtstreeks, gelijk in Israël, noch door de uitspraak van enige Kerk, maar in de consciëntie beide van Overheid en onderdaan aan de ordinantiën Gods gebonden zij'.

to a common political belief the moral bond of political conviction is deepened and strengthened. The loyalty to the party acquires a deeper sense and the danger of an overstrained party discipline is checked by the exclusion of any belief in the infallibility of a human authority.

It cannot be doubtful that in the great struggle between the totalitarian political ideologies and the anti-totalitarian political standpoints the latter are in need of a strong spiritual foundation. Therefore the real formative power of a political party is seriously weakened if the latter lacks a common political standpoint of faith. In the Anglo-saxon countries which hold to the tradition of the dual party system there is little interest in the deeper fundamentals of the party principles. In general, public opinion holds to a partly Christian, partly Humanist anti-totalitarian tradition in politics, and both parties will keep from a frank deviation from this tradition. Bryce observes that by means of its strong organization the party-system of the U.S.A. has greatly contributed to the unification and homogeneity of the population. If the parties had been based on religious or racial differences, the antithetical factors present in the strongly divergent groups of the population would have been strengthened, whereas now they have diminished. But on the other hand Bryce has shown that there is no question of a real political education of the party members by deepening their political conviction. The parties are ruled by an oligarchy and a blind obedience of their members to the party discipline replaces the reflection on the religious foundation of the political standpoint. This is not a reliable basis in the spiritual struggle against political ideologies which threaten the fundamentals of the Western democratic regimes.

On the European continent both the French revolution and the rise of Marxism have stimulated a more profound reflection on the spiritual fundamentals of political party formation. This is why the old English dual party system, with its simple division of the political standpoints into those of liberalism and conservatism, appeared to be unsatisfactory and, from a Christian point of view, unacceptable. The rise of Christian political parties was a result of the insight that in the last instance the struggle between the political standpoints is ruled by an unbridgeable contrast between the religious basic motives. So long as the Christian fundamentals of Western society do not seem to be seriously threatened, this primordial truth may be readily forgotten. But traditional fundamentals are not a safe inheritance. They may be gradually undermined in the national conviction, especially in the present spiritual crisis of Western culture.

Public opinion, as a reflex of the national conviction, is doubtless influenced by the political education of a people, which is the primary task of the parties. By keeping from taking sides in the ultimate questions of political belief, these parties contribute to the secularisation of political conviction, whereby the religious basic motives operative in the anti-Christian political trends acquire free scope. This is the justification of a Christian party-formation on a non-ecclesiastical basis. The alternative is that the Churches take the lead in the political struggle against the anti-Christian political trends. But this must result in a division of the Christian parties according to ecclesiastical groupings. And we have shown that such a grouping contradicts both the inner nature of political parties and that of the Church-institution.

PART III

INTRODUCTION TO THE THEORY OF THE ENKAPTIC INTER-STRUCTURAL INTERLACEMENTS

CHAPTER I

THE FORMS OF ENKAPTIC INTERLACEMENT OF THING-STRUCTURES

§ 1 - THE INTER-STRUCTURAL INTERLACEMENT AND THE LIMITS OF THE COSMOLOGICAL IDEA OF INDIVIDUAL TOTALITY.

When engaging in an inquiry into the individuality-structures of our experiential horizon we began with abstracting them as much as possible from the enkaptical inter-structural interlacements. This appeared to be methodically necessary to get a theoretical insight into their inner nature. Yet it appeared that we were continually confronted with complicated structures that did not permit a provisional abstraction from the interweavings which turned out to be constitutive for themselves. As a general rule we could establish that no single structure of individuality can be realized but in inter-structural intertwinements with other individuality-structures. Guided by our cosmonomic Idea we started from the internal sphere-sovereignty and the mutual irreducibility of the structural types. The cosmological basic principle of sphere-sovereignty first proved to be a fertile idea in the general theory of the modal law-spheres, and it appeared to be equally applicable to the theory of the individuality-structures.

Sphere-sovereignty of modal aspects can only reveal itself within the inter-modal temporal meaning-coherence, and a similar restriction applies to the sphere-sovereignty of structural types of individuality. These types are arranged in an inter-structural enkaptic coherence frustrating any attempt to absolutize them.

The idea of the "universe" in its universalistic conception. PLATO's idea of the relation between micro-, meso- and macro-cosmos.

In tracing this inter-structural coherence the fundamental question arises whether it can be conceived as a final individuality structure embracing all temporal things, occurences, actions and societal relations as a "universe". Or does the individuality-structure remain bound to a diversity which is not enclosed in a temporal individual totality? The dilemma "universalism" versus "individualism" presents itself again, but in a much wider cosmological perspective than in the theory of the societal structures.

PLATO's picture of the world is a universalistic answer to the above-mentioned question. He conceived of the "universe" as a macrocosm or totality-structure also embracing man as a micro-cosm. In this speculative thought [1] the macrocosm was conceived as an animate being on the analogy of man, and the "world-soul" keeping the universe together, as a totality on the analogy of the human soul [2]. This view of the macrocosm admirably fits in with the metaphysical organological conception which tries to conceive the mutual relation between things or societal structures in the metaphysical scheme of the whole and its parts. Its prototype was the Idea of a living being, an *autozooion*.

PLATO's *Timaeus* elaborates this theme in a splendid way and it was already closely connected with the idealistic view of the State of his *Politeia*. In this latter dialogue PLATO construes his ideal State as a connecting link between man as the *microcosm* and the universe as the *macrocosm*. This State is the *mesocosm* embracing all other societal relations as its component parts and arranging them according to the Idea of justice in its concentric relation to the Idea of goodness: Every part should keep to its own social task and thus contribute to the harmony of the whole. The ideal State as the *mesocosm* thus reflects both the order of the microcosm and that of the universe. This universe, formed after the pattern of the Idea of the *αὐτοζῷον*, embracing all living beings, has been ordered into a totality by the world-soul, in which the "world-reason" forms the leading part. It embraces all temporal structures, inclusive of the State, as its component parts.

This conception was a metaphysical view, very far exceeding the conception of a universe generally accepted under the influence of the mechanistic Humanist science-ideal. PLATO's idea of the *macro-cosm* attempted to embrace the complete mean-

---

[1] Cf. Vol. II Part II, pp. 592 ff.

[2] Cf. *Tim.* 30 B; 34 E, 90 (cf. *Phil.* 30; *Laws* 10, 896—898 in Stephen's text.

ing-diversity of the temporal world in a totality which was conceived as a metaphysical being.

The individualistic conception of the idea of the universe. KANT's cosmological idea of the world.

The fundamental difference between this Platonic conception of the universe and that of the modern mechanistic Humanist science-ideal may be strikingly shown by confronting the former with KANT's cosmological idea of the world.

KANT cannot theoretically conceive of the universe in any other way than from a functionalistic mechanical standpoint. But rejecting the metaphysical substance-concept of the Humanistic science-ideal, he also rejects the metaphysical hypostasis of the idea of the universe. In "experience" (*i.e.* the sensory experience of "nature"), in which only phenomena can be known, the cosmos is not given as a totality. Thus in KANT the universe evaporates into a theoretical limiting concept of reason pointing thought only to the totality of transcendental conditions of the experience of the "outer world". This idea is not related to the *individuality-structures* of reality but to the *classical natural scientific concept of function*. Insofar as KANT's cosmological idea of the world is oriented to the *cognitive* ideal of natural science, it is of an evident *individualistic* character. This cognitive ideal does not start from the universe as a totality but from the elementary functional relations of physical interaction.

According to KANT's epistemology, mathematical natural scientific thought finds a limiting or marginal concept of "reason" in the idea of the universe, but not a datum of experience. As a cognitive idea the universe has been mechanized, robbed of its "soul", of its "spirit"; it has become a merely theoretical system of mathematical physical cognitive relations which can never be shut off. Thus the universalistic metaphysical and the individualistic mechanical conceptions of the macrocosm are sharply opposed. The former always opposes a functionalistic mechanical view of the macrocosm, and always considers the universe within the limits of the immanence-standpoint as an animate and spiritualized *totality*. This view is only possible with the aid of a metaphysical concept of substance[1].

The individualistic conception is always determined to con-

---

[1] Cf. also p. 629, note, on FECHNER's cosmological metaphysics.

struc the universe functionalistically from physical relations. Insofar as any rationalistic metaphysics of the mathematical science-ideal[1] is rejected, the totality of the cosmos must evaporate to a subjective limiting concept.

The universe as the interwoven coherence of individuality-structures.

On the Christian transcendence-standpoint this dilemma of universalism versus individualism must be rejected with respect to the conception of the universe as certainly as with respect to the theory of human societal structures. In the light of our cosmonomic Idea there can be no question of a view of the universe as a metaphysical totality displaying the individuality-structure of a "living being". No more can a mechanical conception of the universe be accepted in the sense of a theoretical cognitive ideal identifying the whole of empirical reality with a natural scientific system of physical causal relations.

The meaning-totality of individuality is not to be found in the coherence of the temporal order [2]. Within this coherence individuality is bound to a structural *diversity* which lacks any integration into an all-inclusive whole. The metaphysical speculative view of the universe as a cosmic total being or total relationship embracing all other structures as its component parts must be unconditionally rejected. The divine Revelation in Scripture concerning creation contains no indication of any basis for this speculative conception of immanence-philosophy, which tries to transcend the temporal horizon of human experience. The earth and all the other heavenly bodies have been created in systems of physico-chemically qualified individuality-structures. Natural science is able to *disclose* them in a theoretical sense, but is not entitled to *level* them by means of an absolutized, merely functional view [3]. They cannot be construed from a functionalistic hypothesis of their origin after the manner of the theory of KANT-LAPLACE. Neither can they be conceived as somato-spiritual individual *"Ueberwesen"* (super-beings) with man

---

[1] After the manner of DESCARTES or LEIBNITZ.

[2] Of course this statement does not imply a denial of the modal universality of the functional-physical coherence of the world within its own sphere.

[3] The modal concept of function should always be employed in harmony with the idea of structural individuality when the astronomical picture of the world is at issue.

functioning merely as a "part of the earth" according to his body and mind, in the sense intended by G. TH. FECHNER [1].

They are not shut off in the physico-chemical aspect of reality, but function within their structural type in principle in all the modal law-spheres. They are not entirely apart from the temporal structure of human existence, and do not possess a supra-temporal root of their own, distinct from that of mankind. And they

---

[1] Cf. FECHNER's pronouncement in *Zend-Avesta oder über die Dinge des Himmels und des Jenseits* (1851): 'Just as our bodies belong to the larger, or higher, individual *body* of the earth, our spirits belong to the larger and higher individual *spirit* of the earth. This spirit generally embraces all the spirits of the earthly creatures as subordinated to it in the same way as the body of the earth embraces all earthly bodies of these creatures. The spirit of the earth, however, is not the sum total of the earthly individual spirits but their unified, higher, conscious coherence *embracing them all*. Our individuality, independence, and freedom are only to be understood in a relative sense. They do not suffer because we belong to the spirit of the earth, but rather find their root and ground in the unalterable subordination to it... What is true of the earth which itself is merely a celestial body, also holds good analogously for the other stars. They all are individual animate beings and thus constitute a realm of higher heavenly beings superior to us...

'Just as according to their material aspect all the stars belong to nature as the totality of all that is bodily, all the spirits of the stars belong to the Spirit belonging to the whole of nature, *i.e.* the divine Spirit'. (Quoted from Dr OTTO RICHTER, *Gust. Theod. Fechner, Eine Auswahl aus seinen Schriften*, p. 135/6. ["Wie unsre Leiber dem grössern oder höhern individuellen Leibe der Erde angehören, so unsre Geister dem *grössern und höhern individuellen Geiste der Erde*, welcher überhaupt alle Geister irdischer Geschöpfe ebenso in Unterordnung begreift wie der Leib der Erde alle Leiber derselben. Der Geist der Erde ist aber nicht bloss eine Summe der irdischen Einzelgeister, sondern die alle begreifende, einheitliche, höhere, bewusste Verknüpfung derselben. Unsere Individualität, Selbständigkeit und Freiheit, die aber nur relativ zu fassen, leiden nicht dadurch, dass wir ihm angehören, finden vielmehr Wurzel und Grund darin, indem sie nur immer das Verhältnis der Unterordnung dazu behalten"... "Was von unsrer Erde gilt, welche selbst nur ein Himmelkörper ist, gilt analog von den andern Gestirnen. Sie sind alle individueller Beseelung teilhaft und bilden so ein Reich höherer, uns übergeordneten himmlischer Wesen"... "Wie alle Gestirne nach materieller Seite der Natur als dem Inbegriff alles Körperlichen angehören, so alle Geister der Gestirne *dem Geiste, welcher der ganzen Natur zugehört, d.i.* dem göttlichen Geiste."...]

Here the universalistic conception is carried to its extreme limits and the semi-Platonic view of the macrocosm assumes a distinctly pantheistic tendency.

have been created in a universal order of interweaving coherence with all the other individuality structures.

But this universal order of interlacing coherence of all the temporal individuality-structures that we call *cosmos* or "ordered universe", cannot itself be contained in an all-embracing individuality structure. For an individuality-structure bears the character of a *type* and a structural type pre-supposes a *diversity of types*. The temporal cosmos, however, is the order of coherence which embraces all structural typicality and is the *condition of its possibility*. The speculative conception holds that this cosmos is only one of the many that are *possible*. No wonder that here the cosmic order of inter-structural coherence is supposed to be conceivable as an individuality-structure in its metaphysical misinterpretation. Whoever has seen that the transcendental idea of possibility is entirely determined by the cosmic world-order[1] cannot relapse into such uncritical speculations. The cosmological idea of temporal individuality-structure remains fundamentally limited by the structural diversity. The idea of meaning-modality points above itself to the temporal coherence of all the modal spheres and to the fulness of meaning in the transcendent religious root and to the Origin of the creation. In a similar way the idea of individuality-structure points to that which embraces all such structures and to the religious root and the Origin of all individuality.

The meaning-character of the universal interwoven coherence within the plastic horizon and the reflection of this coherence within the separate individuality-structures.

The analysis of these structures in their expression within the different modal functions has revealed that each of these structures is internally non-self-sufficient. Already the first structural type discussed in Vol. III, Part I, *viz.* that of a linden tree, proved to be incapable of complete isolation and could *not be conceived in itself as an independent substance.*

The qualification of the internal metabolic processes in the tree as *bio*-chemical processes appeals to the cosmic coherence between the tree and its environment (*"Umwelt"*). Outside of this inter-structural coherence the metabolic functions are impossible. The insight into this inter-structural coherence is

[1] Cf. Vol. II, Part II, Ch. III, § 3, pp. 512 ff.

deepened when the micro-structures are taken into account in which the macro-things are founded. The tree's structure seems at first to be simple, but on deeper theoretical analysis it proves to be highly complex because this structure appears to be possible only in the universal inter-structural coherence. The complicated structural interlacements revealed in the natural scientific view of the tree are multiplied when the objective normative functions of the latter are considered. Here this natural thing proves to be included in an extremely complex interwovenness with the structures of temporal human society.

Thus it becomes clear that the universal inter-structural coherence of the cosmos reflects itself in the pheno-typical individuality-structure of this thing. The inter-structural interlacements prove to be fundamentally incapable of isolation. According to its transcendental limiting function the tree is a qualified object of faith, which integrates its individuality-structure into the whole cosmic interwoven coherence. Only in this coherence is the structure *possible* and a *real datum centring* in the religious root of human existence. And the transcendent root of human existence is only really concentrated in Christ, because in Him alone it is *directed* to the true Origin of all things, the Creator of heaven and earth. Thus the meaning-character of created reality maintains itself in an inexhaustible abundance within the plastic horizon of the individuality-structures.

The interwoven coherence of the individuality-structures and the teleological order of the Aristotelian "essential forms".

The temporal order of interlacement of all the individuality-structures cannot at all be conceived in the uniform metaphysical scheme of a teleological world-plan. The idea of a teleological world-order is of Greek origin though Christian scholasticism has accommodated it to the Biblical conception of God's providence. This teleological conception of the cosmos first appeared in Greek thought when the form-motive of the cultural religion acquired primacy in the philosophy of nature.

In the fifth century B.C. it is DIOGENES of Apolonia who applies ANAXAGORAS' basic idea of a teleological world-plan to the interpretation of particular natural phenomena. It is very probable that SOCRATES' idea of a teleological world-order, as it is handed down to us both by XENOPHON's *Memorabilia* and PLATO's *Philebus*, was immediately influenced by ANAXAGORAS and DIOGENES.

And via SOCRATES it became the foundation of the so-called physico-teleological proof of the existence of God as it is found in PLATO and ARISTOTLE. In general it implied a technical-cultural view of nature. This completely suited to the Greek conception of God as the *Demiurg,* the divine Architect, who moulds "matter" after a free project or technical plan.

The teleological order of the Aristotelian essential forms in the scheme of superior and inferior, form and matter, end *(telos)* and means, seems to construe the plastic horizon of experiential reality as an extremely transparant and rational structural totality. But it remains a speculative construction whose simplistic schemes do not correspond to the real extremely complicated states of affairs. When applied to the relations between the individuality-structures, this scheme necessarily leads to a universalistic conception of the temporal cosmos. In reality the cosmic order of inter-structural interweavings, as it reveals itself in the plastic dimension of our experiental horizon, does not display a uniform schematism. But there are different *types of ordering* to be discovered in these interlacements, which show a rich variety and defy any *a-priori* speculative construction. It is this variety of types of ordering which requires a more detailed investigation.

§ 2 - THE CHARACTER OF ENKAPSIS IN CONTRAST TO THE RELATION OF THE WHOLE AND ITS PARTS.

The meaning of the term *enkapsis* in HAERING and HEIDENHAIN.

From the very beginning we have introduced the term "*enkapsis*" to denote the intertwinement of individuality-structures of a different radical-typical or geno-typical character. This terminology requires an explanation since it is used by us in a sense quite different from that attributed to it by those who first introduced it into science and philosophy.

The term "*enkapsis*" was borrowed from the famous anatomist HEIDENHAIN by THEODOR HAERING, who gave it a general philosophical meaning. HEIDENHAIN used the term "*enkapsis*" or "*incapsulation*" to denote the relation between the separate organs and the total organism in the structure of a living creature. His scientific investigations had taught him that the organs of a living body such as the kidneys, the lungs, *etc.* are not simply "parts" of this body in the usual sense of dependent components, but that they are relatively independent individuals. Their growth proves to be a continuous self-propagation, a continuous self-division. On the other hand the total organism reveals itself as an individual whole of relatively independent individualities. Notwithstanding the relative autonomy of these latter it displays a perfectly independent internal unity which lives and works, so to say, in all the individual component parts. For instance, HEIDENHAIN says about the structure of a muscle: 'In a muscle a number of histo-systems of different orders of magnitude are arranged one on top of the other, or to say it in other words, they are shoved into one another *(enkapsis)*: the fibrils, the little columns, the muscle fibres, the flesh fibres, and finally the macroscopic muscle' [1].

This term "*enkapsis*" introduced by HEIDENHAIN is used by HAERING promiscuously with "*Funktionseinheit*" (functional unity) or "*Ganzes mit Gliedern*" (a whole and its members). HAERING supposes he has discovered a general scheme for the unity of individuality in the structural thought denoted by these terms. He defines this scheme as follows: 'Just as the parts do not exist without the whole notwithstanding their relative individual independence, or would at least be different outside of the whole, so, inversely, the whole is not without the parts, but it is at the same time something different, something "new" as compared with the parts. The whole is not at all merely the sum total of its parts, nor a merely external formation of a plurality of parts moulded into some form, but a real qualitative new unity' [2]. He tries to apply this scheme to other "divisions of biology" and to the physico-chemical micro-structures as well as to the "purely psychical" realm, *i.e.* the "*psyche*" as "*ichhafte Funktionseinheit*" (the functional unity of the I-ness). And finally he applies it to the psycho-physical and the "spiritual"-psycho-physical individuality.

Why the term is unserviceable in this meaning.

This conception of the structure of individuality is oriented to a constructive trichotomic schema of *physis*, *psyche* and *spirit*,

---

[1] Quoted by THEODOR L. HAERING, *Ueber Individualität in Natur und Geisteswelt* (B. J. Teubner, Leipzig und Berlin, 1926) p. 46: 'Im Muskel sind mehrfache Histo-systeme verschiedener Grössenordnungen übereinander gelagert, oder, wie man auch sagen kann, in einander geschachtelt (Enkapsis): die Fibrillen, die Säulchen, die Muskelfasern, die Fleischfasern, und schliesslich der makroskopische Muskel'.

[2] *Op. cit.*, p. 47.

rather than to the plastic horizon of experience. The application of this scheme of the unity of individuality to the domain of the "purely psychical" functions proves that this view has nothing to do with our conception of individuality structure. But apart from all these considerations, it should be observed that the term *"enkapsis"* is exclusively used here to denote the immanent relation between the whole of the individuality structure and its parts, although the relative independence of the latter is recognized.

This term, however, is not really appropriate to denote this relation, and had better be replaced by HAERING's own term "unity of individuality". In my opinion the term *"enkapsis"* expresses much rather an interwovenness of individuality-structures that cannot at all be qualified as the relation of a whole and its parts. By this term HEIDENHAIN wished to denote that the organs are relatively independent individuals in the body, consequently more than "parts" in the usual sense. But he could not sufficiently distinguish the figure of *enkapsis* from the relation between the whole and its parts for lack of sufficient insight into the individuality-structure of a thing. Especially the qualifying rôle of the leading function in this structure was not clear to him.

The relative *autonomy* of the organs within the total organism does not mean that they have a natural leading function of their own; for their natural internal distinction is dependent on the leading function of the total organism. HAERING observes: 'Even if one succeeds in keeping a single organ artificially alive outside of the total organism for some length of time, or if one *should* succeed in cultivating it entirely artificially (which up to now has not been possible), this organ would be something fundamentally different from what it is as a member in the whole organism, and not really identical with it' [1].

But the question as to whether, *e.g.*, an animal organ is an independent "thing", cannot be answered experimentally without the *foundation* of an idea of individuality-structures. This

---

[1] *Op. cit.*, p. 47: 'Auch wenn es etwa künstlich gelingt, ein einzelnes Organ eine Zeitlang künstlich ausserhalb des Ganzen am Leben zu erhalten, oder gelänge (was bisher nicht möglich war), gar zu züchten, so ist bezw. wäre es, wie wir sehen werden, in Wahrheit und im Grunde doch ein anderes, als wenn es in diesem Ganzen Glied ist, und mit dem letzteren nicht wirklich identisch'.

point will be considered later on in connection with the experiments in which groups of cells are transplanted or inserted, and with the experiments to cultivate cells of a specific organ or tissue outside of the living total organism. For the present it will suffice to say that an animal organ does not have the natural destination to live apart from the total organism.

The question is not whether, *e.g.*, an organic part artificially kept alive outside of the total organism for a certain length of time, is *different* from what it is in its natural function within the whole. But the question is whether such a part reveals an independent individuality-structure, or remains merely an *animal organ* even in its abnormal condition of an artificially led life. Morbid growth of an organ functioning within the animal body also makes this part *different* from what it was when in a healthy condition. But such a change does not destroy its structural identity. The fact that in its artificial isolation an organ continues to propagate itself in its process of growth is no sufficient reason to call it an independent thing. This fact only proves its *relative autonomy* but not its *sovereignty within its own sphere*, not its independent internal destination. A part may have a relatively autonomous internal sphere of life within the whole, its internal destination as an organic member may leave free scope to this autonomy so that for a short time an organ may even be artificially kept alive outside of the total organism. But this abnormal condition cannot alter its inner nature determined by its natural destination as a part of the whole.

The relation between the whole and its parts within the individuality-structures never has an enkaptic character. Some types of this relation.

A genuine enkaptic structural interlacement, taken in our sense, pre-supposes that the structures of things and events, or those of societal relationships functioning in it, have an independent internal leading function and an internal structural principle of their own.

It is essential to gain an insight into this state of affairs. Therefore a comparison with the relation of the whole and its parts within the separate individuality-structures will be instructive. In the present context we shall restrict ourselves to considering this relation as it presents itself in the thing-structures. Provisionally we leave out of account the fact that, generally speaking, the latter have proved to include enkaptical interlacements between individuality-structures of a more simple character. The complicated structure of what we have called an "enkaptic whole" cannot be understood before we have gained a sufficient insight into the different *types of enkapsis.* In any case an "enkaptic whole" cannot derive its character as a whole from the inter-structural intertwinements which it includes.

Every complete individual thing as an individual totality has its parts, and the relation between the individual totality and its parts, as such, is always determined by the *internal structural principle* of the whole. Two different types of this relation have already been discussed in the first part of this volume, *viz.* that of the *internal homogeneity of the parts in a homogeneous aggregate,* and that of *the internal heterogeneity of the parts in a non-homogeneous total structure* [1]. All the biotically and psychically qualified natural beings, and also the usable objects founded in a technical form, display a non-homogeneous structure. The same thing holds for objective works of art realized in a thing-structure. But the enkaptic structural interlacements between things as such never constitute a relation of the whole and its parts.

The relation between a part and an enkaptic function. The modal functions of a thing are not its parts.

The marble of the "Hermes of Praxiteles" is a physico-chemically qualified aggregate of calc-spar crystals and, as such, no *part* of the work of art proper. It is merely enkaptically bound in the latter through an inter-structural interlacement; it only *functions* in this sculpture and its parts. For the same reason it is not permissible to say that the physico-chemically qualified molecules, as such, are *parts* of the *living organism of the cell.* They lack the subjective vital function and that is why they only function in an enkaptic union in the living organism. The real *parts* of the latter are the nucleus and the protoplasm with their numerous organic-structural component parts.

In all those things whose structure is not that of a homogeneous aggregate, a *part* is essentially qualified by the structure

---

[1] To a certain extent this distinction was known in Greek philosophy since ANAXAGORAS. After him also ARISTOTLE distinguished the ὁμοιομερές, as that which has perfectly similar parts, from the ἀνομοιομερές (the organism as a whole), whose parts are qualitatively different. But here there appears a lack of insight into the individuality-structures determining the relation of the whole and its parts internally.

of the whole. In this case the structure of the whole can never be construed by means of its parts, because the parts, as such, are entirely dependent on the whole. The question what is a part of a non-homogeneous whole cannot be decided by a functional mathematical-physical analysis, but only by an inquiry into the internal individuality-structure of this whole. This fact has always been lost sight of on the functionalistic standpoint.

It should also be borne in mind that the parts of a thing are never to be confounded with its structural functions in the different modal aspects. The physico-chemical functions of a cell are no doubt bound to the molecules of the different kinds of its constitutive matter, but these functions are no living parts of a cell. The parts of a living cell-organism may have relative autonomy within the whole, but just as the "organs" in the body of a poly-cellular animal or of a human being, they do not possess sovereignty within their own sphere as *parts.* Only in a real *enkapsis* does the internal sphere-sovereignty of the individuality-structures become manifest. If a thing with a particular individuality-structure functions enkaptically in a thing with a different structure, this enkaptic interlacement always means a *binding* of the first structure. That is to say the first thing exceeds the boundaries of its internal structural principle in this enkaptic function within another thing. This enkaptic function is not regulated by the thing's own structural law, but by the law of the thing in which the first thing functions enkaptically.

Thus this *enkapsis* leaves the internal sphere-sovereignty of the bound individuality-structure intact. In other words, the enkaptically interwoven thing with an independent individuality structure of its own is influenced by this union with another thing only in such a way that the interwoven thing maintains its internal structural law. In the first part of this volume we have explained that in this enkaptical binding the internal structural principle of the interwoven thing displays variability-types whose basis is no longer to be found in its geno-type. Thus the inter-structural relation of *enkapsis* reveals its fundamental difference from the internal structural relation between the *whole and its parts* in all respects.

§ 3 - THE DIFFERENT TYPES OF ORDERING IN THE ENKAPTICAL INTERLACEMENTS BETWEEN THING-STRUCTURES.

The irreversible enkaptic foundational relation.

As observed, the enkaptic interlacements between the individuality-structures cannot be forced into such a uniform *a-priori* pattern as the Aristotelian form-matter scheme. They display different *types of ordering*. When discussing these types, we should always bear in mind that the structural *a-priori* of the temporal horizon of empirical reality must never be identified with a subjective *a-priori* of our theoretical knowledge. The true individuality-structures and their mutual interlacements can only be detected in our orientation to the integral experiential reality. This subjective investigation, however, remains bound to the guidance of the transcendental structural Idea as the necessary subjective *a priori* of theoretical thought.

Our analysis of the structural principle of a sculpture and of various usable objects was already confronted with a particular type of enkaptical intertwinement [1]. It appeared that, *e.g.*, the natural structure of marble is enkaptically bound in the individuality-structure of a sculpture in such a way that there is an *irreversible foundational relation* between these two structures. The marble may function *freely* in its natural physico-chemically qualified structure, but the marble "*Hermes*", in its structure as an artistic object, is indissolubly bound to the structure of the marble. Its structure is irreversibly founded in the latter. In this enkaptic type of ordering a genuine relation of form and material appeared to be discernible, although not in the sense of the Aristotelian form-matter scheme. For the technical form itself proved to play the rôle of a foundational function in the individuality structure of the object of art. The qualifying function could only be found in the objectified depiction of the aesthetical conception of the god's figure which appeared not at all to be identical with the technical form. Although this type of ordering implies a one-sided and irreversible foundational relation, the enkaptic union in the structure of the artistic object is not indifferent to the natural individuality-structure of the marble as a homogeneous aggregate of calc-spar crystals. For we have seen that in this union the marble begins to display an *opening* and *deepening* of its structure [2], turning it into an aesthetically expressive material in the structure of the object

[1] Cf. Vol. III, Part I, pp. 123 ff.

[2] *Ibid.*, pp. 125, 126, 130, 133.

of art. Within the structure of the "*Hermes*" the marble cannot function as a free natural product. In this inter-structural *enkapsis* the internal nature of the marble has not been destroyed, but it has been opened by the aesthetical-technical formation in a typical way. As a result the physico-chemical functions of the marble not only leave the internal aesthetical harmony *undisturbed*, but they are rendered entirely subservient to the aesthetical expression in the visible macro-image.

In this enkaptic opening the marble material assumes a *variability* type and, conversely, it gives the object of art a *variability type*.

The enkaptic foundational relation between molecule and cell.

The enkaptic type of ordering found in the inter-structural interlacement of marble and an object of art, generally occurs in the intertwinement of micro-things of different radical- or genotypes and of micro- and macro-structures of "natural things" differing in radical type or geno-type. We have already pointed out the interlacement of physico-chemically qualified atoms and molecules with the living cell-organism. The atoms and molecules, as such, appeared not to be *parts* of a living cell-organism, but to be enkaptically bound within the structure of the latter [1].

That this view can really account for the empirical facts established by scientific research will appear from our investigation of the complicated structure of an enkaptical whole in the third chapter. The question as to what are the real parts of a living cell-organism is decided by its internal structure, which has assigned different functions to nucleus and plasm within the living whole. In these two *parts* of a cell-organism, each containing quite a number of organic subordinate parts [2], the atoms are enkaptically bound in a molecular union, but retain their own inner nature and internal sphere-sovereignty. Also in this inter-structural interlacement we discover the typical irrever-

[1] A different view prevails among writers who do not know our idea of individuality-structure nor the modal sphere-sovereignty. Both B. BAVINK and HAERING consider atom and molecule as real parts of a cell. Naturally the mechanistic trend in biology is of the same opinion. In BAVINK this view is dependent on his emergent evolutionistic standpoint.

[2] An instructive picture of the infinitely complex organic articulation of a "simple cell" is to be found, for instance, in FRANCÉ's *Der Organismus* (Drei Masken Verlag, München, 1928).

sible foundational relation together with the typical opening[1] of the bound structure by that of the cell-organism, in which it enkaptically functions.

Not before the process of dissolution starts do the atoms united to molecules regain their freedom, and thereby they lose their typical opening by the vital leading function. The internal organic chemical processes of *assimilation* and *dissimilation* display an undeniable *direction*, and insofar an *anticipatory* character. The resulting chemical combinations formed in this process of a small number of elements (chiefly C, H, O, N.) have for the most part an extremely complicated structure unknown in inorganic chemistry. And what is especially striking is that these combinations *in their phenotypes* are *determined by the individuality-structure of the organism.* It is a well-known fact that each type of "organism" produces its own variability-type of chemical combinations, in particular its own type of *albumen.* The organic catalyzers, the so-called *enzymes*[2] or *ferments* operate according to typical organic, surprisingly rapid procedures quite different from those applied in the laboratory, when organic chemical combinations are synthetically copied[3].

And in a suitable manner and place these enzymes are secreted by the healthy organism in accordance with the vital needs of the whole. The atoms and molecules cannot display this individuality-structure in their own internal physico-chemically qualified micro-structure[4]. The latter remains something ex-

---

[1] But only in the physico-chemical macro-processes, as we shall see subsequently.

[2] From the Greek term *zumè* = ferment.

[3] These chemical processes in the laboratory of course are no free or spontaneous reactions, but are brought about under the purposive leading of the investigator.

[4] M. HEIDENHAIN, *Plasma und Zelle,* 1e Abt. (1907, Jena), p. 33, observes 'dass diejenigen Eiweiszkörper, welche die physiologische Chemie aus den Intercellulairsubstanzen zu gewinnen vermag, also die sogenannten Albuminoïde, zu den Baumateriale der lebenden Stützsubstanz *offenbar in den nämlichen Verhältnisse* stehen wie die eigentlichen Eiweisse zu dem Protoplasma'. 'Früher', he says, 'war es Sitte, von "lebenden Eiweisz" zu reden; in neuerer Zeit hat sich indessen überall die Erkenntnis Bahn gebrochen, das die Eiweiszkörper, welche die Chemie darstellt, nur Trümmer des Protoplasmas sind." [Those endosperms which physiological chemistry is able to obtain from intercellular substances, hence the so-called albuminoids, *apparently bear the same relation to the building materials of the living basic substance as the albumens proper do to protoplasm.* Formerly it was customary to speak of "living albumen"; in

ternal in comparison with the former [1], although the two structures are enkaptically united.

This in itself is not yet contrary to recent biological views according to which "life" reveals itself in a solidary activity permeating the "living mass" to its minutest biotically qualified particles. Nevertheless this view may imply the tendency to level out the boundaries between the living organism as a structural whole and the different molecular structures of matter in which the former is enkaptically *founded*. This is evident from the emphasis which different adherents of this modern vision lay on the assertion that the cell is not the real bearer of life, but that it is much rather the "living mass" in its finest and most delicate structures [2]. We shall see in the third chapter that this assertion is not sufficiently warranted by the experiential facts.

The provisionally quite hypothetical "*protomeries*" (*i.e.*, ultimate particles) of a "living mass" are conceived after the pattern of material molecules. They are often called "bio-molecules" (VERWORN, WOLTERECK). But the very question is whether "life" can manifest itself *within* the internal molecular structures of matter. If so, we are obliged to assume that such structures may display an autonomous biotical qualification. In my opinion this assumption is meaningless and I shall account for this view in the third chapter.

---

modern times the insight has become general that the protein combinations represented by chemistry are only fragments of protoplasm.]

[1] This statement will probably not be capable of experimental proof, because it is concerned with the internal functions of atoms and molecules *within the living cell*. The attempts to examine the internal conditions of a living being more carefully are restricted within very narrow limits, if we do not wish to seriously injure, or even kill, the living organism. A dead body can be subjected to all kinds of experiments, but life remains hidden from our too intensive observation, and will be extinguished when ruthlessly exposed to the light. BOHR conceived this phenomenon as an analogy of what in modern physics is called "complementarity" *(Komplementarität)*, *i.e.* the fact that when *one* aspect of a quantum-physical micro-event is being measured, the other aspects cannot be verified by our measuring observation. This complementarity has found expression in HEISENBERG's so-called "relations of incertitude". Cf. P. JORDAN, *Quantumphysikalische Bemerkungen zur Biologie und Psychologie*, in *Erkenntnis* (hrg. v. RUDOLF CARNAP and HANS REICHENBACH) Bnd. 4 (1934) p. 244. We shall revert to BOHR's opinion in the third chapter.

[2] Cf. M. HEIDENHAIN, *Plasma und Zelle* (Jena, 1907), 1e Abt. p. 58; and R. WOLTERECK, *Grundzüge einer allgemeinen Biologie* (1932) p. 313, opposing the older view of an organism as a cellular system.

Are organisms micro-physical systems? The theory of JORDAN.

The distinction between the enkaptic function and the internal structure of molecules is of fundamental importance for biology in the recent controversy about P. JORDAN's theory according to which the organisms are essentially *micro-physical* systems [1].

JORDAN considers the reactions forming the basis of the most important vital processes to be processes peculiar to the atomic order of magnitude. The latter, which can only be statistically approached, are supposed to *direct* the reactions manifesting themselves in the macroscopic world. The result is that, in contrast with inorganic macro-processes, these reactions proceed "*a-causally*".

To my mind this theory implies a biologizing of the internal atomic structures of matter enkaptically bound in the living organism, rather than a physicalizing of the vital processes. JORDAN realizes that the laws of quantum mechanics that he tries to apply to biology in the same way as BOHR did, cannot form a sufficient basis for this "*Verstärker-theorie*" (theory of intensification). For these laws also apply to the atoms of inorganic *macro-physical systems*, while the latter exhibit an undoubted a-biotic causal character. Thus I suppose JORDAN's theory stands and falls with the premise that the internal atomic and molecular structures of the different kinds of matter which function in enkaptical binding within a living organism, has a typical biotic qualification. This assumption is not justified in my opinion. Therefore I think JORDAN's views have been rightly attacked by various critics.

The theory of the enkaptical interlacements of structures can bring clarity in this debate, if we recognize that the enkaptic physico-chemical function of the atoms and molecules in a living cell-organism is determined by the structure of this living whole. This physico-chemical function bears an opened macro-physical character and is biotically qualified. The internal

---

[1] P. JORDAN, *Die Naturwissenschaften*, Bnd. 20, pp. 815 ff (1932). Cf. also his treatise *Quantenphysikalische Bemerkungen zur Biologie und Psychologie* in *Erkenntnis*, Bnd. 4, pp. 215 ff. This view is contradicted in the same periodical Bnd. 5, pp. 337 ff. by ERWIN BÜNING, *Sind die Organismen mikrophysikalisehe Systeme?* and by O. MEYERHOF in *Die Naturwissenschaften*, Bnd. 22, pp. 311 ff. (1934).

micro-physical structure, on the contrary, retains its physico-chemical qualification.

The qualifying function of a cell of a poly-cellular non-human body depends on the structure of the whole body.

In the light of our theory of the individuality-structures of temporal reality it is, however, no longer possible to speak of a cell in general. This word denotes an undefined general concept which, as such, says nothing of the individuality-structure of the living unit in question. The germ-cell of all higher poly-cellular organisms develops by means of continuous partition into a being of a pre-determined structural type, as the result of a sexual or non-sexual process of propagation. This individuality-structure is that of a plant, or an animal; only the human germ-cell lacks a radical-typical limitation and refers to the mystery of the spiritual centre of human existence, which transcends all temporal structures. In other words, the qualifying function of a non-human germ-cell is entirely dependent on the individuality-structure of the being destined to develop from it genetically. Only the germ-cell of a plant is *biotically* qualified according to its radical type [1].

---

[1] The important facts recently collected by R. FRANCÉ, HABERLANDT, and others, as material for a "psychology of plants" cannot really serve to demonstrate the existence of a *subjective modal feeling* function in plants. Only if the biotic reaction to stimuli and their organic "*Verwertung*" (utilization) is confused with genuine feeling (*e.g.*, in the leaves of the *mimosa pudica*; or in insectivorous plants like *drosera rotundifolia* or sun-dew, and so on), or if the term "psychology" is used in a perfectly undefined sense, can this reaction be called an instance of "the psychical life of plants". But in our general theory of the modal law-spheres we have seen that biotic reactions to stimuli only have their necessary *sensory analogy* in the modal function of feeling. It is true that this sensory analogy is not necessarily bound to a more or less differentiated nerve system, let alone to a central nervous system. In *protozoa* the single cell appears to possess "nervous-like spheres" serviceable to sensory perception. But the latter, however primitive and perhaps unconscious it be, is never reducible to a vegetative biotic reaction.

B. BAVINK, who from the viewpoint of his "emergent evolutionism" defends the so-called "psychology of plants" with all kinds of reservations, has laid bare its real background. This background is the principle of continuity of the Humanistic personality-ideal in its *pan-psychical* form already found in LEIBNITZ (cf. BAVINK's words cited above, 9th ed. 1948, pp. 463 ff., especially pp. 465/6). This constructive principle of continuity should never be confounded with the cosmic, supra-modal

According to its structural type the germ-cell of poly-cellular creatures is not destined to lead an atomistic separate existence. This cell is qualified by the total structure of the more or less differentiated body whose entire architecture is implied in it as a pre-disposition, but certainly not in the mechanical sense of a "pre-formation" [1]. Our observations on the inner nature of the germ-cell of a poly-cellular being hold with even greater emphasis for the soma-cells developing from it. The soma-cells display a structure differentiated in accordance with the organ in which they function within the totality. The relation of the living cell-body to the poly-cellular part and the total body can thus never be identified with that of an inter-structural enkaptic interlacement, but is the relation between a part and its whole.

Structurally the whole is before the parts, but not in the sense of the enkaptic foundational relation that we discovered between molecules and a living cell-organism.

---

continuity, asserting itself both in the modal and in the plastic dimension of our experiental horizon. The so-called "transitional forms" between the vegetable and the animal kingdoms do not justify a pan-psychical view of reality. These "transitional forms" are after all only border-line structures within each of these kingdoms *pre-supposing the radical-typical boundaries.*

[1] Cf. BAVINK, *op. cit.* (9th ed., 1948) p. 377: 'Es ist, als ob sozusagen jeder einzelnen Zelle der Plan des Ganzen, zu dem sie normalerweise gehört, mit auf den Weg gegeben wäre...' [It is as if, so to say, every individual cell has been given the plan of the whole to which it normally belongs...]. This *integrating tendency,* found in a greater or lesser degree in every part of the living organism, convincingly manifests itself *e.g.,* in the familiar regenerative phenomena; and also in H. DRIESCH's experiments with the division of the germ developing from the egg of sea-urchins *(echinoidea)* in their di-cellular or tetra-cellular stages. The separate cells of the developing embryo do not have an internal destination independent of the structure of the total organism. This is proved by the fact that it does not depend on the individual cell whether one of the two partial cells develops into a whole embryo or half of an embryo. The above mentioned experiments have been extended to other classes of animals; and it has appeared that if a cell remains *single,* it develops into a whole embryo; if it remains together with the other cell, it becomes only half of an embryo. The structural plan of the total animal realizes itself in its parts.

The separate cells of a developing embryo have different possibilities of development in connection with this structural plan. Through the operation of external causes these possibilities can be realized in a way deviating from the structural plan. But we shall discuss this phenomenon later.

> The experiments made in connection with the transplantation and implantation of groups of cells, and in connection with the cultivation of free cell-cultures outside of the living organism.

Against our view it would be possible to adduce the important modern experiments made in connection with the transplantation and implantation of groups of cells, and especially the experiments with the cultivation of free cell-groups (*e.g.*, of connective tissue) outside of the living organism. These cultures exhibit essentially different qualities from those which they display within the living organism in which they form a unified whole with other groups of cells [1]. The mechanistic tendency in biology looks upon such experiments as another confirmation of the sole validity of the deterministic causal-physical view of the biotic developmental phenomena. But — apart from the fact that the mechanistic theory simply ignores the *real structural problem* implied in these experiments [2] — these phenomena do not prove that the *separate cells possess an independent natural inner destination different from that of the total organism.* In all these experiments we are confronted with an aberration due to an external cause purposely directed by theoretical research; or with a case of degeneration, no doubt proceeding in conformity with a strict *functional* law, but structurally only to be qualified as deformations, morbid phenomena or abnormalities [3].

Symptoms of organic disease such as sarcoma, and goiter, do not prove the existence of an independent natural leading function of the affected parts within the organism. The modal, causal-functional coherence of the vital phenomena within the physico-chemical law-sphere is not annihilated by the internal structural law of the individuality-structures functioning in this aspect. These individuality-structures cannot even exist without the modal aspects.

This means that our theory of the individuality-structures and their enkaptic interlacements does not render superfluous the biologist's investigations of the causal-functional coherence of the vital phenomena in their physico-chemical aspect. When he orients his researches to this theory he is much rather stimulated to carry on this causal-functional inquiry with the greatest possible energy and devotion. But it will warn him against a functionalistic eradication both of the modal boundaries of the law-spheres and of the individuality-structures. He will discover the harmonious coherence between the modal functional and the structural-typical view of life phenomena in all normal vital processes.

For this harmonious coherence has not been revealed by DRIESCH's neo-vitalism, nor by MEYER's and HALDANE's modern holism.

---

[1] Cf. B. BAVINK, *op. cit.*, pp. 386 ff.

[2] BAVINK also admits this, *op. cit.*, p. 387.

[3] Cf. the interesting treatise on organic deformations by JOH. REINKE, *Ueber Deformation von Pflanzen durch äussere Einflüsse* (Bot. Ztg. Bnd. 62, pp. 81—112).

Both views start from an erroneous idea of the cosmic meaning-coherence [1].

Enkaptic symbiosis and the *correlative enkapsis* between creatures with a subjective vital function and their environment (*"Umwelt"*).

We find a type of ordering quite different from the enkaptic foundational relation discussed above, in certain inter-structural interlacements which in their biological aspect form the field of research of "ecology" (in a wider sense). We first refer to the interlacement between a living being and its environment *(Umwelt)* within a particular radical type. In a certain sense this interlacement seems to display a foundational relation insofar as a plant or animal, as such, cannot live without the substratum of external physical and chemical "conditions", such as light, air, temperature, and so on.

But we can only speak of an *"Umwelt"* (environment) in connection with a living organism. In this enkaptic interwovenness the environment exhibits an objective biotic or objective psychic qualifying function, only *opened* as such by the subjective structure of the living organism. In this sense this structural function has a dependent character.

No *"Umwelt"* exists apart from the vegetable and animal kingdoms. The enkaptic interlacements here intended, in which the individual displays its *pheno-typical variability,* bears a distinctly *correlative character* in the sense of a *relation of mutual interdependence in a different respect.* The type of ordering in such a *correlative enkapsis* is entirely different from that of *symbiosis,* which differentiates itself in the most widely diverging sub-types, and at the same time remains interwoven with the *correlative enkapsis* between living being and *"Umwelt". Symbiosis* shows typical forms of interlacement between individuality-structures both of the same and of a different radical type, but in any case of a different geno-typical character.

There is first the coherence between an individual and a collective whole. It occurs in all those animal and vegetative forms of *symbiosis* in which, in accordance with its *natural* destination, the individual retains a truly independent sphere of existence outside of the collective unit *within which* it functions as

---

[1] Cf. p. 77 of this volume and the third chapter of part III, pp. 731 ff.

a part of the whole[1]. Among these there are also typical *borderline cases* in the so-called animal colonies or *"Tierstöcke"*, which have been found in particular groups of coelenterates, especially coral zoophytes and *synphonophora* (jellyfish). Perhaps the *synphonophora* are the most interesting of them, because numerous clearly differentiated types of polyps are bodily united into a freely moving total body, although from time to time particular polyps detach themselves from the rest and live apart as "medusas" for a certain time and propagate. In this case, too, we must speak of an *enkaptic symbiosis* besides the relation between a part and the whole.

This type of *enkaptic symbiosis* is also found with the *volvox* and the *spongiae,* which form colonies of cells. *Parasitic symbiosis* occurs, *e.g.*, between animals and plants. This is an example of symbiotic *enkapsis* of individuality-structures possessing a different radical type (*e.g.*, between gall-wasps and oaks, *etc.*). But this parasitic type of symbiotic *enkapsis* is also found between animals or plants of different geno-type, and between particular kinds of *virus* and plants or animals. This does certainly not agree with the teleological Aristotelian scheme of form and matter.

Typical collective structures of *enkaptic symbiosis.*

A special collective type of *enkaptic symbiosis* is found in the relation between the collective total structure of a forest, heath, meadow, steppe, *etc.* and the widely different plants and animals living in them. These collectivities are undoubted examples of structural totalities of a vegetative (biotic) qualification which are statically bound to a larger or smaller area.

Within these collective structures we find the relation of the whole to its parts which is entirely determined by the total structure. But not all vegetation found in these collectivities can be qualified as parts of the whole. A pine forest is only qualified as a dense vegetation of pinetrees, a heath as a dense vegetation of heather, *etc.* Some isolated trees in a heath are, as such, not parts of it, but only show the relation of an *enkaptic symbiosis* with the vegetation of the heath.

The same thing holds for the fauna bound to these vegetative collectivities in an *enkaptic symbiosis.*

---

[1] As a "part of the whole" it is not an "individual", but a member of the collective unit with a well-defined structural task.

The individual plants functioning as the variable parts of the whole, within this collective totality retain their own internal structure, which is only interwoven with the collective structure in an *enkaptic symbiosis.*

Both these collectivities, and each separate individual in them form an *enkaptic symbiosis* with the "*Umwelt*". In all these cases we find natural collective centres or nodal points of *enkaptic symbiosis* (the different kinds of landscape embracing *fauna* and *flora*) which, as such, should not be confused with structural wholes proper. These collective structures of *enkaptic symbiosis* are ruled by a law of "biotic balance", *i.e.* the relative numbers of animals and plants living together in them generally maintain a constant average. But this is no reason to identify the enkaptic interweavings with the structural wholes functioning in them.

The enkaptic character of these relations is proved by the fact that the numbers of the various animals and plants in them fluctuate around a certain average, dependent on the "*Umwelt*", and especially on temperature and rainfall. They compensate one another only so long as the climatic vital conditions are not fundamentally changed. This means that this regularity is not an internal structural law of the landscape as a supposed vital whole, but remains entirely dependent on the "*Umwelt*".

The *enkaptic* subject-object relations between animal or vegetable beings and their formations realized in an objective thing-structure.

Another type of inter-structural interlacement is found in the enkaptic subject-object relations between animal or vegetable beings and their objective formations with which they remain vitally united [1].

We cannot call the calc-shells of the molluscs, *e.g.*, genuine *parts* of the latter's living organisms, because they do not have the same structural principle. The calc-formation in its enkaptic union with the animal organism is of an *objective* psychic qualification, but the animal has a *subjective* psychical leading function. The calc-shell may be detached from this enkaptic interlacement. Then its objective qualifying function becomes in-actualized, *i.e.* rendered in-operative [2], although in human

---

[1] Cf. Volume III, pp. 106 ff.

[2] Cf. Volume III, pp. 147 ff.

experience it continues to be conceived as an animal formation. This formation may have an essential function in animal life, but such a function cannot be considered a *part* of the animal organism. Nevertheless, the shell might prove to belong to a real enkaptic whole of a supra-biotic qualification.

The universal interwoven coherence of the thing-structures and the nodal points of these enkaptic interlacements.

Within the realm of the physico-chemically qualified macro-structures there are a whole series of mutually coherent enkaptical interlacements whose counterpart is found in the relations of the whole and its parts (the planets with their satellites, the solar system, spherical groups of stars, the galaxy, and so on). Astronomy has as yet discovered only little with any certainty about their mutual relations and internal nature (especially as regards the more comprehensive systems). The question is whether these interlacements display the type of a *one-sided foundational relation,* or that of a *correlative enkapsis.*

The answer depends on another question: In how far is there a genetic connection within a system or between the different systems?[1] All the realms of thing-structures, however, are enkaptically interwoven in the plastic horizon, both those of the micro-world and those of the macro-world. In this *enkapsis* the foundational type as well as the correlative and symbiotic types of *enkapsis* play a rôle. And in all cases the pheno-typical forms of things reveal themselves as real nodal points of the enkaptic interlacements. All these interlacements are in turn interwoven with those presenting themselves between the structures of temporal human society, insofar as the natural thing-structures and those of cultural formations are related to the temporal societal structures of human life as objects to their subjects.

The enkaptic interlacements of natural things in human societal structures.

We shall consider a mixed farming business to exemplify the enkaptic interlacement between natural things and a human societal

---

[1] Astronomy has to be content with more or less probable hypotheses as regards the theories about such a genetic connection. A purely functional mechanical explanation of the origin of the celestial bodies can only be considered as a "bad kind of speculation". Cf. HOPMAN, *Weltallkunde* (F. Dümmler, 1929) on this genetic problem.

structure, *viz.* that of cattle-rearing combined with agriculture. The fields, pastures, cattle, buildings (with their stock-in-trade) function in this human societal structure, as well as all the usable objects belonging to the farming. The land and the cattle are qualified only as economic objects of the latter as far as their enkaptic function in it is concerned.

The actualizing of the economic function of fields, pastures, and cattle belongs to the internal destination of the farming business, which is, therefore, entirely dependent on this typical subject-object-structure. But the animals functioning as the live-stock of the farm are, as such, *i.e.* in their own internal structure, certainly not of a typically economic qualification. They are natural beings, according to their inner animal nature bound to the pasture (as a vegetative collectivity) in a symbiotic interlacement, and interwoven in a correlative *enkapsis* with their "*Umwelt*". They live in an animal bi-unity when they copulate, and for some time after the birth of the young at least the mother-animal lives in a natural community with the latter.

But these natural structures with their complicated interlacements can, as such, be interwoven with a human industrial relationship *only enkaptically* and thereby be bound in this structure. Insofar as they are productive objects of a farming-business, animals, pastures, and fields do not function as free, *i.e.* wild natural beings, or natural collectivities. Their economic function is typically founded in an objective cultural form whose subjective correlate is constituted by the typical foundational function of the industrial relationship as an organized cultural-economic power-formation. In the enkaptic interlacement between the internal natural structure of the above mentioned objects and their structure as an industrial object, we again find the typical order of the one-sided foundational relation, but with mutually bound interwoven individuality-structures. In this *enkapsis* industrialized natural things display cultural-economic variability types.

The business-organization, binding animals, pastures and fields in their natural structure, is interwoven with a great number of other human societal structures; also the industrial objects are included in these new, extremely complicated enkaptic relations.

This interwoven coherence of human societal structures will now demand our attention.

Chapter II

THE ENKAPTIC INTERWEAVING FORMS OF HUMAN SOCIETAL STRUCTURES

§ 1 - TYPES OF ORDERING IN THE ENKAPTIC INTERLACEMENTS OF HUMAN SOCIETAL STRUCTURES.

Primitive forms of interlacement and their enkaptic foundation in natural communal structures.

Of the various forms of interlacement of human societal structures we have already discussed the primitive organized communities as undifferentiated units. In this case the remarkable thing is that a societal structural whole itself functions as a form of interlacement. We have seen, however, that this is only possible because the various individuality-structures interwoven in the form of a patriarchal "extended family", or a patriarchal or matriarchal sib or clan, people or tribal relationship, *etc.*, have not been differentiated into separate societal relationships. They realize themselves only in one primitive societal form in which one of the interwoven structural principles assumes the leading rôle. This may be the principle of kinship or that of a primitive political structure.

In these primitive interweaving forms we do not find the figure of a genuinely *differentiated enkapsis*. For within the societal structure the prevailing relation is that of the part to its whole; and there is only one undifferentiated societal whole, so that the sphere-sovereignty of the individuality-structures interwoven in the latter cannot manifest itself *within the internal sphere of this social unit*. But this does not at all mean that the figure of a genuine *enkapsis* is completely absent in a primitive society.

We have seen [1] that natural communities, which in every human society are realized in forms determined by a particular

[1] Vol. III, part II, pp. 339 ff and 353 ff.

level of culture, function in these undifferentiated organizational units only enkaptically.

The marriage bond, the natural family in its most narrow sense, and the natural cognate kinship in its broader extent, as realized internal societal structures, cannot be merged as *parts* in the undifferentiated social wholes. On the contrary, the latter appeared to cut across these natural communities, whose internal sphere of life could thereby be seriously affected or partially deformed. The type of enkaptic interlacement in this case can only be that of an irreversible one-sided foundation. The primitive undifferentiated relationships founded in an historical form of organization cannot exist apart from real natural communities. But the latter by no means pre-suppose the existence of the primitive interweaving forms in which they are bound enkaptically and by which they are greatly influenced [1].

The different *types of enkapsis* between communal and inter-communal or inter-individual relationships, and the transcendental societal category of their correlation.

We have seen, however, that undifferentiated organized communities also have an enkaptic function in inter-communal and inter-individual relationships. What particular *type of enkapsis* is found here?

In general the correlativity between communal and inter-communal or inter-individual societal relations has appeared to be of a really transcendental character. We have called it a *transcendental societal category*. In the modal dimension of our experiential horizon this correlation turned out to be ultimately founded in the modal structure of the aspect of social intercourse. This transcendental correlation must retain its validity also in the plastic dimension of this horizon. No single type of community is to be found which lacks its correlate in certain types of inter-communal or inter-individual relations.

This, however, does not mean that every type of community is interwoven with every type of inter-communal or inter-individual relationships in a *correlative type of enkapsis*. The correlation implied in the transcendental social category concerned

[1] Cf. the sib-less condition of society with most of the pygmies and other primitive peoples.

does not tell us anything about the different types of enkaptic interlacement between the individuality-structures in human society. It is quite possible that particular types of community and inter-communal or inter-individual relations display quite different types of intertwinement. Below we shall see that this is really the case.

As to the undifferentiated organized communities and the inter-communal and inter-individual relationships of a primitive society we may, however, establish that their mutual intertwinement doubtless displays the type of a *correlative enkapsis*. There can be no question here of a one-sided foundation of the former in the latter or *vice versa*. On the contrary, these two kinds of primitive societal relationship mutually pre-suppose one another.

Why the enkaptic interlacement between natural communities and inter-communal or inter-individual relationships cannot display the type of a one-sided foundational relation.

Meanwhile the question arises as to whether natural communities do not enter into a foundational enkaptic relation with inter-communal and inter-individual relations. By way of an example we may quite well imagine a family living in temporary isolation in an uninhabited island. It might seem that such a family does not pre-suppose any inter-communal or inter-individual relationship, whereas the latter, if they later on originate from the settlement of other families on the island, seem to pre-suppose the natural communities. But this example has no more force as an argument than the fancied figure of Robinson Crusoe, which served to support an individualistic view of human society. For such a family originated from a normal society and could only form itself in the correlation of communal and inter-communal or inter-individual societal relations.

Compulsory temporary isolation is an abnormal social figure, only possible, as such, under the transcendental norm of the correlation between communal and non-communal relations.

However, there seems to be a more cogent argument for an affirmative answer to the question framed above, *viz.* the supposed genetic character of the relation between natural communities and the other relationships of human society. At first sight the following reasoning seems to be very plausible: In virtue of the genetic origin of mankind, the inter-individual and inter-communal societal relations must necessarily owe their existence to the natural relations in a marriage, a family, and a natural kinship. In this genetic explanation the natural community-structures are not only the basis of all other types of communities, but also of the various types of non-communal relations. At first sight this view seems to be also consonant with the teaching of the Bible about the temporal evolution of mankind from one pair of parents. But there is every reason to doubt whether this genetic way of thought can actually reveal the type of structural interlacement of the inter-communal and inter-individual relations with the biotically founded communities.

The other types of societal structures cannot have developed from natural communities genetically. Anyone who should maintain that they can, would irrevocably lapse into a relativistic evolutionism eradicating the boundaries between the structures of human societal life. We can speak of a genetic coherence between a real marriage bond and the family relationship as far as their genetic form is concerned. In this form their structures, which are of the same radical type but of a different genotype, are realized in an enkaptic interlacement whose type displays a one-sided foundational relation. But the first pair of human beings did not develop from a human marriage bond. It is not marriage or the family, but it is the transcendent root-community of mankind which forms the ultimate basis of temporal human society. The transcendental Idea of origin does not refer to a temporal natural community-structure as the "germ-cell" of all the others, but to the *basis* of all and any societal structures laid at the creation, and transcending all theoretical thought.

In our opinion theoretical speculations on the way in which the first human beings gradually developed into a human society, are not only fruitless but dangerous. This is especially the case with theories of an essentially evolutionistic stamp, which fundamentally falsify the real structural problem.

According to the order of the creation, the biotically founded community-structures of temporal human social life cannot occur outside of a *correlative enkapsis* with inter-individual societal structures. The Biblical account agrees with this order.

Eve was led to Adam not as a natural sister, nor exclusively as a marriage partner, but as a woman in her full temporal existence (in principle comprising all societal structures at the same time). The first formulation of the married order in the Scriptures, therefore, indicates a *correlative enkapsis* of both marriage and family with the inter-individual societal relations outside of the family: "Therefore shall a man leave his father and his mother, and shall cleave unto his wife" (*Gen. 2 : 24*).

According to the order of the creation, marriage pre-supposes that man takes his life-companion in an inter-individual societal relation, and not on the basis of any blood-relationship, so that a veritable conjugal bond may be formed. The view that the natural family and kinship community, founded in blood-relationship, had entirely absorbed temporal human existence at least in the first generation of mankind, not only lacks any Biblical foundation, but is fundamentally contrary to the Scriptures. The positive forms in which the principle of exogamy is realized are doubtless of an historical foundation. But the principle itself is in my opinion already implied in the order of the creation of marriage, as the expression of a correlative inter-structural interlacement between the marriage bond and the external inter-individual relations outside of family and kinship.

The correlative relation between communities on the one hand and inter-communal and inter-individual societal relations on the other, already implied in the modal horizon of social reality, cannot lose its validity in the plastic horizon. But it would have lost its validity, if at any stage in the development of society temporal human existence had merged into marital and family structures without any counterweight in inter-individual societal relations.

It is true that this does not imply a uniform *type of enkapsis*. But at least the intertwinement of natural communities with their inter-communal and inter-individual relations appears to show the *type of correlativity*.

The enkaptic foundational relation between the opened structures of inter-individual relations and those of free associations.

A quite different type of enkaptic interlacement is found between the differentiated types of opened inter-individual relationships and those of free associations. We have seen that free associations really originate from individualized and differentiated inter-individual relationships. This finds expression in the contractual genetic forms of the former and in the constitutive rôle of the established ends and means of an association. Opened inter-individual relationships may occur without the formation of free associations [1], but the reverse is excluded by the very nature of the latter.

This implies that the type of enkaptic interweaving between these two is that of an *irreversible foundational relation.* The transcendental correlativity between inter-individual or inter-communal and communal societal relationships is not thereby affected. The former are always the reverse of communal relations and have no sense without this transcendental correlation. Opened, individualized and differentiated inter-individual societal relationships have their general transcendental correlate in institutional communities of a differentiated character.

But we shall see that this does not mean a typical *correlative enkapsis* in the above defined sense. In addition the irreversible foundational relation in the enkaptic interlacement between individualized inter-individual relationships and free associations itself implies a transcendental correlativity which should not be confounded with the *correlative type of enkapsis.* As we have explained in an earlier context [2], free associations undeniably bind inter-individual societal relations in a more or less intensive way. This is to say that as soon as free associations arise from the latter, the enkaptic interlacement between these two displays a *reciprocal character.*

The foundational (non-genetic) enkaptic relation between natural institutional communal relationships and differentiated organized communities of an institutional character.

It cannot be doubted that the enkaptic interweaving of natural institutional communities with differentiated organized communities of an institutional character displays the type of an irreversible foundational relation. This has already appeared from our discussion of the transcendental societal categories. For the transcendental distinction between these two categories of communities proved to be based on the temporal

---

[1] The formation of trade-unions and enterpreneurial associations, *e.g.*, was for a long time prohibited in consequence of a prevailing liberalist economic policy. The French *Code pénal* contained a special article against the formation of such associations. Not before the Act of 1 July 1901 was complete freedom of association guaranteed. In England the Combination Act of 1800 prohibited the association of labourers. Here freedom of association was not completely acknowledged before 1875.

[2] Cf. vol. III, pp. 593 ff.

order of those modal aspects in which their typical foundational functions are to be discovered.

Nevertheless, this foundational type of *enkapsis* is different from that which we could establish in the interweaving of the opened differentiated inter-individual and inter-communal relationships with free associations. For the latter type turned out to display a *genetic* character, whereas the former appeared to lack this character. In their genetic forms the State and the Church institution do not show any genetic relation with the natural institutional communities.

The foundational enkaptic relation between the organized institutional communities and the non-political inter-individual and inter-communal relationships in an opened and differentiated society.

What type of *enkaptic* interlacement is found between the opened non-political inter-communal and inter-individual relationships and the differentiated institutional communities? In the first edition of this work I thought it must be that of correlativity. The reason was that I did not yet sufficiently distinguish the transcendental category of correlation between communal and inter-communal or inter-individual relations from the particular type of *correlative enkapsis.*

The truth is, however, that the process of disclosure or opening of the non-political inter-communal and inter-individual relations pre-supposes the rise of institutional communities of a differentiated organizational character. For only the latter are able to break decisively through the undifferentiated societal relationships, though this process is greatly favoured by the development of science, technical progress, and international trade. It may be that there is already a real State or Church-institution in existence, whereas the inter-individual relations have not yet been completely emancipated from their binding to undifferentiated communities. We may refer, for example, to the Carolingian State and the medieval Church.

This is to say that the interlacements of the opened inter-individual and non-political inter-communal relationships with the differentiated organized institutions turn out to display the type of a *one-sided foundational relation.* This implies that the same *type of enkapsis* is found in the inter-structural intertwinements between these institutional communities and the free associations. As to the interlacements of the latter with the

State this convincingly appears from the fact that the genetic forms of the free associations in their juridical aspect pre-suppose the rise of a common private law, founded in the principles of freedom and equality of individual men. For we have seen that this legal sphere is bound to the body politic.

Nevertheless, the irreversible foundational relation inherent in the type of *enkapsis* discussed here is not to be conceived apart from the transcendental correlativity in the mutual binding of the societal relationships concerned. What we have observed in this respect with reference to the typical interlacements between the opened inter-individual relations and the free associations equally applies to any other *enkapsis* of this type.

Just as the opened and differentiated inter-individual societal relationships are enkaptically bound by the State, the latter is bound by the former as soon as it participates in the inter-individual intercourse. And the same state of affairs is found in the enkaptic intertwinement between these inter-individual relations and the Church institution.

The general rule concerning the *type* of the enkaptic interlacements concerned is thereby not affected.

The *correlative type of enkapsis* in the inter-structural intertwinements of the State with the international political relationships. International law and State-law.

This rule, however, does not apply to the intertwinements between the body politic and its inter-communal *political* relationships with other States. Here we meet with an indubitable *correlative type of enkapsis.* It makes no sense to assume that the rise of inter-national relations between the States is irreversibly founded in the rise of the separate body politic. And the reverse assumption is equally meaningless. The truth is that the structure of the body politic has always been realized in a plurality of States, so that the rise of the latter implied their international political relations and *vice versa.* The idea of a *civitas maxima,* a world-State embracing all nations without exemption, has up till now been of a speculative character.

From the juridical point of view this state of affairs implies that any attempt to construe the validity of the international public legal order from the constitutional law of the separate States or *vice versa* contains an intrinsic contradiction. KELSEN's opinion that from a scientific viewpoint these alternative constructions are of equal validity is incompatible both with the inner nature of the State and with that of the international political relations. The *hypothesis* of the sovereignty of the constitutional legal order of the State, as the ultimate origin of the validity of international law, is tantamount to the fundamental denial of international law as an inter-communal legal order. And the reverse *hypothesis* results in the denial of the *inner* communal character of the constitutional State-law, which is the very pre-supposition of international public law as an inter-communal legal order.

Types of enkaptic interlacements of the opened, differentiated inter-individual societal relations with each other.

It is difficult to state in a general way in what types of enkaptic order the various differentiated structures of the opened inter-individual and inter-communal relations are interwoven with each other. One thing is certain: the *foundational* type as well as that of *correlative enkapsis* play an important rôle. Thus the fashion in sporting clothes overarches the different branches of sport in the sense that the former is evidently based on the latter. Another example is international trade, which according to its inter-individual and inter-communal relations is one-sidedly founded in traffic. On the other hand the connection between the "free market" and economically qualified competition is clearly an instance of a *correlative type of enkapsis.*

An accurate analysis of the types of inter-structural interlacement of the different historically founded inter-individual and inter-communal relationships would require a separate volume. But the theory of the enkaptic inter-structural intertwinements in this part of our work is only an "introduction", so that we cannot undertake a more detailed analysis.

The *territorial enkapsis* of the other differentiated societal structures in the State.

However, we must draw attention to a special type of enkaptic interlacement, *viz.* that between the State and the other differentiated social structures.

As such this type may include either a correlative or a foundational type of *enkapsis.*

It is that particular type of interlacement which is given in the unavoidable binding of the other differentiated societal relations to the territory of the State. There is nothing like this figure of *territorial enkapsis*[1] to give the State-minded universalistic sociologist the illusion that his construction of the State as the "totality of all human societal relations" (or at least of all organized relationships) is a true picture of reality. He will have to admit that at least the international societal relations, or the organization of the Roman institutional Church, in principle transcending the territorial boundaries of any body politic, simply cannot be understood as "parts" of the "State as a whole". But all the more emphatically will he point out that at least within its territorial boundaries all the other societal structures can only be parts of the State. However, already the undeniable fact that the relations between the State and its citizens may cut straight across the other societal structures, must demonstrate the untenability of this interpretation of *territorial enkapsis*. The members of the same family or kinship may belong to different political nationalities; and all international organizations and inter-individual societal relations overarch the territorial boundaries of the individual States. As far as the internal structures of the other societal relationships are concerned, the enkaptic territorial connection with the State remains of an external nature.

JOHANNES ALTHUSIUS' conception of the parts of the State.

For a real insight into this state of affairs one must have grasped the internal sphere-sovereignty of the societal structures, even in their most complicated enkaptic interlacements with each other. And it is no accident that it was a Calvinistic thinker who broke with the universalistic conception of the State in a period in which BODIN's concept of sovereignty had introduced a new version of this universalistic view. In opposition to the entire medieval-Aristotelian tradition he gave evidence of taking account of the internal structural principles in his theory of human *symbiosis*.

It was the famous Hernborn jurist, JOHANNES ALTHUSIUS, in his *Politica,* who made the following remark, which has too often been overlooked since GIERKE: *'Membra regni seu symbioticae*

---

[1] A *territorial enkapsis* also occurs before the rise of a genuine State wherever a territorial government is to be found.

universalis consociationis, voco, non singulos homines, neque familias, vel collegia prout in privata et publica particulari consociatione, sed provincias et regiones plures inter se consentientes, de uno corpore ex conjunctione et communicatione mutua constituendo' [1].

The foundation of this view, which clearly contradicted the Aristotelian teleological conception of the State's parts, is to be found in the first chapter of his work. Here he summarized his anti-universalistic standpoint with respect to the inter-structural relation between the different types of social relationships as follows: '*Propriae leges sunt cujusque consociationis peculiares, quibus illa regitur. Atque hae in singulis speciebus consociationis aliae et diversae sunt, prout natura cujusque postulat*' [2].

This utterance may be considered the first modern formulation of the principle of internal sphere-sovereignty in the societal relationships, although as to its particular elaboration ALTHUSIUS' theory of human *symbiosis* remained dependent on the historical conditions of his country at that time.

Territorial and personal enkaptic interlacements.

The territorial type of interlacement, characterizing the enkaptic union of all other differentiated societal relations with the State and its parts, forms a contrast with all the other types of interlacement in a differentiated society on account of their merely personal nature. Of course, the territorial type never occurs without personal interlacements; but the personal types would lack the territorial binding when they were not interwoven with the State and its parts.

---

[1] *Politica* (Groningen, 1610) cap. IX, p. 115: 'I do not call "members of the State", or of the universal *symbiotic community*, the separate single human beings, or the families, nor even the colleges according to their being constituted in a particular private and public association, but a number of provinces and districts agreeing to form one whole by mutual conjunction and communication'.

[2] *Ib.*, cap. I: 'Every type of social relationships has its proper laws peculiar to it, whereby it is ruled. And these laws are different and divergent in each kind of social relationship, according to the requirement of the inner nature of each of them'.

§ 2 - THE NODAL POINTS OF THE ENKAPTIC INTERLACEMENTS BETWEEN THE HUMAN SOCIETAL STRUCTURES AND THE PROBLEM OF THE SOURCES OF LAW.

In our introductory examination of the types of interlacement between the thing-structures of reality we discovered the pheno-typical forms of things and collections of things as the real nodal points of these enkaptic relations.

Can we also point out such nodal points of enkaptic interlacements between the human societal structures? In the second part of this volume (ch. 1 § 2) we have explained that this is really possible. The part played by the pheno-typical form given to the structural interlacements of things either by man or by another agent, is allotted in human society to the positive forms [1] in which the societal structures are realized. These forms bear an enkaptic structural character and consequently cannot be conceived in a merely modal-historical sense. But without exception they have a typical historical foundation, which fact is already implied in their character as free forms of positivization.

We have distinguished them in proportion to their having a genetic or an existential character. In the present context we are only concerned with the genetic forms in their relation to the problem of the sources of law.

The positive forms of existence of a marriage bond, of all organized communities, and at least of the contractual inter-individual or inter-communal relationships presuppose positive genetic forms, establishing or constituting these relations. These genetic forms, as such, are nothing but declarations of will directed to this purpose. They are bound by the positive structural norms of all the societal relationships in which the individual community or contractual inter-individual relation to be constituted is destined to function enkaptically. As *real* constituent actions these declarations of will are of course not merely legal actions (this is only their juridical aspect), but they function in all the modal aspects of human society.

---

[1] The important thing in this case is the *positive* character of the societal form, *i.e.* its temporal realization. Here is consequently not meant the social form as a transcendental category of inter-structural interlacements.

Constituent and constituted genetic forms of positive law.

According to their juridical aspect the volitional declarations concerned are actions constituting law, genetic forms of positive law, and, as such, they pre-suppose the competence to form law in a particular sphere. However, not all genetic forms of positive law are constituent declarations of will in the sense of legal actions constituting a particular sphere of law formation. In all organized communities we must distinguish between the *constituent genetic form* and the *constituted forms* for the internal process of law-making. The latter already pre-suppose established organs for the formation of legal norms. The former call these organs into being.

The inter-individual or inter-communal societal relations, as such, offer no starting-point for this distinction unless in a contractual form they give rise to free associations. But the free societal agreements directed to merely coordinated cooperation are at the same time formal sources of specially qualified inter-individual or inter-communal law *intra partes*, civil law, and integrating non-civil social law. The latter is to be found in "general conditions", "customary stipulations" and so on.

The juridical genetic forms in which the legal norms are positivized are always centres of enkaptic structural interlacements within the juridical law-sphere. Internal constitutional State-law, public international law, civil law, non-civil (specifically qualified) inter-individual or inter-communal law, internal law of association, and so on, have genetic juridical forms whereby they are enkaptically interwoven with each other. This is made possible by the functional coherence of all the individuality-structures in the legal order guaranteed by the modal structure of the juridical aspect.

The interlacement of the material spheres of competence in the juridical genetic forms. The clue to the solution of the problem of the sources of law and the error found in the prevailing theories.

This means that in the juridical genetic forms of positive law different material spheres of competence are interwoven with each other, whose internal limits are dependent on the structural principles of the different types of societal relationships in whose internal sphere the legal norms function. Here is the clue to the extremely interesting problem of the character and the mutual coherence of the sources of positive law. This problem is of fundamental importance to the general theory of law and I have discussed it in a number of separate treatises [1]. A great many theories have been put forward dealing with this problem, and their number is still increasing. Without exception they show one basic defect: they do not properly posit the problem. The positivistic as well as the natural law theories, and those of a naturalistic-sociological stamp as well as the historicist views after all ignore the fundamental problem of the individuality structures within the juridical order.

The so-called "naïve" legalistic variety of juridical positivism tightly clings to the genetic forms of law, and elevates one of them *viz.* the statute law of the body politic, to the highest source of validity. All that is not statute law is subsumed under the vague collective concept customary law. And in line with BODIN's theory of sovereignty it is assumed that the validity of the latter depends on a direct or indirect allowance on the part of the legislator.

But this positivism has no inkling of the fact that the fundamental problem of the enkaptic structural interlacements between spheres of competence, differing in a material sense, *lurks exactly in these genetic forms. The political dogma of the* "will of the legislator" as the sole source of validity of law, of the State as the possessor of a juridically unlimited competence (*"Kompetenz-Kompetenz"*) is simply taken for granted.

But there are also theories that have broken with this dogma and recognize an autonomous formation of law in a contractual way and in the non-political organized communities. Yet these theories show a lack of real insight into the individuality structures of the various spheres of law-formation and their enkaptic interlacements in the juridical genetic forms, maintaining the coherence of the juridical order.

As a rule modern students of sociology of law eliminate the

---

[1] Cf. my series of studies in the quarterly Anti-revol. Staatkunde (4e jrg., 1930, pp. 1—67, 224—265 and 325—362) entitled: *De Bronnen van het Stellig Recht in het licht der Wetsidee*; and my paper for the *Ver. v. Wijsbegeerte des Rechts*, entitled: *De Theorie van de Bronnen van het Stellig Recht in het licht der Wetsidee*, published in the Dutch sociological quarterly: *Mensch en Maatschappij* (1932). A complete elaboration of my theory is to be found in the second and third volume of my work *Encyclopedia of Jurisprudence*, which will be published by H. J. Paris (Amsterdam).

juridical problem of competence because it implies a normative viewpoint. And insofar as this problem is taken into account, as in GURVITCH' pluralistic sociological theory of law, it is turned into a historical problem [1]. The prevailing historicistic view of human society excludes any insight into the transcendental structures of individuality of the societal relationships.

The Historical School, which did not yet eliminate the genuine legal genetic forms from the process of law making, had introduced this view. Even GEORG BESELER and OTTO GIERKE, the Germanistic scholars who were the pioneers of the modern theory of the juridical autonomy of associations, kept clinging to the constituted juridical genetic forms of the autonomous social law (the articles of association, the domestic bylaws). They did not penetrate to the internal structural principles of these organized communities delimiting the latter's material internal spheres of competence in law-formation, but held to the traditional teleological view of these communities. In a differentiated human society, however, the genetic forms cannot guarantee the internal independence of law-formation in the various associations of a non-political structure.

The typical character of the juridical genetic forms is not in conflict with their function as centres of structural interlacements within the juridical order.

As law-forming declarations of the will of competent organs the genetic juridical forms are necessarily bound to the typical structure of the internal legal sphere of the organs. A Church-community cannot promulgate a State-Act; an international legal treaty is a typical genetic form of international law; the articles or domestic rules of an association are the typical genetic form of internal associational law, just as a private contract is the

---

[1] According to GURVITCH (*Sociology of Law,* 1947), the material spheres of competence of the different "functional social groups" (inclusive of the State) are of an absolutely variable character. There does not exist a fixed hiërarchy between the legal orders of the particular groups, which holds for all times. The only absolute sovereignty belongs to the legal order of the "supra-functional" and all-inclusive national community and of the inter-national community of mankind. The latter determine the material competence of all functional groups embraced by them. And they do so in a different way in the different phases of historical development. Cf. my *De Strijd om het Souvereiniteitsbegrip in de moderne Rechts- en Staatsleer* (Amsterdam, 1950), pp. 44 ff.

typical genetic form of private inter-individual law *inter partes*, and so on.

But this is not saying that all law positivized in any of these typical (explicit or direct) [1] genetic forms bears the character of the internal law of the juridical sphere concerned. We have already remarked that the genetic form of ecclesiastical rules may contain provisions of a civil juridical nature. It may even occur that an ecclesiastic regulation contains rules of a public legal character, whose formation belongs to the exclusive original competence of the State. In the same way the form of a private contract of purchase or hire may contain specific economically qualified legal rules relating to the contracting parties, general civil-juridical clauses, and social integrating law ("customary stipulations"). The form of a State Act may contain internal constitutional and administrative law as well as international public law, civil law and a reference to non-civil private law. In the form of an agreement between municipalities or provinces both private and public law may be positivized.

From these facts it appears that though a juridical genetic form (a source of law in a formal legal sense) is inseparably bound up with a law-forming-organ [2], this organ is interwoven in various material spheres of competence. In other words, a particular juridical genetic form, such as the direct or indirect volitional declaration of the legislator, can never be the original source of validity of all positive law. The opposite opinion of the legalistic theory is nothing but an uncritical dogmatism. According to its internal structural principle the State never has an

[1] The opposite of *indirect* or *implicit* forms, *i.e.* law-forming declarations of will deduced from the factual, constant behaviour of a competent former of law. In these forms "customary law" takes its origin within the separate (also public legal) spheres of competence. "Custom" is merely an external criterion by which the genesis of a legal norm is known. It is never a juridical genetic form. *Longaevus usus* is never a requirement if a recent constant practice clearly shows the law-forming will. This is to say that not all legal rules which have an indirect genetic form are to be subsumed under customary law.

[2] This is inherent in the juridical basic concept "source of law". This explains why the traditional theory of customary law could only remain unsatisfactory from the time of the classical Roman jurists to the present day, because it did not pay due attention to the question of the competent organ of law-formation. Customary law can no more be formed apart from competent organs than law which has a direct genetic form.

original competence to form internal ecclesiastical law, non-civil inter-individual law or free internal associational law. Neither do the private parties in a social contract, or the organs of an association, have original competence to form civil law. For civil law, in the sense of the State's integrating law relating to private inter-individual relations, appeals to a civil jurisdiction whose organization belongs to the internal structure of the body politic, and as such civil law does not have a specific non-juridical qualification.

The juridical genetic forms interlace original and derivative spheres of competence.

The question as to what belongs to the original competence of a law-forming organ is thus never dependent on the juridical genetic form in which the legal rules are positivized, but exclusively on the internal structural principles of human societal life founded in the divine world-order. These principles lie at the basis of every formation of positive law and make the latter only possible. One and the same genetic form positivizing juridical principles may be an original source of law within one sphere of competence and a derived source of law within another sphere. Thus the articles of association, for instance, are an original source of law as far as the internal law of the society is concerned, but a derived source of law with regard to civil law. The admirable thing in the enkaptic structural interlacements within the juridical order is that the original spheres of competence bind and limit each other. This state of affairs is based on the entire complicated structure of a differentiated human society.

An internal ecclesiastical legal relation, *e.g.*, does not exist "in itself, *i.e.* in isolation, but only in an enkaptic interlacement with constitutional State-law, civil law, free inter-individual law, internal conjugal law, and family law relations, and so on. Therefore every internal juridical relation within a particular sphere of competence has its counterpart in juridical relations within other spheres of competence. Such a juridical relation has inter-structural aspects that are interwoven with each other.

The civil legal counterpart of an internal question of communal law and the criterion of juridical sphere-sovereignty.

This explains why in modern times a question relating to internal communal law, be it of a public or private juridical nature, may have its counterpart in a civil juridical question which can be decided in a civil court. We shall revert to this point in the next section.

But at the same time it is clear that in general the civil legal question can only relate to the external, formal-juridical aspect of such an internal communal legal point of difference and never to its internal material juridical side. The sphere-sovereignty of the individuality-structures of human societal life maintains itself in the most complicated enkaptic interlacements, also in the juridical aspect of temporal reality.

The only possible criterion of this sphere-sovereignty is not of a formal but of an internal structural character: *All law displaying the typical individuality-structure of a particular community or inter-individual or inter-communal relationship, in principle falls within the original material-juridical sphere of competence of such a societal orbit, and is only formally connected (in its genetic form) with the spheres of competence of the other societal orbits.* In a final section we shall summarily consider the significance of this criterion for jurisprudence and juridical-historical research.

§ 3 - A FEW APPLICATIONS OF THE THEORY OF THE ENKAPTIC STRUCTURAL INTERLACEMENTS TO QUESTIONS OF A JURIDICAL HISTORICAL AND A PRACTICAL JURIDICAL NATURE.

The legal history of the medieval Germanic unions.

The legal history of the rich development of the medieval German unions during the initial phase of a process of societal differentiation is a very instructive subject for us to test our new theory of the enkaptic structural interlacements, and to examine the importance of our criterion to distinguish between the original spheres of juridical competence.

It is no accident that the great leaders of the Germanistic tendency in the Historical school, GEORG BESELER and OTTO GIERKE, put up a strong opposition to the absolutization of the system of concepts of the classical Roman *jus civile et gentium* on the part of the Romanistic wing led by PUCHTA. This opposition was especially due to their extensive research in this branch of study. The above-mentioned system of classical Roman juridical concepts was based on a theoretical abstraction of the private civil law-side of juridical life, in its sharp distinction from the public legal relations. It was bound to fail the student of the history of Germanic law before the reception of Roman law, because popular law was interlaced in every direction with the internal communal relations which, under the viewpoint of the differentiated Roman legal system, displayed both a public and a private juridical character.

However, GIERKE's theory of the organized communities was of a universalistic-metaphysical stamp and was unable to give an insight into the real individuality structures of human society. When the intricate structural interlacements in Germanic juridical life in the Middle Ages had to be analysed, this theory was naturally disappointing. These structural interlacements were indeed very complicated and displayed the character of both a *territorial* and a *personal enkapsis.* This appears from the internally interwoven spheres of competence in the local ordinances of a mark. Such an ordinance contained provisions concerning the internal law of the mark qualified by the function of the latter as an economic organization working the common lands and waters. These provisions alternate with regulations concerning weddings and funerals, ecclesiastical affairs and poor-relief, and administrative law. This is a typical interlacement of the mark proper with the secular sheriff's office and the ecclesiastical parish. There were numerous interlacements between ecclesiastical and secular spheres of competence in the ecclesiastical immunities, with feudal relationships and the relations of patronage, the so-called seignorial (or manorial) rights, and so on.

The structural interlacements in the positive organizational form of the late medieval craft-guilds.

Especially when in the later Middle-ages the craft guilds had acquired great political power and in the towns the process of social differentiation began to reveal itself, these guilds displayed very complicated structural interlacements. Repeatedly we find the following differentiated structures in them interwoven with each other:

1. the structure of a private, economically qualified trade-union;
2. that of a coercive organization with a public legal sphere of competence derived from the city government, connected with an economic monopoly, and the so-called guild-ban;
3. the structure of a part of the political organization of a town on a military basis;

4. the structure of an ecclesiastical organized group with (at least as a rule) an altar and church services of its own.

But this enumeration gives much too simple a picture of the structural interlacements in question. For the structures mentioned here are in their turn interwoven with all kinds of features peculiar to an undifferentiated community: the guild as a fraternity *(fraternitas, convivium)* with its common meals and guild-feasts, with its duties of mutual aid and assistance (enkaptically including the families of the members) in all kinds of circumstances. Their strong communal mind, viewed as a normative pattern of behaviour, is reminiscent of the spirit of kinship in the old sibs, and the structural principle of a brotherly and sisterly love-union has the leading function.

The legal historian who examines the relation between city law and guild law should carefully distinguish between the widely different societal structures enkaptically interlaced in the already *differentiated positive* organizational forms of the late-medieval guilds, and at the same time he should do full justice to their close coherence.

Which were the original spheres of competence with their own specific sovereignty and which were the derivative spheres of competence of the craft-guilds in this phase of development? Was the public juridical monopolistic structure really an original and internal constituent part of these partly primitive, partly already differentiated communities? What was the essential relation between the guild as an industrial association in the sense of an economically qualified vocational organization [1], and the guild as an undifferentiated organized community in the sense of a "fraternity"? Is the craft-guild in this stage of development still to be considered as a single communal whole with an undifferentiated inner destination?

These are a series of questions whose very formulation may illustrate the importance of the theory of the enkaptic structural interlacements for the study of legal history. For the current views cannot shed light on the problem of the structural unity of these remarkable communities in the transitional period con-

[1] Such an organization did not put the modern individualistic motive of pecuniary gain in the foreground; the maintenance of professional ethics, the ethics of the craft, was an essential element in a medieval craft-guild. This can be readily conceded to GIERKE. But it does not detract from the economic qualification of the industrial structure of a guild, nor did the factual behaviour of the guilds always correspond to the normative pattern of their ethics.

necting medieval and modern times, notwithstanding the profound research in regard to the historical origin of the craft-guilds.

GIERKE's view of the structure of the craft-guilds.

Among the older investigators GIERKE defines the medieval craft-guild as "a voluntary society or association based on a free, deliberate union which, like other guilds, comprises the entire man, just as nowadays only the family and the State do, and unites its members as brothers" [1].

Apart from the rather inappropriate comparison with a modern family and a State, the writer appears to view the craft-guilds qua talis as undifferentiated communities with an internal unity. But there are important objections to this view insofar as it does not take into account the later structural differentiation of these guilds at the time of their greatest power. It is certain that the oldest guilds mentioned in the documents, *viz.* the Frankish (and probably also the Anglo-saxon) guilds, displayed an undifferentiated structure. There is much to recommend the view that the old guilds, especially those that took the form of a sworn peace-guild, established a kind of artificial sib-relation between the families of the guild-brothers at a time when the orginal sibs (taken in the sense of *agnatic* communities) had already dissolved. The same thing applies to the view that in the late medieval fraternities the idea of the sib survived, deepened by the Christian idea of brotherhood [2].

This view, which does not at all imply that the guild-fraternity *originated* from the old sib relationship, is to my mind quite compatible with SOMMER's and SIEBER's conception that the old guilds were identical with the primitive neighbourhoods (in the

---

[1] O. GIERKE, *Das deutsche Genossenschaftsrecht.* Bnd. I (1868) p. 359: 'Die Zunft (ist) eine auf frei gewollter Vereinigung beruhende Verbindung oder eine gewillkürte Genossenschaft welche gleich anderen Gilden den ganzen Menschen, wie heute nur Familie und Staat, ergriff und ihre Mitglieder gleich Brüdern mit einander vereinte'.

[2] This is by no means a view held by WILDA and L. BRENTANO alone (BRENTANO once again gave an elaborate defence of it in *Eine Geschichte der wirtschaftlichen Entwicklung Englands,* Bnd. I, 1927, pp. 166 ff.); it is also defended by KARL HEGEL, *e.g. (Städte und Gilden der Germanischen Völker im Mittelalter,* Bnd. I, 1891, pp. 134 ff.), who reduced WILDA's thesis to its true proportions and ably defended it against an attack made by VON PAPPENHEIM *(De alt-dänischen Schutzgilden,* 1885, pp. 82 ff.).

sense of undifferentiated organized societies), characterized by mutual aid and assistance in all circumstances.

But the later development of the genuine craft-guilds formed by men of the same industry or trade in medieval towns clearly points to the operation of a differentiating process. Owing to this differentiation the structure of the economically qualified industrial organization, although interwoven with that of the undifferentiated fraternity, began to distinguish itself clearly from the latter. If the primitive neighbourhoods are the foundation of the craft-guilds, the interlacement between the structure of the organization of artisans and the undifferentiated guild-fraternity is easy to explain. For in medieval towns people of the same craft lived together in wards and streets [1].

In this case it would be an example of *territorial enkapsis* [2]. *Enkapsis* — but not identity. Already the connection with the public juridical structure of office, industrial monopoly, and guild-ban could only relate to the economically qualified structure of a vocational organization and not to an undifferentiated fraternity which also comprised the wives and children of the brethren. For, at least in the towns, the vocational brotherhoods *as such* lacked political governmental authority. The natural family-relationships of the guild-brethren were interwoven with the *fraternitas* in a *personal enkapsis*. But the craft-organization could only comprise the fellow-craftsmen (possibly also women), although the women and children were in a specially privileged position when the office was to be obtained (the so-called "*inninge*"), and in particular when it became hereditary.

Was then the vocational organization identical with the organization of the public office, the *magisterium*, whose sphere of competence had originally been derived from the lord of the town and the market? This hypothesis, too, cannot stand the

---

[1] Cf. J. B. AKKERMANN, *Het ontstaan der Ambachtsgilden* (thesis Leiden 1919) p. 158 and the literature cited there; especially F. KEUGEN, *Aemter und Zünfte, Zur Entstehung des Zunftwesens* (1903), pp. 139 ff. and EBERSTADT, *Der Ursprung des Zunftwesens* (2e Aufl., 1915) pp. 282 ff. Official craft and fraternity are clearly distinguished in different guild-regulations, *e.g.*, in the *skra* of the Flessburg shoemakers' and furriers' guild of 1437 and that of the bakers' guild of 1452 (cf. HEGEL, *op. cit.* I, p. 213/4). In the Parisian craft-guilds (with the exception of the butchers' guild) office and guild were always kept apart (cf. AKKERMANN, *op. cit.*, p. 176).

[2] Cf. volume III, pp. 659 ff.

test. In various towns it is possible to point out crafts which originally were not at all connected with the structure of a public office. And the guilds embracing these crafts had not obtained the guild-ban either [1].

But even if from the outset a craft was connected with the public office, the customary identification of craft and office cannot be correct. An industrial organization has its own internal economic-structural qualification, whereas the office was preponderantly concerned with the "public interest" of the town [2]. The connection of craft and office could thus only have an enkaptic character. This fact is of vital importance to our insight into the internal original spheres of competence of guild and city in the regulation of industrial life. In the introduction to OVERVOORDE's and JOOSTING's edition of the sources of law relating to the Utrecht guilds up to 1528, the municipal regulations concerned with these guilds have been classed under different heads, so that the public juridical aspects of this governmental interference are clearly distinguishable from the internal industrial viewpoint of the craft [3].

If we construe the late medieval craft guild only from the fusion of office and guild, we are thus guilty of over-simplification. The craft guild had two internal original spheres of com-

---

[1] *E.g.*, the guilds of the gardeners, those of the weavers, and those of the tailors in Bazel. Cf. AKKERMANN, *op. cit.*, p. 188/9.

[2] But as the object of the seignorial (or manorial) right of the lord of the town or market it no doubt also had to serve his pecuniary interest. GIERKE's idealistic picture of the medieval official character of the craft is too much oblivious of this fact.

[3] *Op. cit.*, XLI and XLII. The council's regulations are classed under the following headings:

1. the boundaries to the monopoly and the relation to alien merchants;
2. protection against the monopoly;
3. the care for public security;
4. market police;
5. regulations concerning taxation;
6. obligatory services to be rendered by the guilds for the benefit of the town *(tocht, waak, brandwezen, i.e.:* military service, watch, fire-brigade);
7. measures for the maintenance of the council's regulations. And lastly the writers mention a number of cases in which the town-council seemed to interfere with the internal industrial sphere, but they immediately try to indicate the public-juridical grounds for this interference.

petence, related to two different structural societal relationships combined in an *enkapsis* without forming an internal unity.

Moreover, the organization of the craft was interwoven with the derived public legal sphere of competence of office and guild-ban, and the guild fraternity was not only interwoven with the organized craft but also with an internal ecclesiastical group-structure and with a political structure (at least when the guild had attained to political power), as a part of the city organization.

If the guild-ban is considered as an essential element of the craft guild in its more restricted sense, one should bear in mind that this element can only be concerned with the positive existential form of the craft-organization in a particular variability type. But this element as such cannot be based on the internal stucture of the industrial organization. In the juridical modal aspect this leads to the insight that it is necessary to make a sharp distinction between the internal sphere-sovereignty of a guild in its two original spheres of competence and the autonomy of a guild in its official public-juridical and its ecclesiastical function.

But GIERKE starts from the idea of an internal unity of the late medieval guild relationship in all its structural aspects, in accordance with the prevailing view, and in spite of the distinction between the guild society as an autonomous organization, and as a part of the town community. GIERKE considers the widely different structures enkaptically interwoven in the organizational forms of the craft-guild, as different "sides" or "purposes" of one and the same *"Genossenschaft"*. Thus the boundaries between the internal structures and the merely enkaptic functions of the guild become completely blurred. He seeks the internal bond (holding all these different "sides" together and permeating them) in the fact that the craft guild was a *"Rechtsgenossenschaft"*, a *"Friedens- und Rechtseinheit"* (a juridical society, a unity for peace and justice) [1].

---

[1] *Op. cit.*, p. 396: 'War die Zunft, wie wir gesehen, eine politische und militärische, eine religiöse und gesellige, eine sittliche, eine wirtschaftliche und eine Vermögenseinheit, so lag das alle diese verschiedenen Seiten *vermittelnde und durchdringende* Band darin, dass sie eine Friedens- und Rechtsgenossenschaft war'. [As we have seen the guild was a political, military, religious, social, moral, industrial and property owning unity: the bond connecting and permeating all these different sides was the fact that the guild was a society for the promotion of peace and justice].

GIERKE's conception that the internal unity of the craft guilds was guaranteed by its juridical organization is untenable.

But this view overlooks the fact that the guild law displayed the same internal structural differences which should render the structural unity of the guild as an organized community extremely problematical in the eyes of the historian. To demonstrate the internal unity of the various guild structures GIERKE tightly clings to the real or supposed juridical genetic forms of guild law ("custom"[1] and "autonomy", "*Weisthum*" and "*Willkür*"). In other words, the nodal points of the enkaptic structural *interlacements* are taken to be the guarantee of the internal structural unity! But the true answer to the question about the relation between the legal spheres of competence of town and guild exactly depends on the insight into the fundamental difference between the internal structural relationships and their enkaptic interlacements with other structures in those juridical genetic forms! When one studies the contents of the guild regulations one is struck by the great structural variety of the provisions in them. These juridical regulations do not at all form an internal unity from the point of view of the material sphere of competence. They only hang together in a formal juridical way, *viz.* insofar as they had the same juridical genetic form and were formally maintained by the same guild organs administering justice.

How could one ever derive a criterion of the internal unity of the craft guilds from this merely formal juridical view-point?

GIERKE himself has to admit the fundamental difference between political and industrial members, and that between fellow craftsmen in the full sense of the word and mere members of the protective guild-relationship[2]. The confusion must have a disastrous effect on the historian's attempt to find the fundamental boundaries of the juridical spheres of competence between city and guild (of course, on the basis of his documentary evidence). For he then unwittingly elevates the public juridical autonomy of the guilds to their original (undifferentiated) sphere of competence, confounding autonomy with sphere sovereignty proper. This sphere of competence is now represented

[1] But "custom" as such is not a juridical genetic form, cf. volume III, p. 666, note 1.

[2] In the first place women and children belonging to the guild as an undifferentiated fraternity.

to have only exterior limits in the demands of the city's public interest[1]. This conclusion has, of course, not been drawn from an unprejudiced examination of the documents, but depends on GIERKE's organological theory of organized communities. It is impossible to interpret the documentary material in a legal historical way independently of a structural theoretical view of human societal life. In the initial period of societal differentiation in the towns a free non-political association could never constitute a public legal sphere of competence. This sphere was in principle derived from the city (or from the lord of the city), although in many towns the so-called guild-movement had led to a preponderant rôle of the craft-guilds in the government of the town. Only as the free organization of a craft, and as an undifferentiated fraternity without a political structure, could the guild possess original spheres of competence. But GIERKE's organological theory of organized communities is not oriented to the real individuality-structures of human society and is consequently unable to distinguish the figure of *enkapsis* from that of the internal unity of an organized community.

Art. 167 of the Dutch constitution. j°. art. 2 of the Judicial Organization Act in the light of the theory of structural interlacements.

There is another important field of research in which we can put our theory of the enkaptic structural interlacements to the test. We mean the question of the internal limits to the spheres of competence of the State's common courts with reference to questions of internal communal law in modern jurisprudence. Just as in the case of the questions of legal history discussed above we are here confronted with problems of a special science. For their solution a supposedly purely special scientific attitude

---

[1] Cf. especially GIERKE's expositions *op. cit.* Bnd. I, pp. 380—383; *e.g.*, p. 381: 'Die wahre Quelle aber auch der obrigkeitlich genehmigten Zunftrechte war genossenschaftliche Beliebung...' *etc.*, and p. 382: 'Da die Zunft eine selbständige Genossenschaft war und folglich nicht nur ein von dem städlichen verschiedenes Vermögen, *sondern auch ein eignes und unabhängiges öffentliches Recht* besass...' (Italics are mine). [p. 381: But the true source also of the guild-law allowed by the magistrates was the will of the association... *etc.* And p. 382: As the guild was an independent society and consequently not merely possessed financial means different from those of the city, *but also possessed an independent public law of its own...*].

of thought will at once prove to be inadequate. If we want to known the basic lines of Dutch jurisprudence[1] with respect to the limits of the material competence of the common courts in civil cases connected with questions of a non-civil nature, we must first study the statute law regulations concerned. In art. 167 of the Dutch Constitution j.° art. 2 of the Judicial Organization Act of 18 April 1827 (Gazette no. 20) we find the "*sedes materiae*", the fundamental legal provisions concerning the so-called "attributive competence" of the common courts. This is the regulation of (derived) material competence containing the nature of the disputes to be subjected to the civil judicature in its various branches.

The famous Dutch statesman and scholar THORBECKE defended the view that the so-called *fundamentum petendi* (*i.e.* the character of the legal relation from which the action originates), is decisive for the question as to what actions for debt belong to the cognizance of the civil judge[2]. This view seems to find support in the literal text of the above-named article of the constitution. But on legal historical grounds jurisprudence invariably interprets it in conformity to the different wording of art. 2. J.O. Act, and accordingly has decided that not the basis but only the object of an action is decisive[3]. In its sentence of the 31st December, 1915, W., 9947, the Supreme Court of the Netherlands formulated this perhaps in a sharper way: "the right to be protected is decisive"[3]. In other words, all claims for *jura in*

[1] 'Jurisprudence' is meant here in the sense of a complex of judicial decisions.

[2] Cf. THORBECKE, *Aanteekening op de Grondwet*, vol. II, pp. 155 ff.

[3] Art. 167 of the Constitution runs as follows: 'Alle twistgedingen over eigendom of daaruit voortspruitende rechten, over schuldvordering en andere burgerlijke rechten behoren bij uitsluiting tot de kennisneming van de rechterlijke macht'. [All disputes about property or the rights proceeding from it, about claims for debt and other civil rights exclusively belong to the cognizance of the common courts (the judicial power)]. Art. 2 J.O. Act: 'De kennisneming en beslissing van alle geschillen over eigendom, of daaruit voortspruitende rechten, over schuldvorderingen of burgerlijke rechten, en de toepassing van alle soort van wettig bepaalde straffen, zijn bij uitsluiting opgedragen aan de rechterlijke macht, volgens de verdelingen van regtsgebied, de regterlijke bevoegdheid en de werkzaamheden bij deze wet geregeld'. [The cognizance and decision of all disputes about property or the rights proceeding from it, about claims for debt or civil rights, and the application of all kinds of legally determined punishments, are exclusively entrusted to the judicial power, according to the divisions of jurisdiction, the judicial competence and the activities governed by this Act.]

rē and debt can be made valid in law before the common civil judge, no matter what the internal character is of the juridical relations from which they arise. This renders art. 2 of the J.O. Act an extremely interesting legal provision from the point of view of the enkaptic structural interlacements in positive law.

The positivistic legal theory, which eradicates the internal structural differences between the juridical relations, would lead to the conclusion that the competence of the common courts is, therefore, not bound within any limits by the internal structure of the juridical relations from which the claims arise. For, according to the constant judicial opinion, the Act does not make any difference in this respect. But the judge does not at all draw this positivistic conclusion from his interpretation of art. 167 of the Constitution j.° art. 2 of the J.O. Act.

The study of the judicial decisions shows that all along the line the structural difference between civil and non-civil law remains of fundamental importance to the question about the kind of cases of which the civil judge has to form an independent judgment. The point is that the civil judge is indeed competent to take cognizance of claims whose *fundamentum petendi* is found in non-civil legal relations. But, according to the constant judicial opinion, he has in principle to refrain from judging of material questions of law concerned with the internal structure of the public administration and with that of non-civil communal and contractual law. In these matters he generally places himself on a formal juridical standpoint while respecting the original spheres of competence belonging to the non-civil legal orbits of law. The parties to the action may try to involve the civil judge in the above mentioned material juridical questions. But his answer is invariably that these questions do not concern civil-legal relations and are therefore withdrawn from the decision of the judge.

And this is not a special viewpoint of Dutch civil jurisdiction. In English judicature, *e.g.*, the same attitude obtains with regard to the internal law of associations. According to the English common law courts, the judicial decision of the "domestic tribunals" of such associations is only assailable in a civil process if the proceedings have been contrary to the principles of "natural justice". These principles are the following: the principle of *"audi et alteram partem"* must have been observed in the internal jurisdiction of an association in its sharpest possible formal sense; no patent partiality can be tolerated in the decisions of the "domestic tribunals", and nothing may be done which is contrary to the articles of association or the domestic by-laws. This is all the more interesting as free associations (especially "clubs") occupy a very important place in social life in England [1].

On the whole the Supreme Court of Germany (the "*Reichsgericht*") takes the same formal view in questions relating to the internal legal relationships of associations which may be interlaced with civil law-suits. Since 1923 [2] an exception was made with respect to the so-called *Zwanggenossenschaften* (coercive associations), such as trade unions, the membership of which is unavoidable if one does not wish to go begging for bread. In the case of such associations the civil judge does examine the material grounds of a decision for the expulsion of a member. The reason is that these organizations had acquired a social position far exceeding their internal legal sphere, and practically decided the fate of their members by expelling the latter. The expelled member's total private social status was at stake in this case. The typical enkaptic structural interlacement of such indirectly compulsory organizations with the structure of the State and the civil legal relations plays a special rôle here. Also from a civil law standpoint it became necessary to accord a more than formal juridical protection to the members from possible abuse of the internal authority of the trade unions. In this case the internal sphere of competence of the civil judge is not really exceeded, as will appear from the sequel.

Formal and material criteria of an illegal act in the judicial decisions relating to art. 1401 of the Dutch Civil Code.

The formal attitude assumed by the Dutch civil judge in questions relating to the internal side of legal relations which as to their inner nature exceed the boundaries of civil law, is all the more striking since the decision of the Supreme Court of the Netherlands of the 31st. of January, 1919 (W. 1036).

---

[1] Cf. W. A. ROBSON, *Justice and Administrative Law* (1928), pp. 169 ff.

[2] Cf. the sentence of the *Reichsgericht* of 20th December 1923 (Entsch. R. G. in Zivilsachen Bnd. 107, p. 386). This decision was based on the following consideration: 'In Fällen wie hier, wo die Zugehörigkeit zum Verein geradezu eine Lebensfrage für die Mitglieder bildet, musz das Gericht eine sachliche Nachprüfung des Ausschlieszungsbeschlusses nach der Richtung gestattet sein, ob nicht in dem Vorgehen des Vereins gegen das Mitglied eine offenbare Unbilligkeit zu finden ist'.

This decision introduced a new criterion of civil wrong which according to art. 1401 of the Dutch Civil Code gives rise to an action for damages. In contradistinction to the English law of torts, this article establishes the liability for any tort causing damages to another person by guilt. The article mentioned speaks of "any unlawful act". Before the year 1919 the Supreme Court understood by this term exclusively actions contrary to an explicitly formulated legal duty or implying an infringement of a person's subjective right. The new criterion, introduced in the decision mentioned, added to these formal kinds of illegal acts every acting "contrary to the due care pertaining to another's person or goods in inter-individual societal intercourse" [1].

It is clear that by the application of this criterion the unlawfulness of a private act is conceived in a *material* sense according to unwritten legal norms, which lack the explicit genetic form of statute law. However, when a civil judge is called upon in a civil law-suit to judge of the lawfulness of an internal juridical decision on the part of a competent organ of an organized community, he does not employ a material, but a formal concept of unlawfulness. This happens if the decision of the material legal question should lead the judge to encroach upon the internal legal sphere determined by the inner structure of the societal relationship concerned. The Supreme Court takes this view (and this example is followed by the lower courts) both with regard to the public administration and the private legal relationships which as such lack a civil legal character. I shall mention some instances of the judicial view in this matter:

> The Hague arrondissement court pronounced the civil judge's incompetence in questions of "faith and confession, practice and conduct of the members of a Church-society in its sentence of 28th February 1888 (about art. 3 of the general regulation of the *Nederl. Herv. Kerk* of 1st May 1852). The same view was taken by the decision of the arrondissement court of Utrecht 18th April 1928 W. 11886 with regard to the property of the Church building and manse of Tienhoven, after the schism in the *Gereformeerde Kerken* which had occurred in the year 1926. In its judgment the court considered that it was not entitled to "express any spiritual, but only civil legal appreciations". On this ground it refused to enter into the matter of the material lawfulness of the synodal decrees in question [2].

---

[1] Naturally "social intercourse" is meant here in a juridical sense.

[2] Cf. the material on this subject collected from judicial decisions and literature by LÉON VAN PRAAG, *Rechtspraak en voornaamste Literatuur*

The same attitude was maintained by the civil courts in the numerous law-suits concerning the property of the Church buildings and manses originating from a second schism in the Reformed Churches. In general the organizational relations in a Church community are judged according to the external rules of the Civil Code relating to free associations. Cf., *e.g.*, the sentence of the Supreme Court of the *Netherlands of 13th July 1946* N.J. 1947, 1. These rules are certainly not applicable to the genuine internal organization of a Church, since the latter lacks the character of a free association. Nevertheless, from the viewpoint of civil law the application of these formal rules is a guarantee against the interference with the genuine internal law of the Church.

With respect to the internal law of free associations the civil judge is repeatedly called upon to decide whether their decisions to expel one or more members are lawful or not. In these cases, too, the judge anxiously sticks to the formal concept of unlawfulness in respect to all questions of genuine internal associational law, *i.e.* he simply inquires whether a decision is formally based on the articles of association.

The *application of the material criterion of unlawfulness, introduced* by the sentence of 1919, to internal administrative actions of the government was in principle rejected by the Supreme Court of the Netherlands in the famous "Strooppot case" of 29th June 1928 W. 11864.

This is all the more important if one considers that the current theory bases the validity of the internal law of an organized community with regard to its members exclusively on an agreement. According to this contractual viewpoint the individual has voluntarily submitted to this law and has been accepted by the other members as one of them. The validity of this agreement is traced back to the Dutch Civil Code (cf. art. 1374, 1st part: "all agreements that have been legally made are law to those who have concluded them"). This positivistic contractual theory is still influenced by the Humanistic doctrine of natural law and its contractual construction of all communities irrespective of their inner nature. It assumes that the whole of civil judicial decisions relating to the "autonomy of private organizations" can be understood without the aid of any material concept of competence, *i.e.* without any insight into the inner structure of the internal communal law. According to this view the civil judge does not need any other legal ground for his non-

---

betr. de Wet op de Recht. Organ. 1e ged. Alg. Begins., pp. 647 ff., suppl. 1e ged. (1930) p. 145, 2e ged. pp. 134 ff., and in the quarterly *Themis* (1920) pp. 174 and 305 ff.

interference in material questions of internal communal law than the old nominalistic principle: *Volenti non fit iniuria,* the familiar adage of the Humanistic theory of natural law.

Neither the contractual construction, nor GIERKE's theory of the formal autonomy of private organized communities can give an account of the constant judicial opinion in question.

But can this individualistic contractual construction really give an account of the civil judicial standpoint in these matters? I deny this. This construction is helpless in the face of cases in which a civil court has to decide material juridical questions not concerning the internal structure of a private organized community, although they are formally governed by provisions of the articles of association or the ecclesiastical legal order.

On this point the older judicial view of the Dutch courts was much more formalistic than the modern. Thus *e.g.*, the decision of the Amsterdam court given on the 22nd June 1880 (W. 4609) is instructive. Some members of a shipyard workers' union had been expelled by the general meeting of the union on the ground of their behaviour alleged to have been "detrimental and disgraceful" to the union. The court decided that they could not even lodge a complaint with a civil judge because of the violation of the principle of *audi et alteram partem,* if the union's articles of association and domestic bylaws did not formally guarantee the observance of this principle. The material decision was concerned with the question as to whether or not the member's behaviour was a case in point as to the ground of the expulsion mentioned. The court considered that this material question belonged to the exclusive competence of the general meeting of the members of the union. An interesting contrast is offered by the decision of a material juridical question by a civil judge in the award of the Utrecht court of the 26th June 1918 W.P.N.R. 2603, in another case of expulsion. A member of a typographical society had been expelled on the ground of art. 7 of the articles of association for 'endangering the reputation' of the society summoned.

The defendant objected that the judge was not competent in this case because only the society's general meeting was competent to decide upon the expulsion of members. But the court rejected this defence, as the claimant did not request the court to rescind the expulsion and to restore him as a member of the association. The claimant only pleaded for damages on the ground of the alleged unlawfulness of the expulsion. Then the court examined the facts adduced by the defendant serving to prove that the reputation of the organization had been endangered.

The claimant, as chairman of a public meeting, had allowed an insulting expression to be used referring to the members of the society. The court decided in a material sense that this expression was "certainly insulting to those to whom it is applied, and that if this is done to all or most of the members of a society, the reputation of that society is certainly injured, at least endangered". Why did the judge employ a material criterion of unlawfulness in this case, whereas he generally places himself on a strictly formal standpoint with respect to juridical questions of an internal associational nature? This must be quite inexplicable to the theory of the formal autonomy of private associations (BESELER, GIERKE, *etc.*) as well as to the contractual theory. Both would have to lead to the conclusion that in the above-mentioned case the civil judge ought to have taken a formal legal standpoint. But if we apply the criterion of "juridical sphere-sovereignty", the matter is clear. In the case of the typographical society the application of the material criterion of unlawfulness does not result in a real encroachment on the internal legal sphere of the association, because the material juridical question in this case was itself of a civil juridical nature and had nothing to do with the typical structure of the society. It was a question of an ordinary "insult" in a civil juridical sense as to which the Civil Code even assigns a separate action for tort (Art. 1408).

The original material spheres of competence cannot be eradicated by human arbitrariness.

Of course, the objection may be raised: it is quite possible that in the future the civil judge alters his present attitude to the material legal questions connected with the inner nature and structure of the organized communities.

Indeed, this is not impossible. In a South-African lawsuit concerning the deposition of the ecclesiastical professor DU PLESSIS, for instance, the judge was induced to a material appreciation of questions of belief and confession in spite of his protestations to the contrary. But even in such cases of a material excess of legal power the strong arm of the State appears to be unable to violate the internal sphere-sovereignty of an organized community, so long as the latter puts up a united resistance for the defence of its original sphere of competence. Of course, the State can temporarily prohibit the formation of private associations. But it cannot arbitrarily change the internal structural principles of the societal relationships and their original spheres of competence. A civil judge's sentence can do no more than pronounce the *civil* unlawfulness of the challenged decision of an internal organ of an organized community, and sentence it to pay damages, or a so-called penal sum.

But *within its original sphere of competence* an organized community can never be compelled to accept a civil judge's decision which exceeds the boundaries of the civil legal sphere.

When the civil judge in final instance, even on wrong grounds, has pronounced the civil unlawfulness of a decision taken by a competent authoritative organ of a private community, the latter has to accept this sentence *in a civil juridical sense* unconditionally. It has to pay the damages imposed by the judge because the latter remained entirely within his material sphere of competence when he fixed them. But the authoritative organ of such a community is not bound to adapt its decision, given within the original sphere of its competence, to the judge's personal opinion on matters outside his material sphere of legal power, even if this opinion would form an *essential ground* of his sentence. He can never give an *official* opinion in such matters.

This is a question of juridical insight into states of affairs which the positivistic juridical theory misinterprets fundamentally. The latter is not based on positive law, which is not of a theoretical character and cannot give a binding theory. But the misconception referred to is the result of a fallacious theory of positive law, on which a legalistic positivism bases its interpretation of the legal rules.

The contractual construction of the internal law of organized communities is an absolute failure in the case of public law. The judicial opinion as to an unlawful action on the part of the government, judged according to the principles of common civil law.

The positivistic contractual theory by means of which current opinion tries to construe the "formal autonomy of a free association" or a Church community from the legal viewpoint, is unable to give a theoretical account of the different structures of positive law. It is completely unable to elucidate the judicial view in cases of a civil wrong on the part of the public administration. Also with reference to the internal public legal aspect of the government's actions, civil judicature employs a strictly formal criterion of unlawfulness and does not apply the material criterion formulated by the Dutch Supreme Court in its famous decision of 1919. In this case the positivistic juridical theory can no longer appeal to the old natural law doctrine of a "social contract" to construe the legal autonomy of the internal sphere of public administration.

Yet in these judicial decisions the same question is at issue that occurs in the case of unlawful actions on the part of the organs of private organisations; *viz.* the civil judge will make a halt before the internal sphere of communal law.

But a positivistic theory has no eye for the internal structural differences between civil law and internal communal law. This theory cannot understand why the material civil legal criterion of unlawfulness, formulated by the Dutch Supreme Court as "contrary to the due care pertaining to another's person or goods, in civil legal intercourse", does not apply to the *internal* communal relationship between government and subjects. It cannot understand why, in respect to the latter, civil jurisdiction restricts the concepts "civil wrong" to a violation on the part of public administrative organs of subjective rights or formal legal duties.

But the truth is that only a material administrative jurisdiction governed by public juridical principles [1] can offer the injured subject redress in cases exceeding the boundaries of a civil legal relation.

Jurisdiction has not been entrusted with the task of theorizing about law, but with that of forming law *in concreto*; in general it shows a very correct intuitive insight into the fundamental structural differences between civil law and internal administrative law. It refuses to judge the internal structure of unlawful governmental actions by means of a material civil law standard. The structure of social reality itself resists such an eradication of the structural boundaries.

The structural interlacement of civil law and internal communal law considered from the standpoint of Art. 1401 of the Dutch Civil Code. The insufficiency of GIERKE's theory of organized communities to account for this interlacement.

How can we understand that the civil judge's formal standpoint with regard to the internal law of organized communities and inter-individual societal relations is really a matter of civil law? The answer will also give us a clearer insight into the fact that the internal communal legal relationships have their civil legal counterpart. This is the reason why they can be submitted to the civil judge's decision, although only from the formal standpoint. GIERKE's organic theory of organized communities has been rightly criticized for its inability to account for the possibility of making a violation of the internal rights of member-

---

[1] We refer once again to PAUL DUEZ, *La Responsabilité de la Puissance Public en dehors du Contrat.*

ship into the object of a civil law-suit against the corporation [1]. If these internal rights are qualified by their inherence in membership *qua talis,* and a member, as such, is merely a part of the whole, how can he bring an action against the whole, just like an outsider? [2]

Indeed, GIERKE'S sharp separation between communal law *(Sozialrecht)* and inter-individual civil law *(Individualrecht),* and his lack of insight into their enkaptic structural interlacements render this state of affairs inexplicable [3]. If, however, there is an unbreakable enkaptic structural interlacement between internal communal law and civil inter-individual law, then every internal communal legal relation must in principle have its external civil juridical counterpart. Then the antinomy pointed out in GIERKE'S theory of organized communities, *viz.* that in a civil law-suit about internal rights of membership a

---

[1] Cf. J. BINDER, *Das Problem der juristischen Persönlichkeit* (1907), p. 112.

[2] GIERKE cannot indicate a material-juridical criterion to delimit the internal law of an organized community, and consequently he is involved in a patent antinomy with respect to the *"reine Mitgliedschaftsverhältnisse"* (pure relations of co-membership) within a private association. On the one hand he writes *(Deutsches Privatrecht* I, p. 534/5) about these legal relations: 'Sie sind freilich, da sie ein selbständiges Dasein ausserhalb des körperschaftlichen Zusammenhanges nicht haben, nur durch, nicht gegen die körperschaftliche Lebensordnung gesichert'. [To be sure they are guaranteed only by, and not against, the order of corporate life, because they do not possess an independent existence outside of the corporate coherence.] But he immediately adds: 'Mithin müssen, bevor die Körperschaft gegen ihr Mitglied der richterlichen Hülfe bedarf oder das Mitglied gegen die Körperschaft den Rechtsweg beschreiten kann, zunächst die durch die Körperschaft selbst gebotenen Mittel der Abhülfe erschöpt sein'. [That is why before the corporation needs judicial aid against its member, or before a member can go to law against the corporation, the means of redress offered by the corporation itself must be completely exhausted.]. Consequently these purely internal juridical relations can after all be made valid against the corporation, though we were first told they could not. Here appears the antinomy. On his standpoint GIERKE cannot see how an internal legal relation in a community has its civil juridical counterpart, which can only be distinguished from the former by means of a material structural criterion. He has at his disposal only the formal criterion of the civil judge's incompetence to an independent examination of the decisions on the part of the organs of a society which are in formal agreement with its articles of association (*op. cit.*, p. 435). We have already shown that this criterion is insufficient.

part is opposed to the whole, will naturally be removed. Human legal subjectivity is not split up into that of an individual and that of a member of a communal whole, as in GIERKE, but functions only in the unbreakable correlation of these two.

When a civil judge applies the formal test of the articles of association and the domestic regulation of a society to the actions performed by the organs within their original sphere of competence, he does so to maintain legal security, a genuine civil juridical principle. And when he subjects a domestic jurisdiction to the test of the principles of *audi et alteram partem,* and of impartiality, he also applies genuine principles of common civil law relating to what in the natural law doctrine was called the complex of unalienable human rights. It is clear that in this sense a civil legal relation is necessarily interwoven with the internal juridical relations of an organized community. The latter are enkaptically bound by civil law to protect the legal status of the human personality as such.

The question relating to an ecclesiastical assessment imposed upon baptismal members of the Dutch Reformed Church brought before a civil court, and the juridical sphere-sovereignty of the Church.

But a civil judge need not restrict himself to a merely formal test of legal questions relating to the internal life of a community, by means of statute law, articles of association and domestic rules, if the material juridical question does not belong to the original sphere of competence of the organized community concerned. In the first place we have seen that not all the provisions originating in the genetic form of such communal law are peculiar to an internal community as regards their material meaning-structure.

In addition to the example given above, I refer to the judicial standpoint in the well-known case relating to the nature of the juridical bond established by baptism between a baptismal member and an institutional Church. This case was concerned with a Church tax to be paid by baptismal members in virtue of the General Rules of the Dutch Reformed Church [1]. The sentence of the Supreme Court of the Netherlands of 29th December 1911 W. 9272 qualified this juridical bond as a civil legal or "secular" relation. The Supreme Court

---

[1] The Dutch Reformed Church *(Nederlandse Hervormde Kerk)* is not identical with the *Gereformeerde Kerken,* which separated from the former in 1886.

declared that this civil juridical bond displays an unbreakable coherence with the "religious or ideal bond". At the same time the ecclesiastical regulation of the rights and duties of the members was called a "*special regulation*" under the "*supreme rule of the general* statute law" to which the former always has to yield, "unless the general statute law itself leaves scope for deviation". The *theoretical* point of view expressed by the Supreme Court here, though not detracting from the correctness of its concrete decision in the given case, was entirely in agreement with the prevailing doctrine most sharply formulated by the earlier mentioned statesman and scholar THORBECKE [1]. According to this doctrine the so-called "visible Church" is an ordinary civil association or society, an ordinary "corporation" in the sense of the Civil Code, as the Supreme Court has it. The internal juridical relations in such a society are simply of a civil legal character. Consequently there can be no question of an internal ecclesiastical law with a particular structure of its own and with an original sphere of competence. In this view private law is only of one kind: it is identical with civil law.

To this prevailing theory A. F. DE SAVORNIN LOHMAN [2], professor of constitutional law at the Free University of Amsterdam, opposed another, according to which the "visible Church" is not at all a society in a civil juridical sense, but an institution. It has a spiritual character of its own and possesses an internal spiritual legal sphere, which should be considered as entirely apart from civil law. As a result the civil juridical rules relating to associations can never be applied here. This view implies that the Dutch Reformed Church cannot at all call in the aid of a civil judge in case a baptismal member refuses to pay the ecclesiastical tax.

Neither of these theories does justice to the structural differences and coherences within the juridical sphere. THORBECKE totally ignores the internal *legal* individuality-structure of the temporal institutional Church and therefore levels all non-public juridical spheres under the *civil legal denominator. LOHMAN, on the other* hand, absolutizes the internal juridical sphere of the Church to an entirely independent sphere of competence which nowhere even touches civil law.

The true state of affairs can only be grasped if we have an insight into the enkaptic structural interlacements between civil law and internal ecclesiastical law, and apply the material criterion of juridical sphere-sovereignty formulated by us.

Then it at once appears that baptism really establishes a juridical bond of an internal ecclesiastical nature, which can only be understood from the point of view of the internal structural principle of the temporal Church institution. But the obligation to pay an "ecclesiastic tax", imposed on the baptismal members in the legal form of

---

[1] Cf. Mr L. H. VAN LENNEP, *De Rechtskracht van de Verordeningen der Christelijke Kerkgenootschappen* (diss. Leiden, 1909), pp. 111 ff.

[2] *De Rechtsbevoegdheid der Kerken*, in the review „*Rechtsgeleerd Magazijn*" (1893), pp. 103 ff.

the General Rules of the Dutch Reformed Church, can never be of an internal ecclesiastical juridical character. This obligation has no internal relation to the typical structural principle of the institutional Church: it is even contrary to this internal structural principle. In a differentiated human society the imposition of a tax not based on the free compliance of a member only belongs to the original competence of the State, as a coercive institution founded in the power of the sword. The Church institution does not possess this competence, at least never in an original sense. The juridical question as to whether or not the baptismal members of the Dutch Reformed Church, as such, are bound to pay an assessment in the "Church tax" can only be answered in accordance with a material civil legal view-point. No doubt parents are perfectly entitled to have their children baptized in a particular Church community and thus to have them incorporated as baptismal members in this latter. For this power is implied in the original competence inherent in their parental authority. But this cannot give rise to any financial obligations on the part of a baptismal member that has not voluntarily joined the Church community, except those that are according to the norms of civil law, *i.e.* only those based on his consent. This consent is only valid in law after his coming of age. By judging such a question according to the civil juridical principles of the law of contract, the civil judge can never encroach upon the internal sphere of competence of the Church.

Respect for the original non-civil juridical spheres of competence does not imply respect for abuse of power.

In the second place the boundaries of the civil legal sphere of competence cannot be in principle exceeded when guarantees are created against evident partiality or abuse of power, irrespective of the question as to whether these guarantees are offered by means of civil legislation or by the law of jurisprudence[1]. Such partiality or abuse of power may arise when the authoritative organs of an organized community or a family exercise their authority contrary to its inner nature and destination so that the civil juridical interests of its members are injured.

This may also occur in the exertion of the marital power in the internal conjugal community. In this case the wife should have an appeal to the civil judge in order to protect her civil legal interests. And the same thing applies to the relation between civil law and the internal sphere of the private, non-civil law of inter-individual relations.

In the non-civil juridical integrating process of private inter-

[1] *I.e.* judge made law.

individual law the "dominating groups" give the lead on the basis of their peculiar position of power in society, without having any legal competence proper. In this case there is no guarantee of their observing the requirements of good faith and equity with respect to the other party. The latter can often only accept the conditions laid down in a one-sided manner (thus, *e.g.*, the agreements made with a transportation company). And this makes it possible to violate the deepened civil-juridical principles of the law of contract *de facto*.

In this case, too, the civil juridical counterpart of the non-civil law formation must not for a moment be lost sight of.

The enkaptic inter-structural interlacements between civil law and non-civil private law prove to be an extremely delicate juridical tissue, and the criterion of the juridical sphere-sovereignty is grasped in its true sense only if we realize the impossibility of isolating the original spheres of competence from one another hermetically. The sovereignty of the modal law-spheres within their own boundaries only functions according to their internal modal meaning in the cosmic coherence of all the modal aspects. In the same way the juridical sphere-sovereignty of the original spheres of competence can only exist in their intricate mutual structural interlacements. Not with a butcher knife, but only with the lancet of a structural analysis can this tissue be theoretically analysed in a proper way.

The limits of the original competence of the legislator in the sphere of civil law.

The above implies that there are also fundamental limits to the original competence of the legislator with respect to the enkaptic binding of non-civil inter-individual commercial or industrial law to the civil legal order.

In this respect it is very instructive to take cognizance of the development of the Dutch Code of Commerce since its introduction in 1838. In line with the French *Code du Commerce* the Dutch legislator intended to codify the law of commerce without having a clear insight into the inner boundaries of a civil legal regulation. Thus he started with a compulsory definition of commercial acts and of the occupation of merchants which restricted the objects of commerce to movables (wares) .

As a consequence the Code did not acknowledge brokers in real estates. Limited liability companies were bound to the purpose of commerce in the sense defined by the Code, *etc.*

Here we meet with a cleár encroachment on the part of the civil legislator upon the internal sphere of competence of commerce and industry. We have seen that civil law, in the sense of private common State-law, does not permit itself to be bound to a specific economic purpose. By its inner nature it lacks any specific qualification of a non-juridical character. It is consequently beyond the civil legal power of the legislator to determine the inner sphere of activity of commerce and industry, and to bind a particular juridical form of association to a commercial purpose whose inner content is defined by the legislator himself. The result of this "*excès de pouvoir*" was that there arose a sharp conflict between the compulsory rules of the Code and non-civil commercial and industrial law. In this conflict both the common courts and the organs of public administration took sides in favour of the latter. And finally the legislator was obliged to join the legal praxis. The limited liability Comp. Act of 2nd July 1928 repealed the binding of these companies to a commercial purpose. The Act of 5th May 1922 repealed the limitative circumscription of the task of brokers. And the Act of 2nd July 1934 repealed the initial articles (2—5) of the Code which had tried to establish compulsory criteria of commercial actions and merchants.

There are many other examples to be adduced of the formation of private industrial or commercial law contrary to compulsory rules of the civil legislator, where the conflict arose from an exceeding of the inner boundaries of civil law on the part of the legislator. But the above may suffice to illustrate our thesis that in the intricate enkaptic. interlacements of the original spheres of competence the latter maintain their internal limits determined by the inner nature and structure of the different societal relationships.

Chapter III

THE ENKAPTIC STRUCTURAL WHOLE AND THE CONCEPT OF SUBSTANCE IN MODERN PHILOSOPHY OF NATURE

INTRODUCTION.

The theory of enkaptic inter-structural interlacements gives rise to a new problem which is of fundamental philosophical importance. It may be formulated as follows: How is it possible that in such interlacements new structural wholes are constituted?

This problem does not permit itself to be evaded any longer. For it has appeared that in itself the figure of *enkapsis* is sharply opposed to the *relation of a whole and its parts.* But if temporal reality were built up only in inter-structural interlacements not embraced by integral structural wholes, it would be impossible to account for the naïve experience of things as individual totalities. For we have seen that not any of these things displays a simple structure of individuality but that they are much rather constituted on the basis of enkaptic interweavings of structures.

Therefore, the theory of the enkaptic structural whole that we shall explain in this chapter turns out to be the indispensable keystone of that of the enkaptic interlacements. This new theory, however, which I developed for the first time in an ample treatise published in the quarterly *Philosophia Reformata* [1], is no more the result of an *a-priori* construction than any other part of the philosophy explained in this work. Rather it has ripened only little by little in a continuous confrontation with empirical, scientifically established states of affairs. In this respect, too, the idea of the enkaptic structural whole is opposed to the *a priori* substance-concept of metaphysics. In the present

---

[1] *Het Substantiebegrip in de Moderne Natuurphilosophie en de Theorie van het Enkaptisch Structuurgeheel* (Phil. Ref. 15th year, 1950), pp. 66—139.

chapter we shall continually confront these two conceptions with each other and with the empirical states of affairs. From this confrontation it will also appear to what degree in modern theoretical biology and philosophy of nature the substance-concept has impeded a satisfactory solution of the structural problems.

§ 1 - A PROVISIONAL DEFINITION OF THE ENKAPTIC STRUCTURAL WHOLE AND AN INVESTIGATION INTO THE TYPES OF ENKAPTIC INTERLACEMENTS IN WHICH IT MAY PRESENT ITSELF.

We shall start with a provisional definition of what we understand by an enkaptic structural whole, in order to delimit the ontological problem implied in it. *We shall speak of a genuine enkaptic structural whole when an interlacement between structures of a different radical- or genotype is realized in one and the same typically qualified form-totality embracing all the interwoven structures in a real enkaptic unity without encroaching upon their inner sphere-sovereignty.*

From our previous investigations it has become evident that the different structures interwoven into such an enkaptic whole cannot be related *to one another* according to the whole-part relation. For in this case the figure of *enkapsis* would be cancelled. The enkaptic structural whole must much rather embrace all the structures interwoven within its internal operational sphere and assign to them their due place within the whole. The enkaptic functions of these structures must be serviceable to the whole, and the leading and qualifying rôle within the latter must be assigned to the highest of the inter-woven structures. Nevertheless the enkaptic total structure may not coalesce with this qualifying structural type.

The enkaptic structural whole and the undifferentiated individuality structures.

One should, however, be on one's guard against identifying this structural whole with an undifferentiated structure of individuality encountered, for instance, in a primitive organized community. For the latter does not réalize any differentiated structure. Here we find only one undifferentiated internal operational sphere which eventually may fulfil at the same time the rôle of a political community, a cult community, a school, a "club", a business, an artificial kinship, *etc.*

In a genuine enkaptic structural whole, on the contrary, we always find different internal operational spheres of the structures interwoven in it, which maintain their inner sphere-sovereignty. And insofar as the qualifying structural principle is of a differentiated character — which appears not to be the case in the human body — the latter's differentiated leading function is at the same time that of the enkaptic whole.

In this enkaptic structural whole the individuality-structures interlaced in its form-totality are to be viewed as belonging to the total-structure only so long as they are united by the latter in a mutual enkaptic bond. As soon as this *enkapsis* is broken the whole is destroyed.

The enkaptic component structure, however, — insofar as it does not play the leading and qualifying rôle in the whole — necessarily embraces two clearly distinct but mutually indissolubly coherent operational spheres, *viz.*:

1. an internal sphere revealing its own inner sphere-sovereignty, and

2. an external-enkaptic sphere originating from the fact that the higher component structure in which it is bound avails itself of the modal functions of the lower structure and orders the latter within its own operational sphere; *all this according to the ordering principle of the enkaptic whole.*

In consequence of this extremely intricate composition the figure of an enkaptic structural whole confronts a structural analysis with the most difficult problems. For in this very figure the relation of *enkapsis* to the *whole-part relation* displays a critical complication which must lead us astray as soon as the former is confounded with the latter.

The theory of *enkapsis,* developed by HEIDENHAIN and THEODOR L. HAERING, which we have discussed in the first chapter of this section, has failed in the face of this very complication of the enkaptic structural whole. It was originally oriented to the relation of the organic whole and its relatively autonomous parts, which HAERING erroneously viewed as an universal pattern of an enkaptic structural totality.

This was a consequence of the methodological error implied in starting from the most intricate state of affairs, such as it presents itself in the enkaptic structural whole, before a due insight has been gained into the figure of *enkapsis* as such.

In my first introduction to the theory of enkaptic inter-structural interlacements, explained in the first (Dutch) edition of this work, I followed the other way round. In my opinion the latter is the only right methodological approach to the problem. It was of a primordial importance to arrive at an insight into the very different *types of enkapsis* which are incompatible with any uniform schematism.

Therefore my first investigations into the problem of the enkaptic interlacements did not yet go into the most intricate question, *viz.* that of the enkaptic whole. It is true that in this way the theory explained in the first edition could not be complete in a systematic sense. Neverthelass, the inductive method followed in this introductory inquiry paved the way for a methodically right approach to the problem to be explained in the present chapter.

It is of the utmost importance to establish that the intricate figure of an enkaptic whole by no means presents itself in *all* enkaptic relations. Let us consider this state of affairs more in detail.

The enkaptic structural whole and the different types of enkaptic interlacement.

In the previous chapters we have examined the different "types of ordering" of these relations. The results of this enquiry will now show us the way to establish in which of these types the figure of an enkaptic structural whole may occur.

This is in the first place that of the *irreversible foundational relation.* We should, however, observe that even this type does not always function in an enkaptic structural totality. This has already appeared from our inquiry into this type of *enkapsis* such as it presents itself within human societal relationships. In a differentiated human society there is no "highest component structure" that can qualify a supposed enkaptic structural whole of human society.

But there is always an enkaptic totality to be found cohering with the irreversible foundational relations encountered in the interlacement of structural types belonging to the three primary "kingdoms" (*viz.* that of physico-chemically qualified kinds of matter and things, and the vegetable and animal kingdoms). In addition it is found in the human bodily structure as the structural whole of man's individual temporal existence. Moreover it presents itself in context with the same type of enkaptic ordering encountered in the different structural types of products of animal and human formation.

Among the other types of *enkapsis* relevant in this context we may mention the different kinds of *enkaptic symbiosis* in which a real *collective structure* is to be discovered. But in my opinion the figure of an enkaptic whole is lacking wherever we meet with the type of *correlative enkapsis,* such as it reveals itself in the interlacement of plants and animals with their "*Umwelt*", and of the latter with the phenotypes of the former. Modern students of botany and zoölogy (WOLTERECK and many other scholars) often speak in this case, too, of an internal structural unity and totality. But to my mind this cannot be right. A plant or animal cannot be a part of its "*Umwelt*" (though no doubt in its particular vital environment also other plants and animals will function), nor *vice versa.* And there is not to be discovered an enkaptic structural whole, in the previously defined sense, embracing both of them in their correlative interwovenness. Only a universalistic biological theory may suppose that such a totality is really given in the universal unity of "life" and its conditions.

We shall now examine the problem of the enkaptic structural whole that presents itself within the three primary kingdoms. Only in the final stage of this investigation — which requires a continuous confrontation with the results of special scientific research — we may hope to find a solution to the problem how such a whole is *ontologically possible.*

For, as observed, the question is not how we can find an *a priori* consistent construction. We should much rather engage in tracing structural states of affairs that reveal themselves in empirical reality itself and which will appear to offer serious difficulties to an accurate structural explanation. Perhaps my provisional conception of the enkaptic structural whole will even turn out to lack the character of a "consistent structural view" when we engage in a more detailed analysis of the ontological problem implied in it. In this case it will require a later revision. But in the first phase of our enquiry I prefer to run the risk of a merely provisional approach if at least I may hope to have accounted for the empirical states of affairs.

§ 2 - THE ENKAPTIC STRUCTURAL WHOLE IN MOLECULAR STRUCTURES OF MATTER AND ATOMICALLY ORDERED CRYSTAL-LATTICES. A CONFRONTATION OF THIS FIGURE WITH THE METAPHYSICAL CONCEPT OF SUBSTANCE AS IT IS USED IN HOENEN'S NEO-THOMISTIC PHILOSOPHY OF INORGANIC NATURE.

The apparent paradox in the basic thesis of chemistry.

Since BOYLE it was considered as a genuine paradox of chemistry that the properties of chemical elements in their different combinations are not perceptible, whereas it must be assumed that they are nevertheless really present.

Meanwhile the further development of atom-theory has shed new light on this question: It is now generally known that the atom's *nucleus* determines the place of an element in the periodical system and thereby at the same time what we have called its physico-chemically qualified geno-type. It is also known that the typical chemical reactions occurring in chemical combinations are only related to the electrons in the periphery of the atom. It is very probable that in the heavier elements these typical reactions are bound to the outermost shell of electrons only. In the chemical combinations of such heavier elements the change occurring in the latter thus remains restricted to the outermost regions of the atoms. The inside shells of electrons, and *a-fortiori* the *nucleus*, do not alter their inner structure[1].

The philosophical structural problem concerning the relation of dissimilar atoms and their molecular combinations.

The philosophic structural problem is naturally not solved by this empirical statement. We are of the opinion that only the theory of the enkaptic interlacements is able to give this solution in a satisfactory way.

In the light of our previous investigations it cannot be doubted that in the chemical combination water, for instance, we are confronted with a genuine irreversible *enkaptic foundational relation.* The atoms are enkaptically bound in the new kind of matter without losing their original genotype. Should we assume that they have become parts of the new matter water? Certainly not. For the combination H_2O is itself the minimal form-totality

---

[1] Cf. B. BAVINK, *op. cit.*, p. 151 and more in detail EMELÉUS-ANDERSON, *Ergebnisse und Probleme der modernen anorganischen Chemie* (transl. by Kurt Karbe, Berlin, 1940), pp. 12 ff.

of the latter. The H atoms and the O atom, on the contrary, remain hydrogen and oxygen, respectively. Their *nuclei,* which determine their chemical structural type, remain unaltered, at least as to their *structural principle*; they do not partake in the combination, they are not ruled by the internal structural principle of the matter water.

This does not exclude the fact that the atoms, as total units, function in enkaptic binding within the new individuality structure. For without their internal connection with the *nuclei* the electrons of the outward atom spheres would not be able to display chemical functions. But they do not become *parts* of the chemical combination *as a new kind of matter.*

About this state of affairs, too, modern chemistry has not left us in uncertainty. The electronic theory of valency[1] has until now been the most comprehensive attempt at an explanation of the chemical combinations, though it is generally acknowledged that it is only an approximative attempt. The more recent and certainly more exact theories based on wave mechanics are provisionally only applicable in a very restricted area of chemistry. We shall avail ourselves of the theory of valency since the other theories imply unconquerable difficulties for those who are not able to comprehend their intricate mathematical apparatus.

According to the former there are three different types of binding of atoms, *viz.* the electronic binding, the covalency binding and the coordination binding[2]. In the first type an electron of the outermost atom sphere passes from one atom or group of atoms into another atom or group of atoms. The two atoms or groups of atoms are held together by their mutual electrostatic attraction.

In the covalency binding two atoms possess common electrons so that at every turn there are present two common electrons — one of each atom — for a simple combination, four for a double binding, *etc.* When the combining atoms or atom groups are not of the same type, the electrons are not equally divided

---

[1] By "valency" chemistry understands the numerical relation in which the different elements combine. Thus, *e.g.*, elements combining with hydrogen in a one-one relation of atoms have a *valence of one*, just like *hydrogen* itself. Elements which bind two *hydrogen* atoms or another element of the valency of one have the *valency of two, etc.*

[2] EMELÉUS-ANDERSON, *op. cit.*, p. 12 and N. V. SIDGWICK, *The Electronic Theory of Valence.*

and the combination displays a so-called dipole moment, *i.e.* a polar structure.

The coordination-binding is as a rule identical with the covalency binding and is only distinct from the latter insofar as the two electrons effecting the combination always belong to either of the two combining atoms only.

So it appears that the combination is always concerned with the electrons of the outermost atomic sphere. The constellation of the *nucleus*, and in the case of the heavier elements also that of the inside shells of electrons, remain unaltered. This latter result of the theory of valency is, at least *in principle*, not affected by the more recent theories oriented to wave mechanics, albeit that these theories were obliged to break with the atomistic view of the former and with its sensory pattern of the atomic constellation. Consequently we may establish that the two *hydrogen* atoms and the *oxygen* atom, in their typical binding within the water-molecule, cannot be considered as *parts* of the new matter water. A part of a whole must display the internal structure of the latter and this is not the case here. We are only warranted to say that there arises a *functional* combination between the atoms, *i.e.* that the latter function *enkaptically* within the chemical combination water.

Meanwhile the question may be asked: Is there not to be found an enkaptic structural whole embracing both the bound *hydrogen* atoms and the *oxygen* atom as its enkaptic parts?

The enkaptic structural whole as a typically qualified form-totality.

In my opinion such an enkaptic whole can indeed be pointed out, *viz.* the molecule as a typical physico-chemically qualified *form-totality*. The latter cannot coalesce with the new matter water as a chemical combination. For we have seen that the *nuclei* of atoms do not combine. Atoms are consequently not parts of the matter water. But they are certainly embraced by the molecule as the minimal form-totality in which the internal structural principle of water can only be realized.

But how is the internal structure of this qualified form-totality to be conceived? The form is here a typically ordered *physico-spatial* figure[1] or configuration, and this typical configuration is

[1] Cf. WOLTERECK's explanation of the concept "ordered spatial figure" in his cited work pp. 97 ff. That the molecule is a physico-chemically

the foundation of the qualifying physico-chemical function of the whole, which coalesces with that of the new matter water.

In the more complicated or higher qualified enkaptic natural totalities of the macro-world, such as, *e.g.*, a mountain, a polycellular plant or animal, the embracing form-whole will be of a different type and will display a macroscopic figure in the sensory space of perception. But a typical founding spatial form, irrespective of its modality and typical qualification, is essential to the structural whole which may rightly be called an *enkaptic structural totality*.

This is, for instance, not so in the case of unordered aggregates, which, notwithstanding certain interactions between their different components, lack the typical *total form of an inner structural whole* [2]. Nor is this state of affairs to be found in the case of total-structures without a specific form such as, *e.g.*, a piece of granite or iron and in general alloys whose typical structural properties (such as hardness, elasticity, malleability and micro-structures) have been examined in detail. On the other hand, we do find the figure of an enkaptic structural whole in the case of inorganic crystals with their 32 classes of typical symmetrical forms, determined by their inner total structure. The same may be said with respect to the characteristic mountain forms, in which the internal totality structures of typical geological formations in the final phase of their development display typical totality figures [3]. The structural properties of such formations (such as shell lime, lithographic slate, chalk, *etc.*) are not deducible from a mere addition of those of the minerals and petrified animal and vegetable remnants enkaptically bound in them.

In any case the enkaptic total structure *as such* must possess a typical embracing form-totality, irrespective of the particular qualification of the latter. For only such a form-totality can do justice both to the enkaptic inter-structural interlacement and

---

qualified form-totality appears from the fact that its micro-figure is constituted by electro-magnetic forces effecting a typical ordering of the atoms in the *energy-space* which is not identical with the objective sensory space of perception.

[2] For example, the upper mud layer of the bottom of a lake, which forms an un-ordered aggregate of all sorts of remnants, animals, bacteria, sand, *etc.*, or a heap of compost.

[3] The distinction between totality-structures without and with a typical form-whole is amply explained by WOLTERECK, *op. cit.*, pp. 78 ff.

to the whole-part relation. The form has appeared to be the nodal point of enkaptic relations. Consequently, if the latter function in the typically qualified form of a *whole* which, as such, cannot coalesce with any of the structures interlaced by it, but assign to each of them their due place[1], then the whole-part relation is guaranteed as well. If such a typical form-totality is lacking, as in the case of a mere *correlative enkapsis,* we cannot speak of an enkaptic structural whole.

In the case of a water-molecule, however, there is no doubt that it can be discovered. For its internal total structure embraces both the atoms combined in its physico-spatial configuration, and the new matter water. And it is really a *physico-chemically qualified* form-totality with a typical spatial ordering of atoms according to their valency. This physical spatial form is indeed the foundation of the typical chemical characteristics of the whole. This fact finds its exact expression in the structural formula H_2O, which pertains to the molecular structure rather than to water as the result of the combination.

Two seemingly incompatible series of data are to be reconciled with each other by the conception of the molecule as an enkaptic whole. The evidence in favour of the continued actual presence of the atoms in a chemical combination and that in favour of the conception that the combination is a new whole.

The above structural analysis can account for two seemingly incompatible series of experimentally established facts. One of them seems to be in favour of the conception that in a molecule or atomically ordered crystal-lattice the atoms remain actually present. The other seems to justify the view that both molecule and crystal-lattice are real wholes.

The strongest, and to my mind convincing, experimental proof of the first conception is the complete immunity of the atomic nuclei — and in the case of the heavier elements also of the more central shells of electrons — to the combination. For from this fact it may be established that the atom does not undergo an *inner* and consequently *essential* structural change. Its alterations appear to be of a *peripheral* character only. This conclusion is corroborated by a series of other data of which we shall mention only the two most important established facts. In

[1] According to the *enkaptic foundational relation* that finds its nodal point in the form-totality.

the first place it has appeared that the duration of a radio-active element's existence is completely independent of its free or bound condition. Secondly we refer to the integral preservation of the typical line-spectra of the elements in the X rays spectrum of the latter. This fact is important in this context since this spectrum does not originate from the periphery but from the more central shells of electrons surrounding the nuclei of heavier atoms.

On the other hand it has been established that the light-spectra of combined atoms do not pass over into this X rays spectrum. But the former do not originate from the more central sphere but from the *periphery* of the nucleus' environment in the atom.

Of these two arguments the one concerning the independent duration of the existence of a radio-active element is doubtless the most important. For in a separate treatise we have shown that the existential duration of an individual whole is determined by the typical temporal order of its individuality-structure [1].

In case of an intrinsical change of the latter the constancy of the existential duration of a radio-active element would thus be inexplicable.

Another evidence, derived from the experimental confirmation of the so-called stoechiometrical laws [2] of chemical combinations concerning mass and weight of the latter, is not so conclusive in my opinion. For the nuclear structure of atoms is not essentially concerned with these experiments.

That in a crystal-lattice the atoms really continue to exist could be proved in a particularly convincing experimental way with the aid of a so-called Laue-diagram [3]. The latter shows the deviation of Röntgen rays through crystal-lattices. Crystals ap-

---

[1] *Het Tijdsprobleem in de Wijsbegeerte der Wetsidee* II (Phil. Reformata 5th year, 1940, pp. 216 ff.).

[2] The Greek word *stoicheion* means "element". The laws intended are the following:

1. the famous law of LAVOISIER, according to which the mass of a combination is equal to the sum of the masses of the component elements;
2. the law of PROUST, *i.e.* the law of constant proportions or of constant composition;
3. the law of DALTON or that of multiple proportions, according to which the total weight of a chemical combination is equal to the sum of the total weights of the component elements, each multiplied by a small integer (1, 2, 3, *etc.*).

[3] This diagram is composed of a number of points regularly ordered around the point of incidence of the chief ray.

peared to have a net-like structural form whose nodal points are occupied by the centra of atoms. The distances between the latter in the different net planes could be calculated in an exact way. From continued investigations it appeared that the intensity of the rays reflected by the crystal-lattice is not only dependent on the ordering of the atoms, but also on the so-called "atomic form-factor", *i.e.* on the inner structural form of each separate atom. This intensity appears to increase in proportion to the number of electrons of the latter.

Also the elementary waves emitted by the electrons of the same atom proved to interfere with each other in dependence upon the atom structure itself, as HARTREE has shown (1928/9). A particularly convincing effect was produced by the recent experiments of KOSSEL and his cooperators. They succeeded in influencing crystals by means of cathode rays and later on also by Röntgen rays in such a way that the *separate atoms* of the crystal-lattice operate as independent sources of radiation[1]. No wonder that in recent theory the actual existence of atoms in a crystal-lattice is accepted as an established fact[2]. It is, however, certainly not right to suppose that this is only a consequence of the classical mechanistic theory, which conceived crystals as mere aggregates of separate atoms. For it should not be forgotten that modern physics and crystallography no longer rest on the classical mechanist foundations. We may only establish that the philosophical structural problem raised by the maintenance of the atomic structures in a crystal-lattice as yet lacks a satisfactory solution.

On the other hand there are a series of experimentally established facts which are doubtless in favour of the conception that a molecule is a typical whole. It has appeared, for example, that the colours of the absorption-spectrum (*i.e.* the spectrum of light dispersed by matter) do not correspond to vibrations whose amplitude may vary *continually,* but are bound to typical quantum conditions. This is certainly not in accordance with the classical atomistic conception of a molecule as a mechanical aggregate of atoms. There are, in addition, other facts which are

---

[1] Cf. F. LAVES, *Fünf und zwanzig Jahre Laue-Diagramme* (Die Naturwissenschaften 25th year, 1937, pp. 705 ff.).

[2] Cf., *e.g.,* F. M. JAEGER, *Lectures on the Principles of Symmetry* (2nd ed. 1920) p. 158: 'These atoms preserve, therefore, apparently their individuality as constituents of such crystalline substances'.

in favour of the opinion that a chemical combination is a new totality. But it is not necessary to sum them up since the older atomistic view has been definitively abandoned by modern physics and chemistry.

The philosophical background of the older conception of the chemical combination as an aggregate of elements.

True, in classical physics and chemistry this atomistic view was generally accepted. Insofar as experimentally established facts were known testifying to the continued existence of atoms in their different combinations, they were considered to be convincing proofs of the rightness of this atomistic conception.

That the latter was not easily relinquished was doubtless due to the influence of the deterministic science-ideal which implicitly or explicitly ruled the theoretical view of empirical reality.

This classical mechanistic view reached its acme in the atom model projected by RUTHERFORD according to which an atom was also conceived as a mechanical system of elementary corpuscles (a kind of solar system with planets in micro-dimensions). But since the rise of quantum physics in the XXth century this conception was factually antiquated. It could only have an after effect in modern atom theory as a sort of atavism. This can for instance be clearly pointed out with respect to BOHR's new atom theory. The latter tried to accommodate the classical pattern of RUTHERFORD to the quantum theory of MAX PLANCK, though this mechanistic model of atom structure had already been involved in insoluble conflicts with the electro-magnetic theory of MAXWELL.

True, BOHR in this way arrived at a formula which in an amazingly exact and elegant way could account for the experimental results with respect to the atom-spectrum. But on the other hand his theory resulted in new anomalies because of its maintaining certain mechanistic conceptions which were in principle incompatible with the foundations of quantum-mechanics. In the present context we cannot go into this subject matter in more detail and may refer the interested reader to some works cited in the foot note[1], in which RUTHERFORD's and BOHR's atom-theories have been subjected to an ample analysis.

---

[1] P. HOENEN S.J., *Philosophie der anorganische Natuur*, pp. 408 ff. LOUIS DE BROGLIE, *La Physique moderne et les Quanta* (éd. Flammarion, 1936), pp. 152 ff.

The neo-Thomistic theory of HOENEN concerning the ontological structure of atom and molecule.

We shall, however, have to pay special attention to the neo-Thomistic theory of HOENEN, emiritus-professor of the Gregorian University in Rome, concerning the ontological structure of atoms, molecules and crystals. The reason is that this theory gives us occasion once again to confront the Aristotelian-Thomistic concept of substance with our idea of an enkaptic structural whole.

HOENEN is of the opinion that the acceptance of a continued actual existence of atoms in molecules or atomically ordered crystal-lattices necessarily must lead to the atomistic conception of the latter as aggregate conditions. To this view he opposes only one alternative: the neo-Thomistic conception which conceives a *mixtum* (*i.e.* a composite) as a new substance in which the elements are no longer present *actually* but only *virtually* or *potentially*. In this condition the properties of the latter may be preserved to a greater or smaller extent, but their substantial form has been destroyed by their combination; the preserved properties have become "accidents" of a new substance that can only possess one single substantial form [1]. This preservation of properties is explained from the affinity of the nature of the elements with that of the *mixtum*, appearing from the genetic connection of the latter with the former. The *mixtum* is thus a "substance", a new totality, consisting of one "primary matter" and one "substantial form", which gives to this primary matter *unity of being*. Its matter is a potentiality with reference to a form. From the Aristotelian view that there is only one primary matter in all natural bodies it may, however, not be concluded that this potentiality is the same with respect to all "forms".

The neo-Thomistic doctrine concerning the "gradation" in the realization of potencies; the conception of a heterogeneous continuum.

The point is that there is a "gradation" in potencies, revealing itself in a combining of elements in such a way that "primary matter" has first a disposition to the elements and only *via* the latter to the "*mixtum*" or composite. The number of these gradations will increase in proportion to the distance between primary matter and the substantial form ultimately assumed by it.

---

[1] Cf. THOMAS AQUINAS, *Summa Theol.* I. qu. 76a, 4 ad 6.

From the unity of substantial form, on the other hand, it may not be concluded that the new substance must necessarily be a homogeneous whole all of whose parts display the same properties. The inner unity of an extended substance does not exclude a diversity of properties in its different parts. This implies the possibility of a "*heterogeneous continuum*". HOENEN applies this neo-scholastical view to the modern theory of atom and molecule, and to that of the crystal forms. According to him the atom is thus a "composite substance" whose true "elements" are protons, neutrons and electrons. It is a "natural minimum" in the Aristotelian sense, *i.e.* according to its "physical nature", determined by its "substantial form", it is not further to be divided into material substances of the same kind. This implies that in case of its splitting up into its most simple components there arise "elementary substances" of a different physical nature. The molecule, as the natural minimum of a chemical combination, and the crystal-lattice are all the same new substances. If they consist of atoms of a different chemical kind, they are to be considered "specific heterogeneous totalities". This is to say, the specific heterogeneous properties of the atoms are preserved to a certain degree in the combination. This preservation of specific atomic properties is nothing but the result of the affinity in "nature" of the combination with the atoms from which it has originated. The fact that medieval scholasticism assumed inorganic composites necessarily to be composed of homogeneous parts is ascribed by HOENEN to a defective experience.

Preservation of the nuclear properties of atoms in a molecule or atomically ordered crystal-lattice is thus not considered by HOENEN to be evidence of a continued actual existence of the atoms in their combination. It is explained by him from the principle of virtual preservation of heterogeneous properties of the components in a heterogeneous composite.

Critique of HOENEN's theory.

The manner in which this neo-Thomistic scholar has tried to conceive the recent results of modern natural science in a Thomistic philosophical frame of thought deserves special attention.

His argument is always strong and clear when he subjects the classical atomistic conception, founded on a mechanistic view of nature, to a fundamental philosophical criticism. It stands to reason that in this respect he may find support in recent ideas which have entered modern physics in connection with the quantum-theory, though it is not to be assumed that physics will in the future return to the Thomistic substance-concept.

On essential points, however, this neo-scholastical theory fails to account for the experimental results in a really satisfactory way.

First, even from a Thomistic viewpoint the immunity of atom nuclei — and in the case of the heavier elements also of the inside shells of electrons — with respect to the combination, cannot be really explained from the scholastical principle concerning virtual preservation of certain heterogeneous properties of atoms. For the nuclear structure of the atom is not simply a specific accidental property. It is much rather *that part of the atom's total structure which determines the particular type of element.* In the Thomistic line of thought this nuclear structure should be viewed as the *substantial form* of the atom since it gives to its "matter" the indispensible "unity of being". In the face of the established fact that this "substantial form" is not destroyed by the combining of the atoms, HOENEN's argument against the actual presence of the latter in the combination is doomed to fail. And thereby this neo-Thomistic theory concerning the structure of a molecule has come into an impasse. For by accepting the actual existence of atoms in the combination, the unity of a molecule as a whole would no longer be tenable from the viewpoint of the Thomistic substance concept.

Also the experimental datum concerning the immunity of the existential duration of a radio-active element with respect to its bound condition in a molecule cannot be accounted for from this point of view. Here, too, there is no question of an accidental property of an element, but its internal structure as an actual whole is at issue. Its internal process of decay is a real *nuclear* alteration giving rise to a new element. It remains completely incomprehensible how this datum might be philosopsically interpreted as a simple change of properties of the composite in which the radio-active element is bound, whereas at the same time the continued actual presence of the bound element is denied.

The same objection must be raised against HOENEN's neo-Thomistic conception of the structure of a crystal-lattice as a *heterogeneous continuum.* This view may perhaps be able to account for the experiental datum concerning the distances of the nodal points of the net-like structural form. But HOENEN does not mention the influence of the "atomic form-factor" upon the intensity of reflection of the incident Röntgen rays discussed above, nor the results of KOSSEL's experiments. Both of these experimental data are not really compatible with a denial of the actual presence of the atoms in the crystals. For they, too, are related to the internal individuality-structure of the bound elements and not to simple accidental properties of the latter.

In addition, the entire neo-scholastical concept of a heterogeneous continuum is hardly compatible with the foundations of modern wave mechanics. The famous French scientist DE BROGLIE has rightly observed that the quantum condition of energy does not agree with the classical conception of physical space as a *continuum*. From this it follows that also the structural form of a crystal is not to be viewed as a real continuum.

The Aristotelian-Thomistic concept of substance implies a *dilemma* which must be deemed unacceptible from the point of view of modern science. It must lead to the conclusion that atoms can only actually exist in a free condition as "substances". If they do not exist as "substances", they cannot actually exist at all. But a free atom no more corresponds to this metaphysical concept than a bound element. Temporal reality is in principle built up in enkaptic structural interlacements which leave no room for absolute metaphysical points of reference.

Here we arrive at the philosophical insufficiency of HOENEN's theory in respect to the structural problems raised by the experimental data of modern physics and chemistry. The substance concept in principle precludes the insight into the relation of *enkapsis*. But thereby it precludes at the same time any possibility of a distinction between the *molecule* — or the atomically ordered crystal-lattice, respectively — as a *typical qualified enkaptic form-totality*, and the *genuine chemical combination* of which the former is only the *bearer*. As a consequence the structural problem concerning the relation between the bound atoms and the molecule or crystal, as typical wholes, is oversimplified. There is no question here of one simple totality-structure which would destroy the internal structure of its components. Rather there are three different structures to be distinguished, functioning in enkaptic interlacement. If only the relation between molecule (or crystal) and its atoms were at issue, and there were no *enkapsis*, the neo-Thomistic dilemma might seem to be inescapable: either the molecule or crystal is a new totality, which destroys the actual existence of the atoms, *or* the former are merely aggregates of atoms.

But since the *enkapsis relation* is at issue in the structural problem concerned, this dilemma is unacceptible *in principle.* A molecule or crystal, as an enkaptic form-totality, is very well able to embrace in a particular manner the interlaced structures of its bound atoms, without destroying the latter in any way in *their internal sphere-sovereignty.* And to my mind only this conception can do justice to the two series of experimental data which at first sight seemed to contradict one another.

The Aristotelian-Thomistic concept of substance is unbreakably bound to the form-matter motive, which rules its philosophical approach to the structural problems: An individual whole can only have one substantial form. The component atoms are consequently obliged to become "matter" of the substantial form of molecule or crystal. For if they should preserve their own substantial form, the "unity of being" of the combination would be impossible[1].

This reasoning is consistent in a logical respect if one starts from the Greek form-matter motive and the metaphysical substance-concept oriented to it. But it is not permissible to impose upon philosophy and science the dilemma *either* to accept the neo-Thomistic solution of the structural problem, *or* to fall back upon the atomistic view of the classical mechanistic theory. By positing this dilemma HOENEN shows a dogmatic attitude in respect to the transcendental presuppositions of theoretic thought. It is true that classical physics, too, held to a substance-concept, albeit in a sense quite different from that of Aristotelian metaphysics. Therefore it may seem that HOENEN's dilemma is stringent when the neo-Thomistic view is only compared with the classical atomistic conception. But a really critical philosophy should not posit such dilemmas as if they were simply founded in a logical alternative. It should always be ready to account for the presuppositions which rule the manner of positing the philosophical problems. It should not mask these presuppositions by

---

[1] *Op. cit.*, p. 325 (with regard to a "living being"): 'In the *mixta* which are living beings the material components, inclusive of the elements, cannot be actually present; a living being cannot be an aggregate of substances since it is a substance; it is a totality; it has the substantial unity inherent in an *ens* (being). If the components were actually present, it would at the same time be *one* and *plural* in substance, *i.e.* in the same respect, which is absurd'. This reasoning is also applied to inorganic combinations (cf. p. 326 of the quoted work).

a dogmatical metaphysics, which is presented as an unprejudiced ontology.

This implies that our conception of the enkaptic structural whole may not be judged after the standard of Thomistic metaphysics or the classical mechanistic view of nature. According to our structural theory both the bound atoms and the new chemical matter are ordered within a typical form-totality, and in my opinion this conception can really account for the experimental data. But it is not permissible to conclude from the neo-Thomistic concept of substance that such an enkaptic structural whole cannot satisfy the ontological requirement of a "unity of being". For the very structure of such an enkaptic form-totality requires the binding of plural structural wholes in an embracing new totality in such a way that the inner proper nature of each of the latter is preserved.

To my mind HOENEN's neo-Thomistic theory is no more able to account satisfactorily for the real structure of a chemical combination than for the dissolution of the latter. The elements which may be detached from the combination must be actually present in the molecule, though in a bound condition. Every theory denying this is obliged to demonstrate from empirical facts that the atoms in the combination display an essential structural change. And we have seen that HOENEN has not succeeded in this proof. But suppose he did succeed in making acceptable a "substantial change" of the elements, then he would not yet have solved the structural problem concerning the dissolution of a combination.

What solution has his theory to offer in respect to the latter question? HOENEN thinks it is implied in the above mentioned conception concerning the gradations in potentiality. If the atoms are "virtually" present in the composite they can reappear actually when the "*mixtum*" is dissolved into its elements: their potentiality is no longer *pure* potentiality, it has already been determined to give these components in these certain quantities, if the composite falls asunder[1].

This theory may doubtless lay claim to our respect because of its sagacity, but we cannot acknowledge it as a real solution of the problem. From a Thomistic point of view the question should be framed as follows: *How can the atoms regain their substantial form in the process of dissolution after having lost it in the*

[1] *Op. cit.*, p. 326.

chemical combination? This is not to be explained from the virtual preservation of some heterogeneous atomic properties within the molecule. For, according to the neo-scholastical conception, the atoms themselves have lost their substantial form in the combination. They have been made into "matter" with reference to the new substantial form of the latter.

But the reappearance of the atom's "substantial form" is not to be explained from the specific "matter" of a *molecule.* An appeal to the genetic affinity between the "nature" of the elements and that of the composite is of no avail here. If indeed from the combination of the elements a new totality arises, which is more than the sum of its parts, the internal structure of the latter is not deducible from that of the elements in a genetic way. Nor can this new totality (*e.g.*, the matter water) fall asunder into its elements, if the "substantial form" of the latter has been really destroyed. There exists no genetic affinity of nature between the composite and its *separate* elements. If HOENEN should really accept this affinity, his conception would not be intrinsically different from the classical atomistic view of the combination that he so sharply combats. In this case he would hold to the opinion that water is nothing but an aggregate of its elements.

'The preservation of properties of the elements after their transition into a *mixtum*', so he observes, 'should be explained by the material cause, as the *ratio sufficiens* of this state of affairs; new properties of the *mixtum* should be explained from the efficient cause, at least insofar as they do not result from the mutual cooperation of the preserved properties' [1]. This reasoning should also hold in the reverse direction with respect to the rise of actual free atoms from the dissolution of the combination. In this way the virtual preservation of certain properties of the elements in the composite can never explain the actual reappearance of the atoms in their proper "substantial form". A "material cause" is no *ratio sufficiens* of this result and HOENEN fails to indicate its *efficient and its "formal" cause.*

The conception of material composites in pre-Thomistic medieval scholasticism.

In medieval scholasticism the Arabian Aristotelians and the older Christian scholastics before THOMAS had already been

---

[1] *Op. cit.*, p. 530.

sharply aware of this state of affairs. Though there are to be found many differences in the details of their conceptions, they almost unanimously assumed a certain actual presence of the substantial forms of the elements in the composite. But, in order to save the unity of the *mixtum* as a "new substance", they denied the preservation of the "substance" of the components. From a scholastic metaphysical point of view the inner contradiction of this solution is obvious. Thus THOMAS could easily show that a plurality of "substantial forms" is incompatible with the "unity of substance".

But does this scholastic controversy not confirm our view that the *vitium originis* is to be sought in an inner contradiction of the substance-concept itself?

It is not the intricate structure of empirical reality which implies this contradiction. Much rather the latter originates from the attempt to conceive this structure in a metaphysical *a priori* way which does not fit it.

§ 3 - THE ENKAPTIC STRUCTURAL WHOLE OF THE LIVING CELL-BODY AND THE SUBSTANCE-CONCEPT IN THEORETICAL BIOLOGY.

Meanwhile our theory of the enkaptic structural whole has to prove its utility in a wider field of structures than that of the inorganic kingdom alone. We have now to pay attention to the structural problems arising in connection with the enkaptic relation between the living organism and the different kinds of matter of the living cell-body.

In the second chapter (part III) we have explained that the atoms and chemical combinations of these kinds of matter cannot be viewed as parts of the living organism of a cell. Rather it appeared that the former are enkaptically bound in the latter according to a particular *type of ordering* of the inter-structural interlacements, *viz.* that of the irreversible foundational relation. In itself a living organism is only an individuality-structure. In its realization it is unbreakably bound to different matter-structures which do not coalesce with it. Thus the problem arises concerning the enkaptic structural whole embracing both the matter-structures and that of the living organism of the cell. If such an enkaptic whole should be lacking, a real cell would lack the inner structural unity of a concrete "thing". For the *enkapsis as such* cannot guarantee this inner unity.

It is thus necessary to distinguish between the *cell-organism* and the *real cell-body.*

Now it cannot be doubted that in the latter there are chemical elements combined in a typical, extremely intricate way. It is also known that only a relatively small number of elements play a rôle in these combinations. In the main there are four which are indispensable, *viz.* hydrogen (H), oxygen (O), carbon (C) and nitrogen (N). As a rule there are also present phosphor, magnesium, calcium, natron, kalium, chlorine, sulphur, iodine and iron. Some elements of the latter group may be lacking, *viz.* calcium, and in vegetable cells also natron and chlorine.

The higher organic combinations of these elements in the plasm and the nuclear sphere of the living cell are, however, extremely complicated and thereby extremely labile. And the assimilatory and dissimilatory processes in which they are constituted and dissolved do not correspond in any respect to the ordinary chemical changes in the inorganic world, or even to the spontaneous decay of radio-active matter. The chief difference is the preservation of the material basic structure of nucleus and plasm, whereas the material combinations used in these processes are in a condition of complete lability. This is why the bio-chemical constellation seems to withdraw itself from a complete physico-chemical determination.

BOHR's biological relation of uncertainty.

In order to isolate completely determined chemical combinations from the cell, it is first necessary to "kill" the relevant regions of the living cell-body. The famous Danish physicist NIELS BOHR has tried to approach this state of affairs by means of an analogous extension of HEISENBERG's relations of uncertainty which occur, *e.g.*, in the case of the determination of position and velocity of an electron, in an electro-magnetic field. An *analogous state of affairs presents itself*, according to BOHR, in bio-physics and bio-chemistry. The determination of the physico-chemical processes occurring in the living cell finds its limit of certitude and exactness in life itself [1]. We have already encountered this conception in an earlier context.

Naturally BOHR's biological relation of incertitude cannot solve the philosophical structural problem with which we are con-

[1] Cf., for example, the explanation of BOHR's view in the review *Naturwissenschaften* 21, 245 (1933).

cerned here. But his conception is doubtless of particular importance as a pregnant formulation of the limits which a mathematical causal explanation encounters in the internal physico-chemical constellation of a living organism.

These limits must be posited by the individuality-structure of the latter. They cannot pertain to the physico-chemically qualified structures of the different kinds of matter functioning in the bio-physical and bio-chemical processes. Only in the case of the highest, extremely complicated organic combinations (such as *globulin, nuclein, albumen, etc.*) it has up till now appeared to be impossible to find fixed structural formulas. But this does not detract from the fact that since WÖHLER's famous synthesis of urine matter (1828) chemistry has succeeded in a synthetical preparation of a great number of organic combinations. And since the discovery of the rôle of catalysators[1] in fermentation-processes, it has even made great progress in disclosing the secret of the way in which the organic production of these matters is accomplished by the living organism, at least insofar as this process is to be approached by means of physico-chemical methods of research. For the central rôle of the organism's vital function in it can never be eliminated in these investigations.

What is the meaning of BOHR's relation of incertitude with respect to the methods of organic chemistry in their application to bio-chemical processes?

The question can be asked: What is the meaning of BOHR's relation of incertitude with respect to the methods of organic chemistry in their application to bio-chemical processes? This question is not to be answered in a satisfactory way without our having gained insight into the philosophical structural problem concerning the relation of a physico-chemical combination, as such, to the genuine *bio*-chemical constellation in the individuality-structure of a living organism.

We must emphatically repeat that by "living organism" we do not understand an individual living being, such as a plant, an animal or a man. Rather we use this term in the sense of a

---

[1] By "catalysator" chemistry understands a substance that produces a chemical reaction in other combinations without partaking itself in this reaction. A fermentation-process turned out to be a catalytic process in which a complex of combinations functions as catalysator. Though the latter are not living "substances", they are produced by a living organism.

typically biotically qualified structure of individuality, functioning within an enkaptic structural whole that will appear to be the body of the living being.

It should not be thought that in this way an *artificial* distinction is introduced which does not correspond to real states of affairs. The distinction concerned hangs unbreakably together with the insight that a "living body" is not built up in a simple or singular structure, and that it cannot coalesce with its "living organism". That this insight corresponds to real states of affairs will appear from what follows.

The Aristotelian-Thomistic substance-concept and the identification of a living organism with the animated body.

The neo-Thomistic view of the relation between the material components and the body of a living being has been summarized in a pregnant way in an utterance of HOENEN's, already quoted in an earlier context [1]. Starting from the Aristotelian concept of substance HOENEN cannot accept the actual presence of material elements and their chemical combinations in a living whole. The living body is not distinguished from its living organism. Instead, the material body is conceived as a specific "matter" (in the metaphysical Aristotelian sense) which is completely animated by a specific "soul" as its "substantial form", giving it "actuality" and "unity of being".

We have seen that this conception starts from an unacceptable dilemma. The acknowledgment of an actual, though bound presence of material components in the living body does not at all imply that the latter would be only an "aggregate" and would lack the totality-structure of an individual whole.

The question as to whether all components of a living body are "living" in a subjective sense, is not to be answered from the viewpoint of an *a priori* metaphysics. It should be answered on the basis of an empirical research. We should only bear in mind that vital phenomena cannot be scientifically conceived apart from the structure in which they present themselves. And as soon as the structural problem proper is at issue, the difference in philosophical insight and religious starting point appears to play a decisive part in the scientific debate.

---

[1] Cf. p. 709 note 1 of this volume.

On the neo-Thomistic standpoint, however, the above-mentioned question is already answered *a priori* by the logical implications of the Aristotelian substance-concept. In this case an empirical research is factually superfluous since it cannot teach us anything about the problem concerned, which is of an exclusively metaphysical nature. This is a kind of *a priori* reasoning which is unacceptable from any specific scientific viewpoint.

The distinction between living and non-living components in a cell-body has urged itself upon biology as a result of empirical research. It rests upon a firm factual basis and as such it has nothing to do with atomistic-mechanistic conceptions of "life".

We have thus to account for these empirical data in our theory of the "enkaptic whole". Naturally we cannot go into a detailed inquiry into the results of modern cytology (*i.e.* the scientific inquiry into the composition of cells). We are not competent to do so and, in addition, we must observe that these results are still increasing continually. Nevertheless, we are obliged to pay attention at least to those scientifically established facts which are of essential importance with respect to the structural problems at issue in the present context.

The cell as the minimal unity capable of independent life.

First of all we have to establish that the cell with its nuclear and plasm-sphere is the smallest unity capable of independent life that has up till now been discovered. It is true that in the bodies of higher, especially of animal beings, and *a fortiori* in the human body, there occur many non-cellular tissues (such as tendons, cuticular formations, *etc.*) which partake of the vital function of the organism in an active sense. In addition it cannot be denied that even in *protozoa* an extra-cellular bifurcation of the genuine cellular plasm has been found in which different bio-physical and -chemical processes occur without any contact-relation with the cellular endo-plasm. This so-called exo-plasm often displays a very intricate structure.

All such exo-plasmatic, consequently non-cellular components doubtless display the typical characteristics of autonomous division, increasement, capability for stimulation *etc.*, albeit to a less intensive degree than plasmatic cellular organs.

But apart from a connection with genuine cells these exo-plasmatic components have appeared to lack viability. In this respect they have no other relation to the living cell-organism than the innumerable smaller living units occurring in the latter itself [1]. For the subjective vital function of these units, too, is dependent on the total cell-organism, as will appear presently. It is true that in *bacteria* and blue-green *algae* a genuine cell-nucleus is not to be found. But they do possess a more diffuse central *cell-sphere* which fulfils the same rôle as a nucleus.

The typical physico-chemical aspect of a cell-structure.

From a physico-chemical viewpoint the first remarkable fact is that by far most of the living cells display the material sub-structure of a so-called colloidal system. This is to say that they do not contain genuine solutions of matter, nor only rude suspensions or emulsions, respectively, but are in a typical intermediate condition of matter division.

It is this colloidal condition which lies at the foundation of that extremely intricate physico-chemical constellation which is found in the internal structure of a cell's living organism.

A colloidal mixture contains a solved matter in such a fine division that this matter acquires an enormous development of surface surpassing the ordinary macroscopic condition millions of times. On the other hand this development of surface does not occur to such an extent that all specific properties which the matter concerned displays in greater dimensions are lost. On these surfaces enormous electric charges are present. This is why colloids are very "sensitive" to changes of electric condition, but also to alterations of temperature, *etc.* [2].

As a colloidal system, protoplasm may pass from a sol- (solution) condition into a gel- (gelatin) condition and *vice versa*. It has also been established that colloidal a-biotic systems very often display a crystalline or semi-crystalline structure. In this structure the form of molecule passes without sharp boundaries into that of micro-crystals (molecular complexes).

Secondly it is a remarkable fact that by far most cells display a so-called *alveolar* form of plasm. This means that the latter is divided into a great number of small bubbles *(alveoli)* covered by membranes. This, too, is of the highest importance to vital processes.

---

[1] Cf. WOLTERECK, *op. cit.*, pp. 313 ff.

[2] Cf. BAVINK, *op. cit.*, p. 340.

The so-called hylocentric, kinocentric and morpho-centric structure of a living cell (WOLTERECK), viewed from the physico-chemical aspect.

The chief point, however, is the typically centered construction of the living cell. For here the genuine internal structural principle of its living organism reveals itself even in its physico-chemical aspect. It is an established fact that the entire process of constructive and destructive metabolism, and also the typical organizing, determining and regulating effects are directed from a *central sphere* in the cell-body. And it is beyond doubt that in any case the *nucleus* (or the diffuse nuclear cell-sphere, respectively) is concerned in this directing rôle, irrespective of the question whether it must itself be viewed as the operating centre or whether it is serviceable only as a sort of store-room for the necessary materials. In addition the more passive part of *chromatin* (*i.e.* the nuclear matter) in the process of cell-division is to be paid attention to.

Secondly, at least in animal plasm, a typical *internal motive centre* is present, *viz.* the so-called *centro-soma.* The entire process of cell-divisions and its preparation, *e.g.,* starts from this centre[1].

In the third place the cell's living organism appears to display a centred structure with respect to the production of typical somatic part-forms. This latter state of affairs is of fundamental importance to the enkaptic structural whole; we shall revert to it.

By this three-fold centred structure the living organism of a cell is fundamentally different from all physico-chemically qualified enkaptic micro-wholes (molecules, crystals)[2]. And this difference is already revealed in its physico-chemical aspect. It seems to be a direct expression of the individuality-structure of a cell's living organism, in which the biotical function has the central rôle of a *qualifying radical function.*

Even the most complicated model of a polypeptid molecule, projected by organic chemistry (E. FISHER) to approach the structure of a so-called "living albumen molecule", lacks this centred construction. It only displays the picture of a bipolar

---

[1] In vegetable cells these *centro-somas* are generally lacking. Cf. E. KÜSTER, *Die Zelle und die Gewebe des pflanzlichen Organismus* (Handbuch der Biologie, hrg. von Bertallanffy, 1942) Bnd. VI, Heft 1, p. 13. WOLTERECK, as a zoologist, generalizes too much.

[2] Cf. WOLTERECK, *op. cit.,* pp. 132 and 133.

binding of amino-acids ordered in the form of a chain with many radicals [1], groups or side-chains. This model may suffice for certain atomistic and materialistic conceptions of the hereditary process, based upon the ordering of genes in the chromosomes of a cell-nucleus. But it fails in principle, if the entire physico-chemical aspect of a living cell-organism is taken into account.

The same holds with respect to the hypothesis of the Russian materialistic biologist KOLZOFF concerning the "molecular components of living albumen substance". According to him these components should be conceived as crystals and the assimilatory processes are supposed to be *crystallization* processes of amino-acids present in the solution, and of other fragments of albumen. This hypothesis, too, is at the utmost able to account for the colloidal material constellation of a plasmatic cell-body. But it can never explain the typical centred structure of a living plasmatic organism. Molecules and crystals, as minimal enkaptic form-totalities of chemical combinations, in principle lack such a concentric construction.

The phenomenon of bi-, or poly-nuclear cells.

Insofar as in *protozoa* a poly-nuclear cell is found, every nucleus appears to be the potential centre of a new cell-body [2]. In many *protozoa* this poly-nuclear condition is only a temporary phenomenon in connection with propagation.

These *protozoa* increase the number of their nuclei by means of a series of nuclear divisions. Finally they fall asunder into as many new individuals as there are nuclei. Consequently the nuclear division here performs the same function as cell-division does with *metazoa* (poly-cellular beings).

Other *protozoa* are characterized by the permanent possession of a plurality of similar nuclei. An *actino-sphaerium* may even contain more than a hundred of them. When the single cell body is then cut in pieces it appears that such pieces of cytoplasm are able to become complete individuals. Each separate nucleus is thus the centre of a particular sphere of proto-plasm.

---

[1] In organic chemistry the term "radical" means an element or atom, or group of these, forming the base of a compound and remaining unaltered during the ordinary chemical changes of a compound.

[2] Cf. on this subject and the immediately following data E. REICHENOW's treatise *Protozoa* in *Handbuch der Biologie* (v. BERTALLANFFY) Bnd. VI, bl. 2, pp. 42 ff.

The poly-nuclear cell-body in this case appears to embrace different centred units each of which can develop into a new cell-body. SACHS called such a potential unit of nucleus and protoplasm-sphere an *energide*.

Finally there exists a form of poly-nuclearity in which the nuclei are dissimilar. All *infusoria, e.g.,* possess at least two nuclei which, because of their very different magnitude, are distinguished as a *large* and a *small* nucleus. The significance of this phenomenon becomes clear when we consider the double function of a nucleus. It is the bearer of heredity factors and it also has a central task in the vital processes. In poly-cellular beings the former function is assigned to the nuclei of genital cells, which have an unlimited capability of propagation, the second task is fulfilled by those of the other soma-cells. In most of the *protozoa* both functions are combined in one nucleus. With *infusoria,* on the other hand, they are assigned to two different nuclei. The small nucleus is the *generative,* the large one is the *somatical* nucleus. The same division of labour, which in poly-cellular beings occurs among particular cells, is carried through in these most organized *protozoa* within the frame of the single cell in respect to the nuclei. Just as the cells of the different organs originate from the genital cells of *metazoa,* the macro-nuclei of the *infusoria* originate from the offspring of the small nuclei.

Thus the phenomenon of bi- or poly-nuclear cells does not detract from the centred structure of the cell-body and its living organism.

The smallest living units within the cell-structure.

The atomistic view may object that a correct comparison between living and in-organic corpuscles implies that one should not start from the living cell as a whole but from the smallest living units. As observed, a cell contains innumerable particles which display the characteristic properties of living plasm: assimilation, autonomous reproduction, growth, division, autonomous reactions to stimulation, *etc.* Starting from this undeniable datum, different biologists have sought for elementary components of living plasm. The latter were introduced under different names, such as bio-molecules (VERWORN), *"Miscellen"* (NÄGELI), vitules (A. MEIJER), protomeries (HEIDENHAIN). *Nobody has, however, succeeded in proving indisputably that such minimal cell-particles are capable of maintaining life apart from a living cell.* In any case neither such endo-plasmatic units nor the earlier mentioned exo-plasmatic living particles can detract from the fact that the cell-organism is the real normal minimal *centre of life.* And it is exactly the centred structure of a living cell-organism and cell-body which in its physico-chemical aspect has not any analogy in the minimal enkaptic form-totalities of inorganic chemical combinations.

Non-living components of the cell-body and their enkaptic binding in the living organism.

On the other hand, not all components present in a cell-body participate in the subjective vital function of the organism. This participation may certainly not be assumed with reference to inorganic combinations, such as water, by far the greatest component of plasmatic matter, or carbonic acid, *etc.* Apart from the Aristotelian metaphysical substance-concept there is no single ground to be adduced in favour of the conception that in the colloidal condition of plasmatic matter such chemical components alter their inner nature and are transformed into "living matter". There can be question only of an enkaptic binding within more intricate or higher qualified structures, respectively.

Nor may the character of living components be ascribed to enzymes or ferments, which in all probability play such an important rôle in processes of assimilation and dissimilation. Though produced by the living organism itself, they operate only as organic catalysts. That they lack the character of living material components was experimentally proved by BUCHNER in 1896. The convincing force of this proof is not affected by the results of later investigations showing that fermentation-processes have a more intricate character than was initially supposed [1]. In any case enzymes seem to be nothing but complicated protein combinations whose synthetical composition has not yet been possible.

Continued research has taught that also the so-called "organizers" are nothing but inductive, non-living material components capable of influencing living cells in a specific way, even after the cells producing them have been killed. We shall revert to this state of affairs later on.

Furthermore we may consider as non-living components of a

[1] Cf. BAVINK, *op. cit.*, pp. 348 ff. and WOLTERECK, *op. cit.*, p. 334.

cell-body the vacuoles present in plasm, the nucleoles[1] (or certain kinds of nucleoles), and other paraplasmatic material particles[2].

Among the non-living components we have also encountered the typical mineral formations of *protozoa* and *protophytes* secreted by protoplasm at the periphery. Their typical structure has already been analyzed in the first part of this volume[3]. We have seen that the Si O_2-formations of *radiolaria,* for example, cannot be considered as aggregative forms of Si O_2 crystals. The reason is that the thousands of specific figures of silicon-acid produced by the plasm of these *protozoa* completely deviate from the well-known in-organic crystal-formations of this mineral. According to their internal structure, these animal formations are doubtless qualified by a *typical psychical object-function,* which expresses itself in their typical figure. But they are themselves already *typical form-totalities* functioning in their turn as *enkaptic components of the living cell-body.*

They are, however, no more to be considered as parts of the living organism of a cell than the enzymes, the "organizers", and the non-living paraplasmatic components.

Real minimal parts of the living organism can only be those particles of plasm and nucleus that actually partake in the *subjective* vital function of the centred living whole.

Do there exist bio-molecules?

Here we are once again confronted with the question: Are these "bio-elements" to be conceived as a specific kind of "molecules" of chemical combinations deserving the name *bio*-molecules?

Molecules composed of dissimilar atoms have appeared to be enkaptic form-totalities of a typical physico-chemical qualification. It is true that the boundaries between molecules and crystals cannot be sharply indicated. In higher organic combinations the minimal form-totalities built up of chains of double molecules may rightly be called quasi-crystalline molecules. But this does not detract from their physico-chemical qualification. The term "bio-molecule" must consequently imply an inner contra-

---

[1] Nucleoles are the numerous nuclear corpuscles within a cell's nucleus.

[2] According to WOLTERECK, p. 356, this is generally accepted in modern biological theory.

[3] Cf. volume III, pp. 85—87.

diction if it is taken in the sense that a molecule of organic matter may be a living unit [1].

It should not be supposed that we are falling back here upon that *a priori* method of reasoning which we have emphatically rejected in our criticism of HOENEN's neo-Thomistic conception. Our thesis is much rather based upon real structural states of affairs which have urged themselves upon empirical research. The point is that a molecule or quasi-crystal of an organic chemical combination, however complicated and labile its inner construction may be, in principle lacks that centred structure which appeared to be essential to an independent living unit. *As to its inner structure* any molecule or crystal is in principle *physico-chemically qualified.*

In a *bio*-physico-chemical constellation, however, there is no question of the *internal structures* of such minimal form-units of chemical combinations. Much rather we are confronted here by *biotically directed* physico-chemical *functions* of material components, which in the metabolical processes are serviceable to the sustenance of a living body as a whole. In this sense these functions belong to the living organism itself, but they are not *internal functions* of the molecules or crystals which are enkaptically bound by the former.

In the light of our structural theory this state of affairs is to be characterized as follows: *In the internal structure of a living organism the physico-chemical constellation is necessarily disclosed or opened by the subjective vital function. It must thus remain completely open, dynamic and labile.*

This entire internal physico-chemical constellation occurs under the typical direction of so-called *bio-impulses.* The latter are never to be explained in a purely physico-chemical sense but are always qualified by the central subjective vital function of the organism as a whole, though they have doubtless a *physico-chemical aspect.* It is an established fact that in the balance of

---

[1] In his repeatedly quoted work WOLTERECK has devoted excellent pages to the relation of a chemical combination to the bio-chemical constellation. Nevertheless he finally accepts the term "bio-molecule", 'because the prefix "bio" clearly expresses that there is no question of molecules in the sense of chemistry but only of something comparable with the latter' (*op. cit.*, p. 318). To my mind the acceptance of this term is not advisable since it favours a conceptual confusion. We shall see later on that it has played WOLTERECK himself a bad trick in his conception of the so-called *matrix* of "living matter".

reception and delivery of energy these bio-impulses are negligible because of their minimal use of energy; it has equally been established that they possess a spontaneous character.

Our structural theory of *enkapsis* can thus completely do justice to BOHR's bio-chemical relation of incertitude. But at the same time the latter is *structurally localized* and *determined* as an *enkaptic relation*. This is to say: the bio-chemical constellation starts exactly at the point where the molecular or quasi-crystalline structures of organic matter *end*. But the latter are not thereby eliminated from the enkaptic whole of the living cell-body; rather they are enkaptically bound in the latter.

Without the formation of molecules or quasi-crystals there could not originate a bio-chemical constellation: the living organism avails itself of *variability-types* of the former, which the different kinds of matter only assume within its internal bio-physical and -chemical sphere.

Recent experimental research has indeed been able to establish that a living body contains molecular-crystalline structures of organic matter. Through a great technical improvement of Röntgen-irradiation this research has succeeded in acquiring Laue-diagrams of living nervous and muscular tissues. Though the illumination of such tissues lasted only for ten minutes at the most, these diagrams appeared to possess sufficient clarity. And at least in the case of nervous tissues irradiation did not diminish the latter's susceptibility to stimulation nor their conductibility [1]. It has now also been established that with regard to their material sub-structure tendons are built up of genuine crystals with large molecules and that these crystals are ordered after the pattern of fibres. At present we know that in muscular contraction myosin-molecules ordered in the form of chains play an active rôle. In such contraction these myosin-molecules pass from a folded-up form, proper to their resting condition, into a more strongly folded shape of supercontraction [2]. But these molecular structures do not teach us anything about the enkaptic functions of these gigantic molecules within the *bio-physical and bio-chemical constellation* of living organisms. The typical bio-impulses directing this contraction can never be explained from a physico-chemically qualified matter construction.

[1] Cf. the interesting treatise of FRANCIS O. SCHMITT, *Erforschung der Feinstruktur tierischer Gewebe mit Hilfe der Röntgenstraleninterferenz-Methoden* in the review *Naturwissenschaften* 25th year, 1937, pp. 709 ff.

[2] *Ibid.*

The problem concerning living protein is an incorrectly posited problem.

Insofar as I may permit myself to have an opinion on this question, I think that the famous problem concerning so-called "living protein" is *insoluble in principle,* since it is wrongly posited. Nevertheless this problem has held bio-chemistry captive up to the present although this branch of science has become much more critical with respect to the requirements of a so-called bio-synthesis than it was in the days of HAECKEL.

Protein-combinations, such as are found in a living body, are only to be viewed as extremely intricate and labile material combinations, which in principle are physico-chemically determined in their inner molecular structure. The discovery of their ultimate structural formulae may never be supposed to be scientifically impossibile. This even remains true notwithstanding the fact (established by Röntgen-analysis) that in the living body these highest organic combinations do not form molecules of a stable magnitude, but only of a variable size. Insofar as here, too, BOHR's relation of incertitude is at issue, it can only pertain to the enkaptic functions of these molecules in the living organism, not to the molecular structures as such. It is true that plasmatic protein with its colloidal properties has up to now only been known as an organic product of living organisms. Nevertheless, as a chemical combination, it may be detached from the latter, and — on the condition of a due protection against micro-organisms — it can be kept intact for an unlimited time. As such it cannot be *qualified* by the subjective vital function of a living organism.

Consequently, suppose that organic chemistry at one time or other succeeds in finding definite structural formulae and also in composing these most intricate combinations synthetically, the genuine bio-chemical constellation would still lack a theoretical explanation. The only result would be the synthesis of "dead" matter.

According to modern conceptions of a possible bio-synthesis the latter is not concerned with composing relatively simple albuminoid materials *(protein).* This was already possible long ago. The point is rather to compose extremely complicated proteins containing, besides amino-acids, other (so-called prosthetical) groups, which can often be split off from albumenoids without any alteration of the latter themselves[1]. In other words, science is

[1] Cf. E. LEHNARTZ, *Die chemischen Voraussetzungen des Lebens* (*Handb. der Biologie,* hrg. v. BERTALANFFY) Bnd. I, Heft 4, p. 120.

looking for the so-called *proteid-molecule* as an element of living plasm, and it hopes to be able to compose this element synthetically. In addition scientists take into account the requirement of this molecule's capability of propagation, implied in the nature of a living unit.

WOLTERECK has summarized the modern program of bio-synthesis as follows: 'The object would be to compose living plasm from colloidal protein substances and to produce in this plasm structures containing such kinds of matter which display a catalytic activity and maintain themselves in the process of cell-division (heredity). On such kinds of matter the determination of all singular properties must depend.'

WOLTERECK acknowledges the possibility that at one time or other it would be possible to compose synthetically such a material combination which would display the characteristic properties of assimilation and dissimilation, growth, movement, division, susceptibility to stimulation, tension, pluriformity, *etc.*

'All this', he observes, 'may be expected with regard to formations composed of non-living labile combinations, as a possible result. For it implies nothing that is fundamentally new. Dissolution and reconstruction, shape production and movement, increase of substance (growth) and division, even restoration (in crystal) and a sort of sensitivity (photo-sensitivity) — all this may occur in the world of inanimate things. It would here only be *brought together.* We may suppose that future bio-chemists will succeed in such a concentration of many properties characteristic of life in one and the same material combination, though this assumption seems improbable' [1]. But on two essential points any attempt at bio-synthesis is doomed to fail: First, such a synthetically construed colloidal system can never maintain its identity in the process of metabolism and exchange of energy, in its movement, dissolution and increase. When non-living complexes alter themselves by producing something new or fall asunder into their elements, they disappear and are replaced by something different. The combination of continual active change with maintenance of the total-system is, according to WOLTERECK, a completely new *biotic* phenomenon. It cannot be produced artificially by the concentration and combination of a-biotic components.

Secondly, such an artificial "living" aggregate or system will

---

[1] *Op. cit.*, p. 521.

never be capable of "experiencing something in itself", even if it could react to all sorts of *stimuli*. For, according to WOLTERECK, we must ascribe some kind of a-psychical experience even to the most simple living beings, though we know such "*Innen-Erregungen*" directly only as feelings and volitional tendencies of an "experiencing I".

This latter assumption, amply elaborated in the final part of WOLTERECK's important work, may be let alone in the present context. As we shall see later on, it is completely dependent upon his irrationalist, emergent evolutionistic starting-point. It remains entirely obscure what is to be understood by "a-psychic experiences" as the "inner side of life".

To my mind WOLTERECK's first argument against the possibility of a bio-synthesis already clinches the matter. For here he implicitly characterizes the typical fundamental difference between a bio-chemical and a physico-chemically qualified constellation. Even in its bio-chemical aspect a living organism displays that remarkable centred totality-structure which maintains itself in the continual change of all material combinations functioning enkaptically in it. This structure has indeed no single analogy in any molecular or crystalline structure of organic matter, nor in a spontaneous falling asunder of a radioactive element, nor in the "growth" of a crystal form in a matrix-lye. This centred structure guarantees to a cell's living organism the preservation of its biotically qualified identity. It has its necessary counter-part in the complete variability of all material combinations in their enkaptic function within this living organism.

How far can physics and chemistry penetrate into a bio-chemical constellation?

Physics and chemistry are able to penetrate into this bio-chemical constellation with their proper methods of inquiry only insofar as they take into account the individuality-structure of a living cell-organism. The applicability of the specific methods of physics and chemistry oriented to the atomic, molecular and crystalline structures of material combinations, is naturally not limited to inorganic matters. These methods much rather find their limit *at that critical point where in the internal physico-chemical sphere of a living organism there is no question any longer of definite material components.*

To trace the real *bio*-physical and *bio*-chemical constellation, physics and chemistry should not seek for the *material results* of a bio-chemical process but rather for *the manner in which these results are produced*[1]. The issue here is concerned with *processes* rather than with their products.

It is beyond doubt that a living organism, in building up and dissolving the body's material components, sets about it in a way quite different from the methods usual in a chemical laboratory. To mention only one characteristic difference: as a rule the organism effects assimilatory and dissimilatory processes by means of ferments or enzymes; the chemist in his laboratory, on the other hand, performs his analysis and synthesis of elements by means of heating. DRIESCH has rightly observed that the most remarkable characteristic of organic metabolism rests on the very use of ferments on the part of a living organism. The characteristic trait is that, by means of regulation, this metabolism is made serviceable to the living whole. In proportion to local and temporal needs there will occur a chemical combining process or a chemical dissolution.

Genuine *bio*-chemistry can consequently never be identical with *organic* chemistry. It can only start after the methods of the latter have been exhausted in an analysis of the material substrates of a living organism and the products of its bio-chemical activity.

It is beyond doubt that both bio-chemistry and bio-physics have to seek for a physico-chemical explanation of the processes occurring within the internal sphere of a living organism. But the typical biotic qualification of these events will always remain the ultimate limit to these methods of explanation. Suppose science seeks for a physical explanation of the remarkable mineral formations performed by *radiolaria* or other kinds of *protozoa*. In the process of producing these forms there occurs a gel- and mineral formation which is exactly limited to certain sectors. Attempting to explain this manner of formation, bio-

[1] DRIESCH remarks in his *Philosophie des Organischen* (2e Aufl. 1921) p. 200: 'die Wirkung des Fermentes, *wenn es einmal da ist, ist chemisch...* Das heiszt nun natürlich nicht, dasz aller Stoffwechsel chemischer Natur sei'. [the effect of a ferment, when it is once present, is chemical... This does naturally not mean that all metabolism is of a chemical nature]. As we shall see later on, DRIESCH does not know a genuine *bio-chemical constellation* in the sense defined earlier. Nevertheless he has sharply observed that only the *process* of forming enzymes has a typical connection with life.

physics cannot do without assuming typical checking field-effects in plasm which remain constant, in contrast to the continual alteration of the material components of the latter and to the complete plasticity of plasm freely moving between the forms produced. But these field-effects really belong to the disclosed or opened bio-physical structure of the living organism. They are directed by the qualifying biotic function of the latter.

From a physical point of view such a biotically qualified "field of formation" belongs to an assumed *given* physical constellation, which itself cannot be explained in a purely physical way. Both such typical field-reactions and the catalytic processes in assimilation and dissimilation are started and directed by bio-impulses. And the latter are accessible to physics and chemistry only *in their physico-chemical aspect,* not in their qualifying *biotic* modality [1].

Biotically qualified field-effects are fundamentally different from electro-magnetic field-effects without such a biotic qualification. This difference is already implied in their non-homogeneous complication and the spontaneous way in which they are started.

Does there exist a specific vital matter?

If this is the real state of affairs, the question may be asked

---

[1] WOLTERECK (*op. cit.*, p. 458) elucidates the difference between enzymes and hormones operating as bio-impulses in a living organism, and the catalysts of non-biotically qualified chemical processes as follows: 'Ein Katalysator beschleunigt oder hemmt eine ohnehin im Gang befindliche Reaktion. Ein Enzym oder Hormon und im weiteren Sinne ein Bioimpuls bestimmt auch die Qualität des Vorgangs. (Dies kann möglicherweise durch Unterdrückung der einen und durch Forderung der anderen Teilvorgänge zustande kommen...). Die biotischen Impulse zeichnen sich dadurch aus, dasz sie einen *Erregungszustand* im Plasma oder Zellverband hervorrufen. Dadurch unterscheiden sie sich sehr von den gewöhnlichen Katalysatoren, die OSTWALD einem mechanischen "Schmiermittel" vergleicht, das den Ablauf bestimmter Reaktionen erleichtert'. [A catalyst accelerates or checks a reaction which is already going on. An enzyme or hormone — and in a broader sense a bio-impulse — also determines the quality of the process. (This may possibly also be brought about by keeping down one part of a process and stimulating the other...) Biotic impulses are characterized by their causing a condition of "*Erregung*" (being stimulated and excited) in plasm or cell. Thereby they are very different from ordinary catalysts, which OSTWALD compares with a mechanical lubricant facilitating the process of certain reactions.].

whether it makes sense to seek any further for a specific "vital matter" as the generator of the bio-chemical constellation, indicated by the terms "*matrix*" (WOLTERECK), "germ-plasm" or "idioplasm" (PLATE)?

This question is answered in the negative both by the mechanistic and the neo-vitalistic trends in modern biological theory.

According to KOLTZOFF, an outstanding materialistic representative of the first trend, the acceptance of such a specific "bio-substance" would necessarily lead to a vitalistic standpoint. This standpoint is supposed to imply that biotic phenomena are different in principle from physico-chemical processes and that "bio-substance" is exempt from physico-chemical laws. But the founder of modern neo-vitalism, the famous biologist and philosopher HANS DRIESCH, emphatically denies the existence of a specific material bio-substance. He assumes that matter can only be "living" so long as some "entelechy" has a controlling influence upon a physico-chemical constellation [1].

The recent conception [2], according to which there does exist a specific "bio-substance", fundamentally distinct from a-biotic and necro-biotic matter, wishes to take an intermediate standpoint between these two extreme trends.

WOLTERECK is one of the most prominent adherents of this view. He is of the opinion that it should already be accepted from the viewpoint of the logical principle of economy in the explanation of phenomena. Against DRIESCH's concept of "entelechy", which we shall consider presently, he observes: 'It seems to me that DRIESCH too quickly substitutes a metaphysical notion for an unknown property of the physical-real plasm without having shown the necessity of this introduction from the exclusion of physical possibilities. The possibility that the unquestionable bio-specificities are caused by a particular physico-chemical situation has anyhow not been refuted. The well-known proofs formulated by DRIESCH in favour of the immaterial autonomy of vital processes do not concern the elementary processes in bio-substance but rather the intricate functions of development, restitution and activity...' [3]. Let us see whether this argument is to the point.

---

[1] *Philosophie des Organischen*, p. 504: 'Eine *chemische* "lebende Substanz" gibt es auf alle Fälle nicht'. [Anyhow, there does not exist a *chemical* "living substance".

[2] The older vitalistic trends will be discussed presently.

[3] *Op. cit.*, p. 331.

§ 4 - THE DILEMMA "MECHANISM OR VITALISM IN BIOLOGY" VIEWED IN THE LIGHT OF THE SUBSTANCE-CONCEPT.

The philosophical back-ground of the mechanistic conception.

The old dilemma, mechanism or vitalism[1], is in the nature of the case unacceptable on our standpoint. The mechanistic view, even nowadays adhered to by most of the biologists concerned with analytical investigations[2], continues to seek for a bio-synthesis by means of protein combinations. According to this standpoint colloid-chemistry has the task to disclose all the "secrets of life". This trend is still entirely inspired by the classical science-ideal striving after perfect domination of nature by means of a complete causal determination even of vital phenomena.

It starts from an *a priori* absolutization of the physico-chemical energy-aspect of empirical reality. Consequently, in principle it denies the irreducible nature of the biotic modality of

---

[1] It is not correct to identify vitalism with the view according to which the biotic aspect has its proper laws and a living organism is characterized by its total structure of individuality. This identification is also found in DRIESCH's *Phil. des Organischen*, pp. 138 ff. The term "vitalists" may only be rightly applied to those who in any way *absolutize* the biotic aspect of a living body. This may occur either at the cost of the non-vital components of the latter, or at the cost of the original and irreducible character of post-biotic modalities, or by elevating the biotic modality to a self-contained *substance*. Naturally, we cannot go here into all nuances of the mechanistic and vitalistic trends. Nor can we go into the divergent recent attempts at overcoming the dilemma by indicating a third possibility (the so-called "*Stufentheorieën*" or emergent evolutionistic theories; the so-called "*mnemism*" of E. HERING and SEMON, *etc.*); or into the attempts at evading the dilemma as a provisionally insoluble problem by restricting themselves to a merely descriptive and "empirical" criterion of organic vital phenomena as "autonomous totality-phenomena" (GURVITCH, UNGERER, BERTALLANFFY, ALVERDES, *etc.)*.

We shall only engage in a more detailed critical analysis of the conceptions of DRIESCH, WOLTERECK and B. BAVINK.

An excellent, though succinct survey of all these views is to be found in E. UNGERER's treatise *Die Erkenntnisgrundlagen der Biologie. Ihre Geschichte, und gegenwärtiger Stand* (Handb. der Biol., Bnd. I, H. 3), pp. 76 ff. Cf. also R. WOLTERECK, *Philosophie des Lebendigen* (1940). The best description of the history of vitalism is to be found in DRIESCH's *Geschichte des Vitalismus.*

[2] Especially by the older scientists, such as WILHELM ROUX, HERBST, RHUMBLER and KOLTZOFF. Cf. RHUMBLER, *Das Lebensproblem* (1930) and his treatise *Das Protoplasma als physikalisches System*, Erg. Physiol. 1914.

experience. It necessarily involves itself in inner antinomies resulting from the absolutization of a modal law-sphere. In addition it handles a deterministic physical concept of causality, which modern physics has already been obliged to relinquish, albeit that it is not permissible to identify all modern mechanistic conceptions with a machine theory of life, as is done by DRIESCH.

A deterministic causal explanation of physico-chemical processes encounters a first limit in the micro-structure of atoms. This has found its natural-scientific formulation in HEISENBERG'S relations of uncertainty mentioned above. BERNARD BAVINK has rightly observed that the acceptance of a second limit in the internal bio-physico-chemical constellation of a living organism, can never contradict the results of modern physics and chemistry. Rather it is only in conflict with the *a priori* mechanistic starting-point of classical natural science, which has appeared to disagree with the structure of empirical reality.

The modal aspect in which the physico-chemical functions of a living organism present themselves does not have a rigid structure. As we have seen, it opens and discloses itself within the individuality-structure of this organism.

Neo-vitalism, too, holds to the mechanistic view of the physico-chemical processes.

This latter state of affairs has also been lost sight of by DRIESCH and his adherents. These neo-vitalists do not detract from the basic tenet of mechanistic theory concerning the complete closeness of any physico-chemical constellation, as a mechanical chain of causes and effects. Their only concern is to withdraw "life" from the rule of the mechanistic concept of causality; they think they have proved experimentally that a living organism is not to be explained from a mere summation of already present physico-chemical elements. This view is based upon DRIESCH'S experimental proofs concerning the typical totality-character of the phenomena of self-regulation, regeneration and heredity occurring in living organisms, and in general of any animal and human action.

Neo-vitalism in contrast to older vitalism.

Older vitalism generally accepted a fundamental difference between organic and in-organic matter. Without any basis in empirical research it proclaimed the *a priori* thesis: "chemistry will never succeed in a synthetical composition of organic kinds of matter". Sometimes it also started from a particular "vital force", though this conception could also be meant in a mechanistic sense [1].

Neo-vitalism distinguishes itself from these older views by the very abandoning of all structures of matter to physico-chemical analysis and determination. It rejects both the *a priori* conception of older kinds of vitalism and the idea of a "vital force" as a particular potency of energy. It intends to base its own vitalistic view only on experimental results. The older idea of specific organic matter, which would be exempt from physico-chemical laws, has been exploded by the methodical physico-chemical analysis of almost the entire realm of organic matter combinations. DRIESCH and his adherents have abandoned this untenable position.

DRIESCH's experimental "proofs" of the existence of "entelechies". The so-called harmonious-equipotential system and totality-causality.

The founder of neo-vitalism has tried to show in an experimental way that organic bio-phenomena are not to be explained by means of the analytical causal method of physics and chemistry. He is of the opinion that these phenomena imply a particular type of causality which he calls "*Ganzheitskausalität*" in contrast to mechanistic "*Einzelkausalität*". The remarkable results of DRIESCH's famous experiments with eggs of sea-hedgehogs appeared to be incompatible with the mechanistic view. They showed that it is possible to take away any one part from the young germ-cells (or, in later phases of development, from separate germ-parts) without affecting the final result: the rise of a complete living individual. One may remove germ-parts or deform the latter (without killing them) by pressing them between two glass sheets. Yet the total ultimate result will be reached. The germ-cells themselves develop by continued division as a "harmonic equipotential system", *i.e.* a system in which all the elements possess an equal disposition to lead to the total final

---

[1] E. UNGERER has shown in his treatise cited above that the theory of a specific vital force was not at all meant by all of its adherents in a metaphysical-vitalistic sense. In JOH. CHR. KEIL's treatise *Ueber die Lebenskraft* (1795), *e.g.*, it was even defended in a mechanistic way. In HERMANN LOTZE's writing *Leben und Lebenskraft* (1842) the concept "vital force" is already fundamentally criticized and rejected.

result in mutual harmonic cooperation. Such systems lie also at the foundation of regenerative processes occurring in the full grown organisms. They do not operate after the pattern of *quantitative* physico-chemical causality but according to a typical *totality*-causality [1]. And the same thing holds with respect to the propagation of organisms. Hereditary phenomena are never explainable from mere material "genes".

Insofar as these arguments intend nothing but elucidating the totality character of a living organism, in all of its manifestations, we can readily accept them. We can also agree with the distinction between quantitative causality and totality-causality though we may derogate from the demonstrating force of the arguments based on DRIESCH's experiments [2].

But this does not imply an acceptance of the neo-vitalistic view as such. It appears that DRIESCH lacks any insight into the modal structures of our experiential horizon. This is why he has recourse to the *substance-concept* to account for the fundamental difference between biotic and physico-chemical functions. "Life" is now conceived phylogenetically as a "super-individual substance" lacking temporal *genesis,* as an invisible immaterial "organic form" in a pseudo-Aristotelian sense, of which all visible individual forms are only materialized products. This substance is called "entelechy". With DRIESCH this term means an intensive (*i.e.* non-spatial) multiplicity manifesting itself, on the one hand, as "psychoid", governing the body when it has already been formed, and, on the other hand, as "form-entelechy", which originates the body as a form-totality [3]. A "*psyche*" can never influence material natural phenomena, so DRIESCH argues; only a "*psychoid*", as *correlate* of the latter, is able to do so.

"What is properly speaking an organic form? What is its *essence,* its *constant "so being"*, what is *substance* in respect to

---

[1] *Phil. des Organischen,* passim.; *Der Begriff der organischen Form* (1919), pp. 54 ff.; *Ordnungslehre* (2e Aufl. 1923), pp. 301 ff.

[2] In the first place these experiments lead only to the results intended by DRIESCH in the initial phases of development of the germ-cells. The experiment with eggs of sea-hedgehogs is not successful in later developmental phases. This is also the case when one cuts the egg not vertically but transversally. Cf. Dr. J. H. F. UMBGROVE, *Leven en Materie* (Nijhoff, 's-Gravenhage, 1943), pp. 54 ff. We must, however, remark that DRIESCH himself has repeatedly acknowledged that his experiments are bound to the initial phases of development of the germ-cells.

[3] *Phil. des Organischen,* pp. 357 ff.

it, *to which* consequently *all properties belong*? Our answer is: The proper *substance* of organic form is our *entelechy:* the latter is the "form", the *εἶδος* in the Aristotelian sense; that which is formed in a visible way is only the transitory product of its operation into matter' [1].

In DRIESCH's *"Ordnungslehre"* the substance-concept is not meant in a metaphysical sense.

Now one should not conclude too quickly that DRIESCH has recourse to metaphysics in order to explain empirical states of affairs. For DRIESCH does not intend to do so. He views his *"entelechy"* primarily as a second *natural factor*, which he tries to conceive in the "purely logical" concepts of his *"Ordnungslehre"*. A metaphysical interpretation of these concepts is only at issue in his *"Wirklichkeitslehre"* and DRIESCH is of the opinion that the latter can only arrive at *probable* conclusions. He wishes only to accept a metaphysics based on the results of empirical research of the natural phenomena and able to account for the *"Ordnungslehre"* [2]. The primary theses (*"Ursetzungen"*) of the latter are, according to DRIESCH, the necessary conditions of an ordered experience of nature, without implying the transcendental idealistic sense ascribed to them by KANT.

DRIESCH in principle rejects any view of metaphysics as an *a priori* and *primordial* basic science (*philosophia prima*). His starting-point (viewed from the immanence-standpoint) is the Cartesian *cogito* [3] (I am conscious of something, or I know something), not the ontological concept of being in its Aristotelian sense, ruled by the Greek form-matter motive. His philosophical basis is not metaphysics, but his *"Ordnungslehre"*. And the latter is certainly influenced by KANT's epistemology, albeit that DRIESCH — in contrast to KANT — ascribes to his ordering concepts or categories also an *intentional* relation to "reality in itself". Properly speaking, the question as to whether *"entelechy"* is an immaterial substance in a metaphysical sense, coördinated with the spatial substance of material body [4], should not be ans-

---

[1] *Der Begriff der organischen Form* (Abh. zur theor. Biol., hrg. von Dr. Julius Schaxel, Heft 3, Berlin, 1919), p. 71.

[2] Cf. *Wirklichkeitslehre* (2e Aufl.), pp. 1—65.

[3] DRIESCH only rejects DESCARTES' metaphysical conclusion from *"cogito"*. Cf. his *Philosophische Gegenwartsfragen* (Leipzig, 1933), p. 23/4: *Excurs über Descartes.*

[4] Apparently DRIESCH has in view the two Cartesian substances.

wered in a categorical sense. It must remain an open question [1]. Nevertheless we shall see that DRIESCH does not maintain this critical standpoint and finally does ascribe a meta-physical sense to his *entelechy* as "substance" [2].

In his opinion we may conceive *entelechy* as an ordering concept, but we cannot have any representation of it. The reason is that all our representations are bound to sensory perception. The latter is only concerned with things and events in time and space, consequently only with *effects of entelechy in matter*. Well then, the concept "substance" or "essential form", as it is used in DRIESCH's *"Ordnungslehre"*, is only meant in the non-metaphysical sense of an "ordering notion". It is a concept belonging to a theory of the general logical relations in which it cannot mean anything but *relatum,* or the constant point of reference of all relations, which itself does not imply any relation [3]. "*Entelechy*", as "form" and "substance", is then to be understood as "the constant bearer of the whole of the properties of the latter", indicating its *essence* as *"bedeutungshaft erfasztes Sosein"* [4].

It is meant here as an "empirical natural factor", *i.e.* a factor to be known from its *phenomenal manifestation.* In our experience it is at least *intended* as "an independent reality, foreign to the experiencing ego". In this context DRIESCH speaks of a "*gleichsam selbständig seiendes Etwas*", apparently to exclude the metaphysical sense of a "thing in itself" [5]. And in this sense he speaks in his *"Ordnungslehre"* of two substances of natural reality, *viz.* matter (mass) and form (entelechy).

But also in this non-metaphysical sense entelechy, as substance, does certainly not mean organic life as an *experiential modality,* as an *aspect* of reality. Much rather it refers to an immate-

---

[1] Cf. *Phil. des Organischen,* pp. 495—519.

[2] This is overlooked by O. HEINICHEN, *Driesch' Philosophy* (Leipzig 1924), p. 160.

[3] *Ordnungslehre,* pp. 311—313. This is why it is called "das *reine* Glied der Relation".

[4] *Ordnungslehre,* p. 90. DRIESCH denies that this is a nominalistic conception of "essence". He observes that he also accepts *universalia in rebus.* But this does not detract from the nominalistic character of his "*Ordnungslehre*". Genuine "realism" always starts from the metaphysical concept of being and never from the Cartesian "I think" or "I am conscious of something", as DRIESCH does. So-called "critical realism" is, therefore, never *genuine* realism, since its starting-point is *subjective.*

[5] *Op. cit.,* p. 156.

rial and constant bearer of properties, which is opposed to the material natural substance as the immaterial independent cause of all its effects in the latter [1]. DRIESCH no more knows a modal biotic aspect of empirical reality than ARISTOTLE or THOMAS did. By means of his substance-concept he tries directly to conceive the (logical) essence of an individual living whole *before having acquired any insight into the modal structures of empirical reality*. This is why this concept, even in its non-metaphysical use, also impedes the insight into the individuality-structures.

DRIESCH's conception of entelechy is fundamentally different from the Aristotelian view.

DRIESCH's conception of entelechy is quite different from the Aristotelian view. The point is that DRIESCH holds to the Cartesian substance-concept, albeit with reserve as to its metaphysical interpretation. This implies a dualistic separation of an immaterial substance and a material one, and a mechanistic conception of the latter as an independent extended corporeal entity [2].

"Body" in DRIESCH is identical with "matter" and is separated as "substance" from the immaterial "entelechy" [3].

---

[1] *Phil. des Organischen*, p. 508: 'In *keiner* Form hängt das *Dasein* des Naturagens Entelechie von irgendetwas Materiellem ab, obschon seine räumlichen *Leistungen*... von gegebenen materiellen Zuständen abhängen'.

[2] DRIESCH was fully aware of the fact that his concept of entelechy lacks the genuine Aristotelian sense. In a footnote on p. 71 of his *Der Begriff der organischen Form* quoted here, he observes: 'Aristotle's εἶδος consequently corresponds *more of less* to our concept of entelechy, it is well known that his ἐντελεχεῖα has a different meaning'. And in his *Phil. des Org.*, p. 170 he remarks: 'We want to use the word entelechy only as a proof of our veneration for this great genius; we accept his word only as a form which we have filled and shall fill with a new content'.

[3] This clearly appears from DRIESCH's remarks *(Phil. d. Org.*, pp. 209—210) with respect to WEISMANN's theory concerning the material continuity of germ-plasm: 'Wörtlich genommen ist diese Behauptung offenbar selbstverständlich, obschon darum nicht unwichtig. Denn da alles Leben sich *an Körpern, d.h. an der Materie,* darstellt, und da die Entwicklung aller Nachkommen *von Teilen der elterlichen Körper, d.h. vom Stoff oder Material der Eltern,* ihren Ursprung nimmt, folgt ohne weiteres, dasz im gewissen Sinne eine stoffliche Kontinuität existiert, so lange es Leben gibt, wenigstens Leben in den uns bekannten Formen'. [Taken to the letter, this thesis is apparently a matter of course, though therefore not unimportant. For any life manifests itself in *bodies, i.e.* in *matter,* and the development of all offspring originates from parts of the paternal bodies, *i.e.* from the paternal *matter or material.* From this it immedia-

ARISTOTLE, on the contrary, views a "natural primary substance" always as a composite of form and matter. With him the "entelechy" of a living body is never itself a "substance". All natural substances are material; their "form" is never an independent being.

DRIESCH's *"entelechy"*, as the immaterial "natural form", potentially contains "also all particular potences of a functional, adaptive, restitutive character to be found in the realized form". It even includes the possibility of all future generations inclusive of the possibility of all future phylogenetic processes of mutation. From a phylogenetic viewpoint there are consequently not *many* entelechies, rather there is only one, *viz.* the "super-personal life", of which all individual entelechies are only temporal and transitory ramifications [1].

„Entelechy" as a metaphysical substance. DRIESCH's view of the scheme act-potence confronted with the Aristotelian conception.

In this context DRIESCH now also expressly raises the *metaphysical* question as to whether this "entelechy" itself develops,

---

tely follows that there exists a material continuity in a certain sense so long as there exists life, at least life in the forms known to us.]

Life and *material body* are thus separated from one another as "substances". DRIESCH does not know *a biotic or psychic function of the body.* "Body", *as such,* to him means an extended material substance, whose spatial figure, however, originates from the operation of an immaterial entelechy-substance.

As to DRIESCH's Cartesian identification of "material substance" with space itself or at least with an extensive material element, I refer, *e.g.*, to *Phil. d. Org.*, p. 497, where we read: 'Anorganische Substanz ist entweder selbst Extensivität, d.h. der Raum als Träger der phänomenalistischen Realität, oder sie ist etwas, das aus absolut einzelnen Elementen, welche im *Extensiven* eines *neben* dem anderen sind, besteht'. [Inorganic substance is either itself extension, *i.e.* space as the bearer of phenomenal reality, or it is something consisting of absolutely singular elements which in extension are next to one another.]

[1] Cf. *Der Begriff der organischen Form*, p. 72: 'Durch die Beziehung einer gegebenen Form und ihrer personalen εἶδος auf Vererbung und Phylogenie wird nun sofort die "Form" im substantialen Sinne ihres eigentlich *personalen Charakters entkleidet:* die sich in der materiellen Produktion von Personen betätigende Entelechie *ist nicht selbst "personal"*, als ob es "viele" Entelechieën gäbe. Das Leben ist *Eines*, eine grosze in Personen, welche von einander abstammen, gegliederte Gesamtheit.' This thesis is explained more amply in DRIESCH's *Logische Studien über Entwicklung* I, p. 9 ff.

in which case it could not be the "constant substance" of the empirical "organic form". His answer is: " 'Here we can only advance by applying the conceptual pair *actus* and *potentia* to two essential sides of the substantial entelechy. As *potentia* it is the constant substance of the "form", but as to its *actus* manifesting itself in matter, it changes in the sense of a development of the type of a non-mechanical evolution' [1]. This statement proves that DRIESCH really ascribes to his entelechy also a metaphysical sense, in spite of his earlier statements that this question should remain "open". For the "constant substance", which is at issue in this context, is no longer meant in the sense of an ordering concept. It is only to be understood as an immaterial "thing in itself".

And at the same time we may establish that also the metaphysical conceptual pair *actus et potentia* is used here in a sense fundamentally different from its Aristotelian meaning. For in ARISTOTLE "potency" (*δύναμις*) is always inherent in "matter". According to DRIESCH, on the contrary, the very entelechy, viewed from the side of "form" and "immaterial constant substance", is a pure "potence", which only in its operating in matter becomes "actus".

DRIESCH denies a typical bio-chemical constellation. The problem concerning the influence of entelechy upon a purely mechanical matter.

Besides the existence of a particular "living matter" DRIESCH also denies the existence of a particular "bio-chemical constellation" in the sense formerly defined by us. Viewed from its physico-chemical side, a living organism is, according to him, nothing but "dead matter", which *as such* possesses a completely closed constellation determined in a mechanical causal way. *From the physico-chemical viewpoint* material organisms with and without entelechy (*i.e.* dead and living organisms) are, therefore, not different in principle [2]. The difference is exclusi-

---

[1] *Der Begriff der organischen Form*, p. 72: 'Hier kommen wir wohl nur dadurch weiter, dasz wir das Begriffspaar *actus* und *potentia* auf zwei Wesens*seiten* der substantialen Entelechie anwenden: Als *potentia* ist sie die beharrliche Substanz der "Form", aber ihrem *actus* nach, welcher sich an Materie betätigt, verändert sie sich im Sinne einer Entwicklung vom Typus nichtmaschineller Evolution'.

[2] This is not in conflict with DRIESCH's conception that, as a "living organism", a body is a material system whose behaviour does not con-

vely to be found in the controlling influence of entelechy upon matter, and this influence is not of a physico-chemical character.

This raises the crucial problem: How can such an immaterial entelechy influence matter in its physico-chemical constellation without breaking through the causally determined mechanistic system of the latter? And inversely: How can a mechanically determined matter influence an immaterial entelechy without encroaching upon the latter's autonomy?

DRIESCH has amply discussed these questions in his large work *Philosophie des Organischen* [1]. In a later treatise, entitled *Logische Studien über Entwicklung,* he has deepened his former view to an important degree.

He assumes four possibilities with respect to a causal method of operation of entelechy:

---

form to mechanical, but to vitalistic laws. (Cf. *Phil. d. Org.* I, pp. 851 ff.; *Leib und Seele* (Leipzig, 3e Aufl. 1923, p. 88). For the body is certainly *not* such an autonomous vital material system *from the physico-chemical point of view.* The latter cannot show us anything but mechanical causal processes. It is only in consequence of the controlling influence of an immaterial entelechy that a living body displays the typical traits of a *vital* material system. But this influence is of a non-physical character and its causality is a *vital* causality which, according to DRIESCH, always presupposes the mechanical causality displayed in the physico-chemical constellation of matter. This clearly appears from his discussion of the relation between the brain as a "physico-chemical system" and the "psyche" which operates by means of this system. In his *Leib und Seele,* pp. 89—90, he observes: 'Das Hirn ist für das Handeln als Naturereignis notwendig, sein Bau in den verschiedenen Tiergruppen bedingt des Handelns besondere Form und Höhe, Hirndefekte bedingen gelegentlich, obschon nicht immer, bestimmte Handlungsdefekte. Aber des Hirns physikalisch-chemische Zuständlichkeit in irgend einem gegebenen Zeitpunkt ist *nicht* der vollständige zureichende Werdegrund, sondern nur ein Teilwerdegrund für das, was an ihm und von ihm aus geschieht; und das *obwohl* in jedem beliebigen Zeitpunkt das Hirn als materielles Ding *seine bestimmte physiko-chemische, oder, in Kürze, mechanistische Kennzeichnung besitzt.*' [The brain is necessary for an action as a natural event, its construction in the different animal groups conditions the particular form and level of action; brain defects condition occasionally, though not always, certain defects in action. But the brain's physico-chemical condition at a given point of time is not the complete sufficient genetic ground, but only a partial genetic ground for what happens in it and proceeds from it; and this *though* in anyone point of time the brain as a material thing possesses *its determined physico-chemical, or, in short, mechanistic* characteristic.]

[1] *Op. cit.*, pp. 153—240.

1. Entelechy is itself able to originate physical movement (energy). In this case, however, the basic law concerning the preservation of energy would be violated.
2. Entelechy removes energy by means of a sort of "turning" of material systems (Descartes, Hartmann), and it functions in this way as an "*arbeitslose Kraft*". Suppose a force is working upon a physical system perpendicularly to the momentary direction of its movement. In this case the work done by this force is zero but the latter is nevertheless able to cause a change in the direction of moving matter particles. We can imagine that entelechy adds such forces to the physical forces of the material system, or withdraws the former from the latter if need be. In this case all particles concerned will be led into different directions without the balance of energy being altered.
3. Entelechy may "suspend" movement by temporarily transforming actual kinetic energy into potential energy. Entelechy may also set free kinetic energy bound by it so that the latter changes into actual energy; and this may occur in a teleological relation to the needs of the living whole.
4. Entelechy imposes a rough building plan upon the material system; but within the frame of this plan it leaves free scope to the physico-chemical movements of the material system. It thus creates within the material system of cells only certain chances ("*naturwirkliche Bedingungsgleichungen*") within which each separate physico-chemical event may freely proceed.

The first of these hypotheses is rejected by Driesch because of its incompatibility with the basic law of the preservation of energy. It would imply a rise of energy from an immaterial source. In this case entelechy would operate in a *quantitative*-causal way by originating a certain quantum of energy. The three remaining hypotheses are equivalent in his opinion as acceptable attempts at an explanation of the method of operating of entelechy. In 1908 he chose the third solution, but later on he preferred the theory of the rough building-plan. The reason was that the latter was supposed to give a satisfactory explanation of the undeniable fact that the vital form-totality is only realized in a rough outline while the position of the individual cells in the separate organs remains accidental. The Russian biologist Gurwitch probably meant something similar by what he called a vital form *(morphe)* which only *regulates* the physico-chemical system without *determining* it[1].

The second and third hypotheses have already been subjected to a decisive criticism by BERNARD BAVINK[2]. First he observes that the physico-chemical laws are not exhausted by the law of the preservation of energy. According to the classical view, apparently adhered to by DRIESCH, a physical system proceeds in conformity to certain differential equations combining the initial condition with the changes of the magnitudes concerned. The law concerning the preservation of energy is only one integral of these equations. DRIESCH might object to this argument that he has also taken into account the law of entropy. But it remains true that the laws of thermo-dynamics alone cannot completely determine the closed physico-chemical system of classical physics and chemistry.

DRIESCH should have shown how an entelechy may be able to alter the direction of a physico-chemical process that is already completely determined by its initial condition and the classical laws of nature. His arguments, however, lead his explanatory attempts into a vicious circle, or they presuppose a physico-chemical function of entelechy itself, contrary to its assumed immaterial nature. In order to illustrate the possibility of an entelechy's influence upon matter, DRIESCH adduces that by means of a machine a human being may lead a physico-chemical process to certain ends without violating physico-chemical laws. This is doubtless true. But man can only bring about this either by means of small quantities of energy inserted by him in the process concerned, or by constructing a machine in such a way that the physico-chemical processes in it must occur in the direction required.

Applied to an entelechy this would mean in the first case that the former itself must produce energy although in minimal quantities. In the second case the argument would result in the assumption that the organism, though originating from entelechy, functions completely as a machine. Both consequences contradict the neo-vitalist view. In addition, if the working of entelechy upon matter is conceived after the pattern of the human direction of a machine, we are once again confronted with the problem: How can a human being influence physico-

[1] GURWITCH, *Biol. Zentrallblatt 32* (1912), p. 458 and *Arch. f. Entwicklungsmechanik*, Bnd. 30, I, p. 139.

[2] *Op. cit.*, pp. 445 ff.

chemical processes? For man himself is a living being in which an entelechy must be at work, if the neo-vitalist conception is true. But the method of working of entelechy was to be explained by its very comparison with the human direction of a machine, so that we move in a vicious circle.

The so-called suspension-theory developed in DRIESCH's third hypothesis in any case supposes the production of some energy on the part of an entelechy. And as to the second hypothesis it should be observed that a force which does not do any work is nevertheless a *physical* force, whereas an entelechy was supposed to be an immaterial cause.

Finally we will briefly consider DRIESCH's fourth hypothesis which BAVINK does not discuss. The so-called building-plan theory is no better than the two former explanatory attempts. This theory, too, supposes *"a physico-chemical realization"* of the rough plan in the material organism, which, as a "close physico-chemical system", is supposed to be completely determined by its initial condition and its self-contained laws. When the building-plan of an architect is realized, this realization can never occur in a purely immaterial way. Rather it needs physico-chemical energy not belonging to the physico-chemical constellation of the building materials. This comparison, too, implies the vicious circle in which we were moving when DRIESCH compared the working of entelechy with the human direction of a machine.

It is the dualistic substance-concept which involves theoretical thought in such insoluble (because wrongly posited) problems. So long as "life" is viewed as an immaterial "substance" working upon a "material substance", the question how such an operation is possible will remain the chief crux of theoretical biology. For the substance-concept itself, whether or not used in an explicitly metaphysical sense, implies an unconquerable antinomy, which we have amply discussed in the first part of this volume. The reason is that it elevates a theoretical abstraction to an independent being.

An entelechy in DRIESCH's neo-vitalist sense cannot exist in temporal reality; for it is nothing but a theoretical abstraction of the biotic modality of experience, absolutized to an "immaterial substance". This concept of entelechy is nothing but the vitalistic counter-part of the mechanistic concept of "matter", which modern physics was obliged to relinquish because of its incompatibility with the micro-structures of energy.

The neo-vitalistic view confronted with the neo-Thomist conception. DRIESCH's philosophy of nature shows a transformation of the Greek basic motive into the Humanistic basic motive of nature and freedom.

The question may be asked why DRIESCH has refrained from reverting to the genuine Aristotelian conception of entelechy. For it cannot be doubted that the latter, revived in the neo-Thomist philosophy of nature, is in different respects in a better position than neo-vitalism. It does not involve itself in the contradictions of a vitalism which is at the same time intended to maintain the basic tenets of the mechanistic view of matter. For it holds that the specific "matter" of a living being has no independent being but, as a *hulè* in the Greek sense, can only occur in the substantial form of a *psyche*. And it equally denies an independent being of the latter but assumes (apart from the Thomist reserve with respect to the human rational soul) that the substantial form of a composite can only be realized in a specific "matter". The Aristotelian-Thomistic view does not know any other matter in a living body than "living" matter, *i.e.* in its frame of thought, *animated* matter.

The answer to the question concerned must be: In his philosophy of organic nature DRIESCH does not start from the Greek basic motive of neo-Thomism. Rather his basic motive is that of nature and freedom in the modern Humanist sense [1]. The Greek idea of *hulè* remained entirely foreign to him. His concept of matter is completely oriented to the modern deterministic science-ideal of classical natural science.

It is true that he continually avails himself of the scheme of *matter and form* and that of *act and potence*. Seemingly he even connects the particular Greek concepts of *anangkè* and *tuchè* [2]

---

[1] This is also implicitly granted by HEINICHEN in his quoted writing (p. 150), when he summarizes DRIESCH's view of the relation between entelechy and causality as follows: 'In der Naturphilosophie gibt es der Begriff der Freiheit nicht, der die Voraussetzung alles Schöpferischen, Neuen ist; es *darf* für die Naturphilosophie keine Freiheit geben, denn im strengen Wortsinne bedeutet Freiheit die Verneinung eindeutiger Bestimmtheit, und es ist unmöglich zu denken, dasz bei gegebenen Umständen *entweder* das eine *oder* das andere geschehen könne." This statement is completely oriented to the classical deterministic view of nature in its dialectical contrast with the Humanist freedom motive.

[2] Cf. what we have observed with respect to these Greek notions in volume I, pp. 61 ff.

with his notion of matter. But in reality all these basic ideas have been fundamentally transformed by the Humanist motive of nature and freedom.

In his *Ordnungslehre* DRIESCH speaks of a basic dualism in the world which he characterizes as the irreconcible contrast between "totality" and "chance" [1]. But his idea of chance is diametrically opposed to the Greek idea of *tuchè* and *anangkè*. When he introduces this notion, he immediately adds: I explicitly define the concept "chance" as *Nichtganzbezogenheit* (*i.e.*, what is not related to a totality) — consequently not, *e.g.*, as "lack of cause" [2]. And then he continues as follows: 'This contrast between totality and chance is the fundamental opposition from which all contrasts usually called "dualistic" derive; *viz.* the contrast between animate and inanimate, form and matter, mind and body, soul and body, *etc.* One may define chance as a concurrence of mutually independent causal series, as *e.g.*, the great embryologist C. E. v. BAER does. But this is only a particular instance of chance which is implied in our completely universal delimitation of this concept' [3].

In "matter" (*i.e.* "inanimate nature") chance rules without restriction *("schlechthin")*, though we have seen that DRIESCH conceives of "matter" in *a rigid mechanically determined way.* Only a few traits of unity and totality are realized in it (*e.g.*, the unity of the three-dimensional physical space in which all matter is supposed to move).

Yet the dualist motive of "totality" and "chance" is not identical with the Humanist basic motive of freedom and nature, which

---

[1] *Ordnungslehre* (2e Aufl.), p. 446 ff.

[2] Cf. also DRIESCH's treatise *Wahrscheinlichkeit und Freiheit* (Phil. Gegenwartsfragen, 1933) p. 170: 'Das zufällige Ereignis ist also nicht "Glied" eines Ganzen, sondern nur "Teil" einer summenhaften Gesamtheit'. [An accidental event is consequently not an "(organic) part" of a whole, but only an "element" of a sum total of elements.] The concept "*summenhafte Gesamtheit*" in DRIESCH's terminology always has an atomistic mechanistic sense.

[3] *Ordnungslehre,* p. 446: 'Dieser Gegensatz zwischen Ganzheit und Zufall ist das grundlegende, auf das alle Gegensätze, die man gelegentlich "dualistisch" zu nennen pflegt, zurückgehen, also der Gegensatz von Belebten und Unbelebten, Form und Materie, Geist und Körper, Seele und Leib und andere. Auch wer, wie z.B. der grosze Embryologe C. E. v. BAER, den Zufall als das Zusammentreffen von einander unabhängiger Kausalreihen definiert, fixiert damit etwas Bestimmtes, was sich unserer ganz allgemeinen Umgrenzung des Zufalls einfügt.'

in its deepest sense rules DRIESCH's entire thought. In his *Wirklichkeitslehre* DRIESCH opposes *genuine freedom* to *univocal determinateness* in the process of genesis. The question as to whether there exists freedom in this sense is called here a metaphysical question of belief which should remain unanswered by philosophy as science [1]. This standpoint differs from KANT's. For KANT answers this question in a positive sense, in his *Critique of Practical Reason,* and he may do so because he does not hold to an exclusively scientific view of philosophy. DRIESCH and KANT agree, however, in the opinion that "freedom" is not a question of scientific demonstration, but of belief. Their difference of opinion concerning the material conception of freedom will be considered presently in a footnote [2].

In any case DRIESCH's philosophy of nature remains entirely enclosed within the frame of determinism. Also his neo-vitalism is not at all intended to place a barrier in the way of the classical science-ideal with its postulate of a closed causal explanation of nature. On the contrary, its true intention was to save the concept of natural law also in the sphere of bio-phenomena, although this concept must assume a different sense here from its mechanistic conception. The concept of totality *(Ganzheit)* remains with DRIESCH an ordering notion pertaining to *natural phenomena.* As such it seems not to be oriented to the freedom-motive of the Humanist personality-ideal, as was the case in German freedom-idealism.

And yet, when we penetrate into the deeper strata of DRIESCH's philosophy of nature, it is hardly to be denied that in the dualist theme of totality and chance, the influence of the dialectical basic motive of freedom and nature is present. DRIESCH's particular idea of totality, in its contrast to that of a mere summation of mechanical elements, is doubtless dependent on the influence of SCHELLING's freedom-idealism upon the philosophy of nature. In DRIESCH the romantic idealist idea of totality has only been transformed into a *second concept of natural causality.* The purpose of this transformation was to save the classical science-ideal with respect to the *bio*-phenomena.

The common origin of DRIESCH's and SCHELLING's idea of totality was the idea of totality developed in KANT's *Kritik der teleologischen Urteilskraft.* In this latter work this notion was only

---

[1] *Wirklichkeitslehre,* p. 93—122.

[2] Cf. p. 749, note 1.

serviceable to the dialectical attempt at bridging the cleft between nature and freedom, if only by way of an "as if"-judgment.

Driesch has intentionally elevated this teleological idea of totality to a new category of natural science, next to the mechanistic categories of classical physics [1]. So it has become a constitutive category of science itself.

Nevertheless, this "ordering notion" continues to betray its origin from the Humanistic freedom-idea by its polar contrast to the mechanistic concept of a determined aggregate of elements. This polar contrast between "mechanism" and "totality" is not to be bridged in Driesch's philosophy of nature. It implies a mechanistic view of "matter" in the sense of classical physics and — as its polar counter-part — an entelechy as "substance" which works upon matter after the pattern of a "totality-causality".

An acceptance of the Aristotelian-Thomistic view of a living whole was thus already excluded by the transcendental basic Idea of Driesch's philosophy.

§ 5 - THE RELATION OF THE MOLECULAR (OR CRYSTALLINE) STRUCTURES OF MATTER TO THE LIVING ORGANISM AND THE LIVING BODY. THE PROBLEM CONCERNING THE "BIO-SUBSTANCE" IN WOLTERECK.

Woltereck's hypothesis concerning a particular bio-substance.

After our critical analysis of the mechanistic and the neo-vitalist standpoints, we shall now consider in more detail Woltereck's earlier mentioned hypothesis concerning a particular "bio-substance". Woltereck has initially bound this hypothesis to the explicit reserve that he accepts it only "until it should be refuted".

---

[1] This scientific transformation of the Kantian notion of a teleological whole was facilitated by the fact that Driesch denies the genuine freedom-character of Kant's practical Idea of liberty. Kant had identified the latter with the Idea of "moral autonomy" of the "pure human will" regulated by the "categorical imperative". According to Driesch, genuine metaphysical freedom is incompatible with any general law imposing itself upon human action. This thesis must consequently include Kant's categorical imperative. In Driesch' opinion genuine freedom is only compatible with a consistent pantheism, in the sense of a "becoming deity" lacking also any determination by a constant divine nature.

It must be evident beforehand that the introduction of this hypothesis can have nothing to do with the older vitalist view of a vital matter. WOLTERECK does not in the least intend to withdraw his hypothetical material bio-substance from physico-chemical scientific research. On the contrary, he blames DRIESCH for having prematurely substituted the "metaphysical notion of "entelechy" for an as yet unknown property of the "physical real *plasm*". He is of the opinion that DRIESCH has not proved the necessity of this substitution by the exclusion of genuine physico-chemical possibilities.

On the other hand his standpoint is equally opposed to the mechanist view according to which bio-phenomena are exclusively explainable from intricate physico-chemical processes. He thinks that his hypothetical material bio-substance is connected with "immaterial and conditional structural constants" ("*Wenn-so-constanten*") as potencies, which as such pass away together with their material bearer.

Physico-chemical bio-phenomena, accessible to sensory perception and logical analysis are, according to him, only the temporal-spatial *outside* of living organisms. The genuine *essence* of the latter is their immaterial *inside*. Biological research may only approach this essential inside by conceiving a vital process as an "inner experience" of the living being.

As we have seen, WOLTERECK considers an artificial bio-synthesis to be impossible *in principle*. He agrees with the opinion that a causal physico-chemical analysis of bio-phenomena encounters an insuperable limit: 'Our causal-material analysis of bio-phenomena', so he observes, 'cannot exceed a certain limit. However wonderful the advances which we owe to experimental analysis..., by clarifying the material hereditary units, the organisers and hormones, and by the discovery of the behaviour and operation of these bearers of impulses, this analysis has reached its ultimate limit; or to be more precise: it *will* have reached this limit when we arrive at a complete knowledge of the field-conditions and field-processes lying at the foundation of this behaviour and operation' [1].

[1] *Op. cit.*, p. 512/3: 'Wir kommen mit der kausal-materiellen Analyse der Lebenserscheinungen über einen bestimmten Punkt nicht hinaus. So wunderful die Fortschritte sind, die wir der experimentellen Analyse... verdanken; mit der Klarstellung von materiellen Erbeinheiten, von Organisatoren und von Hormonen und mit der Enthüllung des Verhaltens

And finally we must remark that WOLTERECK's hypothetical "bio-substance" is no more meant in a metaphysical sense than initially DRIESCH's "entelechy" was. WOLTERECK himself points to the multivocality of the term "substance" in its philosophical use. He explicitly declares that he wants to understand by it nothing but "living mass".

By the latter, however, he decidedly means a specific "living matter", a complex of molecules fundamentally distinct from inanimate matter or dead plasm in consequence of an as yet unknown physico-chemical property, a so-called "primary bio-chemical moment". In addition, this bio-substance is supposed to be characterized by the two basic vital properties of autonomous capability for stimuli and genetic continuity. WOLTERECK *compares this specific physico-chemical condition of his "bio-substance" with that of radio-active elements and aromatic combinations, which are also distinct from other kinds of matter by specific "moments".*

In favour of his hypothesis he first points to the fact that, notwithstanding our lack of knowledge of the "bio-chemical basic moment", we may clearly establish a fundamental difference between the material components of a living cell-body: on the one hand we discover components which *produce* other kinds of matter without passing away themselves; on the other hand we meet with material components which *are produced* without being capable of *producing.*

An intermediate position is taken by *enzymes,* which do not reproduce themselves and consequently cannot be viewed as "living components", but nevertheless do not partake in the chemical processes influenced by them in a regulative sense.

As "living substance" WOLTERECK only regards the producing "chief substance" of all bio-systems. Every bio-system seems to contain three components:

1. units effectuating the processes of dissimilation and assimilation;
2. so-called inductive material units which are operative in a determining, or regulating, or organizing way, respectively (genes, hormones, enzymes, organizers);
3. the "*matrix*" (germ-plasm, idio-plasm, reserve-plasm), *i.e.*

---

und Wirkens dieser Impulsträger ist die fatale Grenze der materiell-kausalen Analyse erreicht, genauer: *wird* sie erreicht sein, wenn wir die ihnen zugrunde liegenden Feldzustände und Feldvorgänge vollständig kennen werden.'

that unknown living basic matter of the cell which remains constant in spite of all changes in the bio-chemical constellation. This "matrix" reproduces itself and potentially guarantees all typical properties of the different species as well as all operative functions of the living cell. And it also produces, if need be, the inductive material components.

The inductive material components in the living cell-body: enzymes, hormones, organisers and genes.

Now we may establish that modern biology has indeed succeeded in showing the presence of inductive material factors in the living cell-body. This result has been reached in a threefold way.

First, physiological chemistry has succeeded in establishing the catalytic operation of enzymes in metabolic processes. In addition, it has established by serological research the function of the specificity of protein combinations produced by living organisms according to their different geno-types. In recent times physiological chemistry has also elucidated the enormous significance of the hormones or internal secretions [1].

The existence of "organizers" has been indisputably shown by so-called "developmental mechanics" founded by WILHELM ROUX. These "organisers" have appeared to exercise a determining influence upon the embryonic development of a living body and its particular organs. Continued research has brought to light that here, too, we are confronted with particular *material* factors.

There is an abundance of experimental material with respect to this subject-matter. We have already mentioned the experiments of SPEMANN and his school with the transplantation of cells from the so-called blastopore, *i.e.* the invagination of the *gastrula* [2] of a developing embryo.

---

[1] Physiological chemistry has already succeeded in synthetically preparing different kinds of hormones (insulin, adrenalin, thyroxin, different genital hormones *etc.*), which have found an extensive application both in medicine and zoology.

[2] By means of division of the animal germ-cell there first arise two cells, then four, thereupon eight, sixteen, *etc.* Finally there arises a solid ball of cells, which is called *morula* (*i.e.* mulberry). By secretion of liquid the latter turns into a hollow ball, called *blastula*, which then further is transformed into the *gastrula*. During the latter process, the so-called gastrulation, there arise two different layers of cells, the inner and outer blastoderm, between which in all higher animals very soon a meso-blastoderm is formed.

It appeared that the fixation of the developmental direction of the separate parts of an embryo occurs the sooner in proportion as the latter's position is nearer to the blastopore. It was already known that in the developmental phase of an embryo a living cell (or groups of cells) has much more genetic potencies than that which is finally *realized.* In the fixation of the ultimate developmental *direction* the neighbouring cell or group of cells appears to exercise a determining influence. This operation occurs in a strict law-conformity and may eventually also deviate from the total building-plan of the organism. The question, *e.g.*, as to whether from one of the two part-cells of the egg of a sea-hedgehog, a complete or the half of an embryo develops, is dependent on a complex of causes. These causes partly lie beyond the internal working-sphere of this single cell, though it is certain that at first the capability or incapability of the internal structure of the egg's protoplasma to *regulation* is decisive here[1]. If the cell is separated from its fellow-cell, then it will produce a complete embryo, if it remains united with the latter it will produce a half one. In this case the developmental law of the separate cells apparently suits the building-plan of the total organism. But under certain conditions it also appeared possible to cause entirely abnormal formations of organs and even a double embryo by means of transplantation of cells.

SPEMANN's disciple H. MANGOLD succeeded in giving rise to an entirely new embryo by transplanting a piece of the blastopore of a gastrula in a tissue of another embryo, *viz.* that tissue which later on develops into abdominal-skin. This new embryo, however, *arising in the place of inplantation, did not merely grow* from the transplanted cell-groups, but for the greater part by far from the cells of the host-embryo. The latter were now determined in a quite different direction! Later on many other experiments with such remarkable "chimera-formations" have occurred. Thereby it has been indisputably established that the cells of the blastopore have the potence of compelling the neighbouring cell-groups to develop the form in question. This was the experimental proof of SPEMANN's hypothesis that the blastopore must contain the organizing centre[2].

---

[1] Cf. DRIESCH, *Phil. d. Org.*, pp. 56 ff.

[2] At a more advanced stage of development, however, the direction of the development appears to be already determined to such a degree that a fundamental change is no longer possible.

It was a matter of course that the mechanist trend conceived these "organizers" as material substances expanding themselves from the centre concerned to the environment. The neo-vitalists, on the contrary, viewed these "organisers" in the nature of the case as effects of the immaterial entelechy. The experiments with abnormal organ- and chimera-formations seemed to contradict this neo-vitalist interpretation. But DRIESCH tried to reconcile these experiments with the neo-vitalist view by means of his building-plan-theory or by assuming "sub-entelechies" which operate without subjecting themselves to the rough building-plan of the whole [1]. Meanwhile, later experiments have shown that the "organisers" are indeed inductive material factors.

HOLTFRETER and other investigators of the Dahlem Institute succeeded in producing the induction of an embryo in the indifferent abdominal tissue of the host-animal by means of dead cellular material originating from the blastopore [2]. Thereby the supposition already made earlier that the embryonic organisers, too, are a kind of hormones (developmental hormones) was nearly elevated to certainty. But, naturally, this did not mean that the rightness of the mechanistic interpretation was experimentally proved. For the determining influence of the material organisers is completely dependent upon the potencies of the living cell-organism of the host-animal.

The third kind of inductive material factors has been brought to light by modern genetics in combination with a microscopic investigation of the cells, especially the germ-cells and their nuclear components. These combined investigations have led to the discovery of the *genes* in the chromosomes [3] of the cell-nucleus, which are viewed as the material bearers of factors of hereditary dispositions.

The existence of these genes and their local distribution in the chromosomes can no longer be doubted. For it has been experimentally proved that in the case of an artificial partial des-

---

[1] *Phil. d. Org.*, p. 483.

[2] Cf. the report of these experiments in the review *Naturwissenschaften*, Bnd. 51 (1932), pp. 972 ff.

[3] Chromosomes are the looplike threads into which, during the process of cell-division, the chromatin (*i.e.* the nuclear matter capable of being coloured) contracts itself. This phenomenon is usually accompanied by a temporary disappearance of the two other important nuclear components, *viz.* the nucleoles (nuclear corpuscles) and later on also the nuclear membrane.

truction of a chromosome in the germ-cells of *Drosophila* also particular properties of the individual had vanished. According to the genetical analysis of MORGAN and his school (whose results have been recorded in the famous chromosome-maps) these properties must have had their seat in the vanished piece of chromatin. MORGAN, who was certainly not an adherent of the mechanistic standpoint, supposed that the genes are fitted into a linear ordering of the chromatin particles of a chromosome. In this case the structure of a polypeptid-molecule urges itself upon us, in which the separate genes are supposed to function as changeable radicals. Other investigators have supposed that genes, too, are a kind of enzyme-like material components which have some connection with the above-mentioned "developmental hormones". It needs no further argument that also the discovery of these genes has nothing to do with a mechanistic interpretation of the hereditary phenomena.

WOLTERECK is of the opinion that the experimental material briefly outlined above may be considered to be a sufficient foundation for his view of the cell-structure which starts from the existence of a material bio-substance.

As we have seen, he distinguished three components in the biochemical constellation of the cell: a "matrix", material components bringing about the processes of assimilation and dissimilation, and inductive material factors of a determining, organizing and regulating character respectively. Now he assumes that this distinction as such has been *proved*; opinions may differ only concerning the question how these three kinds of components *cohere with each other*[1].

In his opinion the best founded hypothesis is the following: In every living being there exists a specific living material substance, *viz.* the "matrix", which differs with the different species of living beings. There exist more simple constellations of matter (radicals), dependent on the matrix, which cause the assimilatory and dissimilatory processes. These radicals are continually changing by partially falling asunder and partially taking up material combinations, *i.e.* by dividing themselves and growing, *etc.* They may be considered to be identical with HEIDENHAIN's "protomeries" or minimal living particles. Finally there exist particular material components (produced by the matrix) which are operative in organizing, differentiating and regulating the

[1] *Op. cit.*, p. 352.

cell-organism. Among these latter the genes have their seat in the nuclear loops of the germ-cells. They are to be looked upon either as micro-grains of chromatin or as radicals within the latter. The localization of the genes is known. As to the material components causing the assimilatory and dissimilatory processes it may be assumed as probable that they are distributed over the whole cell as "protomeries". But as to the matrix we do not know where it has its proper seat [1].

With respect to this question WOLTERECK assumes two possible hypotheses: either the matrix is spread everywhere in the plasm and nucleus of the cell in equal proportions, and it produces, besides other structures and material components, the chromatin threads and the genes; or the matrix is present in a concentrated form in the chromosomes, perhaps in the form of a chain of molecules with many side-chains, radicals, *etc.* more or less loosely combined with the latter. In this case the radicals hanging on it are the genes, which later on produce differentiating impulses.

This latter hypothesis seems to WOLTERECK the best founded supposition because it corresponds more precisely to the results of cytological and genetical research. But he does not want to exclude the possibility that also outside of a cell-nucleus there are determining hereditary material components which might be called "plasmatic matrix".

The question concerning the seat of the "organizers" and "regulators" within a cell-body then remains unanswered. But in any case these material components are also produced by the matrix.

Criticism of WOLTERECK's theory.

It cannot be doubtful that the kernel of WOLTERECK's theory must be sought in the assumption of a "matrix" as a material bio-substance. It is remarkable that he initially introduced the latter only in a hypothetical sense and cautiously bound this hypothesis to the reserve: "*bis zu ihrer Widerlegung*". He even explicitly warned his readers "that an unknown moment" (*viz.* the assumed bio-chemical basic moment of the matrix) "can neither be strictly proved nor refuted", but only "be rendered probable or improbable". Meanwhile this reserve has apparently been abandoned in the continuation of his argument. It is indeed

[1] *Op. cit.*, p. 352.

surprising that later on WOLTERECK speaks of the existence of his "matrix" as an experimentally established or proved fact (*op. cit.*, p. 352).

He does not inform us how his hypothesis concerning a bio-substance has been proved. From the experimental material briefly mentioned above, this proof can certainly not be derived.

On the contrary, we have seen that the material components of a cell whose inductive, determining or regulative functions have been experimentally established, have more and more proved to be *non-living* combinations. As to genes WOLTERECK himself has observed that they cannot be pure living units [1]. And he has also emphatically established that the existence of "bio-molecules", which are supposed to bring about the assimilatory and dissimilatory processes, has never been *proved*.

Thus the question arises: How has WOLTERECK arrived at his hypothesis concerning the "matrix" as a constant bio-substance which would continually reproduce itself? To answer this question we should consider that WOLTERECK himself has identified his "matrix" with the concepts germ-plasm, idio-plasm or hereditary material. He prefers his own term only because the others are more or less burdened by the theories which have availed themselves of them.

WEISMANN's theory concerning the continuity of the germ-plasm.

The term germ-plasm has been introduced by the famous biologist AUGUST WEISMANN, one of the prominent representatives of the older Darwinist theory of evolution. WEISMANN was of the opinion that from the very beginning in the process of embryonic development those cells are separated which later on become the so-called mother-cells or germ-cells. They form the continuous *"Keimbahn"*, as WEISMANN called it, passing through the generations, whereas the body-cells, or the *soma*, are again and again split off, as it were, from the former. The germ-cells of the present generation are thus not produced by the individual bodies in which they are taken up; rather they are the direct products of the germ-cells of the previous generation from which also the soma-cells of the present generation originate. This was the theory concerning the *continuity of germ-plasm*, which notwithstanding the strong opposition it aroused at first,

---

[1] *Op. cit.*, p. 353.

has at present been rather generally accepted. This acceptance was especially owing to the fact that the so-called cell-lineage research succeeded in directly tracing the isolated developmental course of the germ-cells [1].

Meanwhile, DRIESCH has pointed to the fact that all this only concerns empirical data of *descriptive* embryology. The more recent discoveries concerning the restitution of a living organism have made it necessary to add so many reserves to the theory of the "*spezifische Keimbahne*" that it practically loses any significance. For these discoveries have shown that in the earliest phases of development a cell possesses a so-called "masked" prospective potency which may lead to results quite different from what has been factually reached. According to DRIESCH, this new experimental material entitles us to ascribe to all the cells of a *soma* in principle all morphogenetic possibilities. Perhaps it would be possible under certain conditions (as yet unknown) that any soma-cell becomes a germ-cell [2]. This is why DRIESCH is of the opinion that WEISMANN's concept of "*Keimbahn*" has only a descriptive character and cannot be elevated to a fundamental concept.

However this may be, WEISMANN himself has certainly not conceived the "continuous germ-plasm" as a specific "bio-substance", in the sense of WOLTERECK. Much rather the intention of his theory was to provide mechanistic evolutionism with a general foundation. And this evolutionist view in principle rejected the assumption of a specific "bio-substance".

Even if WEISMANN's theory should be considered as *proved* by the research of cell-lineage, this proof can thus certainly not pertain to WOLTERECK's hypothetical "matrix". *The real existence of such a material bio-substance can never be proved in a purely experimental way. For the question as to whether material combinations as such may be qualified by a subjective biotic func-*

---

[1] Cf. BAVINK, *op. cit.*, pp. 406 ff., who apparently assumes that WEISMANN's theory has been *proved* by the results of this research.

[2] *Phil. d. Org.*, p. 210. From a quite different standpoint WEISMANN's theory is rejected by the neo-Lamarckians, such as O. HERTWIG (*Allgemeine Biologie*, 6th and 7th ed. 1923). The latter holds to the transmission of acquired characters in the hereditary process by means of an alteration of the idio-plasm of the egg-cell. This theory is naturally obliged to deny the independence of germ-plasm with respect to the *soma*.

tion necessarily implies a philosophical problem of structure[1]. *And the standpoint chosen with respect to the latter problem in principle determines any theoretical interpretation of the results* of experimental research'.

It is not the continuity of germ-plasm which is at issue here. Rather we are confronted with the question concerning the relation between *typically biotically and typically physico-chemically qualified structures of individuality within an apparently present totality-structure of the living cell-body.*

We are certainly entitled to say that the results of experimental research have made it necessary to distinguish between living and non-living components of a cell. WOLTERECK himself does so emphatically. But the structural problem proper is not thereby solved. Already the way in which a scientific investigator *posits* it, is philosophically conditioned.

The influence of the metaphysical substance-concept upon WOLTERECK's theory of "matrix".

Now it seems to me that WOLTERECK, however reserved he appeared to be with respect to the metaphysical substance-concept, has nevertheless unconsciously been influenced by it. We could establish the same state of affairs with DRIESCH. Even the *term* "substance", however reservedly used, turns out to exercise a kind of magic influence upon many serious scientific theorists. DRIESCH elevated his "entelechy" to a "substance" of the living organic form-totality. WOLTERECK conceived his "matrix" as a "bio-substance", in the sense of a specific "living matter", which in addition was supposed to possess an inner-side as an "experiential centre".

When elaborating his matrix-theory, WOLTERECK appears to return to the hypothesis that the "bio-substance" may display the intricate structure of a polypeptid molecule. And he does so notwithstanding the fact that he himself had emphatically established that such a structural model can never account for the typical *centered* structure of a living cell.

But a molecular theory of "living matter" necessarily implies the tendency to eliminate the typical totality-structure of a living organism. And this consequence decidedly contradicts WOLTERECK's earlier statement that the living cell is the minimal whole capable of life in an independent sense.

---

[1] This is implicitly acknowledged by WOLTERECK himself insofar as he ascribes to his hypothetical matrix an "invisible basic structure".

Now we should bear in mind that until the XXth century the modern concept of matter was itself connected with a mechanistic substance-concept. Classical physics founded by GALILEO and NEWTON held to the metaphysical conception of "matter", as a spatial mechanical substance remaining quantitatively constant in all physico-chemical changes. As soon as this classical substance-concept of matter appeared to be untenable, it was methodically transformed into a mathematical-physical *concept of function,* a functional mass-concept, which as such lacks any ontological connotation as a rigid substantial constant. This mass-concept only pertains to the physico-chemical *energy-aspect* of experiential reality.

Modern chemistry ascribes to the general concept matter only the meaning of a certain system of equilibrium between *protons, neutrons* and *electrons.*

Specific kinds of matter are only known in the atomic structures of chemical elements and in the molecular or crystalline form-structures of their chemical combinations.

These structures have proved to be *physico-chemically qualified,* in the sense of our theory of individuality-structures. *Only by restricting the concept of matter to these typical structures can we ascribe to it a univocal sense, founded in the plastic horizon of human experience.*

As soon as, in line with the Aristotelian idea of *hulè,* "matter" is conceived of as mere potentiality, it can no longer be viewed as a *real* constellation in itself. In this case it must be reduced to a metaphysical *component* of a "composite natural substance", implying a specific "substantial form" as its complement. But neither in the frame of thought of modern natural science nor in that of the Greek and scholastic form-matter theme can it make sense to speak of a specific material *bio*-substance, in contrast to an *in-organic* substance of "dead matter".

WOLTERECK's standpoint regarding this bio-substance is indeed far from clear. On the one hand he emphatically rejects any mechanistic reduction of a living organism to mere material processes. In this context he observes that his hypothesis of a "matrix" only leads to "shifting the indubitable visible particularity of all living bodies into the invisible basic structure in which the spatial and temporal specificities of the organism must be somehow represented and prepared" [1]. *But, on the other*

[1] *Op. cit.,* p. 330.

hand, he parallels the "primary bio-chemical element" by which "living matter" is to be distinct from "dead matter", with the specific properties of radio-active kinds of matter and aromatic combinations. By so doing WOLTERECK apparently overlooks that the characteristic properties of these latter kinds of matter are indubitably *determined by their physico-chemical structure.* The assumption of a specific "living mass" or "*bio*-substance", however, implies an inner contradiction. For, on the one hand, this bio-substance is supposed to have a typical physico-chemical structure (although unknown up to now) by which it is determined as matter; on the other, it must be qualified by a typical biotic moment.

For such a *biotic* qualification must doubtless be assumed if there be any question of a *bio*-substance. ROUX [1] has already repeatedly pointed to the fact that a system of material combinations (A, B, C, D, *etc.*) may chemically effect the rise of a matter X in a continually increasing quantity, but that from a purely chemical point of view it is entirely impossible that X assimilates itself. Such an assimilation can certainly not be a *purely* chemical process.

In WOLTERECK's own explanations the contradiction mentioned reveals itself in the above analysed way: He starts with accepting the living cell in its totality as the minimal unit capable of independent life. But, in consequence of his hypothesis concerning a "bio-substance", he finally arrives at the hypothetical assumption of a molecular structure of a material "matrix", which must explain even the typical centered structure of the living cell-organism [2]. And he does so notwithstanding he himself has emphasized that the causal physico chemical analysis encounters insuperable limits in the bio-chemical constellation!

In this way WOLTERECK, too, has involved himself in the inner antinomies of the substance-concept. Thereby his attempt at overcoming the dilemma vitalism-mechanism was doomed to fail. The course of his argument clearly shows that he, too, had

---

[1] *Ueber die bei der Vererbung von Variationen anzunehmenden Vorgänge* (Vorträge und Aufsätze über Entwicklungsmechanik nr. 19 (1913), p. 4.

[2] For in this way WOLTERECK later on elaborates his thesis "that the indisputibly present bio-specificities are caused by a particular chemico-physical situation" (*op. cit.*, p. 331).

recourse to the substance-concept for lack of insight into the modal structures and the typical individuality-structures of our experiential horizon. DRIESCH elevated "life" to an "immaterial substance" and called it "entelechy". WOLTERECK on the one hand reduces "life" to a particular physico-chemical constellation of a material bio-substance, on the other he sublimates it to an immaterial inner experience of a non-spatial ontical centre. How can we explain this remarkable dualist view?

WOLTERECK'S philosophical standpoint. His dynamical ontological *"Stufentheorie"*.

WOLTERECK'S biological view is only explicable from his later work *Ontologie des Lebendigen* (1940), in which he reveals himself as an adherent of a dynamical *"Stufentheorie"* of reality. This theory tries to overcome the dilemma mechanism-vitalism by means of a genetic monism which nevertheless accepts irreducible levels of becoming. This means that on the one hand the irreducible character of life as a new level of reality is acknowledged, but on the other the process of becoming is conceived as a continuous evolution in which "life" is viewed as an "emergence" of physico-chemical constellations. We have already encountered this "emergent evolutionism" in an earlier context [1]. WOLTERECK is of the opinion that "life" may very well be conceived genetically as an "emergence" of a-biotic matter-combinations; just like the genesis of the different chemical elements may be explained from an increase of the possibilities of a material basic substance, or psychical life as an "emergence" of merely biotic, and "mind" as an "emergence" of psychical life. According to WOLTERECK, the rise of different autonomous "levels of reality" is ruled by "structural constants" which he also calls "autonomous powers", "determinants", "imagoids" or "ideas".

Thereby he involves himself in the antinomy between the assumed constancy of these structural determinants on the one

---

[1] This emergent evolutionism has in recent times been in vogue with many philosophically trained biologists and physicists. L. MORGAN is one of the chief representatives of this view. It is also adhered to by J. H. WOODGER and A. N. WHITEHEAD, by B. BAVINK and WOLTERECK and different other scholars. The *ontological* view of WOLTERECK is strongly influenced by NICOLAI HARTMANN'S *"Schichtentheorie"*.

hand, and the continuity and unity of the process of becoming, on the other. WOLTERECK himself has acknowledged that on his standpoint this antinomy is insoluble: 'As to the living determinants of becoming', he observes, 'and the determinants of value, there exists an unsolved antinomy between the state of affairs meant by the term *validity* and that concerning the "*genesis* of validity". The former requires exemption from time or at least indifference to time, the latter refers to the *genesis* of ideas and values which undeniably arise from human cultural activity and which we surmise in the becoming of organisms' [1].

WOLTERECK rejects the solution of this antinomy presented by Platonism and the modern philosophy of values, which have recourse to a supra-temporal kingdom of Ideas or values. Rather he resigns to the sceptical conclusion: 'we will not succeed in solving the antinomy between the a-temporal validity and the genesis of values.'

The origin of this antinomy, however, is evident. The latter is due to an overstraining of the modal aspect of biotic development in its *subject*-side. We are here confronted with an *irrationalistic evolutionism* that views the *structural laws* as products of *the creative freedom* of a *"Welt-Subjekt"*, which itself is involved in a process of continual development. Here, too, the Humanist basic motive of *nature and freedom* is the ultimate, indeed *religious,* moving power of theoretical thought. The evolutionist basic idea of the latter implies the attempt to conceive "freedom" (in the irrationalist sense of "creative subjective freedom") as the "completion of nature" (*Vollendung der Natur)* [2].

---

[1] *Ontologie des Lebendigen* (1940) § 176: *Die Antinomie zwischen Gelten und Ursprung des Geltens.* In the German text this passage reads as follows: 'Für die lebendigen Werdebestimmer und Wert-determinanten besteht eine ungelöste Antinomie zwischen dem Sachverhalt *Geltung,* der Zeitlosigkeit oder mindestens Zeitindifferenz erfordert, und dem Sachverhalt "*Entstehen von Geltung*" von Ideen und Werten, wie sie aus menschlichem Schaffen unverkennbar hervorgehen und wie wir sie im Werden der Organismen vermuten.'

[2] *Ontologie,* p. 9: 'Eine selbstverständliche Aussage wird für unsere Untersuchung wesentlich werden: Ausdruck, *Gesetze* und *Sinn* gehen nicht auf Ursachen zurück, sondern können nur als *freie* Setzungen verstanden werden. Wenn überhaupt Metaphysisches allem Zweifel entrückt ist, so ist es die *schöpferische Freiheit* des *Sinn*-gebenden Weltsubjekts...

On this standpoint any insight into the modal structures and individuality structures of empirical reality is precluded, just as in the case of DRIESCH.

This appears, moreover, from the following statement of WOLTERECK: 'the spiritual-psychic phenomena, the productive activities and their results belong just as much to life as, *e.g.*, the shell formation or movement of *protozoa*. A temple, a book, a sonata or a strategic plan are bio-phenomena, results of the productive activity of living "subjects of happening". And literally the same assertion holds with respect to the buildings made by termites, the cocoon spun by a caterpillar, the melody of a bird call, the leaf-incision made by a birch-leaf-roller: *Anybody who does not understand this coherence of the phenomena mentioned, because it seems to be paradoxal, will hardly ever completely conceive the real extent and contents of the concept of life*' [1]. (Italics are mine).

Such an utterance clearly testifies to a complete lack of insight into the difference between the modal sense of the biotic aspect and the biotic *analogies* presenting themselves within the modal structures of all post-biotic modalities of experience. In addition this utterance reveals a lack of insight into the difference between the modal structure of the biotic aspect and the typical structures of individuality *functioning within it.* As a

---

Wir werden dabei die Grundlage nicht zu verleugnen haben, von der unser Forschen ausgeht: die Erkenntnis der Einen, Totalen alles Erfahrbare Umfassende Wirklichkeit der "*Natur*" (I italicize). Das kann, wer will, eine "naturalistische" Grundlage nennen.' [A statement which is indeed a matter of course will become of essential importance to our inquiry: Expression, *laws* and *meaning* do not derive from causes but are only to be understood as *free* creations. If any metaphysical state of affairs is beyond all doubt, then it is the *creative freedom* of the World-Subject which *gives meaning*... Besides we should not deny the foundation from which our investigation starts, *viz.* the knowledge of the one total reality of "nature" embracing all that is capable of being experienced. If one wants to do so, this can be called a "naturalistic" foundation.]

[1] *Op. cit.*, p. 52: 'die geistig-seelische Phänomene, Leistungen, Produkte gehören genau so zum Leben wie etwa die Schalenbindung oder die Bewegung von Protoza. Ein Tempel oder ein Buch, eine Sonate oder ein strategischer Plan sind Lebens-erscheinungen, Leistungen lebendiger Geschehens-subjekte; und wörtlich das gleiche gilt für die Bauten von Termiten, für das Gespinst einer Raupe, für die Tonfolge eines Vogelrufs, für den Blattschnitt eines Birkenrollers: *Wem diese Zusammengehörigkeit, weil sie paradox aussieht,* nicht einleuchten will, der wird kaum jemals Umfang und Inhalt des Lebensbegriffes völlig verstehen."

result WOLTERECK falls back into a genuine "biologism" whereby the concept of life loses any defined modal sense [1].

We have seen, however, that a clear insight into the relation between the physico-chemically qualified material combinations and the living organism within the total structure of a cell, depends on a clear insight into the different modal aspects of the latter. And the very insight into the inner nature and the unbreakable inter-modal coherence of these modal aspects is precluded in principle by the acceptance of the substance-concept.

Our critical analysis of the theories of DRIESCH and WOLTERECK has continually confirmed the correctness of this thesis.

A brief resumption of my own view.

When engaging in an inquiry into the intricate structure of a living cell we have made a sharp distinction between three different individuality-structures: first, those of the physico-chemically qualified material combinations, which themselves in their molecular or quasi-crystalline form-minima appeared to be genuine enkaptic structural wholes; secondly, that of the cell's living organism, in which these building-materials are enkaptically bound; thirdly, that of the cell-body as a biotically qualified enkaptic form-totality embracing the other structures in the enkaptic bond of its form.

This distinction was oriented to the vegetable cell. In the case of an animal cell the structure of the living organism is the foundation of a higher structure, *viz.* that of the *sensorium*, which has a psychic qualification. This implies that the enkaptic structural whole of an animal cell-body is also psychically qualified.

The genuine bio-chemical constellation appeared to occur within the structure of a cell's living organism, not in the

---

[1] Also the irrationalistically conceived freedom-motive thereby assumes a patent biologistic sense. Compare the following statement (*op. cit.*, p. 122): 'Der zweite Teil der geäuszerten Erwartung' (*viz.* that the total process of becoming of the world strives after "completion" in the sense of perfection) 'sieht *im Geiste des Menschen* die Möglichkeit einer Welt-vollendung und zwar in einem zukünftigen, geadelten, schöpferisch-freien Geiste. Das ist die "Messias-erwartung" *biologisch gesehen.*' [The second part of the expectation expressed views the possibility of a completion of the world *in the human mind*, and such in a future, noble-minded, creative free spirit. *This is the Messiah-expectation biologically viewed.*] (I italicize the latter words).

molecular or quasi-crystalline structure of the material components of the cell-body. When a cell is killed, the *internal* structure of its building materials is not immediately changed. Only their biotically qualified enkaptic chemical function disappears. This is to say that the bio-chemical constellation is only built up by means of those physico-chemical functions of the material components which are enkaptically bound in the living cell-organism. These functions fall outside of the internal structure of these material components. They are not physico-chemically determined since they are subject to the continual direction of the leading biotic function of the cell-organism. They are as such internal physico-chemical functions of the latter and not of the material molecules.

But this living organism can only realize itself in the enkaptical form-totality of the living cell-body, of which (in the case of a vegetable cell) it is only the *qualifying* component, just as the chemical combination appeared to be the qualifying component of the molecular form-whole.

In the case of an animal cell the higher structure of the *sensorium* binds the lower individuality-structures of the living organism and the cell's material components. This is to say that we are confronted here not only by a *bio*-chemical constellation but in addition by a *physico*-chemical one. This state of affairs explains why an indubitably psychically qualified reaction observed in *protozoa* also displays a physico-chemical and biotic aspect.

This latter state of affairs has been completely misinterpreted from the current dualistic view-point which speaks of a "*psyche*" in distinction from the "*material body*". THEODOR HAERING also appeared to adhere to this view which, with respect to a human being, adds a "spirit" or "mind" to the *psyche*. This is why his conception of an enkaptic whole remained unsuitable. Since "psyche" and "spirit" are conceived here as immaterial entities, irrespective of the question as to whether they are or are not conceived as "substances", this view is involved in insoluble problems. How can a "psyche" or "spirit" influence a material body? DRIESCH, too, appeared to be entangled in this wrongly posited question.

The living organism of a cell is indeed living in all of its inner articulations. It can as such not contain lifeless parts. The cell-*body*, however, cannot be identical with this part-structure of its total existence. As an enkaptic form-totality it also contains the life-less material combinations bound by its living organism, which itself has appeared to be enkaptically founded in this material sub-structure. In an animal cell the structure of the living organism is bound in its turn by that of the *sensorium*, and the latter qualifies the cell-body as an enkaptic form-totality. This does not detract from the fact that in the higher differentiated poly-cellular animals, the differentiated psychic functions are bound to complexes of cells belonging to the central nervous system.

Now the significance of our distinction between the living organism and the body of a cell becomes completely clear. This distinction appears to be not at all artificial, but much rather necessary to account for the real states of affairs within the cell as a whole.

Our previous analysis of the molecular matter-structures has shown that by applying our theory of *enkapsis*, culminating in the idea of the enkaptic structural whole, two series of experimental data could be harmonized which by the application of the substance-concept seemed to contradict each other. The same holds with respect to the structure of a living cell-body.

As long as biology continues to cling to the intrinsically contradictory substance-concept, the vain contest between the mechanistic and the vitalistic views will be continued without any prospect of its definitive decision.

Once again the Aristotelian-Thomisticc substance-concept confronted with the structural problem of the living body.

A return to the Aristotelian-Thomistic substance-concept will be of no avail to vitalism in its relatively justified opposition to the mechanistic view.

For, as observed, this scholastical substance-concept compels any theory which accepts it to neglect or misinterpret the ever increasing series of experimental results which exactly seem to corroborate the mechanistic position. These results have undisputably shown that a living body contains many lifeless components which *in their internal structure* are completely determined in a physico-chemical sense.

We have seen that the neo-Thomist theory cannot account for these experimental results by means of its doctrine concerning a virtual preservation of properties of the material components in a living whole.

The question is not as to whether the material components in their enkaptic function within the living organism play *an essential rôle* in the vital processes of the body. The only question is whether they may participate in the *subjective biotic function* of the latter, *i.e.* whether they can be really *living* components of the body, just like nucleus and plasm, as enkaptically founded organic parts of a living cell, doubtless are *living* parts [1]. In the light of the experimental results this question can only be answered in the negative.

The neo-Thomist philosophy of nature can save its vitalist view only by denying the continued actual existence of the lifeless material components in the living cell-body. But exactly on this critical point the Thomistic substance-concept appears to contradict the structure of reality.

The ontological problem concerning the enkaptic structural whole of the living cell-body. An objection to our theory.

Meanwhile there remains a critical question concerning our theory of the enkaptic structural whole which may be asked from the ontological point of view. We have to consider it cautiously to secure our view against a possible misunderstanding.

From the very beginning we have observed that our conception of an enkaptic structural whole does not imply the consequence that the internal molecular or crystalline structures of the different material components are, *as such,* part-structures of the living body. Such a consequence would certainly contradict our basic tenet that the whole-part relation is exclusively determined by the structure of the whole.

But is our theory not involved in another contradiction? How can an enkaptic structural whole display an *inner unity of structure* though it seems to be constituted only in an intricate system of enkaptic interlacements? Does not the very plurality of structures interwoven within its internal sphere contradict this structural unity?

Our answer to this question is: Such a contradiction can only originate from an erroneous way of positing the intricate

---

[1] It should be borne in mind that the concepts "nucleus" and "protoplasm" are *biologically qualified* notions and do not pertain to physics and chemistry, insofar as the latter are only concerned with lifeless material combinations.

structural problem whereby our theory of the living body as an enkaptic whole is yet again misintepreted as an aggregate-theory. But it might be that our terminological indication of the structural state of affairs has as yet lacked that ultimate exactitude which is necessary to preclude such misunderstandings. A first misunderstanding may arise from indicating the enkaptically *interwoven* structures within the living body as *part*-structures of the latter. Strictly speaking, this initial indication cannot correspond to the real structural state of affairs. For even the fact that the interwoven structures are enkaptically bound by the form-totality of the whole cannot detract from their genuine structural types, which are different from that of the body as a whole.

Therefore we should now abandon this confusing terminology which is certainly inadequate from the ontological point of view. We have temporarily availed ourselves of it because our first concern was to account for the experiential data which could not be explained by applying the Aristotelian-Thomistic substance-concept. These data testified to a plurality of structures bound by a whole. The metaphysical neo-Thomist theory was built up by means of an *a-priori* close reasoning which *from a logical point of view* implied no contradiction so long as the internally contradictory substance-concept itself was taken for *granted.* But the real structural states of affairs proved not to fit in this *a-priori* construction.

When we pay attention to the rôle of the material combinations in a living cell-body, we may formulate the real state of affairs as follows: *A cell cannot live in the molecular or (quasi-) crystalline matter-structures. Nevertheless the latter are actually present in the living cell-body, because its organism can no more live without than within them, and the material sub-structure really functions within its form-totality.*

Any philosophical theory which does not wish to distort the data for the sake of an *a-priori* close reasoning is obliged to account for this state of affairs in a cautious way.

To arrive at complete clarity in respect to the subject-matter of this chapter we shall now engage in a more detailed ontological consideration of the structure of a cell-body as an enkaptic form-totality.

A more detailed ontological consideration of the cell-body as a (typically qualified) enkaptic form-totality.

We have seen that a living cell-organism is enkaptically founded in a very particular mixture of matter and binds the latter within its own individuality-structure. The nodal point of this intertwinement has appeared to be the earlier discussed alveolar-colloidal and centered *form* of the plasm, maintaining itself in the continual process of dissolution and building up of the molecular matter-structures. In this form the material components also disclose those particular variability-types which function in the bio-chemical constellation and are no longer physico-chemically but biotically determined.

But it is the cell-body as a whole which gives the plasmatic matter this particular form; and this form, as the *bodily* form of the living cell-organism, is qualified by the *subjective biotic* function of the enkaptic whole, or, in the case of an animal cell, by the psychic function of the sensorium qualifying the animal cell-body. This biotic or psychical qualification respectively, is immediately obvious in uni-cellular beings: the plasmatic form remains entirely *plastic,* leaving room to contraction and expansion of its surface in all directions and to a mutual removability of the parts. In this way the cell-body is capable of adapting itself to its different biotic or primitive psychic functions, respectively, without being fixed within rigid form-boundaries.

WOLTERECK observes: 'In the *protozoa* and *protophytes* it is immediately evident that the total form is an *expression of the total system,* in this case of the cell. With respect to poly-cellular beings this state of affairs can only be deduced from particular observations and considerations. Also the separate organ-forms of the continuations of the plasm, the cilia, fibres, vacuoles, *etc.* are produced by the total substratum of the system... The living "cell-body" as a whole is the bearer and producer both of all of its part-forms and of the specific total form (figure) of the radiolarium, infusorium, bacterium' [1].

---

[1] *Grundzüge,* p. 117: 'Bei den Protozoem und Protophyten ist ohne weiteres klar — was bei den Vielzelligen erst aus besonderen Beobachtungen und Erwägungen abgeleitet werden kann — das die Gesamtform ein *Ausdruck des ganzen Systems,* hier also der Zelle ist, und dasz auch die einzelnen Organformen der Fortsätze, Zilien, Fasern, Vakuolen u.s.w. vom Gesamtsubstrat des Systems erzeugt werden... Der lebendige "Zell-leib" ist als Ganzes Träger und Produzent sowohl seiner sämtlichen Teil-

The cell-form as an elementary form-totality [1].

The answer to the question as to whether a cell-body is a real structural whole, or a mere aggregate of structures intertwined with one another enkaptically, in the first place depends on the insight into the nature of the cell-*form*. Is the latter indeed an *elementary form-totality* or is it rather a *mere aggregate of differently qualified forms?*

This question becomes of primordial importance if it is borne in mind that it is the very body-*form* in which the different typical structures distinguishable in a cell-body are to be enkaptically interlaced. If it should appear that this form is only composed of molecular matter-configurations, or of the latter and of typical biotically qualified organ-forms, respectively, then there could indeed be no question of a typical form-totality of the body. In this case the typical foundational function of the assumed enkaptic structural whole would be lacking and thereby the latter would turn out to be impossible in an ontological sense.

DRIESCH, WOLTERECK, BERTALANFFY and other famous biological theorists have doubtless the credit of having refuted the aggregate-theory on experimental grounds. The former has shown in particular that the visible figure of poly-cellular plants, animals and the human body is not only built up from organ-forms, tissue-forms and cell-forms but that in addition it is obedient to the *specific form-laws of a totality* [2].

DRIESCH's demonstration of the impossibility of a pure physico-chemical theory of the biotically qualified shape-formation [3] possessed a particular convincing force. The older theory of WEISMANN concerning the predisposition of all full grown organic forms, owing to a material (though invisible) morphogenetic primary structure in the nucleus of the germ-cells, was thereby definitively refuted.

WOLTERECK has particularly demonstrated that also the separate cell-form is to be viewed as an elementary total form in which a typical structural whole expresses itself.

---

formen als der spezifischen Gesamtform (Gestalt) des betreffenden Radiolars, Infusors, Bakteriums.'

[1] Compare in general with respect to the biological form-problem BERTALANFFY's *Kritische Theorie der Formbildung* (Berlin, 1928), and particularly WOLTERECK's *Grundzüge*, p. 114 ff.

[2] *Phil. d. Org.*, pp. 1—180.

[3] *Op. cit.*, pp. 125 ff.

WOLTERECK's investigations into the "biotic elementary forms".

WOLTERECK's investigations devoted to the "biotic elementary forms" are of a particular interest for our theory of the enkaptic structural whole. We shall therefore briefly resume some chief points of his explanations concerned.

Some uni-cellular beings (such as *bacteria*, uni-cellular green and blue-green *algae* and *amoebae*) display a restricted number of almost undifferentiated — and in this sense *simple* — figures. But also many cells of complicated animal and in particular of vegetable bodies display such a simple figure, in which besides cell-membrane and nucleus no particular constant organic forms have developed.

On the other hand, the greater part of tissue-cells and of uni-cellular beings have *differentiated* figures, either as a result of the secretion of complicated forms by the plasm, or by an intricate organic articulation of the cell-body itself.

Especially the flagellated cells deserve our interest. They are known either as independent vegetable, animal and bacterium-beings, or as developmental phases of poly-cellular beings. (Also the sperm-cells are a kind of flagellated cells provided with a scourge-like offshoot).

WOLTERECK calls the morphological structure of these latter the "elementary form *kat' exochèn*" common to all main groups of living beings. This type occurs in very simple figures in *bacteria* and *monads* [1], and with refinedly elaborated organ-forms in the *peridinidiae* [2] with their spiral circulation for the whips, their cellulose shells, complicated eyes, tentacles, *etc.* All these differentiated part-forms are produced by the living cell-body as a whole and are a differentiated morphological expression of its inner structural totality. The same holds as to the specialized tissue-cells of plants and animals, which equally — though not in the same multiplicitly — display part-forms within the frame of their specific total form, such as epithelial cells, muscle-cells, gland-cells, *etc.* Here, too, the total cell-form with all of its particular articulations of inner and outer architecture is a function of the total cell-body.

---

[1] Very small *protozoa* belonging to the flagellates.

[2] So called cilio-flagellates which move forward through the water by means of two dissimilar small scourges. It is not certain whether they belong to the *protozoa* or to the *protophytes*.

In this context WOLTERECK's above-mentioned observation concerning the typical totality character of the form-products of different *protozoa* and *protophytes* [1] is also of particular importance. The typical silico-lattices, -tubes or -radii, *e.g.*, secreted by the cell-body of *radiolaria* and silico-flagellates appeared to display specific total-forms different from species to species. All of them fundamentally deviate from the physico-chemically determined crystal-forms of the mineral *silicon dioxyde* (SiO_2). Nevertheless it must be assumed that in these specific silico-forms, molecular forms of the combination SiO_2 are enkaptically bound. For they remain typical SiO_2 figures.

The production of these typical forms always starts with alterations of the colloidal plasm, which zonally passes from the sol-condition into the gel-condition. The plasmatic zones which have arrived at the latter condition already display the typical physico-spatial relations of the skeletons and shells originating from them in the process of silica-formation. The formation starts from the cell-body in its centred and entirely movable colloidal-fluid figure, and this plastic whole is present both within and between the parts of the produced form.

Similar complicated fixed formations arise in the plasm of calc-algae and *foraminifera* and here, too, the plasm is present within and between the parts of the produced calc-shells. All of the produced parts of the skeletons or shells stand in particular relations of dimension and direction. They cannot be the result of separate physico-chemical operations of material components of the plasm, because, during the production, the parts of the plastic cell-body continually change their position within and between these fixed formations.

Plasmatic, allo-plasmatic and xeno-plasmatic forms. Indifference of this distinction with respect to the form-structure.

Both, uni-cellular and poly-cellular plants and animals may build up specific sensorily perceptible spatial forms with the aid of materials of three kinds, *viz.* either plasmatic matter, or cell-secretions, or finally foreign kinds of matter which the organism has taken up from outside. WOLTERECK, therefore, dis-

---

[1]) Cf. the ample discussion of these formations in E. REICHENAU's treatise *Protozoa* (Handbuch der Biologie, hrg. v. Bertalanffy, Bnd. VI, Heft 2, pp. 53 ff.).

tinguishes three kinds of formations, *viz.* plasmatic, allo-plasmatic and xeno-plasmatic shapes.

Plasmatic forms are found, *e.g.*, in the *pseudo-poda* and motive organs of uni-cellular beings; furthermore in the cotyledons (seed-leaves), nerve-cells and sense-organs of animals. All these organic forms arise from solidified plasm (having passed into the gel-condition).

Allo-plasmatic forms are of two kinds: Either the living cell secretes inorganic kinds of matter (taken up by it in a solved form) in a solid form. Well-known examples are the silico-skeletons and calc-shells of many uni-cellular beings, the silico- and calc-skeletons of sponges, coral polyps, echino-derms, and vertebrates. Or the organism produces organic forms of its own, for example the cellulose coverings of uni- and poly-cellular plants, the chitin of articulate animals and the horny formations (scales, hairs, feathers, *etc.*).

Xeno-plasmatic forms are also found both with uni-cellular and poly-cellular beings. Many *rhizopoda* which are provided with shells, and the simplest kinds of the different groups of *foraminifera* have the potency to collect grains of sand, silico-needles, micro-shells of diatoms, *etc.,* and to form from them coverings surrounding the cell-body. Similar phenomena are found with articulates. Lobsters cover their shells or hindpart with pieces of sea-weed, sponges or snail-houses; larvae of insects build up artificial tubes and "houses" from shell pieces, *etc.*

It is a particularly interesting phenomenon that — especially with *protozoa* — the xeno- and alloplasmatic forms may be similar: with *foraminifera* we find, for instance, tube-like and bottle-like formations consisting either of sand-particles stuck together, or of a porcelain-like calcium mass.

From this it appears that the different nature of the materials cannot be of essential importance to the form-production of the living bodies. The same form may be built up from different kinds of matter (both organic and inorganic). And the same matter may be serviceable to the construction of quite different forms. The only essential thing is the *formative principle* that selects the materials and works them into particular kinds of moulded products.

Now we have seen that the typical products of formation discussed here are not all of them *living parts* of the cell-body. The allo-plasmatic and xeno-plasmatic forms are not typically qualified by a biotic or post-biotic *subject*-function, but by an *ob-*

ject-function of biotic or post-biotic modality. In the living organism, and the animal *sensorium* they can consequently only function *enkaptically*.

But this structural subject-object relation does not detract from the *enkaptic form-totality* of the living cell-body. And the same holds good for the poly-cellular body.

In the first place the foundational form-totality of a living body as such is always an *objective sensory-spatial figure*. The latter doubtless gives expression to the biotic (or psychic) subject-object relation between the living organism (or the animal sensorium) and its non-living form-product. But the latter itself appeared to display a figure which obeys the form-laws of the *cell-body as a whole* and not the laws of crystallization of the materials used.

The internal structural unity of the body is not threatened by the fact that its morphological sensory figure encompasses forms of an objective biotic (or -psychic) qualification. For this morphological sensory figure as a whole implies the very subject-object relation. The vegetable and animal bodily form as such is an objective expression of the body's qualifying function. The non-living form-product is an autogenous *product* of the living body and not separated from the latter, but taken up in its *objective sensory form-totality*. And this form-totality has appeared to be the foundational function of the enkaptic structural whole.

Only after the separation of the non-living form-product from the living body that has produced it, does the form-function of the former cease to belong to the total bodily form. Nevertheless, even in this case this formation retains its objective biotic (or objective psychic) qualification as vegetable or animal form-product, respectively.

The chief point is, therefore, that both the form of a living cell-body as a whole, and that of its organic parts is a morphological expression of an enkaptic structural whole of a higher than physico-chemical qualification.

The different structures interlaced by this enkaptic form-totality are indeed no parts of the total structure. The material components of the body are only *realized* in the morphological interlacements of the structures concerned. This is why no single morphological criterium is suitable to distinguish the different "structural layers" of a living body. But the living body itself is a morphological whole typically qualified by the highest structure enkaptically bound by it. Therefore it is (at least insofar as it is of a vegetable or animal character) a *real thing-structure,* accessible to naïve experience. For the latter does not theoretically distinguish the different structures in whose morphological interlacements the enkaptic form-totality constitutes itself. It immediately grasps the *morphological whole.*

The sensory form-totality, as the foundational function of the living body, does not coalesce with the typical foundational form-functions of the interlaced structures.

It should be noted that the sensory total form of the living body, as an enkaptic whole, does not coalesce with the typical form-functions which have a foundational rôle in the different interlaced structures.

This is immediately evident in the case of the physico-chemically qualified structures of the molecules or crystals of the bodily matter. But the same must be true with respect to the typical foundational function of a body's living organism. The latter has a typical biotic qualification, and its foundational form is of an objective bio-spatial character. As such, it is not able to constitute in itself the enkaptic form-totality, characteristic of the bodily whole, though it certainly binds the different kinds of bodily matter in an enkaptic way within its bio-spatial form.

It is only in the objective sensory space that an enkaptic form-totality can be built up which lies at the foundation of the real whole of a living body, and not merely of the whole of one of the structures interlaced in it. For in this modality of spatial figures all the precedent modalities of spatial forms are objectified in the same analogous sense, so that they cannot obtrude at the cost of the sensory total image of the body.

This sensory total form gives a living body its objective *material* sensory figure, which in the dynamic biotic space is still lacking. It is the objective sensory image of the *materialized* living organism. In the case of an animal body it gives at the same time objective expression to the higher structure of the *sensorium,* and in a human body, in an anticipatory direction, to the *act-structure* of the enkaptic whole. In other words, the sensory total form of the body overlaps the interlaced structures. It gives expression to an enkaptic totality which constitutes itself by means of interstructural intertwinements, without being reducible to the latter. This is a second reason why the enkaptic whole is immediately accessible to naïve experience, since the latter does not penetrate into the interlaced structures themselves, but grasps the continuous whole only. Nevertheless, naïve experience is implicitly aware of the qualifying rôle of the highest structure as to the sensory form-totality.

The sensory-spatial form of the enkaptic whole does certainly not contain the modal nuclear type of individuality of this qualifying structure *as such*, but only that of the body as a typically qualified morphological unity, *realizing* the enkaptic totality in all of its interlaced structural layers. Therefore, it is only the foundational function of this realized whole, and not that of its abstract qualifying structure *in the latter's internal sphere*. The qualifying function of the latter, if present, can only be that of the body, insofar as it is enkaptically bound by the body, and not in its purely internal rôle in this qualifying structure.

The form-type of the living body as variability-type. The living body and its "*Umwelt*".

It is a matter of course that this bodily total form is at the same time the nodal point of enkaptic interlacements between the living being and its "*Umwelt*" and that thus it is co-determined by its relation to the latter. But this state of affairs does not detract from the fact that the bodily form is produced by the living being itself and that, consequently, it is not at all mechanically impressed upon the latter by its vital milieu. In his voluminous *Organographie der Planzen* [1], K. v. GOEBEL has shown with the aid of a wealth of empirical material that the multiplicity of the organ-forms by far surpasses that of the life conditions. This already appears from the great form-diversity of unicellular plants living under completely or nearly equal milieu-relations.

WOLTERECK distinguishes three main groups of morphological types in which the relation to the milieu finds expression:

1. the *suspensoid type* of those living beings which are "suspended" in their milieu (water, air);
2. the *motoroid type* of those which move by swimming or creeping in a particular direction;
3. the *basoid type* of those which with a plane or a pole of their body fasten themselves to the bottom, so that with the other pole they are turned away from the latter.

[1] Vol. I (Jena, 1928).

In each of these types the organic forms are never a mechanical result of adaptation to the milieu, but always co-determined by the structural geno-types of the living beings concerned. The thousandfold abundance of forms within the motoroid type, *e.g.*, is never to be explained one-sidedly from the entirely monotonous milieu of the beings belonging to this type. To become convinced of this state of affairs, as WOLTERECK observes, one need only turn up an atlas of the freely swimming *peridinidiae*, or of diatoms, or of *radiolaria*, in the same part of the ocean.

We can say that WOLTERECK's three basic types of "*Umweltbedingtheit*" are in fact *variability-types*, but that they nevertheless realize themselves *in accordance with the nature of the geno-types*. In this sense they are an expression of the internal structural type of the living body in its relation to the milieu.

WOLTERECK formulates this state of affairs in the frame of his own thought in this way "that the organisms are doubtless autonomous in the production of body-forms, but that beforehand this autonomy implies particular relations to the *Umwelt*" [1].

So it appears that the form-totality of a living-body is a real nodal point of enkaptic interlacements, both as to its internal constitution and as to its outer milieu. But at the same time it remains the *morphological expression of an internal structural whole*.

We have already mentioned the important methodological consequence following from the insight into this state of affairs with respect to the inquiry into the structures interlaced in the body-form. *The criterion of these structural strata can never be of a morphological character, but should be oriented to their internal structural principles. In this way each of these structural layers has its proper internal criterion. But the body, as an enkaptic structural whole, intertwines them in its typically qualified form-totality.*

The objectivistic conception of the body as an absolutization of the objective sensory bodily form.

In this context we finally have to pay attention to the old controversy between the Platonic and the Aristotelian view of the material body which even nowadays continues to influence scholastic thought. PLATO viewed the body as a vehicle *(ochèma)* of the soul. This was obviously an *objectivistic* conception,

---

[1] *Grundzüge*, p. 137.

whereas the Aristotelian view of the animate body was much rather of a subjectivistic character since it ascribed all the "formal" qualities of the body to the soul as its substantial form.

How is it to be explained that the Platonic conception again and again urged itself upon the Augustinian trend in scholasticism with a particular convincing force, in contradistinction to the Aristotelian view?

The answer to this question is already implied in our previous analysis of the body as an enkaptic structural whole. For although this analysis preponderantly pertained to the cell-body, as the simplest example of a living bodily whole, its method is also applicable to the poly-cellular bodies of plants, animals and even of human beings.

The Platonic conception is apparently oriented to the objective sensory form of the body, which is only the foundational function of its structure as an enkaptic whole. If only this objective sensorily perceptible aspect of the body is paid attention to, the *psychic subject-object relation* urges itself upon us with an inner necessity. This sensory figure of the body is doubtless related to a possible subjective sensory perception. If then furthermore the latter is considered to be metaphysically related to a "soul", in the sense of an "immaterial substance", the "material body" is indeed hardly to be conceived in another manner than as a "vehicle" or an objective "organ" of the soul [1]. This means a hypostatization of the objective morphological aspect of the body, which becomes particularly destructive to an insight into the human body as the enkaptic structural whole of the *total temporal human existence.*

In modern existentialistic philosophy we may observe a return to the subjectivistic view of man's corporality, especially with SARTRE and MERLEAU PONTY. Here this view is completely emancipated from the Greek metaphysical substance-concept and the form-matter motive which was its religious starting-point. But, especially in MERLEAU PONTY, "experienced corporality" is considered to belong to a supposed "pre-objective" experiential field,

---

[1] This background of the Platonic conception is particularly clear in the French sociologist and constitutional law theorist MAURICE HAURIOU, whose view of the relation between soul and body has always remained dualistic Platonic. For he based this conception explicitly upon a pure morphological concept of form and consequently rejected the Aristotelian-Thomistic view of the soul as the *substantial form* of the material body.

which is sharply opposed to the objectivistic analytical mode of thought of science. This involves a fundamental misinterpretation both of the subject-object relation of pre-theoretic experience and of the antithetic "*Gegenstand-relation*" of theoretic thought. This leads MERLEAU PONTY to his characterization of human corporality as a "blind adherence" ("*adhésion aveugle*") to the pre-objective world.

CONCLUSION.

The position of man in the temporal world.

So it appears that the theory of the enkaptic structural whole forms the necessary connective link between the theory of the individuality-structures and their temporal interweavings, and what is called a philosophical anthropology.

All our previous investigations have been nothing but a necessary preparation for the latter. They all implicitly tended to the ultimate and doubtless most important problem of philosophical reflection: What is man's position in the temporal cosmos in relation to his divine Origin? This question urged itself upon us at the outset of our inquiry and it returns at the end of this trilogy.

Nevertheless the present work does not yet contain a philosophical anthropology. We have reserved this theme for the third volume of our trilogy *Reformation and Scholasticism in Philosophy*. The reason is that in our opinion the really philosophical problems concerning man's position in the temporal cosmos cannot be rightly posited without a due insight into the transcendental conditions of philosophic thought. And in addition a philosophic anthropology presupposes an inquiry into the different dimensions of the temporal horizon with its modal and individuality structures.

This opinion is certainly not in line with the existentialistic fashion in contemporary European thought. The latter seeks an immediate approach to the innermost sphere of man's temporal existence to interpret the I-ness in its situation in the temporal world from those emotional dispositions (concern, care, dread) which are supposed to be the most fundamental strata of human existence, *i.e.* its "*Existentialen*" ("existentials"). If HEIDEGGER's "existential" of dread is replaced by that of "love" in the sense meant by the Swiss psychiatrist BINSWANGEER (the "meeting" between "I" and "thou"), then this hermeneutic approach to man seems to assume a trustworthy Christian meaning. This existentialism is not interested in the structural investigations which we deem to be a necessary condition of a really warranted philosophical anthropology. As a "supra-scientific" approach to man's existence it believes it has elevated itself above all structural conditions of temporal experience and can penetrate into its subject-matter by means of an immediate "encounter". "Encounter" and "experience" are opposed to one another as "genuine inner knowledge" to "objectifying outer knowledge".

It is disappointing but not surprising that different trends in Christian neo-scholasticism have welcomed this existentialistic anthropology as a "more Biblical" manner of thought in comparison with the proud rationalism and idealism of a former period. For what trend of immanence-philosophy has not been "accommodated" to the Biblical point of view and in this sense proclaimed to be "Biblical"? It was readily forgotten that the genuine Biblical view of "encounter" transcends any *philosophical* approach to temporal human life and that the dialectical opposition between "encounter" and "experience" contradicts the very core of the Biblical Revelation.

It was also forgotten that even with the Christian founder of existentialism, Sören Kierkegaard, existentialistic philosophy and the divine Revelation in Jesus Christ were considered to be separated by an unbridgeable gulf.

The ultimate and central questions about human existence cannot be answered by any philosophy in an autonomous way, since they are of a religious character. They are only answered in the divine Word-Revelation. But our transcendental critique of theoretical thought has shown that this answer has an intrinsic connection with the philosophical questions concerning man's position in the temporal world. For this answer indeed reveals man to himself and gives theoretical thought, as soon as the latter is ruled by its radical moving power, that true concentric direction which precludes any absolutization of temporal aspects. It also lays bare the root of all lack of true self-knowledge and thereby it unmasks the hidden basic motives of any kind of anthropology which holds to the immanence-standpoint.

Consequently, any expectation that an existentialist philosophy might contribute to man's true self-knowledge should be abandoned. This philosophy is no more fit to do so than modern depth-psychology. Naturally I do not mean that this recent philosophic trend has nothing to say to Christian thought. Its great representatives are doubtless serious philosophers, and their ideas deserve special attention as a *manifestation of the spirit of* our time, though the most prominent leaders of this movement have already broken with it.

But it is a veritable *spectaculum miserabile* to see how Christian theologians and philosophers seek their philosophical equipment here and join the existentialistic movement to combat the former invasion of Greek ideas into Christian thought. Apparently they have learned nothing from the history of Christian scholasticism. They reject the radical transcendental critique of philosophical thought because they do not wish to break with the time-honoured spirit of the scholastic accommodation of immanence-philosophy to the Christian doctrine.

But all those who have understood the necessity of an inner reformation of the philosophic attitude of thought from the radical Biblical standpoint, will comprehend why we emphatically warn against any exaggerated expectation concerning a philosophic anthropology. They will also understand our thesis that the central question: Who is man? means both the beginning and the end of philosophical reflection.

The question concerning the human I-ness as the centre of human existence has already appeared in the Prolegomena of our transcendental critique. But that about man's temporal existential form has been seen to imply a series of primordial problems which should be first considered. At least one central point of a truly Christian anthropology must be made perfectly clear. Man, as such, has no temporal qualifying function like temporal things and differentiated societal structures, but at the root of his existence he transcends all temporal structures. Therefore the search for a "substantial essential form" of human nature, in the sense of the Aristotelian-Thomistic metaphysical anthropology, is incompatible with what the Scriptures have revealed to us about created human nature.

In the radical community of the human race according to the divine order of creation, man is not qualified as a "rational-moral "being", but only by his kingly position as the personal religious creaturely centre of the whole earthly cosmos. In him the rational-moral functions also find their concentration and through him the entire temporal world is included both in apostasy and in salvation. All things, beings, and factual relations qualified by a temporal modal function are transitory, the temporal bonds of love included. But man has an eternal destination, not as an abstract "rational soul" or spiritual "mind", but in the fulness of his concrete, individual personality. This puts it beyond any doubt that the various conceptions of "body" and "soul", or of "body", "soul" and "spirit" devised from the immanence-standpoint are in principle unserviceable in a Christian anthropology which starts from the radical basic motive of the Word-Revelation. The all-sided temporal existence of man, *i.e.* his "body", in the full Scriptural sense of the word, can only be understood from the supra-temporal religious centre, *i.e.* the "soul", or the "heart", in its Scriptural meaning. Every conception of the so-called "immortal soul", whose supra-temporal centre of being must be sought in rational-moral functions, remains rooted in the starting-point of immanence-philosophy.

But all this merely relates to the only possible starting-point of a Christian anthropology. Any one who imagines that from our standpoint human existence is no more than a complex of temporal functions centering in the "heart", has an all too simple and erroneous idea of what we understand by "anthropology". What has appeared in the course of our investigations in this third volume is that in temporal human existence we can point to an extremely intricate system of enkaptic structural interlacements, and that these interlacements presuppose a comprehensive series of individuality structures, bound within an enkaptic structural whole. This insight implies new anthropological problems which cannot in any way be considered as solved. But they do not concern the central sphere of human existence, which transcends the temporal horizon. No existentialistic self-interpretation, no "act-psychology", no phenomenology or "metaphysics of the mind" can tell us what the human ego is, but — we repeat it — only the divine Word-Revelation in Christ Jesus. The question: "Who is man?" is unanswerable from the immanence-standpoint. But at the same time it is a problem which will again and again urge itself on apostate thought with relentless insistence, as a symptom of the internal unrest of an uprooted existence which no longer understands itself.

Printed in the USA
CPSIA information can be obtained
at www.ICGtesting.com
LVHW041949041023
759837LV00020B/692